Get Connected.

Guided Examples

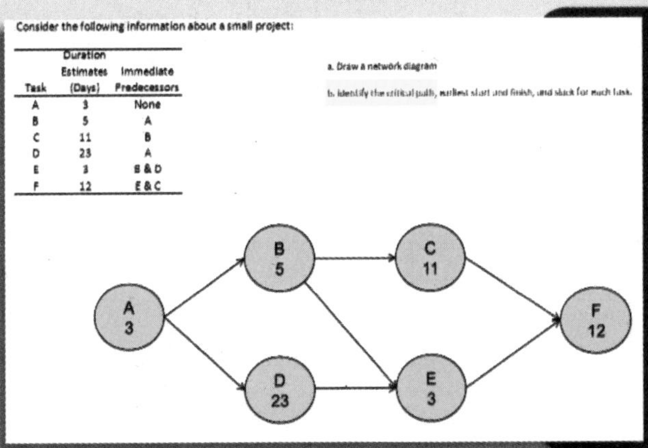

Guided Examples provide students with narrated and animated video tutorials and step-by-step walkthroughs of exercises and examples from the text. Students appreciate the Guided Examples because they can learn to solve a problem when they get stuck doing their homework. There are guided examples for several problems in each chapter of the text.

End-of-Chapter and Test

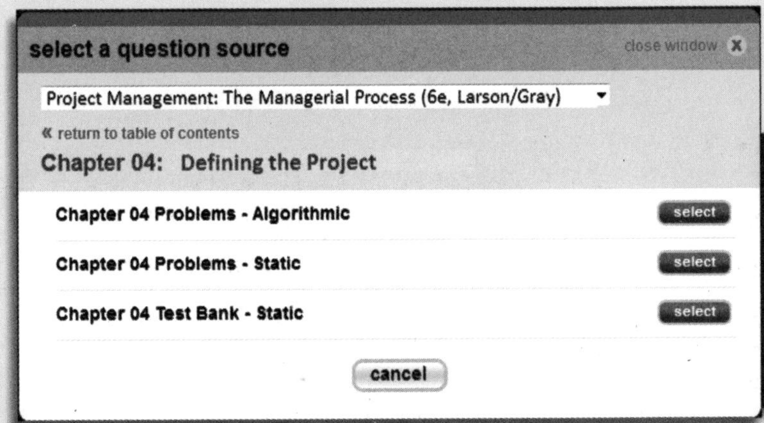

Connect Operations Management includes both static and algorithmic versions of end-of-chapter problems and static test bank questions.

Get Engaged.

eBooks

Connect Plus includes a media-rich eBook that allows the instructor to share notes with students. Students can insert and review their own notes, highlight the text, search for specific information, and interact with media resources. Using an eBook with *Connect Plus* gives students a complete digital solution that allows them to access their materials from any computer.

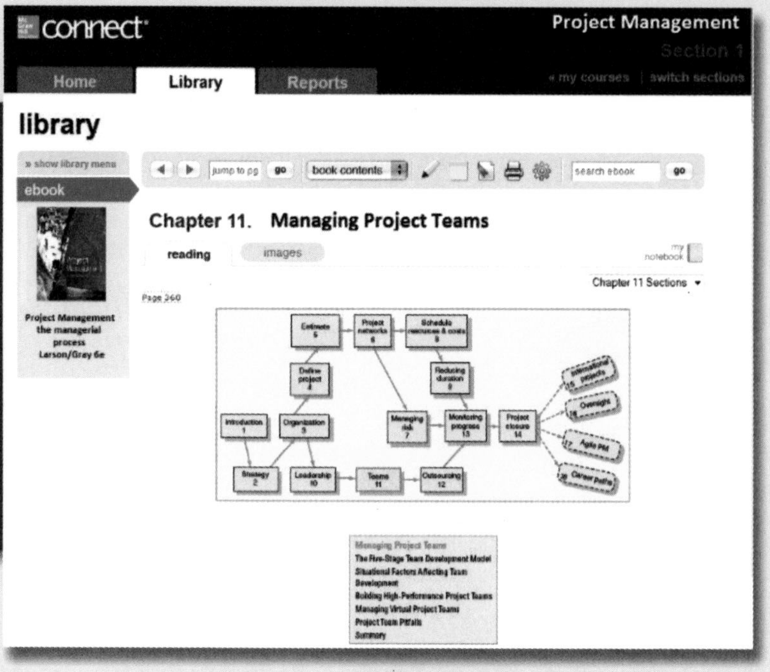

Project Management

The Managerial Process

The McGraw-Hill Series Operations and Decision Sciences

OPERATIONS MANAGEMENT

Beckman and Rosenfield,
Operations, Strategy: Competing in the 21st Century,
First Edition

Benton,
Purchasing and Supply Chain Management,
Second Edition

Bowersox, Closs, Cooper, and Bowersox,
Supply Chain Logistics Management,
Fourth Edition

Brown and Hyer,
Managing Projects: A Team-Based Approach,
First Edition

Burt, Petcavage, and Pinkerton,
Supply Management,
Eighth Edition

Cachon and Terwiesch,
Matching Supply with Demand: An Introduction to Operations Management,
Third Edition

Cooper and Schindler,
Business Research Methods,
Twelfth Edition

Finch,
Interactive Models for Operations and Supply Chain Management,
First Edition

Fitzsimmons, Fitzsimmons, and Bordoloi,
Service Management: Operations, Strategy, Information Technology,
Eighth Edition

Gehrlein,
Operations Management Cases,
First Edition

Harrison and Samson,
Technology Management,
First Edition

Hayen,
SAP R/3 Enterprise Software: An Introduction,
First Edition

Hill,
Manufacturing Strategy: Text & Cases,
Third Edition

Hopp,
Supply Chain Science,
First Edition

Hopp and Spearman,
Factory Physics,
Third Edition

Jacobs, Berry, Whybark, and Vollmann,
Manufacturing Planning & Control for Supply Chain Management,
Sixth Edition

Jacobs and Chase,
Operations and Supply Management: The Core,
Third Edition

Jacobs and Chase,
Operations and Supply Management,
Fourteenth Edition

Jacobs and Whybark,
Why ERP?
First Edition

Larson and Gray,
Project Management: The Managerial Process,
Sixth Edition

Leenders, Johnson, and Flynn,
Purchasing and Supply Management,
Fourteenth Edition

Nahmias,
Production and Operations Analysis,
Sixth Edition

Olson,
Introduction to Information Systems Project Management,
Second Edition

Schroeder, Goldstein, Rungtusanatham,
Operations Management: Contemporary Concepts and Cases,
Sixth Edition

Seppanen, Kumar, and Chandra,
Process Analysis and Improvement,
First Edition

Simchi-Levi, Kaminsky, and Simchi-Levi,
Designing and Managing the Supply Chain: Concepts, Strategies, Case Studies,
Third Edition

Sterman,
Business Dynamics: Systems Thinking and Modeling for Complex World,
First Edition

Stevenson,
Operations Management,
Eleventh Edition

Swink, Melnyk, Cooper, and Hartley,
Managing Operations Across the Supply Chain,
Second Edition

Thomke,
Managing Product and Service Development: Text and Cases,
First Edition

Ulrich and Eppinger,
Product Design and Development,
Fourth Edition

Zipkin,
Foundations of Inventory Management,
First Edition

QUANTITATIVE METHODS AND MANAGEMENT SCIENCE

Hillier and Hillier,
Introduction to Management Science: A Modeling and Case Studies Approach with Spreadsheets,
Fifth Edition

Stevenson and Ozgur,
Introduction to Management Science with Spreadsheets,
First Edition

Project Management

The Managerial Process

Sixth Edition

Erik W. Larson
Oregon State University

Clifford F. Gray
Oregon State University

Mc Graw Hill Education

PROJECT MANAGEMENT: THE MANAGERIAL PROCESS, SIXTH EDITION

This book is printed on acid-free paper.

1 2 3 4 5 6 7 8 9 0 QVS/QVS 1 0 9 8 7 6 5 4 3

ISBN 978-0-07-809659-4
MHID 0-07-809659-6

Managing Director: *Douglas Reiner*
Senior Brand Manager: *Thomas Hayward*
Executive Director of Development: *Ann Torbert*
Senior Development Editor: *Wanda Zeman*
Digital Development Editor: *Meg Maloney, Kevin Shanahan*
Dir. of Digital Content Development: *Doug Ruby*
Senior Marketing Manager: *Heather Kazakoff*
Content Production Manager: *Faye Schilling*
Content Project Manager: *Heather Ervolino*
Buyer: *Nichole Birkenholz*
Media Project Manager: *Sivakumar Munuswamy*
Compositor: *Aptara®, Inc.*
Typeface: *10.5/12 Times New Roman MT Std*
Printer: *Quad/Graphics*

Library of Congress Cataloging-in-Publication Data

Gray, Clifford F.
Project management : the managerial process / Erik W. Larson, Clifford F. Gray.—Sixth edition.
pages cm
Previous editions published as: Project management : the managerial process / Clifford F. Gray, Erik W. Larson.
ISBN 978-0-07-809659-4 (alk. paper)
1. Project management. 2. Time management. 3. Risk management. I. Larson, Erik W., 1952- II. Title.
HD69.P75G72 2014
658.4′04—dc23

2013027472

www.mhhe.com

About the Authors

Erik W. Larson

ERIK W. LARSON is professor of project management at the College of Business, Oregon State University. He teaches executive, graduate, and undergraduate courses on project management and leadership. His research and consulting activities focus on project management. He has published numerous articles on matrix management, product development, and project partnering. He has been honored with teaching awards from both the Oregon State University MBA program and the University of Oregon Executive MBA program. He has been a member of the Portland, Oregon, chapter of the Project Management Institute since 1984. In 1995 he worked as a Fulbright scholar with faculty at the Krakow Academy of Economics on modernizing Polish business education. He was a visiting professor at Chulalongkorn University in Bangkok, Thailand, and at Baden-Wuerttemberg Cooperative State University in Bad Mergentheim, Germany. He received a B.A. in psychology from Claremont McKenna College and a Ph.D. in management from State University of New York at Buffalo. He is a certified project management professional (PMP) and Scrum Master.

Clifford F. Gray

CLIFFORD F. GRAY is professor emeritus of management at the College of Business, Oregon State University. He continues to teach undergraduate and graduate project management courses overseas and in the United States; he has personally taught more than 100 executive development seminars and workshops. His research and consulting interests have been divided equally between operations management and project management; he has published numerous articles in these areas, plus a text on project management. He has also conducted research with colleagues in the International Project Management Association. Cliff has been a member of the Project Management Institute since 1976 and was one of the founders of the Portland, Oregon, chapter. He was a visiting professor at Kasetsart University in Bangkok, Thailand, in 2005. He was the president of Project Management International, Inc. (a training and consulting firm specializing in project management) 1977–2005. He received his B.A. in economics and management from Millikin University, M.B.A. from Indiana University, and doctorate in operations management from the College of Business, University of Oregon. He is certified Scrum Master.

"Man's mind, once stretched by a new idea, never regains its original dimensions."

Oliver Wendell Holmes, Jr.

To my family who have always encircled me with love and encouragement—my parents (Samuel and Charlotte), my wife (Mary), my sons and their wives (Kevin and Dawn, Robert and Sally) and their children (Ryan, Carly, Connor and Lauren).

C.F.G.

"We must not cease from exploration and the end of all exploring will be to arrive where we begin and to know the place for the first time."

T. S. Eliot

To Ann whose love and support has brought out the best in me. And, to our girls Mary, Rachel, and Tor-Tor for the joy and pride they give me. Finally, to my muse, Neil, for the faith and inspiration he instills.

E.W.L

Preface

Our motivation in writing this text continues to be to provide a realistic, socio-technical view of project management. In the past, textbooks on project management focused almost exclusively on the tools and processes used to manage projects and not the human dimension. This baffled us since people not tools complete projects! While we firmly believe that mastering tools and processes is essential to successful project management, we also believe that the effectiveness of these tools and methods is shaped and determined by the prevailing culture of the organization and interpersonal dynamics of the people involved. Thus, we try to provide a holistic view that focuses on both of these dimensions and how they interact to determine the fate of projects.

The role of projects in organizations is receiving increasing attention. Projects are the major tool for implementing and achieving the strategic goals of the organization. In the face of intense, worldwide competition, many organizations have reorganized around a philosophy of innovation, renewal, and organizational learning to survive. This philosophy suggests an organization that is flexible and project driven. Project management has developed to the point where it is a professional discipline having its own body of knowledge and skills. Today it is nearly impossible to imagine anyone at any level in the organization who would not benefit from some degree of expertise in the process of managing projects.

Audience

This text is written for a wide audience. It covers concepts and skills that are used by managers to propose, plan, secure resources, budget, and lead project teams to successful completions of their projects. The text should prove useful to students and prospective project managers in helping them understand why organizations have developed a formal project management process to gain a competitive advantage. Readers will find the concepts and techniques discussed in enough detail to be immediately useful in new-project situations. Practicing project managers will find the text to be a valuable guide and reference when dealing with typical problems that arise in the course of a project. Managers will also find the text useful in understanding the role of projects in the missions of their organizations. Analysts will find the text useful in helping to explain the data needed for project implementation as well as the operations of inherited or purchased software. Members of the Project Management Institute will find the text is well structured to meet the needs of those wishing to prepare for PMP (Project Management Professional) or CAPM (Certified Associate in Project Management) certification exams. The text has in-depth coverage of the most critical topics found in PMI's *Project Management Body of Knowledge* (PMBOK). People at all levels in the organization assigned to work on projects will find the text useful not only in providing them with a rationale for the use of project management processes but also because of the insights they will gain on how to enhance their contributions to project success.

Our emphasis is not only on how the management process works, but more importantly, on *why* it works. The concepts, principles, and techniques are universally applicable. That is, the text does not specialize by industry type or project scope. Instead, the text is written for the individual who will be required to manage a variety of projects in a variety of different organizational settings. In the case of some small projects, a few of the steps of the techniques can be omitted, but the conceptual framework applies to all organizations in which projects are important to survival. The approach can be used in pure project organizations such as construction, research organizations, and engineering consultancy firms. At the same time, this approach will benefit organizations that carry out many small projects while the daily effort of delivering products or services continues.

Content

In this and other editions we continue to resist the forces that engender scope creep and focus only on essential tools and concepts that are being used in the real world. We have been guided by feedback from practitioners, teachers, and students. Some changes are minor and incremental, designed to clarify and reduce confusion. Other changes are significant. They represent new developments in the field or better ways of teaching project management principles. Below are major changes to the sixth edition.

- Computer exercises and MS Project examples have been updated to MS Project 2010, and 2013 including video tutorials to help students master the basics of MS Project.
- Terms and concepts have been updated to be consistent with the fifth edition of the *Project Management Body of Knowledge* (2013).
- The chapters on Agile Project Management and Careers in Project Management have been expanded.
- Chapter 6 utilizes a new example that clarifies the differences between free and total slack. Chapters 1, 2, 4, 5 and 14 have been updated.
- A description of the Activity on Arrow (AoA) method for calculating networks has been deleted from the text and is now available only in the Instructor's Manual.
- New student exercises and cases have been added to many chapters.
- The Blue Zuma computer exercise in Appendix 2 has been replaced by the new Red Zuma exercise.
- The Snapshot from Practice boxes feature a number of new examples of project management in action as well as new Research Highlights that continue to promote practical application of project management.
- The Instructor's Manual contains a listing of current YouTube videos that correspond to key concepts and Snapshots from Practice.

Overall the text addresses the major questions and issues the authors have encountered over their 60 combined years of teaching project management and consulting with practicing project managers in domestic and foreign environments. The following questions represent the issues and problems practicing project managers find consuming most of their effort: What is the strategic role of projects in contemporary organizations? How are projects prioritized? What organizational and managerial styles will improve chances of project success? How do project managers orchestrate the complex network of relationships involving vendors, subcontractors, project team members, senior management, functional managers, and customers that affect project success? What factors contribute to the development of a high-performance project team? What project management system can be set up to gain some measure of control? How do managers prepare for a new international project in a foreign culture? How does one pursue a career in project management?

Project managers must deal with all these concerns to be effective. All of these issues and problems represent linkages to an integrative project management view. The chapter content of the text has been placed within an overall framework that integrates these topics in a holistic manner. Cases and snapshots are included from the experiences of practicing managers. The future for project managers appears to be promising. Careers will be determined by success in managing projects.

Student Learning Aids

The text website (www.mhhe.com/larsongray6e) includes study outlines, online quizzes, PowerPoint slides, videos, Microsoft Project Video Tutorials and web links. The trial version of Microsoft Project software is included on its own CD-ROM free with the text.

Acknowledgments

We would like to thank Lacey McNeely for updating the Test Bank and Online Quizzes; Charlie Cook for revising the PowerPoint slides; Oliver F. Lehmann for providing access to PMBOK study questions; and Pinyarat Sirisomboonsuk for accuracy checking the text and Instructor's Resource Manual content.

Next, it is important to note that the text includes contributions from numerous students, colleagues, friends, and managers gleaned from professional conversations. We want them to know we sincerely appreciate their counsel and suggestions. Almost every exercise, case, and example in the text is drawn from a real-world project. Special thanks to managers who graciously shared their current project as ideas for exercises, subjects for cases, and examples for the text. Shlomo Cohen, John A. Drexler, Jim Moran, John Sloan, Pat Taylor, and John Wold, whose work is printed, are gratefully acknowledged. Special gratitude is due Robert Breitbarth of Interact Management, who shared invaluable insights on prioritizing projects. University students and managers deserve special accolades for identifying problems with earlier drafts of the text and exercises.

We are indebted to the reviewers of past editions who shared our commitment to elevating the instruction of project management. The reviewers include Paul S. Allen, Rice University; Denis F. Cioffi, George Washington University; Joseph D. DeVoss, DeVry University; Edward J. Glantz, Pennsylvania State University; Michael Godfrey, University of Wisconsin–Oshkosh; Robert Key, University of Phoenix; Dennis Krumwiede, Idaho State University; Nicholas C. Petruzzi, University of Illinois–Urbana/Champaign; William R. Sherrard, San Diego State University; S. Narayan Bodapati, Southern Illinois University at Edwardsville; Warren J. Boe, University of Iowa; Burton Dean, San Jose State University; Kwasi

Amoako-Gyampah, University of North Carolina–Greensboro; Owen P. Hall, Pepperdine University; Bruce C. Hartman, University of Arizona; Richard Irving, York University; Robert T. Jones, DePaul University; Richard L. Luebbe, Miami University of Ohio; William Moylan, Lawrence Technological College of Business; Edward Pascal, University of Ottawa; James H. Patterson, Indiana University; Art Rogers, City University; Christy Strbiak, U.S. Air Force Academy; David A. Vaughan, City University; and Ronald W. Witzel, Keller Graduate School of Management. Nabil Bedewi, Georgetown University; Scott Bailey, Troy University; Michael Ensby, Clarkson University; Eldon Larsen, Marshall University; Steve Machon, DeVry University–Tinley Park; William Matthews, William Patterson University; Erin Sims, DeVry University–Pomona; Kenneth Solheim, DeVry University–Federal Way; and Oya Tukel, Cleveland State University. Gregory Anderson, Weber State University; Dana Bachman, Colorado Christian University; Alan Cannon, University of Texas, Arlington; Susan Cholette, San Francisco State; Michael Ensby, Clarkson University; Charles Franz, University of Missouri, Columbia; Raouf Ghattas, DeVry University; Robert Groff, Westwood College; Raffael Guidone, New York City College of Technology; George Kenyon, Lamar University; Elias Konwufine, Keiser University; Rafael Landaeta, Old Dominion University; Muhammad Obeidat, Southern Polytechnic State University; Linda Rose, Westwood College; Oya Tukel, Cleveland State University; and Mahmoud Watad, William Paterson University.

In the sixth edition we continue to commit to improving the text content and improving instruction of project management. We are grateful to those reviewers who provided helpful critiques and insights on the fifth edition, which helped us prepare this revision. The reviewers for the sixth edition include Victor Allen, Lawrence Technological University; Mark Angolia, East Carolina University; Alan Cannon, University of Texas at Arlington; Robert Cope, Southeastern Louisiana University; Kenneth DaRin, Clarkson University; Ron Darnell, Amberton University; Jay Goldberg, Marquette University; Mark Huber, University of Georgia; Marshall Issen, Clarkson University; Charles Lesko, East Carolina University; Lacey McNeely, Oregon State University; Donald Smith, Texas A&M University; Peter Sutanto, Prairie View A&M University; Jon Tomlinson, University of Northwestern Ohio. We thank you for your many thoughtful suggestions and for making our book better. Of course we accept responsibility for the final version of the text.

In addition, we would like to thank our colleagues in the College of Business at Oregon State University for their support and help in completing this project. In particular, we recognize Prem Mathew and Ping-Hung Hsieh for their helpful advice and suggestions. We also wish to thank the many students who helped us at different stages of this project, most notably Neil Young, Saajan Patel, Katherine Knox, Dat Nguyen, Lacey McNeely and David Dempsey. Mary Gray deserves special credit for editing and working under tight deadlines on earlier editions. Special thanks go to Pinyarat ("Minkster") Sirisomboonsuk for her help in preparing the last four editions.

Finally, we want to extend our thanks to all the people at McGraw-Hill/Higher Education for their efforts and support. First, we would like to thank Thomas Hayward and Wanda Zeman for providing editorial direction, guidance, and management of the book's development for the sixth edition. And we would also like to thank Jane Mohr, Heather Ervolino, Nichole Birkenholz, Arpana Kumari, and Janean Utley for managing the final production, design, supplement, and media phases of the sixth edition.

Erik W. Larson

Clifford F. Gray

Note to Student

You will find the content of this text highly practical, relevant, and current. The concepts discussed are relatively simple and intuitive. As you study each chapter we suggest you try to grasp not only how things work, but why things work. You are encouraged to use the text as a handbook as you move through the three levels of competency:

I know.

I can do.

I can adapt to new situations.

Project management is both people and technical oriented. Project management involves understanding the cause-effect relationships and interactions among the sociotechnical dimensions of projects. Improved competency in these dimensions will greatly enhance your competitive edge as a project manager.

The field of project management is growing in importance and at an exponential rate. It is nearly impossible to imagine a future management career that does not include management of projects. Résumés of managers will soon be primarily a description of the individual's participation in and contributions to projects.

Good luck on your journey through the text and on your future projects.

Chapter-by-Chapter Revisions for the Sixth Edition

Chapter 1: Modern Project Management

- New Snapshot: *Project Management in Action 2013.*
- Makes stronger case for why project management is essential skill set for anyone's career.
- New Snapshot: *A Dozen Examples of Projects Given to Recent College Graduates.*

Chapter 2: Organization Strategy and Project Selection

- New Snapshot: *Does IBM's Watson's Jeopardy Project Represent a Change in Strategy?*
- New Snapshot: *HP's Strategy Revision.*
- Expanded discussion on the importance of project sponsors.
- Revamped description of how project risks are assessed during the proposal phase.
- New case: *Fund Raising Project Selection Case.*

Chapter 3: Organization: Structure and Culture

- New Snapshot: *Google-y.*
- New case: *Horizon Consulting.*

Chapter 4: Defining the Project

- A new central example of a Work Breakdown Structure (WBS).
- Discussion of Process Breakdown Structure (PBS).
- Inclusion of "power/interest" map for assessing stakeholders.

Chapter 5: Estimating Project Times and Costs

- New Snapshot: *Reducing Estimating Error.*
- Introduction to Reference Class Forecasting methodology.
- New case: *Post Graduation Adventure.*

Chapter 6: Developing a Project Schedule

- A new central example that clarifies the differences between free and total slack.
- A description of the Activity on Arrow (AoA) method for calculating networks has been deleted from the text and is now available only in the Instructor's Manual.

Chapter 7: Managing Risk

- New Snapshot: *Playing Soccer in the Desert.*
- New case: *Sustaining Project Risk Management during Implementation.*

Chapter 8 Appendix 1: The Critical-Chain Approach

- New Snapshot: *Critical Chain Applied to Airplane Part Arrivals.*

Chapter 9: Reducing Project Duration

- New Snapshot: *Smartphone Wars.*

Chapter 10: Leadership: Being an Effective Project Manager

- New case: *The Blue Sky Project.*
- New ethical dilemmas mini-case: *Old Princeton Landing.*

Chapter 11: Managing Project Teams

- Expanded discussion on project vision.

Chapter 12: Outsourcing: Managing Interorganizational Relations

- New Snapshot: *The Boeing 787 Dreamliner.*
- New Snapshot: *U.S. Department of Defense's Value Engineering Awards 2013.*
- New case: *Shell Case Fabricators.*

Chapter 15: International Projects

- More extensive discussion of financial risks associated with international projects.
- New Snapshot: *Project X–Namibia, Africa.*
- New exercise assessing relative safety of different countries.

Chapter 17: An Introduction to Agile Project Management

- Elaborates on the role of product owner in Scrum.
- Includes all the principles of Agile Manifesto.
- Introduces the use of Sprint and Release Burndown charts to monitor progress on Agile projects.
- Discusses the use of hybrid models that combine elements of Agile and Waterfall.

Chapter 18: Project Management Career Paths

- New Snapshot: *Ron Parker.*
- Discussion on how to take advantage of opportunities at a university to develop project management skills.
- Expanded discussion of the value of certification.
- New Snapshot: *Grooming the Next Generation at Intel.*

Appendix 2: Computer Project Exercises

- The Blue Zuma computer exercise in Appendix 2 has been replaced by a new Red Zuma exercise.
- A video tutorial that demonstrates step by step how to complete and answer the original Blue Zuma exercise is available online for students.

Brief Contents

Preface vii

1. Modern Project Management 2
2. Organization Strategy and Project Selection 24
3. Organization: Structure and Culture 66
4. Defining the Project 100
5. Estimating Project Times and Costs 128
6. Developing a Project Plan 160
7. Managing Risk 204
8. Scheduling Resources and Costs 250
9. Reducing Project Duration 304
10. Leadership: Being an Effective Project Manager 338
11. Managing Project Teams 374
12. Outsourcing: Managing Interorganizational Relations 418
13. Progress and Performance Measurement and Evaluation 456
14. Project Closure 510
15. International Projects 538
16. Oversight 572
17. An Introduction to Agile Project Management 590
18. Project Management Career Paths 614

APPENDIX

One Solutions to Selected Exercises 627

Two Computer Project Exercises 641

GLOSSARY 658
ACRONYMS 667
PROJECT MANAGEMENT EQUATIONS 668
INDEX 669

Contents

Preface vii

Chapter 1
Modern Project Management 2

What Is a Project? 6
The Project Life Cycle 8
The Project Manager 9
Being Part of a Project Team 10
Current Drivers of Project Management 11
Project Governance 15
Alignment of Projects with Organizational Strategy 16
Project Management Today: A Socio-Technical Approach 17
Summary 18

Chapter 2
Organization Strategy and Project Selection 24

The Strategic Management Process: An Overview 26
Four Activities of the Strategic Management Process 29
The Need for a Project Portfolio Management System 32
Problem 1: The Implementation Gap 32
Problem 2: Organization Politics 33
Problem 3: Resource Conflicts and Multitasking 34
A Portfolio Management System 36
Classification of the Project 36
Selection Criteria 37
Financial Criteria 37
Nonfinancial Criteria 39
Applying a Selection Model 42
Sources and Solicitation of Project Proposals 43
Ranking Proposals and Selection of Projects 44
Managing the Portfolio System 46
Balancing the Portfolio for Risks and Types of Projects 48
Summary 49
Appendix 2.1: Request for Proposal (RFP) 63

Chapter 3
Organization: Structure and Culture 66

Project Management Structures 67
Organizing Projects within the Functional Organization 68
Organizing Projects as Dedicated Teams 71
Organizing Projects within a Matrix Arrangement 74
Different Matrix Forms 75
What Is the Right Project Management Structure? 79
Organization Considerations 79
Project Considerations 79
Organizational Culture 81
What Is Organizational Culture? 81
Identifying Cultural Characteristics 83
Implications of Organizational Culture for Organizing Projects 86
Summary 89

Chapter 4
Defining the Project 100

Step 1: Defining the Project Scope 102
Employing a Project Scope Checklist 102
Step 2: Establishing Project Priorities 106
Step 3: Creating the Work Breakdown Structure 108
Major Groupings Found in a WBS 108
How WBS Helps the Project Manager 109
A Simple WBS Development 109
Step 4: Integrating the WBS with the Organization 113
Step 5: Coding the WBS for the Information System 113
Process Breakdown Structure 116
Responsibility Matrices 117
Project Communication Plan 118
Summary 122

Chapter 5
Estimating Project Times and Costs 128

Factors Influencing the Quality of Estimates 130
Estimating Guidelines for Times, Costs, and Resources 131

Top-Down versus Bottom-Up Estimating 133
Methods for Estimating Project Times and Costs 135
Top-Down Approaches for Estimating Project Times and Costs 135
Bottom-Up Approaches for Estimating Project Times and Costs 139
A Hybrid: Phase Estimating 141
Level of Detail 143
Types of Costs 144
Refining Estimates 146
Creating a Database for Estimating 149
Summary 150
Appendix 5.1: Learning Curves for Estimating 155

Chapter 6

Developing a Project Plan 160

Developing the Project Network 161
From Work Package to Network 162
Constructing a Project Network 164
Terminology 164
Basic Rules to Follow in Developing Project Networks 164
Activity-on-Node (AON) Fundamentals 165
Network Computation Process 169
Forward Pass—Earliest Times 169
Backward Pass—Latest Times 171
Determining Slack (or Float) 173
Using the Forward and Backward Pass Information 175
Level of Detail for Activities 176
Practical Considerations 176
Network Logic Errors 176
Activity Numbering 176
Use of Computers to Develop Networks 177
Calendar Dates 180
Multiple Starts and Multiple Projects 180
Extended Network Techniques to Come Closer to Reality 180
Laddering 180
Use of Lags to Reduce Schedule Detail and Project Duration 180
An Example Using Lag Relationships—The Forward and Backward Pass 185
Hammock Activities 186
Summary 187

Chapter 7

Managing Risk 204

Risk Management Process 205
Step 1: Risk Identification 207
Step 2: Risk Assessment 210
Probability Analysis 213
Step 3: Risk Response Development 214
Mitigating Risk 214
Avoiding Risk 215
Transferring Risk 216
Retaining Risk 216
Contingency Planning 216
Technical Risks 218
Schedule Risks 220
Cost Risks 220
Funding Risks 221
Opportunity Management 221
Contingency Funding and Time Buffers 222
Budget Reserves 223
Management Reserves 223
Time Buffers 224
Step 4: Risk Response Control 224
Change Control Management 225
Summary 229
Appendix 7.1: PERT and PERT Simulation 239

Chapter 8

Scheduling Resources and Costs 250

Overview of the Resource Scheduling Problem 251
Types of Resource Constraints 253
Classification of a Scheduling Problem 255
Resource Allocation Methods 255
Assumptions 255
Time-Constrained Project: Smoothing Resource Demand 255
Resource-Constrained Projects 257
Computer Demonstration of Resource-Constrained Scheduling 262
The Impacts of Resource-Constrained Scheduling 268
Splitting Activities 268
Benefits of Scheduling Resources 270
Assigning Project Work 270
Multiproject Resource Schedules 271
Using the Resource Schedule to Develop a Project Cost Baseline 273
Why a Time-Phased Budget Baseline Is Needed 273
Creating a Time-Phased Budget 274
Summary 279
Appendix 8.1: The Critical-Chain Approach 293

Chapter 9
Reducing Project Duration 304

Rationale for Reducing Project Duration 305
Options for Accelerating Project Completion 307
Options When Resources Are Not Constrained 308
Options When Resources Are Constrained 310
Project Cost–Duration Graph 313
Explanation of Project Costs 313
Constructing a Project Cost–Duration Graph 314
Determining the Activities to Shorten 314
A Simplified Example 316
Practical Considerations 318
Using the Project Cost–Duration Graph 318
Crash Times 319
Linearity Assumption 319
Choice of Activities to Crash Revisited 319
Time Reduction Decisions and Sensitivity 320
What if Cost, Not Time, Is the Issue? 321
Summary 323

Chapter 10
Leadership: Being an Effective Project Manager 338

Managing versus Leading a Project 339
Managing Project Stakeholders 340
Influence as Exchange 344
Task-Related Currencies 345
Position-Related Currencies 346
Inspiration-Related Currencies 346
Relationship-Related Currencies 346
Personal-Related Currencies 347
Social Network Building 347
Mapping Dependencies 347
Management by Wandering Around (MBWA) 349
Managing Upward Relations 350
Leading by Example 352
Ethics and Project Management 355
Building Trust: The Key to Exercising Influence 357
Qualities of an Effective Project Manager 359
Summary 362

Chapter 11
Managing Project Teams 374

The Five-Stage Team Development Model 377
Situational Factors Affecting Team Development 378
Building High-Performance Project Teams 380
Recruiting Project Members 380
Conducting Project Meetings 383
Establishing a Team Identity 387
Creating a Shared Vision 388
Managing Project Reward Systems 391
Orchestrating the Decision-Making Process 392
Managing Conflict within the Project 394
Rejuvenating the Project Team 398
Managing Virtual Project Teams 399
Project Team Pitfalls 403
Groupthink 403
Bureaucratic Bypass Syndrome 404
Team Spirit Becomes Team Infatuation 404
Going Native 404
Summary 405

Chapter 12
Outsourcing: Managing Interorganizational Relations 418

Outsourcing Project Work 419
Best Practices in Outsourcing Project Work 423
Well-Defined Requirements and Procedures 424
Extensive Training and Team-Building Activities 426
Well-Established Conflict Management Processes in Place 427
Frequent Review and Status Updates 427
Co-Location When Needed 429
Fair and Incentive-Laden Contracts 430
Long-Term Outsourcing Relationships 431
The Art of Negotiating 432
1. Separate the People from the Problem 433
2. Focus on Interests, Not Positions 434
3. Invent Options for Mutual Gain 435
4. When Possible, Use Objective Criteria 435
Dealing with Unreasonable People 436
A Note on Managing Customer Relations 437
Summary 440
Appendix 12.1: Contract Management 449

Chapter 13
Progress and Performance Measurement and Evaluation 456

Structure of a Project Monitoring Information System 457
The Project Control Process 458
Monitoring Time Performance 459

Development of an Earned Value Cost/Schedule System 462
What Costs Are Included in Baselines? 465
Methods of Variance Analysis 465
Developing a Status Report: A Hypothetical Example 467
Assumptions 467
Baseline Development 467
Development of the Status Report 468
Indexes to Monitor Progress 473
Performance Indexes 473
Project Percent Complete Indexes 474
Technical Performance Measurement 475
Software for Project Cost/Schedule Systems 475
Additional Earned Value Rules 476
Forecasting Final Project Cost 476
Other Control Issues 479
Scope Creep 479
Baseline Changes 481
The Costs and Problems of Data Acquisition 482
Summary 483
Appendix 13.1: The Application of Additional Earned Value Rules 499
Appendix 13.2: Obtaining Project Performance Information from MS Project 2010 506

Chapter 14
Project Closure 510

Types of Project Closure 512
Wrap-up Closure Activities 513
Creating the Final Report 516
Post-Implementation Evaluation 517
Team Evaluation 517
Individual, Team Member, and Project Manager Performance Reviews 520
Retrospectives 522
Why Retrospectives? 522
Initiating the Retrospective Review 523
Use of an Independent Facilitator 524
Selection of a Facilitator 524
Roles of a Facilitator 524
Managing a Retrospective 525
Overseeing a Post-Project Retrospective 526
Utilization of Retrospectives 529
Archiving Retrospectives 529
Concluding Retrospective Notes 530
Summary 530
Appendix 14.1: Project Closeout Checklist 533
Appendix 14.2: Euro Conversion—Project Closure Checklist 535

Chapter 15
International Projects 538

Environmental Factors 540
Legal/Political 540
Security 541
Geography 542
Economic 542
Infrastructure 544
Culture 545
Project Site Selection 547
Cross-Cultural Considerations: A Closer Look 548
Adjustments 549
Working in Mexico 552
Working in France 553
Working in Saudi Arabia 555
Working in China 556
Working in the United States 557
Summary Comments about Working in Different Cultures 559
Culture Shock 560
Coping with Culture Shock 562
Selection and Training for International Projects 563
Summary 566

Chapter 16
Oversight 572

Project Oversight 573
Importance of Oversight to the Project Manager 574
Portfolio Project Management 574
Project Office 574
Phase Gate Methodology 577
Organization Project Management in the Long Run 582
Organization Project Management Maturity 582
The Balanced Scorecard Model 586
Summary 586

Chapter 17
An Introduction to Agile Project Management 590

Traditional versus Agile Methods 591
Agile PM 594
Agile PM in Action: Scrum 596
Roles and Responsibilities 598
Scrum Meetings 598
Product and Sprint Backlogs 600
Sprint and Release Burndown Charts 601

Applying Agile PM to Large Projects 603
Limitations and Concerns 604
Summary 606

Chapter 18
Project Management Career Paths 614

Career Paths 615
Pursuing a Career 618
Professional Training and Certification 619
More on Certification 620
Gaining Visibility 621
Mentors 622
Success in Key Projects 623
Summary 624

Appendix 1: **Solutions to Selected Exercises 627**
Appendix 2: **Computer Project Exercises 641**

Glossary 658

Acronyms 667

Project Management Equations 668

Index 669

CHAPTER ONE

Modern Project Management

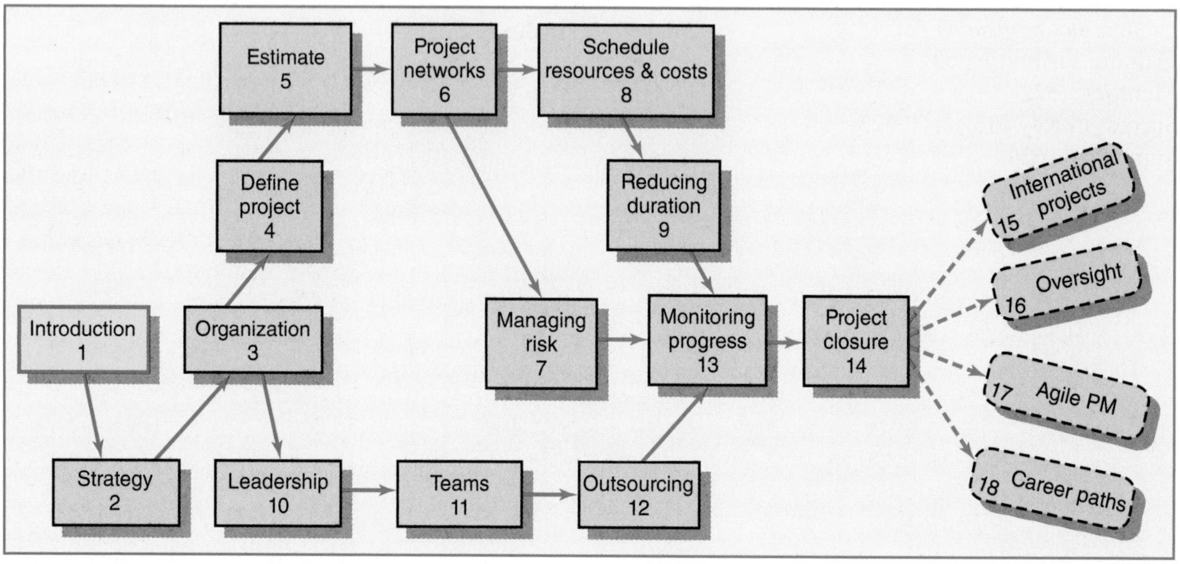

Modern Project Management

What Is a Project?

Current Drivers of Project Management

Project Governance

Project Management Today—A Socio-Technical Approach

Summary

Text Overview

All of mankind's greatest accomplishments—from building the great pyramids to discovering a cure for polio to putting a man on the moon—began as a project.

This is a good time to be reading a book about project management. Business leaders and experts have proclaimed that project management is critical to sustainable economic growth. New jobs and competitive advantage are achieved by constant innovation, developing new products and services, and improving both productivity and quality of work. This is the world of project management. Project management provides people with a powerful set of tools that improves their ability to plan, implement, and manage activities to accomplish specific organizational objectives. But project management is more than just a set of tools; it is a results-oriented management style that places a premium on building collaborative relationships among a diverse cast of characters. Exciting opportunities await people skilled in project management.

The project approach has long been the style of doing business in the construction industry, U.S. Department of Defense contracts, and Hollywood as well as big consulting firms. Now project management has spread to all avenues of work. Today, project teams carry out everything from port expansions to hospital restructuring to upgrading information systems. They are creating next generation, fuel efficient vehicles, developing sustainable sources of energy, and exploring the farthest reaches of outer space. The impact of project management is most profound in the electronics industry, where the new folk heroes are young professionals whose Herculean efforts lead to the constant flow of new hardware and software products.

Project management is not limited to the private sector. Project management is also a vehicle for doing good deeds and solving social problems. Endeavors such as providing emergency aid to areas hit by natural disasters, devising a strategy for reducing crime and drug abuse within a city, or organizing a community effort to renovate a public playground would and do benefit from the application of modern project management skills and techniques.

Perhaps the best indicator of demand for project management can be seen in the rapid expansion of the Project Management Institute (PMI), a professional organization for project managers. PMI membership has grown from 93,000 in 2002 to more than 434,000 currently. See the PMI Snapshot from Practice, for information regarding professional certification in project management.

It's nearly impossible to pick up a newspaper or business periodical and not find something about projects. This is no surprise! Approximately \$2.5 trillion (about 25 percent of the U.S. gross national product) are spent on projects each year in the United States alone. Other countries are increasingly spending more on projects. Millions of people around the world consider project management the major task in their profession.

SNAPSHOT FROM PRACTICE — The Project Management Institute*

The Project Management Institute (PMI) was founded in 1969 as an international society for project managers. Today PMI has members from more than 180 countries and more than 424,600 members. PMI professionals come from virtually every major industry, including aerospace, automotive, business management, construction, engineering, financial services, information technology, pharmaceuticals, health care, and telecommunications.

PMI provides certification as a ***Project Management Professional (PMP)***—someone who has documented sufficient project experience, agreed to follow the PMI code of professional conduct, and demonstrated mastery of the field of project management by passing a comprehensive examination. The number of people earning PMP status has grown dramatically in recent years. In 1996 there were fewer than 3,000 certified project management professionals. By June of 2013 there were more than 537,400 Professional credential holders.

Just as the CPA exam is a standard for accountants, passing the PMP exam may become the standard for project managers. Some companies are requiring that all their project managers be PMP certified. Moreover, many job postings are restricted to PMPs. Job seekers, in general, are finding that being PMP certified is an advantage in the marketplace.

PMI added a certification as a *Certified Associate in Project Management (CAPM)*. CAPM is designed for project team members and entry-level project managers, as well as qualified undergraduate and graduate students who want a credential to recognize their mastery of the project management body of knowledge. CAPM does not require the extensive project management experience associated with the PMP. For more details on PMP and CAPM, "Google" PMI to find the current Web site for the Project Management Institute.

* *PMI Today*, June 2013, p. 4

Most of the people who excel at managing projects never have the title of project manager. They include accountants, lawyers, administrators, scientists, contractors, public health officials, teachers, and community advocates whose success depends upon being able to lead and manage project work. For some, the very nature of their work is project driven. Projects may be cases for lawyers, audits for accountants, events for artists, and renovations for contractors. For others, projects may be a small, but critical part of their work. For example, a high school teacher who teaches four classes a day is responsible for coaching a group of students to compete in a national debate competition. A store manager who oversees daily operations is charged with developing an employee retention program. A sales account executive is given the additional assignment of team lead to launch daily deals into a new city. A public health official who manages a clinic is also responsible for organizing a Homeless Youth Connect event. For these and others, project management is not a title, but a critical job requirement. It is hard to think of a profession or a career path that would not benefit from being good at managing projects.

Not only is project management critical to most careers, the skill set is transferable across most businesses and professions. At its core, project management fundamentals are universal. The same project management methodology that is used to develop a new product can be adapted to create new services, organize events, refurbish aging operations, and so forth. In a world where it is estimated that each person is likely to experience three to four career changes, managing projects is a talent worthy of development.

SNAPSHOT FROM PRACTICE — A Dozen Examples of Projects Given to Recent College Graduates

1. Business information: Join a project team charged with installing new data security system.
2. Physical education: Design and develop a new fitness program for senior citizens that combines principles of yoga and aerobics.
3. Marketing: Execute a sales program for new home air purifier.
4. Industrial engineering: Manage a team to create a value chain report for every aspect of key product from design to customer delivery.
5. Chemistry: Develop a quality control program for organization's drug production facilities.
6. Management: Implement a new store layout design.
7. Pre-med neurology student: Join project team linking mind mapping to an imbedded prosthetic that will allow blind people to function near normally.
8. Sports communication: Join Olympic project team that will promote women's sport products for the 2016 Games in Reo de Janeiro, Brazil.
9. Systems engineer: Become a project team member of a project to develop data mining of medical papers and studies related to drug efficacy.
10. Accounting: Work on an audit of a major client.
11. Public health: Research and design a medical marijuana educational program.
12. English: Create a web-based user manual for new electronics product.

© Troels Graugaard/E+/Getty Images

The significance of project management can also be seen in the classroom. Twenty years ago major universities offered one or two classes in project management, primarily for engineers. Today, most universities offer multiple sections of project management classes, with the core group of engineers being supplemented by business students majoring in marketing, management information systems

(MIS), and finance, as well as students from other disciplines such as oceanography, health sciences, computer sciences, and liberal arts. These students are finding that their exposure to project management is providing them with distinct advantages when it comes time to look for jobs. More and more employers are looking for graduates with project management skills. See the nearby Snapshot from Practice for examples of projects given to recent college graduates. The logical starting point for developing these skills is understanding the uniqueness of a project and of project managers.

What Is a Project?

What do the following headlines have in common?

Millions watch Olympic Opening Ceremony
Citywide WiFi system set to go live
Hospitals respond to new Health Care Reforms
Apple's new iPhone hits the market
City receives stimulus funds to expand light rail system

All of these events represent projects.

© Lars Baron/Getty Images

The Project Management Institute provides the following definition of a project:

> A **project** is a temporary endeavor undertaken to create a unique product, service, or result.

Like most organizational effort, the major goal of a project is to satisfy a customer's need. Beyond this fundamental similarity, the characteristics of a project help differentiate it from other endeavors of the organization. The major characteristics of a project are as follows:

1. An established objective.
2. A defined life span with a beginning and an end.
3. Usually, the involvement of several departments and professionals.
4. Typically, doing something that has never been done before.
5. Specific time, cost, and performance requirements.

First, projects have a defined objective—whether it is constructing a 12-story apartment complex by January 1 or releasing version 2.0 of a specific software package as quickly as possible. This singular purpose is often lacking in daily organizational life in which workers perform repetitive operations each day.

Second, because there is a specified objective, projects have a defined endpoint, which is contrary to the ongoing duties and responsibilities of traditional jobs. In many cases, individuals move from one project to the next as opposed to staying in one job. After helping to install a security system, an IT engineer may be assigned to develop a database for a different client.

Third, unlike much organizational work that is segmented according to functional specialty, projects typically require the combined efforts of a variety of specialists. Instead of working in separate offices under separate managers, project participants, whether they be engineers, financial analysts, marketing professionals, or quality control specialists, work closely together under the guidance of a project manager to complete a project.

The fourth characteristic of a project is that it is nonroutine and has some unique elements. This is not an either/or issue but a matter of degree. Obviously, accomplishing something that has never been done before, such as building a electric automobile or landing two mechanical rovers on Mars, requires solving previously unsolved problems and breakthrough technology. On the other hand, even basic construction projects that involve established sets of routines and procedures require some degree of customization that makes them unique.

Finally, specific time, cost, and performance requirements bind projects. Projects are evaluated according to accomplishment, cost, and time spent. These triple constraints impose a higher degree of accountability than you typically find in most jobs. These three also highlight one of the primary functions of project management, which is balancing the trade-offs between time, cost, and performance while ultimately satisfying the customer.

What a Project Is Not Projects should not be confused with everyday work. A project is not routine, repetitive work! Ordinary daily work typically requires doing the same or similar work over and over, while a project is done only once; a new product or service exists when the project is completed. Examine the list in Table 1.1 that compares routine, repetitive work and projects. Recognizing the difference is important because too often resources can be used up on daily operations which may not contribute to longer range organization strategies that require innovative new products.

Program versus Project In practice the terms project and program cause confusion. They are often used synonymously. *A* **program** *is a group of related projects*

TABLE 1.1
Comparison of Routine Work with Projects

Routine, Repetitive Work	Projects
Taking class notes	Writing a term paper
Daily entering sales receipts into the accounting ledger	Setting up a sales kiosk for a professional accounting meeting
Responding to a supply-chain request	Developing a supply-chain information system
Practicing scales on the piano	Writing a new piano piece
Routine manufacture of an Apple iPod	Designing an iPod that is approximately 2 × 4 inches, interfaces with PC, and stores 10,000 songs
Attaching tags on a manufactured product	Wire-tag projects for GE and Wal-Mart

designed to accomplish a common goal over an extended period of time. Each project within a program has a project manager. The major differences lie in scale and time span.

Program management is the process of *managing* a group of ongoing, interdependent, related *projects* in a coordinated way to achieve strategic objectives. For example, a pharmaceutical organization could have a program for curing cancer. The cancer program includes and coordinates *all* cancer projects that continue over an extended time horizon (Gray, 2011). Coordinating all cancer projects under the oversight of a cancer team provides benefits not available from managing them individually. This cancer team also oversees the selection and prioritizing of cancer projects that are included in their special "Cancer" portfolio. Although each project retains its own goals and scope, the project manager and team are also motivated by the higher program goal. Program goals are closely related to broad strategic organization goals.

The Project Life Cycle

Another way of illustrating the unique nature of project work is in terms of the **project life cycle.** Some project managers find it useful to use the project life cycle as the cornerstone for managing projects. The life cycle recognizes that projects have a limited life span and that there are predictable changes in level of effort and focus over the life of the project. There are a number of different life-cycle models in project management literature. Many are unique to a specific industry or type of project. For example, a new software development project may consist of five phases: definition, design, code, integration/test, and maintenance. A generic cycle is depicted in Figure 1.1.

The project life cycle typically passes sequentially through four stages: defining, planning, executing, and delivering. The starting point begins the moment the project is given the go-ahead. Project effort starts slowly, builds to a peak, and then declines to delivery of the project to the customer.

1. **Defining stage:** Specifications of the project are defined; project objectives are established; teams are formed; major responsibilities are assigned.
2. **Planning stage:** The level of effort increases, and plans are developed to determine what the project will entail, when it will be scheduled, whom it will benefit, what quality level should be maintained, and what the budget will be.

FIGURE 1.1
Project Life Cycle

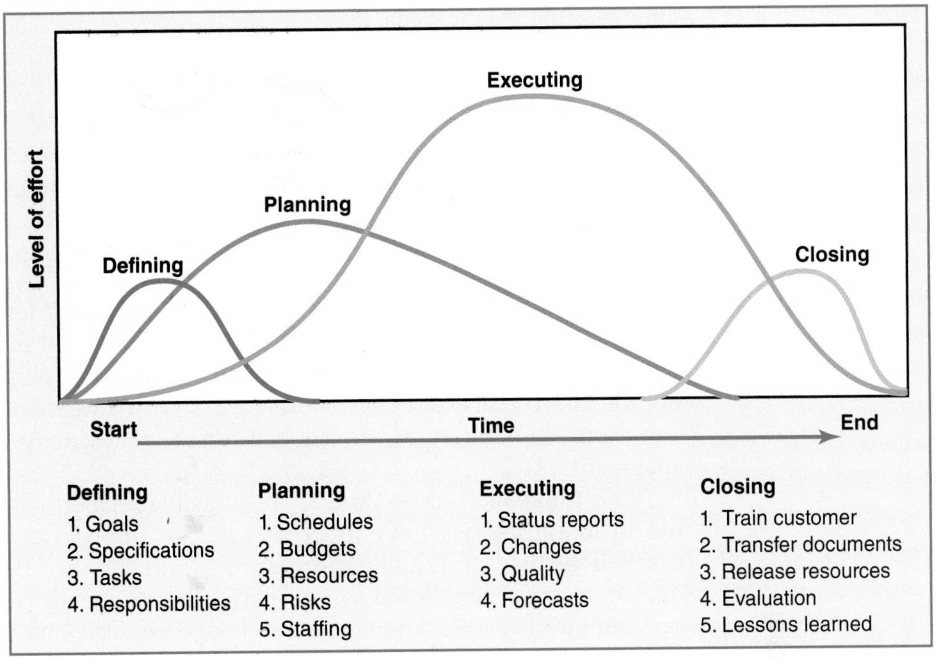

3. **Executing stage:** A major portion of the project work takes place—both physical and mental. The physical product is produced (a bridge, a report, a software program). Time, cost, and specification measures are used for control. Is the project on schedule, on budget, and meeting specifications? What are the forecasts of each of these measures? What revisions/changes are necessary?
4. **Closing stage:** Closing includes three activities: delivering the project product to the customer, redeploying project resources, and post-project review. Delivery of the project might include customer training and transferring documents. Redeployment usually involves releasing project equipment/materials to other projects and finding new assignments for team members. Post-project reviews include not only assessing performance but also capturing lessons learned.

In practice, the project life cycle is used by some project groups to depict the timing of major tasks over the life of the project. For example, the design team might plan a major commitment of resources in the defining stage, while the quality team would expect their major effort to increase in the latter stages of the project life cycle. Because most organizations have a portfolio of projects going on concurrently, each at a different stage of each project's life cycle, careful planning and management at the organization and project levels are imperative.

The Project Manager

At first glance project managers perform the same functions as other managers. That is, they plan, schedule, motivate, and control. However, what makes them unique is that they manage temporary, nonrepetitive activities, to complete a fixed life project. Unlike functional managers, who take over existing operations, project managers create a project team and organization where none existed before. They must decide what and how things should be done instead of simply managing set processes. They must meet the challenges of each phase of the project life cycle, and even oversee the dissolution of their operation when the project is completed.

Project managers must work with a diverse troupe of characters to complete projects. They are typically the direct link to the customer and must manage the tension between customer expectations and what is feasible and reasonable. Project managers provide direction, coordination, and integration to the project team, which is often made up of part-time participants loyal to their functional departments. They often must work with a cadre of outsiders—vendors, suppliers, subcontractors—who do not necessarily share their project allegience.

Project managers are ultimately responsible for performance (frequently with too little authority). They must ensure that appropriate trade-offs are made between the time, cost, and performance requirements of the project. At the same time, unlike their functional counterparts, project managers generally possess only rudimentary technical knowledge to make such decisions. Instead, they must orchestrate the completion of the project by inducing the right people, at the right time, to address the right issues and make the right decisions.

While project management is not for the timid, working on projects can be an extremely rewarding experience. Life on projects is rarely boring; each day is different from the last. Since most projects are directed at solving some tangible problem or pursuing some useful opportunity, project managers find their work personally meaningful and satisfying. They enjoy the act of creating something new and innovative. Project managers and team members can feel immense pride in their accomplishment, whether it is a new bridge, a new product, or needed service. Project managers are often stars in their organization and well compensated.

Good project managers are always in demand. Every industry is looking for effective people who can get the right things done on time. Clearly, project management is a challenging and exciting profession. This text is intended to provide the necessary knowledge, perspective, and tools to enable students to accept the challenge.

Being Part of a Project Team

Most people's first exposure to project management occurs while working as part of a team assigned to complete a specific project. Sometimes this work is full-time, but in most cases, people work part-time on one or more projects. They must learn how to juggle their day-to-day commitments with additional project responsibilities. They may join a team with a long history of working together, in which case roles and norms are firmly established. Alternatively, their team may consist of strangers from different departments and organizations. As such, they endure the growing pains of a group evolving into a team. They need to be a positive force in helping the team coalesce into an effective project team.

Not only are there people issues, but project members are also expected to use project management tools and concepts. They develop or are given a project charter or scope statement that defines the objectives and parameters of the project. They work with others to create a project schedule and budget that will guide project execution. They need to understand project priorities so they can make independent decisions. They must know how to monitor and report project progress. Although much of this book is written from the perspective of a project manager, the tools, concepts, and methods are critical to everyone working on a project. Project members need to know how to avoid the dangers of scope creep, manage the critical path, engage in timely risk management, negotiate, and utilize virtual tools to communicate.

Current Drivers of Project Management

Q8

Project management is no longer a special-need management. It is rapidly becoming a standard way of doing business. See Snapshot from Practice: Project Management in Action: 2013. An increasing percentage of the typical firm's effort is being devoted to projects. The future promises an increase in the importance and the role of projects in contributing to the strategic direction of organizations. Several reasons why this is the case are briefly discussed below.

Compression of the Product Life Cycle

One of the most significant driving forces behind the demand for project management is the shortening of the product life cycle. For example, today in high-tech industries the product life cycle is averaging 6 months to 3 years. Only 30 years ago, life cycles of 10 to 15 years were not uncommon. *Time to market* for new products with short life cycles has become increasingly important. A common rule of thumb in the world of high-tech product development is that a six-month project delay can result in a 33 percent loss in product revenue share. Speed, therefore, becomes a competitive advantage; more and more organizations are relying on cross-functional project teams to get new products and services to the market as quickly as possible.

Knowledge Explosion

The growth in new knowledge has increased the complexity of projects because projects encompass the latest advances. For example, building a road 30 years ago was a somewhat simple process. Today, each area has increased in complexity, including materials, specifications, codes, aesthetics, equipment, and required specialists. Similarly, in today's digital, electronic age it is becoming hard to find a new product that does not contain at least one microchip. Product complexity has increased the need to integrate divergent technologies. Project management has emerged as an important discipline for achieving this task.

Triple Bottom Line (planet, people, profit)

The threat of global warming has brought sustainable business practices to the forefront. Businesses can no longer simply focus on maximizing profit to the detriment of the environment and society. Efforts to reduce carbon imprint and utilize renewable resources are realized through effective project management. The impact of this movement towards sustainability can be seen in changes in

SNAPSHOT FROM PRACTICE Project Management in Action: 2013

© Frederic J. Brown/AFP/Getty Images

Businesses thrive and survive based on their ability to manage projects that produce products and services that meet market needs. Below is a small sample of projects that are important to their company's future.

ORGANIZATION: PROCTER AND GAMBLE

Project: Global Ordering, Shipping, and Billing Project

The project goal is to improve customer service, processes, and organization structure. The global team relied on virtual communication, while closely managing risk and milestone dates. The new system is designed to allow P&G to make real-time decisions, enabling the company to collect and respond to consumer/retailer feedback to create more compelling promotions to increase sales. The system should also improve efficiencies in supply chains by, for example, identifying the best warehouses to ship products to.

—*PMI Today,* 2012 PMI Project of the Year Finalists, December 2012, p. 7

ORGANIZATION: OAKLAND A'S BASEBALL TEAM

Project: Cisco Stadium

In November 2006, the future of the Oakland A's looked bright as the team announced plans to build a new ballpark in Fremont, CA. Upon announcing plans to build a ballpark, the Oakland A's sold the naming rights to the ballpark to Cisco Systems for $4 million/year over 30 years. The ballpark design mimicked classic ballparks of the past, while combining the most advanced technology in the world. Those plans have since been derailed as opposition increased from major retailers and homeowners near the stadium site. The A's have spent the past five years pursuing other options including building the ballpark in Oakland, near the coliseum, or possibly in San Jose, CA. The A's need the new stadium to turn around lagging attendance, which has been at or near the bottom among major league baseball clubs.

—*Oakland Tribune,* 8/1/12

the objectives and techniques used to complete projects. See Snapshot from Practice: Dell Children's Becomes World's First "Green" Hospital.

Corporate Downsizing

The last decade has seen a dramatic restructuring of organizational life. Downsizing (or rightsizing if you are still employed) and sticking to core competencies

ORGANIZATION: CHINA SUNERGY CO., LTD

Project: Sanliurfa Solar Park, Turkey

The Chinese company, Sunergy, has entered into a joint agreement with Seul Energy, a leading solar developer, to develop a 500kw solar park in Sanliurfa, Turkey. The plants will incorporate state of the art technology and new types of solar cells. The project is the beginning of an ambitious program designed to meet the expected growth in demand for energy in Central Asia.

—www.prnewswire.com/news-releases/china, accessed 1/5/13

ORGANIZATION: THE WALT DISNEY COMPANY

Project: *Star Wars Episode 7*

Disney spent over $4 billion to purchase Lucasfilm, which included exclusive past and future rights to the popular Star Wars franchise. Preproduction work on the newest Star Wars feature is scheduled to begin in 2013 with a projected release date in 2015. The Star Wars investment is seen by industry experts as an effort by Disney to broaden its pop culture reach and re-establish Disney films in the sci-fi/fantasy genre after the failure of space epic *John Carter* and *Mars Needs Moms*.

—*businessweek.com*, 11/11/12

ORGANIZATION: DISH NETWORK

Project: Hopper

Dish Network made a splash at the 2013 Consumer Electronics Show by showing off the latest generation of Hopper, a whole-home HD DVR system. Hopper includes commercial skipping technology and the ability to move programs onto iPads and other mobile devices. The announcement cemented Dish's position as one of the leaders in the "TV Everywhere" movement in which favorite shows and movies can be accessed from any device at any location. Dish is counting on Hopper and related products to compete against DirecTV and deep-pocketed cable and telecom providers.

—*Ces.cnet.com*, 1/8/13

ORGANIZATION: BILL & MELINDA GATES FOUNDATION

Project: Drought-Tolerant Maize for Africa

The goal of the project is to help farmers in Sub-Saharan Africa living in drought-susceptible areas increase their maize (corn) productivity. Getting the improved maize varieties into the hands of African farmers is the product of over two decades of research and involves a broad coalition of partners, from governments and NGOs to seed dealers and farmers. More than 2 million smallholder farmers in Africa are already realizing the benefits of higher yields. By 2016, the drought-tolerant maize project is expected to boost maize yields by as much as 30%, benefiting up to 40 million people in Africa.

—*gatesfoundation.org*, accessed 1/9/13

ORGANIZATION: FIAT, ITALY

Project: 2013 Fiat 500 EV

Available Spring 2013, the EV is a totally electric version of the popular Fiat 500 line. The EV sports a 100-hp electric motor powered by lithium batteries with 87 miles of electric range. Fiat needs to prove that it is a forward looking company and provide another reason to buy the 500 other than styling or the sales curve will plunge once the cuteness fails. Success will depend upon overcoming customer range anxiety and the risk that governments will stop supporting electric vehicles with attractive subsidies.

—*caranddriver.com*, accessed 1/20/13

ORGANIZATION: SONY, JAPAN

Project: Sony PlayStation 4 (PS4)

It's been seven years since Sony released the highly successful PlayStation 3, and the Internet is buzzing with rumors of a fourth-generation PlayStation. The PS4 reportedly will feature a tablet-style controller and state of the art graphics. At stake is Sony's position in the $10 billion-plus gaming industry.

—*sonyps4.com*, accessed 1/11/13

have become necessary for survival for many firms. Middle management is a mere skeleton of the past. In today's flatter and leaner organizations, where change is a constant, project management is replacing middle management as a way of ensuring that things get done. Corporate downsizing has also led to a change in the way organizations approach projects. Companies outsource significant segments of project work, and project managers have to manage not only their own people but also their counterparts in different organizations.

SNAPSHOT FROM PRACTICE — Dell Children's Becomes World's First "Green" Hospital*

Dateline 1/7/2009, Austin Texas: Dell Children's Medical Center becomes the first hospital in the world to receive platinum LEED (Leadership in Energy & Environmental Design) certification. Platinum certification is the highest award granted by the U.S. Green Building Council.

Dell Children's occupies nearly one-half million square feet on 32 acres that were once part of Austin's old Mueller Airport. Its environmentally sensitive design not only conserves water and electricity, but positively impacts the hospital's clinical environment by improving air quality, making natural sunlight readily available, and reducing a wide range of pollutants.

In order to receive LEED certification, buildings are rated in five key areas: sustainable site development, water savings, energy efficiency, materials selection, and environmental quality. Listed below are some of the accomplishments in each LEED category:

Sustainable Site

- 47,000 tons of Mueller Airport runway material was reused on site.
- About 40 percent fly ash instead of Portland cement in concrete yields a drop in carbon dioxide emissions equivalent to taking 450 cars off the road.
- 925 tons of construction waste was recycled on site.

Water Efficiency and Water Conservation

- Reclaimed water is used for irrigation; xeriscaped landscaping uses native plants, which require less water.
- Low-flow plumbing fixtures.

Energy Efficiency and Energy Conservation

- An on-site natural gas turbine supplies all electricity, which is 75 percent more efficient than coal-fired plants.
- Converted steam energy from a heating/cooling plant supplies all chilled water needs.

Indoor Environment Quality and Lighting

- Most interior spaces are within 32 feet of a window.
- Motion and natural light sensors shut off unneeded lights.

Conservation of Materials and Resources

- Use of local and regional materials saves fuel for shipping.
- Special paints and flooring emit low levels of volatile organic compounds (VOCs).

"Even before the first plans were drawn up, we set our sight on creating a world-class children's hospital, and becoming the first LEED Platinum hospital in the world was definitely part of that," said Robert Bonar, president and CEO, Dell Children's Medical Center of Central Texas. "Our motivation to pursue LEED Platinum was not just environmental. Being a 'green' hospital has profound, measurable effect on healing. What's good for the environment and good for our neighbors is also good for our patients."

* *Austin Business Journal*, 1-11-2009; www.dellchildrens.net/about_us/news/2009/01/08.

Increased Customer Focus

Increased competition has placed a premium on customer satisfaction. Customers no longer simply settle for generic products and services. They want customized products and services that cater to their specific needs. This mandate requires a much closer working relationship between the provider and the receiver. Account executives and sales representatives are assuming more of a project manager's role as they work with their organization to satisfy the unique needs and requests of clients.

Increased customer attention has also prompted the development of customized products and services. For example, 15 years ago buying a set of golf clubs was a relatively simple process: You picked out a set based on price and feel. Today, there are golf clubs for tall players and short players, clubs for players who tend to slice the ball and clubs for those who hook the ball, high-tech clubs with the latest metallurgic discovery guaranteed to add distance, and so forth. Project management is critical both to development of customized products and services and to sustaining lucrative relationships with customers.

Small Projects Represent Big Problems

The velocity of change required to remain competitive or simply keep up has created an organizational climate in which hundreds of projects are implemented concurrently. This climate has created a multiproject environment and a plethora of new problems. Sharing and prioritizing resources across a portfolio of projects is a major challenge for senior management. Many firms have no idea of the problems involved with inefficient management of small projects. Small projects typically carry the same or more risk as do large projects. Small projects are perceived as having little impact on the bottom line because they do not demand large amounts of scarce resources and/or money. Because so many small projects are going on concurrently and because the perception of the inefficiency impact is small, measuring inefficiency is usually nonexistent. Unfortunately, many small projects soon add up to large sums of money. Many customers and millions of dollars are lost each year on small projects in product and service organizations. Small projects can represent hidden costs not measured in the accounting system.

Organizations with many small projects going on concurrently face the most difficult project management problems. A key question becomes one of how to create an organizational environment that supports multiproject management. A process is needed to prioritize and develop a portfolio of small projects that supports the mission of the organization.

In summary, there are a variety of environmental forces interacting in today's business world that contribute to the increased demand for good project management across all industries and sectors. Project management appears to be ideally suited for a business environment requiring accountability, flexibility, innovation, speed, and continuous improvement. These environment and other factors have created the necessity for major oversight of all organization projects.

Project Governance

Competing in a global market influenced by rapid change, innovation, and time to market means organizations manage more and more projects. Some means for coordinating and managing projects in this changing environment is needed. Centralization of project management processes and practices has been the practical outcome. For example, Google, Apple, General Electric, and Sony all have over 1,000 projects being implemented concurrently every day of the year across borders and differing cultures. *Questions: How do these organizations oversee the management of all these projects? How were these projects selected? How do they ensure performance measurement and accountability? How can project management continually improve?* Centralization entails governance of all project processes and practices to improve project management.

Governance is designed to improve project management in the whole organization over the long haul. The rationale for integration of project management was to provide senior management with:

- An overview of all project management activities;
- A big picture of how organizational resources are being used;
- An assessment of the risk their portfolio of projects represents;

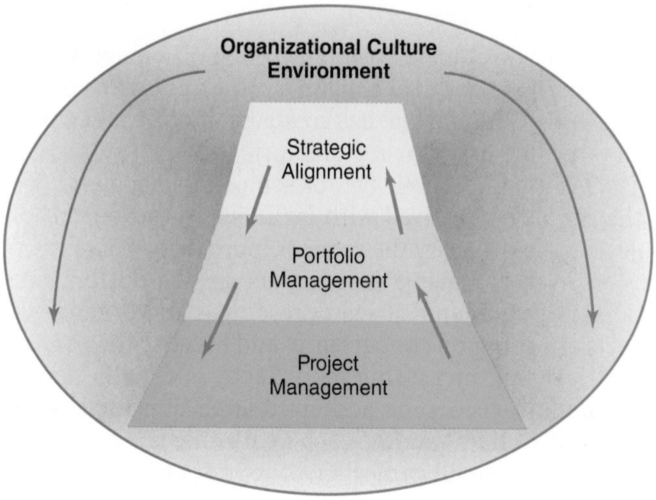

FIGURE 1.2
Integrated Management of Projects

- A rough metric for measuring the improvement of managing projects relative to others in the industry;
- Linkages of senior management with actual project execution management.

Full insight of all components of the organization is crucial for aligning internal business resources with the requirements of the changing environment. Governance enables management to have greater flexibility and better control of all project management activities.

Operationally, what does project management integration mean? It necessitates combining all of the major dimensions of project management under one umbrella. Each dimension is connected in one seamless, integrated domain. Governance means applying a set of knowledge, skills, tools, and techniques to a collection of projects in order to move the organization toward its strategic goals. This integrative movement represents a major thrust of project driven organizations across all industries. See Figure 1.2, Integrated Management of Projects.

Alignment of Projects with Organizational Strategy

Today, projects are the *modus operandi* for implementing strategy. Yet in some organizations, selection and management of projects often fail to support the strategic plan of the organization. Strategic plans are written by one group of managers, projects selected by another group, and projects implemented by another. These independent decisions by different groups of managers create a set of conditions leading to conflict, confusion, and frequently an unsatisfied customer. Under these conditions, resources of the organization are wasted in non-value-added activities/projects.

Since projects are the modus operandi, strategic alignment of projects is of major importance to conserving and effective use of organization resources. Selection criteria need to ensure each project is prioritized and contributes to strategic goals. Anything less is a waste of scarce organizational resources—people, capital, and equipment. Ensuring alignment requires a selection process that is systematic, open, consistent, and balanced. All of the projects selected become part of a project portfolio that balances the total risk for the organization. Management of the project portfolio ensures that only the most valuable projects are approved and managed across the entire organization.

Project Management Today: A Socio-Technical Approach

Senior management is often involved in selecting projects but seldom involved in implementing them. Implementing the project is the challenge.

There are two dimensions within the actual execution of projects (see Figure 1.3, The Technical and Sociocultural Dimensions of the Project Management Process). The first dimension is the technical side of the management process, which consists of the formal, disciplined, purely logical parts of the process. This technical dimension includes planning, scheduling, and controlling projects. Clear project scope statements are written to link the project and customer and to facilitate planning and control. Creation of the deliverables and work breakdown structures facilitates planning and monitoring the progress of the project. The work breakdown structure serves as a database that links all levels in the organization, major deliverables, and all work—right down to the tasks in a work package. Effects of project changes are documented and traceable. Thus, any change in one part of the project is traceable to the source by the integrated linkages of the system. This integrated information approach can provide all project managers and the customer with decision information appropriate to their level and needs. A successful project manager will be well trained in the technical side of managing projects.

The second and opposing dimension is the sociocultural side of project management. In contrast to the orderly world of project planning, this dimension involves the much messier, often contradictory and paradoxical world of implementation. It centers on creating a temporary social system within a larger organizational environment that combines the talents of a divergent set of professionals working to complete the project. See Research Highlight: Works Well with Others. Project managers must shape a project culture that stimulates teamwork and high levels of

FIGURE 1.3
The Socio-Technical Dimensions of the Project Management Process

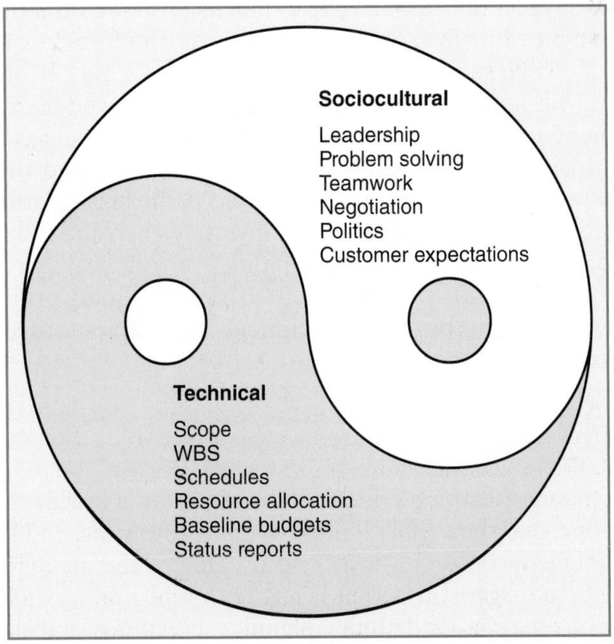

Research Highlight — Works Well with Others*

The phrase "works well with others" has long been a staple on grade school report cards; now, in the IT world, it's the No. 1 criterion for management candidates. In a nationwide survey conducted in 1999, 27 percent of chief information officers (CIOs) cited strong interpersonal skills as the single most important quality for reaching management levels. Advanced technical skills came in second, receiving 23 percent of the response.

The project was sponsored by RHI Consulting, which provides information technology professionals on a project basis. An independent research firm was hired to administer the survey. Over 1,400 CIOs responded to the questionnaire.

Survey respondents were also asked:

In 2005, how frequently will employees in your IT department work on project-based teams with members of other departments throughout the company?

Their responses:		
	Very frequently	57%
	Somewhat frequently	26%
	Somewhat infrequently	10%
	Very infrequently	6%
	Never	1%

Greg Scileppi, RHI Consulting's executive director, recommends that IT professionals develop their interpersonal skills. "The predominance of project teams has created a corresponding need for strong communication and team-player abilities. Technical staff put these skills to test daily as they work with employees at all levels to create and implement IT solutions ranging from simple troubleshooting to corporate web initiatives and system wide upgrades."

* Joanita M. Nellenbach, "People Skills Top Technical Knowledge, CIOs Insist," *PMNetwork* (August 1999), pp. 7–8.

personal motivation as well as a capacity to quickly identify and resolve problems that threaten project work. Things rarely go as planned and project managers must be able to steer the project back on track or alter directions when necessary.

The socio-cultural dimension also involves managing the interface between the project and external environment. Project managers have to assuage and shape expectations of customers, sustain the political support of top management, negotiate with their functional counterparts, monitor subcontractors, and so on. Overall, the manager must build a cooperative social network among a divergent set of allies with different standards, commitments, and perspectives.

Some suggest that the technical dimension represents the "science" of project management while the sociocultural dimension represents the "art" of managing a project. To be successful, a manager must be a master of both. Unfortunately, some project managers become preoccupied with the planning and technical dimension of project management. Often their first real exposure to project management is through project management software, and they become infatuated with network charts, Gantt diagrams, and performance variances; they attempt to manage a project from a distance. Conversely, there are other managers who manage projects by the "seat of their pants," relying heavily on team dynamics and organizational politics to complete a project. Good project managers balance their attention to both the technical and sociocultural aspects of project management.

Summary

Project management is a critical skill set in today's world. A project is defined as a nonroutine, one-time effort limited by time, resources, and performance specifications designed to meet customer needs. One of the distinguishing characteristics of project management is that it has both a beginning and an end and typically consists of four phases: defining, planning, executing, and closing. Effective project management begins with selecting and prioritizing projects that support the firm's mission and strategy. Successful implementation requires both technical and social skills. Project managers have to plan and budget projects as well as orchestrate the contributions of others.

Text Overview

This text is written to provide the reader with a comprehensive, integrative understanding of the project management process. The text focuses both on the science of project management and the art of managing projects. Following this introductory chapter, Chapter 2 focuses on how organizations go about evaluating and selecting projects. Special attention is devoted to the importance of aligning project selection to the mission and strategy of the firm. The organizational environment in which projects are implemented is the focus of Chapter 3. The discussion of matrix management and other organizational forms is augmented by a discussion of the role the culture of an organization plays in the implementation of projects.

The next six chapters focus on developing a plan for the project; after all, project success begins with a good plan. Chapter 4 deals with defining the scope of the project and developing a work breakdown structure (WBS). The challenge of formulating cost and time estimates is the subject of Chapter 5. Chapter 6 focuses on utilizing the information from the WBS to create a project plan in the form of a timed and sequenced network of activities.

Risks are a potential threat to every project, and Chapter 7 examines how organizations and managers identify and manage risks associated with project work. Resource allocation is added to the plan in Chapter 8 with special attention devoted to how resource limitations impact the project schedule. After a resource schedule is established, a project time-phased budget is developed. Finally, Chapter 9 examines strategies for reducing ("crashing") project time either prior to the initiation of the project or in response to problems or new demands placed on the project.

Chapters 10 through 12 focus on project implementation and the sociocultural side of project management, beginning with Chapter 10, which focuses on the role of the project manager as a leader and stresses the importance of managing project stakeholders within the organization. Chapter 11 focuses on the core project team; it combines the latest information on team dynamics with leadership skills/techniques for developing a high-performance project team. Chapter 12 continues the theme of managing project stakeholders by discussing how to outsource project work and negotiate with contractors, customers, and suppliers.

Chapter 13 focuses on the kinds of information managers use to monitor project progress, with special attention devoted to the key concept of earned value. The project life cycle is completed with Chapter 14, which covers closing out a project and the important assessment of performance and lessons learned. Four "supplemental" chapters are included to augment the project management core. Implementation of project management in multicultural, international environments is the subject of Chapter 15. Chapter 16 focuses the need for organizational oversight and how it impacts the management of projects. The emergence of agile project management, a more flexible team approach to managing complex projects where requirements cannot be clearly defined before the project begins, is the subject of Chapter 17. Finally, Chapter 18 concludes with coverage of career issues in the field of project management.

Throughout this text you will be exposed to the major aspects of the project management system. However, a true understanding of project management comes not from knowing what a scope statement is, or the critical path, or partnering with contractors, but from comprehending how the different elements of the project management system interact to determine the fate of a project. If, by the end of this text, you come to appreciate and begin to master both the technical and sociocultural dimensions of project management, you should have a distinct competitive advantage over others aspiring to work in the field of project management.

Key Terms

Program, *7*
Project, *6*
Project life cycle, *8*
Project Management Professional (PMP), *4*

Review Questions

1. Define a project. What are five characteristics that help differentiate projects from other functions carried out in the daily operations of the organization?
2. What are some of the key environmental forces that have changed the way projects are managed? What has been the effect of these forces on the management of projects?
3. Why is the implementation of projects important to strategic planning and the project manager?
4. The technical and sociocultural dimensions of project management are two sides to the same coin. Explain.
5. What is the impact of governance on managing an individual project? Why is this approach important in today's environment?

Exercises

1. Review the front page of your local newspaper, and try to identify all the projects contained in the articles. How many were you able to find?
2. Individually identify what you consider to be the greatest achievements accomplished by mankind in the last five decades. Now share your list with three to five other students in the class, and come up with an expanded list. Review these accomplishments in terms of the definition of a project. What does your review suggest about the importance of project management?
3. Individually identify projects assigned in previous terms. Were both sociocultural and technical elements factors in the success or difficulties in the projects?
4. Check out the Project Management Institute's home page at *www.pmi.org*.
   a. Review general information about PMI as well as membership information.
   b. See if there is a PMI chapter in your state. If not, where is the closest one?
   c. Use the search function at the PMI home page to find information on Project Management Body of Knowledge (PMBOK). What are the major knowledge areas of PMBOK?
   d. Explore other links that PMI provides. What do these links tell you about the nature and future of project management?

Note: If you have any difficulty accessing any of the Web addresses listed here or elsewhere in the text, you can find up-to-date addresses on the home page of Dr. Erik Larson, coauthor of this text: http://business.oregonstate.edu/faculty-and-staff-bios/erik-larson

References

Ball Parks of Baseball, "Cisco Field," *http://www.ballparksofbaseball.com/future/CiscoField.htm* (accessed June 2, 2009).

Benko, C., and F. W. McFarlan, *Connecting the Dots* (Boston: HBS Press, 2003).

Cohen, D. J., and R. J. Graham, *The Project Manager's MBA* (San Francisco: Jossey-Bass, 2001).

Darnell, R., "The Emerging Role of the Project Manager," *PM Network,* Vol. 11, No. 7 (1997).

Derby, Charles, and Ofer Zwikael, "The Secret of (Defining) Success," *PM Network*, Vol. 26, No. 8, August 2012, pp. 20–22.

Gray, Clifford, "Program Management, A Primer," *PM World Today*, Vol. 13, No. 8, August 2011, pp. 1–7.

Jonas, D., "Empowering Project Portfolio Managers: How Management Involvement Impacts Project Management Performance," *International Journal of Project Management,* Vol. 28, No. 8 (2010), pp. 818–831.

Koh, Aileen, and Lynn Crawford, "Portfolio Management: The Australian Experience," *Project Management Journal,* Vol. 43, No. 6 (2012), pp. 33–41.

Peters, T., *PM Network,* January 2004, Vol. 18, No. 1, p. 19.

Project Management Institute, *Leadership in Project Management Annual* (Newton Square, PA: PMI Publishing, 2006).

Project Management Institute, *A Guide to the Project Management Body of Knowledge (PMBOK),* (Newton Square, PA: PMI Publishing, 2013).

Project Management Institute, *PMI Today,* July 2011, p. 11.

The Standish Group, *CHAOS Summary 2009*, pp. 1–4.

Stewart, T. A., "The Corporate Jungle Spawns a New Species: The Project Manager," *Fortune* (September 1996), pp. 14–15.

Case

A Day in the Life

Rachel, the project manager of a large information systems project, arrives at her office early to get caught up with work before her co-workers and project team arrive. However, as she enters the office she meets Neil, one of her fellow project managers, who also wants to get an early start on the day. Neil has just completed a project overseas. They spend 10 minutes socializing and catching up on personal news.

CHAPTER TWO

Organization Strategy and Project Selection

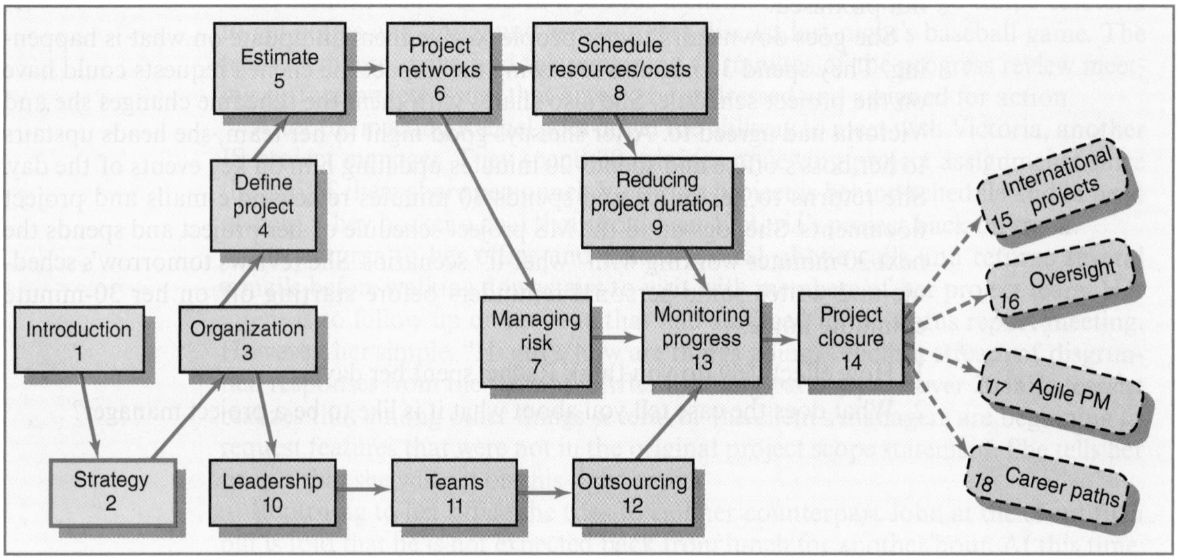

Organization Strategy and Project Selection

The Strategic Management Process: An Overview

The Need for a Project Portfolio Management System

A Portfolio Management System

Selection Criteria

Applying a Selection Model

Managing the Portfolio System

Summary

Appendix 2.1: Request for Proposal (RFP)

Strategy is implemented through projects. Every project should have a clear link to the organization's strategy.

Strategy is fundamentally deciding how the organization will compete. Organizations use projects to convert strategy into new products, services, and processes needed for success. For example, Intel's major strategy is one of differentiation. Its projects target innovation and time to market. Currently, Intel is directing its strategy toward specialty chips for products other than computers, such as autos, security, cell phones, air controls. Another goal is to reduce project cycle times. Intel, NEC, General Electric, and AT&T have reduced their cycle times by 20–50 percent. Projects and project management play the key role in supporting strategic goals. It is vital for project managers to think and act strategically.

Aligning projects with the strategic goals of the organization is crucial for project success. Today's economic climate is unprecedented by rapid changes in technology, global competition, and financial uncertainty. These conditions make strategy/project alignment even more essential for success. Ensuring a strong link between the strategic plan and projects is a difficult task that demands constant attention from top and middle management.

The larger and more diverse an organization, the more difficult it is to create and maintain this strong link. Companies today are under enormous pressure to manage a process that clearly aligns projects to organization strategy. Ample evidence still suggests that many organizations have not developed a process that clearly aligns project selection to the strategic plan. The result is poor utilization of the organization's resources—people, money, equipment, and core competencies. Conversely, organizations that have a coherent link of projects to strategy have more cooperation across the organization, perform better on projects, and have fewer projects.

How can an organization ensure this link and alignment? The answer requires integration of projects with the strategic plan. Integration assumes the existence of a strategic plan and a process for prioritizing projects by their contribution to the plan. A crucial factor to ensure the success of integrating the plan with projects lies in the creation of a process that is open and transparent for all participants to review. This chapter presents an overview of the importance of strategic planning and the process for developing a strategic plan. Typical problems encountered when strategy and projects are not linked are noted. A generic methodology that ensures integration by creating very strong linkages of project selection and priority to the strategic plan is then discussed. The intended outcomes are clear organization focus, best use of scarce organization resources (people, equipment, capital), and improved communication across projects and departments.

SNAPSHOT FROM PRACTICE HP's Strategy Revision*

August 18, 2011, Hewlett Packard announced a dramatic change in strategy. Leo Apotheker, CEO of the world's largest seller of personal computers, decided to exit the low margin PC unit. He wanted to redirect HP to *business software, networking, and storage,* which carry higher margins. Unfortunately, Apotheker failed to communicate the strategic change effectively, lost credibility, and was dismissed. He was replaced by Meg Whitman, while controversy over the company's haphazard direction continued.

THE PC MARKET

Fundamentally, the PC has become a commodity. Although the HP personal computer unit represents nearly a third of total revenue and about 19 percent of HP's profit, growth and profits are slowing. Increased competition from Asia, for example, Lenovo, will continue to erode margins. More importantly, increasing use of smartphones and tablets is already cannibalizing the PC market.

FUTURE MARKETS

In HP's words, their new corporatewide mission *is to provide seamless, secure, context-aware experiences for a connected world.** Business software, networking, and storage can be nicely connected for a grand corporate strategy to meet the new mission.

IBM, Google, Oracle, and Microsoft already dominate the software industry. They and others are all moving to collect and use unstructured data to enhance decision making and/or client requests across numerous industries. All are developing better search engines to sort through any manner of data for information relevant to the search. These dominant players leave HP in a catch-up mode.

HP's plan to compete requires quick action. Executing the software strategy will require purchasing smaller firms or developing collaborative relationships to acquire specific expertise. HP has made two purchases to buttress the new strategy. Autonomy Corporation, UK, will concentrate on mining and searching large structured and unstructured data. Their purchase of Vertica provides an analytics platform for large structured and unstructured data. We can expect to see more purchases that connect software, storage, and networking, which will complement HP's current expertise in the server business.

EXECUTING STRATEGY

HP faces risks. HP has bet the farm on this revised strategy that looks similar to what IBM started over a decade ago. IBM has spent billions and ten years of development to perfect their systems (see previous Watson Snapshot). HP is in a "follower" position. This means gaining market share from tough rivals such as IBM, Apple, Google, Oracle, and Cisco. Can HP afford to go face-to-face with others in stronger cash positions? Can HP sell off its PC division at a reasonable price?

HP must move quickly to catch up. Executing the new mission statement presents numerous leadership challenges. The changes in HP strategies over the last 15 years have caused confusion and a loss of employee loyalty. Additional changes in organizational culture, along with many new mission critical projects, will place further stress on the organization. HP must be vigilant in selecting, prioritizing, and balancing organizational risk for all projects. HP needs to communicate a coherent strategy that can be executed consistently over time.

Although there are outsiders who have praised or criticized the new strategy, we must wait and see how the details unfold. HP's strategic moves will make interesting case studies for years to come.

* *HP website,* HP newsroom.

This step typically includes an analysis of "who are the customers" and "what are their needs as they (the *customers*) see them."

The next step is an assessment of the internal and external environments. What are the internal strengths and weaknesses of the enterprise? Examples of internal strengths or weaknesses could be core competencies, such as technology, product quality, management talent, low debt, and dealer networks. Managers can alter internal strengths and weaknesses. Opportunities and threats usually represent external forces for change such as technology, industry structure, and competition. Competitive benchmarking tools are sometimes used here to assess current and future directions. Opportunities and threats are the flip sides of each other. That is, a threat can be perceived as an opportunity, or vice versa. Examples of perceived external threats could be a slowing of the economy, a maturing life cycle, exchange rates, or government regulation. Typical opportunities are increasing demand, emerging markets, and demographics. Managers or individual firms have limited opportunities to influence such external environmental factors; however, in recent years notable exceptions have been new technologies such as Apple using the iPod to create a market to sell music. The keys are to attempt to forecast fundamental industry changes and stay in a proactive mode rather than a reactive one. This assessment of the external and internal environments is known as the SWOT analysis (strengths, weaknesses, opportunities, and threats).

From this analysis, critical issues and strategic alternatives are identified. Critical analysis of the strategies includes asking questions: Does the strategy take advantage of our core competencies? Does the strategy exploit our competitive advantage? Does the strategy maximize meeting customers' needs? Does the strategy fit within our acceptable risk range? These strategic alternatives are winnowed down to a critical few that support the basic mission.

Strategy formulation ends with cascading objectives or projects assigned to lower divisions, departments, or individuals. Formulating strategy might range around 20 percent of management's effort, while determining *how* strategy will be implemented might consume 80 percent.

Set Objectives to Achieve Strategies

Objectives translate the organization strategy into specific, concrete, measurable terms. Organizational objectives set targets for all levels of the organization. Objectives pinpoint the direction managers believe the organization should move toward. Objectives answer in detail *where* a firm is headed and *when* it is going to get there. Typically, objectives for the organization cover markets, products, innovation, productivity, quality, finance, profitability, employees, and consumers. In every case, objectives should be as operational as possible. That is, objectives should include a time frame, be measurable, be an identifiable state, and be realistic. Doran created the memory device shown in Exhibit 2.1, which is useful when writing objectives.[2]

Each level below the organizational objectives should support the higher-level objectives in more detail; this is frequently called cascading of objectives. For example, if a firm making leather luggage sets an objective of achieving a 40 percent increase in sales through a research and development strategy, this charge is passed to the marketing, production, and R&D departments. The R&D department accepts the firm's strategy as their objective, and their strategy becomes the design and development of a new "pull-type luggage with hidden retractable wheels." At this point the objective becomes a project to be implemented—to develop the retractable wheel luggage for market within six months within a budget of $200,000. In summary, organizational objectives drive your projects.

EXHIBIT 2.1
Characteristics of Objectives

S	**Specific**	Be specific in targeting an objective
M	**Measurable**	Establish a measurable indicator(s) of progress
A	**Assignable**	Make the objective assignable to one person for completion
R	**Realistic**	State what can realistically be done with available resources
T	**Time related**	State when the objective can be achieved, that is, duration

[2] Doran, G. T., "There's a Smart Way to Write Management Goals and Objectives," *Management Review,* November 1981, pp. 35–36.

Implement Strategies through Projects

Implementation answers the question of *how* strategies will be realized, given available resources. The conceptual framework for strategy implementation lacks the structure and discipline found in strategy formulation. Implementation requires action and completing tasks; the latter frequently means mission-critical projects. Therefore, implementation must include attention to several key areas.

First, completing tasks requires allocation of resources. Resources typically represent funds, people, management talents, technological skills, and equipment. Frequently, implementation of projects is treated as an "addendum" rather than an integral part of the strategic management process. However, multiple objectives place conflicting demands on organizational resources. Second, implementation requires a formal and informal organization that complements and supports strategy and projects. Authority, responsibility, and performance all depend on organization structure and culture. Third, planning and control systems must be in place to be certain project activities necessary to ensure strategies are effectively performed. Fourth, motivating project contributors will be a major factor for achieving project success. Finally, areas receiving more attention in recent years are portfolio management and prioritizing projects. Although the strategy implementation process is not as clear as strategy formulation, all managers realize that, without implementation, success is impossible. Although the four major steps of strategic management process have not been altered significantly over the years, the view of the time horizon in the strategy formulation process has been altered radically in the last two decades. Global competition and rapid innovation require being highly adaptive to short-run changes while being consistent in the longer run.

The Need for a Project Portfolio Management System

Implementation of projects without a strong **priority system** linked to strategy creates problems. Three of the most obvious problems are discussed below. A **project portfolio** system can go a long way to reduce, or even eliminate, the impact of these problems.

Problem 1: The Implementation Gap

In organizations with short product life cycles, it is interesting to note that frequently participation in strategic planning and implementation includes participants from all levels within the organization. However, in perhaps 80 percent of the remaining product and service organizations, top management pretty much formulates strategy and leaves strategy implementation to functional managers. Within these broad constraints, more detailed strategies and objectives are developed by the functional managers. The fact that these objectives and strategies are made *independently* at different levels by functional groups within the organization hierarchy causes manifold problems.

Some symptoms of organizations struggling with strategy disconnect and unclear priorities are presented here.

- Conflicts frequently occur among functional managers and cause lack of trust.
- Frequent meetings are called to establish or renegotiate priorities.
- People frequently shift from one project to another, depending on current priority. Employees are confused about which projects are important.

- People are working on multiple projects and feel inefficient.
- Resources are not adequate.

Because clear linkages do not exist, the organizational environment becomes dysfunctional, confused, and ripe for ineffective implementation of organization strategy and, thus, of projects. The **implementation gap** refers to the lack of understanding and consensus of organization strategy among top and middle-level managers.

A scenario the authors have seen repeated several times follows. Top management picks their top 20 projects for the next planning period, without priorities. Each functional department—marketing, finance, operations, engineering, information technology, and human resources—selects projects from the list. Unfortunately, independent department priorities across projects are not homogenous. A project that rates first in the IT department can rate 10th in the finance department. Implementation of the projects represents conflicts of interest with animosities developing over organization resources.

If this condition exists, how is it possible to effectively implement strategy? The problem is serious. One study found that only about 25 percent of *Fortune 500* executives believe there is a strong linkage, consistency, and/or agreement between the strategies they formulate and implementation. In another study of Deloitte Consulting, Jeff MacIntyre reports, "Only 23 percent of nearly 150 global executives considered their project portfolios aligned with the core business."[3] Middle managers considered organizational strategy to be under the purview of others or not in their realm of influence. It is the responsibility of senior management to set policies that show a distinct link between organizational strategy and objectives and projects that implement those strategies. The research of Fusco suggests the implementation gap and prioritizing projects are still overlooked by many organizations. He surveyed 280 project managers and found that 24 percent of their organizations did not even publish or circulate their objectives; in addition, 40 percent of the respondents reported that priorities among competing projects were not clear, while only 17 percent reported clear priorities.[4]

Problem 2: Organization Politics

Politics exist in every organization and can have a significant influence on which projects receive funding and high priority. This is especially true when the criteria and process for selecting projects are ill-defined and not aligned with the mission of the firm. Project selection may be based not so much on facts and sound reasoning, but rather on the persuasiveness and power of people advocating projects.

The term **"sacred cow"** is often used to denote a project that a powerful, high-ranking official is advocating. Case in point, a marketing consultant confided that he was once hired by the marketing director of a large firm to conduct an independent, external market analysis for a new product the firm was interested in developing. His extensive research indicated that there was insufficient demand to warrant the financing of this new product. The marketing director chose to bury the report and made the consultant promise never to share this information with anyone. The director explained that this new product was the "pet idea" of the new

[3] MacIntyre, J., *PM Network*, vol. 20 (11) November 2006, pp. 32–35.

[4] Fusco, J. C., "Better Policies Provide the Key to Implementing Project Management," *Project Management Journal*, vol. 28 (3) 1997, pp. 38–41.

Each project proposal is then evaluated by its relative contribution/value added to the selected criteria. Values of 0 to a high of 10 are assigned to each criterion for each project. This value represents the project's fit to the specific criterion. For example, project 1 appears to fit well with the strategy of the organization since it is given a value of 8. Conversely, project 1 does nothing to support reducing defects (its value is 0). Finally, this model applies the management weights to each criterion by importance using a value of 1 to 3. For example, ROI and strategic fit have a weight of 3, while urgency and core competencies have weights of 2. Applying the weight to each criterion, the priority team derives the weighted total points for each project. For example, project 5 has the highest value of 102 $[(2 \times 1) + (3 \times 10) + (2 \times 5) + (2.5 \times 10) + (1 \times 0) + (1 \times 8) + (3 \times 9) = 102]$ and project 2 has a low value of 27. If the resources available create a cutoff threshold of 50 points, the priority team would eliminate projects 2 and 4. (Note: Project 4 appears to have some urgency, but it is not classified as a "must" project. Therefore, it is screened with all other proposals.) Project 5 would receive first priority, project *n* second, and so on. In rare cases where resources are severely limited and project proposals are similar in weighted rank, it is prudent to pick the project placing less demand on resources. Weighted multiple criteria models similar to this one are rapidly becoming the dominant choice for prioritizing projects.

At this point in the discussion it is wise to stop and put things into perspective. While selection models like the one above may yield numerical solutions to project selection decisions, models should not make the final *decisions*—the people using the models should. No model, no matter how sophisticated, can capture the total reality it is meant to represent. Models are tools for guiding the evaluation process so that the decision-makers will consider relevant issues and reach a meeting of the minds as to which projects should be supported and not supported. This is a much more subjective process than calculations suggest.

Applying a Selection Model

Project Classification It is not necessary to have exactly the same criteria for the different types of projects discussed above (strategic and operations). However, experience shows most organizations use similar criteria across all types of projects, with perhaps one or two criteria specific to the type of project—e.g., strategic breakthrough versus operational.

Regardless of criteria differences among different types of projects, the most important criterion for selection is the project's fit to the organization strategy. Therefore, this criterion should be consistent across all types of projects and carry a high priority relative to other criteria. This uniformity across all priority models used can keep departments from suboptimizing the use of organization resources. Anyone generating a project proposal should classify their proposal by type, so the appropriate criteria can be used to evaluate their proposal.

Selecting a Model In the past, financial criteria were used almost to the exclusion of other criteria. However, in the last two decades we have witnessed a dramatic shift to include multiple criteria in project selection. Concisely put, profitability alone is simply not an adequate measure of contribution; however, it is still an important criterion, especially for projects that enhance revenue and market share such as breakthrough R&D projects.

Today, senior management is interested in identifying the potential mix of projects that will yield the best use of human and capital resources to maximize return on investment in the long run. Factors such as researching new technology, public image, ethical position, protection of the environment, core competencies, and strategic fit might be important criteria for selecting projects. Weighted scoring criteria seem the best alternative to meet this need.

Weighted scoring models result in bringing projects to closer alignment with strategic goals. If the scoring model is published and available to everyone in the organization, some discipline and credibility are attached to the selection of projects. The number of wasteful projects using resources is reduced. Politics and "sacred cow" projects are exposed. Project goals are more easily identified and communicated using the selection criteria as corroboration. Finally, using a weighted scoring approach helps project managers understand how their project was selected, how their project contributes to organization goals, and how it compares with other projects. Project selection is one of the most important decisions guiding the future success of an organization.

Criteria for project selection are the area where the power of your portfolio starts to manifest itself. New projects are aligned with the strategic goals of the organization. With a clear method for selecting projects in place, project proposals can be solicited.

Sources and Solicitation of Project Proposals

As you would guess, projects should come from anyone who believes his or her project will add value to the organization. However, many organizations restrict proposals from specific levels or groups within the organization. This could be an opportunity lost. Good ideas are not limited to certain types or classes of organization stakeholders. Encourage and keep solicitations open to all sources—internal and external sponsors.

Figure 2.4A provides an example of a proposal form for an automatic vehicular tracking (Automatic Vehicle Location) public transportation project. Figure 2.4B presents a preliminary risk analysis for a 500-acre wind farm. Many organizations use risk analysis templates to gain a quick insight of a project's inherent risks. Risk factors depend on the organization and type of projects. This information is useful in balancing the project portfolio and identifying major risks when executing the project. Project risk analysis is the subject of Chapter 7.

In some cases organizations will solicit ideas for projects when the knowledge requirements for the project are not available in the organization. Typically, the organization will issue an RFP (Request for Proposal) to contractors/vendors with adequate experience to implement the project. In one example, a hospital published an RFP that asked for a bid to design and build a new operating room that uses the latest technology. Several architecture firms submitted bids to the hospital. The bids for the project were evaluated internally against other potential projects. When the project was accepted as a go, other criteria were used to select the best qualified bidder. See Appendix 2.1 of this chapter for a complete description of requests for proposal (RFP).

FIGURE 2.5
Project Screening Process

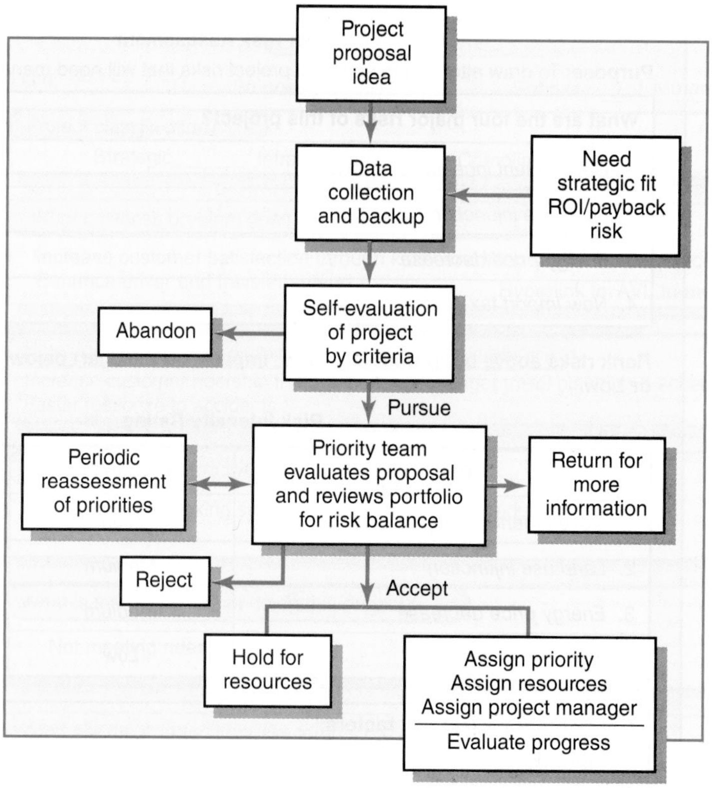

creates an opportunity to fix field problems, has no effect on sales, and will have major impact on customer service. On these three objectives, project 26 would receive a score of 265 [99 + 0 + (2 × 83)]. Individual weighted scores are totaled for each project and are used to prioritize projects.

Responsibility for Prioritizing

Prioritizing can be an uncomfortable exercise for managers. But prioritizing projects is a major responsibility for senior management. Prioritizing means discipline, accountability, responsibility, constraints, reduced flexibility, and loss of power. Top management commitment means more than giving a blessing to the priority system; it means management will have to rank and weigh, in concrete terms, the objectives and strategies they believe to be most critical to the organization. This public declaration of commitment can be risky if the ranked objectives later prove to be poor choices, but setting the course for the organization is top management's job. The good news is, if management is truly trying to direct the organization to a strong future position, a good project priority system supports their efforts and develops a culture in which everyone is contributing to the goals of the organization.

Managing the Portfolio System

Managing the portfolio takes the selection system one step higher in that the merits of a particular project are assessed within the context of existing projects. At the same time it involves monitoring and adjusting selection criteria to reflect

FIGURE 2.6
Priority Screening Analysis

			Project number			
Must objectives		**Must meet if impacts**	**...26**	**27**	**28**	**29**
All activities meet current legal, safety, and environmental standards		Yes-Meets objective No-Does not meet obj N/A-No impact	**n/a**			
All new products will have a complete market analysis		Yes-Meets objective No-Does not meet obj N/A-No impact	**yes**			
Want objectives	**Relative Importance 1-100**	**Single project impact definitions**	**Weighted score**	**Weighted score**	**Weighted score**	**Weighted score**
Provides immediate response to field problems	**99**	0 Does not address 1 = Opportunity to fix 2 Urgent problem	**99**			
Create $5 million in new sales by 20xx	**88**	0 < $100,000 1 = $100,000–500,000 2 > $500,000	**0**			
Improve external customer service	**83**	0 Minor impact 1 = Significant impact 2 Major impact	**166**			
↓						
Total weighted score						
Priority						

the strategic focus of the organization. This requires constant effort. The priority system can be managed by a small group of key employees in a small organization. Or, in larger organizations, the priority system can be managed by the project office or a governance team of senior managers.

Senior Management Input

Management of a portfolio system requires two major inputs from senior management. First, senior management must provide guidance in establishing selection criteria that strongly align with the current organization strategies. Second, senior management must annually decide how they wish to balance the available organizational resources (people and capital) among the different types of projects. A preliminary decision of balance must be made by top management (e.g., 20 percent compliance, 50 percent strategic, and 30 percent operational) before project selection takes place, although the balance may be changed when the projects submitted are reviewed. Given these inputs the priority team or project office can carry out its the authors prefer multi-weighted scoring models. These models keep project selection highly focused on alignment with organization strategy. Weighted scoring models require major effort in establishing the criteria and weights.

Key Terms

Implementation gap, 33
Net present value, 37
Organization politics, 33
Payback, 37
Priority system, 32
Priority team, 40
Project portfolio, 32
Project screening matrix, 41
Sacred cow, 33
Strategic management process, 28

Review Questions

1. Describe the major components of the strategic management process.
2. Explain the role projects play in the strategic management process.
3. How are projects linked to the strategic plan?
4. The portfolio of projects is typically represented by compliance, strategic, and operations projects. What impact can this classification have on project selection?
5. Why does the priority system described in this chapter require that it be open and published? Does the process encourage bottom-up initiation of projects? Does it discourage some projects? Why?
6. Why should an organization not rely only on ROI to select projects?
7. Discuss the pros and cons of the checklist versus the weighted factor method of selecting projects.

Exercises

1. You manage a hotel resort located on the South Beach on the Island of Kauai in Hawaii. You are shifting the focus of your resort from a traditional fun-in-the-sun destination to eco-tourism. (Eco-tourism focuses on environmental awareness and education.) How would you classify the following projects in terms of compliance, strategic, and operational?

   a. Convert the pool heating system from electrical to solar power.
   b. Build a 4-mile nature hiking trail.
   c. Renovate the horse barn.
   d. Launch a new promotional campaign with Hawaii Airlines.
   e. Convert 12 adjacent acres into a wildlife preserve.
   f. Update all the bathrooms in condos that are 10 years old or older.
   g. Change hotel brochures to reflect eco-tourism image.
   h. Test and revise disaster response plan.
   i. Introduce wireless Internet service in café and lounge areas.

   How easy was it to classify these projects? What made some projects more difficult than others? What do you think you now know that would be useful for managing projects at the hotel?

2.* Two new software projects are proposed to a young, start-up company. The Alpha project will cost $150,000 to develop and is expected to have annual net cash flow of $40,000. The Beta project will cost $200,000 to develop and is expected to have annual net cash flow of $50,000. The company is very concerned about their cash flow. Using the payback period, which project is better from a cash flow standpoint? Why?

3. A five-year project has a projected net cash flow of $15,000, $25,000, $30,000, $20,000, and $15,000 in the next five years. It will cost $50,000 to implement the project. If the required rate of return is 20 percent, conduct a discounted cash flow calculation to determine the NPV.
4. You work for the 3T company, which expects to earn at least 18 percent on its investments. You have to choose between two similar projects. Below is the cash information for each project. Your analysts predict that inflation rate will be a stable 3 percent over the next 7 years. Which of the two projects would you fund if the decision is based only on financial information? Why?

Omega Year	Inflow	Outflow	Netflow	Alpha Year	Inflow	Outflow	Netflow
Y0	0	$225,000	−225,000	Y0	0	$300,000	−300,000
Y1	0	190,000	−190,000	Y1	$ 50,000	100,000	−50,000
Y2	$ 150,000	0	150,000	Y2	150,000	0	150,000
Y3	220,000	30,000	190,000	Y3	250,000	50,000	200,000
Y4	215,000	0	215,000	Y4	250,000	0	250,000
Y5	205,000	30,000	175,000	Y5	200,000	50,000	150,000
Y6	197,000	0	197,000	Y6	180,000	0	180,000
Y7	100,000	30,000	70,000	Y7	120,000	30,000	90,000
Total	1,087,000	505,000	582,000	Total	1,200,000	530,000	670,000

5.* You are the head of the project selection team at SIMSOX. Your team is considering three different projects. Based on past history, SIMSOX expects at least a rate of return of 20 percent. Your financial advisors predict inflation to remain at 3 percent into the foreseeable future.

Given the following information for each project, which one should be SIMSOX first priority? Should SIMSOX fund any of the other projects? If so, what should be the order of priority based on return on investment?

Project: **Dust Devils**

Year	Investment	Revenue Stream
0	$500,000	0
1		50,000
2		250,000
3		350,000

Project: **Ospry**

Year	Investment	Revenue Stream
0	$250,000	0
1		75,000
2		75,000
3		75,000
4		50,000

* The solution to these exercises can be found in Appendix One.

Project: **Voyagers**

Year	Investment	Revenue Stream
0	$75,000	0
1		15,000
2		25,000
3		50,000
4		50,000
5		150,000

6. You are the head of the project selection team at Broken Arrow records. Your team is considering three different recording projects. Based on past history, Broken Arrow expects at least a rate of return of 20 percent. Your financial advisors predict inflation to remain at 2 percent into the foreseeable future.

   Given the following information for each project, which one should be Broken Arrow's first priority? Should Broken Arrow fund any of the other projects? If so, what should be the order of priority based on return on investment?

Recording Project: **Time Fades Away**

Year	Investment	Revenue Stream
0	$600,000	0
1		600,000
2		75,000
3		20,000
4		15,000
5		10,000

Recording Project: **On the Beach**

Year	Investment	Revenue Stream
0	$400,000	0
1		400,000
2		100,000
3		25,000
4		20,000
5		10,000

Recording Project: **Tonight's the Night**

Year	Investment	Revenue Stream
0	$200,000	0
1		200,000
2		125,000
3		75,000
4		20,000
5		10,000

7. The Custom Bike Company has set up a weighted scoring matrix for evaluation of potential projects. Below are five projects under consideration.
   a. Using the scoring matrix below, which project would you rate highest? Lowest?
   b. If the weight for "Strong Sponsor" is changed from 2.0 to 5.0, will the project selection change? What are the three highest weighted project scores with this new weight?
   c. Why is it important that the weights mirror critical strategic factors?

Project Screening Matrix

Criteria / Weight	Strong sponsor	Supports business strategy	Urgency	10% of sales from new products	Competition	Fill market gap	Weighted total
	2.0	5.0	4.0	3.0	1.0	3.0	
Project 1	9	5	2	0	2	5	
Project 2	3	7	2	0	5	1	
Project 3	6	8	2	3	6	8	
Project 4	1	0	5	10	6	9	
Project 5	3	10	10	1	8	0	

References

Adler, P. S., et al., "Getting the Most Out of Your Product Development Process," *Harvard Business Review,* vol. 74 (2), pp. 134–52.

Benko, C., and F. W. McFarlan, *Connecting the Dots: Aligning Projects With Objectives in Unpredictable Times* (Boston: Harvard Business School Press, 2003).

Bigelow, D., "Want to Ensure Quality? Think Project Portfolio Management," *PM Network,* vol. 16 (1) April 2002, pp. 16–17.

Bloomberg Businessweek, "IBM Wants to Put Watson in Your Pocket," September 17–23, 2012, pp. 41–42.

Boyer, C., "Make Profit Your Priority," *PM Network,* vol. 15 (10) October 2003, pp. 37–42.

Cohen, D., and R. Graham, *The Project Manager's MBA* (San Francisco: Jossey-Bass, 2001), pp. 58–59.

Crawford, L., B. Hobbs, and J. R. Turne, "Aligning Capability with Strategy: Categorizing of Projects to Do the Right Projects and Do Them Right," *Project Management Journal,* vol. 37 (2) June 2006, pp. 38–50.

Descamps, J. P., "Mastering the Dance of Change: Innovation as a Way of Life," *Prism,* Second Quarter, 1999, pp. 61–67.

Doran, G. T., "There's a Smart Way to Write Management Goals and Objectives," *Management Review,* November 1981, pp. 35–36.

Floyd, S. W., and B. Woolridge, "Managing Strategic Consensus: The Foundation of Effectiveness Implementation," *Academy of Management Executives,* vol. 6 (4) 1992, pp. 27–39.

Foti, R., "Louder Than Words," *PM Network,* December 2002, pp. 22–29. Also see Foti, R., "Make Your Case, Not All Projects Are Equal," *PM Network,* vol. 31(7) 2003, pp. 35–43.

Frank, L., "On Demand," *PM Network,* vol. 18 (4) April 2004, pp. 58–62.

Friedman, Thomas L., *Hot, Flat, and Crowded* (New York: Farrar, Straus, and Giroux, 2008).

Fusco, J. C., "Better Policies Provide the Key to Implementing Project Management," *Project Management Journal,* vol. 28 (3) 1997, pp. 38–41.

Helm, J., and K. Remington, "Effective Project Sponsorship: An Evaluation of the Executive Sponsor in Complex Infrastructure Projects by Senior Project Managers," *Project Management Journal,* vol. 36 (1) September 2005, pp. 51–61.

Hutchens, G., "Doing the Numbers," *PM Network,* vol. 16 (4) March 2002, p. 20.

Johnson, R. E., "Scrap Capital Project Evaluations," *Chief Financial Officer,* May 1998, p. 14.

Kaplan, R. S., and D. P. Norton, "The Balanced Scorecard—Measures That Drive Performance," *Harvard Business Review,* January–February 1992, pp. 73–79. Also see Kaplan, Robert, http;//balancedscorecard.org.

Kenny, J., "Effective Project Management for Strategic Innovation and Change in an Organizational Context," *Project Management Journal,* vol. 34 (1) 2003, pp. 45–53.

Kharbanda, O. P., and J. K. Pinto, *What Made Gertie Gallop: Learning from Project Failures* (New York: Van Nostrand Reinhold, 1996), pp. 106–11, 263–83.

Korte, R. F., and T. J. Chermack, "Changing Organizational Culture with Scenario Planning," *Futures,* vol. 39 (6) August 2007, pp. 645–56.

Leifer, R., C. M. McDermott, G. C. O'Connor, L. S. Peters, M. Price, and R. W. Veryzer, *Radical Innovation: How Mature Companies Can Outsmart Upstarts* (Boston: Harvard Business School Press, 2000).

MacIntyre, J., *PM Network,* vol. 20 (11) November 2006, pp. 32–35.

Magretta, Joan, *Understanding Michael Porter: The Essential Guide to Competition and Strategy* (Boston: Harvard Business Press Book, 2011).

Matheson, D., and J. Matheson, *The Smart Organization* (Boston: Harvard Business School Press, 1998), pp. 203–09.

Milosevic, D. Z., and S. Srivannaboon, "A Theoretical Framework for Aligning Project Management with Business Strategy," *Project Management Journal,* vol. 37 (3) August 2006, pp. 98–110.

Morris, P. W., and A. Jamieson, "Moving from Corporate Strategy to Project Strategy," *Project Management Journal,* vol. 36 (4) December 2005, pp. 5–18.

Motta, Silva, and Rogério Hermida Quintella, "Assessment of Non-Financial Criteria in the Selection of Investment Projects for Seed Capital Funding: The Contribution of Scientometrics and Patentometrics," *Journal of Technology Management Innovation,* vol. 7 (3) 2012.

PMI, "PMI's Pulse of the Profession," March 2012, Project Management Institute, p. 7.

Raskin, P., et al., *Great Transitions: The Promise and Lure of the Times Ahead,* retrieved 6-3-08. See *www.gtinitiative.org/documents/Great_Transitions.pdf*

Schwartz, Peter, and Doug Randall, "An Abrupt Climate Change Scenario and its Implications for United States National Security," Global Business Network, Inc., October 2003.

Shenhar, A., "Strategic Project Leadership: Focusing Your Project on Business Success," *Proceedings of the Project Management Institute Annual Seminars & Symposium,* San Antonio, Texas, October 3–10, 2002, CD. Also see Shenhar, Aaron, *Reinventing Project Management* (Harvard Business School, 2007).

Smith, D. K., and R. C. Alexander, *Fumbling the Future: How Xerox Invented, Then Ignored the First Personal Computer* (New York: Macmillan, 1988).

Swanson, S., "All Things Considered," *PM Network,* vol. 25 (2) February 2011, pp. 36–40.

Woodward, H., "Winning in a World of Limited Project Spending," *Proceedings of the Project Management Institute Global Congress North America,* Baltimore, Maryland, September 18–12, 2003, CD.

Case

Hector Gaming Company

Hector Gaming Company (HGC) is an educational gaming company specializing in young children's educational games. HGC has just completed their fourth year of operation. This year was a banner year for HGC. The company received a large influx of capital for growth by issuing stock privately through an investment banking firm. It appears the return on investment for this past year will be just over 25 percent with zero debt! The growth rate for the last two years has been approximately 80 percent each year. Parents and grandparents of young children have been buying HGC's products almost as fast as they are developed. Every member of the 56-person firm is enthusiastic and looking forward to helping the firm grow to be the largest and best educational gaming company in the world. The founder of the firm, Sally Peters, has been written up in *Young Entrepreneurs* as "the young entrepreneur to watch." She has been able to develop an organization culture in which all stakeholders are committed to innovation, continuous improvement, and organization learning.

Last year, 10 top managers of HGC worked with McKinley Consulting to develop the organization's strategic plan. This year the same 10 managers had a retreat in Aruba to formulate next year's strategic plan using the same process suggested by McKinley Consulting. Most executives seem to have a consensus of where the firm should go in the intermediate and long term. But there is little consensus on how this should be accomplished. Peters, now president of HGC, feels she may be losing control. The frequency of conflicts seems to be increasing. Some individuals are always requested for any new project created. When resource conflicts occur among projects, each project manager believes his or her project is most important. More projects are not meeting deadlines and are coming in over budget. Yesterday's management meeting revealed some top HGC talent have been working on an international business game for college students. This project does not fit the organization vision or market niche. At times it seems everyone is marching to his or her own drummer. Somehow more focus is needed to ensure everyone agrees on *how* strategy should be implemented, given the resources available to the organization.

Yesterday's meeting alarmed Peters. These emerging problems are coming at a bad time. Next week HGC is ramping up the size of the organization, number of new products per year, and marketing efforts. Fifteen new people will join HGC next month. Peters is concerned that policies be in place that will ensure the new people are used most productively. An additional potential problem looms on the horizon. Other gaming companies have noticed the success HGC is having in their niche market; one company tried to hire a key product development employee away from HGC. Peters wants HGC to be ready to meet any potential competition head on and to discourage any new entries into their market. Peters knows HGC is project driven; however, she is not as confident that she has a good handle on how such an organization should be managed—especially with such a fast growth rate and potential competition closer to becoming a reality. The magnitude of emerging problems demands quick attention and resolution.

Peters has hired you as a consultant. She has suggested the following format for your consulting contract. You are free to use another format if it will improve the effectiveness of the consulting engagement.

What is our major problem?

Identify some symptoms of the problem.

What is the major cause of the problem?

Provide a detailed action plan that attacks the problem. Be specific and provide examples that relate to HGC.

Case

Film Prioritization

The purpose of this case is to give you experience in using a project priority system that ranks proposed projects by their contribution to the organization's objectives and strategic plan.

COMPANY PROFILE

The company is the film division for a large entertainment conglomerate. The main office is located in Anaheim, California. In addition to the feature film division, the conglomerate includes theme parks, home videos, a television channel, interactive games, and theatrical productions. The company has been enjoying steady growth over the past 10 years. Last year total revenues increased by 12 percent to $21.2 billion. The company is engaged in negotiations to expand its theme park empire to mainland China and Poland. The film division generated $274 million in revenues, which was an increase of 7 percent over the past year. Profit margin was down 3 percent to 16 percent because of the poor response to three of the five major film releases for the year.

COMPANY MISSION

The mission for the firm:

> Our overriding objective is to create shareholder value by continuing to be the world's premier entertainment company from a creative, strategic, and financial standpoint.

The film division supports this mission by producing four to six high-quality, family entertainment films for mass distribution each year. In recent years, the CEO of the company has advocated that the firm take a leadership position in championing environmental concerns.

COMPANY "MUST" OBJECTIVES

Every project must meet the must objectives as determined by executive management. It is important that selected film projects not violate such objectives of high strategic priority. There are three must objectives:

1. All projects meet current legal, safety, and environmental standards.
2. All film projects should receive a PG or lower advisory rating.
3. All projects should not have an adverse effect on current or planned operations within the larger company.

COMPANY "WANT" OBJECTIVES

Want objectives are assigned weights for their relative importance. Top management is responsible for formulating, ranking, and weighting objectives to ensure that projects support the company's strategy and mission. The following is a list of the company's want objectives:

1. Be nominated for and win an academy award for Best Animated Feature or Best Picture of the Year.
2. Generate additional merchandise revenue (action figures, dolls, interactive games, music CDs).
3. Raise public consciousness about environmental issues and concerns.
4. Generate profit in excess of 18 percent.
5. Advance the state of the art in film animation, and preserve the firm's reputation.
6. Provide the basis for the development of a new ride at a company-owned theme park.

ASSIGNMENT

You are a member of the priority team in charge of evaluating and selecting film proposals. Use the provided evaluation form to formally evaluate and rank each proposal. Be prepared to report your rankings and justify your decisions.

PROJECT PROPOSAL 6: KEIKO—ONE WHALE OF A STORY

The story of Keiko, the famous killer whale, will be told by an imaginary offspring Seiko, who in the distant future is telling her children about their famous grandfather. The big-budget film will integrate actual footage of the whale within a realistic animated environment using state-of-the-art computer imagery. The story will reveal how Keiko responded to his treatment by humans.

Probability	80%	50%	20%
ROI	6%	18%	25%

PROJECT PROPOSAL 7: GRAND ISLAND

The true story of a group of junior-high biology students who discover that a fertilizer plant is dumping toxic wastes into a nearby river. The moderate-budget film depicts how students organize a grassroots campaign to fight local bureaucracy and ultimately force the fertilizer plant to restore the local ecosystem.

Probability	80%	50%	20%
ROI	9%	15%	20%

Case

Fund Raising Project Selection case

The purpose of this "case exercise" is to provide you with experience in using a project selection process that ranks proposed projects by their contribution to an organization's mission and strategy.

FUND RAISING PROJECT

Assume you are a member of a class on project management. Each student will join a team of 5–7 students who will be responsible for creating, planning and executing a fund raising project for a designated charity. The fund raising project has two goals: (1) raise money for a worthy cause and (2) provide an opportunity for all team members to practice project management skills and techniques.

In addition to completing the project a number of deliverables are required to complete this assignment. These deliverables include:

a) Project Proposal
b) Implementation Plan
c) Risk Management Plan
d) Status Report
e) Project Reflections Presentation
f) Project Retrospective/Audit

Approved projects will receive $250 seed money to be reimbursed upon completion of the project.

"MUST" OBJECTIVES

Every project must meet the "must" objectives as determined by the instructor. There are four must objectives:

1. All projects must be safe, legal and comply with university policies.
2. All projects must be capable of earning at least $500.

3. All projects must be able to be completed within nine weeks.
4. All projects must provide an opportunity for every member of the project team to experience and learn about project management.

Among the factors to consider for the last objective would be the extent there is meaningful work for every member of the team, the degree of coordination required, the extent the team will have to work with external stakeholders, and the complexity of the project.

"WANT" OBJECTIVES

In addition to the must objectives, there are "want" objectives that the instructor would like to achieve. The following is a list of these objectives:

1. Earn more than $500 for a charity
2. Increase public awareness of the charity
3. Provide a resume worthy experience for students
4. Be featured on local TV news
5. Be fun to do

ASSIGNMENT

You are a member of the class priority team in charge of evaluating and approving fund raising projects. Use the provided proposal evaluation form to formally evaluate and rank each proposal. Be prepared to report your rankings and justify your decision. You should assume that these projects would be held at your university or college.

FUND RAISING PROPOSALS

PROJECT PROPOSAL 1: HOOPS FOR HOPE

The project is a three-on-three basketball tournament to raise money for the Down Syndrome Association. The tournament will consist of three brackets: Co-ed, Male, and Female teams. There will be a $40 entry fee per team and additional funds will be derived from the sale of commemorative T-shirts ($10). Winning teams will receive gift baskets consisting of donations from local businesses and restaurants. The event will be held at the university recreational center.

PROJECT PROPOSAL 2: SINGING FOR SMILES

The project will hold a karaoke competition with celebrity judges at a popular campus night spot. Funds will be raised by $5 admission at the door and a raffle for prizes donated by local businesses. Funds will be donated to Smile Train, an international organization that performs cleft lip surgery at a cost of $250 per child. The event will feature pictures of children born with cleft lips and with every $50 earned a piece of a picture puzzle will be added until the original picture is covered with a smiling face.

PROJECT PROPOSAL 3: HALO FOR HEROES

The project will be a Halo video game competition to be held over the weekend utilizing the College's big screen electronic classrooms. Teams of 4 players will play each other in a single elimination tournament with the grand prize being a Sony Play Station 3 donated by a local video game store. Entry fee is 24$ per team and individual players will be able to play in a loser's bracket for 5$. All proceeds will go to the National Military Family Association.

PROJECT PROPOSAL 4: RAFFLE FOR LIFE

Organize a raffle contest. Raffle tickets will be sold for 3$ a piece with the winning ticket worth $300. Each of the six team members will be responsible for selling 50 raffle tickets. All profits will go to the American Cancer Society.

PROJECT PROPOSAL 5: HOLD'EM FOR HUNGER

Organize a Texas Hold'em poker tournament at a campus dining facility. It will cost 20$ to enter the tournament with a $15 buy-in in fee. Prizes include $300, $150, and $50 gift certificates to a large department store. Gift certificates purchased from entry fees. All players will be eligible to win two donated tickets to Men and Women basketball games. Funds raised will go to local county food shelter.

PROJECT PROPOSAL 6: BUILD YOUR OWN BOX

The purpose of this project is to raise awareness of plight of homeless. Students will donate ten dollars to participate in building and living in a cardboard city on the university quad for one night. Building materials will be provided by local recycling centers and hardware stores. Hot soup will be provided by the team at midnight to all participants. Proceeds for go to the local homeless shelter.

Project Priority Evaluation Form

Must objectives		Must meet if impacts	1	2	3	4	5	6	7
Be safe, legal, & comply with University Policies		Y = yes N = no							
Earn at least $500		Y = yes N = no							
Can be completed within 9 weeks		Y = yes N = no							
Opportunity to learn Project Management		Y = yes N = no							
Want objectives	**Relative Importance 1–100**	**Single project impact definitions**							
Earning potential	**90**	0: 500–750 1: 750–1500 2: >$1500 3: >$2000							
Fun	**30**	0: None 1: Some fun 2: A lot of fun							
Increase awareness of charity	**30**	0: No potential 1: Low potential 2: High potential							
Resume worthy	**40**	0: No potential 1: Low potential 2: High potential							
Be featured on local TV news	**40**	0: No potential 1: Low potential 2: High potential							
		Total weighted score							
		Priority							

Appendix 2.1

Request for Proposal (RFP)

Once an organization selects a project, the customer or project manager is frequently responsible for developing a request for proposal (RFP) for the project or sections of the project.

The responsible project manager will require input data from all stakeholders connected to the activities covered in the RFP. The RFP will be announced to external contractors/vendors with adequate experience to implement the project. For example, government projects frequently advertise with a "request for proposal" to outside contractors for roads, buildings, airports, military hardware, space vehicles. Similarly, businesses use RFPs to solicit bids for building a clean room, developing a new manufacturing process, delivering software for insurance billing, conducting a market survey. In all of these examples, requirements and features must be in enough detail that contractors have a clear description of the final deliverable that will meet the customer's needs. In most cases the RFP also specifies an expected format for the contractor's bid proposal so the responses of different contractors can be fairly evaluated. Although we typically think of RFPs for external contractors, in some organizations RFPs are used internally; that is, the organization sends out an RFP to different divisions or departments.

The content of the RFP is extremely important. In practice, the most common error is to offer an RFP that lacks sufficient detail. This lack of detail typically results in conflict issues, misunderstandings, often legal claims between the contractor and owner, and, in addition, an unsatisfied customer. All RFPs are different, but the outline in Figure A2.1 is a good starting point for the development of a detailed RFP. Each step is briefly described next.

1. Summary of needs and request for action. The background and a simple description of the final project deliverable are given first. For example, through simulated war games, the U.S. Navy has found their giant warships of the past are too vulnerable against today's technology (an example is the Silkworm antiship missiles). In addition, the Navy's mission has shifted to supporting ground forces and peacekeeping missions, which require getting closer to shore. As a result, the Navy is revamping ships for near-shore duty. The Navy will select three designs for further refinement from the responses to its RFP. In general, it is expected that the new ship will be capable of at least 55 knots, measure between 80 and 250 feet in length, and be fitted with radar absorbing panels to thwart guided missiles.

FIGURE A2.1
Request for Proposal

1. Summary of needs and request for action
2. Statement of work (SOW) detailing the scope and major deliverables
3. Deliverable specifications/requirements, features, and tasks
4. Responsibilities—vendor and customer
5. Project schedule
6. Costs and payment schedule
7. Type of contract
8. Experience and staffing
9. Evaluation criteria

2. Statement of work (SOW) detailing the scope and major deliverables. For example, if the project involves a market research survey, the major deliverables could be design, data collection, data analysis, and providing recommendations by February 21, 2014, for a cost not to exceed $300,000.

3. Deliverable specifications/requirements, features, and tasks. This step should be very comprehensive so bid proposals from contractors can be validated and later used for control. Typical specifications cover physical features such as size, quantity, materials, speed, and color. For example, an IT project might specify requirements for hardware, software, and training in great detail. Tasks required to complete deliverables can be included if they are known.

4. Responsibilities—vendor and customer. Failing to spell out the responsibilities for both parties is notorious for leading to serious problems when the contractor implements the project. For example, who pays for what? (If the contractor is to be on site, will the contractor be required to pay for office space?) What are the limits and exclusions for the contractor? (For example, who will supply test equipment?) What communication plan will be used by the contractor and owner? If escalation of an issue becomes necessary, what process will be used? How will progress be evaluated? Well-defined responsibilities will avoid many unforeseen problems later.

5. Project schedule. This step is concerned with getting a "hard" schedule which can be used for control and evaluating progress. Owners are usually very demanding in meeting the project schedule. In today's business environment, time-to-market is a major "hot button" that influences market share, costs, and profits. The schedule should spell out what, who, and when.

6. Costs and payment schedule. The RFP needs to set out very clearly how, when, and the process for determining costs and conditions for progress payments.

7. Type of contract. Essentially there are two types of contracts—fixed-price and cost-plus. Fixed-price contracts agree on a price or lump sum in advance, and it remains as long as there are no changes to the scope provisions of the agreement. This type is preferred in projects that are well defined with predictable costs and minimal risks. The contractor must exercise care estimating cost because any underestimating of costs will cause the contractor's profit to be reduced. In cost-plus contracts the contractor is reimbursed for all or some of the expenses incurred during performance of the contract. This fee is negotiated in advance and usually involves a percent of total costs. "Time and materials" plus a profit factor are typical of cost-plus contracts. Both types of contracts can include incentive clauses for superior performance in time and cost, or in some cases, penalties—for example, missing the opening date of a new sports stadium.

8. Experience and staffing. The ability of the contractor to implement the project may depend on specific skills; this necessary experience should be specified, along with assurance such staff will be available for this project.

9. Evaluation criteria. The criteria for evaluating and awarding the project contract should be specified. For example, selection criteria frequently include methodology, price, schedule, and experience; in some cases these criteria are weighted. Use of the outline in Figure A2.1 will help to ensure key items in the proposal are not omitted. A well-prepared RFP will provide contractors with sufficient guidelines to prepare a proposal that clearly meets the project and customer's needs.

SELECTION OF CONTRACTOR FROM BID PROPOSALS

Interested contractors respond to project RFPs with a written bid proposal. It is likely that several contractors will submit bid proposals to the customer.

The final step in the RFP process is to select the contractor who best meets the requirements requested in the RFP. The selection criteria given in the RFP are used to evaluate which contractor is awarded the contract to implement the project. Losing contractors should be given an explanation of the key factors that led to the selection of the winning contractor/vendor; appreciation for their participation and effort should be acknowledged. See Figure A2.2, Contractor Evaluation Template, adapted from one used in practice.

FIGURE A2.2 Contractor Evaluation Template

Contractor Evaluation Template	**Maximum Weight**	**Proposal 1**	**Proposal 2**	**Proposal 3**	**Proposal 4**
Contractor qualifications	Weight = 10				
Technical skills available	Weight = 20				
Understanding of contract and conditions	Weight = 5				
Financial strength to implement project	Weight = 15				
Understanding of proposal specifications	Weight = 10				
Innovativeness and originality of proposal	Weight = 5				
Reputation for delivering on time and budget	Weight = 15				
Price	Weight = 20				
Total	**100**				

CHAPTER THREE

Organization: Structure and Culture

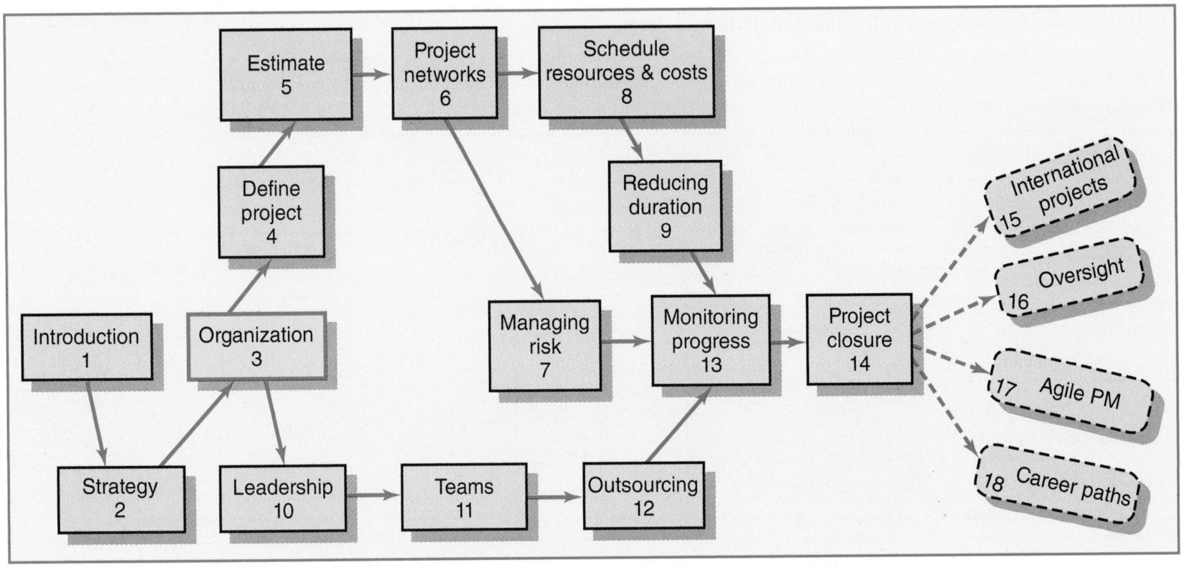

Organization: Structure and Culture

Project Management Structures

What Is the Right Project Management Structure?

Organizational Culture

Implications of Organizational Culture for Organizing Projects

Summary

Matrix management works, but it sure is difficult at times. All matrix managers must keep up their health and take Stress-Tabs.

—A Project Manager

Once management approves a project then the question becomes, how will the project be implemented? This chapter examines three different project management structures used by firms to implement projects: functional organization, dedicated project teams, and matrix structure. Although not exhaustive, these structures and their variant forms represent the major approaches for organizing projects. The advantages and disadvantages of each of these structures are discussed as well as some of the critical factors that might lead a firm to choose one form over others.

Whether a firm chooses to complete projects within the traditional functional organization or through some form of matrix arrangement is only part of the story. Anyone who has worked for more than one organization realizes that there are often considerable differences in how projects are managed within certain firms even with similar structures. Working in a matrix system at AT&T is different from working in a matrix environment at Hewlett-Packard. Many researchers attribute these differences to the organizational culture at AT&T and Hewlett-Packard. A simple explanation of *organizational culture* is that it reflects the "personality" of an organization. Just as each individual has a unique personality, so each organization has a unique culture. Toward the end of this chapter, we examine in more detail what organizational culture is and the impact that the culture of the parent organization has on organizing and managing projects.

Both the project management structure and the culture of the organization constitute major elements of the enterprise environment in which projects are implemented. It is important for project managers and participants to know the "lay of the land" so that they can avoid obstacles and take advantage of pathways to complete their projects.

Project Management Structures

A project management system provides a framework for launching and implementing project activities within a parent organization. A good system appropriately balances the needs of both the parent organization and the project by defining the interface between the project and parent organization in terms of authority, allocation of resources, and eventual integration of project outcomes into mainstream operations. With this in mind, we will start the discussion of project management structures.

FIGURE 3.2
Dedicated Project Team

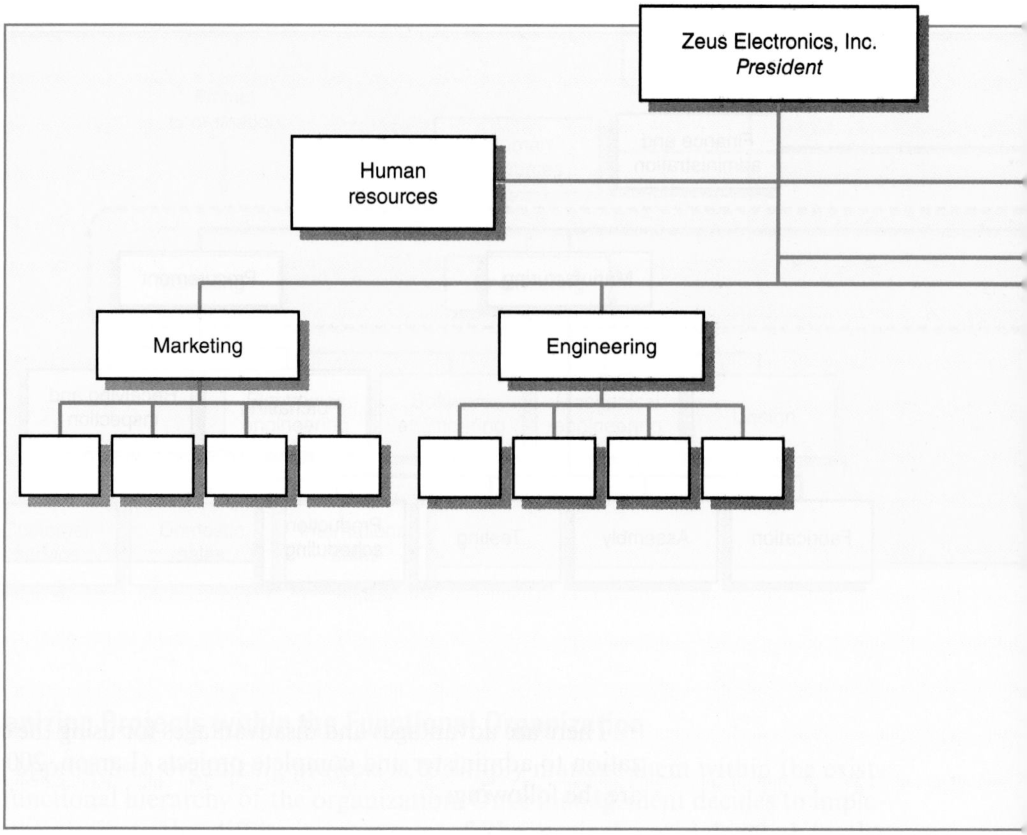

for different units. For example, the marketing department may consider the project urgent while the operations people considered it only of secondary importance. Imagine the tension if the marketing people have to wait for the operations people to complete their segment of the project before they proceed.

2. **Poor Integration.** There may be poor integration across functional units. Functional specialists tend to be concerned only with their segment of the project and not with what is best for the total project.

3. **Slow.** It generally takes longer to complete projects through this functional arrangement. This is in part attributable to slow response time—project information and decisions have to be circulated through normal management channels. Furthermore, the lack of horizontal, direct communication among functional groups contributes to rework as specialists realize the implications of others' actions after the fact.

4. **Lack of Ownership.** The motivation of people assigned to the project can be weak. The project may be seen as an additional burden that is not directly linked to their professional development or advancement. Furthermore, because they are working on only a segment of the project, professionals do not identify with the project.

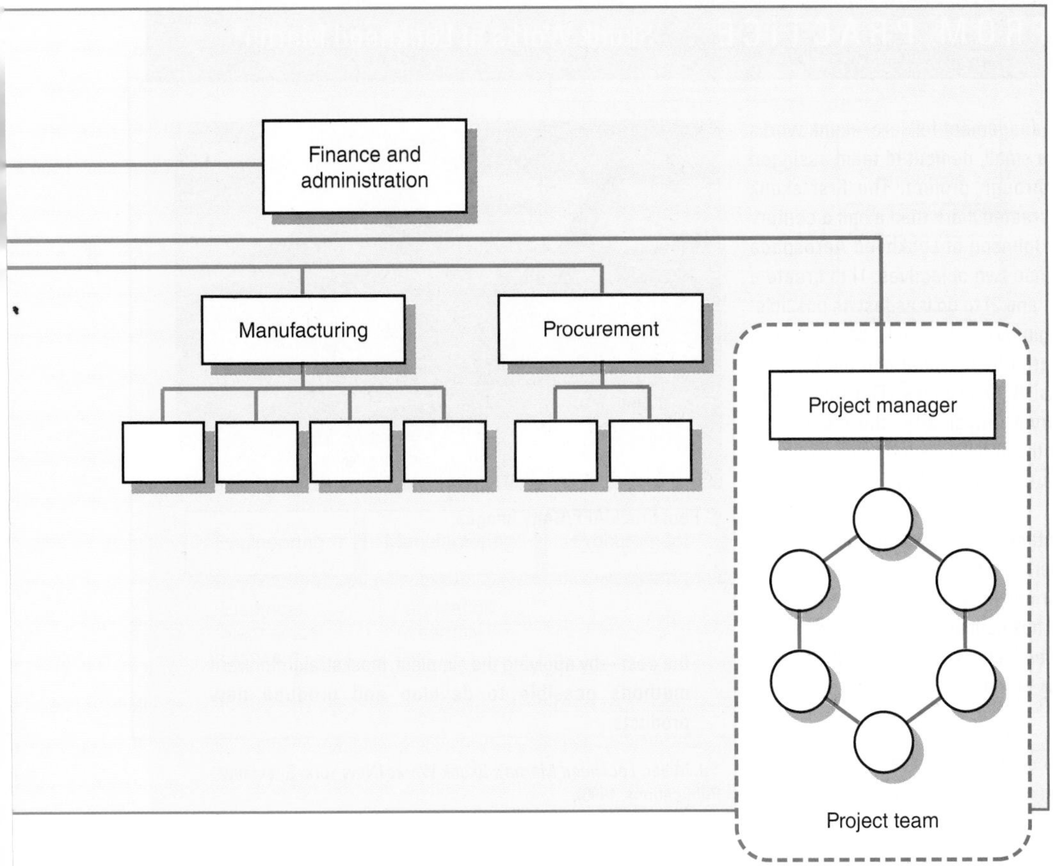

Organizing Projects as Dedicated Teams

At the other end of the structural spectrum is the creation of **dedicated project teams.** These teams operate as separate units from the rest of the parent organization. Usually a full-time project manager is designated to pull together a core group of specialists who work full time on the project. The project manager recruits necessary personnel from both within and outside the parent company. The subsequent team is physically separated from the parent organization and given marching orders to complete the project (see Figure 3.2).

The interface between the parent organization and the project teams will vary. In some cases, the parent organization maintains a tight rein through financial controls. In other cases, firms grant the project manager maximum freedom to get the project done as he sees fit. Lockheed Martin has used this approach to develop next-generation jet airplanes. See Snapshot from Practice: Skunk Works.

In the case of firms where projects are the dominant form of business, such as a construction firm or a consulting firm, the entire organization is designed to support project teams. Instead of one or two special projects, the organization consists of sets of quasi-independent teams working on specific projects. The main responsibility of traditional functional departments is to assist and support these project teams. For example, the marketing department is directed at generating

SNAPSHOT FROM PRACTICE The Birth of the Mac*

One of the advantages of creating dedicated project teams is that project participants from different functional areas can develop into a highly cohesive work team that is strongly committed to completing the project. While such teams often produce Herculean efforts in pursuit of project completion, there is a negative dimension to this commitment that is often referred to in the literature as **projectitis.** A we–they attitude can emerge between project team members and the rest of the organization. The project team succumbs to *hubris* and develops a holier-than-thou attitude that antagonizes the parent organization. People not assigned to the project become jealous of the attention and prestige being showered on the project team, especially when they believe that it is their hard work that is financing the endeavor. The tendency to assign project teams exotic titles such as "Silver Bullets" and "Tiger Teams," as well as give them special perks, tends to intensify the gap between the project team and the parent organization.

© Apic/Getty Images

Such appears to have been the case with Apple's highly successful Macintosh development team. Steve Jobs, who at the time was both the chairman of Apple and the project manager for the Mac team, pampered his team with perks including at-the-desk massages, coolers stocked with freshly squeezed orange juice, a Bosendorfer grand piano, and first-class plane tickets. No other employees at Apple got to travel first class. Jobs considered his team to be the elite of Apple and had a tendency to refer to everyone else as "Bozos" who "didn't get it." Engineers from the Apple II division, which was the bread and butter of Apple's sales, became incensed with the special treatment their colleagues were getting.

One evening at Ely McFly's, a local watering hole, the tensions between Apple II engineers seated at one table and those of a Mac team at another boiled over. Aaron Goldberg, a long-time industry consultant, watched from his barstool as the squabbling escalated. "The Mac guys were screaming, 'We're the future!' The Apple II guys were screaming, 'We're the money!' Then there was a geek brawl. Pocket protectors and pens were flying. I was waiting for a notebook to drop, so they would stop and pick up the papers."

Although comical from a distance, the discord between the Apple II and Mac groups severely hampered Apple's performance during the 1980s. John Sculley, who replaced Steve Jobs as chairman of Apple, observed that Apple had evolved into two "warring companies" and referred to the street between the Apple II and Macintosh buildings as "the DMZ" (demilitarized zone).

* J. Carlton, *Apple: The Inside Story of Intrigue, Egomania, and Business Blunders* (New York: Random House, 1997), pp. 13–14; J. Sculley, *Odyssey: Pepsi to Apple . . . A Journey of Adventure, Ideas, and the Future* (New York: Harper & Row, 1987), pp. 270–79.

help is not formally sanctioned by the organization discourage this from happening.

4. **Difficult Post-Project Transition.** Assigning full-time personnel to a project creates the dilemma of what to do with personnel after the project is completed. If other project work is not available, then the transition back to their original functional departments may be difficult because of their prolonged absence and the need to catch up with recent developments in their functional area.

Organizing Projects within a Matrix Arrangement

One of the biggest management innovations to emerge in the past 40 years has been the matrix organization. **Matrix** management is a hybrid organizational form in which a horizontal project management structure is "overlaid" on the normal functional hierarchy. In a matrix system, there are usually two chains of command, one along functional lines and the other along project lines. Instead of delegating segments of a project to different units or creating an autonomous team, project participants report simultaneously to both functional and project managers.

Companies apply this matrix arrangement in a variety of different ways. Some organizations set up temporary matrix systems to deal with specific projects, while "matrix" may be a permanent fixture in other organizations. Let us first look at its general application and then proceed to a more detailed discussion of finer points. Consider Figure 3.4. There are three projects currently under way: A, B, and C. All three project managers (PM A-C) report to a director of project management, who supervises all projects. Each project has an administrative assistant, although the one for project C is only part time.

Project A involves the design and expansion of an existing production line to accommodate new metal alloys. To accomplish this objective, project A has assigned to it 3.5 people from manufacturing and 6 people from engineering. These individuals are assigned to the project on a part-time or full-time basis, depending on the project's needs during various phases of the project. Project B involves the development of a new product that requires the heavy representation of engineering, manufacturing, and marketing. Project C involves forecasting changing needs of an existing customer base. While these three projects, as well as others, are being completed, the functional divisions continue performing their basic, core activities.

The matrix structure is designed to optimally utilize resources by having individuals work on multiple projects as well as being capable of performing normal functional duties. At the same time, the matrix approach attempts to achieve greater integration by creating and legitimizing the authority of a project manager. In theory, the matrix approach provides a dual focus between functional/technical expertise and project requirements that is missing in either the project team or functional approach to project management. This focus can most easily be seen in the relative input of functional managers and project managers over key project decisions (see Table 3.1).

Different Matrix Forms

In practice there are really different kinds of matrix systems, depending on the relative authority of the project and functional managers (Larson & Gobeli, 1985; Bowen et al., 1994). Here is a thumbnail sketch of the three kinds of matrices:

- **Weak matrix**—This form is very similar to a functional approach with the exception that there is a formally designated project manager responsible for coordinating project activities. Functional managers are responsible for

TABLE 3.1
Division of Project Manager and Functional Manager Responsibilities in a Matrix Structure

Project Manager	Negotiated Issues	Functional Manager
What has to be done?	Who will do the task?	How will it be done?
When should the task be done?	Where will the task be done?	
How much money is available to do the task?	Why will the task be done?	How will the project involvement impact normal functional activities?
How well has the total project been done?	Is the task satisfactorily completed?	How well has the functional input been integrated?

FIGURE 3.4
Matrix Organization Structure

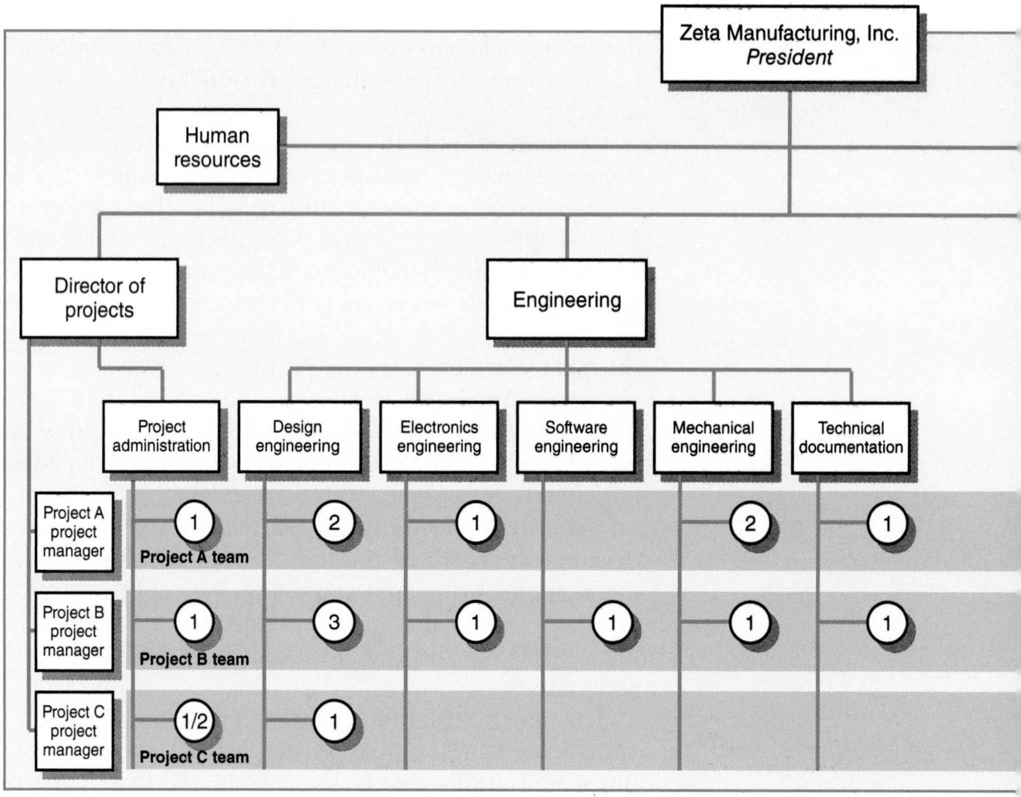

managing their segment of the project. The project manager basically acts as a staff assistant who draws the schedules and checklists, collects information on status of work, and facilitates project completion. The project manager has indirect authority to expedite and monitor the project. Functional managers call most of the shots and decide who does what and when the work is completed.

- **Balanced matrix**—This is the classic matrix in which the project manager is responsible for defining what needs to be accomplished while the functional managers are concerned with how it will be accomplished. More specifically, the project manager establishes the overall plan for completing the project, integrates the contribution of the different disciplines, sets schedules, and monitors progress. The functional managers are responsible for assigning personnel and executing their segment of the project according to the standards and schedules set by the project manager. The merger of "what and how" requires both parties to work closely together and jointly approve technical and operational decisions.
- **Strong matrix**—This form attempts to create the "feel" of a project team within a matrix environment. The project manager controls most aspects of the project, including scope trade-offs and assignment of functional personnel. The project manager controls when and what specialists do and has final say on major project decisions. The functional manager has title over her people and is

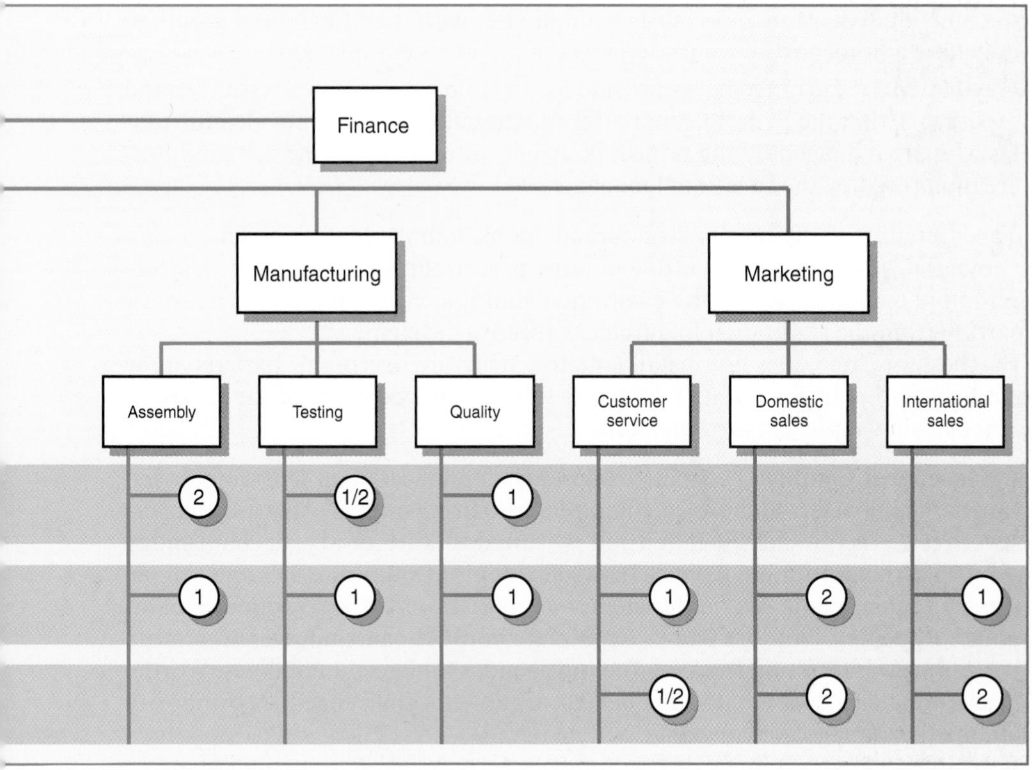

consulted on a need basis. In some situations a functional manager's department may serve as a "subcontractor" for the project, in which case they have more control over specialized work. For example, the development of a new series of laptop computers may require a team of experts from different disciplines working on the basic design and performance requirements within a project matrix arrangement. Once the specifications have been determined, final design and production of certain components (i.e., power source) may be assigned to respective functional groups to complete.

Matrix management both in general and in its specific forms has unique strengths and weaknesses (Larson & Gobeli, 1987). The advantages and disadvantages of matrix organizations in general are noted below, while only briefly highlighting specifics concerning different forms:

1. **Efficient.** Resources can be shared across multiple projects as well as within functional divisions. Individuals can divide their energy across multiple projects on an as-needed basis. This reduces duplication required in a projectized structure.
2. **Strong Project Focus.** A stronger project focus is provided by having a formally designated project manager who is responsible for coordinating and integrating contributions of different units. This helps sustain a holistic approach to problem solving that is often missing in the functional organization.

3. **Easier Post-Project Transition.** Because the project organization is overlaid on the functional divisions, specialists maintain ties with their functional group, so they have a homeport to return to once the project is completed.
4. **Flexible.** Matrix arrangements provide for flexible utilization of resources and expertise within the firm. In some cases functional units may provide individuals who are managed by the project manager. In other cases the contributions are monitored by the functional manager.

The strengths of the matrix structure are considerable. Unfortunately, so are the potential weaknesses. This is due in large part to the fact that a matrix structure is more complicated and the creation of multiple bosses represents a radical departure from the traditional hierarchical authority system.

Furthermore, one does not install a matrix structure overnight. Experts argue that it takes 3–5 years for a matrix system to fully mature. So many of the problems described below represent growing pains.

1. **Dysfunctional Conflict.** The matrix approach is predicated on tension between functional managers and project managers who bring critical expertise and perspectives to the project. Such tension is viewed as a necessary mechanism for achieving an appropriate balance between complex technical issues and unique project requirements. While the intent is noble, the effect is sometimes analogous to opening Pandora's box. Legitimate conflict can spill over to a more personal level, resulting from conflicting agendas and accountabilities. Worthy discussions can degenerate into heated arguments that engender animosity among the managers involved.
2. **Infighting.** Any situation in which equipment, resources, and people are being shared across projects and functional activities lends itself to conflict and competition for scarce resources. Infighting can occur among project managers, who are primarily interested in what is best for their project.
3. **Stressful.** Matrix management violates the management principle of unity of command. Project participants have at least two bosses—their functional head and one or more project managers. Working in a matrix environment can be extremely stressful. Imagine what it would be like to work in an environment in which you are being told to do three conflicting things by three different managers.
4. **Slow.** In theory, the presence of a project manager to coordinate the project should accelerate the completion of the project. In practice, decision making can get bogged down as agreements have to be forged across multiple functional groups. This is especially true for the balanced matrix.

When the three variant forms of the matrix approach are considered, we can see that advantages and disadvantages are not necessarily true for all three forms of matrix. The Strong matrix is likely to enhance project integration, diminish internal power struggles, and ultimately improve control of project activities and costs. On the downside, technical quality may suffer because functional areas have less control over their contributions. Finally, projectitis may emerge as the members develop a strong team identity.

The Weak matrix is likely to improve technical quality as well as provide a better system for managing conflict across projects because the functional manager assigns personnel to different projects. The problem is that functional control is often maintained at the expense of poor project integration. The Balanced matrix can achieve better balance between technical and project requirements, but it is a very delicate system to manage and is more likely to succumb to many of the problems associated with the matrix approach.

What Is the Right Project Management Structure?

There is empirical evidence that project success is directly linked to the amount of autonomy and authority project managers have over their projects (Gray et al., 1990; Larson & Gobeli, 1988; Larson & Gobeli, 1987). However, most of this research is based on what is best for managing specific projects. It is important to remember what was stated in the beginning of the chapter—that the best system balances the needs of the project with those of the parent organization. So what project structure should an organization use? This is a complicated question with no precise answers. A number of issues need to be considered at both the organization and project level.

Organization Considerations

At the organization level, the first question that needs to be asked is how important is project management to the success of the firm? What percentage of core work involves projects? If over 75 percent of work involves projects, then an organization should consider a fully projectized organization. If an organization has both standard products and projects, then a matrix arrangement would appear to be appropriate. If an organization has very few projects, then a less formal arrangement is probably all that is required. Dedicated teams could be created on an as-needed basis and the organization could outsource project work.

A second key question is resource availability. Remember, matrix evolved out of the necessity to share resources across multiple projects and functional domains while at the same time creating legitimate project leadership. For organizations that cannot afford to tie up critical personnel on individual projects, a matrix system would appear to be appropriate. An alternative would be to create a dedicated team but outsource project work when resources are not available internally.

Within the context of the first two questions, an organization needs to assess current practices and what changes are needed to more effectively manage projects. A strong project matrix is not installed overnight. The shift toward a greater emphasis on projects has a host of political implications that need to be worked through, requiring time and strong leadership. For example, we have observed many companies that make the transition from a functional organization to a matrix organization begin with a weak functional matrix. This is due in part to resistance by functional and department managers toward transferring authority to project managers. With time, these matrix structures eventually evolve into a project matrix. Many organizations have created Project Management Offices to support project management efforts. See Snapshot from Practice: POs: Project Offices.

Project Considerations

At the project level, the question is how much autonomy the project needs in order to be successfully completed. Hobbs and Ménard (1993) identify seven factors that should influence the choice of project management structure:

- Size of project.
- Strategic importance.

SNAPSHOT FROM PRACTICE POs: Project Offices*

Project offices (POs) were originally developed as a response to the poor track record many companies had in completing projects on time, within budget, and according to plan. They were often established to help matrix systems mature into more effective project delivery platforms.

Today, POs come in many different shapes and forms. One interesting way of classifying POs was set forth by Casey and Peck, who describe certain POs in terms of being (1) a weather station, (2) a control tower, or (3) a resource pool. Each of these models performs a very different function for its organization.

- **Weather Station.** The primary function of the weather station PO is to track and monitor project performance. It is typically created to satisfy top management's need to stay on top of the portfolio of projects under way in the firm. Staff provides an independent forecast of project performance. The questions answered for specific projects include:
  - How are our projects progressing? Which ones are on track? Which ones are not?
  - How are we doing in terms of cost? Which projects are over or under budget?
  - What are the major problems confronting projects? Are contingency plans in place? What can the organization do to help the project?
- **Control Tower.** The primary function of the control tower PO is to improve project execution. It considers project management as a profession to be protected and advanced. Staff at the PO identify best practices and standards for project management excellence. They work as consultants and trainers to support project managers and their teams.
- **Resource Pool.** The goal of the resource pool PO is to provide the organization with a cadre of trained project managers and professionals. It operates like an academy for continually upgrading the skills of a firm's project professionals. In addition to training, this kind of PO also serves to elevate the stature of project management within the organization.

* W. Casey and W. Peck, "Choosing the Right PMO Setup," *PM Network,* vol. 15, no. 2(2001), pp. 40–47.

- Novelty and need for innovation.
- Need for integration (number of departments involved).
- Environmental complexity (number of external interfaces).
- Budget and time constraints.
- Stability of resource requirements.

The higher the levels of these seven factors, the more autonomy and authority the project manager and project team need to be successful.[1] This translates into using either a dedicated project team or a project matrix structure. For example, these structures should be used for large projects that are strategically critical and are new to the company, thus requiring much innovation. These structures would also be appropriate for complex, multidisciplinary projects that require input from many departments, as well as for projects that require constant contact with customers to assess their expectations. Dedicated project teams should also be used for urgent projects in which the nature of the work requires people working steadily from beginning to end.

Many firms that are heavily involved in project management have created a flexible management system that organizes projects according to project requirements. For example, Chaparral Steel, a mini-mill that produces steel bars and beams from scrap metal, classifies projects into three categories: advanced

[1] For a more sophisticated discussion of contingency factors related to managing specific projects see: A. J. Shenhar and D. Dvir, *Reinventing Project Management: The Diamond Approach to Successful Growth and Innovation* (Boston: Harvard Press, 2007).

development, platform, and incremental. Advanced development projects are high-risk endeavors involving the creation of a breakthrough product or process. Platform projects are medium-risk projects involving system upgrades that yield new products and processes. Incremental projects are low-risk, short-term projects that involve minor adjustments in existing products and processes. At any point in time, Chaparral might have 40–50 projects underway, of which only one or two are advanced, three to five are platform projects, and the remainder are small, incremental projects. The incremental projects are almost all done within a weak matrix with the project manager coordinating the work of functional subgroups. A strong matrix is used to complete the platform projects, while dedicated project teams are typically created to complete the advanced development projects. More and more companies are using this "mix and match" approach to managing projects.

Organizational Culture

The decision for combining a discussion of project management structures and organizational cultures in this chapter can be traced to a conversation we, the authors, had with two project managers who work for a medium-sized information technology firm.

The managers were developing a new operating platform that would be critical to the future success of their company. When they tried to describe how this project was organized, one manager began to sketch out on a napkin a complicated structure involving 52 different teams, each with a project leader and a technical leader! In response to our further probing to understand how this system worked, the manager stopped short and proclaimed, "The key to making this structure work is the culture in our company. This approach would never work at company Y, where I worked before. But because of our culture here we are able to pull it off."

This comment, our observations of other firms, and research suggest there is a strong connection between project management structure, organizational culture, and project success.[2] We have observed organizations successfully manage projects within the traditional functional organization because the culture encouraged cross-functional integration. Conversely we have seen matrix structures break down because the culture of the organization did not support the division of authority between project managers and functional managers. We have also observed companies relying on independent project teams because the dominant culture would not support the innovation and speed necessary for success.

What Is Organizational Culture?

Organizational culture refers to a system of shared norms, beliefs, values, and assumptions which binds people together, thereby creating shared meanings (Deal & Kennedy, 1982). This system is manifested by customs and habits that exemplify the values and beliefs of the organization. For example, egalitarianism may be expressed in the informal dress worn at a high-tech firm. Conversely, mandated uniforms at a department store reinforce respect for the hierarchy.

[2] See, for example: Kerzner, H., *In Search of Excellence in Project Management* (New York: Von Nostrand Reinhold, 1997); Matheson, D., and J. Matheson, *The Smart Organization* (Boston: HBS Press, 1998).

Culture reflects the personality of the organization and, similar to an individual's personality, can enable us to predict attitudes and behaviors of organizational members. Culture is also one of the defining aspects of an organization that sets it apart from other organizations even in the same industry.

Research suggests that there are 10 primary characteristics which, in aggregate, capture the essence of an organization's culture:[3]

1. **Member identity**—the degree to which employees identify with the organization as a whole rather than with their type of job or field of professional expertise.
2. **Team emphasis**—the degree to which work activities are organized around groups rather than individuals.
3. **Management focus**—the degree to which management decisions take into account the effect of outcomes on people within the organization.
4. **Unit integration**—the degree to which units within the organization are encouraged to operate in a coordinated or interdependent manner.
5. **Control**—the degree to which rules, policies, and direct supervision are used to oversee and control employee behavior.
6. **Risk tolerance**—the degree to which employees are encouraged to be aggressive, innovative, and risk seeking.
7. **Reward criteria**—the degree to which rewards such as promotion and salary increases are allocated according to employee performance rather than seniority, favoritism, or other nonperformance factors.
8. **Conflict tolerance**—the degree to which employees are encouraged to air conflicts and criticisms openly.
9. **Means versus end orientation**—the degree to which management focuses on outcomes rather than on techniques and processes used to achieve those results.
10. **Open-systems focus**—the degree to which the organization monitors and responds to changes in the external environment.

As shown in Figure 3.5, each of these dimensions exists on a continuum. Assessing an organization according to these 10 dimensions provides a composite picture of the organization's culture. This picture becomes the basis for feelings of shared understanding that the members have about the organization, how things are done, and the way members are supposed to behave.

Culture performs several important functions in organizations. An organization's culture *provides a sense of identity* for its members. The more clearly an organization's shared perceptions and values are stated, the more strongly people can identify with their organization and feel a vital part of it. Identity generates commitment to the organization and reasons for members to devote energy and loyalty to the organization.

A second important function is that culture *helps legitimize the management system* of the organization. Culture helps clarify authority relationships. It provides reasons why people are in a position of authority and why their authority should be respected.

[3] Harrison, M. T., and J. M. Beyer, *The Culture of Organizations* (Englewood Cliffs, NJ: Prentice Hall, 1993); O'Reilly, C. A., J. Chatman, and D. F. Caldwell, "People and Organizational Culture: A Profile Comparison Approach to Assessing Person-Organization Fit," *Academy of Management Journal*, vol. 34, no. 3. September 1991, pp. 487–516; and Schein, E., *Organizational Culture and Leadership: A Dynamic View* (San Francisco, CA: Jossey-Bass, 2010).

FIGURE 3.5
Key Dimensions Defining an Organization's Culture

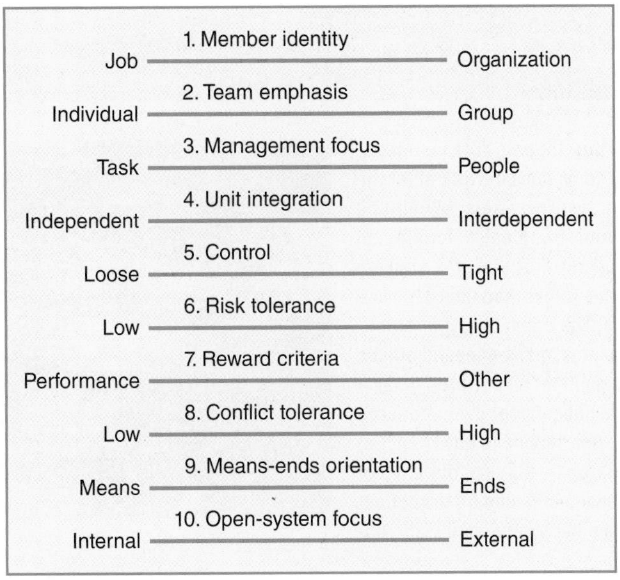

Most importantly, organizational culture *clarifies and reinforces standards of behavior.* Culture helps define what is permissible and inappropriate behavior. These standards span a wide range of behavior from dress code and working hours to challenging the judgment of superiors and collaborating with other departments. Ultimately, culture *helps create social order* within an organization. Imagine what it would be like if members didn't share similar beliefs, values, and assumptions—chaos! The customs, norms, and ideals conveyed by the culture of an organization provide the stability and predictability in behavior that is essential for an effective organization. See Snapshot from Practice: Google-y for an example of this.

Although our discussion of organizational culture may appear to suggest one culture dominates the entire organization, in reality this is rarely the case. "Strong" or "thick" are adjectives used to denote a culture in which the organization's core values and customs are widely shared within the entire organization. Conversely, a "thin" or "weak" culture is one that is not widely shared or practiced within a firm.

Even within a strong organizational culture, there are likely to be subcultures often aligned within specific departments or specialty areas. As noted earlier in our discussion of project management structures, it is not uncommon for norms, values, and customs to develop within a specific field or profession such as marketing, finance, or operations. People working in the marketing department may have a different set of norms and values than those working in finance.

Countercultures sometimes emerge within organizations that embody a different set of values, beliefs, and customs—often in direct contradiction with the culture espoused by top management. How pervasive these subcultures and countercultures are affect the strength of the culture of the organization and the extent to which culture influences members' actions and responses.

Identifying Cultural Characteristics

Deciphering an organization's culture is a highly interpretative, subjective process that requires assessment of both current and past history. The student of culture cannot simply rely on what people report about their culture. The physical

SNAPSHOT FROM PRACTICE Google-y*

In 2012 Google Inc. topped *Fortune* magazine's list of best companies to work at for the third time in the past five years. When one enters the 24-hour Googleplex located in Mountain View, California, you feel that you are walking through a new-age college campus rather than the corporate office of a billion-dollar business. The collection of interconnected low-rise buildings with colorful, glass-encased offices feature upscale trappings—free gourmet meals three times a day, free use of an outdoor wave pool, indoor gym and large child care facility, private shuttle bus service to and from San Francisco and other residential areas—that are the envy of workers across the Bay area. These perks and others reflect Google's culture of keeping people happy and thinking in unconventional ways.

© Proehl Studios/Corbis

The importance of corporate culture is no more evident than in the fact that the head of Human Resources, Stacy Savides Sullivan, also has the title of Chief Culture Officer. Her task is to try to preserve the innovative culture of a start-up as Google quickly evolves into a mammoth international corporation. Sullivan characterizes Google culture as "team-oriented, very collaborative and encouraging people to think nontraditionally, different from where they ever worked before—work with integrity and for the good of the company and for the good of the world, which is tied to our overall mission of making information accessible to the world." Google goes to great lengths to screen new employees to not only make sure that they have outstanding technical capabilities but also that they are going to fit Google's culture. Sullivan goes on to define a Google-y employee as somebody who is "flexible, adaptable, and not focusing on titles and hierarchy, and just gets stuff done."

Google's culture is rich with customs and traditions not found in corporate America. For example, project teams typically have daily "stand-up" meetings seven minutes after the hour. Why seven minutes after the hour? Because Google co-founder Sergey Brin once estimated that it took seven minutes to walk across the Google campus. Everybody stands to make sure no one gets too comfortable and no time is wasted during the rapid-fire update. As one manager noted, "The whole concept of the stand-up is to talk through what everyone's doing, so if someone is working on what you're working on, you can discover and collaborate not duplicate."

Another custom is "dogfooding." This is when a project team releases the functional prototype of a future product to Google employees for them to test drive. There is a strong norm within Google to test new products and provide feedback to the developers. The project team receives feedback from thousands of Google-ys. The internal focus group can log bugs or simply comment on design or functionality. Fellow Google-ys do not hold back on their feedback and are quick to point out things they don't like. This often leads to significant product improvements.

* Walters, H., "How Google Got Its New Look," *BusinessWeek,* May 10, 2010; Goo, S. K., "Building a 'Googley' Workforce," *Washington Post,* October 21, 2006; Mills, E., "Meet Google's Culture Czar," *CNET News.com,* April 27, 2007.

environment in which people work, as well as how people act and respond to different events that occur, must be examined. Figure 3.6 contains a worksheet for diagnosing the culture of an organization. Although by no means exhaustive, the checklist often yields clues about the norms, customs, and values of an organization:

1. **Study the physical characteristics of an organization.** What does the external architecture look like? What image does it convey? Is it unique? Are the buildings and offices the same quality for all employees? Or are modern buildings and fancier offices reserved for senior executives or managers from a specific department? What are the customs concerning dress? What symbols does the

FIGURE 3.6
Organizational Culture Diagnosis Worksheet

Power Corp.

I. Physical Characteristics:
Architecture, office layout, décor, attire

Corporate HQ is 20 story modern building—president on top floor. Offices are bigger in the top floors than lower floors. Formal business attire (white shirts, ties, power suits, . . .). Power appears to increase the higher up you are.

II. Public Documents:
Annual reports, internal newsletters, vision statements

At the heart of the Power Corp. way is our vision . . . to be the global energy company most admired for its people, partnership, and performance.

Integrity. We are honest with others and ourselves. We meet the highest ethical standards in all business dealings. We do what we say we will do.

III. Behavior:
Pace, language, meetings, issues discussed, decision-making style, communication patterns, rituals

Hierarchical decision-making, pace brisk but orderly, meetings start on time and end on time, subordinates choose their words very carefully when talking to superiors, people rarely work past 6:00 P.M., president takes top performing unit on a boat cruise each year . . .

IV. Folklore:
Stories, anecdotes, heroines, heroes, villains

Young project manager was fired after going over his boss's head to ask for additional funds.

Stephanie C. considered a hero for taking complete responsibility for a technical error.

Jack S. was labeled a traitor for joining chief competitor after working for Power Corp. for 15 years.

organization use to signal authority and status within the organization? These physical characteristics can shed light on who has real power within the organization, the extent to which the organization is internally differentiated, and how formal the organization is in its business dealings.

2. **Read about the organization.** Examine annual reports, mission statements, press releases, and internal newsletters. What do they describe? What principles are espoused in these documents? Do the reports emphasize the people who work for the organization and what they do or the financial performance of the firm? Each emphasis reflects a different culture. The first demonstrates concern for the people who make up the company. The second may suggest a concern for results and the bottom line.
3. **Observe how people interact within the organization.** What is their pace—is it slow and methodical or urgent and spontaneous? What rituals exist within the organization? What values do they express? Meetings can often yield insightful information. Who are the people at the meetings? Who does the talking? To whom do they talk? How candid is the conversation? Do people speak for the organization or for the individual department? What is the focus of the meetings? How much time is spent on various issues? Issues that are discussed repeatedly and at length are clues about the values of the organization's culture.
4. **Interpret stories and folklore surrounding the organization.** Look for similarities among stories told by different people. The subjects highlighted in recurring stories often reflect what is important to an organization's culture. For example, many of the stories that are repeated at Versatec, a Xerox subsidiary that makes

graphic plotters for computers, involve their flamboyant cofounder, Renn Zaphiropoulos. According to company folklore, one of the very first things Renn did when the company was formed was to assemble the top management team at his home. They then devoted the weekend to handmaking a beautiful teak conference table around which all future decisions would be made. This table came to symbolize the importance of teamwork and maintaining high standards of performance, two essential qualities of the culture at Versatec. Try to identify who the heroes and villains are in the folklore company. What do they suggest about the culture's ideals? Returning to the Versatec story, when the company was eventually purchased by Xerox many employees expressed concern that Versatec's informal, play hard/work hard culture would be overwhelmed by the bureaucracy at Xerox. Renn rallied the employees to superior levels of performance by arguing that if they exceeded Xerox's expectations they would be left alone. Autonomy has remained a fixture of Versatec's culture long after Renn's retirement.

It is also important to pay close attention to the basis for promotions and rewards. What do people see as the keys to getting ahead within the organization? What contributes to downfalls? These last two questions can yield important insights into the qualities and behaviors which the organization honors as well as the cultural taboos and behavioral land mines that can derail a career. For example, one project manager confided that a former colleague was sent to project management purgatory soon after publicly questioning the validity of a marketing report. From that point on, the project manager was extra careful to privately consult the marketing department whenever she had questions about their data.

With practice an observer can assess how strong the dominant culture of an organization is and the significance of subcultures and countercultures. Furthermore, learners can discern and identify where the culture of an organization stands on the 10 cultural dimensions presented earlier and, in essence, begin to build a cultural profile for a firm. Based on this profile, conclusions can be drawn about specific customs and norms that need to be adhered to as well as those behaviors and actions that violate the norms of a firm.

Implications of Organizational Culture for Organizing Projects

Project managers have to be able to operate in several, potentially diverse, organizational cultures. First, they have to interact with the culture of their parent organization as well as the subcultures of various departments (e.g., marketing, accounting). Second, they have to interact with the project's client or customer organizations. Finally, they have to interact in varying degrees with a host of other organizations connected to the project. These organizations include suppliers and vendors, subcontractors, consulting firms, government and regulatory agencies, and, in many cases, community groups. Many of these organizations are likely to have very different cultures. Project managers have to be able to read and speak the culture they are working in to develop strategies, plans, and responses that are likely to be understood and accepted. Still, the emphasis of this chapter is on the relationship between organizational culture and project management structure, and it is necessary to defer further discussion of these implications until Chapters 10–12, which focus on leadership, team building, and outsourcing.

FIGURE 3.7
Cultural Dimensions of an Organization Supportive of Project Management

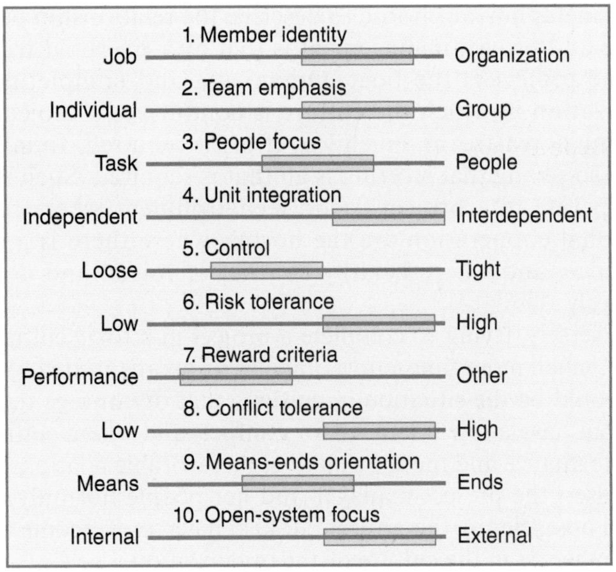

Earlier we stated that we believe there are strong relationships among project management structure, organizational culture, and successful project management. To explore these relationships further, let us return to the dimensions that can be used to characterize the culture of an organization. When examining these dimensions we could hypothesize that certain aspects of the culture of an organization would support successful project management while other aspects would deter or interfere with effective management. Figure 3.7 attempts to identify which cultural characteristics create an environment conducive to completing most complex projects involving people from different disciplines.

Note that, in many cases, the ideal culture is not at either extreme. For example, a fertile project culture would likely be one in which management balances its focus on the needs of both the task and the people. An optimal culture would balance concern with output (ends) and processes to achieve those outcomes (means). In other cases, the ideal culture would be on one end of a dimension or the other. For example, because most projects require collaboration across disciplines, it would be desirable that the culture of the organization emphasize working in teams and identifying with the organization, not just the professional domain. Likewise, it is important that the culture support a certain degree of risk taking and a tolerance for constructive conflict.

One organization that appears to fit this ideal profile is 3M. 3M has received acclaim for creating an entrepreneurial culture within a large corporate framework. The essence of its culture is captured in phrases that have been chanted often by 3Mers throughout its history: "Encourage experimental doodling." "Hire good people and leave them alone." "If you put fences around people, you get sheep. Give people the room they need." Freedom and autonomy to experiment are reflected in the "15 percent rule," which encourages technical people to spend up to 15 percent of their time on projects of their own choosing and initiative. This fertile culture has contributed to 3M's branching out into more than 60,000 products and 35 separate business units (Collins & Porras, 1994).

The metaphor we choose to describe the relationship between organizational culture and project management is that of a riverboat trip. Culture is the river and the project is the boat. Organizing and completing projects within an organization in which the culture is conducive to project management is like paddling downstream: much less effort is required. In many cases, the current can be so strong that steering is all that is required. Such is the case for projects that operate in a project-friendly environment where team-work and cross-functional cooperation are the norms, where there is a deep commitment to excellence, and where healthy conflict is voiced and dealt with quickly and effectively.

Conversely, trying to complete a project in a toxic culture is like paddling upstream: much more time, effort, and attention are needed to reach the destination. This would be the situation in cultures that discourage teamwork and cooperation, that have a low tolerance for conflict, and where getting ahead is based less on performance and more on cultivating favorable relationships with superiors. In such cases, the project manager and her people not only have to overcome the natural obstacles of the project but also have to overcome the prevailing negative forces inherent in the culture of the organization.

The implications of this metaphor are important. Greater project authority and time are necessary to complete projects that encounter a strong, negative cultural current. Conversely, less formal authority and fewer dedicated resources are needed to complete projects in which the cultural currents generate behavior and cooperation essential to project success.

The key issue is the degree of interdependency between the parent organization and the project team. In cases where the prevalent organizational culture supports the behaviors essential to project completion, a weaker, more flexible project management structure can be effective. For example, one of the major reasons Chaparral Steel is able to use a functional matrix to successfully complete incremental projects is that its culture contains strong norms for cooperation (Bowen et al., 1994). See the Research Highlight: The Secret of Success for another example of how culture supports successful project management.

When the dominant organization culture inhibits collaboration and innovation, it is advisable to insulate the project team from the dominant culture. Here it becomes necessary to create a self-sufficient project team. If a dedicated project team is impossible because of resource constraints, then at least a project matrix should be used where the project manager has dominant control over the project. In both cases, the managerial strategy is to create a distinct team subculture in which a new set of norms, customs, and values evolve that will be conducive to project completion.

Under extreme circumstances this project culture could even represent a counterculture in that many of the norms and values are the antithesis of the dominant, parent culture. Such was the case when IBM decided to develop their personal computer quickly in 1980 (Smith & Reinertsen, 1995). They knew that the project could get bogged down by the overabundance of computer knowledge and bureaucracy in the company. They also realized that they would have to work closely with suppliers and make use of many non-IBM parts if they were to get to the market quickly. This was not the IBM way at the time, so IBM established the PC project team in a warehouse in Boca Raton, Florida, far from corporate headquarters and other corporate development facilities that existed within the organization.

Research Highlight — The Secret of Success*

In *The Secret of Success: The Double Helix of Formal and Informal Structures in an R&D Laboratory* Polly Rizova revealed the results of a year-long investigation into the inner workings of a Fortune 500 R&D Lab. Through interviews with key participants and analysis of social networking data, Rizova assessed the efficacy of six high-tech development projects.

Four critical success factors emerged from her research. One element that is crucial to success is a heavy reliance on open and unrestricted patterns of communication, coupled with a low degree of formal reporting. In other words, team members freely interacted with each other regardless of title, experience, or discipline. A second key is having individuals on the project who are highly respected across the laboratory for their exceptional technical skills and experience. Similarly, it is also vital to have individuals involved in the project who are highly respected for their organizational expertise and experience. Having both "technical stars" and "organizational stars" on the project team were essential to success. The final factor is a strong and sustained support for the project from the company's corporate management. What's more, her analysis revealed interactive nature of the four conditions; namely that no one condition was likely to produce successful outcomes on its own, but only when put together in a way in which they reinforce each other. Here the culture of the laboratory was seen as the key catalyst.

Rizova describes a matrix system in which people work on multiple projects simultaneously but with a different wrinkle. Individuals occupy different positions and play different roles depending upon the project. For example, it is common for a senior engineer to be the manager of one project and a researcher on another that is led by his or her subordinate. In essence one must "boss" his or her own boss. At first glance this formal structure should create destructive tensions. However, Rizova argues that the organizational culture of the lab is the glue that keeps things running smoothly.

She described a culture in which the social norms of cooperation, respect, and civility are upheld and reproduced. It is a culture characterized by trust and a strong drive toward superior individual and organizational learning and achievement. The culture is captured in the comments of researchers:

> That is one of the nicest things around here. Your opinions are listened to. Superiors consider our advice. You will find that most of the projects here are a team effort.
>
> What I like most is the positive thinking and the "whatever it takes" attitude. Personality conflicts can be devastating. Here everyone helps you and supports you. There is no "I" in the word team.
>
> Very friendly environment. . . . I met new people and learned a lot from them. They do not mind sharing their expertise.

* Polly S. Rizova, *The Secret of Success: The Double Helix of Formal and Informal Structures in an R&D Laboratory* (Stanford, CA: Stanford University Press, 2007).

Summary

This chapter examined two major characteristics of the parent organization that affect the implementation and completion of projects. The first is the formal structure of the organization and how it chooses to organize and manage projects. Although the individual project manager may have very little say as to how the firm chooses to manage projects, he or she must be able to recognize the options available as well as the inherent strengths and weaknesses of different approaches.

Three basic project management structures were described and assessed as to their weaknesses and strengths. Only under unique circumstances can a case be made for managing a project within the normal functional hierarchy. When thinking only in terms of what is best for the project, the creation of an independent project team is clearly favored. However, the most effective project management system appropriately balances the needs of the project with those of the parent organization. Matrix structures emerged out of the parent organization's need to share personnel and resources across multiple projects and operations while creating legitimate project focus. The matrix approach is a hybrid organizational form that combines elements of both the functional and project team forms in an attempt to realize the advantages of both.

The second major characteristic of the parent organization that was discussed in this chapter is the concept of organizational culture. Organizational culture is the pattern of beliefs and expectations shared by an organization's members. Culture includes the behavioral norms, customs, shared values, and the "rules of the game" for getting along and getting ahead within the organization. It is important for project managers to be "culture sensitive" so that they can develop appropriate strategies and responses and avoid violating key norms that would jeopardize their effectiveness within the organization.

The interaction between project management structure and organizational culture is a complicated one. We have suggested that in certain organizations, culture encourages the implementation of projects. In this environment the project management structure used plays a less decisive role in the success of the project. Conversely, for other organizations in which the culture stresses internal competition and differentiation, just the opposite may be true. The prevailing norms, customs, and attitudes inhibit effective project management, and the project management structure plays a more decisive role in the successful implementation of projects. At a minimum, under adverse cultural conditions, the project manager needs to have significant authority over the project team; under more extreme conditions firms should physically relocate dedicated project teams to complete critical projects. In both cases, the managerial strategy should be to insulate project work from the dominant culture so that a more positive "subculture" can emerge among project participants.

The project management structure of the organization and the culture of the organization are major elements of the environment in which a project is initiated. Subsequent chapters will examine how project managers and professionals work within this environment to successfully complete projects.

Key Terms

Balanced matrix, *76*
Dedicated project team, *71*
Matrix, *74*
Organizational culture, *81*
Projectized organization, *72*
Project office (PO), *80*
Strong matrix, *76*
Weak matrix, *75*

Review Questions

1. What are the relative advantages and disadvantages of the functional, matrix, and dedicated team approaches to managing projects?
2. What distinguishes a weak matrix from a strong matrix?
3. Under what conditions would it be advisable to use a strong matrix instead of a dedicated project team?
4. How can project management offices (POs) support effective project management?
5. Why is it important to assess the culture of an organization before deciding what project management structure should be used to complete a project?
6. Other than culture, what other organizational factors should be used to determine which project management structure should be used?
7. What do you believe is more important for successfully completing a project—the formal project management structure or the culture of the parent organization?

Exercises

1. Going to college is analogous to working in a matrix environment in that most students take more than one class and must distribute their time across multiple classes. What problems does this situation create for you? How does it affect your performance? How could the system be better managed to make your life less difficult and more productive?
2. You work for LL Company, which manufactures high-end optical scopes for hunting rifles. LL Company has been the market leader for the past 20 years and has decided to diversify by applying its technology to develop a top-quality binocular. What kind of project management structure would you recommend they use for this project? What information would you like to have to make this recommendation, and why?
3. You work for Barbata Electronics. Your R&D people believe they have come up with an affordable technology that will double the capacity of existing MP3 players and uses audio format that is superior to MP3. The project is code named KYSO (Knock Your Socks Off). What kind of project management structure would you recommend they use for the KYSO project? What information would you like to have to make this recommendation and why?
4. This chapter discussed the role of values and beliefs in forming an organization's culture. The topic of organization culture is big business on the Internet. Many companies use their Web pages to describe their mission, vision, and corporate values and beliefs. There also are many consulting firms that advertise how they help organizations to change their culture. The purpose of this exercise is for you to obtain information pertaining to the organizational culture for two different companies. You can go about this task by very simply searching on the key words "organizational culture" or "corporate vision and values." This search will identify numerous companies for you to use to answer the following questions. You may want to select companies that you would like to work for in the future.
   a. What are the espoused values and beliefs of the companies?
   b. Use the worksheet in Figure 3.6 to assess the Web page. What does the Web page reveal about the culture of this organization? Would this culture be conducive to effective project management?
5. Use the cultural dimensions listed in Figure 3.5 to assess the culture of your school. Instead of employees, consider students, and instead of management, use faculty. For example, member identity refers to the degree to which students identify with the school as a whole rather than their major or option. Either as individuals or in small groups rate the culture of your school on the 10 dimensions.
   a. What dimensions were easy to evaluate and which ones were not?
   b. How strong is the culture of your school?
   c. What functions does the culture serve for your school?
   d. Do you think the culture of your school is best suited to maximizing your learning? Why or why not?
   e. What kind of projects would be easy to implement in your school and what kind of projects would be difficult given the structure and culture of your school? Explain your answer.
6. You work as an analyst in the marketing department for Springfield International (SI). SI uses a weak matrix to develop new services. Management has created an extremely competitive organizational culture that places an emphasis

upon achieving results above everything else. One of the project managers that you have been assigned to help has been pressuring you to make his project your number one priority. He also wants you to expand the scope of your work on his project beyond what your marketing manager believes is necessary or appropriate. The project manager is widely perceived as a rising star within SI. Up to now you have been resisting the project manager's pressure and complying with your marketing manager's directives. However, your most recent interchange with the project manager ended by his saying, "I'm not happy with the level of help I am getting from you and I will remember this when I become VP of Marketing." How would you respond and why?

References

Block, T. R., and J. D. Frame, *The Project Office—A Key to Managing Projects Effectively* (Menlo Park, CA: Crisp Publications, 1998).

Block, T. R., and J. D. Frame, "Today's Project Office: Gauging Attitudes," *PM Network,* August 2001.

Bowen, H. K., K. B. Clark, C. A. Holloway, and S. C. Wheelwright, *The Perpetual Enterprise Machine* (New York: Oxford University Press, 1994).

Brown, S., and K. R. Eisenhardt, "Product Development: Past Research, Present Findings, and Future Directions," *Academy of Management Review,* 20 (2) 1995, pp. 343–78.

Cameron, K. S., and R. E. Quinn, *Diagnosing and Changing Organizational Culture: Based on the Competing Values Framework* (Upper Saddle River, NJ: Prentice Hall, 2011).

Carlton, J., *Apple: The Inside Story of Intrigue, Egomania, and Business Blunders* (New York: Random House, 1997), pp. 13–14.

Casey, W., and W. Peck, "Choosing the Right PMO Setup," *PM Network,* 15 (2) 2001, pp. 40–47.

Collins, J. C., and J. I. Porras, *Built to Last: The Successful Habits of Visionary Companies* (New York: HarperCollins, 1994), pp. 150–58.

Deal, T. E., and A. A. Kennedy, *Corporate Cultures: The Rites and Rituals of Corporate Life* (Reading, MA: Addison-Wesley, 1982).

De Laat, P. B., "Matrix Management of Projects and Power Struggles: A Case Study of an R&D Laboratory," *IEEE Engineering Management Review,* Winter 1995.

Filipczak, B., "Beyond the Gates of Microsoft," *Training,* September 1992, pp. 37–44.

Gallagher, R. S., *The Soul of an Organization: Understanding the Values That Drive Successful Corporate Cultures* (Chicago: Dearborn Trade Publishing, 2002).

Graham, R. J., and R. L. Englund, *Creating an Environment for Successful Projects: The Quest to Manage Project Management* (San Francisco: Jossey-Bass, 1997).

Gray, C., S. Dworatschek, D. H. Gobeli, H. Knoepfel, and E. W. Larson, "International Comparison of Project Organization Structures: Use and Effectiveness," *International Journal of Project Management,* vol. 8, no. 1, February 1990, pp. 26–32.

Harrison, M. T., and J. M. Beyer, *The Culture of Organizations* (Englewood Cliffs, NJ: Prentice Hall, 1993).

Hobbs, B., and P. Ménard, "Organizational Choices for Project Management," in Paul Dinsmore (ed.), *The AMA Handbook of Project Management* (New York: AMACOM, 1993).

Hobday, M., "The Project-Based Organization: An Ideal Form for Managing Complex Products and Systems?" *Research Policy,* vol. 29, no. 17, 2000.

Jassawalla, A. R., and H. C. Sashittal, "Cultures that Support Product-Innovation Processes," *Academy of Management Executive,* 15 (3) 2002, pp. 42–54.

Johnson, C. L., M. Smith, and L. K. Geary, *More Than My Share in All* (Washington, D.C.: Smithsonian Institute Publications, 1990).

Kerzner, H., *In Search of Excellence in Project Management* (New York: Von Nostrand Reinhold, 1997).

Kerzner, H., "Strategic Planning for the Project Office," *Project Management Journal,* 34 (2) 2003, pp. 13–25.

Larson, E. W., "Project Management Structures" in *The Wiley Handbook for Managing Projects,* P. Morris & J. Pinto (eds.) (New York: Wiley, 2004), pp. 48–66.

Larson, E. W., and D. H. Gobeli, "Matrix Management: Contradictions and Insights," *California Management Review,* vol. 29, no. 4, Summer 1987, p. 137.

Larson, E. W., and D. H. Gobeli, "Organizing for Product Development Projects," *Journal of Product Innovation Management,* vol. 5, 1988, pp. 180–90.

Larsson, U. (ed.), *Cultures of Creativity: The Centennial Exhibition of the Nobel Prize* (Canton, MA: Science History Publications, 2001).

Laslo, Z., and A. I. Goldberg, "Matrix Structures and Performance: The Search for Optimal Adjustments to Organizational Objectives?" *IEEE Transactions in Engineering Management,* vol. 48, no. 12, 2001.

Lawrence, P. R., and J. W. Lorsch, *Organization and Environment* (Homewood, IL: Irwin, 1969).

Majchrzak, A., and Q. Wang, "Breaking the Functional Mind-Set in Process Organizations," *Harvard Business Review,* Sept.–Oct. 1996, pp. 93–99.

Miller, J., *Lockheed Martin's Skunk Works* (New York: Speciality Publications, 1996).

Olson, E. M., O. C. Walker, Jr., and R. W. Ruekert, "Organizing for Effective New Product Development: The Moderating Role of Product Innovativeness," *Journal of Marketing,* vol. 59 (January), 1995, pp. 48–62.

O'Reilly, C. A., J. Chatman, and D. F. Caldwell, "People and Organizational Culture: A Profile Comparison Approach to Assessing Person-Organization Fit," *Academy of Management Journal,* vol. 34, no. 3, September 1991, pp. 487–516.

Pettegrew, A. M., "On Studying Organizational Culture," *Administrative Science Quarterly,* vol. 24, no. 4, 1979, pp. 570–81.

Powell, M., and J. Young, "The Project Management Support Office" in *The Wiley Handbook for Managing Projects,* P. Morris and J. Pinto (eds.) (New York: Wiley, 2004), pp. 937–69.

Rebello, K., "Inside Microsoft," *Business Weekly,* July 15, 1996, pp. 56–67.

Rizova, P., *The Secret of Success: The Double Helix of Formal and Informal Structures in an R&D Laboratory* (Stanford, CA: Stanford University Press, 2007).

Schein, E., *Organizational Culture and Leadership: A Dynamic View* (San Francisco, CA: Jossey-Bass, 2010).

Sculley, J., *Odyssey: Pepsi to Apple . . . A Journey of Adventure, Ideas, and the Future* (New York: Harper & Row, 1987), pp. 270–79.

Shenhar, A. J., "From Theory to Practice: Toward a Typology of Project Management Styles," *IEEE Transactions in Engineering Management,* 41 (1) 1998, pp. 33–48.

Shenhar, A. J., D. Dvir, T. Lechler, and M. Poli, "One Size Does Not Fit All—True for Projects, True for Frameworks," *Frontiers of Project Management Research and Application,* Proceedings of PMI Research Conference, Seattle, 2002, pp. 99–106.

Smith, P. G., and D. G. Reinertsen, *Developing Products in Half the Time* (New York: Van Nostrand Reinhold, 1995).

Stuckenbruck, L. C., *Implementation of Project Management* (Upper Darby, PA: Project Management Institute, 1981).

Youker, R., "Organizational Alternatives for Project Management," *Project Management Quarterly,* vol. 8, March 1977, pp. 24–33.

Case

Moss and McAdams Accounting Firm

Bruce Palmer had worked for Moss and McAdams (M&M) for six years and was just promoted to account manager. His first assignment was to lead an audit of Johnsonville Trucks. He was quite pleased with the five accountants who had been assigned to his team, especially Zeke Olds. Olds was an Army vet who returned to school to get a double major in accounting and computer sciences. He was on top of the latest developments in financial information systems and had a reputation for coming up with innovative solutions to problems.

M&M was a well-established regional accounting firm with 160 employees located across six offices in Minnesota and Wisconsin. The main office, where Palmer worked, was in Green Bay, Wisconsin. In fact, one of the founding members, Seth Moss, played briefly for the hometown NFL Packers during the late 1950s. M&M's primary services were corporate audits and tax preparation. Over the last two years the partners decided to move more aggressively into the consulting business. M&M projected that consulting would represent 40 percent of their growth over the next five years.

M&M operated within a matrix structure. As new clients were recruited, a manager was assigned to the account. A manager might be assigned to several accounts, depending on the size and scope of the work. This was especially true in the case of tax preparation projects, where it was not uncommon for a manager to be assigned to 8 to 12 clients. Likewise, senior and staff accountants were assigned to multiple account teams. Ruby Sands was the office manager responsible for assigning personnel to different accounts at the Green Bay office. She did her best to assign staff to multiple projects under the same manager. This wasn't always possible, and sometimes accountants had to work on projects led by different managers.

M&M, like most accounting firms, had a tiered promotion system. New CPAs entered as junior or staff accountants. Within two years, their performance was reviewed and they were either asked to leave or promoted to senior accountant. Sometime during their fifth or sixth year, a decision was made to promote them to account manager. Finally, after 10 to 12 years with the firm, the manager was considered for promotion to partner. This was a very competitive position. During the last five years, only 20 percent of account managers at M&M had been promoted to partner. However, once a partner, they were virtually guaranteed the position for life and enjoyed significant increases in salary, benefits, and prestige. M&M had a reputation for being a results-driven organization; partner promotions were based on meeting deadlines, retaining clients, and generating revenue. The promotion team based its decision on the relative performance of the account manager in comparison to his or her cohorts.

One week into the Johnsonville audit, Palmer received a call from Sands to visit her office. There he was introduced to Ken Crosby, who recently joined M&M after working nine years for a Big 5 accounting firm. Crosby was recruited to manage special consulting projects. Sands reported that Crosby had just secured a major consulting project with Springfield Metals. This was a major coup for the firm: M&M had competed against two Big 5 accounting firms for the project. Sands went on to explain that she was working with Crosby to put together his team. Crosby insisted that Zeke Olds be assigned to his team. Sands told him that this would be impossible because Olds was already assigned to work on the Johnsonville audit. Crosby persisted, arguing that Olds's expertise was essential to the Springfield project. Sands decided to work out a compromise and have Olds split time across both projects.

At this time Crosby turned to Palmer and said, "I believe in keeping things simple. Why don't we agree that Olds works for me in the mornings and you in the afternoons. I'm sure we can work out any problems that come up. After all, we both work for the same firm."

SIX WEEKS LATER

Palmer could scream whenever he remembered Crosby's words, "After all, we both work for the same firm." The first sign of trouble came during the first week of the new arrangement when Crosby called, begging to have Olds work all of Thursday on his project. They were conducting an extensive client visit, and Olds was critical to the assessment. After Palmer reluctantly agreed, Crosby said he owed him one. The next week when Palmer called Crosby to request that he return the favor, Crosby flatly refused and said any other time but not this week. Palmer tried again a week later and got the same response.

At first Olds showed up promptly at 1:00 P.M. at Palmer's office to work on the audit. Soon it became a habit to show up 30 to 60 minutes late. There was always a good reason. He was in a meeting in Springfield and couldn't just leave, or an urgent task took longer than planned. One time it was because Crosby took his entire team out to lunch at the new Thai restaurant—Olds was over an hour late because of slow service. In the beginning Olds would usually make up the time by working after hours, but Palmer could tell from conversations he overheard that this was creating tension at home.

What probably bothered Palmer the most were the e-mails and telephone calls Olds received from Crosby and his team members during the afternoons when he was supposed to be working for Palmer. A couple of times Palmer could have sworn that Olds was working on Crosby's project in his (Palmer's) office.

Palmer met with Crosby to talk about the problem and voice his complaints. Crosby acted surprised and even a little bit hurt. He promised things would change, but the pattern continued.

Palmer was becoming paranoid about Crosby. He knew that Crosby played golf with Olds on the weekends and could just imagine him badmouthing the Johnsonville project and pointing out how boring auditing work was. The sad fact was that there probably was some truth to what he was saying. The Johnsonville project was getting bogged down, and the team was slipping behind schedule. One of the contributing factors was Olds's performance. His work was not up to its usual standards. Palmer approached Olds about this, and Olds became defensive. Olds later apologized and confided that he found it difficult switching his thinking from consulting to auditing and then back to consulting. He promised to do better, and there was a slight improvement in his performance.

The last straw came when Olds asked to leave work early on Friday so that he could take his wife and kids to a Milwaukee Brewers baseball game. It turned out Springfield Metals had given Crosby their corporate tickets, and he decided to treat his team with box seats right behind the Brewers dugout. Palmer hated to do it, but he had to refuse the request. He felt guilty when he overheard Olds explaining to his son on the telephone why they couldn't go to the game.

Palmer finally decided to pick up the phone and request an urgent meeting with Sands to resolve the problem. He got up enough nerve and put in the call only to be told that Sands wouldn't be back in the office until next week. As he put the receiver down, he thought maybe things would get better.

TWO WEEKS LATER

Sands showed up unexpectedly at Palmer's office and said they needed to talk about Olds. Palmer was delighted, thinking that now he could tell her what had been going on. But before he had a chance to speak, Sands told him that Olds had come to see her yesterday. She told him that Olds confessed that he was having a hard time working on both Crosby's and Palmer's projects. He was having difficulty concentrating on the auditing work in the afternoon because he was thinking about some of the consulting issues that had emerged during the morning. He was putting in extra hours to try to meet both of the projects' deadlines, and this was creating problems at home. The bottom line was that he was stressed out and couldn't deal with the situation. He asked that he be assigned full-time to Crosby's project. Sands went on to say that Olds didn't blame Palmer, in fact he had a lot of nice things to say about him. He just enjoyed the consulting work more and found it more challenging. Sands concluded by saying, "I told him I understood, and I would talk to you about the situation and see what could be done. Frankly, I think we should pull him from your project and have him work full-time on Crosby's project. What do you think?"

1. If you were Palmer at the end of the case, how would you respond?
2. What, if anything, could Palmer have done to avoid losing Olds?
3. What advantages and disadvantages of a matrix type organization are apparent from this case?
4. What could the management at M&M do to more effectively manage situations like this?

Case

Horizon Consulting

Patti Smith looked up at the bright blue Carolina sky before she entered the offices of Horizon Consulting. Today was Friday, which meant she needed to prepare for the weekly status report meeting. Horizon Consulting is a **custom software development company** that offers fully integrated **mobile application services** for **iPhone™, Android™, Windows Mobile®** and **BlackBerry®** platforms. Horizon was founded by James Thrasher, a former Marketing executive, who quickly saw the potential for digital marketing via smartphones. Horizon enjoyed initial success in sports marketing, but quickly expanded to other industries. A key to their success was the decline in cost for developing smartphone applications which expanded the client base. The decline in cost was primarily due to learning curve and ability to build customized solutions on established platforms.

Patti Smith was a late bloomer who went back to college after working in the restaurant business for nine years. She and her former husband had tried unsuccessfully to operate a vegetarian restaurant in Golden, Colorado. After her divorce, she returned to University of Colorado where she majored in Management Information Systems with a minor in Marketing. While she enjoyed her marketing classes much more than her MIS classes, she felt the IT know-how acquired would give her an advantage in the job market. This turned out to be true as Horizon hired her to be an Account Manager soon after graduation.

Patti Smith was hired to replace Stephen Stills who had started the restaurant side of the business at Horizon. Stephen was "let go" according to one Account Manager for being a *prima donna* and hoarding resources. Patti's clients ranged from high-end restaurants to hole in wall Mom and Pop shops. She helped develop smartphone apps that let users make reservations, browse menus, receive alerts on daily specials, provide customer feedback, order take-out and in some cases order delivery. As an Account Manager she worked with clients to assess their needs, develop a plan, and create customized smartphone apps.

Horizon appeared to be a good fit for Patti. She had enough technical training to be able to work with software engineers and help guide them to produce client-ready products. At the same time she could relate to the restaurateurs and enjoyed working with them on web design and digital marketing.

Horizon was organized into three departments: Sales, Software Development, and Graphics, with Account Managers acting as project managers. Account Managers generally came from Sales, and would divide their time between projects and making sales pitches to potential new clients. Horizon employed a core group of software engineers and designers, supplemented by contracted programmers when needed.

The first step in developing a smartphone application involved the Account Manager meeting with the client to define the requirements and vision for the application. The Account Manager would then work with a Graphic User Interface (GUI) designer to come up with a preliminary story board of how the application would function and look. Once the initial concept and requirements were approved the Account Manager was assigned two pairs of software engineers. The first pair (app engineers) would work on the smartphone side of the application while the second pair would work on the client side of the application. Horizon preferred to have software engineers work in tandem so they could check each other's work. The two app engineers would typically work full time on the application until it was completed while the other engineers would work on multiple projects as needed. Likewise, GUI designers would work on the project at certain key stages in the product development cycle when their expertise was needed.

The head of Graphics manages the GUI designers' schedule while the head of Software manages the software engineer assignments. At the end of each project Account Managers submitted performance reviews of their team. The Director of Sales was responsible for the Account Managers' performance reviews based on customer satisfaction, generation of sales, and project performance.

Horizon believed in iterative development and every two to three weeks Account Managers were expected to demonstrate the latest version of applications to clients. This led to useful feedback and in many cases redefining the scope of the project. Often clients wanted to add more functionality to their application once they realized what the software could do. Depending upon the complexity of the application and changes introduced once the project was under way, it typically took Horizon two to four months to deliver a finished product to a client.

Patti was currently working on three projects. One was for Shanghai Wok, a busy Chinese mom and pop restaurant located in downtown Charlotte, North Carolina. The owners of Shanghai Wok wanted Horizon to create a smartphone app that would allow customers to order and pay in advance for meals they would simply pick up at a walk-up window. The second project was for Taste of India that operated in Kannapolis, North Carolina. They wanted Horizon to create a phone app that would allow staff at the nearby bio-tech firms to order food that would be delivered on-site during lunch and dinner hours. The last project was for Nearly Normal, a vegetarian restaurant which wanted to send out e-mail alerts to subscribers that would describe in detail their daily fresh specials.

James Thrasher was an admirer of Google and encouraged a playful but focused environment at work. Employees were allowed to decorate their work spaces, bring pets to work, and play ping pong or pool when they needed a break. Horizon paid its employees well but the big payoff was the annual Christmas bonus. This bonus was based on overall company profits, which were distributed proportionately based on pay grade and performance reviews. It was not uncommon for employees to receive a 10–15 percent boost in pay at the end of the year.

STATUS REPORT MEETING

As was her habit Patti entered the status report meeting room early. David Briggs was in the midst of describing the game-winning catch John Lorsch had made in last night's softball game. Horizon sponsored a co-ed city league softball team which most of the Account Managers played on. Patti had been coaxed to play to ensure that the requisite number of "females" were on the field. She balked at the idea at first; softball wasn't really her sport, but she was glad she did. Not only was it fun, but it gave her a chance to get to know the other managers.

James Thrasher entered the room and everyone settled down to business. He started off as he always did by asking if anybody had important news to bring to everyone's attention. Jackson Browne slowly raised his hand and said, "I am afraid I do. I just received notification from Apple IOS that they have rejected our TAT app." TAT was a phone app that Jackson was the project lead on that allowed subscribers to reserve and see in real time what swimming lanes were available at a prestigious athletic club. This announcement was followed by a collective groan. Before an Apple app could go operational it had to be submitted and approved by Apple. Usually this was not a problem, but lately Apple had been rejecting apps for a variety of reasons. Jackson went on to circulate the list of changes that had to be made before Apple would approve the app. The group studied the list, and in some cases ridiculed the new requirements.

Ultimately, James Thrasher asked Jackson how long it would take to make the necessary changes and resubmit the app for approval. Jackson felt it would probably take two to three weeks at most. Thrasher asked who the engineers that worked on this project were. Patti's heart fell. One of the app engineers who had developed the TAT app was working on her Shanghai Wok project. She knew what was going to happen next. Thrasher announced, "OK everyone, it only makes sense that these engineers are the best ones to finish what they had started so they are all going to have to be reassigned back to the TAT project. Those affected are going to have to get together after this meeting and figure how you are going to replace them." The meeting then proceeded as planned with each account manager reporting the status of their projects, and sharing relevant issues with the group.

POST-MEETING

As everyone filed out, Patti looked around to see who else was in her same boat. There were three other Account Managers as well as Jackson Browne. Resource assignments were a reoccurring issue at Horizon given the nature of their work. Horizon had developed a policy where decisions were made based on project priority. Each project was assigned a Green, Blue or Purple designation based on the company priority. Priority status was based on the extent the project contributed to the mission of the firm. The Shanghai Wok project given its limited size and scope was a Purple project, which was the lowest ranking. The list of available software engineers was displayed on the big screen. Patti was only familiar with a few of the names.

Leigh Taylor who had the only Green project immediately selected Jason Wheeler from the list. She had used him before and was confident in his work. Tom Watson and Samantha Stewart both had Blue Projects and both needed to replace a mobile app engineer. They both immediately jumped on the name of Prem Mathew, claiming he was the best person for their project. After some friendly jousting, Tom said, "OK, Sam, you can have him; I remember when you helped me out on the Argos project; besides my project is just beginning. I'll take Shin Chen." Everyone looked at Patti; she started by saying, "You know, I am only familiar with a few of these names; I guess I'll go with Mike Thu." Jackson interjected, "Hey everyone, I am really sorry this happened, and I am sure Mike is a good programmer, but I recommend you work with Axel Gerthoff. I have used him before, and he is a very quick study and a joy to work with." This was a relief to Patti and she quickly took his advice. They left to submit a report to Thrasher detailing the decisions they each had made and the impact on their project.

1. How successful was the post-meeting?
2. What factors contributed to the success or failure of this meeting?
3. What kind of project management structure does Horizon use? Is it the right structure? Explain.

CHAPTER FOUR

Defining the Project

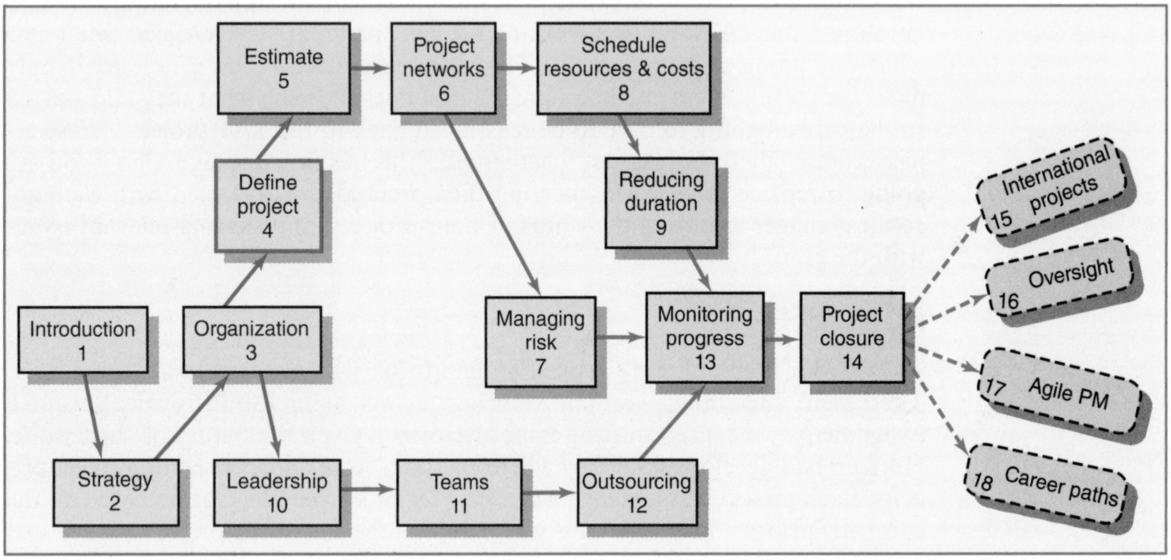

Defining the Project

Step 1: Defining the Project Scope
Step 2: Establishing Project Priorities
Step 3: Creating the Work Breakdown Structure
Step 4: Integrating the WBS with the Organization
Step 5: Coding the WBS for the Information System
Responsibility Matrices
Project Communication Plan
Summary

S*elect a dream*
U*se your dream to set a goal*
C*reate a plan*
C*onsider resources*
E*nhance skills and abilities*
S*pend time wisely*
S*tart! Get organized and go*

. . . it is one of those acro-whatevers,
*said Pooh.**

Project managers in charge of a single small project can plan and schedule the project tasks without much formal planning and information. However, when the project manager must manage several small projects or a large complex project, a threshold is quickly reached in which the project manager can no longer cope with the detail.

This chapter describes a disciplined, structured method for selectively collecting information to use through all phases of the project life cycle, to meet the needs of all stakeholders (e.g., customer, project manager), and to measure performance against the strategic plan of the organization. The method suggested is a selective outline of the project called the *work breakdown structure*. The early stages of developing the outline serve to ensure that all tasks are identified and that participants of the project have an understanding of what is to be done. Once the outline and its detail are defined, an integrated information system can be developed to schedule work and allocate budgets. This baseline information is later used for control.

In addition, the chapter presents a variant of the work breakdown structure called the *process breakdown structure* as well as responsibility matrices that are used for smaller, less complex projects. With the work of the project defined through the *work breakdown structure,* the chapter concludes with the process of creating a communication plan used to help coordinate project activities and follow progress.

The five generic steps described herein provide a structured approach for collecting the project information necessary for developing a work breakdown structure. These steps and the development of project networks found in the next chapters all take place concurrently, and several iterations are typically required to develop dates and budgets that can be used to manage the project. The old saying "We can control only what we have planned" is true; therefore, defining the project is the first step.

* Roger E. Allen and Stephen D. Allen, *Winnie-the-Pooh on Success* (New York: Penguin, 1997), p. 10.

SNAPSHOT FROM PRACTICE

Big Bertha II versus the USGA's COR Requirement*

© Time & Life Pictures/Getty Images

In 1991 Callaway Golf Equipment introduced their Big Bertha driver and revolutionized the golf equipment business. Big Bertha—named after the World War I German long-distance cannon—was much larger than conventional woods and lacked a hosel (the socket in the head of the club into which the shaft is inserted) so that the weight could be better distributed throughout the head. This innovative design gave the clubhead a larger sweet spot, which allowed a player to strike the golf ball off-center and not suffer much loss in distance or accuracy. Callaway has maintained its preeminent position in the golf industry by utilizing space-age technology to extend the accuracy and distance of golf equipment.

In 2000 Callaway introduced the Big Bertha ERC II forged titanium driver. The driver was technologically superior to any driver on the market. However, there was one big problem. The new version of Bertha did not conform to the coefficient of restitution (COR) requirement established by the United States Golf Association (USGA). As a result it was barred from use by golfers in North America who intended to play by USGA's Rules of Golf.

The USGA believed that the rapid technological advances in golf equipment made by Callaway Golf and other golf manufacturers were threatening the integrity of the game. Players were hitting balls so much farther and straighter that golf courses around the world were being redesigned to make them longer and more difficult.

So in 1998 the USGA established performance thresholds for all new golf equipment. In order to prevent manufacturers from developing more powerful clubs, the USGA limited the COR of new golf equipment to 0.83. The COR was calculated by firing a golf ball at a driver out of a cannon-like machine at 109 miles per hour. The speed that the ball returned to the cannon could not exceed 83 percent of its initial speed (90.47 mph). The USGA called the ratio of incoming to outgoing velocity the coefficient of restitution (COR). The intent of the USGA COR threshold was to limit the distance that golf balls could be hit since studies indicated that 0.01 increase in COR resulted in two extra yards of carry. The Big Bertha ERC II's COR was 0.86.

After numerous efforts to get USGA to change its technical requirements, Callaway's engineers went back to the drawing board and in 2002 introduced Great Big Bertha II, which conformed to USGA's 0.83 COR restriction.

* John E. Gamble. "Callaway Golf Company: Sustaining Advantage in a Changing Industry," in A. A. Thompson, J. E. Gamble, and A. J. Strickland, *Strategy: Winning in the Marketplace,* Boston: McGraw-Hill/Irwin, 2004, pp. C204–C228.

SNAPSHOT FROM PRACTICE Scope Statement

PROJECT OBJECTIVE

To construct a high-quality, custom home within five months at cost not to exceed $500,000.

DELIVERABLES

- A 2,200-square-foot, 2½-bath, 3-bedroom, finished home.
- A finished garage, insulated and sheetrocked.
- Kitchen appliances to include range, oven, microwave, and dishwasher.
- High-efficiency gas furnace with programmable thermostat.

MILESTONES

1. Permits approved—March 5
2. Foundation poured—March 14
3. Drywall in. Framing, sheathing, plumbing, electrical, and mechanical inspections passed—May 25
4. Final inspection—June 7

TECHNICAL REQUIREMENTS

1. Home must meet local building codes.
2. All windows and doors must pass NFRC class 40 energy ratings.
3. Exterior wall insulation must meet an "R" factor of 21.
4. Ceiling insulation must meet an "R" factor of 38.
5. Floor insulation must meet an "R" factor of 25.
6. Garage will accommodate two large-size cars and one 20-foot Winnebago.
7. Structure must pass seismic stability codes.

LIMITS AND EXCLUSIONS

1. The home will be built to the specifications and design of the original blueprints provided by the customer.
2. Owner is responsible for landscaping.
3. Refrigerator is not included among kitchen appliances.
4. Air conditioning is not included but prewiring is included.
5. Contractor reserves the right to contract out services.
6. Contractor is responsible for subcontracted work.
7. Site work limited to Monday through Friday, 8:00 A.M. to 6:00 P.M.

CUSTOMER REVIEW

John and Joan Smith

The checklist on pages 102–103 is generic. Different industries and companies will develop unique checklists and templates to fit their needs and specific kinds of projects. A few companies engaged in contracted work refer to scope statements as "statements of work" (SOW). Other organizations use the term *project charter.* However, the term **project charter** has emerged to have a special meaning in the world of project management. A project charter refers to a document that authorizes the project manager to initiate and lead the project. This document is issued by upper management and provides the project manager with written authority to use organizational resources for project activities. Often the charter will include a brief scope description as well as such items as risk limits, customer needs, spending limits, and even team composition.

Many projects suffer from **scope creep,** which is the tendency for the project scope to expand over time—usually by changing requirements, specifications, and priorities. Scope creep can be reduced by carefully writing your scope statement. A scope statement that is too broad is an invitation for scope creep. Scope creep can have a positive or negative effect on the project, but in most cases scope creep means added costs and possible project delays. Changes in requirements, specifications, and priorities frequently result in cost overruns and delays. Examples are abundant—Denver airport baggage handling system; Boston's new freeway system ("The Big Dig"); China's fast train in Shanghai; and the list goes on. On software development projects, scope creep is manifested in bloated products in which added functionality undermines ease of use.

Finally, the matrix is useful midway in the project for approaching a problem that must be solved.

One caveat must be mentioned; during the course of a project, priorities may change. The customer may suddenly need the project completed one month sooner, or new directives from top management may emphasize cost saving initiatives. The project manager needs to be vigilant in order to anticipate and confirm changes in priorities and make appropriate adjustments.

Step 3: Creating the Work Breakdown Structure

Major Groupings Found in a WBS

Once the scope and deliverables have been identified, the work of the project can be successively subdivided into smaller and smaller work elements. The outcome of this hierarchical process is called the **work breakdown structure (WBS).** Use of WBS helps to assure project managers that all products and work elements are identified, to integrate the project with the current organization, and to establish a basis for control. Basically, the WBS is an outline of the project with different levels of detail.

Figure 4.3 shows the major groupings commonly used in the field to develop a hierarchical WBS. The WBS begins with the project as the final deliverable. Major

FIGURE 4.3
Hierarchical Breakdown of the WBS

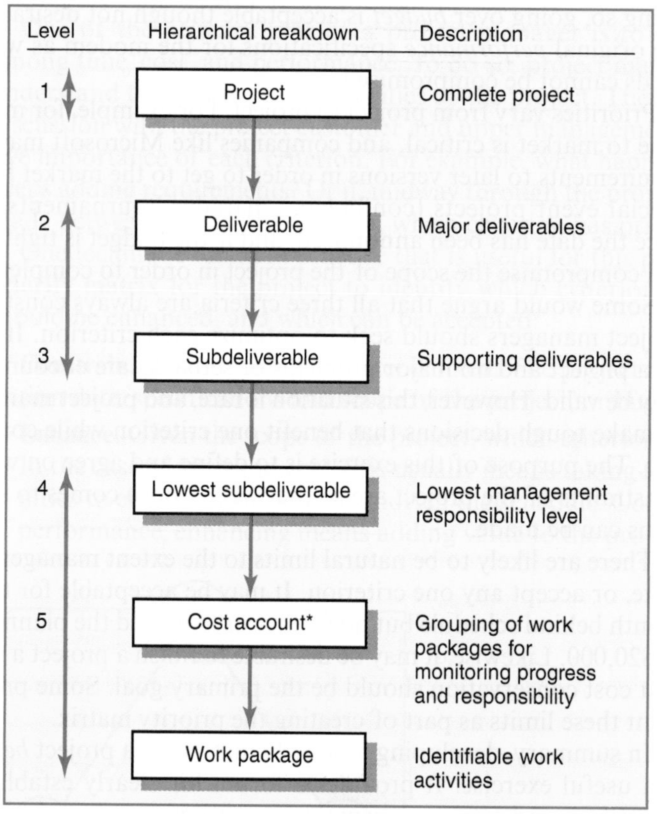

* This breakdown groups work packages by type of work within a deliverable and allows assignment of responsibility to an organizational unit. This extra step facilitates a system for monitoring project progress (discussed in Chapter 13).

project work deliverables/systems are identified first; then the subdeliverables necessary to accomplish the larger deliverables are defined. The process is repeated until the subdeliverable detail is small enough to be manageable and where one person can be responsible. This subdeliverable is further divided into work packages. Because the lowest subdeliverable usually includes several work packages, the work packages are grouped by type of work—for example, design and testing. These groupings within a subdeliverable are called cost accounts. This grouping facilitates a system for monitoring project progress by work, cost, and responsibility.

How WBS Helps the Project Manager

The WBS defines all the elements of the project in a hierarchical framework and establishes their relationships to the project end item(s). Think of the project as a large work package that is successively broken down into smaller work packages; the total project is the summation of all the smaller work packages. This hierarchical structure facilitates evaluation of cost, time, and technical performance at all levels in the organization over the life of the project. The WBS also provides management with information appropriate to each level. For example, top management deals primarily with major deliverables, while first-line supervisors deal with smaller subdeliverables and work packages.

Each item in the WBS needs a time and cost estimate. With this information it is possible to plan, schedule, and budget your project. The WBS also serves as a framework for tracking cost and work performance.

As the WBS is developed, organizational units and individuals are assigned responsibility for executing work packages. This integrates the work and the organization. In practice, this process is sometimes called the organization breakdown structure (OBS), which will be further discussed later in the chapter.

Use of the WBS provides the opportunity to "roll up" (sum) the budget and actual costs of the smaller work packages into larger work elements so that performance can be measured by organizational units and work accomplishment.

The WBS can also be used to define communication channels and assist in understanding and coordinating many parts of the project. The structure shows the work and organizational units responsible and suggests where written communication should be directed. Problems can be quickly addressed and coordinated because the structure integrates work and responsibility.

A Simple WBS Development

Figure 4.4 shows a simplified WBS to develop a new prototype tablet computer. At the top of the chart (level 1) is the project end item—the E-Slim Tablet x-13 Prototype. The subdeliverables levels (2–5) below level 1 represent further decomposition of work. The levels of the structure can also represent information for different levels of management. For example, level 1 information represents the total project objective and is useful to top management; levels 2, 3, and 4 are suitable for middle management; and level 5 is for first-line managers.

In Figure 4.4 level 2 indicates there are two major deliverables—Hardware and CPU, or central processing unit. (There are likely to be other major

FIGURE 4.4 Work Breakdown Structure

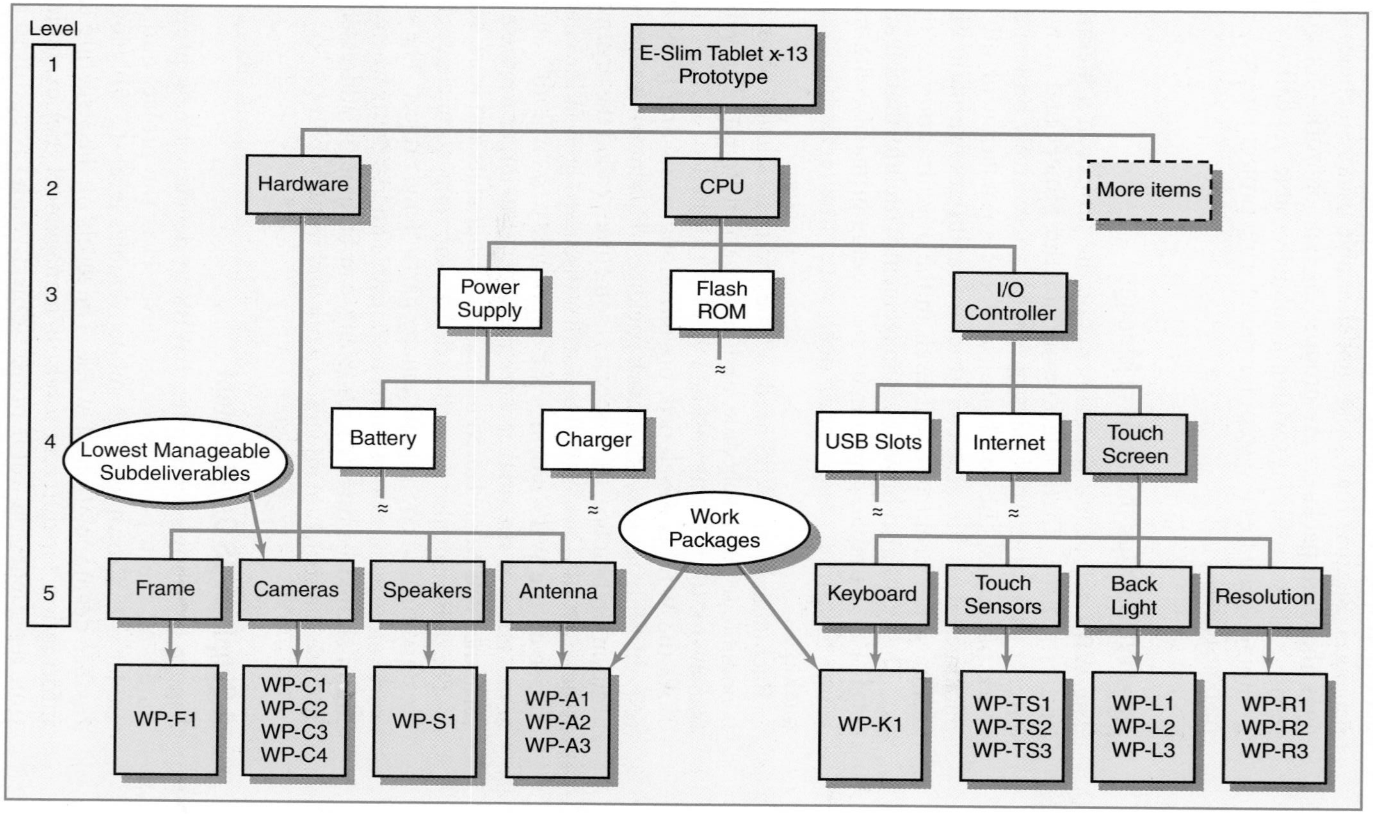

deliverables such as software, but for illustrative purposes we are limiting our focus to just two major deliverables.) At level 3, the CPU is connected to three deliverables—Power Supply, Flash ROM, and I/O Controller. The I/O Controller has three subdeliverables at level 4—USB Slots, Internet, and Touch Screen. The many subdeliverables for USB Slots and Internet have not been decomposed. The Touch Screen (shaded) has been decomposed down to level 5 and to the work package level.

Note that level 2, Hardware, skips levels 3 and 4 because the final subdeliverables can be pushed down to the lowest manageable level 5; skipping levels 3 and 4 suggests little coordination is needed and skilled team members are already familiar with the work needed to complete the level 5 subdeliverables. For example, Hardware requires four subdeliverables at level 5—Frame, Cameras, Speakers, and Antenna. Each subdeliverable includes work packages that will be completed by an assigned organizational unit. Observe that the Cameras subdeliverable includes four work packages—WP-C1, 2, 3, and 4. The Back Light, a subdeliverable of Touch Screen, includes three work packages—WP-L 1, 2, and 3.

The lowest level of the WBS is called a **work package.** Work packages are short-duration tasks that have a definite start and stop point, consume resources, and represent cost. Each work package is a control point. A work package manager is responsible for seeing that the package is completed on time, within budget, and according to technical specifications. Practice suggests a work package should not exceed 10 workdays or one reporting period. If a work package has a duration exceeding 10 days, check or monitoring points should be established within the duration, say, every three to five days, so progress and problems can be identified before too much time has passed. Each work package of the WBS should be as independent of other packages of the project as possible. No work package is described in more than one subdeliverable of the WBS.

There is an important difference from start to finish between the last work breakdown subdeliverable and a work package. Typically, a work breakdown subdeliverable includes the outcomes of more than one work package from perhaps two or three departments. Therefore, the subdeliverable does not have a duration of its own and does not consume resources or cost money directly. (In a sense, of course, a duration for a particular work breakdown element can be derived from identifying which work package must start first [earliest] and which package will be the latest to finish; the difference from start to finish becomes the duration for the subdeliverable.) The higher elements are used to identify deliverables at different phases in the project and to develop status reports during the execution stage of the project life cycle. Thus, the work package is the basic unit used for planning, scheduling, and controlling the project.

To review, each work package in the WBS

1. Defines work (what).
2. Identifies time to complete a work package (how long).
3. Identifies a time-phased budget to complete a work package (cost).
4. Identifies resources needed to complete a work package (how much).
5. Identifies a single person responsible for units of work (who).
6. Identifies monitoring points for measuring progress (how well).

Creating a WBS from scratch can be a daunting task. Project managers should take advantage of relevant examples from previous projects to begin the process.

FIGURE 4.5 Integration of WBS and OBS

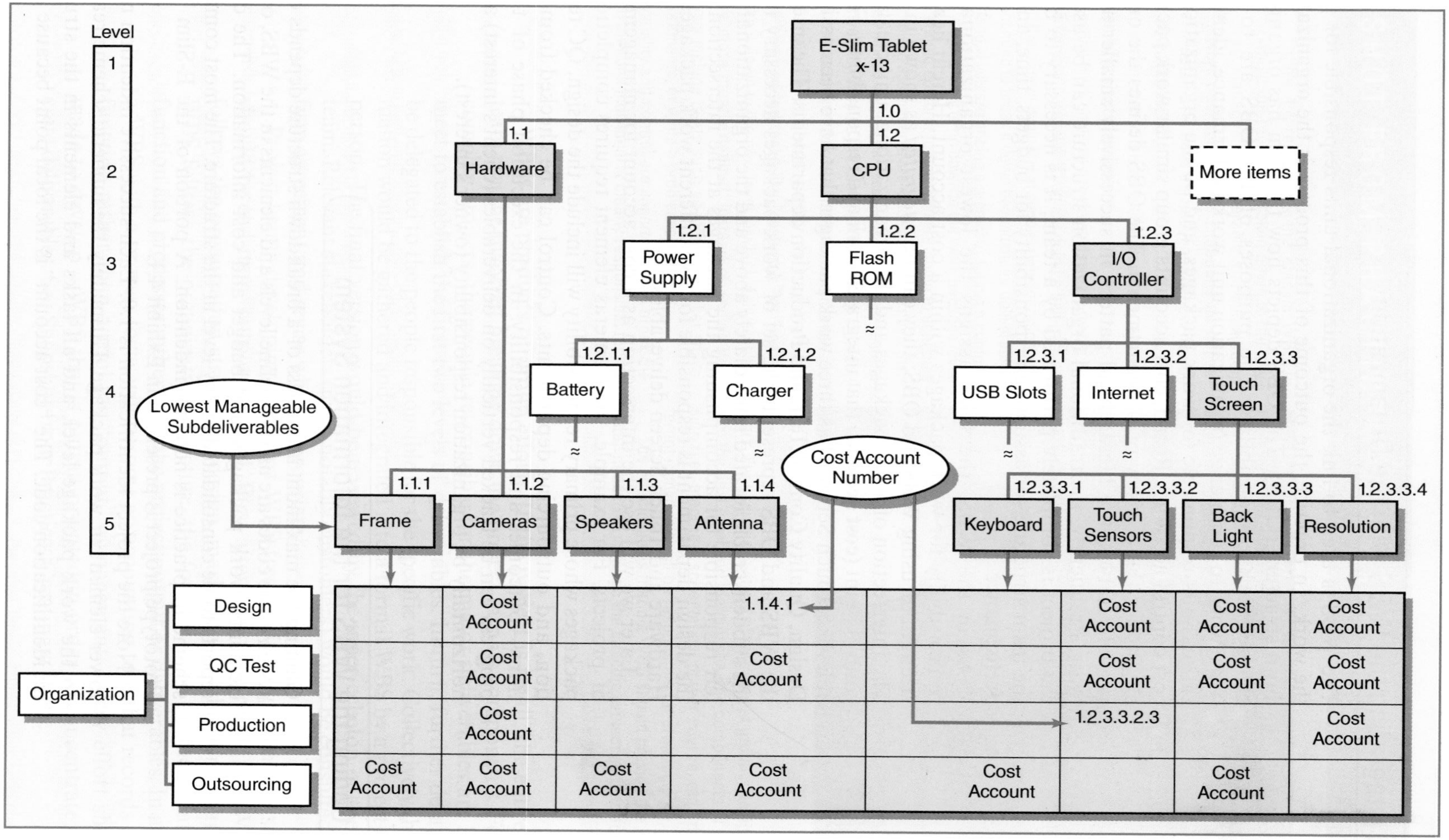

EXHIBIT 4.1
Coding the WBS

	Task Mode	Task Name
1		**1 E-Slim Tablet x-13 Prototype**
2		**1.1 Hardware**
3		1.1.1 Cameras
4		1.1.2 Speakers
5		1.1.3 Antenna
6		**1.2 CPU**
7		**1.2.1 Power supply**
8		1.2.1.1 Battery (more items)
9		1.2.1.2 Charger (more items)
10		**1.2.2 Flash Rom (more items)**
11		1.2.2.1 I/O controller
12		1.2.2.2 USB slots (more items)
13		1.2.2.3 Internet (more items)
14		**1.2.3 Touch screen**
15		**1.2.3.1 Keyboard**
16		1.2.3.1.1 Work package
17		**1.2.3.2 Touch sensors**
18		1.2.3.2.1 Work package
19		1.2.3.2.2 Work package
20		1.2.3.2.3 Work package
21		1.2.3.3 Back light (more items)
22		1.2.3.4 Resolution (more items)

work assignments, time, cost, and technical performance come together at this point.

This coding system can be extended to cover large projects. Additional schemes can be added for special reports. For example, adding a "23" after the code could indicate a site location, an elevation, or a special account such as labor. Some letters can be used as special identifiers such as "M" for materials or "E" for engineers. You are not limited to only 10 subdivisions (0–9); you can extend each subdivision to large numbers—for example, .1−.99 or .1−.9999. If the project is small, you can use whole numbers. The following example is from a large, complex project:

3R−237A−P2−33.6

where 3R identifies the facility, 237A represents elevation and the area, P2 represents pipe two inches wide, and 33.6 represents the work package number. In practice most organizations are creative in combining letters and numbers to minimize the length of WBS codes.

FIGURE 4.7 Responsibility Matrix for a Market Research Project

	Project Team				
Task	Richard	Dan	Dave	Linda	Elizabeth
Identify target customers	R	S		S	
Develop draft questionnaire	R	S	S		
Pilot-test questionnaire		R		S	
Finalize questionnaire	R	S	S	S	
Print questionnaire					R
Prepare mailing labels					R
Mail questionnaires					R
Receive and monitor returned questionnaires				R	S
Input response data			R		
Analyze results		R	S	S	
Prepare draft of report	S	R	S	S	
Prepare final report	R		S		

R = Responsible
S = Supports/assists

example, Figure 4.8 is an RM for a larger, more complex project to develop a new piece of automated equipment. Notice that within each cell a numeric coding scheme is used to define the nature of involvement on that specific task. Such an RM extends the WBS/OBS and provides a clear and concise method for depicting responsibility, authority, and communication channels.

Responsibility matrices provide a means for all participants in a project to view their responsibilities and agree on their assignments. They also help clarify the extent or type of authority exercised by each participant in performing an activity in which two or more parties have overlapping involvement. By using an RM and by defining authority, responsibility, and communications within its framework, the relationship between different organizational units and the work content of the project is made clear.

Project Communication Plan

Once the project deliverables and work are clearly identified, following up with an internal communication plan is vital. Stories abound of poor communication as a major contributor to project failure. Having a robust communications plan can go a long way toward mitigating project problems and can ensure that customers, team members, and other stakeholders have the information to do their jobs.

The communication plan is usually created by the project manager and/or the project team in the early stage of project planning.

Communication is a key component in coordinating and tracking project schedules, issues, and action items. The plan maps out the flow of information to

FIGURE 4.8 Responsibility Matrix for the Conveyor Belt Project

	Organization							
Deliverables	Design	Development	Documentation	Assembly	Testing	Purchasing	Quality Assur.	Manufacturing
Architectural designs	1	2			2		3	3
Hardware specifications	2	1				2	3	
Kernel specifications	1	3						3
Utilities specifications	2	1			3			
Hardware design	1			3		3		3
Disk drivers	3	1	2					
Memory management	1	3			3			
Operating system documentation	2	2	1					3
Prototypes	5		4	1	3	3	3	4
Integrated acceptance test	5	2	2		1		5	5

1 Responsible
2 Support
3 Consult
4 Notification
5 Approval

5. Develop a WBS for a local stage play. Be sure to identify the deliverables and organizational units (people) responsible. How would you code your system? Give an example of the work packages in one of your cost accounts. Develop a corresponding OBS which identifies who is responsible for what.
6. Use an example of a project you are familiar with or are interested in. Identify the deliverables and organizational units (people) responsible. How would you code your system? Give an example of the work packages in one of your cost accounts.
7. Develop a communication plan for an airport security project. The project entails installing the hardware and software system that (1) scans a passenger's eyes, (2) fingerprints the passenger, and (3) transmits the information to a central location for evaluation.
8. Go to an Internet search engine (e.g., Google) and type in "project communication plan." Check three or four that have ".gov" as their source. How are they similar or dissimilar? What would be your conclusion concerning the importance of an internal communication plan?
9. Your roommate is about to submit a scope statement for a spring concert sponsored by the entertainment council at Western Evergreen State University (WESU). WESU is a residential university with over 22,000 students. This will be the first time in six years since WESU sponsored a spring concert. The entertainment council has budgeted $40,000 for the project. The event is to occur on June 5th. Since your roommate knows you are taking a class on project management she has asked you to review her scope statement and make suggestions for improvement. She considers the concert a resume-building experience and wants to be as professional as possible. Below is a draft of her scope statement. What suggestions would you make and why?

WESU Spring Music Concert

Project Objective

To organize and deliver a 6-hour music concert

Deliverables

- Concert security
- Contact local newspapers and radio stations
- Separate beer garden
- Six hours of musical entertainment
- Design a commemorative concert t-shirt
- Local sponsors
- Food venues
- Event insurance
- Safe environment

Milestones

1. Secure all permissions and approvals
2. Sign big-name artist
3. Contact secondary artists
4. Secure vendor contracts
5. Advertising campaign
6. Plan set-up
7. Concert
8. Clean-up

Technical Requirements

1. Professional sound stage and system
2. At least five performing acts
3. Restroom facilities
4. Parking
5. Compliance with WESU and city requirements/ordinances

Limits and Exclusions

- Seating capacity for 8,000 students.
- Performers are responsible for travel arrangement to and from WESU.
- Performers must provide own liability insurance.
- Performers and security personnel will be provided lunch and dinner on the day of the concert.
- Vendors contribute 25 percent of sales to concert fund.
- Concert must be over at 12:15 A.M.

Customer Review: WESU

References

Ashley, D. B., et al., "Determinants of Construction Project Success," *Project Management Journal,* 18 (2) June 1987, p. 72.

Chilmeran, A. H., "Keeping Costs on Track," *PM Network,* 19 (2) 2004, pp. 45–51.

Gary, L. "Will Project Scope Cost You—Or Create Value?" *Harvard Management Update,* January 2005.

Gobeli, D. H., and E. W. Larson, "Project Management Problems," *Engineering Management Journal,* 2, 1990, pp. 31–36.

Ingebretsen, M., "Taming the Beast," *PM Network,* July 2003, pp. 30–35.

Katz, D. M., "Case Study: Beware 'Scope Creep' on ERP Projects," *CFO.com,* March 27, 2001.

Kerzner, H., *Project Management: A Systems Approach to Planning,* 8th ed. (New York: Van Nostrand Reinhold, 2003).

Lewis, J. P., *Project Planning, Scheduling and Controlling,* 3rd ed. (Burr Ridge, IL: McGraw-Hill, 2000).

Luby, R. E., D. Peel, and W. Swahl, "Component-Based Work Breakdown Structure," *Project Management Journal,* 26 (2) December 1995, pp. 38–44.

Murch, R., *Project Management: Best Practices for IT Professionals* (Upper Darby, NJ: Prentice Hall, 2001).

Pinto, J. K., and D. P. Slevin, "Critical Success Factors Across the Project Life Cycle," *Project Management Journal,* 19 (3) June 1988, p. 72.

Pitagorsky, G., "Realistic Project Planning Promotes Success," *Engineer's Digest,* 29 (1) 2001.

PMI Standards Committee, *Guide to the Project Management Body of Knowledge* (Newton Square, PA: Project Management Institute, 2000).

Posner, B. Z., "What It Takes to Be a Good Project Manager," *Project Management Journal,* 18 (1) March 1987, p. 52.

Raz, T., and S. Globerson, "Effective Sizing and Content Definition of Work Packages," *Project Management Journal,* 29 (4) 1998, pp. 17–23.

The Standish Group, *CHAOS Summary 2009,* pp. 1–4.

Tate, K., and K. Hendrix, "Chartering IT Projects," *Proceedings, 30th Annual, Project Management Institute* (Philadelphia, PA. 1999), CD.

CHAPTER FIVE

Estimating Project Times and Costs

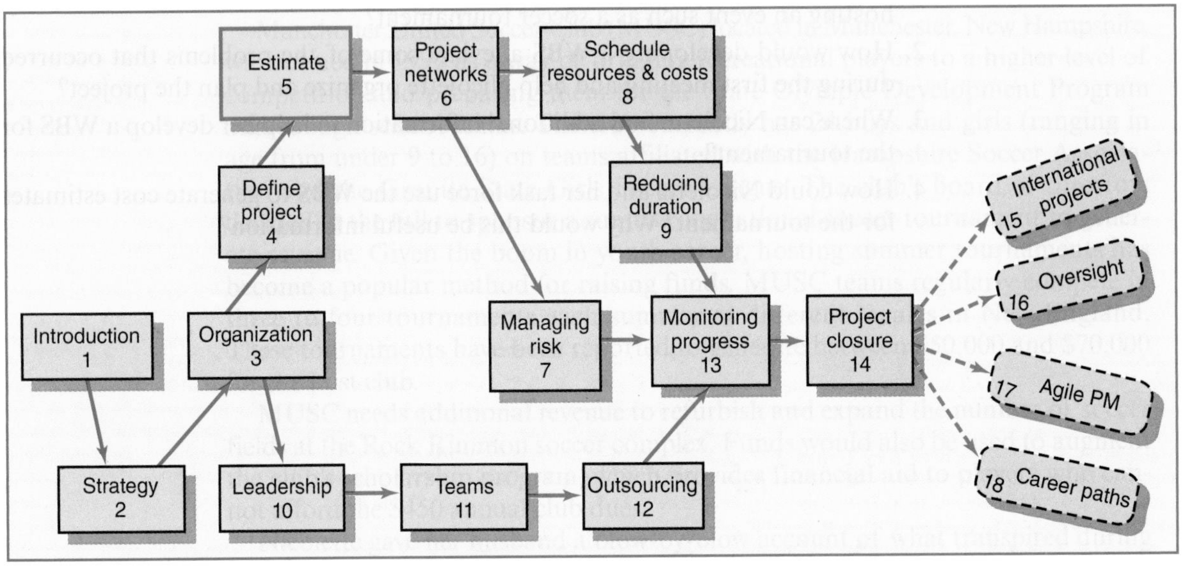

Estimating Project Times and Costs

Factors Influencing the Quality of Estimates

Estimating Guidelines for Times, Costs, and Resources

Top-Down versus Bottom-Up Estimating

Methods for Estimating Project Times and Costs

Level of Detail

Types of Costs

Refining Estimates

Creating a Database for Estimating

Summary

Appendix 5.1: Learning Curves for Estimating

*Project estimation is indeed a yardstick for project cost control. And if the yardstick is faulty, you start on the "wrong foot." . . . we exhort you not to underestimate the estimate.**

Given the urgency to start work on the project, managers sometimes minimize or avoid the effort to follow through on estimating project time and cost. This attitude is a huge mistake and costly. There are important reasons to make the effort and incur the cost of estimating for your project. Exhibit 5.1 summarizes some key reasons.

Estimating is the process of forecasting or approximating the time and cost of completing project deliverables. Estimating processes are frequently classified as top-down and bottom-up. Top-down estimates are usually done by senior management. Management will often derive estimates from analogy, group consensus, or mathematical relationships. Bottom-up estimates are typically performed by the people who are doing the work. Their estimates are based on estimates of elements found in the work breakdown structure.

All project stakeholders prefer accurate cost and time estimates, but they also understand the inherent uncertainty in all projects. Inaccurate estimates lead to false expectations and consumer dissatisfaction. Accuracy is improved with greater effort, but is it worth the time and cost—estimating costs money! Project estimating becomes a trade-off, balancing the benefits of better accuracy against the costs for securing increased accuracy.

Cost, time, and budget estimates are the lifeline for control; they serve as the standard for comparison of actual and plan throughout the life of the project. Project status reports depend on reliable estimates as the major input for measuring variances and taking corrective action. Ideally, the project manager, and in most cases the customer, would prefer to have a database of detailed schedule and cost estimates for every work package in the project. Regrettably, such detailed data gathering is not always possible or practical and other methods are used to develop project estimates.

EXHIBIT 5.1
Why Estimating Time and Cost Are Important

- Estimates are needed to support good decisions.
- Estimates are needed to schedule work.
- Estimates are needed to determine how long the project should take and its cost.
- Estimates are needed to determine whether the project is worth doing.
- Estimates are needed to develop cash flow needs.
- Estimates are needed to determine how well the project is progressing.
- Estimates are needed to develop time-phased budgets and establish the project baseline.

* O. P. Kharbanda and J. K. Pinto, *What Made Gertie Gallop: Learning from Project Failures* (New York: Von Nostrand Reinhold, 1996), p. 73.

TABLE 5.1
Conditions for Preferring Top-Down or Bottom-Up Time and Cost Estimates

Condition	Top-Down Estimates	Bottom-Up Estimates
Strategic decision making	X	
Cost and time important		X
High uncertainty	X	
Internal, small project	X	
Fixed-price contract		X
Customer wants details		X
Unstable scope	X	

However, there are sound reasons for using top-down or bottom-up estimates. Table 5.1 depicts conditions that suggest when one approach is preferred over another.

Top-down estimates usually are derived from someone who uses experience and/or information to determine the project duration and total cost. However, these estimates are sometimes made by top managers who have very little knowledge of the component activities used to complete the project. For example, a mayor of a major city making a speech noted that a new law building would be constructed at a cost of $23 million and would be ready for occupancy in two and one-half years. Although the mayor probably asked for an estimate from someone, the estimate could have come from a luncheon meeting with a local contractor who wrote an estimate (guesstimate) on a napkin. This is an extreme example, but in a relative sense this scenario is frequently played out in practice. See Snapshot from Practice: Council Fumes, for another example of this. The question actually is, *do these estimates represent low-cost, efficient methods*? Seldom. The fact that the estimate came from the top can influence people responsible to "do what it takes to make the estimate."

If possible and practical, you want to push the estimating process down to the work package level for bottom-up estimates that establish low-cost, efficient methods. This process can take place after the project has been defined in detail. Good sense suggests project estimates should come from the people most knowledgeable about the estimate needed. The use of several people with relevant experience with the task can improve the time and cost estimate. The **bottom-up** approach at the work package level can serve as a check on cost elements in the WBS by rolling up the work packages and associated cost accounts to major deliverables. Similarly, resource requirements can be checked. Later, the time, resource, and cost estimates from the work packages can be consolidated into time-phased networks, resource schedules, and budgets that are used for control.

The bottom-up approach also provides the customer with an opportunity to compare the low-cost, efficient method approach with any imposed restrictions. For example, if the project completion duration is imposed at two years and your bottom-up analysis tells you the project will take two and one-half years, the client can now consider the trade-off of the low-cost method versus compressing the project to two years—or in rare cases canceling the project. Similar trade-offs can be compared for different levels of resources or increases in technical performance. The assumption is any movement away from the low-cost, efficient method will increase costs—e.g., overtime. The preferred approach in defining the project is to make rough top-down estimates, develop the WBS/OBS, make bottom-up estimates, develop schedules and budgets, and reconcile differences between top-down and bottom-up estimates. Hopefully, these steps will be done *before* final

SNAPSHOT FROM PRACTICE Council Fumes as Tram Tale Unfolds*

Portland, Oregon's, Willamette riverfront development has exploded with seven condominium towers and a new health sciences center under construction. The health science complex is to be linked with Oregon Health Sciences University (OHSU), which is high on a nearby hill, with an aerial cable tram.

The aerial tram linking the waterfront district to OHSU is to support the university expansion, to increase biotechnology research, and to become Portland's icon equivalent to Seattle's Space Needle. All of the hype turned south when news from a hearing suggested that the real budget for the tram construction, originally estimated at $15 million, is going to be about $55–$60 million, nearly triple the original estimate. The estimate could even go higher. Commissioners want to find out why city staff knowingly relied on flawed estimates. Mike Lindberg, president of the nonprofit Aerial Transportation Inc., acknowledged "the $15 million number was not a good number. It was simply a guesstimate." Commissioner Erik Sten said, "Those numbers were presented as much more firm than they appear to have been. . . . It appears the actual design wasn't costed out. That's pretty shoddy."

© Cliff Gray

* *The Oregonian,* January 13, 2006, by Frank Ryan, pages A1 and A14, and April 2, 2006, page A1.

negotiation with either an internal or external customer. In conclusion, the ideal approach is for the project manager to allow enough time for both the top-down and bottom-up estimates to be worked out so a complete plan based on reliable estimates can be offered to the customer. In this way false expectations are minimized for all stakeholders and negotiation is reduced.

Methods for Estimating Project Times and Costs

Top-Down Approaches for Estimating Project Times and Costs

At the strategic level top-down estimating methods are used to evaluate the project proposal. Sometimes much of the information needed to derive accurate time and cost estimates is not available in the initial phase of the project—for example, design is not finalized. In these situations top-down estimates are used until the tasks in the WBS are clearly defined.

Consensus Methods

This method simply uses the pooled experience of senior and/or middle managers to estimate the total project duration and cost. This typically involves a meeting where experts discuss, argue, and ultimately reach a decision as to their best guess estimate. Firms seeking greater rigor will use the Delphi Method to make these macro estimates. See Snapshot from Practice: The Delphi Method.

It is important to recognize that these first top-down estimates are only a rough cut and typically occur in the "conceptual" stage of the project. The top-down

TABLE 5.2
Simplified Basic Function Point Count Process for a Prospective Project or Deliverable

	Complexity Weighting			
Element	**Low**	**Average**	**High**	**Total**
Number of *inputs*	____ × 2 +	____ × 3 +	____ × 4	= ____
Number of *outputs*	____ × 3 +	____ × 6 +	____ × 9	= ____
Number of *inquiries*	____ × 2 +	____ × 4 +	____ × 6	= ____
Number of *files*	____ × 5 +	____ × 8 +	____ × 12	= ____
Number of *interfaces*	____ × 5 +	____ × 10 +	____ × 15	= ____

historical data by type of software project for the industry—for example, MIS systems. In the U.S. software industry, one-person month represents on average five function points. A person working one month can generate on average (across all types of software projects) about five function points. Of course each organization needs to develop its own average for its specific type of work. Such historical data provide a basis for estimating the project duration. Variations of this top-down approach are used by companies such as IBM, Bank of America, Sears Roebuck, HP, AT&T, Ford Motors, GE, DuPont and many others. See Table 5.2 and Table 5.3 for a simplified example of function point count methodology.

From historical data the organization developed the weighting scheme for complexity found in Table 5.2. Function points are derived from multiplying the number of kinds of elements by weighted complexity.

Table 5.3 shows the data collected for a specific task or deliverable: Patient Admitting and Billing—the number of inputs, outputs, inquiries, files, and interfaces along with the expected complexity rating. Finally, the application of the element count is applied and the function point count total is 660. Given this count and the fact that one-person month has historically been equal to 5 function points, the job will require 132 person months (660/5 = 132). Assuming you have 10 programmers who can work on this task, the duration would be approximately 13 months. The cost is easily derived by multiplying the labor rate per month times 132 person months. For example, if the monthly programmer

TABLE 5.3
Example: Function Point Count Method

Software Project 13: Patient Admitting and Billing

15	Inputs	Rated complexity as low	(2)
5	Outputs	Rated complexity as average	(6)
10	Inquiries	Rated complexity as average	(4)
30	Files	Rated complexity as high	(12)
20	Interfaces	Rated complexity as average	(10)

Application of Complexity Factor

Element	Count	Low	Average	High	Total
Inputs	15	× 2			= 30
Outputs	5		× 6		= 30
Inquiries	10		× 4		= 40
Files	30			× 12	= 360
Interfaces	20		× 10		= 200
				Total	660

rate is \$4,000, then the estimated cost would be \$528,000 (132 × 4,000). Although function point metrics are useful, their accuracy depends on adequate historical data, currency of data, and relevancy of the project/deliverable to past averages.

Learning Curves

Some projects require that the same task, group of tasks, or product be repeated several times. Managers know intuitively that the time to perform a task improves with repetition. This phenomenon is especially true of tasks that are labor intensive. In these circumstances the pattern of improvement phenomenon can be used to predict the reduction in time to perform the task. From empirical evidence across *all* industries, the pattern of this improvement has been quantified in the **learning curve** (also known as improvement curve, experience curve, and industrial progress curve), which is described by the following relationship:

Each time the output quantity doubles, the unit labor hours are reduced at a constant rate.

In practice the improvement ratio may vary from 60 percent, representing very large improvement, to 100 percent, representing no improvement at all. Generally, as the difficulty of the work decreases the expected improvement also decreases and the improvement ratio that is used becomes greater. One significant factor to consider is the proportion of labor in the task in relation to machine-paced work. Obviously, a lower percentage of improvement can occur only in operations with high labor content. Appendix 5.1 at the end of the chapter provides a detailed example of how the improvement phenomenon can be used to estimate time and cost for repetitive tasks.

The main disadvantage of top-down approaches to estimating is simply that the time and cost for a specific task are not considered. Grouping many tasks into a common basket encourages errors of omission and the use of imposed times and costs.

Micro estimating methods are usually more accurate than macro methods.

Bottom-Up Approaches for Estimating Project Times and Costs

Template Methods

If the project is similar to past projects, the costs from past projects can be used as a starting point for the new project. Differences in the new project can be noted and past times and costs adjusted to reflect these differences. For example, a ship repair drydock firm has a set of standard repair projects (i.e., templates for overhaul, electrical, mechanical) that are used as starting points for estimating the cost and duration of any new project. Differences from the appropriate standardized project are noted (for times, costs, and resources) and changes are made. This approach enables the firm to develop a potential schedule, estimate costs, and develop a budget in a very short time span. Development of such templates in a database can quickly reduce estimate errors.

Parametric Procedures Applied to Specific Tasks

Just as parametric techniques such as cost per square foot can be the source of top-down estimates, the same technique can be applied to specific tasks. For example, as part of an MS Office conversion project, 36 different computer workstations needed to be converted. Based on past conversion projects, the project

SNAPSHOT FROM PRACTICE Estimate Accuracy

The smaller the element of a work package, the more accurate the overall estimate is likely to be. The extent of this improvement varies by type of project. The table below is developed to reflect this observation. For example, information technology projects that determine their time and cost estimates in the conceptual stage can expect their "actuals" to err up to 200 percent over cost and duration and, perhaps, as much as 30 percent under estimates. Conversely, estimates for buildings, roads, etc., made after the work packages are clearly defined, have a smaller error in actual costs and times of 15 percent over estimate and 5 percent less than estimate. Although these estimates vary by project, they can serve as ballpark numbers for project stakeholders selecting how project time and cost estimates will be derived.

Time and Cost Estimate Accuracy by Type of Project

	Bricks and Mortar	**Information Technology**
Conceptual stage	+60% to −30%	+200% to −30%
Deliverables defined	+30% to −15%	+100% to −15%
Work packages defined	+15% to −5%	+50% to −5%

For example, when the project need is determined, a macro estimate of the project cost and duration is made so analysis and decisions can be made. Simultaneously a detailed estimate is made for deriving project specifications and a macro estimate for the remainder of the project. As the project progresses and specifications are solidified, a detailed estimate for design is made and a macro estimate for the remainder of the project is computed. Clearly, as the project progresses through its life cycle and more information is available, the reliability of the estimates should be improving. See Snapshot from Practice: Estimating Accuracy.

Phase estimating is preferred by those working on projects where the final product is not known and the uncertainty is very large—for example, the integration of wireless phones and computers. The commitment to cost and schedule is only necessary over the next phase of the project and commitment to unrealistic future schedules and costs based on poor information is avoided. This progressive macro/micro method provides a stronger basis for using schedule and cost estimates to manage progress during the next phase.

Unfortunately your customer—internal or external—will want an accurate estimate of schedule and cost the moment the decision is made to implement the project. Additionally, the customer who is paying for the project often perceives phase estimating as a blank check because costs and schedules are not firm over most of the project life cycle. Even though the reasons for phase estimating are sound and legitimate, most customers have to be sold on its legitimacy. A major advantage for the customer is the opportunity to change features, re-evaluate, or even cancel the project in each new phase. In conclusion, phase estimating is very useful in projects that possess huge uncertainties concerning the final nature (shape, size, features) of the project.

See Figure 5.4 for a summary of the differences between top-down and bottom-up estimates.

FIGURE 5.4
Top-Down and Bottom-Up Estimates

	Top-Down Estimates	Bottom-Up Estimates
Intended Use	Feasibility/conceptual phase Rough time/cost estimate Fund requirements Resource capacity planning	Budgeting Scheduling Resource requirements Fund timing
Preparation Cost	1/10 to 3/10 of a percent of total project cost	3/10 of a percent to 1.0 percent of total project cost
Accuracy	Minus 20%, to plus 60%	Minus 10%, to plus 30%
Method	Consensus Ratio Apportion Function point Learning curves	Template Parametric WBS packages Range estimates

Obtaining accurate estimates is a challenge. Committed organizations accept the challenge of coming up with meaningful estimates and invest heavily in developing their capacity to do so. Accurate estimates reduce uncertainty and support a discipline for effectively managing projects.

Level of Detail

Level of detail is different for different levels of management. At any level the detail should be no more than is necessary and sufficient. Top management interests usually center on the total project and major milestone events that mark major accomplishments—e.g., "Build Oil Platform in the North Sea" or "Complete Prototype." Middle management might center on one segment of the project or one milestone. First-line managers' interests may be limited to one task or work package. One of the beauties of WBS is the ability to aggregate network information so each level of management can have the kind of information necessary to make decisions.

Getting the level of detail in the WBS to match management needs for effective implementation is crucial, but the delicate balance is difficult to find. See Snapshot from Practice: Level of Detail. The level of detail in the WBS varies with the complexity of the project; the need for control; the project size, cost, duration; and other factors. If the structure reflects excessive detail, there is a tendency to break the work effort into department assignments. This tendency can become a barrier to success, since the emphasis will be on departmental outcomes rather than on deliverable outcomes. Excessive detail also means more unproductive paperwork. Note that if the level of the WBS is increased by one, the number of cost accounts may increase geometrically. On the other hand, if the level of detail is not adequate, an organization unit may find the structure falls short of meeting its

Research Highlight

Mega Projects: A Special Case

The record of cost estimates for mega projects is not stellar. Popular examples of large cost overruns include the Sydney Opera House, the Chunnel connecting England and France, and Boston's artery/tunnel "Big Dig." In a study of government-approved infrastructure projects, Bent Flyvbjerg found costs for bridges and tunnels, for road, and for rail to be underestimated 33.8%, 20.4%, and 44.7%, respectively, from initial baseline estimates to reality.[1]

Flyvbjerg suggested "... government officials should not trust cost estimates presented by project promoters whose main ambition is to build a project for their private or political gain. These estimates tend to be overly optimistic. Advocates know that high costs reduce the likelihood of funding." The issue comes down to how to mitigate these influences in our estimates.

One approach lies in using an "external view" based on actual outcomes of similar projects completed in the past. It is called **Reference Class Forecasting** (RCF) and uses Flyvbjerg's research approach.

© Michael Dwyer/Alamy

REFERENCE CLASS FORECASTING METHODOLOGY

Fundamentally, his method is simple and straightforward and involves three major steps:

1. *Select a reference class of projects similar to your potential project,* for example, cargo ships or bridges.
2. *Collect and arrange outcome data as a distribution.* Create a distribution of cost overruns as a percent of original project estimate (low to high).
3. *Use the distribution data to arrive at a realistic forecast.* Compare the original cost estimate for the project with the reference class projects. (For example, ask advocate what strong evidence do you have that your project will not follow the projects in the reference class?)

APPLICATION

Flyvbjerg's seminal studies served as an impetus for the use of Reference Class Forecasting. For example, the UK Department for Transport and HM Treasury employs the method as part of project appraisal for large transportation projects under their jurisdiction. The American Planning Association (APA) recommends the RCF method and strongly suggests planners should never rely solely on conventional forecasting techniques when making forecasts. The AACE International (the Association for the Advancement of Cost Engineering) recommends the use of RCF as a validation of cost estimates. Reference class forecasting can easily be applied to projects such as sport events, research and development, information technology systems, power plants and dams, construction, sport arenas, movies, energy exploration, space exploration, and many more classes.[2]

BENEFITS

The benefits of reference class forecasting are compelling:

- Outside empirical data mitigates human bias.
- Political, strategic, and promoter forces have difficulty ignoring outside reference class forecast information.
- Serves as reality check for funding large projects.
- Helps executives avoid unsound optimism.
- Leads to improved accountability.
- Provides basis for project contingency funds.

FUTURE APPLICATION BEYOND INFRASTRUCTURE

Given cost overruns in nine out of ten mega projects, inaccuracies have to be reduced to improve chances of funding. The use of Reference Class Forecasting is increasing as governments and organizations require the method be used to temper project advocate estimates and reduce inaccuracies.

[1] See for example: Lovallo, D., and D. Kahneman, "Delusions of Success: How Optimism Undermines Executives' Decisions," *Harvard Business Review*, July 2003, pp. 56–63; Buehler, R., D. Griffen, and M. Ross, "Exploring the 'Planning Fallacy': Why People Underestimate Their Task Completion Times," *Journal of Personality and Social Psychology*, 67 (3), pp. 366–381.

[2] Flyvbjerg, Bent, "From Nobel Prize to Project Management: Getting Risks Right," *Project Management Journal*, August 2006, pp. 5–15.

of independent testers to the schedule and budget. Finally, organizations adjust estimates to take into account abnormal conditions. For example, if soil samples reveal excessive ground water, then they adjust foundation costs and times.

There will always be some mistakes, omissions, and adjustments that will require additional changes in estimates. Fortunately every project should have a change management system in place to accommodate these situations and any impact on the project baseline. Change management and contingency funds will be discussed later in Chapter 7.

Creating a Database for Estimating

The best way to improve estimates is to collect and archive data on past project estimates and actuals. Saving historical data—estimates and actuals—provides a knowledge base for improving project time and cost estimating. Creating an estimating database is a "best practice" among leading project management organizations.

Some organizations have large estimating departments of professional estimators—e.g., Boeing, IBM—that have developed large **time and cost databases.** Others collect these data through the project office. This database approach allows the project estimator to select a specific work package item from the database for inclusion. The estimator then makes any necessary adjustments concerning the materials, labor, and equipment. Of course any items not found in the database can be added to the project—and ultimately to the database if desired. Again, the quality of the database estimates depends on the experience of the estimators, but over time the data quality should improve. Such structured databases serve as feedback for estimators and as benchmarks for cost and time for each project. In addition, comparison of estimate and actual for different projects can suggest the degree of risk inherent in estimates. See Figure 5.7 for the structure of a database similar to those found in practice.

FIGURE 5.7
Estimating Database Templates

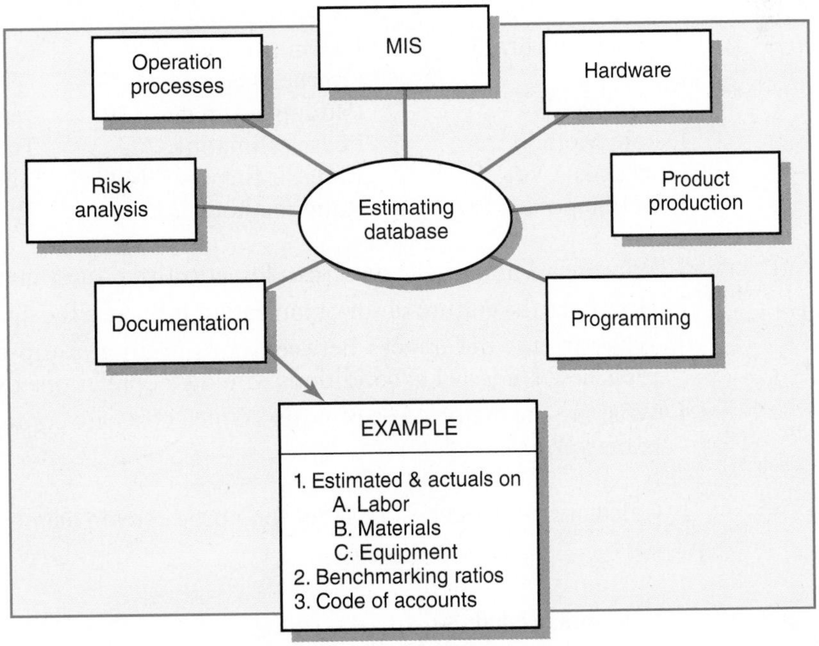

Summary

Quality time and cost estimates are the bedrock of project control. Past experience is the best starting point for these estimates. The quality of estimates is influenced by other factors such as people, technology, and downtimes. The key for getting estimates that represent realistic average times and costs is to have an organization culture that allows errors in estimates without incriminations. If times represent average time, we should expect that 50 percent will be less than the estimate and 50 percent will exceed the estimate. The use of teams that are highly motivated can help in keeping task times and costs near the average. For this reason, it is crucial to get the team to buy into time and cost estimates.

Using top-down estimates is good for initial and strategic decision making or in situations where the costs associated with developing better estimates have little benefit. However, in most cases the bottom-up approach to estimating is preferred and more reliable because it assesses each work package, rather than the whole project, section, or deliverable of a project. Estimating time and costs for each work package facilitates development of the project schedule and a time-phased budget, which are needed to control the project as it is implemented. Using the estimating guidelines will help eliminate many common mistakes made by those unacquainted with estimating times and costs for project control. Establishing a time and cost estimating database fits well with the learning organization philosophy.

The level of time and cost detail should follow the old saying of "no more than is necessary and sufficient." Managers must remember to differentiate between committed outlays, actual costs, and scheduled costs. It is well known that upfront efforts in clearly defining project objectives, scope, and specifications vastly improve time and cost estimate accuracy.

Finally, how estimates are gathered and how they are used can affect their usefulness for planning and control. The team climate, organization culture, and organization structure can strongly influence the importance attached to time and cost estimates and how they are used in managing projects.

Key Terms

Apportionment, *137*
Bottom-up estimates, *134*
Delphi Method, *136*
Direct costs, *144*
Function points, *137*
Learning curves, *139*
Overhead costs, *145*
Padding estimates, *130*
Phase estimating, *141*
Range estimating, *140*
Ratio methods, *136*
Reference Class Forecasting, *148*
Template method, *139*
Time and cost databases, *145*
Top-down estimates, *134*

Review Questions

1. Why are accurate estimates critical to effective project management?
2. How does the culture of an organization influence the quality of estimates?
3. What are the differences between bottom-up and top-down estimating approaches? Under what conditions would you prefer one over the other?
4. What are the major types of costs? Which costs are controllable by the project manager?

Exercises

1. Calculate the direct cost of labor for a project team member using the following data:

   Hourly rate: \$40/hr

   Hours needed: 80

   Overhead rate: 40%

2. Mrs. Tolstoy and her husband, Serge, are planning their dream house. The lot for the house sits high on a hill with a beautiful view of the Appalachian Mountains. The plans show the size of the house to be 2,900 square feet. The average price for a lot and house similar to this one has been \$120 per square foot. Fortunately, Serge is a retired plumber and feels he can save money by installing the plumbing himself. Mrs. Tolstoy feels she can take care of the interior decorating.

   The following average cost information is available from a local bank that makes loans to local contractors and disperses progress payments to contractors when specific tasks are verified as complete.

24%	Excavation and framing complete
8%	Roof and fireplace complete
3%	Wiring roughed in
6%	Plumbing roughed in
5%	Siding on
17%	Windows, insulation, walks, plaster, and garage complete
9%	Furnace installed
4%	Plumbing fixtures installed
10%	Exterior paint, light fixtures installed, finish hardware installed
6%	Carpet and trim installed
4%	Interior decorating
4%	Floors laid and finished

   a. What is the estimated cost for the Tolstoy's house if they use contractors to complete all of the house?

   b. Estimate what the cost of the house would be if the Tolstoys use their talents to do some of the work themselves.

3. Below is a project WBS with cost apportioned by percents. If the total project cost is estimated to be \$600,000, what are the estimated costs for the following deliverables?

   a. Design?

   b. Programming?

   c. In-house testing?

   What weaknesses are inherent in this estimating approach?

4. Firewall Project XT. Using the "complexity weighting" scheme shown in Exercise 5.3 and the function point complexity weighted table shown below, estimate the total function point count. Assume historical data suggest five function points equal one person a month and six people can work on the project.

Complexity Weight Table

Number of inputs	10	Rated complexity low
Number of outputs	20	Rated complexity average
Number of inquiries	10	Rated complexity average
Number of files	30	Rated complexity high
Number of interfaces	50	Rated complexity high

   a. What is the estimated project duration?

   b. If 20 people are available for the project, what is the estimated project duration?

   c. If the project must be completed in six months, how many people will be needed for the project?

EXERCISE 5.3
WBS Figure

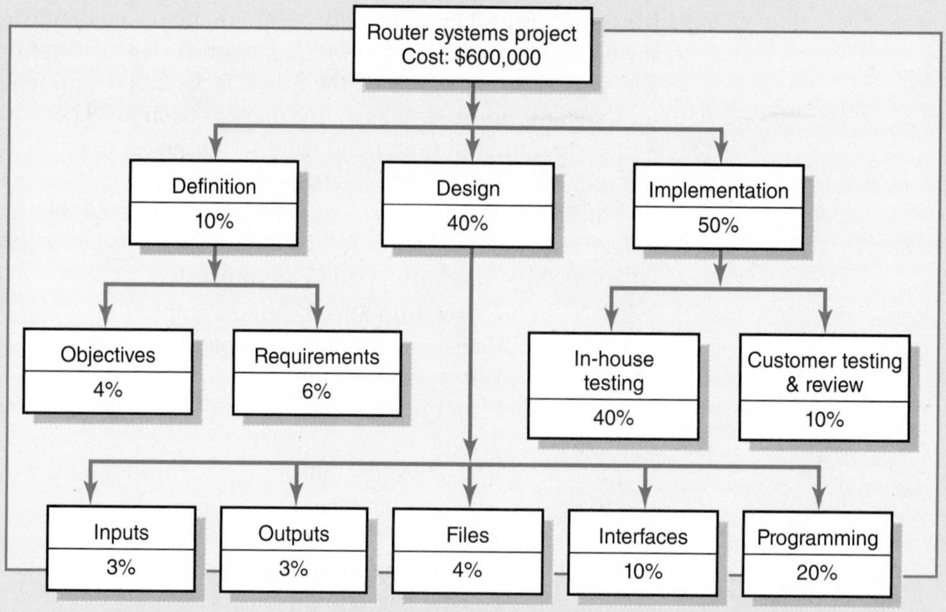

References

Buehler, R., D. Griffen, and M. Ross, "Exploring the 'Planning Fallacy': Why People Underestimate Their Task Completion Times," *Journal of Personality and Social Psychology,* vol. 67 (3), pp. 366–381.

Dalkey, N. C., D. L. Rourke, R. Lewis, and D. Snyder, *Studies in the Quality of Life: Delphi and Decision Making* (Lexington, MA: Lexington Books, 1972).

Flyvbjerg, Bent, "From Nobel Prize to Project Management: Getting Risks Right," *Project Management Journal,* August 2006, pp. 5–15; Flyvbjerg, Bent, "Curbing Optimism Bias and Strategic Misrepresentation in Planning: Reference Class Forecasting in Practice," *European Planning Studies,* vol. 16, No. 1 (January 2008), pp. 3–21; and Flyvbjerg, Bent, N. Bruzelius, and W. Rothengatter, *Mega Projects and Risk: An Anatomy of Ambition* (Cambridge Press, 2003).

Gray, N. S., "Secrets to Creating the Elusive 'Accurate Estimate,'" *PM Network,* 15 (8) August 2001, p. 56.

Jeffery, R., G. C. Low, and M. Barnes, "A Comparison of Function Point Counting Techniques," *IEEE Transactions on Software Engineering,* 19 (5) 1993, pp. 529–32.

Jones, C., *Applied Software Measurement* (New York: McGraw-Hill, 1991).

Jones, C., *Estimating Software Costs* (New York: McGraw-Hill, 1998).

Kharbanda, O. P., and J. K. Pinto, *What Made Gertie Gallop: Learning from Project Failures* (New York: Von Nostrand Reinhold, 1996).

Lovallo, D., and D. Kahneman, "Delusions of Success: How Optimism Undermines Executives' Decisions," *Harvard Business Review,* July 2003, pp. 56–63.

Magne, E., K. Emhjellenm, and P. Osmundsen, "Cost Estimation Overruns in the North Sea," *Project Management Journal* 34 (1) 2003, pp. 23–29.

McLeod, G., and D. Smith, *Managing Information Technology Projects* (Cambridge, MA: Course Technology, 1996).

Milosevic, D. Z., *Project Management ToolBox* (Upper Saddle River, NJ: John Wiley, 2003), p. 229.

Pressman, R. S., *Software Engineering: A Practitioner's Approach,* 4th ed. (New York: McGraw-Hill, 1997).

Symons, C. R., "Function Point Analysis: Difficulties and Improvements," *IEEE Transactions on Software Engineering,* 14 (1) 1988, pp. 2–11.

Case

Sharp Printing, AG

Three years ago the Sharp Printing (SP) strategic management group set a goal of having a color laser printer available for the consumer and small business market for less than $200. A few months later the senior management met off-site to discuss the new product. The results of this meeting were a set of general technical specifications along with major deliverables, a product launch date, and a cost estimate based on prior experience.

Shortly afterward, a meeting was arranged for middle management explaining the project goals, major responsibilities, the project start date, and importance of meeting the product launch date within the cost estimate. Members of all departments involved attended the meeting. Excitement was high. Although everyone saw the risks as high, the promised rewards for the company and the personnel were emblazoned in their minds. A few participants questioned the legitimacy of the project duration and cost estimates. A couple of R&D people were worried about the technology required to produce the high-quality product for less than $200. But given the excitement of the moment, everyone agreed the project was worth doing and doable. The color laser printer project was to have the highest project priority in the company.

Lauren was selected to be the project manager. She had 15 years of experience in printer design and manufacture, which included successful management of several projects related to printers for commercial markets. Since she was one of those uncomfortable with the project cost and time estimates, she felt getting good bottom-up time and cost estimates for the deliverables was her first concern. She quickly had a meeting with the significant stakeholders to create a WBS identifying the work packages and organizational unit responsible for implementing the work packages. Lauren stressed she wanted time and cost estimates from those who would do the work or were the most knowledgeable, if possible. Getting estimates from more than one source was encouraged. Estimates were due in two weeks.

The compiled estimates were placed in the WBS/OBS. The corresponding cost estimate seemed to be in error. The cost estimate was $1,250,000 over the senior management estimate; this represents about a 20 percent overrun! The time estimate from the developed project network was only four months over the top management time estimate. Another meeting was scheduled with the significant

TABLE A5.2
Learning Curves Cumulative Values

Units	60%	65%	70%	75%	80%	85%	90%	95%
1	1.000	1.000	1.000	1.000	1.000	1.000	1.000	1.000
2	1.600	1.650	1.700	1.750	1.800	1.850	1.900	1.950
3	2.045	2.155	2.268	2.384	2.502	2.623	2.746	2.872
4	2.405	2.578	2.758	2.946	3.142	3.345	3.556	3.774
5	2.710	2.946	3.195	3.459	3.738	4.031	4.339	4.662
6	2.977	3.274	3.593	3.934	4.299	4.688	5.101	5.538
7	3.216	3.572	3.960	4.380	4.834	5.322	5.845	6.404
8	3.432	3.847	4.303	4.802	5.346	5.936	6.574	7.261
9	3.630	4.102	4.626	5.204	5.839	6.533	7.290	8.111
10	3.813	4.341	4.931	5.589	6.315	7.116	7.994	8.955
12	4.144	4.780	5.501	6.315	7.227	8.244	9.374	10.62
14	4.438	5.177	6.026	6.994	8.092	9.331	10.72	12.27
16	4.704	5.541	6.514	7.635	8.920	10.38	12.04	13.91
18	4.946	5.879	6.972	8.245	9.716	11.41	13.33	15.52
20	5.171	6.195	7.407	8.828	10.48	12.40	14.64	17.13
22	5.379	6.492	7.819	9.388	11.23	13.38	15.86	18.72
24	5.574	6.773	8.213	9.928	11.95	14.33	17.10	20.31
25	5.668	6.909	8.404	10.19	12.31	14.80	17.71	21.10
30	6.097	7.540	9.305	11.45	14.02	17.09	20.73	25.00
35	6.478	8.109	10.13	12.72	15.64	19.29	23.67	28.86
40	6.821	8.631	10.90	13.72	17.19	21.43	26.54	32.68
45	7.134	9.114	11.62	14.77	18.68	23.50	29.37	36.47
50	7.422	9.565	12.31	15.78	20.12	25.51	32.14	40.22
60	7.941	10.39	13.57	17.67	22.87	29.41	37.57	47.65
70	8.401	11.13	14.74	19.43	25.47	33.17	42.87	54.99
80	8.814	11.82	15.82	21.09	27.96	36.80	48.05	62.25
90	9.191	12.45	16.83	22.67	30.35	40.32	53.14	69.45
100	9.539	13.03	17.79	24.18	32.65	43.75	58.14	76.59
120	10.16	14.16	19.57	27.02	37.05	50.39	67.93	90.71
140	10.72	15.08	21.20	29.67	41.22	56.78	77.46	104.7
160	11.21	15.97	22.72	32.17	45.20	62.95	86.80	118.5
180	11.67	16.79	24.14	34.54	49.03	68.95	95.96	132.1
200	12.09	17.55	25.48	36.80	52.72	74.79	105.0	145.7
250	13.01	19.28	28.56	42.08	61.47	88.83	126.9	179.2
300	13.81	20.81	31.34	46.94	69.66	102.2	148.2	212.2
350	14.51	22.18	33.89	51.48	77.43	115.1	169.0	244.8
400	15.14	23.44	36.26	55.75	84.85	127.6	189.3	277.0
450	15.72	24.60	38.48	59.80	91.97	139.7	209.2	309.0
500	16.26	25.68	40.58	63.68	98.85	151.5	228.8	340.6
600	17.21	27.67	44.47	70.97	112.0	174.2	267.1	403.3
700	18.06	29.45	48.04	77.77	124.4	196.1	304.5	465.3
800	18.82	31.09	51.36	84.18	136.3	217.3	341.0	526.5
900	19.51	32.60	54.46	90.26	147.7	237.9	376.9	587.2
1,000	20.15	34.01	57.40	96.07	158.7	257.9	412.2	647.4
1,200	21.30	36.59	62.85	107.0	179.7	296.6	481.2	766.6
1,400	22.32	38.92	67.85	117.2	199.6	333.9	548.4	884.2
1,600	23.23	41.04	72.49	126.8	218.6	369.9	614.2	1001.
1,800	24.06	43.00	76.85	135.9	236.8	404.9	678.8	1116.
2,000	24.83	44.84	80.96	144.7	254.4	438.9	742.3	1230.
2,500	26.53	48.97	90.39	165.0	296.1	520.8	897.0	1513.
3,000	27.99	52.62	98.90	183.7	335.2	598.9	1047.	1791.

expected. Skilled labor cost is NOK 300 per hour. Desired profit for all projects is 25 percent of total costs.

A. How many labor hours should the eighth satellite require?
B. How many labor hours for the whole project of eight satellites?
C. What price would you ask for the project? Why?
D. Midway through the project your design and production people realize that a 75 percent improvement curve is more appropriate. What impact does this have on the project?
E. Near the end of the project Deutsch Telefon AG has requested a cost estimate for four satellites identical to those you have already produced. What price will you quote them? Justify your price.

CHAPTER SIX

Developing a Project Plan

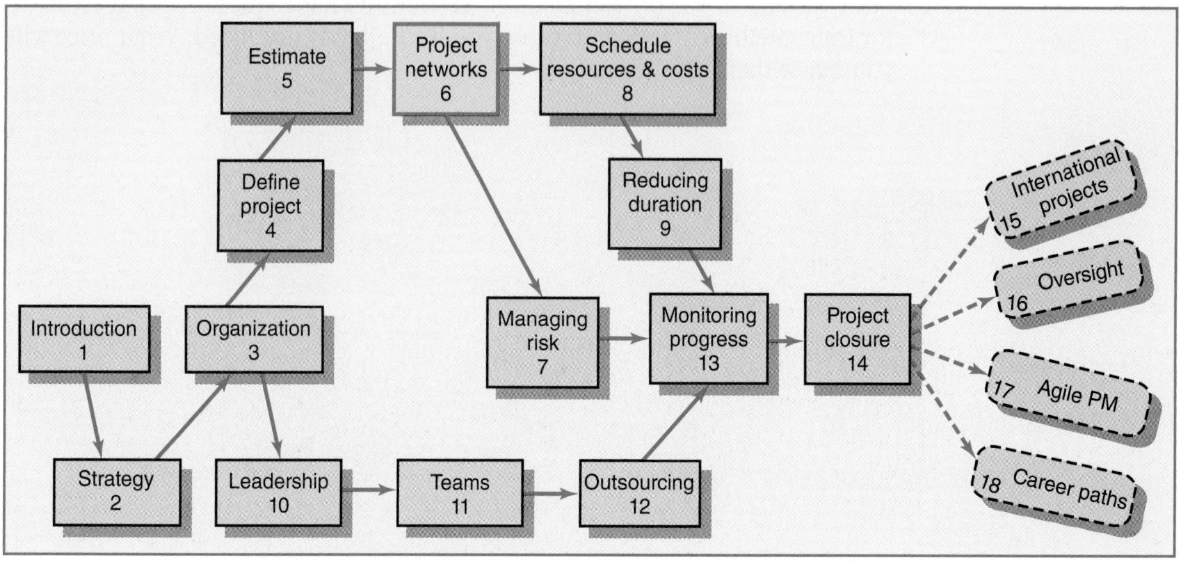

Developing a Project Plan

Developing the Project Network

From Work Package to Network

Constructing a Project Network

Activity-on-Node (AON) Fundamentals

Network Computation Process

Using the Forward and Backward Pass Information

Level of Detail for Activities

Practical Considerations

Extended Network Techniques to Come Closer to Reality

Summary

I keep six honest serving-men (they taught me all I knew); their names are What and Why and When and How and Where and Who.

Rudyard Kipling

Developing the Project Network

The project network is the tool used for planning, scheduling, and monitoring project progress. The network is developed from the information collected for the WBS and is a graphic flow chart of the project job plan. The network depicts the project activities that must be completed, the logical sequences, the interdependencies of the activities to be completed, and in most cases the times for the activities to start and finish along with the longest path(s) through the network—the *critical path*. The network is the framework for the project information system that will be used by the project managers to make decisions concerning project time, cost, and performance.

Developing the project networks takes time for someone or some group to develop; therefore, they cost money! Are networks really worth the struggle? The answer is definitely yes, except in cases where the project is considered trivial or very short in duration.[1] The network is easily understood by others because the network presents a graphic display of the flow and sequence of work through the project. Once the network is developed, it is very easy to modify or change when unexpected events occur as the project progresses. For example, if materials for an activity are delayed, the impact can be quickly assessed and the whole project revised in only a few minutes with the computer. These revisions can be communicated to all project participants quickly (for example, via e-mail or project website).

The project network provides other invaluable information and insights. It provides the basis for scheduling labor and equipment. It enhances communication that melds all managers and groups together in meeting the time, cost, and performance objectives of the project. It provides an estimate of project duration rather than picking a project completion date from a hat or someone's preferred date. The network gives the times when activities can start and finish and when they can be delayed. It provides the basis for budgeting the cash flow of the project. It identifies which activities are "critical" and,

[1] This process could be clarified and improved by using a simple responsibility matrix (see Chapter 3).

method. Today, the activity-on-node method has come to dominate nearly all project network plans. For this reason, we have limited our discussion to AON methods. Figure 6.2 shows a few typical uses of building blocks for the AON network construction. An **activity** is represented by a *node* (box). The node can take many forms, but in recent years the node represented as a rectangle (box) has dominated. The dependencies among activities are depicted by *arrows* between the rectangles (boxes) on the AON network. The arrows indicate how the activities are related and the sequence in which things must be accomplished. The length and slope of the arrow are arbitrary and set for convenience of drawing the network. The letters in the boxes serve here to identify the activities while you learn the fundamentals of network construction and analysis. In practice, activities have identification numbers and descriptions.

There are three basic relationships that must be established for activities included in a project network. The relationships can be found by answering the following three questions for each activity:

1. Which activities must be completed immediately *before* this activity? These activities are called *predecessor* activities.

FIGURE 6.2
Activity-on-Node Network Fundamentals

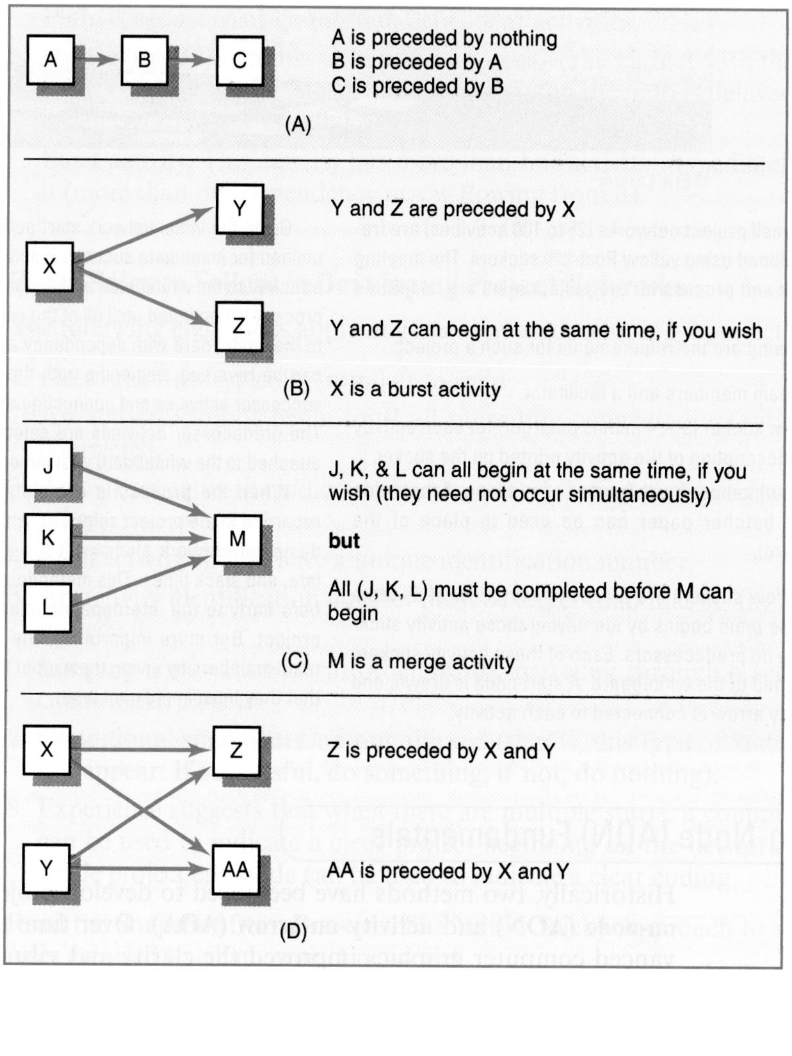

2. Which activities must immediately *follow* this activity? These activities are called *successor* activities.
3. Which activities can occur *while* this activity is taking place? This is known as a *concurrent* or *parallel* relationship.

Sometimes a manager can use only questions 1 and 3 to establish relationships. This information allows the network analyst to construct a graphic flow chart of the sequence and logical interdependencies of project activities.

Figure 6.2A is analogous to a list of things to do where you complete the task at the top of the list first and then move to the second task, etc. This figure tells the project manager that activity A must be completed before activity B can begin, and activity B must be completed before activity C can begin.

Figure 6.2B tells us that activities Y and Z cannot begin until activity X is completed. This figure also indicates that activities Y and Z can occur concurrently or simultaneously if the project manager wishes; however, it is not a necessary condition. For example, pouring a concrete driveway (activity Y) can take place while landscape planting (activity Z) is being accomplished, but land clearing (activity X) must be completed before activities Y and Z can start. Activities Y and Z are considered *parallel* activities. Parallel paths allow concurrent effort, which may shorten time to do a series of activities. Activity X is sometimes referred to as a *burst* activity because more than one arrow bursts from the node. The number of arrows indicates how many activities immediately follow activity X.

Figure 6.2C shows us activities J, K, and L can occur simultaneously if desired, and activity M cannot begin until activities J, K, and L are all completed. Activities J, K, and L are parallel activities. Activity M is called a *merge* activity because more than one activity must be completed before M can begin. Activity M could also be called a milestone—a significant accomplishment.

In Figure 6.2D, activities X and Y are parallel activities that can take place at the same time; activities Z and AA are also parallel activities. But activities Z and AA cannot begin until activities X and Y are both completed. Given these fundamentals of AON, we can practice developing a simple network. Remember, the arrows can cross over each other (e.g., Figure 6.2D), be bent, or be any length or slope. Neatness is not a criterion for a valid, useful network—only accurate inclusion of all project activities, their dependencies, and time estimates.

Information for a simplified project network is given in Table 6.1. This project represents a new automated warehouse system for picking frozen food package orders and moving them to a staging area for delivery to stores.

TABLE 6.1
Network Information

AUTOMATED WAREHOUSE
Order Picking System

Activity	Description	Preceding Activity
A	Define Requirements	None
B	Assign Team	A
C	Design Hardware	A
D	Code Software	B
E	Build and Test Hardware	C
F	Develop Patent Request	C
G	Test Software	D
H	Integrate Systems	E, F, G

FIGURE 6.5 Activity-on-Node Network

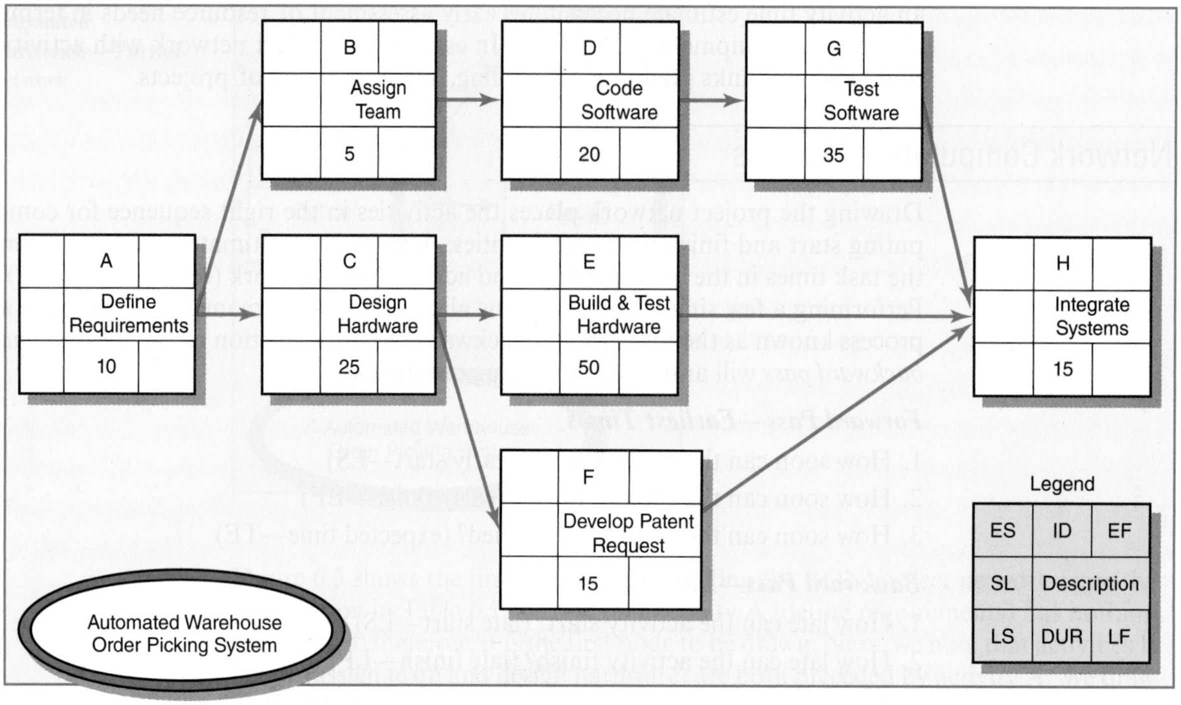

Figure 6.5 shows the network with the activity time estimate found in the node (see "DUR" for duration in the legend). For example, activity A (define requirements) has an activity duration of 10 workdays, and activity E (build and test hardware) has a duration of 50 days. The forward pass begins with the project start time, which is usually time zero. (Note: Calendar times can be computed for the project later in the planning phase.)

In our Automated Warehouse example, the early start time for the first activity (activity A) is zero. This time is found in the upper left corner of the activity A node in Figure 6.6. The early finish for activity A is 10 days (EF = ES + DUR or 0 + 10 = 10). Next, we see that activity A is the predecessor for activities B (assign team) and C (design hardware). Therefore, the earliest activities B and C can begin is the instant in time when activity A is completed; this time is 10 days. You can now see in Figure 6.6 that activities B and C have an early start (ES) of 10 days. Using the formula EF = ES + DUR, the early finish (EF) times for activities B and C are 15 and 35 days. Following the same process of moving along each network path, the early start and finish times for selected activities are shown here:

Activity D: ES = 15	EF = 15 + 20 = 35	Activity F: ES = 35	EF = 35 + 15 = 50
Activity E: ES = 35	EF = 35 + 50 = 85	Activity G: ES = 35	EF = 35 + 35 = 70

Activity H (integrate system) is a merge activity because it is preceded by more than one activity. The early start (ES) of a merge activity depends on the early finish (EF) of all activities that merge to it. In this project activity H is preceded by activities E, F, and G. Which activity controls the ES of activity H? The answer is

FIGURE 6.6 **Activity-on-Node Network Forward Pass**

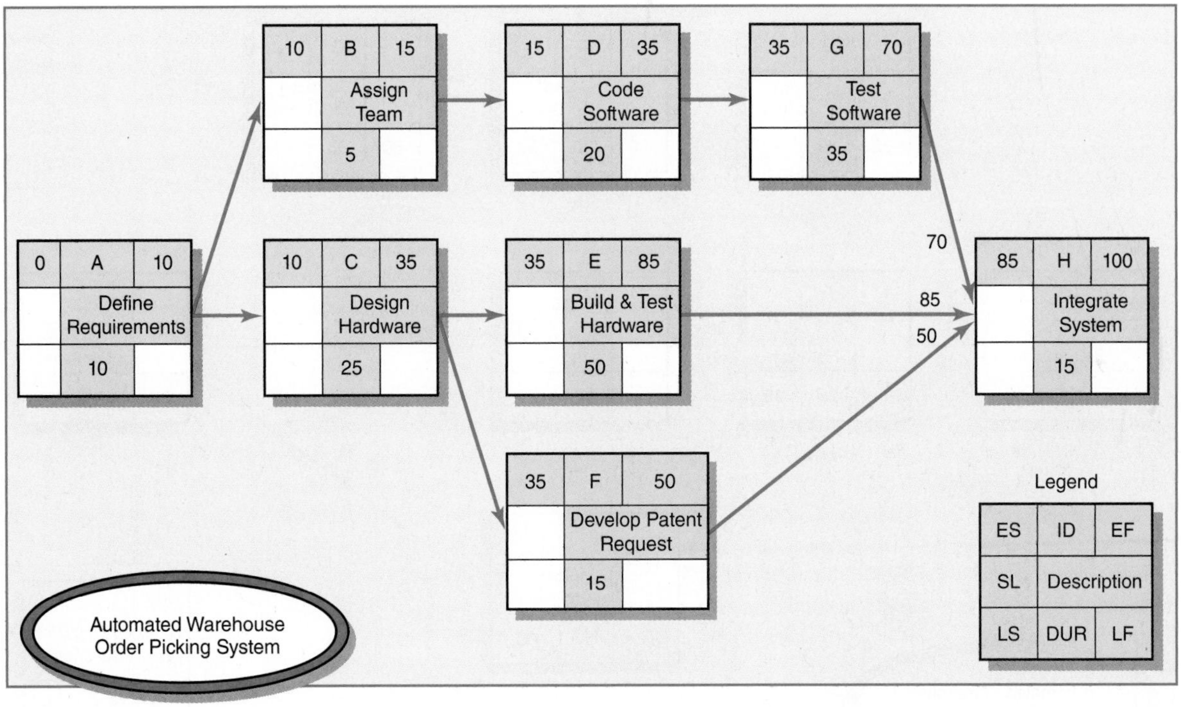

activity E. In Figure 6.6 the EF times are 85, 50, and 70. Since 85 days is the largest EF time, activity E controls the ES for Activity H, which is 85. If activity E is delayed, activity H will be delayed. The early finish for activity H or the project is 100 days (EF = ES + DUR or 85 + 15 = 100).

The forward pass requires that you remember just three things when computing early activity times:

1. You *add* activity times along each path in the network (ES + DUR = EF).
2. You carry the early finish (EF) to the next activity where it becomes its early start (ES), *unless*
3. If the next succeeding activity is a *merge* activity, you select the *largest* early finish number (EF) of *all* its immediate predecessor activities.

The three questions derived from the forward pass have been answered; that is, early start (ES), early finish (EF), and the project expected duration (TE) times have been computed. The backward pass is the next process to learn.

Backward Pass—Latest Times

The backward pass starts with the last project activity(ies) on the network. You trace backward on each path *subtracting* activity times to find the late start (LS) and late finish (LF) times for each activity. Before the backward pass can be computed, the late finish for the last project activity(ies) must be selected. In early planning stages, this time is usually set equal to the early finish (EF) of the last project activity (or in the case of multiple finish activities, the activity with the largest EF). In some cases an imposed project duration deadline exists, and this

FIGURE 6.7 Activity-on-Node Network Backward Pass

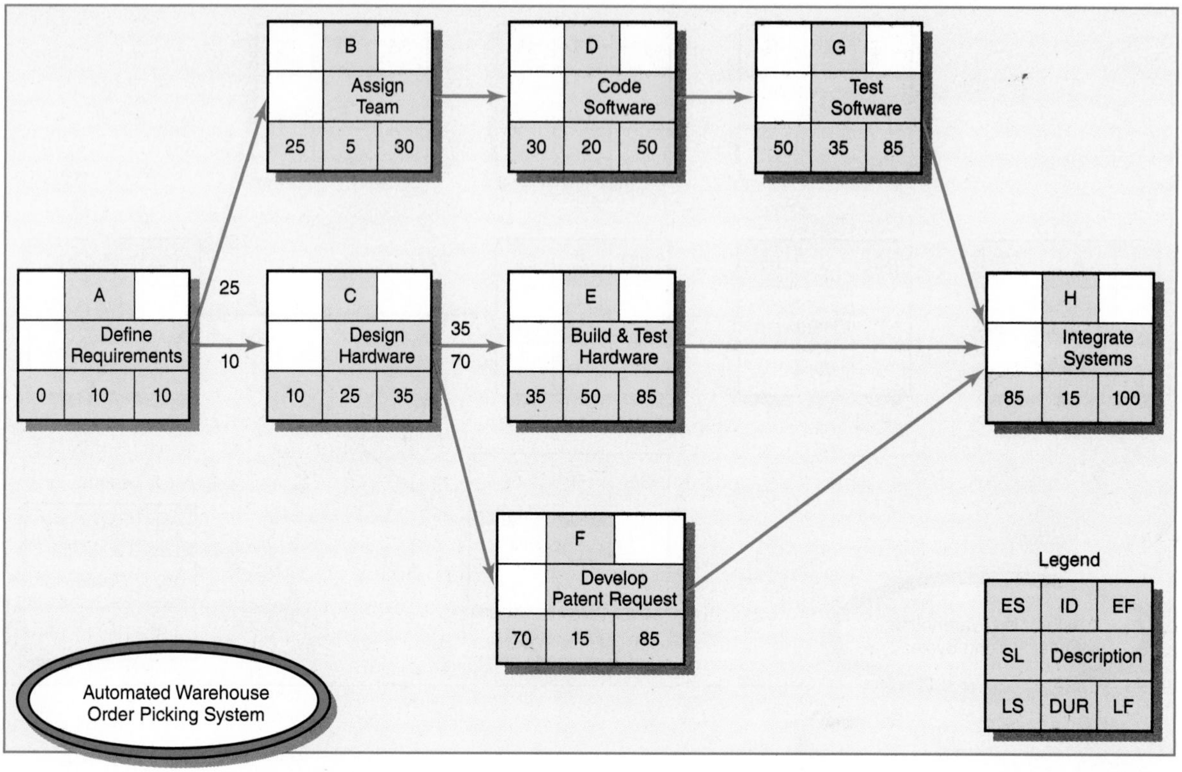

date will be used. Let us assume for planning purposes we can accept the EF project duration (TE) equal to 100 workdays. The LF for activity H becomes 100 days (EF = LF) (see Figure 6.7).

The backward pass is similar to the forward pass; you need to remember three things:

1. You *subtract* activity times along each path starting with the project end activity (LF − DUR = LS).
2. You carry the LS to the next preceding activity to establish its LF, *unless*
3. If the next preceding activity is a *burst* activity; in this case you select the *smallest* LS of all its immediate successor activities to establish its LF.

Let's apply these rules to our Automated Warehouse example. Beginning with activity H (integrate systems) and a LF of 100 workdays, the LS for activity H is 85 days (LF − DUR = LS or 100 − 15 = 85). The LS for activity H becomes the LF for activities E, F, and G. Moving backward on the network the late starts for E, F, and G are shown here (LS = LF − DUR):

Activity E: LS = 85−50 = 35	Activity G: 85−35 = 50
Activity F: LS = 85−15 = 70	

At this point we see that activity C is a *burst* activity that ties to (precedes) activities E and F. The late finish for activity C is controlled by the LS of activities E and F. The *smallest* LS of activities E and F (LS's = 35 and 70) is activity E. This establishes the LF for activity C. The LS for activity C becomes 10. Moving backward to the first project activity, we note it is also a *burst* activity that links to activities B and C. The LF of activity A is controlled by activity C that has the smallest LS of 10 days. Given a LF of 10 days, the LS for activity is time period zero (LS = 10 − 10 = 0). The backward pass is complete, and the latest activity times are known. Figure 6.8 shows the completed network with all the early, late, and slack times included. Slack can be important to managing your project.

Determining Slack (or Float)

Total Slack

When the forward and backward passes have been computed, it is possible to determine which activities can be delayed by computing "slack" or "float." **Total slack** *tells us the amount of time an activity can be delayed and not delay the project.* Stated differently, *total slack is the amount of time an activity can exceed its early finish date without affecting the project end date or an imposed completion date.*

Total slack or float for an activity is simply the difference between the LS and ES (LS − ES = SL) or between LF and EF (LF − EF = SL). For example, in Figure 6.8 the total slack for activity D is 15 workdays, for activity F is 35 days, and for activity E is zero. If total slack of one activity in a path is used, the ES for all activities that follow in the chain will be delayed and their slack reduced. Use of total slack *must be coordinated* with all participants in the activities that follow in the chain.

FIGURE 6.8 Forward and Backward Passes Completed with Slack Times

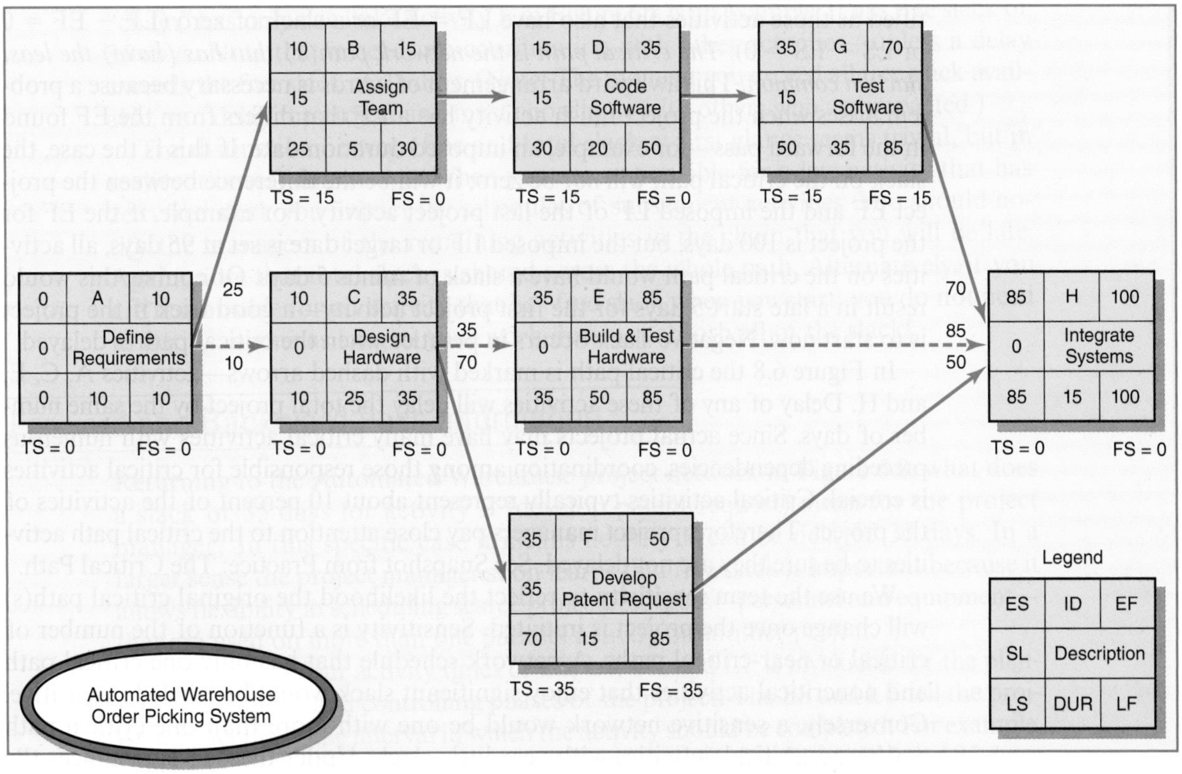

the activity can start as early as day 35 or finish as late as day 85. Conversely, activity C (design hardware), must start on day 10, or the project will be delayed.

When the critical path is known, it is possible to tightly manage the resources of the activities on the critical path so no mistakes are made that will result in delays. In addition, if for some reason the project must be expedited to meet an earlier date, it is possible to select those activities, or combination of activities, that will cost the least to shorten the project. Similarly, if the critical path is delayed and the time must be made up by shortening some activity or activities on the critical path to make up any negative slack, it is possible to identify the activities on the critical path that cost the least to shorten. If there are other paths with very little slack, it may be necessary to shorten activities on those paths also.

Level of Detail for Activities

Time-phasing work and budgets of the project mandate careful definition of the activities that make up the project network. Typically an activity represents one or more tasks from a work package. How many tasks you include in each activity sets the level of detail. In some cases it is possible to end up with too much information to manage, and this can result in increased overhead costs. Managers of small projects have been able to minimize the level of detail by eliminating some of the preliminary steps to drawing networks. Larger firms also recognize the cost of information overload and are working to cut down the level of detail in networks and in most other dimensions of the project.

Practical Considerations

Network Logic Errors

Project network techniques have certain logic rules that must be followed. One rule is that conditional statements such as "if test successful build proto, if failure redesign" are not permitted. The network is not a decision tree; it is a project plan that we assume will materialize. If conditional statements were allowed, the forward and backward pass would make little sense. Although in reality a plan seldom materializes as we expect in every detail, it is a reasonable initial assumption. You shall see that once a network plan is developed, it is an easy step to make revisions to accommodate changes.

Another rule that defeats the project network and computation process is *looping*. Looping is an attempt by the planner to return to an earlier activity. Recall that the activity identification numbers should always be higher for the activities following an activity in question; this rule helps to avoid the illogical precedence relationships among the activities. An activity should only occur once; if it is to occur again, the activity should have a new name and identification number and should be placed in the right sequence on the network. Figure 6.9 shows an illogical loop. If this loop were allowed to exist, this path would perpetually repeat itself. Many computer programs catch this type of logic error.

Activity Numbering

Each activity needs a unique identification code—a letter or a number. In practice very elegant schemes exist. Most schemes number activities in ascending order, that is, each succeeding activity has a larger number so that the flow of the project activities is toward project completion. It is customary to leave gaps between num-

FIGURE 6.9
Illogical Loop

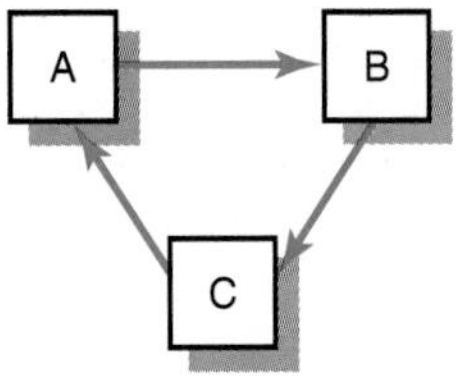

bers (1, 5, 10, 15 . . .). Gaps are desirable so you can add missing or new activities later. Because it is nearly impossible to draw a project network perfectly, numbering networks is frequently not done until after the network is complete.

In practice you will find computer programs that accept numeric, alphabetic, or a combination of activity designations. Combination designations are often used to identify cost, work skill, departments, and locations. As a general rule, activity numbering systems should be ascending and as simple as possible. The intent is to make it as easy as you can for project participants to follow work through the network and locate specific activities.

Use of Computers to Develop Networks

All of the tools and techniques discussed in this chapter can be used with computer software currently available. Two examples are shown in Figures 6.10 and 6.11. Figure 6.10 presents a generic AON computer output for the Automated Warehouse Picking System project. Observe that these computer outputs use numbers to identify activities. The critical path is identified by the nodes (activities) 2, 4, 6, and 9. The activity description is shown on the top line of the activity node. The activity start time and identification are on the second line. The finish time and duration are on the third line of the node. The project starts on January 1 and is planned to finish May 20. Note this sample computer network has included non-work days of holidays and weekends.

Figure 6.11 presents an early start **Gantt chart.**[2] Bar charts are popular because they present an easy-to-understand, clear picture on a time-scaled horizon. They are used during planning, resource scheduling, and status reporting. The format is a two-dimensional representation of the project schedule, with activities down the rows and time across the horizontal axis. In this computer output the shaded bars represent the activity durations. The extended lines from the bars represent slack. For example, "test software" (ID # 8) has a duration of 35 days (shaded area of the bar) and 15 days slack (represented by the extended line). The bar also indicates test software has an early start of February 19 and would finish April 8, but can finish as late as April 29 because it has 15 days of slack. When calendar dates are used on the time axis, Gantt charts provide a clear overview of the project schedule and can often be found posted on the walls of project offices. Unfortunately, when projects have many dependency relationships, the dependency lines soon become overwhelming and defeat the simplicity of the Gantt chart.

Project management software can be a tremendous help in the hands of those who understand and are familiar with the tools and techniques discussed in this text. However, there is nothing more dangerous than someone using the software with little or no knowledge of how the software derives its output. Mistakes in input are very common and require someone skilled in the concepts, tools, and information system to recognize that errors exist so false actions are avoided.

[2] Gantt charts were introduced over 100 years ago by Henry Gantt.

FIGURE 6.10 Automated Warehouse Order Picking System Network

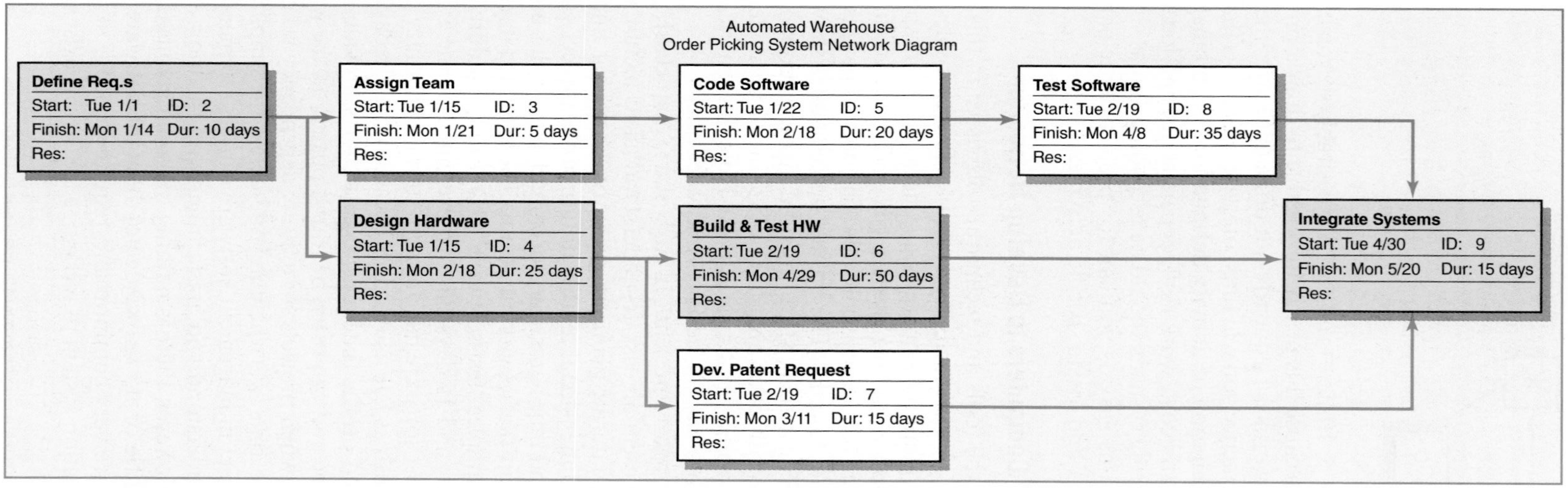

FIGURE 6.11 **Automated Order Warehouse Picking System Bar Chart**

Automated Warehouse Order Picking System Schedule Table

ID	Duration	Task Name	Start	Finish	Late Start	Late Finish	Free Slack	Total Slack
2	10	Define Req.s	Tue 1/1	Mon 1/14	Tue 1/1	Tue 1/15	0 days	0 days
3	5	Assign Team	Tue 1/15	Mon 1/21	Tue 2/5	Mon 2/11	0 days	15 days
4	25	Design Hardware	Tue 1/15	Mon 2/18	Tue 1/15	Mon 2/18	0 days	0 days
5	20	Code Software	Tue 1/22	Mon 2/18	Tue 2/12	Mon 3/11	0 days	15 days
6	50	Build and Test HW	Tue 2/19	Mon 4/29	Tue 2/19	Mon 4/29	0 days	0 days
7	15	Dev. Patent Request	Tue 2/19	Mon 3/11	Tue 4/9	Mon 4/29	35 days	35 days
8	35	Test Software	Tue 2/19	Mon 4/8	Tue 3/12	Mon 4/29	15 days	15 days
9	15	Integrate Systems	Tue 4/30	Mon 5/20	Tue 4/30	Mon 5/20	0 days	0 days

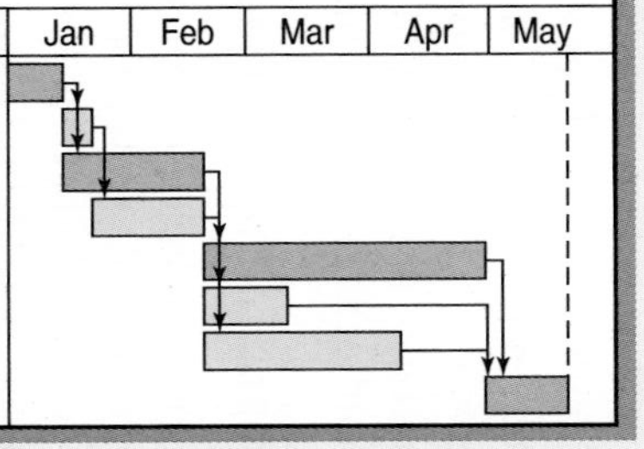

Calendar Dates

Ultimately you will want to assign calendar dates to your project activities. If a computer program is not used, dates are assigned manually. Lay out a calendar of workdays (exclude non-workdays), and number them. Then relate the calendar workdays to the workdays on your project network. Most computer programs will assign calendar dates automatically after you identify start dates, time units, non-workdays, and other information.

Multiple Starts and Multiple Projects

Some computer programs require a common start and finish event in the form of a node—usually a circle or rectangle—for a project network. Even if this is not a requirement, it is a good idea because it avoids "dangler" paths. Dangler paths give the impression that the project does not have a clear beginning or ending. If a project has more than one activity that can begin when the project is to start, each path is a dangler path. The same is true if a project network ends with more than one activity; these unconnected paths are also called danglers. Danglers can be avoided by tying dangler activities to a common project start or finish node.

When several projects are tied together in an organization, using a common start and end node helps to identify the total planning period of all projects. Use of pseudo or dummy wait activities from the common start node allows different start dates for each project.

Extended Network Techniques to Come Closer to Reality

The method for showing relationships among activities in the last section is called the finish-to-start relationship because it assumes all immediate preceding connected activities must be completed before the next activity can begin. In an effort to come closer to the realities of projects, some useful extensions have been added. The use of *laddering* was the first obvious extension practitioners found very useful.

Laddering

The assumption that all immediate preceding activities must be 100 percent complete is too restrictive for some situations found in practice. This restriction occurs most frequently when one activity overlaps the start of another and has a long duration. Under the standard finish-to-start relationship, when an activity has a long duration and will delay the start of an activity immediately following it, the activity can be broken into segments and the network drawn using a *laddering* approach so the following activity can begin sooner and not delay the work. This segmenting of the larger activity gives the appearance of steps on a ladder on the network, thus the name. The classic example used in many texts and articles is laying pipe, because it is easy to visualize. The trench must be dug, pipe laid, and the trench refilled. If the pipeline is one mile long, it is not necessary to dig one mile of trench before the laying of pipe can begin or to lay one mile of pipe before refill can begin. Figure 6.12 shows how these overlapping activities might appear in an AON network using the standard finish-to-start approach.

Use of Lags to Reduce Schedule Detail and Project Duration

The use of *lags* has been developed to offer greater flexibility in network construction. *A lag is the minimum amount of time a dependent activity must be*

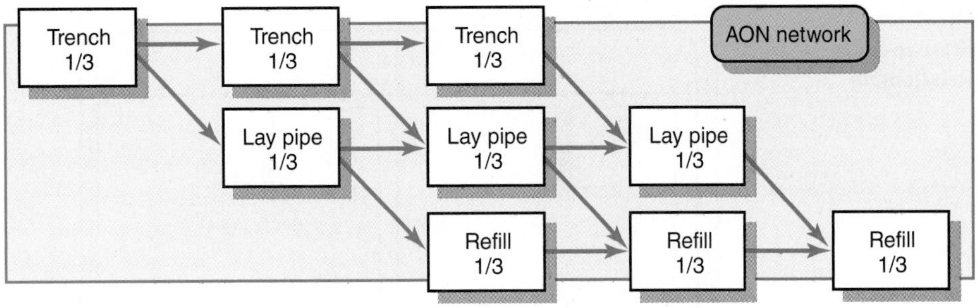

FIGURE 6.12
Example of Laddering Using Finish-to-Start Relationship

delayed to begin or end. The use of lags in project networks occurs for two primary reasons:

1. When activities of long duration delay the start or finish of successor activities, the network designer normally breaks the activity into smaller activities to avoid the long delay of the successor activity. Use of lags can avoid such delays and reduce network detail.
2. Lags can be used to constrain the start and finish of an activity.

The most commonly used relationship extensions are start-to-start, finish-to-finish, and combinations of these two. These relationship patterns are discussed in this section.

Finish-to-Start Relationship

The finish-to-start relationship represents the typical, generic network style used in the early part of the chapter. However, there are situations in which the next activity in a sequence must be delayed even when the preceding activity is complete. For example, removing concrete forms cannot begin until the poured cement has cured for two time units. Figure 6.13 shows this **lag relationship** for AON networks. Finish-to-start lags are frequently used when ordering materials. For example, it may take 1 day to place orders but take 19 days to receive the goods. The use of finish-to-start allows the activity duration to be only 1 day and the lag 19 days. This approach ensures the activity cost is tied to placing the order only rather than charging the activity for 20 days of work. This same finish-to-start lag relationship is useful to depict transportation, legal, and mail lags.

The use of finish-to-start lags should be carefully checked to ensure their validity. Conservative project managers or those responsible for completion of activities have been known to use lags as a means of building in a "slush" factor to reduce the risk of being late. A simple rule to follow is that the use of finish-to-start lags must be justified and approved by someone responsible for a large section of the project. The legitimacy of lags is not usually difficult to discern. The legitimate use of the additional relationship shown can greatly enhance the network by more closely representing the realities of the project.

Start-to-Start Relationship

An alternative to segmenting the activities as we did earlier is to use a start-to-start relationship. Typical start-to-start relationships are shown in Figure 6.14.

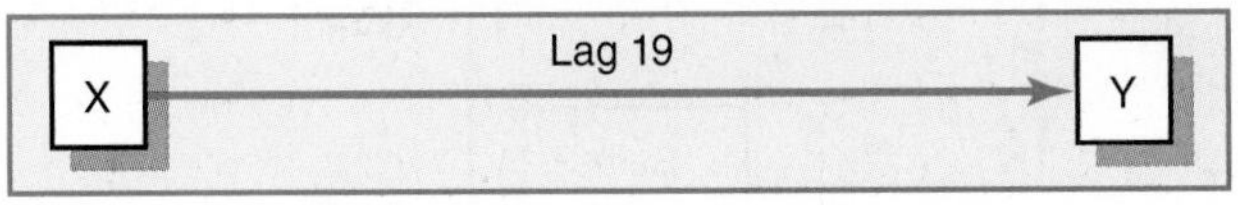

FIGURE 6.13
Finish-to-Start Relationship

FIGURE 6.14
Start-to-Start Relationship

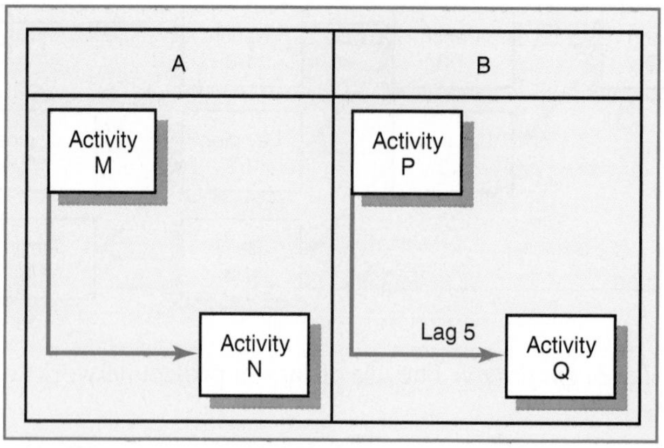

Figure 6.14A shows the start-to-start relationship with zero lag, while Figure 6.14B shows the same relationship with a lag of five time units. It is important to note that the relationship may be used with or without a lag. If time is assigned, it is usually shown on the dependency arrow of an AON network.

In Figure 6.14B, activity Q cannot begin until five time units after activity P begins. This type of relationship typically depicts a situation in which you can perform a portion of one activity and begin a following activity before completing the first. This relationship can be used on the pipe-laying project. Figure 6.15 shows the project using an AON network. The start-to-start relationship reduces network detail and project delays by using lag relationships.

It is possible to find compression opportunities by changing finish-to-start relations to start-to-start relationships. A review of finish-to-start critical activities may point out opportunities that can be revised to be parallel by using start-to-start relationships. For example, in place of a finish-to-start activity "design house, then build foundation," a start-to-start relationship could be used in which the foundation can be started, say, five days (lag) after design has started—assuming the design of the foundation is the first part of the total design activity. This start-to-start relationship with a small lag allows a sequential activity to be worked on in parallel and to compress the duration of the critical path. This same concept is frequently found in projects in which concurrent engineering is used to speed completion of a project. **Concurrent engineering,** which is highlighted in the Snapshot from Practice: Concurrent Engineering, basically breaks activities into

FIGURE 6.15
Use of Lags to Reduce Project Duration

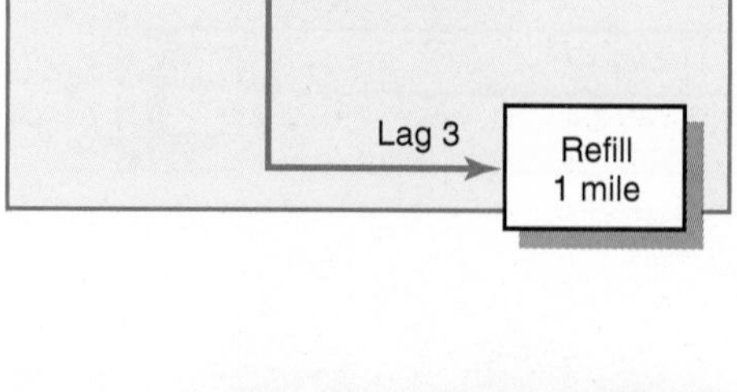

SNAPSHOT FROM PRACTICE Concurrent Engineering*

In the old days, when a new product development project was initiated by a firm, it would start its sequential journey in the research and development department. Concepts and ideas would be worked out and the results passed to the engineering department, which sometimes reworked the whole product. This result would be passed to manufacturing, where it might be reworked once more in order to ensure the product could be manufactured using existing machinery and operations. Quality improvements were initiated after the fact once defects and improvement opportunities were discovered during production. This sequential approach to product development required a great deal of time, and it was not uncommon for the final product to be totally unrecognizable when compared to original specifications.

Given the emphasis on speed to the market, companies have abandoned the sequential approach to product development and have adopted a more holistic approach titled concurrent engineering. In a nutshell, *concurrent engineering* entails the active involvement of all the relevant specialty areas throughout the design and development process. The traditional chainlike sequence of finish-to-start relationships is replaced by a series of start-to-start lag relationships as soon as meaningful work can be initiated for the next phase. Figure 6.16 summarizes the dramatic gains in time to market achieved by this approach.

FIGURE 6.16 New Product Development Process

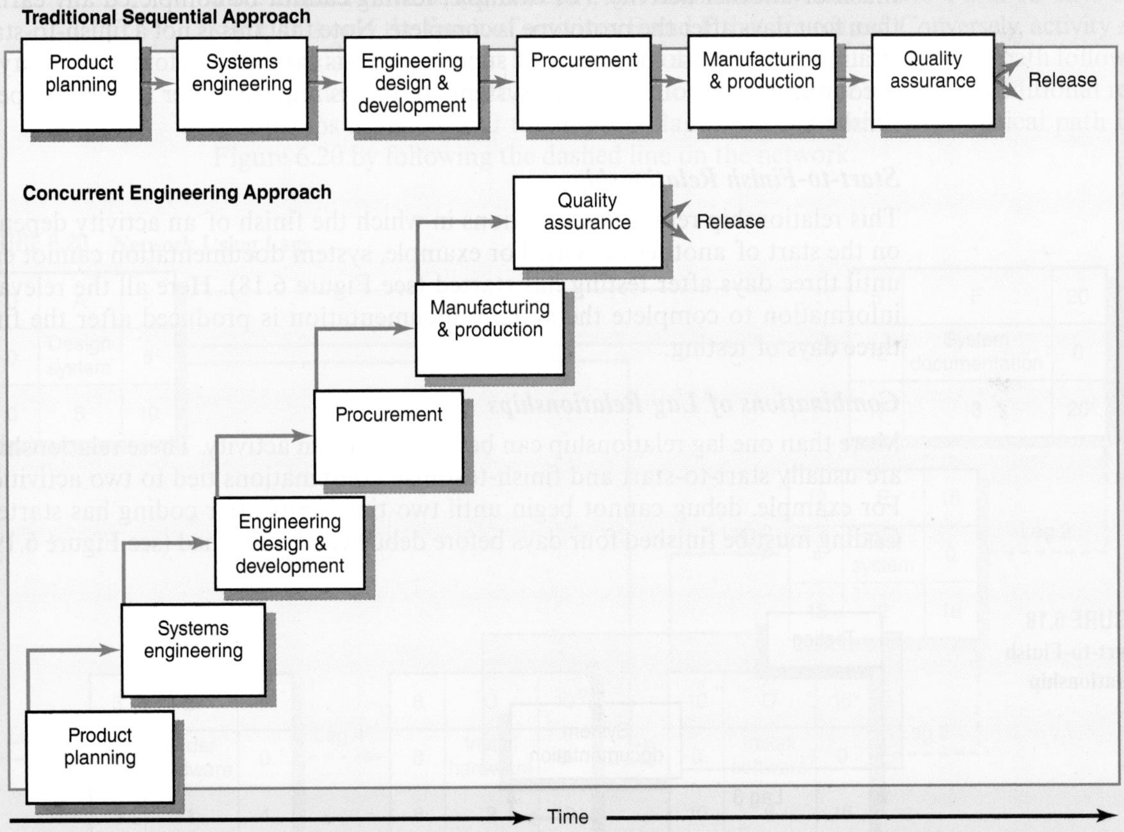

Within the world of project management this approach is also called *Fast Tracking*. General Motors used this approach to design the very first American hybrid car, the Chevy Volt. From the very beginning specialists from marketing, engineering, design, manufacturing, quality assurance, and other relevant departments were involved in every stage of the project. Not only did the project meet all of its objectives, it was completed ahead of schedule.

*"Chevrolet Volt Hits Road, Ahead of Schedule," *The New York Times*, June 25, 2009; retrieved online June 2, 2011.

If a lag relationship exists, each activity must be checked to see if the start or finish is constrained. For example, in the forward pass the EF of activity E (test system) (18) is controlled by the finish of activity D (install software) and the lag of two time units (16 + lag 2 = 18). Finally, in the backward pass, the LS of activity A (design system) is controlled by activity B (order hardware) and the lag relationship to activity A (3 − 3 = 0).

Hammock Activities

Another of the extended techniques uses a **hammock activity.** This type of activity derives its name because it spans over a segment of a project. The hammock activity duration is determined *after* the network plan is drawn. Hammock activities are frequently used to identify the use of fixed resources or costs over a segment of the project. Typical examples of hammock activities are inspection services, consultants, or construction management services. A hammock activity derives its duration from the time span between other activities. For example, a special color copy machine is needed for a segment of a tradeshow publication project. A hammock activity can be used to indicate the need for this resource and to apply costs over this segment of the project. This hammock is linked from the start of the first activity in the segment that uses the color copy machine to the end of the last activity that uses it. The hammock duration is simply the difference between the EF for the last activity and the ES of the first activity. The duration is computed after the forward pass and hence has no influence on other activity times. Figure 6.21 provides an

FIGURE 6.21 Hammock Activity Example

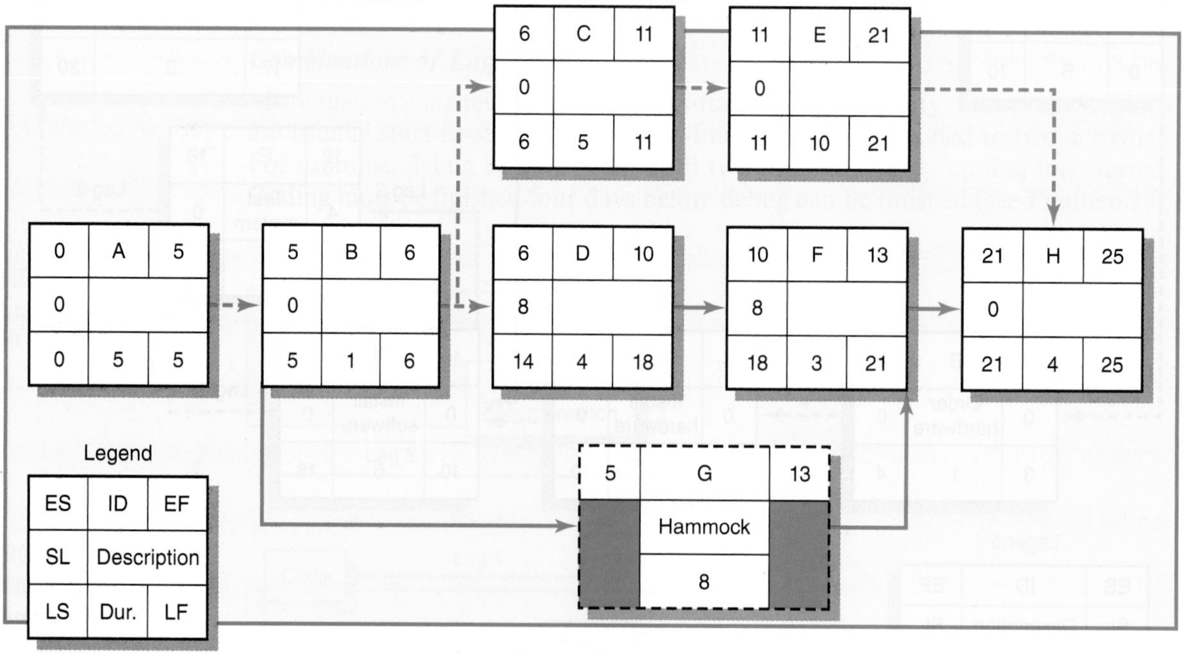

example of a hammock activity used in a network. The duration for the hammock activity is derived from the early start of activity B and the early finish of activity F; that is, the difference between 13 and 5, or 8 time units. The hammock duration will change if any ES or EF in the chain-sequence changes. Hammock activities are very useful in assigning and controlling indirect project costs.[3]

Another major use of hammock activities is to aggregate sections of a project. This is similar to developing a subnetwork, but the precedence is still preserved. This approach is sometimes used to present a "macro network" for upper management levels. Using a hammock activity to group activities can facilitate getting the right level of detail for specific sections of a project.

Summary

Many project managers feel the project network is their most valuable exercise and planning document. Project networks sequence and time-phase the project work, resources, and budgets. Work package tasks are used to develop activities for networks. Every project manager should feel comfortable working in an AON environment. The AON method uses nodes (boxes) for activities and arrows for dependencies. The forward and backward passes establish early and late times for activities. Although most project managers use computers to generate networks and activity times, they find a keen understanding of network development and the ability to compute activity times is invaluable in the field. Computers break down; input errors give false information; some decisions must be made without computer "what if" analysis. Project managers who are well acquainted with network development and AON methods and who are able to compute activity times will encounter fewer problems than project managers less well acquainted. Project networks help to ensure there are no surprises.

Several extensions and modifications have been appended to the original AON method. Lags allow the project planner to more closely replicate the actual conditions found in practice. The use of lags can result in the start or finish of an activity becoming critical. Some computer software simply calls the whole activity critical rather than identifying the start or finish as being critical. Caution should be taken to ensure that lags are not used as a buffer for possible errors in estimating time. Finally, hammock activities are useful in tracking costs of resources used for a particular segment of a project. Hammock activities can also be used to reduce the size of a project network by grouping activities for simplification and clarity. All of the discussed refinements to the original AON methodology contribute toward better planning and control of projects.

[3] In order to designate G as a Hammock activity in MS Project 2012 you would copy and paste for activity G the start date of activity B and the finish date for activity F (http://support.microsoft.com/kb/141733).

Key Terms

Activity, *164*
Activity-on-arrow (AOA), *165*
Activity-on-node (AON), *165*
Burst activity, *164*
Concurrent engineering, *182*
Critical path, *164*
Early and late times, *163*
Free slack, *175*
Gantt chart, *177*
Hammock activity, *186*
Lag relationship, *181*
Merge activity, *164*
Parallel activity, *164*
Sensitivity, *174*
Total slack, *173*

Review Questions

1. How does the WBS differ from the project network?
2. How are WBS and project networks linked?
3. Why bother creating a WBS? Why not go straight to a project network and forget the WBS?
4. Why is slack important to the project manager?
5. What is the difference between free slack and total slack?
6. Why are lags used in developing project networks?
7. What is a hammock activity, and when is it used?

Exercises

Creating a Project Network

1. Here is a partial work breakdown structure for a wedding. Use the method described in the Snapshot from Practice: The Yellow Sticky Approach to create a network for this project.

Note: Do not include summary tasks in the network (i.e., 1.3, Ceremony, is a summary task; 1.2, Marriage license, is not a summary task). Do not consider who would be doing the task in building the network. For example, do not arrange "hiring a band" to occur after "florist" because the same person is responsible for doing both tasks. Focus only on technical dependencies between tasks.

Hint: Start with the last activity (wedding reception), and work your way back to the start of the project. Build the logical sequence of tasks by asking the following question: In order to have or do this, what must be accomplished immediately before this? Once completed, check forward in time by asking this question: Is this task(s) the only thing that is needed immediately before the start of the next task?

Work Breakdown Structure

1. Wedding project
   - 1.1 Decide on date
   - 1.2 Marriage license
   - 1.3 Ceremony
     - *1.3.1 Rent church*
     - *1.3.2 Florist*
     - *1.3.3 Create/print programs*

- *1.3.4 Hire photographer*
- *1.3.5 Wedding ceremony*

1.4 Guests

- *1.4.1 Develop guest list*
- *1.4.2 Order invitations*
- *1.4.3 Address and mail invitations*
- *1.4.4 Track RSVPs*

1.5 Reception

- *1.5.1 Reserve reception hall*
- *1.5.2 Food and beverage*
  - *1.5.2.1 Choose caterer*
  - *1.5.2.2 Decide on menu*
  - *1.5.2.3 Make final order*
- *1.5.3 Hire band*
- *1.5.4 Decorate reception hall*
- *1.5.5 Wedding reception*

Drawing AON Networks

2. Draw a project network from the following information. What activity(s) is a burst activity? What activity(s) is a merge activity?

ID	Description	Predecessor
A	Survey site	None
B	Install drainage	A
C	Install power lines	A
D	Excavate site	B, C
E	Pour foundation	D

3.* Draw a project network from the following information. What activity(s) is a burst activity? What activity(s) is a merge activity?

ID	Description	Predecessor
A	Identify topic	None
B	Research topic	A
C	Draft paper	B
D	Edit paper	C
E	Create graphics	C
F	References	C
G	Final draft	D, E, F

* The solution to this exercise can be found in Appendix One.

4. Draw a project network from the following information. What activity(s) is a burst activity? What activity(s) is a merge activity?

ID	Description	Predecessor
A	Contract signed	None
B	Survey designed	A
C	Target market identified	B
D	Data collection	B, C
E	Develop presentation	B
F	Analyze results	D
G	Demographics	C
H	Presentation	E, F, G

5. Draw a project network from the following information. What activity(s) is a burst activity? What activity(s) is a merge activity?

ID	Description	Predecessor
A	Order review	None
B	Order standard parts	A
C	Produce standard parts	A
D	Design custom parts	A
E	Software development	A
F	Manufacture custom parts	C, D
G	Assemble	B, F
H	Test	E, G

AON Network Times

6. From the following information, develop an AON project network. Complete the forward and backward pass, compute activity slack, and identify the critical path. How many days will the project take?

ID	Description	Predecessor	Time
A	Survey site	None	2
B	Install drainage	A	5
C	Install power lines	A	3
D	Excavate site	B, C	4
E	Pour foundation	D	3

7. The project information for the custom order project of the Air Control Company is presented here. Draw a project network for this project. Compute the early and late activity times and the slack times. Identify the critical path.

ID	Activity	Predecessor	Time
A	Order review	None	2
B	Order standard parts	A	15
C	Produce standard parts	A	10
D	Design custom parts	A	13
E	Software development	A	18
F	Manufacture custom hardware	C, D	15
G	Assemble	B, F	10
H	Test	E, G	5

8. You have signed a contract to build a garage for the Simpsons. You will receive a $500 bonus for completing the project within 15 working days. The contract also contains a penalty clause in which you will lose $100 for each day the project takes longer than 15 working days.

   Draw a project network given the information below. Complete the forward and backward pass, compute the activity slack, and identify the critical path. Do you expect to receive a bonus or a penalty on this project?

ID	Description	Predecessor	Time (days)
A	Pour foundation	None	3
B	Erect frame	A	4
C	Roof	B	4
D	Windows	B	1
E	Doors	B	1
F	Electrical	B	3
G	Rough-in frame	C, D, E, F	2
H	Door opener	E, F	1
I	Paint	G, H	2
J	Cleanup	I	1

9. You are creating a customer database for the Modesto Nuts minor league baseball team. Draw a project network given the information below. Complete the forward and backward pass, compute activity slack, and identify the critical path.

   How long will this project take? How sensitive is the network schedule? Calculate the free slack and total slack for all noncritical activities.

ID	Description	Predecessor	Time (days)
A	Systems design	None	2
B	Subsystem A design	A	1
C	Subsystem B design	A	1
D	Subsystem C design	A	1
E	Program A	B	2
F	Program B	C	2
G	Program C	D	2
H	Subsystem A test	E	1
I	Subsystem B test	F	1
J	Subsystem C test	G	1
K	Integration	H, I, J	2
L	Integration test	K	1

10. J. Wold, project manager of Print Software, Inc., wants you to prepare a project network; compute the early, late, and slack activity times; determine the planned project duration; and identify the critical path. His assistant has

collected the following information for the Color Printer Drivers Software Project:

ID	Description	Predecessor	Time
A	External specifications	None	8
B	Review design features	A	2
C	Document new features	A	3
D	Write software	A	60
E	Program and test	B	60
F	Edit and publish notes	C	2
G	Review manual	D	2
H	Alpha site	E, F	20
I	Print manual	G	10
J	Beta site	H, I	10
K	Manufacture	J	12
L	Release and ship	K	3

11.* A large eastern city is requesting federal funding for a park-and-ride project. One of the requirements in the request application is a network plan for the design phase of the project. Catherine Walker, the chief engineer, wants you to develop a project network plan to meet this requirement. She has gathered the activity time estimates and their dependencies shown here. Show your project network with the activity early, late, and slack times. Mark the critical path.

ID	Description	Predecessor	Time
A	Survey	None	5
B	Soils report	A	20
C	Traffic design	A	30
D	Lot layout	A	5
E	Approve design	B, C, D	80
F	Illumination	E	15
G	Drainage	E	30
H	Landscape	E	25
I	Signing	E	20
J	Bid proposal	F, G, H, I	10

12. You are creating a customer database for the Winston-Salem Warthogs minor league baseball team. Draw a project network given the information below. Complete the forward and backward pass, compute activity slack, and identify the critical path.

* The solution to this exercise can be found in Appendix One.

How long will this project take? How sensitive is the network schedule? Calculate the free slack and total slack for all noncritical activities.

ID	Description	Predecessor	Time (days)
A	Systems design	None	2
B	Subsystem A design	A	1
C	Subsystem B design	A	2
D	Subsystem C design	A	1
E	Program A	B	2
F	Program B	C	10
G	Program C	D	2
H	Subsystem A test	E	1
I	Subsystem B test	F	1
J	Subsystem C test	G	1
K	Integration	H, I, J	2
L	Integration test	K	1

13.* You are completing a group term paper. Given the project network that follows, complete the forward and backward pass, compute activity slack, and identify the critical path. Use this information to create a Gantt chart for the project. Be sure to show slack for noncritical activities.

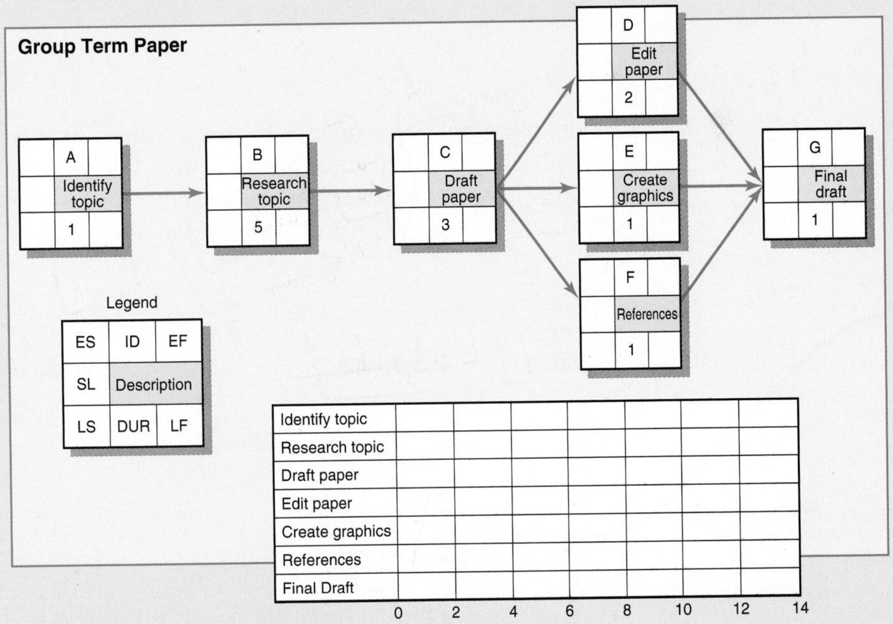

* The solution to this exercise can be found in Appendix One.

14. You are conducting a market research project for FUN Inc. Given the project network that follows, complete the forward and backward pass, compute activity slack, and identify the critical path. Use this information to create a Gantt chart for the project. Be sure to show slack for noncritical activities.

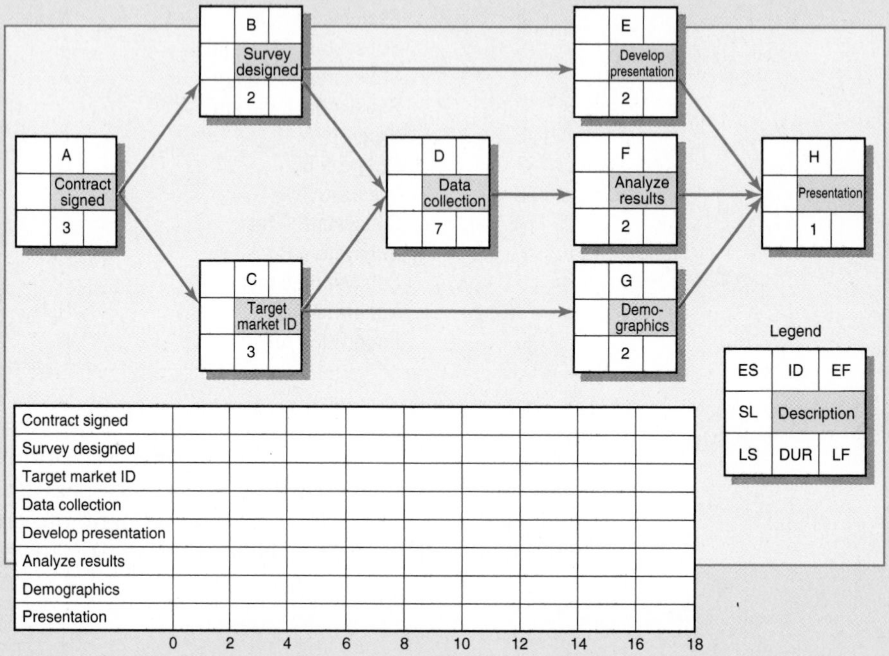

Computer Exercises

15. The planning department of an electronics firm has set up the activities for developing and production of a new MP3 Player. Given the information below, develop a project network using Microsoft Project. Assume a five-day workweek and the project starts on January 4, 2013.

Activity ID	Description	Activity Predecessor	Activity Time (weeks)
1	Staff	None	2
2	Develop market program	1	3
3	Select channels of distribution	1	8
4	Patent	1	12
5	Pilot production	1	4
6	Test market	5	4
7	Ad promotion	2	4
8	Set up for production	4, 6	16

The project team has requested that you create a network for the project, and determine if the project can be completed in 45 weeks.

16. Using Microsoft Project, set up the network and determine the critical path for Phase 1 of the project. The project workweek will be 5 days (M—F).

Whistler Ski Resort Project

Given the fact that the number of skiing visitors to Whistler, B.C., Canada has been increasing at an exciting rate, thanks to the 2010 Winter Olympics, the Whistler Ski Association has been considering construction of another ski lodge and ski complex. The results of an economic feasibility study just completed by members of the staff show that a winter resort complex near the base of Whistler Mountain could be a very profitable venture. The area is accessible by car, bus, train, and air. The board of directors has voted to build the ten-million dollar complex recommended in the study. Unfortunately, due to the short summer season, the complex will have to be built in stages. The first stage (year 1) will contain a day lodge, chair lift, rope tow, generator house (for electricity), and a parking lot designed to accommodate 400 cars and 30 buses. The second and third stages will include a hotel, ice rink, pool, shops, two additional chair lifts, and other attractions. The board has decided that stage one should begin no later than April 1 and be completed by October 1, in time for the next skiing season. You have been assigned the task of project manager, and it is your job to coordinate the ordering of materials and construction activities to ensure the project's completion by the required date.

After looking into the possible sources of materials, you are confronted with the following time estimates. Materials for the chair lift and rope tow will take 30 days and 12 days, respectively, to arrive once the order is submitted. Lumber for the day lodge, generator hut, and foundations will take 9 days to arrive. The electrical and plumbing materials for the day lodge will take 12 days to arrive. The generator will take 12 days to arrive. Before actual construction can begin on the various facilities, a road to the site must be built; this will take 6 days. As soon as the road is in, clearing can begin concurrently on the sites of the day lodge, generator house, chair lift, and rope tow. It is estimated that the clearing task at each site will take 6 days, 3 days, 36 days, and 6 days, respectively. The clearing of the main ski slopes can begin after the area for the chair lift has been cleared; this will take 84 days.

The foundation for the day lodge will take 12 days to complete. Construction of the main framework will take an additional 18 days. After the framework is completed, electrical wiring and plumbing can be installed concurrently. These should take 24 and 30 days, respectively. Finally, the finishing construction on the day lodge can begin; this will take 36 days.

Installation of the chair lift towers (67 days) can begin once the site is cleared, lumber delivered, and the foundation completed (6 days). Also, when the chair lift site has been cleared, construction of a permanent road to the upper towers can be started; this will take 24 days. While the towers are being installed, the electric motor to drive the chair lift can be installed; the motor can be installed in 24 days. Once the towers are completed and the motor installed, it will take 3 days to install the cable and an additional 12 days to install the chairs.

Installation of the towers for the rope tow can begin once the site is cleared and the foundation is built and poured; it takes 4 days to build the foundation, pour the concrete and let it cure, and 20 days to install the towers for the rope tow. While the towers are being erected, installation of the electric motor to drive the rope tow can begin; this activity will take 24 days. After the towers and motor are installed, the rope tow can be strung in 1 day. The parking lot can be cleared once the rope tow is finished; this task will take 18 days.

The foundation for the generator house can begin at the same time as the foundation for the lodge; this will take 6 days. The main framework for the generator house can begin once the foundation is completed; framing will take 12 days. After the house is framed, the diesel generator can be installed in 18 days. Finishing construction on the generator house can now begin and will take 12 more days.

Assignment:

1. Identify the critical path on your network.
2. Can the project be completed by October 1?

Optical Disk Preinstallation Project

17. The optical disk project team has started gathering the information necessary to develop the project network—predecessor activities and activity times in weeks. The results of their meeting are found in the following table.

Activity	Description	Duration	Predecessor
1	Define scope	6	None
2	Define customer problems	3	1
3	Define data records and relationships	5	1
4	Mass storage requirements	5	2, 3
5	Consultant needs analysis	10	2, 3
6	Prepare installation network	3	4, 5
7	Estimate costs and budget	2	4, 5
8	Design section "point" system	1	4, 5
9	Write request proposal	5	4, 5
10	Compile vendor list	3	4, 5
11	Prepare mgmt. control system	5	6, 7
12	Prepare comparison report	5	9, 10
13	Compare system "philosophies"	3	8, 12
14	Compare total installation	2	8, 12
15	Compare cost of support	3	8, 12
16	Compare customer satisfaction level	10	8, 12
17	Assign philosophies points	1	13
18	Assign installation cost	1	14
19	Assign support cost	1	15
20	Assign customer satisfaction points	1	16
21	Select best system	1	11, 17, 18, 19, 20
22	Order system	1	21

The project team has requested that you create a network for the project, and determine if the project can be completed in 45 weeks.

Lag Exercises

18. From the following information, draw the project network. Compute the early, late, and slack times for each activity. Identify the critical path. (Hint: Draw the finish-to-start relationships first.)

ID	Duration	Finish-to-Start Predecessor	Finish-to-Start Lag	Additional Lag Relationships	Lag
A	5	None	0	None	0
B	10	A	0	None	0
C	15	A	0	Start-finish C to D	20
D	5	B	5	Start-start D to E	5
				Finish-finish D to E	25
E	20	B	0	Finish-finish E to F	0
F	15	D	0	None	0
G	10	C	10	Finish-finish G to F	10
H	20	F	0	None	0

19. Given the following information, draw the project network. Compute the early, late, and slack times for the project network. Which activities on the critical path have only the start or finish of the activity on the critical path?

ID	Duration	Finish-to-Start Predecessor	Finish-to-Start Lag	Additional Lag Relationships	Lag
A	2	None	0	None	0
B	4	A	0	None	0
C	6	A	0	Finish-finish C to F	7
D	8	A	0	None	0
E	18	B	0	Finish-finish E to G	9
		C	10		
F	2	D	0	None	
G	5	F	0	Start-start G to H	10
H	5	None	0	None	0
I	14	E	0	Finish-finish I to J	5
J	15	G, H	0	None	0

20.* Given the information in the following lag exercises, compute the early, late, and slack times for the project network. Which activities on the critical path have only the start or finish of the activity on the critical path?

* The solution to this exercise can be found in Appendix One.

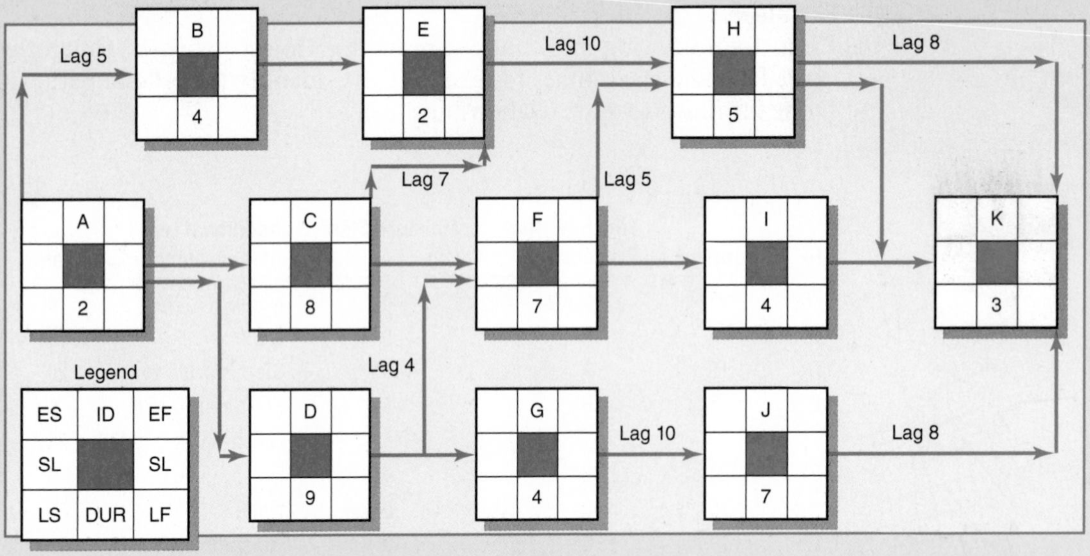

21. Given the network below, compute the early, late, and slack time for each activity.

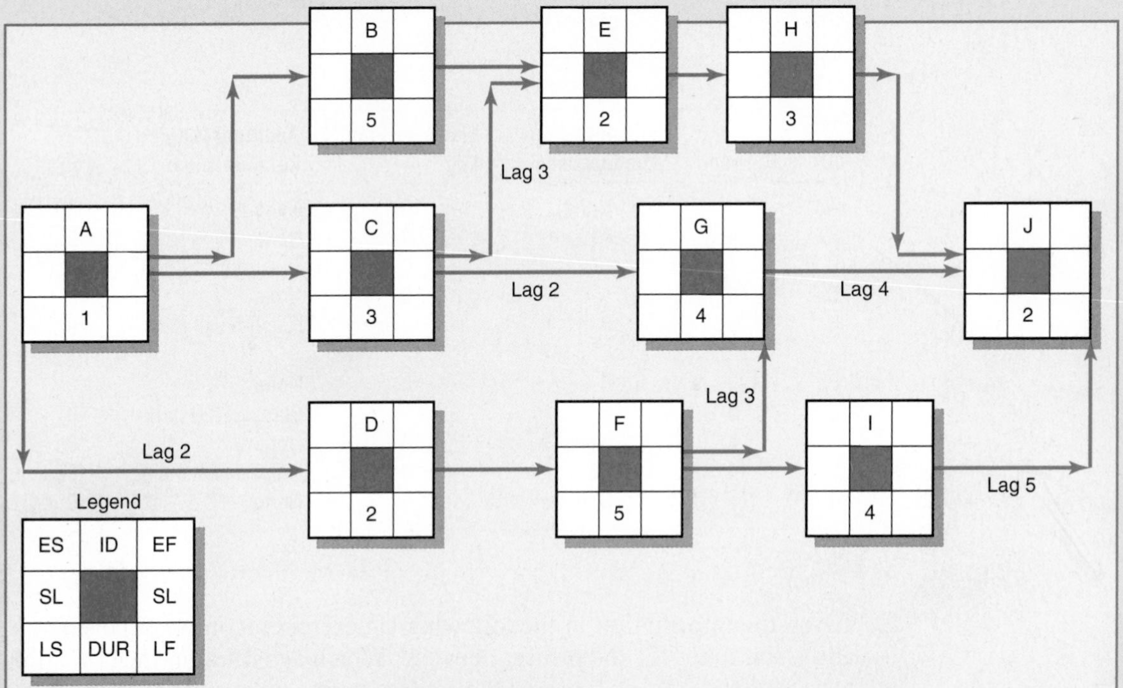

The ES for Activity C is ____
The LS for Activity E is ____
The LS for Activity G is ____

The slack for the start of Activity G is ____
The slack for the start of Activity B is ____
The slack for the start of Activity E is ____

The slack for the finish of Activity H is ____
The slack for the finish of Activity F is ____
The slack for the finish of Activity G is ____

CyClon Project

22. The CyClon project team has started gathering information necessary to develop a project network-predecessor activities and activity time in days. The results of their meeting are found in the following table:

Activity	Description	Duration	Predecessor
1	***CyClon Project***		
2	Design	10	
3	Procure prototype parts	10	2
4	Fabricate parts	8	2
5	Assemble prototype	4	3, 4
6	Laboratory test	7	5
7	Field test	10	6
8	Adjust design	6	7
9	Order stock components	10	8
10	Order custom components	15	8
11	Assemble test production unit	10	9, 10
12	Test unit	5	11
13	Document results	3	12

Part A. Create a network based on the above information. How long will the project take? What is the critical path?

Part B. Upon further review the team recognizes that they missed three finish-to-start lags. Procure prototype parts will involve only 2 days of work but it will take 8 days for the parts to be delivered. Likewise, Order stock components will take 2 days of work and 8 days for delivery and Order custom components 2 days of work and 13 days for delivery.

Reconfigure the CyClon schedule by entering the three finish-to-start lags. What impact did these lags have on the original schedule? On the amount of work required to complete the project?

Part C. Management is still not happy with the schedule and wants the project completed as soon as possible. Unfortunately, they are not willing to approve additional resources. One team member pointed out that the network contained only finish-to-start relationships and that it might be possible to reduce project duration by creating start-to-start lags. After much deliberation the team concluded that the following relationships could be converted into start-to-start lags:

- Procure prototype parts could start 6 days after the start of Design.
- Fabricate parts could start 9 days after the start of Design.
- Laboratory test could begin 1 day after the start of Assemble prototype.
- Field test could start 5 days after the start of Laboratory test.
- Adjust design could begin 7 days after the start of Field test.
- Order stock and Order custom components could begin 5 days after Adjust design.
- Test unit could begin 9 days after the start of Assemble test production unit.
- Document results could start 3 days after the start of Test unit.

Reconfigure the CyClon schedule by entering all nine start-to-start lags. What impact did these lags have on the original schedule (Part A)? How long will the project take? Is there a change in the critical path? Is there a change in the sensitivity of the network? Why would management like this solution?

References

Gantt, H. L., *Work, Wages and Profit*, published by *The Engineering Magazine*, New York, 1910; republished as *Work, Wages and Profits* (Easton, PA: Hive Publishing Company, 1974).

Kelly, J. E., "Critical Path Planning and Scheduling: Mathematical Basis," *Operations Research,* 9 (3) May–June 1961, pp. 296–321.

Levy, F. K., G. L. Thompson, and J. D. West, "The ABCs of the Critical Path Method," *Harvard Business Review,* 41 (5) 1963, pp. 98–108.

Rosenblatt, A., and G. Watson, "Concurrent Engineering," *IEEE Spectrum,* July 1991, pp. 22–37.

Turtle, Q. C., *Implementing Concurrent Project Management* (Englewood Cliffs, NJ: Prentice Hall), 1994.

Case

Advantage Energy Technology Data Center Migration*

Brian Smith, network administrator at Advanced Energy Technology (AET), has been given the responsibility of implementing the migration of a large data center to a new office location. Careful planning is needed because AET operates in the highly competitive petroleum industry. AET is one of five national software companies that provide an accounting and business management package for oil jobbers and gasoline distributors. A few years ago, AET jumped into the "application service provider" world. Their large data center provides clients with remote access to AET's complete suite of application software systems. Traditionally, one of AET's primary competitive advantages has been the company's trademark IT reliability. Due to the complexity of this project, Brian will have to use a parallel method of implementation. Although this will increase project costs, a parallel approach is essential if reliability is not to be compromised.

Currently, AET's data center is located on the second floor of a renovated old bank building in downtown Corvallis, Oregon. The company is moving to a new, one-level building located in the recently developed industrial complex at the Corvallis International Airport. On February 1, Brian is formally assigned the task by the Vice-President of Operations, Dan Whitmore, with the following guidelines:

- From start to finish, it is anticipated the entire project will take three to four months to complete.
- It is essential that AET's 235 clients suffer no downtime.

Whitmore advises Brian to come back to the Executive Committee on February 15, with a presentation on the scope of the project that includes costs, "first-cut" timeline, and proposed project team members.

Brian had some preliminary discussions with some of AET's managers and directors from each of the functional departments and then arranged for a full-day scope meeting on February 4 with a few of the managers and technical

* Prepared by James Moran, a project management instructor at the College of Business, Oregon State University.

representatives from operations, systems, facilities, and applications. The scope team determined the following:

- Three to four months is a feasible project timeline and first-cut cost estimate is \$80,000–\$90,000 (this includes the infrastructure upgrade of the new site).
- Critical to the "no-downtime" requirement is the need to completely rely on AET's remote disaster recovery "hot" site for full functionality.
- Brian will serve as project manager of a team consisting of one team member each from facilities, operations/systems, operations/telecommunications, systems & applications, and customer service.

Brian's Executive Committee report was positively received and, after a few modifications and recommendations, he was formally charged with responsibility for the project. Brian recruited his team and scheduled their first team meeting (March 1) as the initial task of his project planning process.

Once the initial meeting is conducted Brian can hire the contractors to renovate the new data center. During this time Brian will figure out how to design the network. Brian estimates that screening and hiring a contractor will take about one week and that the network design will take about two weeks. The new center requires a new ventilation system. The manufacturer's requirements include an ambient temperature of 67 degrees to keep all of the data servers running at optimal speeds. The ventilation system has a lead time of three weeks. Brian will also need to order new racks to hold the servers, switches, and other network devices. The racks have a two-week delivery time.

The data center supervisor requested that Brian replace all of the old power supplies and data cables. Brian will need to order these as well. Because Brian has a great relationship with the vendor, they guarantee that it will take only one week lead time for the power supplies and the data cables. Once the new ventilation system and racks arrive, Brian can begin installing them. It will take one week to install the ventilation system and three weeks to install the racks. The renovation of the new data center can begin as soon as the contractors have been hired. The contractors tell Brian that construction will take 20 days. Once the construction begins and after Brian installs the ventilation system and racks, the city inspector must approve the construction of the raised floor.

The city inspector will take two days to approve the infrastructure. After the city inspection and after the new power supplies and cables have arrived, Brian can install the power supplies and run the cables. Brian estimates that it will take five days to install the power supplies and one week to run all of the data cables. Before Brian can assign an actual date for taking the network off line and switching to the hot remote site, he must get approval from each of the functional units ("Switchover Approval"). Meetings with each of the functional units will require one week. During this time he can initiate a power check to ensure that each of the racks has sufficient voltage. This will require only one day.

Upon completion of the power check, he can take one week to install his test servers. The test servers will test all of the primary network functions and act as a safeguard before the network is taken off line. The batteries must be charged, ventilation installed, and test servers up and running before management can be assured that the new infrastructure is safe, which will take two days. Then they will sign off the Primary Systems check, taking one day of intense meetings. They will also set an official date for the network move.

Brian is happy that everything has gone well thus far and is convinced that the move will go just as smoothly. Now that an official date is set, the network will be

CHAPTER SEVEN

Managing Risk

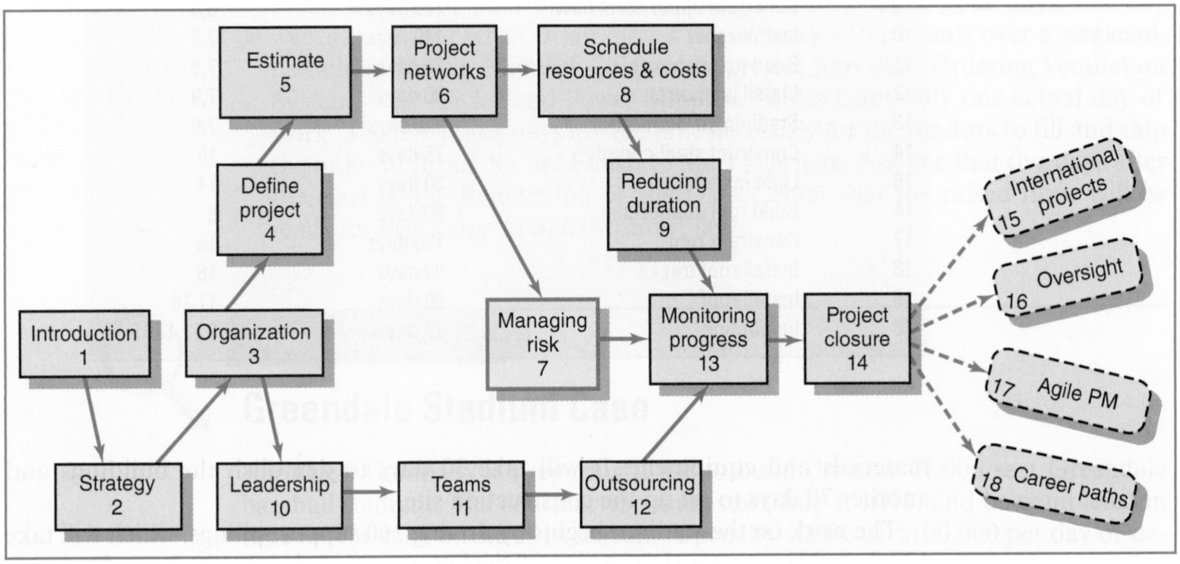

Managing Risk

Risk Management Process

Step 1: Risk Identification

Step 2: Risk Assessment

Step 3: Risk Response Development

Contingency Planning

Opportunity Management

Contingency Funding and Time Buffers

Step 4: Risk Response Control

Change Control Management

Summary

Appendix 7.1: PERT and PERT Simulation

You've got to go out on a limb sometimes because that's where the fruit is.

Will Rogers

Every project manager understands risks are inherent in projects. No amount of planning can overcome *risk,* or the inability to control chance events. In the context of projects, **risk** is an uncertain event or condition that, if it occurs, has a positive or negative effect on project objectives. A risk has a cause and, if it occurs, a consequence. For example, a cause may be a flu virus or change in scope requirements. The event is that team members get stricken with the flu or the product has to be redesigned. If either of these uncertain events occurs, it will impact the cost, schedule, and quality of the project.

Some potential risk events can be identified before the project starts—such as equipment malfunction or change in technical requirements. Risks can be anticipated consequences, like schedule slippages or cost overruns. Risks can be beyond imagination like the 2008 financial meltdown.

While risks can have positive consequences such as unexpected price reduction in materials, the primary focus of this chapter is on what can go wrong and the risk management process.

Risk management attempts to recognize and manage potential and unforeseen trouble spots that may occur when the project is implemented. Risk management identifies as many risk events as possible (what can go wrong), minimizes their impact (what can be done about the event before the project begins), manages responses to those events that do materialize (contingency plans), and provides contingency funds to cover risk events that actually materialize.

For a humorous, but ultimately embarrassing example of poor risk management see Snapshot from Practice: Giant Popsicle Gone Wrong.

Risk Management Process

Figure 7.1 presents a graphic model of the risk management challenge. The chances of a risk event occurring (e.g., an error in time estimates, cost estimates, or design technology) are greatest during the early stages of a project. This is when uncertainty is highest and many questions remain unanswered. As the project progresses toward completion, risk declines as the answers to critical issues (Will the technology work? Is the timeline feasible?) are resolved. The cost impact of a risk event, however, increases over the life of the project. For example, the risk event of a design flaw occurring after a prototype has been made has a greater cost or time impact than if the flaw were discovered during the planning phase of the project.

The cost of mismanaged risk control early on in the project is exemplified by the ill-fated 1999 NASA Mars Climate Orbiter. Investigations revealed that Lockheed

SNAPSHOT FROM PRACTICE Giant Popsicle Gone Wrong*

An attempt to erect the world's largest Popsicle in New York City ended with a scene straight out of a disaster film, but much stickier.

The 25-foot-tall, $17\frac{1}{2}$-ton treat of frozen juice melted faster than expected, flooding Union Square in downtown Manhattan with kiwi-strawberry–flavored fluid.

Bicyclists wiped out in the stream of goo. Pedestrians slipped. Traffic was, well, frozen. Firefighters closed off several streets and used hoses to wash away the thick, sweet slime.

The Snapple Company, a leading maker of soft beverages, had been trying to promote a new line of frozen treats by setting a record for the world's largest Popsicle, but called off the stunt before the frozen giant was pulled fully upright by a construction crane.

Authorities said they were worried the $2\frac{1}{2}$-story popsicle would collapse.

Organizers were not sure why it melted so quickly. "We planned for it. We just didn't expect for it to happen so fast," said Snapple spokeswoman Lauren Radcliffe. She said the company would offer to pay the city for the clean-up costs.

* Associated Press, June 23, 2005.

Martin botched the design of critical navigation software. While flight computers on the ground did calculations based on pounds of thrust per second, the spacecraft's computer software used metric units called newtons. A check to see if the values were compatible was never done.

"Our check and balances processes did not catch an error like this that should have been caught," said Ed Weiler, NASA's associate administrator for space science.

FIGURE 7.1
Risk Event Graph

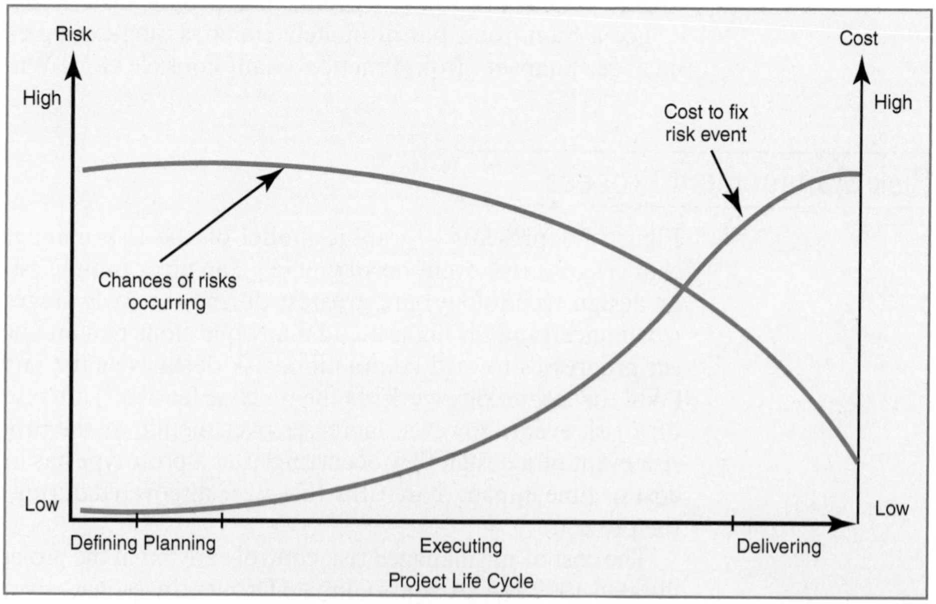

FIGURE 7.2
The Risk Management Process

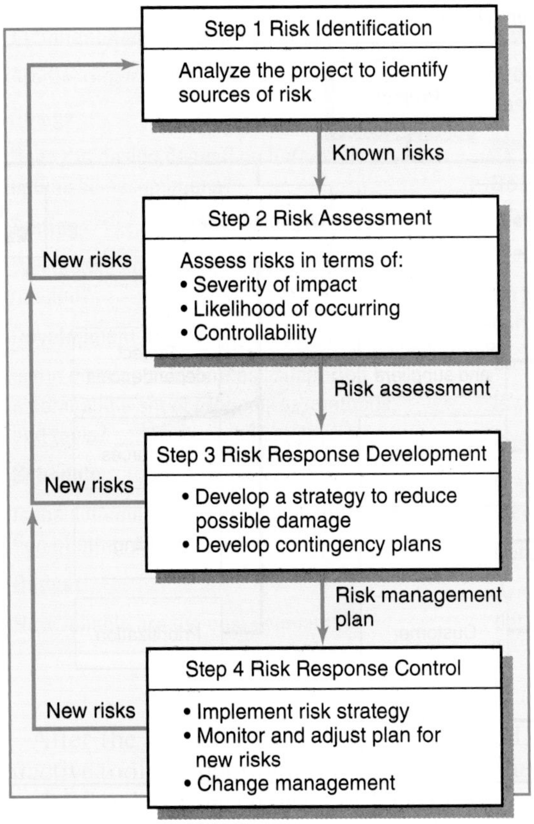

"That is the bottom line" (*Orlando Sentinel,* 1999). If the error had been discovered early the correction would have been relatively simple and inexpensive. Instead the error was never discovered, and after the nine-month journey to the Red Planet, the $125-million probe approached Mars at too low an altitude and burned up in the planet's atmosphere. Following the 1999 debacle, NASA instituted a more robust risk management system which has produced a string of successful missions to Mars, including the dramatic landing of the *Curiosity* rover in August 2012.[1]

Risk management is a proactive approach rather than reactive. It is a preventive process designed to ensure that surprises are reduced and that negative consequences associated with undesirable events are minimized. It also prepares the project manager to take action when a time, cost, and/or technical advantage is possible. Successful management of project risk gives the project manager better control over the future and can significantly improve chances of reaching project objectives on time, within budget, and meeting required technical (functional) performance.

The sources of project risks are unlimited. There are sources external to the organization, such as inflation, market acceptance, exchange rates, and government regulations. In practice, these risk events are often referred to as "threats" to differentiate them from those that are not within the project manager's or team's responsibility area. (Later we will see budgets for such risk events are placed in a "management reserve" contingency budget.) Since such external risks are usually considered before the decision to go ahead with the project, they will be excluded from the discussion of project risks. However, external risks are extremely important and must be addressed.

The major components of the risk management process are depicted in Figure 7.2. Each step will be examined in more detail in the remainder of the chapter.

Step 1: Risk Identification

The risk management process begins by trying to generate a list of all the possible risks that could affect the project. Typically the project manager pulls together, during the planning phase, a risk management team consisting of core team members and other relevant stakeholders. Research has demonstrated that groups

[1] E. Landau, "Mars Landing Went 'Flawlessly,' Scientists Say," *CNN.com,* accessed August 14, 2012.

IT project managers can access "best practices" papers detailing other companies' experiences converting software systems. Inquiries should not be limited to recorded data. Savvy project managers tap the wisdom of others by seeking the advice of veteran project managers.

The risk identification process should not be limited to just the core team. Input from customers, sponsors, subcontractors, vendors, and other stakeholders should be solicited. Relevant stakeholders can be formally interviewed or included on the risk management team. Not only do these players have a valuable perspective, but by involving them in the risk management process they also become more committed to project success.[2]

One of the keys to success in risk identification is attitude. While a "can do" attitude is essential during implementation, project managers have to encourage critical thinking when it comes to risk identification. The goal is to find potential problems before they happen.

The RBS and risk profiles are useful tools for making sure no stones are left unturned. At the same time, when done well the number of risks identified can be overwhelming and a bit discouraging. Initial optimism can be replaced with griping and cries of "what have we gotten ourselves into?" It is important that project managers set the right tone and complete the risk management process so members regain confidence in themselves and the project.

Step 2: Risk Assessment

Step 1 produces a list of potential risks. Not all of these risks deserve attention. Some are trivial and can be ignored, while others pose serious threats to the welfare of the project. Managers have to develop methods for sifting through the list of risks, eliminating inconsequential or redundant ones and stratifying worthy ones in terms of importance and need for attention.

Scenario analysis is the easiest and most commonly used technique for analyzing risks. Team members assess the significance of each risk event in terms of:

- Probability of the event.
- Impact of the event.

Simply stated, risks need to be evaluated in terms of the likelihood the event is going to occur and the impact or consequences of its occurrence. The risk of a project manager being struck by lightning at a work site would have major negative impact on the project, but the likelihood is so low it is not worthy of consideration. Conversely, people do change jobs, so an event like the loss of key project personnel would have not only an adverse impact but also a high likelihood of occurring in some organizations. If so, then it would be wise for that organization to be proactive and mitigate this risk by developing incentive schemes for retaining specialists and/or engaging in cross-training to reduce the impact of turnover.

The quality and credibility of the risk analysis process requires that different levels of risk probabilities and impacts be defined. These definitions vary and should be tailored to the specific nature and needs of the project. For example, a relatively simple scale ranging from "very unlikely" to "almost certainly" may

[2] The Delphi Method (see p. 136) is a popular technique for involving stakeholders.

FIGURE 7.5 Defined Conditions for Impact Scales of a Risk on Major Project Objectives (Examples for negative impacts only)

	Relative or Numerical Scale				
Project Objective	1 Very Low	2 Low	3 Moderate	4 High	5 Very High
Cost	Insignificant cost increase	< 10% cost increase	10–20% cost increase	20–40% cost increase	> 40% cost increase
Time	Insignificant time increase	< 5% time increase	5–10% time increase	10–20% time increase	> 20% time increase
Scope	Scope decrease barely noticeable	Minor areas of scope affected	Major areas of scope affected	Scope reduction unacceptable to sponsor	Project end item is effectively useless
Quality	Quality degradation barely noticeable	Only very demanding applications are affected	Quality reduction requires sponsor approval	Quality reduction unacceptable to sponsor	Project end item is effectively useless

suffice for one project, whereas another project may use more precise numerical probabilities (e.g., 0.1, 0.3, 0.5, . . .).

Impact scales can be a bit more problematic since adverse risks affect project objectives differently. For example, a component failure may cause only a slight delay in project schedule but a major increase in project cost. If controlling cost is a high priority, then the impact would be severe. If, on the other hand, time is more critical than cost, then the impact would be minor.

Because impact ultimately needs to be assessed in terms of project priorities, different kinds of impact scales are used. Some scales may simply use rank-order descriptors, such as "low," "moderate," "high," and "very high," whereas others use numeric weights (e.g., 1–10). Some may focus on the project in general while others focus on specific project objectives. The risk management team needs to establish up front what distinguishes a 1 from a 3 or "moderate" impact from "severe" impact. Figure 7.5 provides an example of how impact scales could be defined given the project objectives of cost, time, scope, and quality.

Documentation of scenario analyses can be seen in various risk assessment forms used by companies. Figure 7.6 is a partial example of a risk assessment form used on an IS project involving the upgrade from Windows 7 to Windows 8.

Notice that in addition to evaluating the severity and probablity of risk events the team also assesses when the event might occur and its detection difficulty. Detection difficulty is a measure of how easy it would be to detect that the event was going to occur in time to take mitigating action, that is, how much warning would we have? So in the Windows 8 conversion example, the detection scale would range from 5 = no warning to 1 = lots of time to react.

Step 3: Risk Response Development

When a risk event is identified and assessed, a decision must be made concerning which response is appropriate for the specific event. Responses to risk can be classified as mitigating, avoiding, transferring, sharing, or retaining.

Mitigating Risk

Reducing risk is usually the first alternative considered. There are basically two strategies for mitigating risk: (1) reduce the likelihood that the event will occur and/or (2) reduce the impact that the adverse event would have on the project. Most risk teams focus first on reducing the likelihood of risk events since, if successful, this may eliminate the need to consider the potentially costly second strategy.

Testing and prototyping are frequently used to prevent problems from surfacing later in a project. An example of testing can be found in an information systems project. The project team was responsible for installing a new operating system in their parent company. Before implementing the project, the team tested the new system on a smaller isolated network. By doing so they discovered a variety of problems and were able to come up with solutions prior to implementation. The team still encountered problems with the installation but the number and severity were greatly reduced.

Often identifying the root causes of an event is useful. For example, the fear that a vendor will be unable to supply customized components on time may be attributable to (1) poor vendor relationships, (2) design miscommunication, and (3) lack of motivation. As a result of this analysis the project manager may decide to take his counterpart to lunch to clear the air, invite the vendor to attend design meetings, and restructure the contract to include incentives for on-time delivery.

Other examples of reducing the probability of risks occurring are scheduling outdoor work during the summer months, investing in up-front safety training, and choosing high-quality materials and equipment.

When the concerns are that duration and costs have been underestimated, managers will augment estimates to compensate for the uncertainties. It is common to use a ratio between old and new project to adjust time or cost. The ratio typically serves as a constant. For example, if past projects have taken 10 minutes per line of computer code, a constant of 1.10 (which represents a 10 percent increase) would be used for the proposed project time estimates because the new project is more difficult than prior projects.

An alternative mitigation strategy is to reduce the impact of the risk if it occurs. For example, a bridge-building project illustrates risk reduction. A new bridge project for a coastal port was to use an innovative, continuous cement-pouring process developed by an Australian firm to save large sums of money and time. The major risk was that the continuous pouring process for each major section of the bridge could not be interrupted. Any interruption would require that the whole cement section (hundreds of cubic yards) be torn down and started over. An assessment of possible risks centered on delivery of the cement from the cement factory. Trucks could be delayed, or the factory could break down. Such risks would result in tremendous rework costs and delays. Risk was reduced by having two additional portable cement plants built nearby on different highways within 20 miles of the bridge project in case the main factory supply was interrupted. These two portable plants carried raw materials for a whole bridge section, and extra trucks were on immediate

SNAPSHOT FROM PRACTICE From Dome to Dust*

On March 26, 2000, the largest concrete domed structure in the world was reduced to a pile of rubble in a dramatic implosion lasting less than 20 seconds. According to Mark Loizeaux, whose Maryland-based Controlled Demolition Inc. was hired to bring the 24-year-old Seattle Kingdome down, "We don't blow things up. We use explosives as an engine, but gravity is the catalyst that will bring it down."

Destroying the Kingdome was the most complicated of the 7,000 demolitions Loizeaux's company has undertaken. Nearly three months of preparations were needed to implode the dome at a total cost of $9 million. The Kingdome was considered to be one of the strongest structures in the world containing over 25,000 tons of concrete with each of its 40 vaulted ribs incorporating seven lengths of two-and-one-quarter-inch reinforcing steel bar.

Strands of orange detonating cord—basically dynamite in a string that explodes at the lightning pace of 24,000 feet per second— connected six pielike divisions of the Kingdome to a nearby control center.

Throughout each section, Controlled Demolition workers drilled nearly 1,000 holes and packed them with high-velocity gelatin explosives the size of hot dogs. Large charges were placed about one-third of the way up each dome rib, smaller charges were put farther up the ribs. When the detonation button was pushed, blasting caps set off a chain reaction of explosions in each section reducing the stadium to rubble.

While the actual implosion was a technical tour-de-force, risk management was a critical part of the project's success. To minimize damage to surrounding buildings, the explosive charges were wrapped in a layer of chain-link fencing covered with thick sheets of geotextile polypropylene fabric to contain flying concrete. Nearby buildings were protected in various manners depending on the structure and proximity to the Dome. Measures included sealing air-handling units, taping seams on doors and windows, covering floors and windows with plywood and draping reinforced polyethylene sheeting around the outside.

© Tim Matsui/Getty Images

To help absorb the impact, air-conditioning units removed from the interior were stacked with other material to create a barrier around the perimeter of the work area.

Hundreds of police officers and security personnel were used to cordon off an area extending roughly 1,000 feet from the Dome from overzealous spectators. Traffic was closed for a larger area. Accommodations were provided for people and pets who lived within the restricted zone.

Eight water trucks, eight sweeper units, and more than 100 workers were deployed immediately after the blast to control dust and begin the cleanup.

As a side note, one-third of the concrete will be crushed and used in the foundation of a new $430 million outdoor football stadium which is being built in its place. The rest of the concrete will be carted away and used in roadbeds and foundations throughout the Seattle area.

* *New York Times*—Sunday Magazine (March 19, 2000); *Seattle Times* (March 27, 2000) website.

standby each time continuous pouring was required. Similar risk reduction scenarios are apparent in system and software development projects where parallel innovation processes are used in case one fails.

The Dome to Dust Snapshot from Practice details the steps Controlled Demolition took to minimize damage when they imploded the Seattle Kingdome.

Avoiding Risk

Risk avoidance is changing the project plan to eliminate the risk or condition. Although it is impossible to eliminate all risk events, some specific risks may be avoided before you launch the project. For example, adopting proven technology instead of experimental technology can eliminate technical failure. Choosing an Australian supplier as opposed to an Indonesian supplier would virtually eliminate the chance that political unrest would disrupt the supply of critical materials. Likewise, one could eliminate the risk of choosing the wrong software by developing web applications using both ASAP.NET and PHP. Choosing to move a concert indoors would eliminate the threat of inclement weather.

Transferring Risk

Passing risk to another party is common; this transfer does not change risk. Passing risk to another party almost always results in paying a premium for this exemption. Fixed-price contracts are the classic example of transferring risk from an owner to a contractor. The contractor understands his or her firm will pay for any risk event that materializes; therefore, a monetary risk factor is added to the contract bid price. Before deciding to transfer risk, the owner should decide which party can best control activities that would lead to the risk occurring. Also, is the contractor capable of absorbing the risk? Clearly identifying and documenting responsibility for absorbing risk is imperative.

Another more obvious way to transfer risk is insurance. However, in most cases this is impractical because defining the project risk event and conditions to an insurance broker who is unfamiliar with the project is difficult and usually expensive. Of course, low-probability and high-consequence risk events such as acts of God are more easily defined and insured. Performance bonds, warranties, and guarantees are other financial instruments used to transfer risk.

On large, international construction projects like petrochemical plants and oil refineries, host countries are insisting on contracts that enforce Build-Own-Operate-Transfer (BOOT) provisions. Here the prime project organization is expected not only to build the facility, but also to take over ownership until its operation capacity has been proven and all the debugging has occurred before final transfer of ownership to the client. In such cases, the host country has transferred financial risk of ownership until the project has been completed and capabilities proven.

Retaining Risk

In some cases a conscious decision is made to accept the risk of an event occurring. Some risks are so large it is not feasible to consider transferring or reducing the event (e.g., an earthquake or flood). The project owner assumes the risk because the chance of such an event occurring is slim. In other cases risks identified in the budget reserve can simply be absorbed if they materialize. The risk is retained by developing a contingency plan to implement if the risk materializes. In a few cases a risk event can be ignored and a cost overrun accepted should the risk event occur.

The more effort given to risk response before the project begins, the better the chances are for minimizing project surprises. Knowing that the response to a risk event will be retained, transferred, or mitigated greatly reduces stress and uncertainty. Again, control is possible with this structured approach.

Contingency Planning

A **contingency plan** is an alternative plan that will be used if a possible foreseen risk event becomes a reality. The contingency plan represents actions that will reduce or mitigate the negative impact of the risk event. A key distinction between a risk response and a contingency plan is that a response is part of the actual implementation plan and action is taken before the risk can materialize, while a contingency plan is not part of the initial implementation plan and only goes into effect after the risk is recognized.

Like all plans, the contingency plan answers the questions of what, where, when, and how much action will take place. The absence of a contingency plan, when a risk event occurs, can cause a manager to delay or postpone the decision to implement a remedy. This postponement can lead to panic, and acceptance of the first remedy suggested. Such after-the-event decision making under pressure can be potentially dangerous and costly. Contingency planning evaluates alternative remedies for possible foreseen events before the risk event occurs and selects the best plan among alternatives. This early contingency planning facilitates a smooth transition to the remedy or work-around plan. The availability of a contingency plan can significantly increase the chances for project success.

Conditions for activating the implementation of the contingency plan should be decided and clearly documented. The plan should include a cost estimate and identify the source of funding. All parties affected should agree to the contingency plan and have authority to make commitments. Because implementation of a contingency plan embodies disruption in the sequence of work, all contingency plans should be communicated to team members so that surprise and resistance are minimized.

Here is an example: A high-tech niche computer company intends to introduce a new "platform" product at a very specific target date. The project's 47 teams all agree delays will not be acceptable. Their contingency plans for two large component suppliers demonstrate how seriously risk management is viewed. One supplier's plant sits on the San Andreas Fault, which is prone to earthquakes. The contingency plan has an alternative supplier, who is constantly updated, producing a replica of the component in another plant. Another key supplier in Toronto, Canada, presents a delivery risk on their due date because of potential bad weather. This contingency plan calls for a chartered plane (already contracted to be on standby) if overland transportation presents a delay problem. To outsiders these plans must seem a bit extreme, but in high-tech industries where time to market is king, risks of identified events are taken seriously.

Risk response matrices such as the one shown in Figure 7.8 are useful for summarizing how the project team plans to manage risks that have been identified.

FIGURE 7.8 Risk Response Matrix

Risk Event	Response	Contingency Plan	Trigger	Who Is Responsible
Interface problems	Mitigate: Test prototype	Work around until help comes	Not solved within 24 hours	Nils
System freezing	Mitigate: Test prototype	Reinstall OS	Still frozen after one hour	Emmylou
User backlash	Mitigate: Prototype demonstration	Increase staff support	Call from top management	Eddie
Equipment malfunctions	Mitigate: Select reliable vendor Transfer: Warranty	Order replacement	Equipment fails	Jim

SNAPSHOT FROM PRACTICE Playing Soccer in the Desert

The average soccer ("football") fan was probably stunned in 2010 when it was announced that the 2022 World Cup would be hosted by the tiny Emirate state of Qatar.* This was a real coup for Qatar, a constitutional monarchy with a population of only 1.7 million people. It is estimated Qatar's successful bid will require spending over $100 billion on World Cup–related infrastructure projects. Those projects include nine new eco-friendly stadiums, roads, bridges, ports, railways, as well as service facilities for the fans and players.

The biggest question on people's minds is how can you play soccer in the desert where typical summer temperatures in Qatar hover around 122 degrees (50° C)! Qatar promised FIFA (Federation Internationale de Football Association) that their World Cup stadiums could be regulated at below 80 degrees (27° C), comfortably below the 86 degrees (30° C) in which FIFA's medical committee says players become fatigued after 51 minutes of play. The simplest answer would be to construct only indoor stadiums. However, FIFA rules mandate that World Cup matches be played under an open roof. In fact, this risk was the largest concern FIFA had in awarding Qatar the 2022 FIFA World Cup. For this reason Qatar plans to build nine fully air-conditioned open-air stadiums.

To persuade the selection committee that it was possible to keep fans and players comfortable despite the heat, Qatar arranged a demonstration of the cooling technology they planned to use. Engineers built a prototype for a small test stadium. The test occurred on a day when the outside temperature was 114 degrees (46° C); the inside temperature was a comfortable 73 degrees (23° C)! The test was successful. Power would come from a nearby solar farm. While there will be risks associated with scaling the technology to larger stadiums, the selection committee was confident that it can work.

Qatar is considering other strategies to beat the heat. For example, Saud Abdul Ghani, head of the Mechanical Engineering department at the University of Qatar, proposes using remote-control artificial clouds over the stadiums to cool things down.** He will use a solar-powered engine to suspend a man-made, ultra-light, carbon fiber cloud over the stadium in an attempt to drop the temperature and to reduce the risk of overloading internal air conditioning. Success of such a cloud would be a significant innovation and major cost saving.

The eyes of the world are on Qatar as it moves toward the 2022 Soccer Cup event.

* http://www.reuters.com/article/2012/02/09/us-contract-qatar-idUSTRE8180GJ20120209, retrieved September 12, 2012.
** Peter Alegi, http://www.footballiscominghome.info/the-hosts/artificial-clouds-2022/, retrieved September 12, 2012.

To read how this approach was critical to securing the 2022 World Cup bid, see the Snapshot from Practice: Playing Soccer in the Desert.

Schedule Risks

Often organizations will defer the threat of a project coming in late until it surfaces. Here contingency funds are set aside to expedite or "crash" the project to get it back on track. Crashing, or reducing project duration, is accomplished by shortening (compressing) one or more activities on the critical path. This comes with additional costs and risk. Techniques for managing this situation are discussed in Chapter 9. Some contingency plans can avoid costly procedures. For example, schedules can be altered by working activities in parallel or using start-to-start lag relationships. Also, using the best people for high-risk tasks can relieve or lessen the chance of some risk events occurring.

Cost Risks

Projects of long duration need some contingency for price changes—which are usually upward. The important point to remember when reviewing price is to avoid the trap of using one lump sum to cover price risks. For example, if inflation has been running about 3 percent, some managers add 3 percent for all resources used in the project. This lump-sum approach does not address exactly where price protection is needed and fails to provide for tracking and control. On cost sensitive projects, price risks should be evaluated item by item. Some purchases and contracts will not change over the life of the project. Those that may change should be identified and estimates made of the magnitude of change. This approach ensures control of the contingency funds as the project is implemented.

Funding Risks

What if the funding for the project is cut by 25 percent or completion projections indicate that costs will greatly exceed available funds? What are the chances of the project being canceled before completion? Seasoned project managers recognize that a complete risk assessment must include an evaluation of funding supply. This is especially true for publicly funded projects. Case in point was the ill-fated ARH-70 Arapaho helicopter which was being developed for the U.S. Army by BellAircraft. Over 300 million dollars had been invested to develop a new age combat and reconnaissance helicopter, when in October 2008, the Defense Department recommended that the project be canceled. The cancellation reflected a need to cut costs and a switch toward using unmanned aircraft for surveillance as well as attack missions.

Just as government projects are subject to changes in strategy and political agenda, business firms frequently undergo changes in priorities and top management. The pet projects of the new CEO replace the pet projects of the former CEO. Resources become tight and one way to fund new projects is to cancel other projects.

Severe budget cuts or lack of adequate funding can have a devastating effect on a project. Typically, when such a fate occurs, there is a need to scale back the scope of the project to what is possible. "All-or-nothing projects" are ripe targets to budget cutters. This was the case of the Arapaho helicopter once the decision was made to move away from manned reconnaissance aircraft. Here the "chunkability" of the project can be an advantage. For example, freeway projects can fall short of the original intentions but still add value for each mile completed.

On a much smaller scale, similar funding risks may exist for more mundane projects. For example, a building contractor may find that due to a sudden downturn in the stock market the owners can no longer afford to build their dream house. Or an IS consulting firm may be left empty handed when a client files for bankruptcy. In the former case the contractor may have as a contingency selling the house on the open market, while unfortunately the consulting firm will have to join the long line of creditors.

Opportunity Management

For the sake of brevity, this chapter has focused on negative risks—what can go wrong on a project. There is a flip side—what could go right on a project? This is commonly referred to as a positive risk or opportunity. An **opportunity** is an event that can have a positive impact on project objectives. For example, unusually favorable weather can accelerate construction work, or a drop in fuel prices may create savings that could be used to add value to a project. Essentially the same process that is used to manage negative risks is applied to positive risks. Opportunities are identified, assessed in terms of likelihood and impact, responses are determined, and even contingency plans and funds can be established to take advantage of the opportunity if it occurs. The major exception between managing negative risks and opportunity is in the responses. The project management profession has identified four different types of response to an opportunity:[4]

Exploit. This tactic seeks to eliminate the uncertainty associated with an opportunity to ensure that it definitely happens. Examples include assigning your best personnel to a critical burst activity to reduce the time to completion or revising a design to enable a component to be purchased rather than developed internally.

Share. This strategy involves allocating some or all of the ownership of an opportunity to another party who is best able to capture the opportunity for the benefit of the project. Examples include establishing continuous improvement incentives for external contractors or joint ventures.

Enhance. Enhance is the opposite of mitigation in that action is taken to increase the probability and/or the positive impact of an opportunity. Examples include choosing site location based on favorable weather patterns or choosing raw materials that are likely to decline in price.

Accept. Accepting an opportunity is being willing to take advantage of it if it occurs, but not taking action to pursue it.

While it is only natural to focus on negative risks, it is sound practice to engage in active opportunity management as well.

Contingency Funding and Time Buffers

Contingency funds are established to cover project risks—identified and unknown. When, where, and how much money will be spent is not known until the risk event occurs. Project "owners" are often reluctant to set up project contingency funds that seem to imply the project plan might be a poor one. Some perceive the contingency fund as an add-on slush fund. Others say they will face the risk when it materializes. Usually such reluctance to establish contingency reserves can be overcome with documented risk identification, assessment, contingency plans, and plans for when and how funds will be disbursed.

The size and amount of contingency reserves depend on uncertainty inherent in the project. Uncertainty is reflected in the "newness" of the project, inaccurate time and cost estimates, technical unknowns, unstable scope, and problems not anticipated. In practice, contingencies run from 1 to 10 percent in projects similar to past projects. However, in unique and high-technology projects it is not uncommon to find contingencies running in the 20 to 60 percent range. Use and rate of consumption of reserves must be closely monitored and controlled. Simply picking a percentage of the baseline, say, 5 percent, and calling it the contingency reserve is not a sound approach. Also, adding up all the identified contingency allotments and throwing them into one pot is not conducive to sound control of the reserve fund.

[4] PMBOK, 5th ed. (Newton Square, PA: PMI, 2013), pp. 345–6.

In practice, the contingency reserve fund is typically divided into budget and management reserve funds for control purposes. Budget reserves are set up to cover identified risks; these reserves are those allocated to specific segments or deliverables of the project. Management reserves are set up to cover unidentified risks and are allocated to risks associated with the total project. The risks are separated because their use requires approval from different levels of project authority. Because all risks are probabilistic, the reserves are not included in the baseline for each work package or activity; they are only activated when a risk occurs. If an identified risk does not occur and its chance of occurring is past, the fund allocated to the risk should be deducted from the budget reserve. (This removes the temptation to use budget reserves for other issues or problems.) Of course if the risk does occur, funds are removed from the reserve and added to the cost baseline.

It is important that contingency allowances be independent of the original time and cost estimates. These allowances need to be clearly distinguished to avoid time and budget game playing.

Budget Reserves

These reserves are identified for specific work packages or segments of a project found in the baseline budget or work breakdown structure. For example, a reserve amount might be added to "computer coding" to cover the risk of "testing" showing a coding problem. The reserve amount is determined by costing out the accepted contingency or recovery plan. The budget reserve should be communicated to the project team. This openness suggests trust and encourages good cost performance. However, distributing budget reserves should be the responsibility of both the project manager and the team members responsible for implementing the specific segment of the project. If the risk does not materialize, the funds are removed from the budget reserve. Thus, budget reserves decrease as the project progresses.

Management Reserves

These reserve funds are needed to cover major unforeseen risks and, hence, are applied to the total project. For example, a major scope change may appear necessary midway in the project. Because this change was not anticipated or identified, it is covered from the management reserve. Management reserves are established *after* budget reserves are identified and funds established. These reserves are independent of budget reserves and are controlled by the project manager and the "owner" of the project. The "owner" can be internal (top management) or external to the project organization. Most management reserves are set using historical data and judgments concerning the uniqueness and complexity of the project.

Placing technical contingencies in the management reserve is a special case. Identifying possible technical (functional) risks is often associated with a new, untried, innovative process or product. Because there is a chance the innovation may not work out, a fallback plan is necessary. This type of risk is beyond the control of the project manager. Hence, technical reserves are held in the management reserve and controlled by the owner or top management. The owner and project manager decide when the contingency plan will be implemented and the reserve funds used. It is assumed there is a high probability these funds will never be used.

TABLE 7.1
Contingency Fund Estimate (Thousands of Dollars)

Activity	Budget Baseline	Budget Reserve	Project Budget
Design	$500	$15	$515
Code	900	80	980
Test	20	2	22
Subtotal	$1,420	$97	$1,517
Management reserve	—	—	50
Total	$1,420	$97	$1,567

Table 7.1 shows the development of a contingency fund estimate for a hypothetical project. Note how budget and management reserves are kept separate; control is easily tracked using this format.

Time Buffers

Just as contingency funds are established to absorb unplanned costs, managers use time buffers to cushion against potential delays in the project. And like contingency funds, the amount of time is dependent upon the inherent uncertainty of the project. The more uncertain the project the more time should be reserved for the schedule. The strategy is to assign extra time at critical moments in the project. For example, buffers are added to

A. activities with severe risks.
B. merge activities that are prone to delays due to one or more preceding activities being late.
C. noncritical activities to reduce the likelihood that they will create another critical path.
D. activities that require scarce resources to ensure that the resources are available when needed.

In the face of overall schedule uncertainty, buffers are sometimes added to the end of the project. For example, a 300-working-day project may have a 30-day project buffer. While the extra 30 days would not appear on the schedule, it is available if needed. Like management reserves, this buffer typically requires the authorization of top management. A more systematic approach to buffer management is discussed in the Chapter 8 Appendix on critical chain project management.

Step 4: Risk Response Control

Typically the results of the first three steps of the risk management process are summarized in a formal document often called the risk register. A **risk register** details all identified risks, including descriptions, category, and probability of occurring, impact, responses, contingency plans, owners, and current status. The register is the backbone for the last step in the risk management process: risk control. Risk control involves executing the risk response strategy, monitoring triggering events, initiating contingency plans, and watching for new risks. Establishing a change management system to deal with events that require formal changes in the scope, budget, and/or schedule of the project is an essential element of risk control.

Project managers need to monitor risks just like they track project progress. Risk assessment and updating needs to be part of every status meeting and progress report system. The project team needs to be on constant alert for new, unforeseen risks. Management needs to be sensitive that others may not be forthright in acknowledging new risks and problems. Admitting that there might be a bug in the design code or that different components are not compatible reflects poorly on individual performance. If the prevailing organizational culture is one where mistakes are punished severely, then it is only human nature to protect oneself. Similarly, if bad news is greeted harshly and there is a propensity to "kill the messenger," then participants will be reluctant to speak freely. The tendency to suppress bad news is compounded when individual responsibility is vague and the project team is under extreme pressure from top management to get the project done quickly.

Project managers need to establish an environment in which participants feel comfortable raising concerns and admitting mistakes. The norm should be that mistakes are acceptable, hiding mistakes is intolerable. Problems should be embraced not denied. Participants should be encouraged to identify problems and new risks. Here a positive attitude by the project manager toward risks is a key.

On large, complex projects it may be prudent to repeat the risk identification/assessment exercise with fresh information. Risk profiles should be reviewed to test to see if the original responses held true. Relevant stakeholders should be brought into the discussion and the risk register needs to be updated. While this may not be practical on an ongoing basis, project managers should touch base with them on a regular basis or hold special stakeholder meetings to review the status of risks on the project.

A second key for controlling the cost of risks is documenting responsibility. This can be problematic in projects involving multiple organizations and contractors. Responsibility for risk is frequently passed on to others with the statement, "That is not my worry." This mentality is dangerous. Each identified risk should be assigned (or shared) by mutual agreement of the owner, project manager, and the contractor or person having line responsibility for the work package or segment of the project. It is best to have the line person responsible approve the use of budget reserve funds and monitor their rate of usage. If management reserve funds are required, the line person should play an active role in estimating additional costs and funds needed to complete the project. Having line personnel participate in the process focuses attention on the management reserve, control of its rate of usage, and early warning of potential risk events. If risk management is not formalized, responsibility and responses to risk will be ignored—*it is not my area.*

The bottom line is that project managers and team members need to be vigilant in monitoring potential risks and identify new land mines that could derail a project. Risk assessment has to be part of the working agenda of status meetings and when new risks emerge they need to be analyzed and incorporated into the risk management process.

Change Control Management

A major element of the risk control process is change management. Every detail of a project plan will not materialize as expected. Coping with and controlling project changes present a formidable challenge for most project managers. Changes come from many sources such as the project customer, owner, project

FIGURE 7.9
Change Control Process

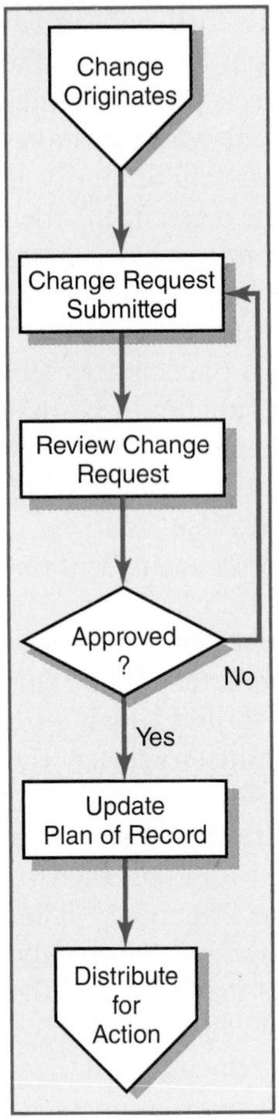

manager, team members, and occurrence of risk events. Most changes easily fall into three categories:

1. Scope changes in the form of design or additions represent big changes; for example, customer requests for a new feature or a redesign that will improve the product.
2. Implementation of contingency plans, when risk events occur, represent changes in baseline costs and schedules.
3. Improvement changes suggested by project team members represent another category.

Because change is inevitable, a well-defined change review and control process should be set up early in the project planning cycle.

Change management systems involve reporting, controlling, and recording changes to the project baseline. (Note: Some organizations consider change control systems part of configuration management.) In practice most change management systems are designed to accomplish the following:

1. Identify proposed changes.
2. List expected effects of proposed change(s) on schedule and budget.
3. Review, evaluate, and approve or disapprove changes formally.
4. Negotiate and resolve conflicts of change, conditions, and cost.
5. Communicate changes to parties affected.
6. Assign responsibility for implementing change.
7. Adjust master schedule and budget.
8. Track all changes that are to be implemented.

As part of the project communication plan, stakeholders define up front the communication and decision-making process that will be used to evaluate and accept changes. The process can be captured in a flow diagram like the one presented in Figure 7.9. On small projects this process may simply entail approval of a small group of stakeholders. On larger projects more elaborate decision-making processes are established, with different processes being used for different kinds of change. For example, changes in performance requirements may require multiple sign-offs, including the project sponsor and client, while switching suppliers may be authorized by the project manager. Regardless of the nature of the project, the goal is to establish the process for introducing necessary changes in the project in a timely and effective manner.

Of particular importance is assessing the impact of the change on the project. Often solutions to immediate problems have adverse consequences on other aspects of a project. For example, in overcoming a problem with the exhaust system for a hybrid automobile, the design engineers contributed to the prototype exceeding weight parameters. It is important that the implications of changes are assessed by people with appropriate expertise and perspective. On construction projects this is often the responsibility of the architecture firm, while "software architects" perform a similar function on software development efforts.

Organizations use change request forms and logs to track proposed changes. An example of a simplified change request form is depicted in Figure 7.10. Typically change request forms include a description of the change, the impact of not approving the change, the impact of the change on project scope/schedule/cost, and defined signature paths for review as well as a tracking log number.

FIGURE 7.10
Sample Change Request

Project name *Irish/Chinese culture exchange* Project sponsor *Irish embassy*
Request number *12* Date *June 6, 2xxx*
Originator *Jennifer McDonald* Change requested by *Chinese culture office*

Description of requested change

1. *Request river dancers to replace small Irish dance group.*
2. *Request one combination dance with river dancers and China ballet group.*

Reason for change

River dancers will enhance stature of event. The group is well known and loved by Chinese people.

Areas of impact of proposed change–describe each on separate sheet

- [X] Scope
- [ ] Schedule
- [X] Cost
- [ ] Risk
- [ ] Other ________

Disposition	Priority	Funding Source
[ ] Approve	[ ] Emergency	[ ] Mgmt. reserve
[X] Approve as amended	[X] Urgent	[ ] Budget reserve
[ ] Disapprove	[ ] Low	[X] Customer
[ ] Deferred		[ ] Other

Sign-off Approvals

Project manager	*William O'Mally*	Date	*June 12, 2xxx*
Project sponsor	*Kenneth Thompson*	Date	*June 13, 2xxx*
Project customer	*Hong Lee*	Date	*June 18, 2xxx*
Other		Date	

An abridged version of a change request log for a construction project is presented in Figure 7.11. These logs are used to monitor change requests. They typically summarize the status of all outstanding change requests and include such useful information as source and date of the change, document codes for related information, cost estimates, and the current status of the request.

Every approved change must be identified and integrated into the plan of record through changes in the project WBS and baseline schedule. The plan of record is the current official plan for the project in terms of scope, budget, and schedule. The plan of record serves as a change management benchmark for future change requests as well as the baseline for evaluating project progress.

If the change control system is not integrated with the WBS and baseline, project plans and control will soon self-destruct. Thus, one of the keys to a successful

FIGURE 7.11 Change Request Log

Owner Requested Change Status Report—Open Items							OSU—Weatherford
			Dates				
Rc#	Description	Reference Document	Date Rec'd	Date Submit	Amount	Status	Comments
51	Sewer work offset				−188,129	OPEN	FUNDING FROM OTHER SOURCE
52	Stainless Plates at restroom Shower Valves	ASI 56	1/5/2013	3/30/2013	9,308	APPROVED	
53	Waterproofing Options	ASI 77	1/13/2013		169,386	OPEN	
54	Change Electrical floor box spec change	RFI 113	12/5/2013	3/29/2013	2,544	SUBMIT	
55	VE Option for Style and rail doors	Door samples	1/14/2013		−20,000	ROM	
56	Pressure Wash C tower	Owner request	3/15/2013	3/30/2013	14,861	SUBMIT	
57	Fire Lite glass in stairs	Owner request			8,000	QUOTE	ROM BASED ON FIRELITE NT
58	Cyber Café added tele/OFOI equipment	ASI 65	1/30/2013	3/29/2013	4,628	APPROVED	
59	Additional Dampers in C wing	ASI 68	2/4/2013	3/29/2013	1,085	SUBMIT	
60	Revise Corridor ceilings	ASI 72	2/13/2013	3/31/2013	−3,755	SUBMIT	

OPEN—Requires estimate
ROM—Rough order magnitude
QUOTE—Subcontractor quotes
SUBMIT—RC letter submitted
APPROVED—RC letter approved
REVISE—RC letter to be reviewed
ASI—Architect's supplemental instructions
RFI—Request for information

change control process is document, document, document! The benefits derived from change control systems are the following:

1. Inconsequential changes are discouraged by the formal process.
2. Costs of changes are maintained in a log.
3. Integrity of the WBS and performance measures is maintained.
4. Allocation and use of budget and management reserve funds are tracked.
5. Responsibility for implementation is clarified.
6. Effect of changes is visible to all parties involved.
7. Implementation of change is monitored.
8. Scope changes will be quickly reflected in baseline and performance measures.

Clearly, change control is important and requires that someone or some group be responsible for approving changes, keeping the process updated, and communicating changes to the project team and relevant stakeholders. Project control depends heavily on keeping the change control process current. This historical record can be used for satisfying customer inquiries, identifying problems in post-project audits, and estimating future project costs.

Summary

To put the processes discussed in this chapter in proper perspective one should recognize that the essence of project management is risk management. Every technique in this book is really a risk management technique. Each in its own way tries to prevent something bad from happening. Project selection systems try to reduce the likelihood that projects will not contribute to the mission of the firm. Project scope statements, among other things, are designed to avoid costly misunderstandings and reduce scope creep. Work breakdown structures reduce the likelihood that some vital part of the project will be omitted or that the budget estimates are unrealistic. Teambuilding reduces the likelihood of dysfunctional conflict and breakdowns in coordination. All of the techniques try to increase stakeholder satisfaction and increase the chances of project success.

From this perspective managers engage in risk management activities to compensate for the uncertainty inherent in project management and that things never go according to plan. Risk management is proactive not reactive. It reduces the number of surprises and leads to a better understanding of the most likely outcomes of negative events.

Although many managers believe that in the final analysis, risk assessment and contingency depend on subjective judgment, some standard method for identifying, assessing, and responding to risks should be included in all projects. The very process of identifying project risks forces some discipline at all levels of project management and improves project performance.

Contingency plans increase the chance that the project can be completed on time and within budget. Contingency plans can be simple "work-arounds" or elaborate detailed plans. Responsibility for risks should be clearly identified and documented. It is desirable and prudent to keep a reserve as a hedge against project risks. Budget reserves are linked to the WBS and should be communicated to the project team. Control of management reserves should remain with the owner, project manager, and line person responsible. Use of contingency reserves should be closely monitored, controlled, and reviewed throughout the project life cycle.

Experience clearly indicates that using a formal, structured process to handle possible foreseen and unforeseen project risk events minimizes surprises, costs, delays, stress, and misunderstandings. Risk management is an iterative process that occurs throughout the lifespan of the project. When risk events occur or changes are necessary, using an effective change control process to quickly approve and record changes will facilitate measuring performance against schedule and cost. Ultimately successful risk management requires a culture in which threats are embraced not denied and problems are identified not hidden.

Key Terms

Avoiding risk, *215*
Budget reserve, *223*
Change management system, *226*
Contingency plan, *216*
Management reserve, *223*
Mitigating risk, *214*
Opportunity, *221*
Retaining risk, *216*
Risk, *205*
Risk breakdown structure (RBS), *208*
Risk profile, *209*
Risk register, *224*
Risk severity matrix, *213*
Scenario analysis, *210*
Time buffer, *224*
Transferring risk, *216*

Review Questions

1. Project risks can/cannot be eliminated if the project is carefully planned. Explain.
2. The chances of risk events occurring and their respective costs increasing change over the project life cycle. What is the significance of this phenomenon to a project manager?
3. What is the difference between avoiding a risk and accepting a risk?
4. What is the difference between mitigating a risk and contingency planning?
5. Explain the difference between budget reserves and management reserves.
6. How are the work breakdown structure and change control connected?
7. What are the likely outcomes if a change control process is not used? Why?
8. What are the major differences between managing negative risks versus positive risks (opportunities)?

Exercises

1. Gather a small team of students. Think of a project most students would understand; the kinds of tasks involved should also be familiar. Identify and assess major and minor risks inherent to the project. Decide on a response type. Develop a contingency plan for two to four identified risks. Estimate costs. Assign contingency reserves. How much reserve would your team estimate for the whole project? Justify your choices and estimates.
2. You have been assigned to a project risk team of five members. Because this is the first time your organization has formally set up a risk team for a project, it is hoped that your team will develop a process that can be used on all future projects. Your first team meeting is next Monday morning. Each team member has been asked to prepare for the meeting by developing, in as much detail as possible, an outline that describes how you believe the team should proceed in handling project risks. Each team member will hand out their proposed outline at the beginning of the meeting. Your outline should include but not be limited to the following information:
   a. Team objectives.
   b. Process for handling risk events.
   c. Team activities.
   d. Team outputs.
3. The Manchester United Soccer Tournament project team (review the Manchester United case at the end of Chapter 4) has identified the following potential risks to their project:
   a. Referees failing to show up at designated games.
   b. Fighting between teams.
   c. Pivotal error committed by a referee that determines the outcome of a game.
   d. Abusive behavior along the sidelines by parents.
   e. Inadequate parking.
   f. Not enough teams sign up for different age brackets.
   g. Serious injury.

   How would you recommend that they respond (i.e., avoid, accept, . . .) to these risks and why?
4. Search the World Wide Web (WWW) using the key words: "best practices, project management." What did you find? How might this information be useful to a project manager?

References

Atkinson, W., "Beyond the Basics," *PM Network,* May 2003, pp. 38–43.

Baker, B., and R. Menon, "Politics and Project Performance: The Fourth Dimension of Project Management," *PM Network,* 9 (11) November 1995, pp. 16–21.

Carr, M. J., S. L. Konda, I. Monarch, F. C. Ulrich, and C. F. Walker, "Taxonomy-Based Risk Identification," *Technical Report CMU/SEI-93-TR 6, Software Engineering Institute,* Carnegie Mellon University, Pittsburgh, 1993.

Ford, E. C., J. Duncan, A. G. Bedeian, P. M. Ginter, M. D. Rousculp, and A. M. Adams, "Mitigating Risks, Visible Hands, Inevitable Disasters, and Soft Variables: Management Research that Matters to Managers," *Academy of Management Executive,* 19 (4) November 2005, pp. 24–38.

Gray, C. F., and R. Reinman, "PERT Simulation: A Dynamic Approach to the PERT Technique," *Journal of Systems Management,* March 1969, pp. 18–23.

Hamburger, D. H., "The Project Manager: Risk Taker and Contingency Planner," *Project Management Journal,* 21 (4) 1990, pp. 11–16.

Hulett, D. T., "Project Schedule Risk Assessment," *Project Management Journal,* 26 (1) 1995, pp. 21–31.

Ingebretson, M., "In No Uncertain Terms," *PM Network,* 2002, pp. 28–32.

"Math Mistake Proved Fatal to Mars Orbiter," *The Orlando Sentinel,* November 23, 1999.

Meyer, A. D., C. H. Loch, and M. T. Pich, "Managing Project Uncertainty: From Variation to Chaos," *MIT Sloan Management Review,* Winter 2002, pp. 60–67.

Pavlik, A., "Project Troubleshooting: Tiger Teams for Reactive Risk Management," *Project Management Journal,* 35 (4) December 2004, pp. 5–14.

Pinto, J. K., *Project Management: Achieving Competitive Advantage* (Upper Saddle River, NJ: Pearson, 2007).

Project Management Body of Knowledge (Newton Square, PA: Project Management Institute, 2013).

Schuler, J. R., "Decision Analysis in Projects: Monte Carlo Simulation," *PM Network,* 7 (1) January 1994, pp. 30–36.

Smith, P. G., and G. M. Merritt, *Proactive Risk Management: Controlling Uncertainty in Product Development* (New York: Productivity Press, 2002).

Smith, P. G., and D. G. Reinertsen, *Developing Products in Half the Time* (New York: Van Nostrand Reinhold, 1995).

Snizek, J. A., and R. A. Henry, "Accuracy and Confidence in Group Judgment," *Organizational Behavior and Human Decision Processes,* 4 (3) 1989, pp. 1–28.

Case

Alaska Fly-Fishing Expedition*

You are sitting around the fire at a lodge in Dillingham, Alaska, discussing a fishing expedition you are planning with your colleagues at Great Alaska Adventures (GAA). Earlier in the day you received a fax from the president of BlueNote, Inc. The president wants to reward her top management team by taking them on an all-expense-paid fly-fishing adventure in Alaska. She would like GAA to organize and lead the expedition.

* This case was prepared with the assistance of Stuart Morigeau.

6. Garage will accommodate two cars and one 28-foot-long Winnebago.
7. Structure must pass seismic stability codes.

LIMITS AND EXCLUSIONS

1. The home will be built to the specifications and design of the original blueprints provided by the customer.
2. Owner is responsible for landscaping.
3. Refrigerator is not included among kitchen appliances.
4. Air conditioning is not included, but house is prewired for it.
5. SFC reserves the right to contract out services.

CUSTOMER REVIEW

"Bolo" and Izabella Czopek.

Case

Trans LAN Project

Trans Systems is a small, information systems consulting firm located in Meridian, Louisiana. Trans has just been hired to design and install a local area network (LAN) for the city of Meridian's social welfare agency. You are the manager for the project, which includes one Trans professional and two interns from a local university. You have just finished a preliminary scope statement for the project (see below). You are now brainstorming potential risks associated with the project.

1. Identify potential risks associated with this project. Try to come up with at least five different risks.
2. Use a risk assessment form similar to Figure 7.6 to analyze identified risks.
3. Develop a risk response matrix similar to Figure 7.8 to outline how you would deal with each of the risks.

PROJECT SCOPE STATEMENT

PROJECT OBJECTIVE

To design and install a new local area network (LAN) within one month with a budget not to exceed $90,000 for the Meridian Social Service Agency with minimum disruption to ongoing operations.

DELIVERABLES

- Twenty workstations and twenty laptop computers.
- Server with dual-core processors.
- Two color laser printers.
- Windows R2 server and workstation operating system (Windows 7).
- Migration of existing databases and programs to new system.
- Four hours of introduction training for client's personnel.

- Sixteen hours of training for client network administrator.
- Fully operational LAN system.

MILESTONES

1. Hardware January 22.
2. Setting users' priority and authorization January 26.
3. In-house whole network test completed February 1.
4. Client site test completed February 2.
5. Training completed February 16.

TECHNICAL REQUIREMENTS

1. Workstations with 17-inch flat panel monitors, dual-core processors, 4 GB RAM, 8X DVD+RW, wireless card, Ethernet card, 500 GB hard drive.
2. Laptops with 12-inch display monitor, dual-core processors, 2GB RAM, 8X DVD+RW, wireless card, Ethernet card, 500 GB hard drive and weigh less than 4½ lbs.
3. Wireless network interface cards and Ethernet connections.
4. System must support Windows Vista/Windows 7 platforms.
5. System must provide secure external access for field workers.

LIMITS AND EXCLUSIONS

1. On-site work to be done after 8:00 P.M. and before 7:00 A.M. Monday through Saturday.
2. System maintenance and repair only up to one month after final inspection.
3. Warranties transferred to client.
4. Only responsible for installing software designated by the client two weeks before the start of the project.
5. Client will be billed for additional training beyond that prescribed in the contract.

CUSTOMER REVIEW

Director of the city of Meridian's Social Service Agency.

Case

XSU Spring Concert

You are a member of the X State University (XSU) student body entertainment committee. Your committee has agreed to sponsor a spring concert. The motive behind this concert is to offer a safe alternative to Hasta Weekend. Hasta Weekend is a spring event in which students from XSU rent houseboats and engage in heavy partying. Traditionally this occurs during the last weekend in May. Unfortunately, the partying has a long history of getting out of hand, sometimes leading to fatal accidents. After one such tragedy last spring, your committee wants to offer an alternative experience for those who are eager to celebrate the change in weather and the pending end of the school year.

You have just finished a preliminary scope statement for the project (see below). You are now brainstorming potential risks associated with the project.

1. Identify potential risks associated with this project. Try to come up with at least five different risks.
2. Use a risk assessment form similar to Figure 7.6 to analyze identified risks.
3. Develop a risk response matrix similar to Figure 7.8 to outline how you would deal with each of the risks.

PROJECT SCOPE STATEMENT

PROJECT OBJECTIVE

To organize and deliver an eight-hour concert at Wahoo Stadium at a cost not to exceed $50,000 on the last Saturday in May.

DELIVERABLES

- Local advertising.
- Concert security.
- Separate Beer Garden.
- Eight hours of music and entertainment.
- Food venues.
- Souvenir concert t-shirts.
- Secure all licenses and approvals.
- Secure sponsors.

MILESTONES

1. Secure all permissions and approvals by January 15.
2. Sign big-name artist by February 15.
3. Complete artist roster by April 1.
4. Secure vendor contracts by April 15.
5. Setup completed on May 27.
6. Concert on May 28.
7. Cleanup completed by May 31.

TECHNICAL REQUIREMENTS

1. Professional sound stage and system.
2. At least one big-name artist.
3. At least seven performing acts.
4. Restroom facilities for 10,000 people.
5. Parking available for 1,000 cars.
6. Compliance with XSU and city requirements/ordinances.

LIMITS AND EXCLUSIONS

1. Performers responsible for travel arrangements to and from XSU.
2. Vendors contribute a set percentage of sales.
3. Concert must be over by 11:30 P.M.

CUSTOMER REVIEW

The president of XSU student body.

Case

Sustaining Project Risk Management during Implementation

BACKGROUND

Bill (Senior VP of product development): Carlos [project manager], we have to talk. I am concerned about the way we manage project risk here at Futuronics. I just came from an international "Future Mote Devices" meeting at UC Berkeley. [Note: A *mote* is a very small [e.g., 2–3mm square], wireless sensing pod that may be placed on land or in water to measure and communicate data.] The project management sessions receiving most attention addressed risk in product development projects. They described our management of project risk to the letter—failure to sustain risk management *after the project gets rolling*. It seems someone has to get burned before risk management is taken seriously.

Much to my surprise, almost every project manager there admitted their firms have a problem sustaining team members' interest in managing risk after the project is on its way. The old saying, "If you don't manage risk, you pay the price later," generated horror stories from a few who paid the price. We spent some time brainstorming ways to handle the problem at the project level, but there were very few concrete suggestions. The meeting gave me a wakeup call. Carlos, we need to tackle this problem or some new or known risk event could put us both out of a job. The similarities between their horror stories and some of our past mistakes are scary.

Since here at Futuronics we only develop new products that are at least seven years beyond anything on the market, the level of both "known risk events and unknown risk" is far higher than in most other organizations. Managing project risk is important to every project, but here at Futuronics every new product project is loaded with risks. Carlos, I'm willing to work with you to improve our management of project risk at Futuronics.

Carlos: Bill, I am aware of the problem. The PMI Roundtables I attend also talk to the difficulty of keeping teams and other stakeholders willing to revisit risk once the project is on its way. [PMI Roundtables are monthly meetings of practicing PMs across industries designed to address project management problems.] I also heard war stories at a recent project management roundtable meeting. I have some notes from the meeting right here.

It all started with the leader's question: "How many project managers actually manage risk over the complete project life cycle?"

PM 1: We all work through the risk management process well before the project begins. We have the process template of risk identification, assessment, response, control, risk register, and contingency down pat. We just don't follow through after the project begins. I think interest dies. Have you ever tried to get project stakeholders to come to a risk meeting when the project is moving relatively well?

PM 2: A recent e-mail from one of our stakeholders said, "We'll deal with it [risk] when it happens."

PM 3: I agree. Interest seems to move from future oriented to reactionary. Also, risk management seems to degenerate into issue (concerns and problems) management versus real risk management.

PM 4: I ask team members, "What is the risk of not managing risk over the life of the project?" Sometimes this question nudges a few to respond positively, especially if risks have changed or new ones are perceived. I use a failed project where a solid risk management process would have avoided the project failure. I explain all of the risk management processes that would have helped to improve the risk elements—risk identification, triggers, responsibility, transfer, accept, etc.

PM 5: Risk is not a line item in the budget or schedule. Maybe it is in the contingency budget to cover "unknowns of unknowns." I have to watch that management doesn't try to squeeze out the contingency budget for something else.

Carlos continued to share with his boss that there were many more comments, but very few gave much guidance. Carlos then shared his idea:

Carlos: Colette is our best trainer, especially in transition management, and she would be a great choice for following through on this problem. Her training classes on upfront risk management are excellent. Should we ask her to present a session?

Bill: You are right, Carlos, Collette is ideal. She is smart and a great team motivator. Ask her, but give her some kind of direction for focus.

A few days later, Carlos sent out a memo:

Colette, this is to follow up on our lunch conversation yesterday discussing sustaining risk management after the project is on its way. Given the nature of our futuristic company, we should stress the point that our product development projects carry many more inherent risks than do traditional projects. I suggest the training classes should drill down on concrete actions and policies that will encourage interest of team members and other project stakeholders in sustaining risk management practices during project execution.

Colette, we appreciate your taking on this project. When you have developed your training session, please give me a copy so I can schedule and support your efforts.

Regards, Carlos

CHALLENGE

Divide the class into teams of three or more participants.

Colette needs your help to develop her training program. You may wish to consider the questions listed below to initiate ideas.

- Why do project stakeholders lose interest in project risk after the project is underway?
- What are the dangers of not keeping on top of risk management during implementation?
- What kind of business is Futuronics in?

Brainstorm specific actions that will encourage project stakeholders to continue to scan and track the project environment for risk events. Suggest three concrete actions or scenarios that will encourage project stakeholders to change their behavior and truly support risk management while projects are being implemented. The following outline headings may be helpful in developing possible actions that would improve/enhance stakeholder support.

- Improving the risk management process
- Organization actions
- Motivating participation

Appendix 7.1

PERT and PERT Simulation

PERT—PROGRAM EVALUATION AND REVIEW TECHNIQUE

In 1958 the Special Office of the Navy and the Booze, Allen, and Hamilton consulting firm developed PERT (program evaluation and review technique) to schedule the more than 3,300 contractors of the Polaris submarine project and to cover uncertainty of activity time estimates.

PERT is almost identical to the critical path method (CPM) technique except it assumes each activity duration has a range that follows a statistical distribution. PERT uses three time estimates for each activity. Basically, this means each activity duration can range from an optimistic time to a pessimistic time, and a weighted average can be computed for each activity. Because project activities usually represent work, and because work tends to stay behind once it gets behind, the PERT developers chose an approximation of the *beta distribution* to represent activity durations. This distribution is known to be flexible and can accommodate empirical data that do not follow a normal distribution. The activity durations can be skewed more toward the high or low end of the data range. Figure A7.1A depicts a *beta distribution* for activity durations that is skewed toward the right and is representative of work that tends to stay late once it is behind. The distribution for the project duration is represented by a normal (symmetrical) distribution shown in Figure A7.1B. The project distribution represents the sum of the weighted averages of the activities on the critical path(s).

Knowing the weighted average and variances for each activity allows the project planner to compute the probability of meeting different project durations. Follow the steps described in the hypothetical example given next. (The jargon is difficult

FIGURE A7.1 Activity and Project Frequency Distributions

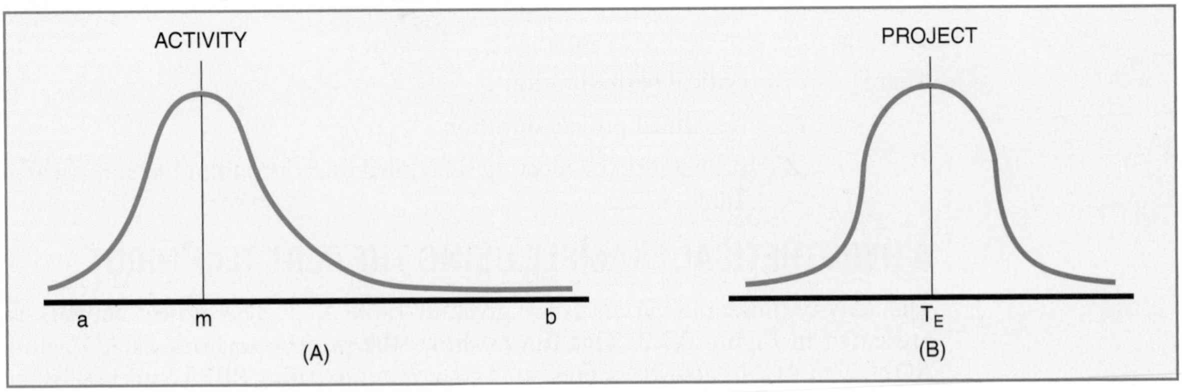

for those not familiar with statistics, but the process is relatively simple after working through a couple of examples.)

The weighted average activity time is computed by the following formula:

$$t_e = \frac{a + 4m + b}{6} \tag{7.1}$$

where t_e = weighted average activity time

a = optimistic activity time (1 chance in 100 of completing the activity earlier under *normal* conditions)

b = pessimistic activity time (1 chance in 100 of completing the activity later under *normal* conditions)

m = most likely activity time

When the three time estimates have been specified, this equation is used to compute the weighted average duration for each activity. The average (deterministic) value is placed on the project network as in the CPM method and the early, late, slack, and project completion times are computed as they are in the CPM method.

The variability in the activity time estimates is approximated by the following equations: Equation 7.2 represents the standard deviation for the *activity.* Equation 7.3 represents the standard deviation for the *project.* Note the standard deviation of the activity is squared in this equation; this is also called variance. This sum includes only activities on the critical path(s) or path being reviewed.

$$\sigma_{t_e} = \left(\frac{b - a}{6}\right) \tag{7.2}$$

$$\sigma_{T_E} = \sqrt{\Sigma\sigma^2_{t_e}} \tag{7.3}$$

Finally, the average project duration (T_E) is the sum of all the average activity times along the critical path (sum of t_e), and it follows a normal distribution.

Knowing the average project duration and the variances of activities allows the probability of completing the project (or segment of the project) by a specific time to be computed using standard statistical tables. The equation below (Equation 7.4) is used to compute the "Z" value found in statistical tables (Z = number of standard deviations from the mean), which, in turn, tells the probability of completing the project in the time specified.

$$Z = \frac{T_S - T_E}{\sqrt{\Sigma\sigma^2_{t_e}}} \tag{7.4}$$

where T_E = critical path duration

T_S = scheduled project duration

Z = probability (of meeting scheduled duration) found in statistical Table A7.2

A HYPOTHETICAL EXAMPLE USING THE PERT TECHNIQUE

The activity times and variances are given in Table A7.1. The project network is presented in Figure A7.2. This figure shows the project network as AOA and AON. The AON network is presented as a reminder that PERT can use AON networks as well as AOA.

TABLE A7.1 Activity Times and Variances

Activity	a	m	b	t_e	$[(b-a)/6]^2$
1–2	17	29	47	30	25
2–3	6	12	24	13	9
2–4	16	19	28	20	4
3–5	13	16	19	16	1
4–5	2	5	14	6	4
5–6	2	5	8	5	1

FIGURE A7.2 Hypothetical Network

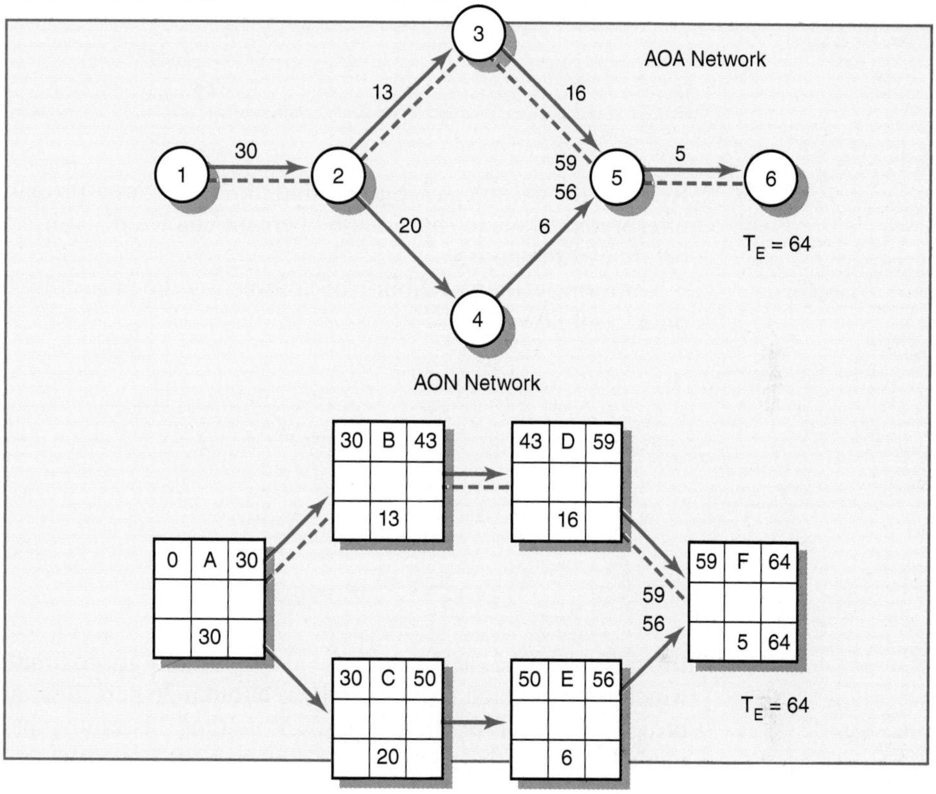

The expected project duration (T_E) is 64 time units; the critical path is 1-2-3-5-6. With this information, the probability of completing the project by a specific date can easily be computed using standard statistical methods. For example, what is the probability the project will be completed before a scheduled time (T_S) of 67? The normal curve for the project would appear as shown in Figure A7.3.

Using the formula for the Z value, the probability can be computed as follows:

$$
\begin{aligned}
Z &= \frac{T_S - T_E}{\sqrt{\Sigma\sigma_{t_e}^2}} \\
&= \frac{67 - 64}{\sqrt{25 + 9 + 1 + 1}} \\
&= \frac{+3}{\sqrt{36}} \\
&= +0.50 \\
P &= 0.69
\end{aligned}
$$

FIGURE A7.3
Possible Project Durations

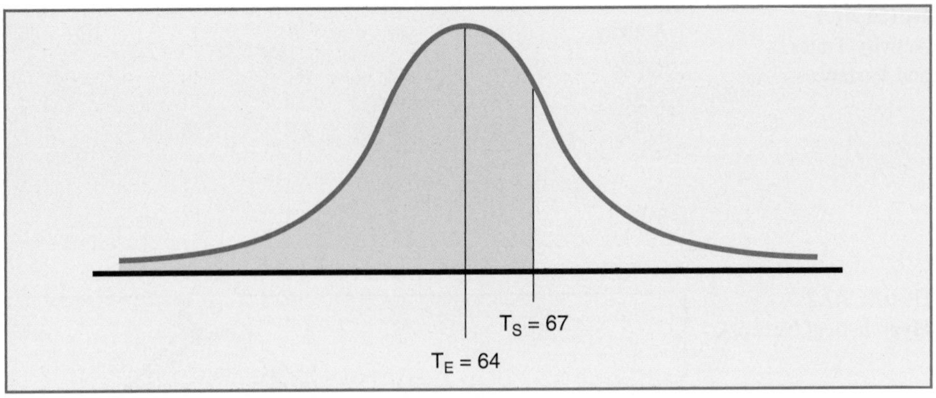

Reading from Table A7.2, a Z value of $+0.5$ gives a probability of 0.69, which is interpreted to mean there is a 69 percent chance of completing the project on or before 67 time units.

Conversely, the probability of completing the project by time period 60 is computed as follows:

$$
\begin{aligned}
Z &= \frac{60 - 64}{\sqrt{25 + 9 + 1 + 1}} \\
&= \frac{-4}{\sqrt{36}} \\
&= -0.67 \\
P &\approx 0.26
\end{aligned}
$$

From Table A7.2, a Z value of -0.67 gives an approximate probability of 0.26, which is interpreted to mean there is about a 26 percent chance of completing the project on or before 60 time units. Note that this same type of calculation can be made for any path or segment of a path in the network.

TABLE A7.2
***Z* Values and Probabilities**

Z Value	Probability	*Z* Value	Probability
−3.0	.001	+0.0	.500
−2.8	.003	+0.2	.579
−2.6	.005	+0.4	.655
−2.4	.008	+0.6	.726
−2.2	.014	+0.8	.788
−2.0	.023	+1.0	.841
−1.8	.036	+1.2	.885
−1.6	.055	+1.4	.919
−1.4	.081	+1.6	.945
−1.2	.115	+1.8	.964
−1.0	.159	+2.0	.977
−0.8	.212	+2.2	.986
−0.6	.274	+2.4	.992
−0.4	.345	+2.6	.995
−0.2	.421	+2.8	.997

When such probabilities are available to management, trade-off decisions can be made to accept or reduce the risk associated with a particular project duration. For example, if the project manager wishes to improve the chances of completing the project by 64 time units, at least two choices are available. First, management can spend money up front to change conditions that will reduce the duration of one or more activities on the critical path. A more prudent, second alternative would be to allocate money to a contingency fund and wait to see how the project is progressing as it is implemented.

EXERCISES

1. Given the project information below, what is the probability of completing the National Holiday Toy project in 93 time units?

Act. ID	Description	Predecessor	Optm. (*a*)	Most likely (*m*)	Pess. (*b*)	Act time t_e	Variance $[(b-a)/6]^2$	Critical
1	Design package	None	6	12	24			
2	Design product	1	16	19	28			
3	Build package	1	4	7	10			
4	Secure patent	2	21	30	39			
5	Build product	2	17	29	47			
6	Paint	3, 4, 5	4	7	10			
7	Test market	6	13	16	19			

2. The Global Tea and Organic Juice companies have merged.

   The following information has been collected for the "Consolidation Project."

Activity	Description	Predecessor	*a* opt	*m* ml	*b* pess
1	Codify accounts	None	16	19	28
2	File articles of unification	None	30	30	30
3	Unify price and credit policy	None	60	72	90
4	Unify personnel policies	None	18	27	30
5	Unify data processing	1	17	29	47
6	Train accounting staff	1	4	7	10
7	Pilot run data processing	5	12	15	18
8	Calculate P & L and balance sheet	6, 7	6	12	24
9	Transfer real property	2	18	27	30
10	Train salesforce	3	20	35	50
11	Negotiate with unions	4	40	55	100
12	Determine capital needs	8	11	20	29
13	Explain personnel policies	11	14	23	26
14	Secure line of credit	9, 12	13	16	19
15	End	10, 13, 14	0	0	0

   1. Compute the expected time for each activity.
   2. Compute the variance for each activity.

3. Compute the expected project duration.
4. What is the probability of completing the project by day 112? Within 116 days?
5. What is the probability of completing "Negotiate with Unions" by day 90?

3. The expected times and variances for the project activities are given below. What is the probability of completing the project in 25 periods?

ID	Description	Predecessor	t_e	Variance $[(b-a)/6]^2$
1	Pilot production	None	6	3
2	Select channels of distrib.	None	7	4
3	Develop mktg. program	None	4	2
4	Test market	1	4	2
5	Patent	1	10	5
6	Full production	4	16	10
7	Ad promotion	3	3	2
8	Release	2,5,6,7	2	1

Case

International Capital, Inc.—Part A

International Capital, Inc. (IC), is a small investment banking firm that specializes in securing funds for small- to medium-sized firms. IC is able to use a standardized project format for each engagement. Only activity times and unusual circumstances change the standard network. Beth Brown has been assigned to this client as project manager partner and has compiled the network information and activity times for the latest client as follows:

Activity	Description	Immediate Predecessor
A	Start story draft using template	—
B	Research client firm	—
C	Create "due diligence" rough draft	A, B
D	Coordinate needs proposal with client	C
E	Estimate future demand and cash flows	C
F	Draft future plans for client company	E
G	Create and approve legal documents	C
H	Integrate all drafts into first-draft proposal	D, F, G
I	Line up potential sources of capital	G, F
J	Check, approve, and print final legal proposal	H
K	Sign contracts and transfer funds	I, J

	Time in Workdays		
Activity	**Optimistic**	**Most Likely**	**Pessimistic**
A	4	7	10
B	2	4	8
C	2	5	8
D	16	19	28
E	6	9	24
F	1	7	13
G	4	10	28
H	2	5	14
I	5	8	17
J	2	5	8
K	17	29	45

MANAGERIAL REPORT

Brown and other broker partners have a policy of passing their plan through a project review committee of colleagues. This committee traditionally checks that all details are covered, times are realistic, and resources are available. Brown wishes you to develop a report that presents a planned schedule and expected project completion time in workdays. Include a project network in your report. The average duration for a sourcing capital project is 70 workdays. IC partners have agreed it is good business to set up projects with a 95 percent chance of attaining the plan. How does this project stack up with the average project? What would the average have to be to ensure a 95 percent chance of completing the project in 70 workdays?

Case

Advantage Energy Technology Data Center Migration—Part B

In Chapter 6, Brian Smith, network administrator at Advanced Energy Technology (AET), was given the responsibility of implementing the migration of a large data center to a new office location.

Careful planning was needed because AET operates in the highly competitive petroleum industry. AET is one of five national software companies that provide an accounting and business management package for oil jobbers and gasoline distributors. A few years ago, AET jumped into the "application service provider" world. Their large data center provides clients with remote access to AET's complete suite of application software systems. Traditionally, one of AET's primary competitive advantages has been the company's trademark IT reliability. Due to the complexity of this project, the Executive Committee insisted that preliminary analysis of the anticipated completion date be conducted.

Brian compiled the following information, in preparation for some PERT analysis:

	Task Name	Time in Workdays Optimistic Dur.	Most Likely Dur.	Pessimistic Dur.	Immediate Predecessor	Critical Path
1	**AET DATA CENTER MIGRATION**	54	68	92		
2	Team meeting	0.5	1	1.5		✓
3	Hire contractors	6	7	8	2	
4	Network design	12	14	16	2	
5	**Ventilation system**	—	—	—	—	
6	Order ventilation system	18	21	30	2	
7	Install ventilation system	5	7	9	6	
8	**New racks**	—	—	—	—	
9	Order new racks	13	14	21	2	✓
10	Install racks	17	21	25	9	✓
11	**Power supplies and cables**	—	—	—	—	
12	Order power supplies & cables	6	7	8	2	
13	Install power supplies	5	5	11	12, 16	
14	Install cables	6	8	10	12, 16	✓
15	Renovation of data center	19	20	27	3, 4	
16	City inspection	1	2	3	3, 7, 10	✓
17	**Switchover Meetings**	—	—	—	—	
18	Facilities	7	8	9	14	
19	Operations/systems	5	7	9	14	
20	Operations/telecommunications	6	7	8	14	
21	Systems & applications	7	7	13	14	
22	Customer service	5	6	13	14	✓
23	Power check	0.5	1	1.5	13, 14, 15	✓
24	Install test servers	5	7	9	18, 19, 20, 21, 22, 23	✓
25	Management safety check	1	2	3	7, 23, 24	✓
26	Primary systems check	1.5	2	2.5	25	✓
27	Set date for move	1	1	1	26	✓
28	Complete move	1	2	3	27	✓

1. Based on these estimates and the resultant expected project duration of 69 days, the executive committee wants to know what is the probability of completing the project before a scheduled time (T_S) of 68 days?
2. The significance of this project has the executive committee very concerned. The committee has decided that more analysis of the duration of each activity is needed. Prior to conducting that effort, they asked Brian to calculate what the expected project duration would have to be to ensure a 93 percent chance of completion within 68 days.

ADVANTAGE ENERGY TECHNOLOGY (AET)—ACCOUNTS PAYABLE SYSTEM

The AET sales department has been concerned about a new start-up company that is about to release an accounts payable system. Their investigation indicates that this new package will provide features which will seriously compete with AET's current Accounts Payable system and some cases, exceed what AET offers.

Tom Wright, senior applications developer at AET, has been given the responsibility of analyzing, designing, developing, and delivering a new accounts payable system (A/P) for AET customers.

Complicating the issue is the concern of the sales department about AET's recent inability to meet promised delivery dates. They have convinced CEO (Larry Martain) that a significant marketing effort will have to be expended to convince the clients they should wait for the AET product rather than jump to a package provided by a new entry to the petroleum software business. Companion to this effort is the importance of the performance of the software development group.

Consequently, Tom has decided to take the following action: tighten up the estimating effort by his developers; incorporate some new estimating procedures; and use some PERT techniques to generate probabilities associated with his delivery dates.

Tom's planning team made a first-cut at the set of activities and associated durations:

		Time in Workdays				
	Task Name	**Optimistic Dur.**	**Most Likely Dur.**	**Pessimistic Dur.**	**Immediate Predecessor**	**Critical Path**
1	**ACCOUNTS PAYABLE SYSTEM**					
2	Planning meeting	1	1	2		✓
3	Team assignments	3	4	5	2	✓
4	**Program specification**					
5	Customer requirements	8	10	12	3	✓
6	Feasibility study	3	5	7	5	
7	Systems analysis	6	8	10	5	✓
8	Prelim budget & schedule	1	2	3	7	✓
9	Functional specification	3	5	7	7	✓
10	Prelim design	10	12	14	9	✓
11	Configuration & perf needs	3	4	5	10	✓
12	Hardware requirements	4	6	8	11	✓
13	System specification	5	7	9	10	
14	Detailed design	12	14	16	12, 13	✓
15	Program specification	8	10	12	14	✓
16	Programming—first phase	27	32	37	15	✓
17	Documentation	14	16	18	10	
18	**Prototype**					
19	Development	5	7	9	16	✓
20	User testing & feedback	12	14	16	19	✓
21	Programming—second phase	10	12	14	16	
22	Beta testing	18	20	22	21	
23	Final documentation pkg	9	10	11	17, 20	✓
24	Training pkg	4	5	6	21SS, 23	✓
25	Product release	3	5	7	22, 23, 24	✓

SS = Start to Start lag

3. Based on these estimates and the critical path, the project duration is estimated at 149 days. But, an AET salesperson in the Southeast Region has discovered that the competing A/P package (with significant improvements) is scheduled for delivery in approximately 145 days. The sales force is very anxious to beat

that delivery time. The executive committee asks Tom for an estimated probability of reducing his expected project duration by two days.

4. The executive committee is advised by Tom that after all the estimating was completed, he determined that one of his two critical systems analysts might have to move out of the area for critical family reasons. Tom is still very confident that with some staff rearrangements, assistance from a subcontractor, and some "hands on" activities on his part he can still meet the original delivery date, based on 149 days.

   This news is very disconcerting to the committee and the sales staff. At this point, the committee decides that based on the most recent delivery performance of AET, a modified, comfortable delivery date should be communicated to AET clients—one that Tom and his staff are very likely to meet. Consequently, Tom is asked to calculate what the expected project duration would have to be to ensure a 98 percent chance of completion within 160 days—that is a "published, drop dead date" that can be communicated to the clients.

CHAPTER EIGHT

Scheduling Resources and Costs

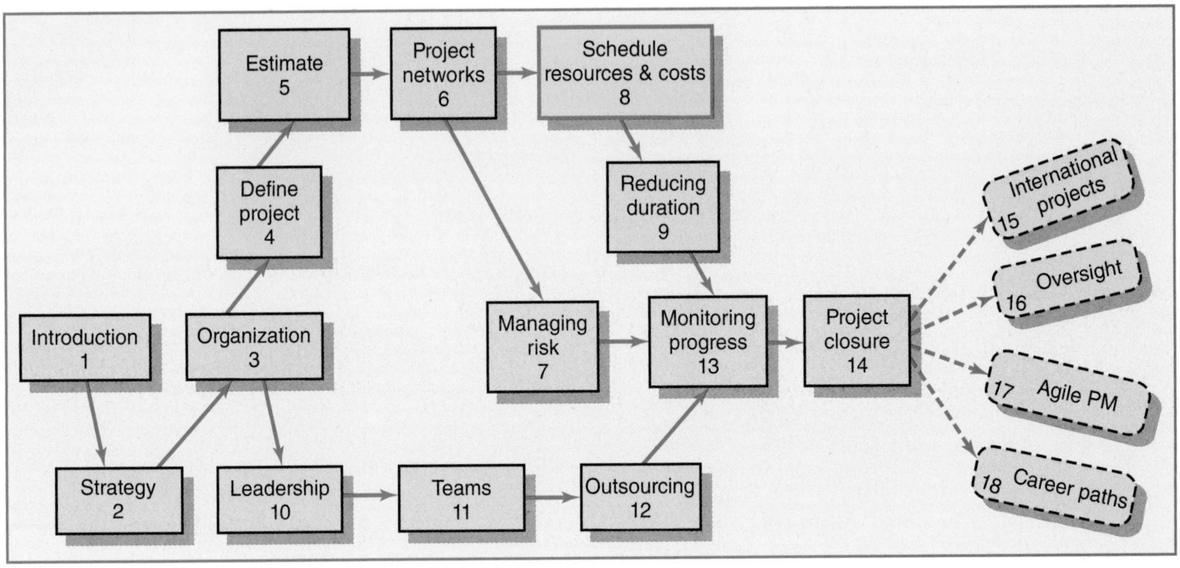

Scheduling Resources and Costs

Overview of the Resource Scheduling Problem

Types of Resource Constraints

Classification of a Scheduling Problem

Resource Allocation Methods

Computer Demonstration of Resource-Constrained Scheduling

Splitting Activities

Benefits of Scheduling Resources

Assigning Project Work

Multiproject Resource Schedules

Using the Resource Schedule to Develop a Project Cost Baseline

Summary

Appendix 8.1: The Critical-Chain Approach

Project network times are not a schedule until resources have been assigned. Cost estimates are not a budget until they have been time-phased.

We have consistently stressed that up-front planning results in big payoffs. For those who have diligently worked through the earlier planning processes chapters, you are nearly ready to launch your project. This chapter completes the final two planning tasks that become the master plan for your project—resource and cost scheduling. (See Figure 8.1.) This process uses the resource schedule to assign **time-phased** costs that provide the project budget *baseline*. Given this time-phased baseline, comparisons can be made with actual and planned schedule and costs. This chapter first discusses the process for developing the project resource schedule. This resource schedule will be used to assign the time-phased budgeted values to create a project budget baseline.

There are always more project proposals than there are available resources. The priority system needs to select projects that best contribute to the organization's objectives, within the constraints of the resources available. If all projects and their respective resources are computer scheduled, the feasibility and impact of adding a new project to those in process can be quickly assessed. With this information the project priority team will add a new project only if resources are available to be formally committed to that specific project. This chapter examines methods of scheduling resources so the team can make realistic judgments of resource availability and project durations. The project manager uses the same schedule for implementing the project. If changes occur during project implementation, the computer schedule is easily updated and the effects easily assessed.

Overview of the Resource Scheduling Problem

After staff and other resources were assigned to her project, a project manager listed the following questions that still needed to be addressed:

- Will the assigned labor and/or equipment be adequate and available to deal with my project?
- Will outside contractors have to be used?

FIGURE 8.1
Project Planning Process

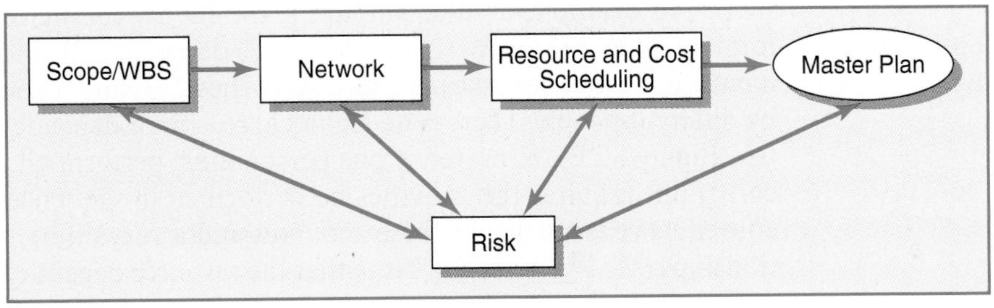

- Do unforeseen resource dependencies exist? Is there a new critical path?
- How much flexibility do we have in using resources?
- Is the original deadline realistic?

Clearly, this project manager has a good understanding of the problems she is facing. Any project scheduling system should facilitate finding quick, easy answers to these questions.

The planned network and activity project duration times found in previous chapters fail to deal with resource usage and availability. The time estimates for the work packages and network times were made independently with the implicit assumption that resources would be available. This may or may not be the case.

If resources are adequate but the demand varies widely over the life of the project, it may be desirable to even out resource demand by delaying noncritical activities (using slack) to lower peak demand and, thus, increase resource utilization. This process is called **resource smoothing.**

On the other hand, if resources are not adequate to meet peak demands, the late start of some activities must be delayed, and the duration of the project may be increased. This process is called *resource-constrained scheduling.* One research study of more than 50 projects by Woodworth and Willie (1975) found that planned project network durations were increased 38 percent when resources were scheduled.

The consequences of failing to schedule limited resources are costly and project delays usually manifest themselves midway in the project when quick corrective action is difficult. An additional consequence of failing to schedule resources is ignoring the peaks and valleys of resource usage over the duration of the project. Because project resources are usually overcommitted and because resources seldom line up by availability and need, procedures are needed to deal with these problems. This chapter addresses methods available to project managers for dealing with resource utilization and availability through resource leveling and resource-constrained scheduling.

Up to now the start and sequence of activities has been based solely on technical or logical considerations. For example, a project network for framing a house might show three activities in a sequence: (1) pour foundation, (2) build frame, and (3) cover roof. A network for a new software project could place the activities in the network, as a sequence of (1) design, (2) code, and (3) test. In other words, you cannot logically perform activity 2 until 1 is completed, and so on. The project network depicts technical constraints (see Figure 8.2A). The network assumes the personnel and equipment are available to perform the required work. This is often not the case!

The absence or shortage of resources can drastically alter technical constraints. A project network planner may assume adequate resources and show activities occurring in parallel. However, parallel activities hold potential for resource conflicts. For example, assume you are planning a wedding reception that includes four activities—(1) plan, (2) hire band, (3) decorate hall, and (4) purchase refreshments. Each activity takes one day. Activities 2, 3, and 4 could be done in parallel by different people. There is no technical reason or dependency of one on another (see Figure 8.2B). However, if one person must perform all activities, the resource constraint requires the activities be performed in sequence or series. Clearly the consequence is a delay of these activities and a very different set of network relationships (see Figure 8.2C). Note that the resource dependency takes priority over

FIGURE 8.2
Constraint Examples

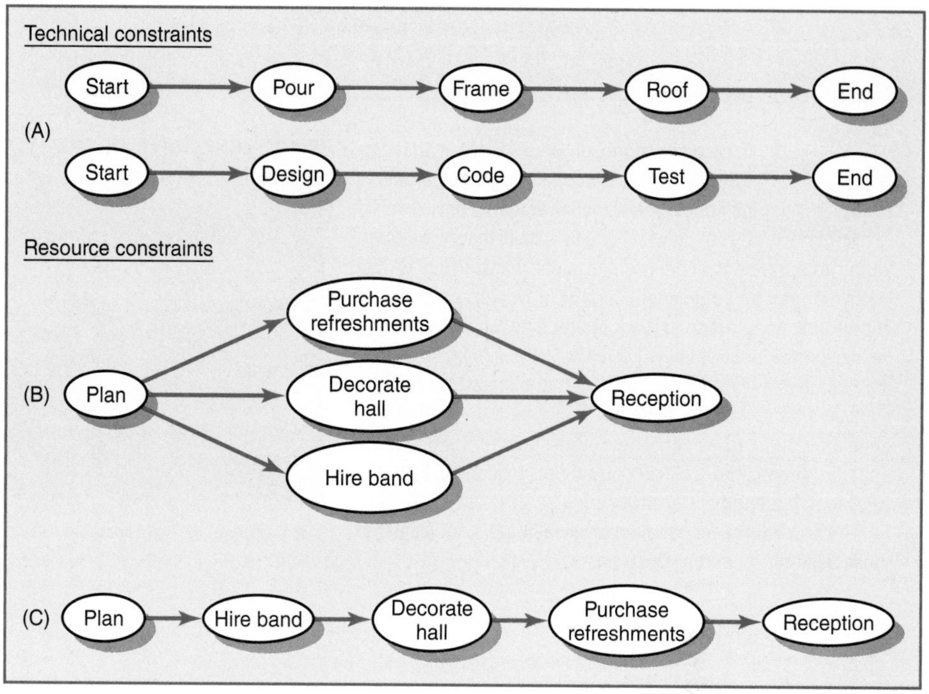

the technological dependency but *does not violate the technological dependency;* that is, hire, decorate, and purchase may now have to take place in sequence rather than concurrently, but they must all be completed before the reception can take place.

The interrelationships and interactions among time and resource constraints are complex for even small project networks. Some effort to examine these interactions before the project begins frequently uncovers surprising problems. Project managers who do not consider resource availability in moderately complex projects usually learn of the problem when it is too late to correct. A deficit of resources can significantly alter project dependency relationships, completion dates, and project costs. Project managers must be careful to schedule resources to ensure availability in the right quantities and at the right time. Fortunately, there are computer software programs that can identify resource problems during the early project planning phase when corrective changes can be considered. These programs only require activity resource needs and availability information to schedule resources.

See the Snapshot from Practice: Working in Tight Places for a third constraint that impinges on project schedules.

Types of Resource Constraints

Resources are people, equipment, and material that can be drawn on to accomplish something. In projects the availability or unavailability of resources will often influence the way projects are managed.

1. ***People.*** This is the most obvious and important project resource. Human resources are usually classified by the skills they bring to the project—for example,

SNAPSHOT FROM PRACTICE Working in Tight Places

In rare situations, physical factors cause activities that would normally occur in parallel to be constrained by contractual or environmental conditions. For example, in theory the renovation of a sailboat compartment might involve four to five tasks that can be done independently. However, since space allows only one person to work at one time, all tasks have to be performed sequentially. Likewise, on a mining project it may be physically possible for only two miners to work in a shaft at a time. Another example would be the erection of a communication tower and nearby groundwork. For safety considerations, the contract prohibits groundwork within 2,000 feet of the tower construction.

The procedures for handling physical factors are similar to those used for resource constraints.

© Digital Vision/PunchStock

programmer, mechanical engineer, welder, inspector, marketing director, supervisor. In rare cases some skills are interchangeable, but usually with a loss of productivity. The many differing skills of human resources add to the complexity of scheduling projects.

*2. **Materials.*** Project materials cover a large spectrum: for example, chemicals for a scientific project, concrete for a road project, survey data for a marketing project.

Material availability and shortages have been blamed for the delay of many projects. When it is known that a lack of availability of materials is important and probable, materials should be included in the project network plan and schedule. For example, delivery and placement of an oil rig tower in a Siberian oil field has a very small time window during one summer month. Any delivery delay means a one-year, costly delay. Another example in which material was the major resource scheduled was the resurfacing and replacement of some structures on the Golden Gate Bridge in San Francisco. Work on the project was limited to the hours between midnight and 5:00 A.M. with a penalty of $1,000 per minute for any work taking place after 5:00 A.M. Scheduling the arrival of replacement structures was an extremely important part of managing the five-hour work-time window of the project. Scheduling materials has also become important in developing products where time-to-market can result in loss of market share.

*3. **Equipment.*** Equipment is usually presented by type, size, and quantity. In some cases equipment can be interchanged to improve schedules, but this is not typical. Equipment is often overlooked as a constraint. The most common oversight is to assume the resource pool is more than adequate for the project. For example, if a project needs one earthmoving tractor six months from now and the organization owns four, it is common to assume the resource will not delay the pending project. However, when the earthmoving tractor is due on-site in six months, all four machines in the pool might be occupied on other projects. In multiproject environments it is prudent to use a common resource pool for all projects. This approach forces a check of resource availability across all projects and reserves the equipment for specific project needs in the future. Recognition of equipment constraints before the project begins can avoid high crashing or delay costs.

Classification of a Scheduling Problem

Most of the scheduling methods available today require the project manager to classify the project as either *time constrained* or *resource constrained.* Project managers need to consult their priority matrix (see Figure 4.2) to determine which case fits their project. One simple test to determine if the project is time or resource constrained is to ask, "If the critical path is delayed, will resources be added to get back on schedule?" If the answer is yes, assume the project is time constrained; if no, assume the project is resource constrained.

A **time-constrained project** is one that must be completed by an imposed date. If required, resources can be added to ensure the project is completed by a specific date. Although time is the critical factor, resource usage should be no more than is necessary and sufficient.

A **resource-constrained project** is one that assumes the level of resources available cannot be exceeded. If the resources are inadequate, it will be acceptable to delay the project, but as little as possible.

In scheduling terms, time constrained means time (project duration) is fixed and resources are flexible, while resource constrained means resources are fixed and time is flexible. Methods for scheduling these projects are presented in the next section.

Resource Allocation Methods

Assumptions

Ease of demonstrating the allocation methods available requires some limiting assumptions to keep attention on the heart of the problem. The rest of the chapter depends entirely on the assumptions noted here. First, splitting activities will not be allowed. This means once an activity is placed in the schedule, assume it will be worked on continuously until it is finished; hence, an activity cannot be started, stopped for a period of time, and then finished. Second, the level of resources used for an activity cannot be changed. These limiting assumptions do not exist in practice, but simplify learning. It is easy for new project managers to deal with the reality of splitting activities and changing the level of resources when they meet them on the job.

Time-Constrained Projects: Smoothing Resource Demand

Scheduling time-constrained projects focuses on resource *utilization.* When demand for a specific resource type is erratic, it is difficult to manage, and utilization may be very poor. Practitioners have attacked the utilization problem using resource leveling techniques that balance demand for a resource.

Basically, all **leveling** techniques delay noncritical activities by using positive slack to reduce peak demand and fill in the valleys for the resources. An example will demonstrate the basic procedure for a time-constrained project. See Figure 8.3.

For the purpose of demonstration, the Botanical Garden project uses only one resource (backhoes); all backhoes are interchangeable. The top bar chart shows the activities on a time scale. The dependencies are shown with the vertical connecting arrows. The horizontal arrows following activities represent activity slack (for example, irrigation requires six days to complete and has six days slack). The number of backhoes needed for each task is shown in the shaded activity

FIGURE 8.3 Botanical Garden

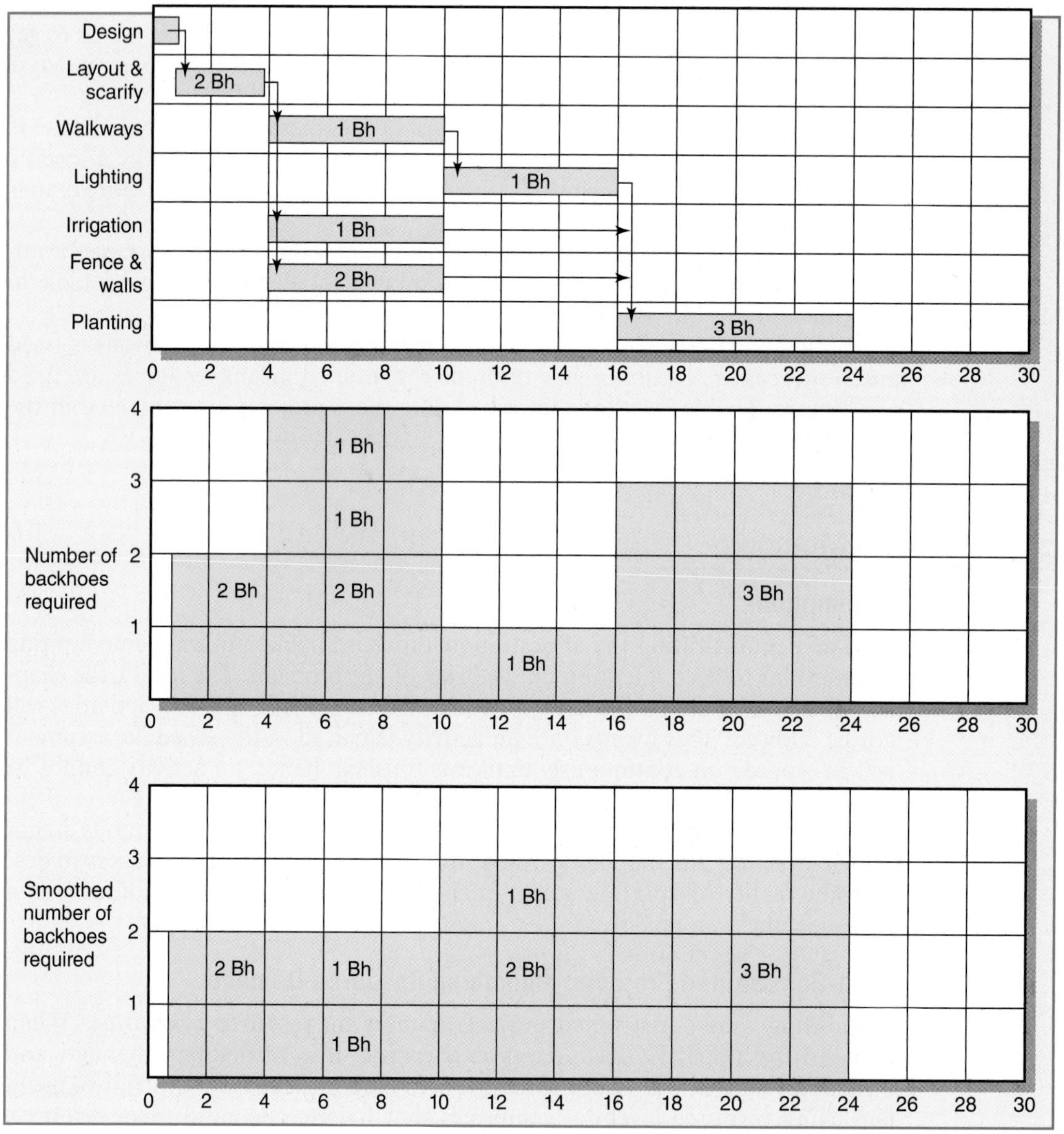

duration block (rectangle). After the land has been scarified and the plan laid out, work can begin on the walkways, irrigation, and fencing and retaining walls simultaneously. The middle chart shows the resource profile for the backhoes. For periods 4 through 10, four backhoes are needed.

Because this project is declared time constrained, the goal will be to reduce the peak requirement for the resource and thereby increase the utilization of the resource. A quick examination of the ES (early start) resource load chart suggests only two activities have slack that can be used to reduce the peak—fence and walls provide the best choice for smoothing the resource needs. Another choice could be irrigation, but it would result in an up and down resource profile. The choice will probably center on the activity that is perceived as having the least risk of being late. The smoothed resource loading chart shows the results of delaying the fence and walls activity. Note the differences in the resource profiles. The important point is the resources needed over the life of the project have been reduced from four to three (25 percent). In addition the profile has been smoothed, which should be easier to manage.

The Botanical Garden project schedule reached the three goals of smoothing:

- The peak of demand for the resource was reduced.
- Resources over the life of the project have been reduced.
- The fluctuations in resource demand were minimized.

The latter improves the utilization of resources. Backhoes are not easily moved from location to location. There are costs associated with changing the level of resources needed. The same analogy applies to the movement of people back and forth among projects. It is well known that people are more efficient if they can focus their effort on one project rather than multitasking their time among, say, three projects.

The downside of leveling is a loss of flexibility that occurs from reducing slack. The risk of activities delaying the project also increases because slack reduction can create more critical activities and/or near-critical activities. Pushing leveling too far for a perfectly level resource profile is risky. Every activity then becomes critical.

The Botanical Garden example gives a sense of the time-constrained problem and the smoothing approach. However, in practice the magnitude of the problem is very complex for even small projects. Manual solutions are not practical. Fortunately, the software packages available today have very good routines for leveling project resources. Typically, they use activities that have the most slack to level project resources. The rationale is those activities with the most slack pose the least risk. Although this is generally true, other risk factors such as reduction of flexibility to use reassigned resources on other activities or the nature of the activity (easy, complex) are not addressed using such a simple rationale. It is easy to experiment with many alternatives to find the one that best fits your project and minimizes risk of delaying the project.

Resource-Constrained Projects

When the number of people and/or equipment is not adequate to meet peak demand requirements and it is impossible to obtain more, the project manager faces a resource-constrained problem. Something has to give. The trick is to prioritize and allocate resources to minimize project delay without exceeding the resource limit or altering the technical network relationships.

The resource scheduling problem is a large combinatorial one. This means even a modest-size project network with only a few resource types might have several thousand feasible solutions. A few researchers have demonstrated *optimum* mathematical solutions to the resource allocation problem but only for small networks and very few resource types (Arrow and Hurowicz, 1977; Talbot and Patterson, 1979; Woodworth and Shanahan, 1988). The massive data requirements for larger problems make pure mathematical solutions (e.g., linear programming) impractical. An alternative approach to the problem has been the use of **heuristics** (rules of thumb) to solve large combinatorial problems. These practical decision or priority rules have been in place for many years.

Heuristics do not always yield an optimal schedule, but they are very capable of yielding a "good" schedule for very complex networks with many types of resources. The efficiency of different rules and combinations of rules has been well documented (Pascoe, 1965; Fendly, 1968). However, because each project is unique, it is wise to test several sets of heuristics on a network to determine the priority allocation rules that minimize project delay. The computer software available today makes it very easy for the project manager to create a good resource schedule for the project. A simple example of the heuristic approach is illustrated here.

Heuristics allocate resources to activities to minimize project delay; that is, heuristics prioritize which activities are allocated resources and which activities are delayed when resources are not adequate.

The parallel method is the most widely used approach to apply heuristics, which have been found to consistently minimize project delay over a large variety of projects. The parallel method is an iterative process that starts from the beginning of project time and, when resources needed exceed the resources available, retains activities first by the priority rules:

1. Minimum slack.
2. Smallest duration.
3. Lowest activity identification number.

Those not able to be scheduled without delaying others are pushed out farther in time. However, do not attempt to move activities that have already started. When considering activities not to delay, consider the resources each activity uses. In any period when two or more activities require the same resource, the priority rules are applied. For example, if in period 5 three activities are eligible to start (i.e., have the same ES) and require the same resource, the first activity placed in the schedule would be the activity with the least slack (rule 1). However, if all activities have the same slack, the next rule would be invoked (rule 2), and the activity with the smallest duration would be placed in the schedule first. In very rare cases, when all eligible activities have the same slack and the same duration, the tie is broken by the lowest activity identification number (rule 3), since each activity has a unique ID number.

When a resource limit has been reached, the early start (ES) for succeeding activities not yet in the schedule will be delayed (and all successor activities not having free slack) and their slack reduced. In subsequent periods the procedure is repeated until the project is scheduled. The procedure is demonstrated next; see Figure 8.4. The shaded areas in the resource loading chart represent the "scheduling interval" of the *time-constrained* schedule (ES through LF). You can schedule the resource any place *within* the interval and not delay the project. Scheduling the activity beyond the LF will delay the project.

The Parallel Method:

Period	Action
	—— See Figure 8.4 ——
0–1	Only activity 1 is eligible. It requires 2 programmers. Load activity 1 into schedule.
1–2	No activities are eligible to be scheduled.
2–3	Activities 2, 3, and 4 are eligible to be scheduled. Activity 3 has the least slack (0)—apply rule 1. Load Activity 3 into schedule. Activity 2 is next with slack of 2; however, activity 2 requires 2 programmers and only 1 is available. Delay activity 2. Update: ES = 3, slack = 1. The next eligible activity is activity 4, since it only requires 1 programmer. Load activity 4 into schedule.
	—— See Figure 8.5 ——
3–4	Activity 2 is eligible but exceeds limit of 3 programmers in pool. Delay activity 2. Update: ES = 4, slack = 0.
4–5	Activity 2 is eligible but exceeds limit of 3 programmers in pool. Delay activity 2. Update: ES = 5, LF = 11, slack = −1. Delay activity 7. Update: ES = 11, LF = 13, slack = −1.
5–6	Activity 2 is eligible but exceeds limit of 3 programmers in pool. Delay activity 2. Update: ES = 6, LF = 12, slack = −2. Delay activity 7. Update: ES = 12, LF = 14, slack = −2.
6–7	Activities 2, 5, and 6 are eligible with slack of −2, 2, and 0, respectively. Load activity 2 into schedule (rule 1). Because activity 6 has 0 slack, it is the next eligible activity. Load activity 6 into schedule (rule 1). The programmer limit of 3 is reached. Delay activity 5. Update: ES = 7, slack = 1.
7–8	Limit is reached. No programmers available. Delay activity 5. Update: ES = 8, slack = 0.
8–9	Limit is reached. No programmers available. Delay activity 5. Update: ES = 9, LF = 11, slack = −1.
9–10	Limit is reached. No programmers available. Delay activity 5. Update: ES = 10, LF = 12, slack = −2.
10–11	Activity 5 is eligible. Load activity 5 into schedule. (Note: Activity 6 does not have slack because there are no programmers available—3 maximum.)
11–12	No eligible activities.
12–13	Activity 7 is eligible. Load activity 7 into schedule.

The programmers are limited to three. Follow the actions described in Figures 8.4 and 8.5. Note how the limit of three programmers starts to delay the project.

Observe how it is necessary to update each period to reflect changes in activity early start and slack times so the heuristics can reflect changing priorities. When using the parallel scheduling method, the network in Figure 8.5 on page 261 reflects the new schedule date of 14 time units, rather than the time-constrained

FIGURE 8.4 Resource-Constrained Schedule through Period 2–3

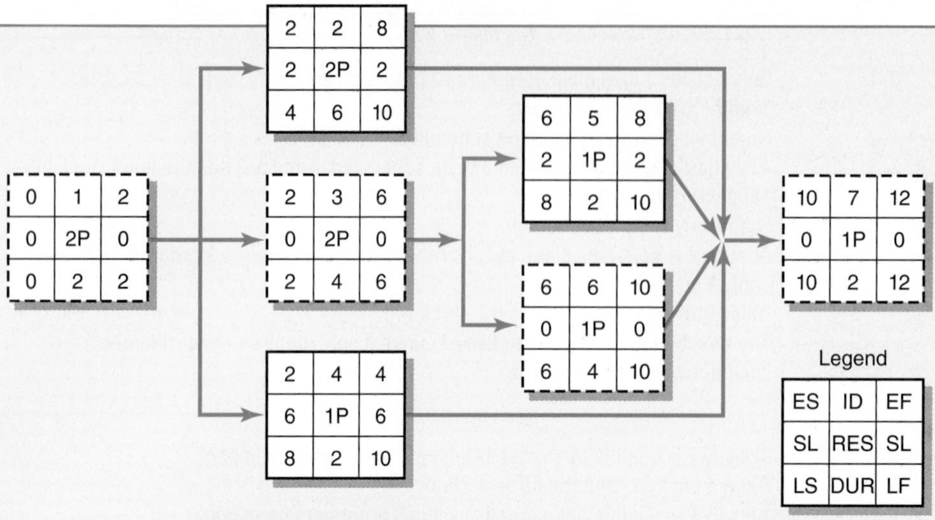

ES resource load chart

ID	RES	DUR	ES	LF	SL	0	1	2	3	4	5	6	7	8	9	10	11	12	13 14
1	2P	2	0	2	0	2	2												
2	2P	6	2	10	2			2	2	2	2	2	2						
3	2P	4	2	6	0			2	2	2	2								
4	1P	2	2	10	6			1	1										
5	1P	2	6	10	2							1	1						
6	1P	4	6	10	0							1	1	1	1				
7	1P	2	10	12	0											1	1		
Total resource load						2P	2P	5P	5P	4P	4P	4P	4P	1P	1P	1P	1P		

Resource-constrained schedule through period 2–3

ID	RES	DUR	ES	LF	SL	0	1	2	3	4	5	6	7	8	9	10	11	12	13 14
1	2P	2	0	2	0	2	2												
2	2P	6	~~2~~ 3	10	~~2~~ 1			X											
3	2P	4	2	6	0			2	2	2	2								
4	1P	2	2	10	6			1	1										
5	1P	2	6	10	2														
6	1P	4	6	10	0														
7	1P	2	10	12	0														
Total resource load						2P	2P	3P	3P	2P	2P								
Resource available						3P	3P	3P	3P	3P	3P	3P	3P	3P	3P	3P	3P		

FIGURE 8.5 Resource-Constrained Schedule through Period 5–6

Resource-constrained schedule through period 5–6

ID	RES	DUR	ES	LF	SL	0–1	1–2	2–3	3–4	4–5	5–6	6–7	7–8	8–9	9–10	10–11	11–12	12–13	13–14
1	2P	2	0	2	0	2	2												
2	2P	6	~~2~~ ~~3~~ ~~4~~ ~~5~~ 6	~~10~~ ~~11~~ 12	~~2~~ ~~1~~ ~~0~~ ~~-1~~ -2			X	X	X	X								
3	2P	4	2	6	0			2	2	2	2								
4	1P	2	2	10	6			1	1										
5	1P	2	6	10	2														
6	1P	4	6	10	0														
7	1P	2	~~10~~ ~~11~~ 12	~~12~~ ~~13~~ 14	~~0~~ ~~-1~~ -2											X	X		
			Total resource load			2P	2P	3P	3P	2P	2P								
			Resource available			3P	3P	3P	3P	3P	3P	3P	3P	3P	3P	3P	3P		

Final resource-constrained schedule

ID	RES	DUR	ES	LF	SL	0–1	1–2	2–3	3–4	4–5	5–6	6–7	7–8	8–9	9–10	10–11	11–12	12–13	13–14
1	2P	2	0	2	0	2	2												
2	2P	6	~~2~~ ~~3~~ ~~4~~ ~~5~~ 6	~~10~~ ~~11~~ 12	~~2~~ ~~1~~ ~~0~~ ~~-1~~ -2			X	X	X	X	2	2	2	2	2	2		
3	2P	4	2	6	0			2	2	2	2								
4	1P	2	2	6	~~6~~ 2			1	1	SL	SL								
5	1P	2	~~6~~ ~~7~~ ~~8~~ ~~9~~ 10	~~10~~ ~~11~~ 12	~~2~~ ~~1~~ ~~0~~ ~~-1~~ -2							X	X	X	X	1	1		
6	1P	4	6	10	0							1	1	1	1				
7	1P	2	~~10~~ ~~11~~ 12	~~12~~ ~~13~~ 14	~~0~~ ~~-1~~ -2											X	X	1	1
			Total resource load			2P	2P	3P	3P	2P	2P	3P	3P	3P	3P	3P	3P	1P	1P
			Resource available			3P	3P	3P	3P	3P	3P	3P	3P	3P	3P	3P	3P	3P	3P

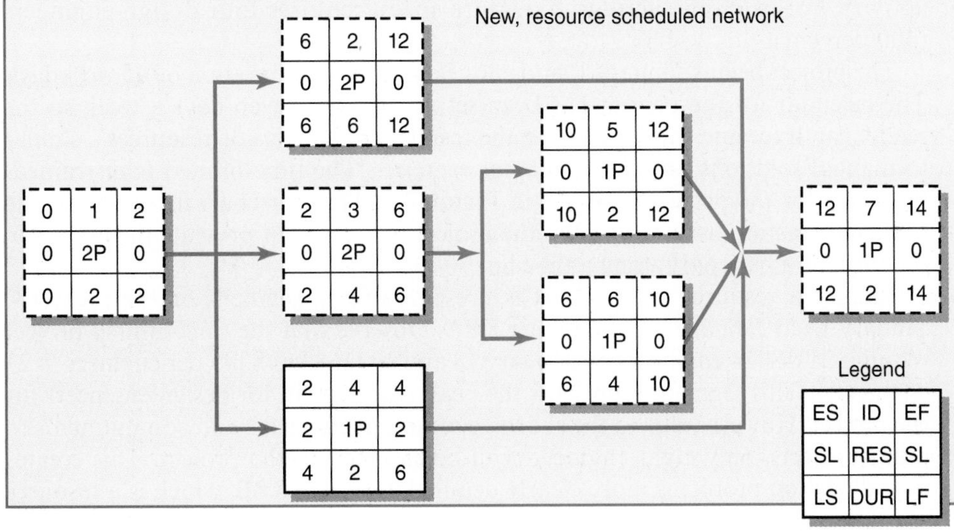

project duration of 12 time units. The network has also been revised to reflect new start, finish, and slack times for each activity. Note that activity 6 is still critical and has a slack of 0 time units because no resources are available (they are being used on activities 2 and 5). Compare the slack for each activity found in Figures 8.4 and 8.5; slack has been reduced significantly. Note that activity 4 has only 2 units of slack rather than what appears to be 6 slack units. This occurs because only three programmers are available, and they are needed to satisfy the resource requirements of activities 2 and 5. Note that the number of critical activities (1, 2, 3, 5, 6, 7) has increased from four to six.

This small example demonstrates the scenario of scheduling resources in real projects and the resulting increase in the risk of being late. In practice this is not a trivial problem! Managers who fail to schedule resources usually encounter this scheduling risk when it is too late to work around the problem, resulting in a project delay.

Since manually using the parallel method is impractical on real-world projects because of size, project managers will depend on software programs to schedule project resources.

Computer Demonstration of Resource-Constrained Scheduling

Fortunately, project management software is capable of assessing and resolving complicated resource-constrained schedules using heuristics similar to what was described above. We will use the EMR project to demonstrate how this is done using MS Project. It is important to note that the software is not "managing" the project. The software is simply a tool the project manager uses to view the project from different perspectives and conditions. See the Snapshot from Practice: Assessing Resource Allocation on page 269 for more tips on assessing resource problems.

EMR is the name given to the development of a handheld electronic medical reference guide to be used by emergency medical technicians and paramedics. Figure 8.6 contains a time-limited network for the design phase of the project. For the purpose of this example, we assume that only design engineers are required for the tasks and that the design engineers are interchangeable. The number of engineers required to perform each task is noted in the network, where 500 percent means five design engineers are needed for the activity. For example, activity 5, feature specs, requires four design engineers (400 percent).

The project begins January 1, and ends February 14, a duration of 45 workdays. The calendar for the project has been set up to work seven days a week so the reader can trace and more easily see the results and impacts of resources—similar to manual solutions present in chapter exercises. The time-limited (constrained) bar chart for the project is shown in Figure 8.7. This bar chart incorporates the same information used to develop the project network, but presents the project in the form of a bar chart along a time line.

Finally, a resource usage chart is presented for a segment of the project—January 15 to January 23; see Figure 8.8A. Observe that the time-limited project requires 21 design engineers on January 18 and 19 (168 hrs/8 hrs per engineer = 21 engineers). This segment represents the peak requirement for design engineers for the project. However, due to the shortage of design engineers and commitments to other projects, only eight engineers can be assigned to the project. This creates overallocation problems more clearly detailed in Figure 8.8B, which is a resource

FIGURE 8.6 EMR Project Network View Schedule before Resources Leveled

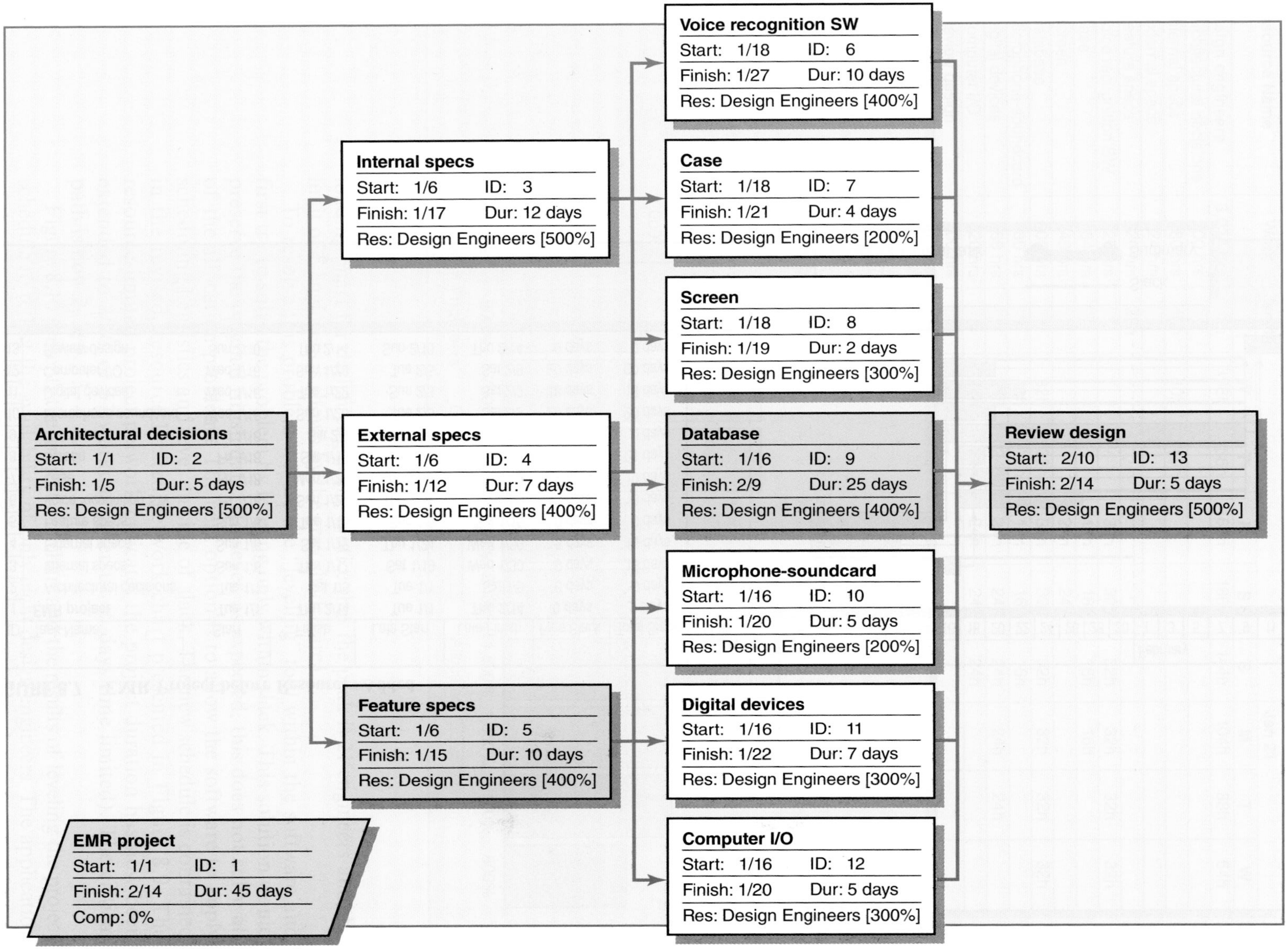

specification activities. All three activities were originally scheduled to start immediately after activity 1, architectural decisions.

This is impossible, since the three activities collectively require 14 engineers. The software chooses to schedule activity 5 first because this activity is on the original critical path and has zero slack (heuristic rule # 1). Next, and concurrently, activity 4 is chosen over activity 3 because activity 4 has a shorter duration (heuristic rule # 2); internal specs, activity 3, is delayed due to the limitation of 8 design engineers. Notice that the original critical path no longer applies because of the resource dependencies created by having only eight design engineers. See Figure 8.9 for the original planned critical path.

Compare the bar chart in Figure 8.10 with the time-limited bar chart in Figure 8.7. For example, note the different start dates for activity 8 (screen). In the time-limited plan (Figure 8.7), the start date for activity 8 is 1/18, while the start date in the resource limited schedule (Figure 8.10) is 2/16, almost a month later!

While resource bar graphs are commonly used to illustrate overallocation problems, we prefer to view resource usage tables like the one presented in Figure 8.8A. This table tells you when you have an overallocation problem and identifies activities that are causing the overallocation.

The Impacts of Resource-Constrained Scheduling

Like leveling schedules, the limited resource schedule usually reduces slack, reduces flexibility by using slack to ensure delay is minimized, and increases the number of critical and near-critical activities. Scheduling complexity is increased because resource constraints are added to technical constraints; start times may now have two constraints. The traditional critical path concept of sequential activities from the start to the end of the project is no longer meaningful. The resource constraints can break the sequence and leave the network with a set of disjointed critical activities. Conversely, parallel activities can become sequential. Activities with slack on a time-constrained network can change from critical to noncritical.

Splitting Activities

Splitting tasks is a scheduling technique used to get a better project schedule and/or to increase resource utilization. A planner splits the continuous work included in an activity by interrupting the work and sending the resource to another activity for a period of time and then having the resource resume work on the original activity. Splitting can be a useful tool if the work involved does not include large start-up or shutdown costs—for example, moving equipment from one activity location to another. The most common error is to interrupt "people work," where there are high conceptual start-up and shutdown costs. For example, having a bridge designer take time off to work on the design problem of another project may cause this individual to lose four days shifting conceptual gears in and out of two activities. The cost may be hidden, but it is real. Figure 8.11 depicts the nature of the splitting problem. The original activity has been split into three separate activities: A, B, and C. The shutdown and start-up times lengthen the time for the original activity.

Some have argued that the propensity to deal with resource shortages by splitting is a major reason why projects fail to meet schedule (c.f., Goldratt, 1997;

SNAPSHOT FROM PRACTICE — Assessing Resource Allocation

One of the strengths of today's project management software is the ability to identify and provide options for resolving resource allocation problems. A project manager who uses MS Project to plan projects shared with us the following checklist for dealing with resource conflicts after preliminary assignment of resources has been made.

1. Assess whether you have overallocation problems (see *Red* in the resource sheet view).
2. Identify where and when conflicts occur by examining the resource usage view.
3. Resolve the problem by
   a. Replacing overallocated resources with appropriate resources that are available. Then ask if this solves the problem.

   If not:

   b. Use the leveling tool and choose the level within slack option.
      i Does this solve the problem? (Are resources still overallocated?)
      ii Check the sensitivity of the network and ask if this is acceptable.

   If not:

   c. Consider splitting tasks.
      i Make sure to readjust task durations to take into account additional start-up and shutdown time.
4. If 3 does not work then either:
   a. Use level tool default option and ask if you can live with the new completion date.

   If not:

   b. Negotiate for additional resources to complete the project. If not possible
   c. Consider reducing project scope to meet deadline.

While this checklist makes specific references to MS Project, the same steps can be used with most project management software.

Newbold, 1997). We agree. Planners should avoid the use of splitting as much as possible, except in situations where splitting costs are known to be small or when there is no alternative for resolving the resource problem. Computer software offers the splitting option for each activity; use it sparingly. See Snapshot from Practice: Assessing Resource Allocation.

FIGURE 8.11
Splitting Activities

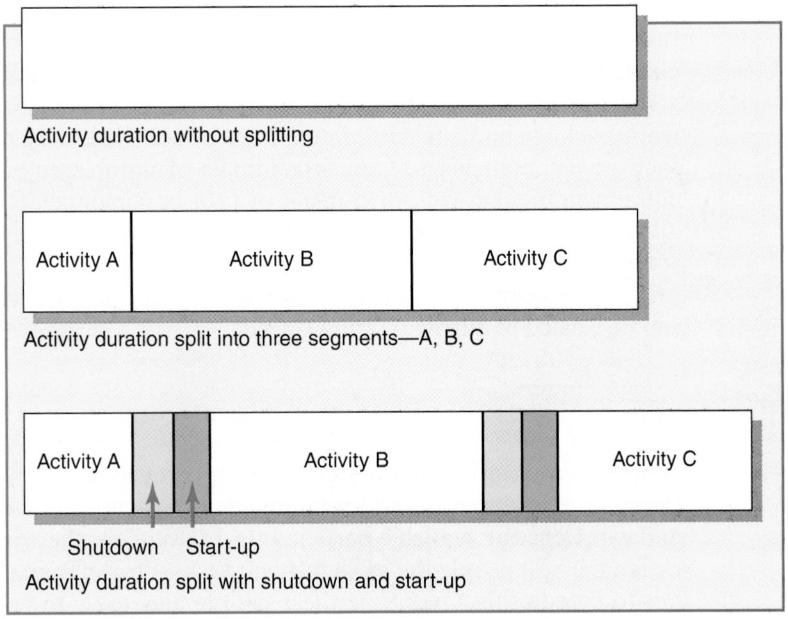

SNAPSHOT FROM PRACTICE U.S. Forest Service Resource Shortage

A major segment of work in managing U.S. Forest Service (USFS) forests is selling mature timber to logging companies that harvest the timber under contract conditions monitored by the Service. The proceeds are returned to the federal government. The budget allocated to each forest depends on the two-year plan submitted to the U.S. Department of Agriculture.

Olympic Forest headquarters in Olympia, Washington, was developing a two-year plan as a basis for funding. All of the districts in the forest submitted their timber sale projects (numbering more than 50) to headquarters, where they were compiled and aggregated into a project plan for the whole forest. The first computer run was reviewed by a small group of senior managers to determine if the plan was reasonable and "doable." Management was pleased and relieved to note all projects appeared to be doable in the two-year time frame until a question was raised concerning the computer printout. "Why are all the columns in these projects labeled 'RESOURCE' blank?" The response from an engineer was, "We don't use that part of the program."

The discussion that ensued recognized the importance of resources in completing the two-year plan and ended with a request to "try the program with resources included." The new output was startling. The two-year program turned into a three-and-a-half-year plan because of the shortage of specific labor skills such as road engineer and environmental impact specialist. Analysis showed that adding only three skilled people would allow the two-year plan to be completed on time. In addition, further analysis showed hiring only a few more skilled people, beyond the three, would allow an extra year of projects to also be compressed into the two-year plan. This would result in additional revenue of more than $3 million. The Department of Agriculture quickly approved the requested extra dollars for additional staff to generate the extra revenue.

Benefits of Scheduling Resources

It is important to remember that, if resources are truly limited and activity time estimates are accurate, the resource-constrained schedule *will* materialize as the project is implemented—*not* the time-constrained schedule! Therefore, failure to schedule limited resources can lead to serious problems for a project manager. The benefit of creating this schedule *before* the project begins leaves time for considering reasonable alternatives. If the scheduled delay is unacceptable or the risk of being delayed too high, the assumption of being resource constrained can be reassessed. Cost-time trade-offs can be considered. In some cases priorities may be changed. See Snapshot from Practice: U.S. Forest Service Resource Shortage.

Resource schedules provide the information needed to prepare time-phased work package budgets with dates. Once established, they provide a quick means for a project manager to gauge the impact of unforeseen events such as turnover, equipment breakdowns, or transfer of project personnel. Resource schedules also allow project managers to assess how much flexibility they have over certain resources. This is useful when they receive requests from other managers to borrow or share resources. Honoring such requests creates goodwill and an "IOU" that can be cashed in during a time of need.

Assigning Project Work

When making individual assignments, project managers should match, as best they can, the demands and requirements of specific work with the qualifications and experience of available participants. In doing so, there is a natural tendency to assign the best people the most difficult tasks. Project managers need to be careful not to overdo this. Over time these people may grow to resent the fact that they

SNAPSHOT FROM PRACTICE Managing Geeks*

Eric Schmidt, after a successful career at Sun Microsystems, took over struggling Novell, Inc., and helped turn it around within two years. Four years later he became the CEO of Google. One of the keys to his success is his ability to manage the technical wizards who develop the sophisticated systems, hardware, and software that are the backbone of electronically driven companies. He uses the term "geek" (and he can, since he is one, with a Ph.D. in computer science) to describe this group of technologists who rule the cyberworld.

Schmidt has some interesting ideas about assigning geeks to projects. He believes that putting geeks together in project teams with other geeks creates productive peer pressure. Geeks care a great deal about how other geeks perceive them. They are good at judging the quality of technical work and are quick to praise as well as criticize each other's work. Some geeks can be unbearably arrogant, but Schmidt claims that having them work together on projects is the best way to control them—by letting them control each other.

At the same time, Schmidt argues that too many geeks spoil the soup. By this he means that, when there are too many geeks on a development team, there is a tendency for intense technical navel gazing. Members lose sight of deadlines, and delays are inevitable. To combat this tendency, he recommends using geeks only in small groups. He urges breaking up large projects into smaller, more manageable projects so that small teams of geeks can be assigned to them. This keeps the project on time and makes the teams responsible to each other.

* Russ Mitchel, "How to Manage Geeks," *Fast Company* (May 31, 1999), pp. 175–80.

are always given the toughest assignments. At the same time, less experienced participants may resent the fact that they are never given the opportunity to expand their skill/knowledge base. Project managers need to balance task performance with the need to develop the talents of people assigned to the project.

Project managers not only need to decide who does what but who works with whom. A number of factors need to be considered in deciding who should work together. First, to minimize unnecessary tension, managers should pick people with compatible work habits and personalities but who complement each other (i.e., one person's weakness is the other person's strength). For example, one person may be brilliant at solving complex problems but sloppy at documenting his or her progress. It would be wise to pair this person with an individual who is good at paying attention to details. Experience is another factor. Veterans should be teamed up with new hires—not only so they can share their experience but also to help socialize the newcomers to the customs and norms of the organization. Finally, future needs should be considered. If managers have some people who have never worked together before but who have to later on in the project, they may be wise to take advantage of opportunities to have these people work together early on so that they can become familiar with each other. Finally, see the Snapshot in Practice: Managing Geeks for some interesting thoughts about how Novell, Inc., puts together teams.

Multiproject Resource Schedules

For clarity we have discussed key resource allocation issues within the context of a single project. In reality resource allocation generally occurs in a multiproject environment where the demands of one project have to be reconciled with the needs of other projects. Organizations must develop and manage systems for efficiently allocating and scheduling resources across several projects with different priorities, resource requirements, sets of activities, and risks. The system must be dynamic and capable of accommodating new projects as well as reallocating resources once project work is completed. While the same resource issues and principles that apply to a single project also apply to this multiproject environment, application and solutions are more complex, given the interdependency among projects.

The following lists three of the more common problems encountered in managing multiproject resource schedules. Note that these are macro manifestations of single-project problems that are now magnified in a multiproject environment:

1. **Overall schedule slippage.** Because projects often share resources, delays in one project can have a ripple effect and delay other projects. For example, work on one software development project can grind to a halt because the coders scheduled for the next critical task are late in completing their work on another development project.
2. **Inefficient resource utilization.** Because projects have different schedules and requirements, there are peaks and valleys in overall resource demands. For example, a firm may have a staff of 10 electricians to meet peak demands when, under normal conditions, only 5 electricians are required.
3. **Resource bottlenecks.** Delays and schedules are extended as a result of shortages of critical resources that are required by multiple projects. For example, at one Lattice Semiconductor facility, project schedules were delayed because of competition over access to test equipment necessary to debug programs. Likewise, several projects at a U.S. forest area were extended because there was only one silviculturist on the staff.

To deal with these problems, more and more companies create project offices or departments to oversee the scheduling of resources across multiple projects. One approach to multiple project resource scheduling is to use a first come–first served rule. A project queue system is created in which projects currently underway take precedence over new projects. New project schedules are based on the projected availability of resources. This queuing tends to lead to more reliable completion estimates and is preferred on contracted projects that have stiff penalties for being late. The disadvantages of this deceptively simple approach are that it does not optimally utilize resources or take into account the priority of the project. See the Snapshot from Practice: Multiple Project Resource Scheduling.

Many companies utilize more elaborate processes for scheduling resources to increase the capacity of the organization to initiate projects. Most of these methods approach the problem by treating individual projects as part of one big project and adapting the scheduling heuristics previously introduced to this "megaproject." Project schedulers monitor resource usage and provide updated schedules based on progress and resource availability across all projects. One major improvement in project management software in recent years is the ability to prioritize resource allocation to specific projects. Projects can be prioritized in ascending order (e.g., 1, 2, 3, 4, . . .), and these priorities will override scheduling heuristics so that resources go to the project highest on the priority list. (Note: This improvement fits perfectly with organizations that use project priority models similar to those described in Chapter 2.) Centralized project scheduling also makes it easier to identify resource bottlenecks that stifle progress on projects. Once identified, the impact of the bottlenecks can be documented and used to justify acquiring additional equipment, recruiting critical personnel, or delaying the project.

Finally, many companies are using outsourcing as a means for dealing with their resource allocation problems. In some cases, a company will reduce the number of projects they have to manage internally to only core projects and outsource

SNAPSHOT FROM PRACTICE Multiple Project Resource Scheduling

The case for a central source to oversee project resource scheduling is well known by practitioners. Here is a synopsis of a conversation with one middle manager.

Interviewer: Congratulations on acceptance of your multi-project scheduling proposal. Everyone tells me you were very convincing.

Middle Manager: Thanks. Gaining acceptance was easy this time. The board quickly recognized we have no choice if we are to keep ahead of competition by placing our resources on the right projects.

Interviewer: Have you presented this to the board before?

Middle Manager: Yes, but not this company. I presented the same spiel to the firm I worked for two years ago. For their annual review meeting I was charged to present a proposal suggesting the need and benefits of central capacity resource planning for managing the projects of the firm.

I tried to build a case for bringing projects under one umbrella to standardize practices and to forecast and assign key people to mission critical projects. I explained how benefits such as resource demands would be aligned with mission critical projects, proactive resource planning, and a tool for catching resource bottlenecks and resolving conflicts.

Almost everyone agreed the idea was a good one. I felt good about the presentation and felt confident something was going to happen. But the idea never really got off the ground; it just faded into the sunset.

With hindsight, managers really did not trust colleagues in other departments, so they only gave half-hearted support to central resource planning. Managers wanted to protect their turf and ensure that they would not have to give up power. The culture there was simply too inflexible for the world we live in today. They are still struggling with constant conflicts among projects.

I'm glad I made the switch to this firm. The culture here is much more team-oriented. Management is committed to improving performance.

noncritical projects to contractors and consulting firms. In other cases, specific segments of projects are outsourced to overcome resource deficiencies and scheduling problems. Companies may hire temporary workers to expedite certain activities that are falling behind schedule or contract project work during peak periods when there are insufficient internal resources to meet the demands of all projects. The ability to more efficiently manage the ebbs and flows of project work is one of the major driving forces behind outsourcing today.

Using the Resource Schedule to Develop a Project Cost Baseline

Once resource assignments have been finalized we are able to develop a baseline budget schedule for the project. Using your project schedule, you can *time-phase* work packages and assign them to their respective scheduled activities to develop a budget schedule over the life of your project. Understanding the reason for time-phasing your budget is very important. Without a time-phased budget good project schedule and cost control are impossible.

Why a Time-Phased Budget Baseline Is Needed

The need for a time-phased budget baseline is demonstrated in the following scenario. The development of a new product is to be completed in 10 weeks at an estimated cost of $400,000 per week for a total cost of $4 million. Management wants a status report at the end of five weeks. The following information has been collected:

- Planned costs for the first five weeks are $2,000,000.
- Actual costs for the first five weeks are $2,400,000.

How are we doing? It would be easy to draw the conclusion there is a $400,000 cost overrun. But we really have no way of knowing. The $400,000 may represent money spent to move the project ahead of schedule. Assume another set of data at the end of five weeks:

- Planned costs for the first five weeks are $2,000,000.
- Actual costs for the first five weeks are $1,700,000.

Is the project costing $300,000 less than we expected? Perhaps. But the $300,000 may represent the fact that the project is behind schedule and work has not started. Could it be the project is behind schedule and over cost? We cannot tell from these data. The many systems found in the real world that use only planned funds (a constant burn rate) and actual costs can provide false and misleading information. There is no way to be certain how much of the physical work has been accomplished. *These systems do not measure how much work was accomplished for the money spent! Hence, without time-phasing cost to match your project schedule, it is impossible to have reliable information for control purposes.*

Creating a Time-Phased Budget

By using information from your WBS and resource schedule, you can create a time-phased cost baseline. Remember from the WBS for the PC Project in Chapters 4 and 5 we integrated the WBS and OBS organization breakdown structure so the work packages could be tracked by deliverable and organization responsible. See Figure 8.12 for an example of the PC Prototype Project arranged by deliverable and organization unit responsible. For each intersection point of the WBS/OBS matrix, you see work package budgets and the total cost. The total cost at each intersection is called a cost or control account. For example, at the intersection of the Read/write head deliverable and the Production department we see there are three work packages with a total budget of $200,000. The sum of all cost accounts in a column should represent the total costs for the deliverable. Conversely, the sum of the cost accounts in a row should represent the costs or budget for the organizational unit responsible to accomplish the work. You can continue to "roll up" costs on the WBS/OBS to total project costs. This WBS provides the information you can use to time phase work packages and assign them to their respective scheduled activities over the life of the project.

Recall, from the development of your work breakdown structure for each work package, the following information needed to be developed:

1. Define work (what).
2. Identify time to complete a work package (how long).
3. Identify a time-phased budget to complete a work package (cost).
4. Identify resources needed to complete a work package (how much).
5. Identify a single person responsible for units of work (who).
6. Identify monitoring points for measuring progress (how well).

Number three, time-phasing the work package, is critical for the final step of creating your budget baseline. The process of time-phasing work packages, which is illustrated next, is demonstrated in Figure 8.13. The work package has a duration of three weeks. Assuming labor, materials, and equipment are tracked separately, the work package costs for labor are distributed over the three weeks as they are expected to occur—$40,000, $30,000, and $50,000 for each week, respectively. When

FIGURE 8.12 **Direct Labor Budget Rollup ($000)**

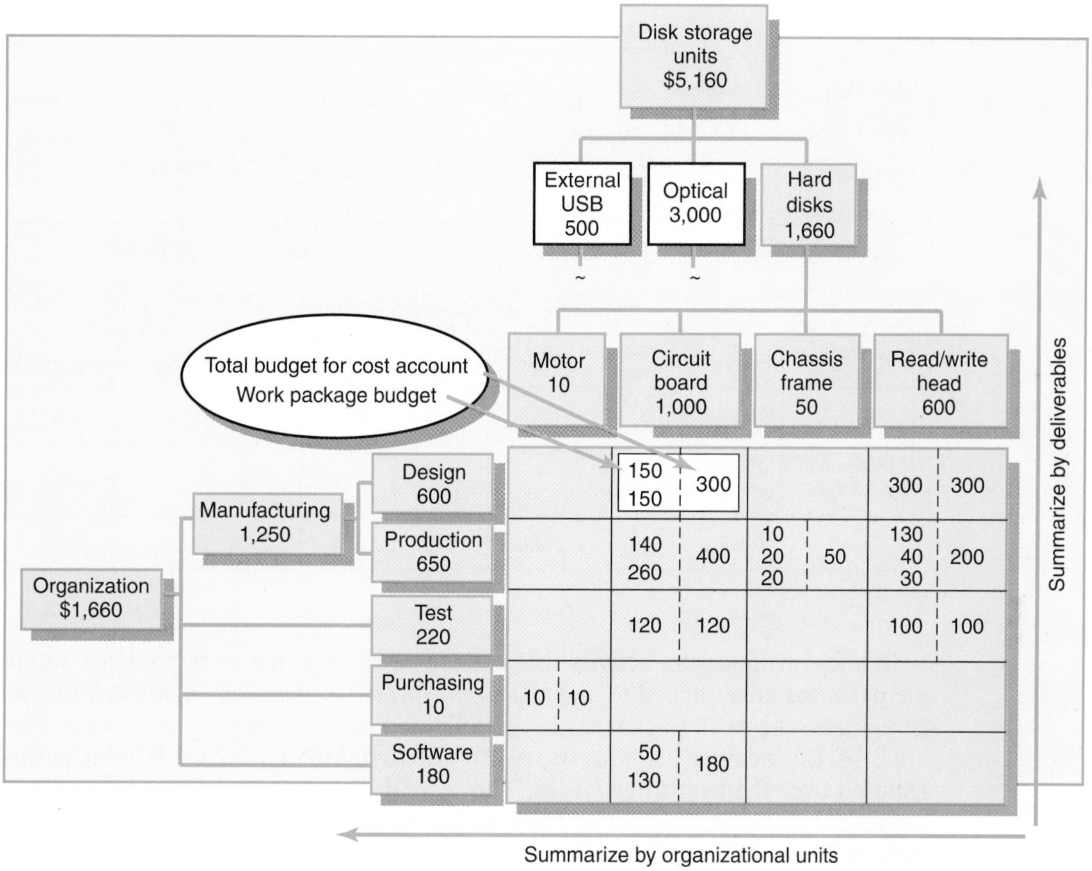

the three-week work package is placed in the network schedule, the costs are distributed to the time-phased budget for the same three scheduled weeks. Fortunately, most single WPs become an activity and the process of distributing costs is relatively simple. That is, the relationship is one-for-one. Such budget timing is directly from the work package to the activity.

FIGURE 8.13 **Time-Phased Work Package Budget (labor cost only)**

Time-Phased Work Package Budget
Labor cost only

Work Package Description *Test*

Page *1* of *1*

Work Package ID ***1.1.3.2.3***

Project *PC Prototype*

Deliverable *Circuit board*

Date *3/24/xx*

Responsible organization unit *Test*

Estimator *CEG*

Work Package Duration *3* weeks

Total labor cost *$120,000*

Time-Phased Labor Budget ($000)

Work Package	Resource	Labor rate	Work Periods--Weeks					
			1	2	3	4	5	Total
Code ***1.1.3.2.3***	Quality testers	$xxxx/ week	$40	$30	$50			$120

FIGURE 8.14
Two Time-Phased Work Packages (labor cost only)

Time-Phased Work Package Budget
Labor cost only

Work Package Description *Software*
Page *1* of *1*
Work Package ID ***1.1.3.2.4.1 and 1.1.3.2.4.2***
Project *PC Prototype*
Deliverable *Circuit board*
Date *3/24/xx*
Responsible organization unit *Software*
Estimator *LGG*
Work Package Duration *4* weeks
Total labor cost *$180,000*

Time-Phased Labor Budget ($000)

Work Package	Resource	Labor rate	Work Periods--Weeks					
			1	2	3	4	5	Total
Code ***1.1.3.2.4.1***	Program'rs	$2,000/ week	$20	$15	$15			$50
Integration ***1.1.3.2.4.2***	System/ program'rs	$2,500/ week			$60	$70		$130
Total			$20	$15	$75	$70		$180

In a few instances an activity will include more than one work package, where the packages are assigned to *one responsible person or department and deliverable.* In this case the work packages are consolidated into one activity. As seen in Figure 8.14, this activity includes two WPs. The first, WP-1.1.3.2.4.1 (Code), is distributed over the first three weeks. The second, WP-1.1.3.2.4.2 (Integration), is sequenced over weeks 3 and 4. The activity duration is four weeks. When the activity is placed in the schedule, the costs are distributed starting with the schedule start—$20,000, $15,000, $75,000, and $70,000, respectively.

These time-phased budgets for work packages are lifted from your WBS and are placed in your project schedule as they are expected to occur over the life of the project. The outcome of these budget allocations is the project *cost* baseline (also called **planned value**—PV), which is used to determine cost and schedule variances as the project is implemented.

Figure 8.15 shows the Patient Entry Project network schedule, which is used to place the time-phased work packages' budgets in the baseline. Figure 8.16 presents the project time-phased budget for the Patient Entry Project and the cumulative graph of the project budget baseline. In this figure you can see how the time-phased work package costs were placed into the network and how the cumulative project budget graph for a project is developed. Notice that costs do not have to be distributed linearly, but the costs should be placed as you expect them to occur.

You have now developed complete time and cost plans for your project. These project baselines will be used to compare planned schedule and costs using an integrative system called *earned value*. The application and use of project baselines to measure performance are discussed in detail in Chapter 13. With your project budget baseline established, you are also able to generate cash flow statements for your project like the one presented in Figure 8.17. Such statements prepare the firm to cover costs over the lifespan of the project. Finally, with resource assignments finalized you are able to generate resource usage schedules for your project (see Figure 8.18). These schedules map out the full deployment of personnel and equipment and can be used to generate individual work schedules.

FIGURE 8.15 **Patient Entry Project Network**

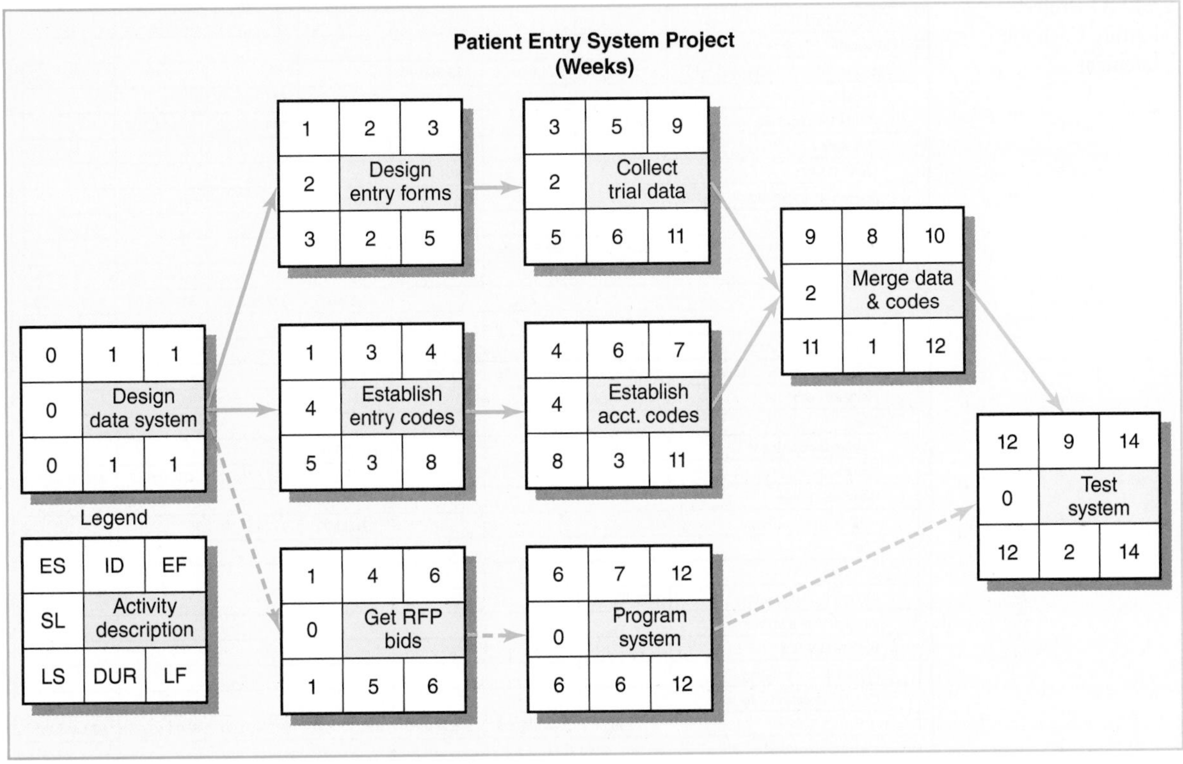

FIGURE 8.16 **Patient Entry Time-Phased Work Packages Assigned**

($000) Week

ID	Dur.	Task	Budget	1	2	3	4	5	6	7	8	9	10	11	12	13	14
1	1	Design data system	5	5													
2	2	Design entry forms	4		2	2											
3	3	Establish entry codes	6		2	2	2										
4	5	Get RFP bids	3		2				1								
5	6	Collect trial data	6				1	1	1	1	1	1					
6	3	Establish account codes	5					2	2	1							
7	6	Program system	12							2		4	2		4		
8	1	Merge data & codes	4										4				
9	2	Test system	7													4	3
		Week total	52	5	6	4	3	3	4	4	1	5	6	0	4	4	3
		Cumulative		5	11	15	18	21	25	29	30	35	41	41	45	49	52

FIGURE 8.17
CEBOO Project Monthly Cash Flow Statement

	January	February	March	April	May	June	July
CEBOO Project							
Hardware							
Hardware specifications	$11,480.00	$24,840.00	$3,360.00				
Hardware design			$23,120.00	$29,920.00	$14,960.00		
Hardware documentation					$14,080.00	$24,320.00	
Prototypes							
Order GXs							
Assemble preproduction models							
Operating system							
Kernel specifications	$5,320.00	$9,880.00					
Drivers							
OC drivers				$3,360.00	$12,320.00	$11,760.00	$12,880.00
Serial VO drivers							
Memory management							
Operating system documentation		$10,240.00	$21,760.00				
Network interface							
Utilities							
Utilities specifications				$8,400.00			
Routine utilities				$5,760.00	$21,120.00	$20,160.00	$10,560.00
Complex utilities							
Utilities documentation				$7,680.00	$17,920.00		
Shell							
System integration							
Architectural decisions	$20,400.00						
Integration first phase							
System H/S test							
Project documentation							
Integration acceptance test							
Total	$37,200.00	$44,960.00	$48,240.00	$55,120.00	$80,400.00	$56,240.00	$23,440.00

FIGURE 8.18
CEBOO Project Weekly Resource Usage Schedule

	12/30	1/6	1/13	1/20	1/27	2/03
I. Suzuki	24 hrs	40 hrs	40 hrs	40 hrs	40 hrs	40 hrs
Hardware specifications				24 hrs	40 hrs	40 hrs
Hardware design						
Hardware documentation						
Operating system documentation						
Utilities documentation						
Architectural decisions	24 hrs	40 hrs	40 hrs	16 hrs		
J. Lopez	24 hrs	40 hrs	40 hrs	40 hrs	40 hrs	40 hrs
Hardware specifications				12 hrs	20 hrs	20 hrs
Hardware design						
Prototypes						
Kernel specifications				12 hrs	20 hrs	20 hrs
Utilities specifications						
Architectural decisions	24 hrs	40 hrs	40 hrs	16 hrs		
Integration first phase						
J.J. Putz				24 hrs	40 hrs	40 hrs
Hardware documentation						
Kernel specifications				24 hrs	40 hrs	40 hrs
Operating system documentation						
Utilities documentation						
Project documentation						
R. Sexon				24 hrs	40 hrs	40 hrs
Hardware specifications				24 hrs	40 hrs	40 hrs
Prototypes						
Assemble preproduction models						
OC drivers						
Complex utilities						
Integration first phase						
System H/S test						
Integration acceptance test						

Summary

Usage and availability of resources are major problem areas for project managers. Attention to these areas in developing a project schedule can point out resource bottlenecks before the project begins. Project managers should understand the ramifications of failing to schedule resources. The results of resource scheduling are frequently significantly different from the results of the standard CPM method.

With the rapid changes in technology and emphasis on time-to-market, catching resource usage and availability problems before the project starts can save the costs of crashing project activities later. Any resource deviations from plan and schedule that occur when the project is being implemented can be quickly recorded and the effect noted. Without this immediate update capability, the real negative effect of a change may not be known until it happens. Tying resource availability to a multiproject, multiresource system supports a project priority process that selects projects by their contribution to the organization's objectives and strategic plan.

Assignment of individuals to projects may not fit well with those assigned by computer software routines. In these cases overriding the computer solution to accommodate individual differences and skills is almost always the best choice.

The project resource schedule is important because it serves as your time baseline, which is used for measuring time differences between plan and actual. The resource schedule serves as the basis for developing your time-phased project cost budget baseline. The baseline (planned value, PV) is the sum of the cost accounts, and each cost account is the sum of the work packages in the cost account. Remember, if your budgeted costs are not time-phased, you really have no reliable way to measure performance. Although there are several types of project costs, the cost baseline is usually limited to direct costs (such as labor, materials, equipment) that are under the control of the project manager; other indirect costs can be added to project costs separately.

Key Terms

Heuristic, *258*
Leveling, *256*
Planned value (PV), *276*
Resource-constrained projects, *255*
Resource smoothing, *252*
Splitting, *268*
Time-constrained projects, *255*
Time-phased budget baseline, *251*

Review Questions

1. How does resource scheduling tie to project priority?
2. How does resource scheduling reduce flexibility in managing projects?
3. Present six reasons scheduling resources is an important task.
4. How can outsourcing project work alleviate the three most common problems associated with multiproject resource scheduling?
5. Explain the risks associated with leveling resources, compressing or crashing projects, and imposed durations or "catch-up" as the project is being implemented.
6. Why is it critical to develop a time-phased baseline?

Exercises

1. Given the network plan that follows, compute the early, late, and slack times. What is the project duration? Using any approach you wish (e.g., trial and error), develop a loading chart for resources, Electrical Engineers (EE), and resource, Mechanical Engineers (ME). Assume only one of each resource exists. Given your resource schedule, compute the early, late, and slack times for your project. Which activities are now critical? What is the project duration now? Could something like this happen in real projects?

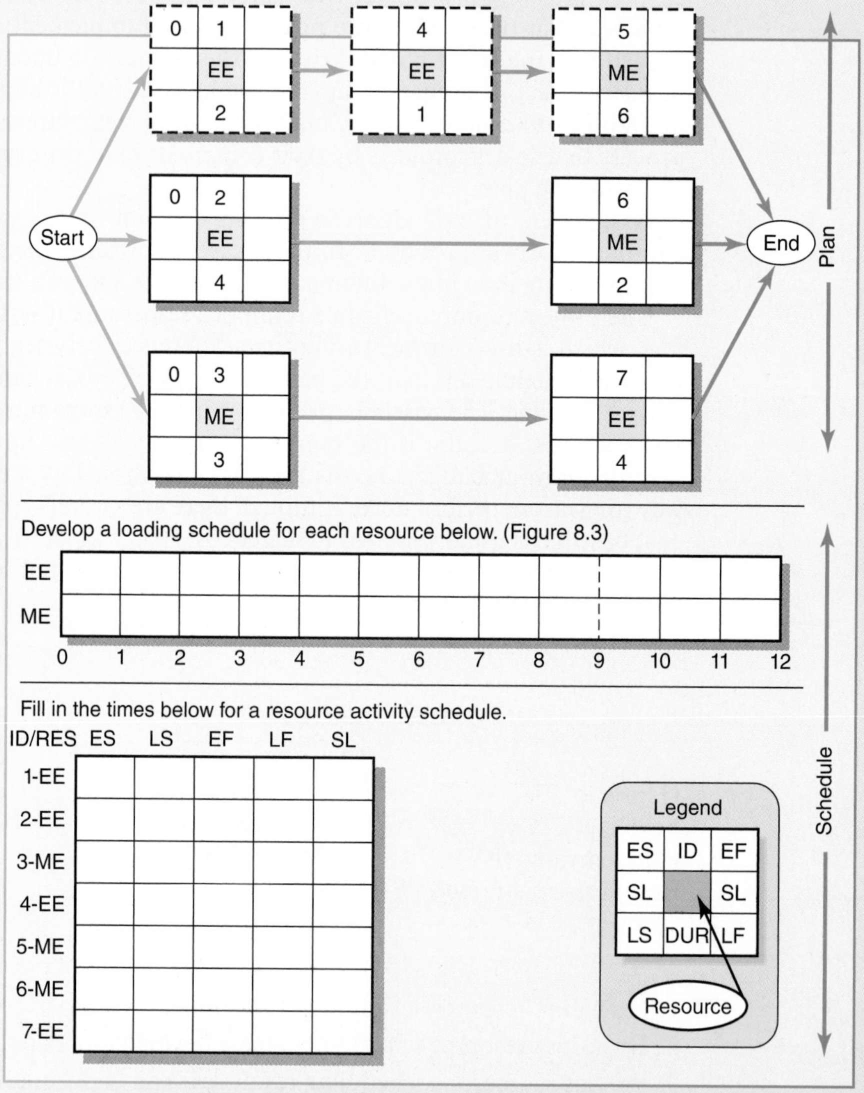

2. Given the network plan that follows, compute the early, late, and slack times. What is the project duration? Using any approach you wish (e.g., trial and error), develop a loading chart for resources Carpenters (C) and Electricians (E). Assume only one Carpenter is available and two Electricians are available.

Given your resource schedule, compute the early, late, and slack times for your project. Which activities are now critical? What is the project duration now?

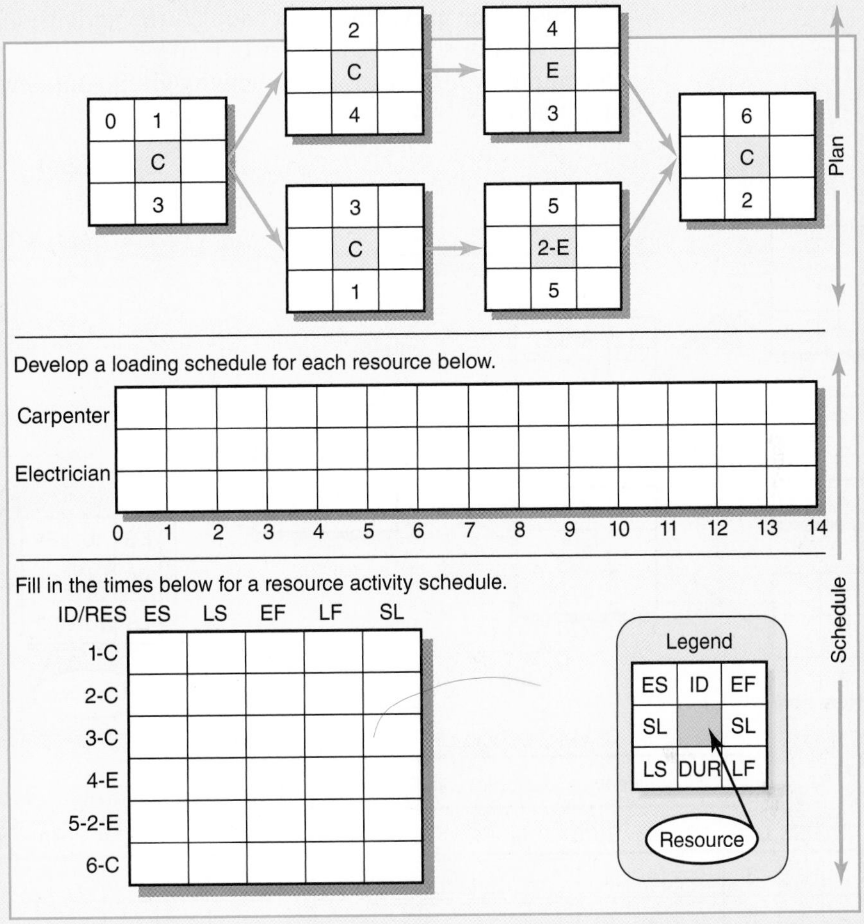

3. Compute the early, late, and slack times for the activities in the network that follows, assuming a time-constrained network. Which activities are critical? What is the time-constrained project duration?

   Note: Recall, in the schedule resource load chart the *time-constrained* scheduling interval (ES through LF) has been shaded. Any resource scheduled beyond the shaded area will delay the project.

   Assume you have only three resources and you are using a computer that uses software that schedules projects by the parallel method and following heuristics. Schedule only one period at a time!

   Minimum slack

   Smallest duration

   Lowest identification number

Keep a log of each activity change and update you make each period—e.g., period 0–1, 1–2, 2–3, etc. (Use a format similar to the one on page 259.) The log should include any changes or updates in ES and slack times each period, activities scheduled, and activities delayed. (Hint: Remember to maintain the technical dependencies of the network.) Use the resource load chart to assist you in scheduling (see pages 260–261—Figures 8.4 and 8.5).

List the order in which you scheduled the activities of the project. Which activities of your schedule are now critical?

Recompute your slack for each activity given your new schedule. What is the slack for activity 1? 4? 5?

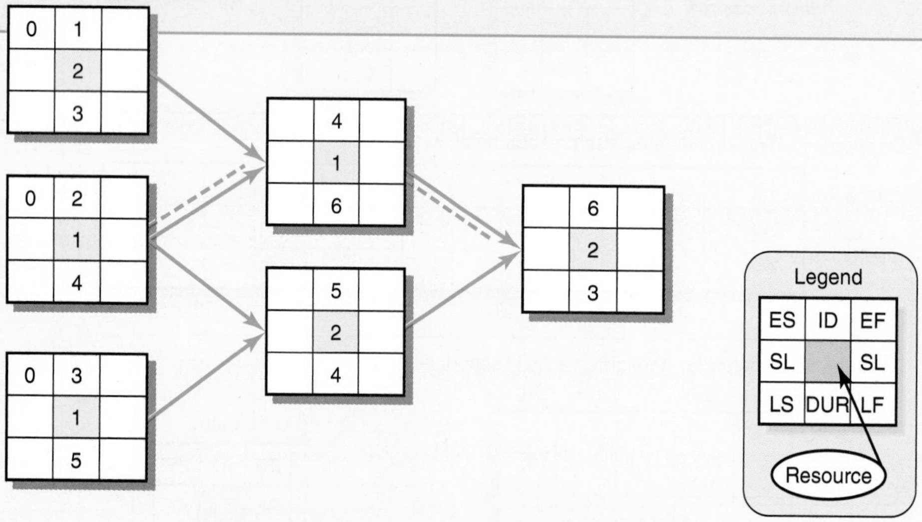

Scheduled resource load chart with ES and slack updates

ID	RES	DUR	ES	LF	SL	0–1	1–2	2–3	3–4	4–5	5–6	6–7	7–8	8–9	9–10	10–11	11–12	12–13	13–14	14–15
1	2	3	0	4	1															
2	1	4	0	4	0															
3	1	5	0	6	1															
4	1	6	4	10	0															
5	2	4	5	10	1															
6	2	3	10	13	0															
Resources scheduled																				
Resources available						3	3	3	3	3	3	3	3	3	3	3	3	3	3	3

4.*You have prepared the following schedule for a project in which the key resources is a tractor. There are three tractors available to the project. Activities A and D require one tractor to complete while activities B, C, E and F require 2 tractors.

Develop a resource-constrained schedule in the loading chart that follows. Use the parallel method and heuristics given. Be sure to update each period as the computer would do. Record the early start (ES), late finish (LF) and slack (SL) for the new schedule.

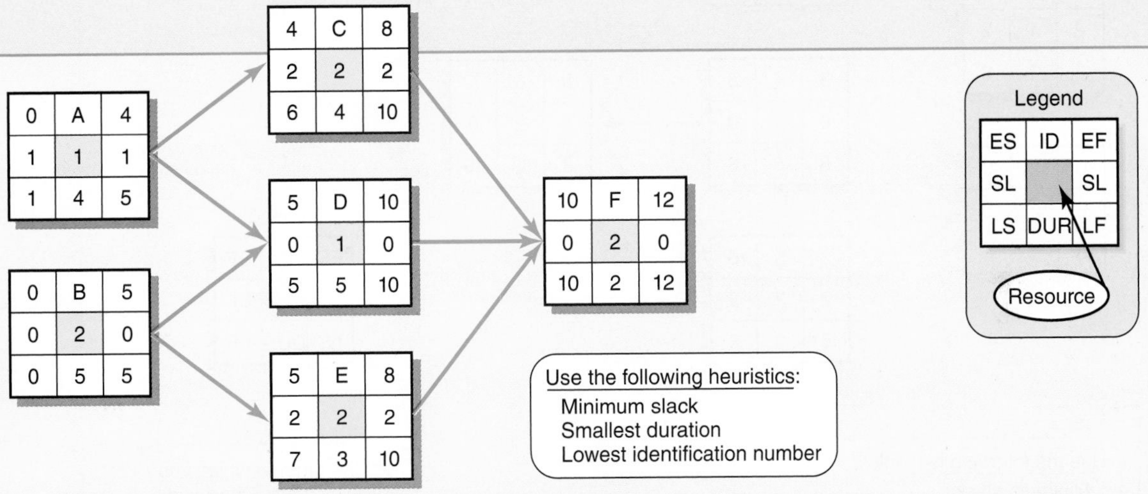

ID	RES	DUR	ES	LF	SL	0	1	2	3	4	5	6	7	8	9	10	11	12	13	14
A	1	4																		
B	2	5																		
C	2	4																		
D	1	5																		
E	2	3																		
F	2	2																		
Resources scheduled																				
Resources available						3	3	3	3	3	3	3	3	3	3	3	3	3	3	3

*The solution to this exercise can be found in Appendix 1.

5. Develop a resource schedule in the loading chart that follows. Use the parallel method and heuristics given. Be sure to update each period as the computer would do. Note: activities 2, 3, 5, and 6 use two of the resource skills. Three of the resource skills are available. How has slack changed for each activity? Has the risk of being late changed? How?

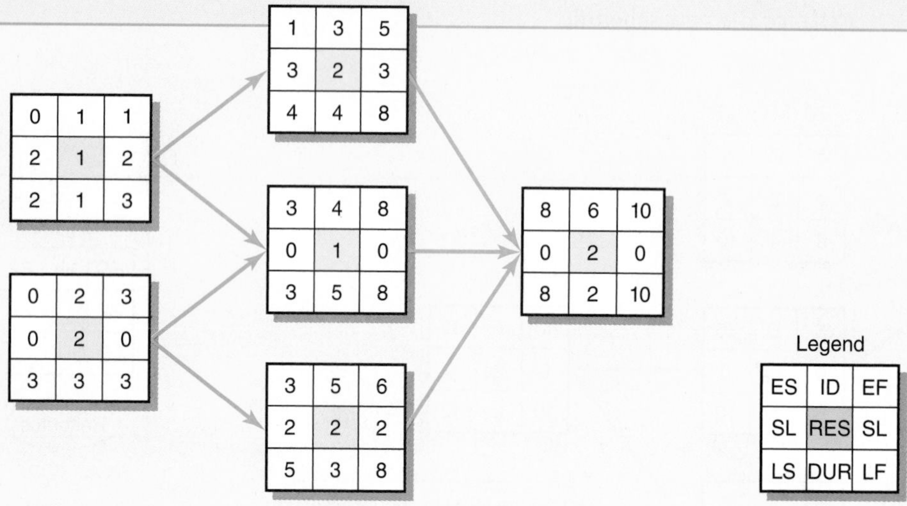

Use the following heuristics:
- Minimum slack
- Smallest duration
- Lowest identification number

List the order in which your activities are scheduled
/_____/_____/_____/
/_____/_____/_____/

ID	RES	DUR	ES	LF	SL	0	1	2	3	4	5	6	7	8	9	10	11	12	13
1	1	1	0	3															
2	2	3	0	3															
3	2	4	1	8															
4	1	5	3	8															
5	2	3																	
6	2	2																	
Resources scheduled																			
Resources available						3	3	3	3	3	3	3	3	3	3	3	3	3	

What is the schedule slack for 1_____, 3_____, and 4_____?
Which activities are critical now? ____________________

6. You have prepared the following schedule for a project in which the key resource is a backhoe. This schedule is contingent on having 3 backhoes. You receive a call from your partner, Brooker, who desperately needs 1 of your backhoes.

You tell Brooker you would be willing to let him have the backhoe if you are still able to complete your project in 11 months.

Develop a resource schedule in the loading chart that follows to see if it is possible to complete the project in 11 months with only 2 backhoes. Be sure to record the order in which you schedule the activities using scheduling heuristics. Activities 5 and 6 require 2 backhoes, while activities 1, 2, 3, and 4 require 1 backhoe. No splitting of activities is possible. Can you say yes to Brooker's request?

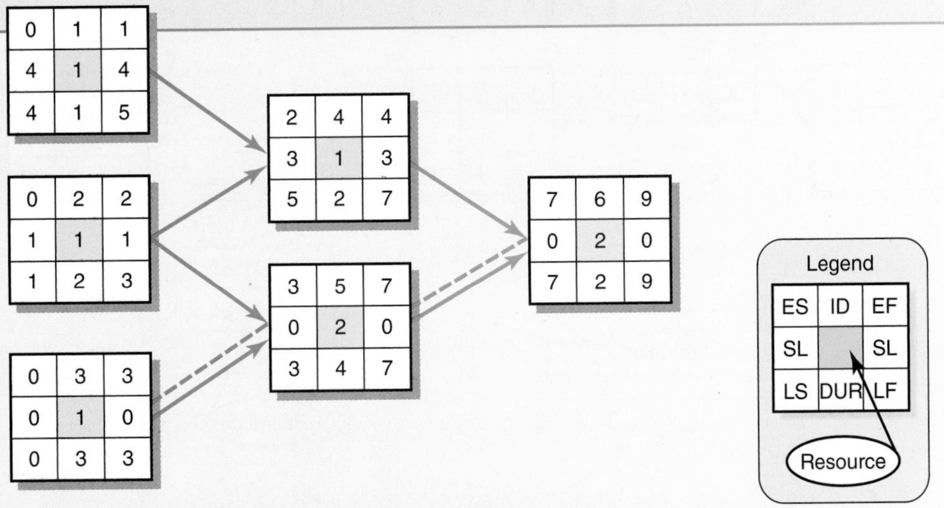

Schedule the resource load chart with ES and Slack updates

ID	RES	DUR	ES	LF	SL	0	1	2	3	4	5	6	7	8	9	10	11	12	13
1	1	1	0	5	4														
2	1	2	0	3	1														
3	1	3	0	3	0														
4	1	2	2	7	3														
5	2	4	3	7	0														
6	2	2	7	9	0														
Resources scheduled																			
Resources available						2	2	2	2	2	2	2	2	2	2	2	2	2	

7.*You are one of three carpenters assigned to complete a short construction project. Right before the start of the project, one of your fellow carpenters was hospitalized and will not be available to work on the project.

Develop a resource-constrained schedule in the loading chart that follows to see how long the project will take with only 2 carpenters. Be sure to record the

*The solution to this exercise can be found in Appendix 1.

order in which you schedule the activities using the scheduling heuristics. Activities A, B, C, D, E, G, and H require 2 carpenters to complete. Activity F requires only 1 carpenter. No splitting of activities is possible.

You will receive a bonus if the project is completed within 15 days. Should you start planning how you will spend your bonus?

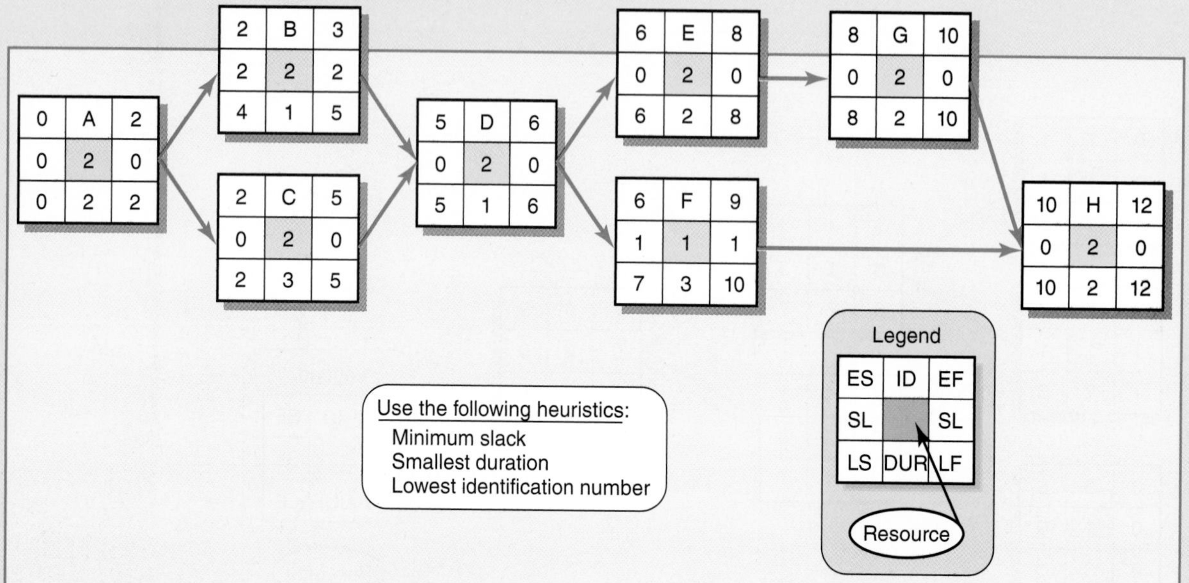

ID	RES	DUR	ES	LF	SL	0	1	2	3	4	5	6	7	8	9	10	11	12	13	14	15	16	17
A	2	2																					
B	2	1																					
C	2	3																					
D	2	1																					
E	2	2																					
F	1	3																					
G	2	2																					
H	2	2																					
Resources scheduled																							
Resources available						2	2	2	2	2	2	2	2	2	2	2	2	2	2	2	2	2	2

8. Given the time-phased work packages, complete the baseline budget form for the project.

Time-phased budget ($ 000)

Week

Task	Budget	1	2	3	4	5	6	7	8	9	10
Activity 1	4	4									
Activity 2	6		1	3	2						
Activity 3	10		2	4	2	2					
Activity 4	8						2	3	3		
Activity 5	3									2	1
Total	31										
Cumulative											

9. Given the time-phased work packages and network, complete the baseline budget form for the project.

Market Survey Project

WBS Work Package Cost by Week

WP Design	4	5	2			
WP Survey	2	2	4	4	4	5
WP Report	3	3	2			

Project Network

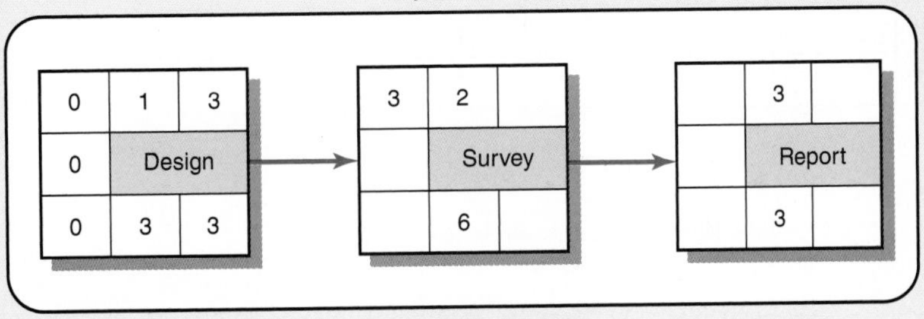

Time-Phased Budget

Week

Task	Budget	1	2	3	4	5	6	7	8	9	10	11	12
Design	11	4	5	2									
Survey	21												
Report	8												
Total	40												
Cumulative													

10.* Given the time-phased work packages and network, complete the baseline budget form for the project.

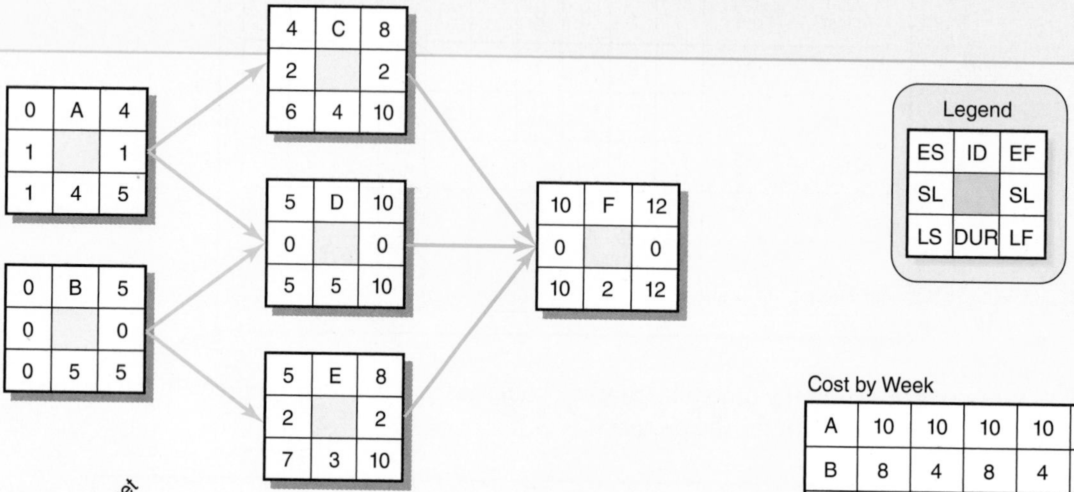

Cost by Week

A	10	10	10	10	
B	8	4	8	4	8
C	12	12	12	12	
D	6	2	2	2	6
E	8	8	12		
F	20	20			

ID	Budget	0	1	2	3	4	5	6	7	8	9	10	11	12
A	40													
B	32													
C	48													
D	18													
E	28													
F	40													
Total	206													
Cumulative														

*The solution to this exercise can be found in Appendix 1.

11. Given the time-phased work packages and network, complete the baseline budget form for the project.

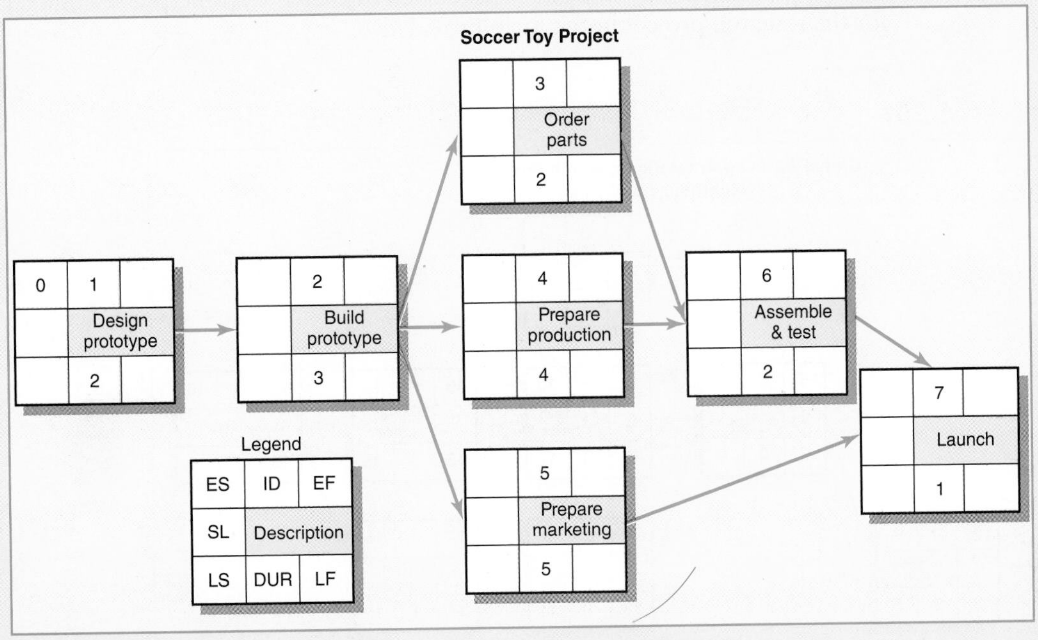

Soccer Toy Project

Cost by Week ($000)

	←1	←2	←3	←4	←5
Design prototype	12	12			
Build prototype	10	10	10		
Order parts	5	5			
Prepare production	16	10	22	16	
Prepare marketing	6	6	0	6	12
Assemble & test	18	18			
Launch	12				

Time-phased Budget ($000)

Week

	Budget	0	1	2	3	4	5	6	7	8	9	10	11	12	13
Design prototype	24														
Build prototype	30														
Order parts	10														
Prepare prod'n	64														
Prepare market'g	30														
Assemble & test	36														
Launch	12														
Total	206														
Cumulative															

12. The National Oceanic Research Institute is planning a research study on global warming in Antarctica. The 16-month network schedule is presented below. It is followed by budgets for each activity. Create a time-phased budget for the research project in the form provided.

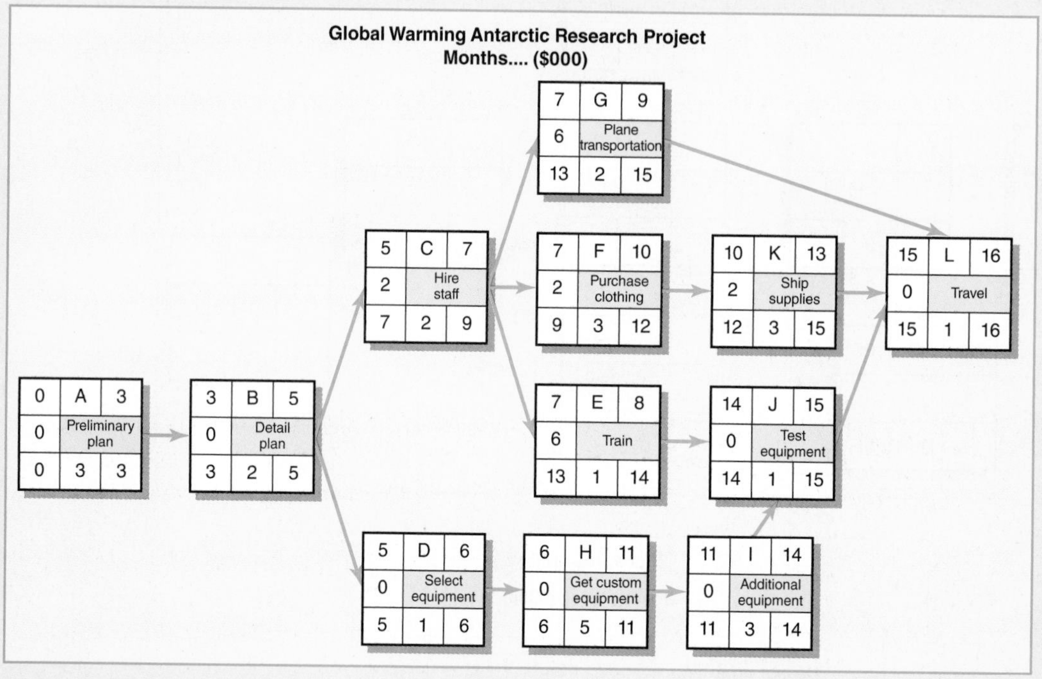

Global Warming Antarctic Research Project
Activity Time Phased Work Packages by Month ($000)

	Task	Duration	Budget	0	1	2	3	4	5	6
A	Preliminary plan	3	3	1	1	1				
B	Detail plan	2	2	1	1					
C	Hire staff	2	4	4						
D	Select equipment	1	5	5						
E	Train	1	3	3						
F	Purchase clothing	3	9	3	0	6				
G	Plane transportation	2	60	5	55					
H	Get custom equipment	5	36	5	5	10	10	6		
I	Additional equipment	3	20	10	5	5				
J	Test equipment	1	6	6						
K	Ship all supplies	5	15	3	3	0	0	9		
L	Travel	1	9	9						
	Total budget		172							

References

Arrow, K. J., and L. Hurowicz, *Studies in Resource Allocation Process* (New York: Cambridge University Press, 1997).

Brucker, P., A. Drexl, R. Mohring, L. Newmann, and E. Pesch, "Resource-constrained Project Scheduling: Notation, Classification, Models and Methods," *European Journal of Operational Research,* Vol. 112, 1999, pp. 3–42.

Burgess, A. R., and J. B. Kellebrew, "Variations in Activity Level on Cyclical Arrow Diagrams," *Journal of Industrial Engineering,* Vol. 13, March–April 1962, pp. 76–83.

Charnes, A., and W. W. Cooper, "A Network Interpretation and Direct Sub Dual Algorithm for Critical Path Scheduling," *Journal of Industrial Engineering,* July–August 1962.

Demeulemeester, E. L., and W. S. Herroelen, *Project Scheduling: A Research Handbook* (Norwell, Mass: Kluwer Academic Publishers, 2002).

Fendly, L. G., "Towards the Development of a Complete Multi Project Scheduling System," *Journal of Industrial Engineering,* Vol. 19, 1968, pp. 505–15.

Goldratt, E., *Critical Chain* (Great Barrington, MA: North River Press, 1997).

Newbold, R. C., "Leveraging Project Resources: Tools for the Next Century," *Proceedings of 28th Annual Project Management Institute, 1997 Seminars and Symposium* (Newtown, PA: Project Management Institute, 1997), pp. 417–21.

Pascoe, T. L., "An Experimental Comparison of Heuristic Methods for Allocating Resources," Ph.D. dissertation, University of Cambridge, United Kingdom, 1965.

Reinersten, D., "Is It Always a Bad Idea to Add Resources to a Late Project?" *Electric Design,* October 30, 2000, pp. 17–18.

Talbot, B. F., and J. H. Patterson, "Optimal Methods for Scheduling Under Resource Constraints," *Project Management Journal,* December 1979.

Wiest, J. D., "A Heuristic Model for Scheduling Large Projects with Unlimited Resources," *Management Science,* Vol. 18, February 1967, pp. 359–77.

Woodworth, B. M., and C. J. Willie, "A Heuristic Algorithm for Resource Leveling in Multiproject, Multiresource Scheduling," *Decision Sciences,* Vol. 6, July 1975, pp. 525–40.

Woodworth, B. M., and S. Shanahan, "Identifying the Critical Sequence in a Resource Constrained Project," *International Journal of Project Management,* Vol. 6, 1988, pp. 89–96.

Case

Power Train, Ltd.

We have smashing systems for reporting, tracking, and controlling costs on design projects. Our planning of projects is better than any I have seen at other companies. Our scheduling seemed to serve us well when we were small and we had only a few projects. Now that we have many more projects and schedule using multiproject software, there are too many occasions when the right people are not assigned to the projects deemed important to our success. This situation is costing us big money, headaches, and stress!

Claude Jones, VP, Design and Operations

HISTORY

Power Train, Ltd. (PT), was founded in 1970 by Daniel Gage, a skilled mechanical engineer and machinist. Prior to founding PT he worked for three years as design engineer for a company that designed and built transmissions for military tanks and trucks. It was a natural transition for Dan to start a company designing and building power trains for farm tractor companies. Today, Dan is no longer active in the management of PT but is still revered as its founder. He and his family still own 25 percent of the company, which went public in 1998. PT has been growing at a 6 percent clip for the last five years but expects industry growth to level off as supply exceeds demand.

Today, PT continues its proud tradition of designing and building the best-quality power trains for manufacturers of farm tractors and equipment. The company employs 178 design engineers and has about 1,800 production and support staff. Contract design projects for tractor manufacturers represent a major portion of PT's revenue. At any given time, about 45 to 60 design projects are going on concurrently. A small portion of their design work is for military vehicles. PT only accepts military contracts that involve very advanced, new technology and are cost plus.

A new phenomenon has attracted management of PT to look into a larger market. Last year a large Swedish truck manufacturer approached PT to consider designing power trains for its trucks. As the industry consolidates, the opportunities for PT should increase because these large firms are moving to more outsourcing to cut infrastructure costs and stay very flexible. Only last week a PT design engineer spoke to a German truck manufacturing manager at a conference. The German manager was already exploring outsourcing of drive trains to Porsche and was very pleased to be reminded of PT's expertise in the area. A meeting is set up for next month.

CLAUDE JONES

Claude Jones joined PT in 1999 as a new MBA from the University of Edinburgh. He worked as a mechanical engineer for U.K. Hydraulics for five years prior to returning to school for the MBA. "I just wanted to be part of the management team and where the action is." Jones moved quickly through the ranks. Today he is the vice president of design and operations. Sitting at his desk, Jones is pondering the conflicts and confusion that seem to be increasing in scheduling people to projects. He gets a real rush at the thought of designing power trains for large trucks; however, given their current project scheduling problems, a large increase in business would only compound their problems. Somehow these conflicts in scheduling have to be resolved before any serious thought can be given to expanding into design of power transmissions for truck manufacturers.

Jones is thinking of the problems PT had in the last year. The MF project is the first to come to mind. The project was not terribly complex and did not require their best design engineers. Unfortunately, the scheduling software assigned one of the most creative and expensive engineers to the MF project. A similar situation, but reversed, happened on the Deer project. This project involved a big customer and new hydrostatic technology for small tractors. In this project the scheduling software assigned engineers who were not familiar with small tractor transmissions. Somehow, thinks Jones, the right people need to be scheduled to the right projects. Upon reflection, this problem with scheduling has been increasing since PT went to multiproject scheduling. Maybe a project office is needed to keep on top of these problems.

A meeting with the information technology team and software vendors was positive but not very helpful because these people are not really into detailed scheduling problems. The vendors provided all sorts of evidence suggesting the heuristics used—least slack, shortest duration, and identification number—are absolutely efficient in scheduling people and minimizing project delays. One project software vendor, Lauren, kept saying their software would allow PT to customize the scheduling of projects and people to almost any variation selected. Lauren repeated over and over, "If the standard heuristics do not meet your requirements, create your own heuristics that do." Lauren even volunteered to assist in setting up the system. But she is not willing to spend time on the problem until PT can describe to her exactly what criteria will be used (and their sequence) to select and schedule people to projects.

WHAT NEXT?

Potential expansion into the truck power train business is not feasible until the confusion in project scheduling is solved or reduced significantly. Jones is ready to tackle this problem, but he is not sure where to start.

Appendix 8.1

The Critical-Chain Approach

In practice, project managers carefully manage slack on sensitive resource-limited projects. If possible, they will add slack at the end of the project by committing to a completion date that goes beyond the scheduled date. For example, the plans say the project should be completed on April 1, although the official completion date is May 1. Other managers take a more aggressive approach to managing slack within the schedule. They use an early start schedule and prohibit use of slack on any activity or work package to be used unless authorized by the project manager. Progress by percent complete and by remaining time are carefully monitored. Activities that are beating estimated completion times are reported so that succeeding activities can start ahead of schedule. This ensures that the time gained is used to start a succeeding activity earlier and time is not wasted. The overall intent is to create and save slack as a time buffer to complete the project early or to cover delay problems that may creep up on critical activities or paths.

Eliyahu Goldratt, who championed the "theory of constraints" in his popular book *The Goal,* advocates an alternative approach to managing slack.[1] He has coined the term "critical-chain" to recognize that the project network may be constrained by both resource and technical dependencies. Each type of constraint can create task dependencies, and in the case of resource constraints, new task dependencies can be created! Remember how resource constraints shifted the critical path? If not, visit Figure 8.5 again. The critical chain refers to the longest string of dependencies that exist on the project. Chain is used instead of path, since the latter tends to be associated with just technical dependencies not resource dependencies.

[1] E. Goldratt, *The Goal* (Great Barrington, MA: North River Press, 1997).

SNAPSHOT FROM PRACTICE — Critical Chain Applied to Airplane Part Arrivals*

In the past Spirit Aero Systems, manufacturer of airplane parts, were forced to delay product development projects as a result of missing parts for assemblies. Spirit management cycled through several approaches, such as lean, value chain, cycle time reduction, knowledge based engineering, to reduce the problem. Although each yielded minor improvements, the impacts were not substantial. Rework, overtime, delay costs, and vendor expediting costs continued to have significant impact on costs, meeting commitments, and reputation. Spirit turned to critical chain management methodology in a pilot project.

Joseph Zenisek, the critical chain manager, said the choice of critical chain was "a game changer for us." Spirit applied the critical chain approach to assembly of newly designed pylons (brackets) used for failure destruction testing of casings for a jet engine project. Zenisek credited success to three key factors:

- Creating a rule to never start a work package until all parts and staff are available.
- Ensuring part buffers to cover work packages by vigilantly monitoring assembly parts that use a large number of parts or where rate or number used is high.
- Developing a small engineering team to manage vendors and buffers to ensure that delivery of over 300 parts arrived on time.

The critical chain program led to impressive results. The parts and staffing rule cut down on late deliveries and rework on partially completed work packages caused by missing parts. The result was a reduction of 50 percent in overtime. Reducing delays reduced assembly cycle time by 18 percent. Work in process and work packages were also reduced since availability of buffer parts avoided delays. The critical chain method led to better resource management and reduced stress.

Given the success of the critical chain program, Spirit intends to expand the application of the critical chain method to new product development projects for their clients.

*Peter Fretty, "E Is in the Air," *PMNetwork,* February 2012, Vol. 26, No. 2, pp. 50–56.

All buffers reduce the risk of the project duration being late and increase the chance of early project completion.[2] See Snapshot from Practice: Critical Chain Applied to Airplane Part Arrivals.

CRITICAL-CHAIN VERSUS TRADITIONAL SCHEDULING APPROACH

To illustrate how CCPM affects scheduling let's compare it with the traditional approach to project scheduling. We will first resolve resource problems the way described in Chapter 8 and then the CCPM method. Figure A8.1A shows the *planned* Air Control project network without any concern for resources. That is, activities are assumed to be independent and resources will be made available and/or are interchangeable.

Figure A8.1B depicts the bar chart for the project. The dark blue bars represent the durations of critical activities; the light blue bars represent the durations of noncritical activities; the gray bars represent slack. Note that the duration is 45 days and the critical path is represented by activities 1, 4, 6, 7, and 8.

Parallel activities hold potential for resource conflicts. This is the case in this project. Ryan is the resource for activities 3 and 6. If you insert Ryan in the bar chart in Figure A8.1B for activities 3 and 6, you can see activity 3 overlaps activity 6 by five days—an impossible situation. Because Ryan cannot work two activities

[2] For more information on buffers see: L. P. Leach, "Critical Chain Project Management Improves Project Performance," *Project Management Journal*, 30 (2) 1999, pp. 39–51.

FIGURE A8.1A **Air Control Project: Time Plan without Resources**

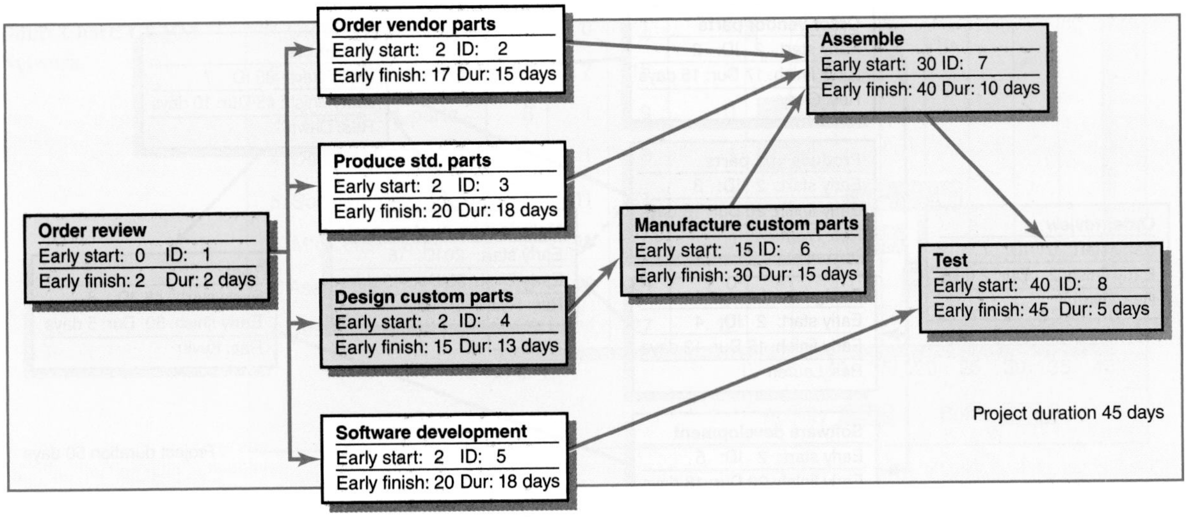

FIGURE A8.1B
Air Control Project: Time Plan without Resources

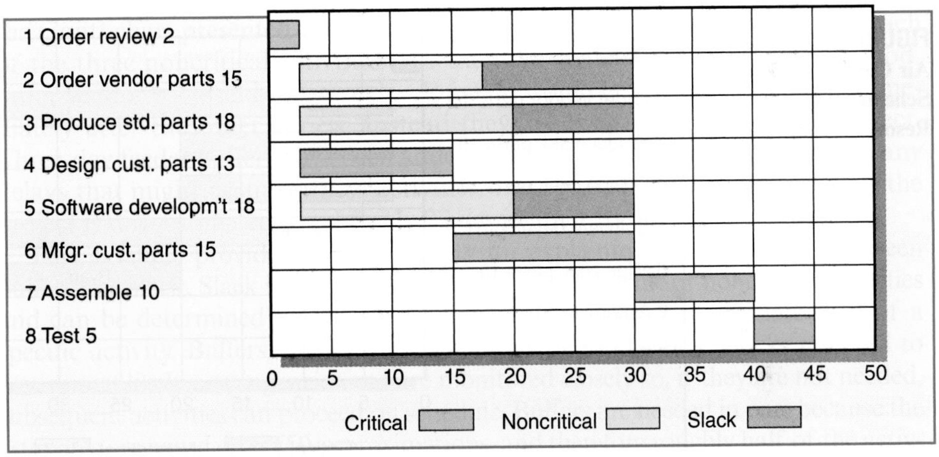

simultaneously and no other person can take his place, a resource dependency exists. The result is that two activities (3 and 6) that were assumed to be independent now become dependent. Something has to give! Figure A8.2A shows the Air Control project network with the resources included. A pseudo-dashed arrow has been added to the network to indicate the resource dependency. The bar chart in Figure A8.2B reflects the revised schedule resolving the overallocation of Ryan. Given the new schedule, slack for some activities has changed. More importantly, the critical path has changed. It is now 1, 3, 6, 7, 8. The resource schedule shows the new project duration to be 50 days rather than 45 days.

Now let's apply the CCPM approach to the Air Control project. Figure A8.3 details many of the changes. First, notice that task estimates now represent approximations of the 50/50 rule. Second, observe that not all of the activities on the critical chain are technically linked. Manufacture custom parts is included because of previously defined resource dependency. Third, a project time buffer is added at the end of schedule. Finally, feeder buffers are inserted at each point where a noncritical activity merges with the critical chain.

Three years ago management decided to add 10 percent time to all activity estimates because almost all projects were coming in late. One thought was people were simply working too hard and needed some relief. This approach did not work! Projects still came in late. Next, management decided to take away the extra time for activities and add 10 percent for project estimates to ensure project durations would be met. Again, nothing improved and projects continued to come in late. Recently, the firm hired a consultant who promoted critical chain scheduling, which was implemented for all projects in her division. Almost all failed to perform.

Pinyarat explained, "The estimates were basically impossible. The activity durations got squeezed down to less than the 50 percent guideline. We were late on nearly every task. In addition, I was not allowed to put in a big enough project buffer, which only added to projects being late. One colleague who was working on six projects gave up and quit; he said he was killing himself and saw no hope of things getting better. My projects are not the only ones having big problems. Some people had no idea why anyone would use CCPM scheduling. To quote one of my best programmers: 'They ask for an estimate and then they cut it 50 percent or more.' What kind of game is this? Apparently they don't trust us."

A week later, to Pinyarat's surprise, she was called to the IT manager's office. Pinyarat imagined numerous bad scenarios of how the meeting would go—even to the remote possibility of being fired! The manager wanted the division to straighten out their project management practices and stop this business of nearly all IT projects being late. There are rumors of cleaning house or outsourcing IT work.

The manager believed Pinyarat, who passed the PMP exam, had the best chance of turning things around. He said, "Pinyarat, I'm nearing the desperate level; top management is reaching the end of the rope with our division. We need to turn this around for both our sakes. Give me a plan that I can sponsor within the week."

Pinyarat explained to her friend a few of her ideas—like squeezing estimates too far. But she said she would take any ideas she can get from anyone.

Give Pinyarat a report that identifies the key problems and a plan of action she can present to her sponsor. Limit your report to 800 words or less.

APPENDIX REFERENCES

Budd, C. S., and M. J. Cooper, "Improving On-time Service Delivery: The Case of Project as Product," *Human Systems Management,* 24 (1) 2005, pp. 67–81.

Goldratt, *Critical Chain* (Great Barrington, MA: North River Press, 1997).

Herroelen, W., R. Leus, and E. Demeulemeester, "Critical Chain Project Scheduling: Do Not Oversimplify," *Project Management Journal,* Vol. 33 (4) 2002, pp. 48–60.

Leach, L. P., "Critical Chain Project Management," *Proceedings of 29th Annual Project Management Institute, 1998, Seminars and Symposium* (Newtown, PA: Project Management Institute, 1998), pp. 1239–44.

Levine, H. A., "Shared Contingency: Exploring the Critical Chain," *PM Network,* October 1999, pp. 35–38.

Newbold, R. C., *Project Management in the Fast Lane: Applying the Theory of Constraints* (Boca Raton, FL: St. Lucie Press, 1998).

Noreen, E., D. Smith, and J. Mackey, *The Theory of Constraints and Its Implication for Management Accounting* (Great Barrington, MA: North River Press, 1995).

Raz, T., R. Barnes, and D. Dvir, "A Critical Look at Critical Chain Project Management," *Project Management Journal,* December 2003, pp. 24–32.

Sood, S., "Taming Uncertainty: Critical-Chain Buffer Management Helps Minimize Risk in the Project Equation," *PM Network,* March 2003, pp. 57–59.

Zalmanson, E., "Readers Feedback," *PM Network,* Vol. 15 (1) 2001, p. 4.

CHAPTER NINE

Reducing Project Duration

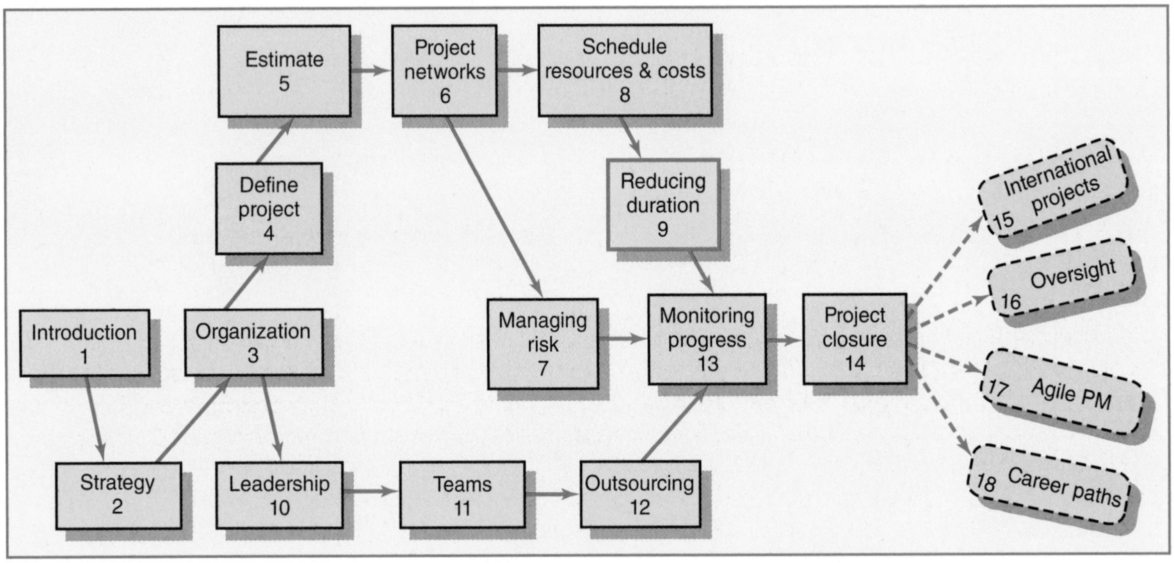

Reducing Project Duration

Rationale for Reducing Project Duration
Options for Accelerating Project Completion
Project Cost–Duration Graph
Constructing a Project Cost–Duration Graph
Practical Considerations
What if Cost, Not Time, Is the Issue?
Summary

In skating over thin ice our safety is in our speed.

—Ralph Waldo Emerson

Imagine the following scenarios:

- After finalizing your project schedule, you realize the estimated completion date is two months beyond what your boss publicly promised an important customer.
- Five months into the project, you realize that you are already three weeks behind the drop-dead date for the project.
- Four months into a project top management changes its priorities and now tells you that money is not an issue. Complete the project ASAP!

What do you do?

This chapter addresses strategies for reducing project duration either prior to setting the baseline for the project or in the midst of project execution. Choice of options is based on the constraints surrounding the project. Here the project priority matrix introduced in Chapter 4 comes into play. For example, there are many more options available for reducing project time if you are not resource constrained than if you cannot spend more than your original budget. We will begin first by examining the reasons for reducing project duration followed by a discussion of different options for accelerating project completion. The chapter will conclude with the classic time-cost framework for selecting which activities to "crash." Crash is a term that has emerged in the Project Management lexicon for shortening the duration of an activity or project beyond when it can be normally done.

Rationale for Reducing Project Duration

There are many good reasons for attempting to reduce the duration of a project. One of the more important reasons today is time to market. Intense global competition and rapid technological advances have made speed a competitive advantage. To succeed, companies have to spot new opportunities, launch project teams, and bring new products or services to the marketplace in a flash. Perhaps in no industry does speed matter as much as in the electronics industry. For example, a rule of thumb for moderate- to high-technology firms is that a six-month delay in bringing a product to market can result in a loss of market share of about 35 percent. In these cases, high-technology firms typically assume that the time savings and avoidance of lost profits are worth any additional costs to reduce time without any formal analysis. See the Snapshot from Practice: Smartphone Wars for more on this.

Business survival depends not only upon rapid innovation but also adaptability. Global recession and energy crises have stunned the business world, and those

Even in situations where cost is transferred to customers there is pressure to reduce cost. Cost overruns make for unhappy customers and can damage future business opportunities. Budgets can be fixed or cut, and when contingency funds are exhausted, then cost overruns have to be made up with remaining activities.

As discussed earlier, shortening project duration may come at the expense of overtime, adding additional personnel, and using more expensive equipment and/or materials. Conversely, sometimes cost savings can be generated by extending the duration of a project. This may allow for a smaller workforce, less-skilled (expensive) labor, and even cheaper equipment and materials to be used. Below are some of the more commonly used options for cutting costs.

Reduce Project Scope

Just as scaling back the scope of the project can gain time, delivering less than what was originally planned also produces significant savings. Again, calculating the savings of a reduced project scope begins with the work breakdown structure. However, since time is not the issue, you do not need to focus on critical activities. For example, on over-budget movie projects it is not uncommon to replace location shots with stock footage to cut costs.

Have Owner Take on More Responsibility

One way of reducing project costs is identifying tasks that customers can do themselves. Homeowners frequently use this method to reduce costs on home improvement projects. For example, to reduce the cost of a bathroom remodel, a homeowner may agree to paint the room instead of paying the contractor to do it. On IS projects, a customer may agree to take on some of the responsibility for testing equipment or providing in-house training. Naturally, this arrangement is best negotiated before the project begins. Customers are less receptive to this idea if you suddenly spring it on them. An advantage of this method is that, while costs are lowered, the original scope is retained. Clearly this option is limited to areas in which the customer has expertise and the capability to pick up the tasks.

Outsourcing Project Activities or Even the Entire Project

When estimates exceed budget, it not only makes sense to re-examine the scope but also search for cheaper ways to complete the project. Perhaps instead of relying on internal resources, it would be more cost effective to outsource segments or even the entire project, opening up work to external price competition. Specialized subcontractors often enjoy unique advantages, such as material discounts for large quantities, as well as equipment that not only gets the work done more quickly but also less expensively. They may have lower overhead and labor costs. For example, to reduce costs of software projects, many American firms outsource work to firms overseas where the salary of a software engineer is one-third that of an American software engineer. However, outsourcing means you have less control over the project and will need to have clearly definable deliverables.

Brainstorming Cost Savings Options

Just as project team members can be a rich source of ideas for accelerating project activities, they can offer tangible ways for reducing project costs. For example, one project manager reported that his team was able to come up with over $75,000 worth of cost saving suggestions without jeopardizing the scope of the project. Project managers should not underestimate the value of simply asking if there is a cheaper, better way.

Summary

The need for reducing the project duration occurs for many reasons such as imposed duration dates, time-to-market considerations, incentive contracts, key resource needs, high overhead costs, or simply unforeseen delays. These situations are very common in practice and are known as cost-time trade-off decisions. This chapter presented a logical, formal process for assessing the implications of situations that involve shortening the project duration. Crashing the project duration increases the *risk* of being late. How far to reduce the project duration from the normal time toward the optimum depends on the *sensitivity* of the project network. A sensitive network is one that has several critical or near-critical paths. Great care should be taken when shortening sensitive networks to avoid increasing project risks. Conversely, insensitive networks represent opportunities for potentially large project cost savings by eliminating some overhead costs with little downside risk.

Alternative strategies for reducing project time were discussed within the context of whether or not the project is resource limited. Project acceleration typically comes at a cost of either spending money for more resources or compromising the scope of the project. If the latter is the case, then it is essential that all relevant stakeholders be consulted so that everyone accepts the changes that have to be made. One other key point is the difference in implementing time-reducing activities in the midst of project execution versus incorporating them into the project plan. You typically have far fewer options once the project is underway than before it begins. This is especially true if you want to take advantage of the new scheduling methodologies such as fast-tracking and critical-chain. Time spent up front considering alternatives and developing contingency plans will lead to time savings in the end.

Key Terms

Crashing, *314*
Crash point, *315*
Crash time, *314*
Direct costs, *314*
Fast-tracking, *310*
Indirect costs, *313*
Outsourcing, *309*
Project cost–duration graph, *313*

Review Questions

1. What are five common reasons for crashing a project?
2. What are the advantages and disadvantages of reducing project scope to accelerate a project? What can be done to reduce the disadvantages?
3. Why is scheduling overtime a popular choice for getting projects back on schedule? What are the potential problems for relying on this option?
4. Identify four indirect costs you might find on a moderately complex project. Why are these costs classified as indirect?
5. How can a cost–duration graph be used by the project manager? Explain.
6. Reducing the project duration increases the risk of being late. Explain.
7. It is possible to shorten the critical path and save money. Explain how.

Exercises

1. Draw a project network from the following information.

Activity	Predecessor	Duration
A	None	2
B	A	4
C	A	3
D	A	2
E	B	3
F	C	6
G	C, D	5
H	E, F	6
I	G	5
J	H, I	5

Activities B and H can be shortened to a minimum of 2 weeks. Which activity would you shorten to reduce the project duration by 2 weeks? Why?

2.* Use the information contained below to compress one time unit per move using the least cost method. Reduce the schedule until you reach the crash point of the network. For each move identify what activity(s) was crashed the adjusted total cost.

Act.	Crash Cost (Slope)	Maximum Crash Time	Normal Time	Normal Cost
A	0	0	1	100
B	100	2	3	150
C	50	1	4	200
D	60	1	3	200
E	70	2	4	200
F	90	1	3	150

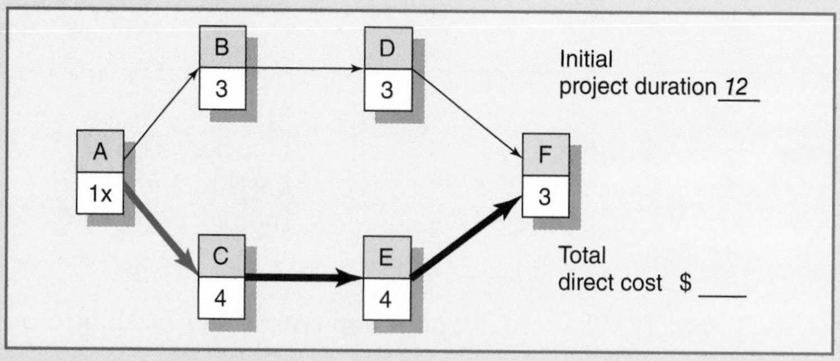

3. Assume the network and data that follow. Compute the total direct cost for each project duration. If the indirect costs for each project duration are $400 (19 time units), $350 (18), $300 (17), and $250 (16), compute the total project cost for each duration. Plot the total direct, indirect, and project costs for each of these durations on a cost-time graph. What is the optimum cost-time schedule for the project? What is this cost?

* The solution to this exercise can be found in Appendix One.

Act.	Crash Cost (Slope)	Maximum Crash Time	Normal Time	Normal Cost
A	20	1	3	50
B	60	2	5	60
C	40	1	3	70
D	0	0	10	50
E	50	3	6	100
F	100	3	7	90
G	70	1	5	50
				$470

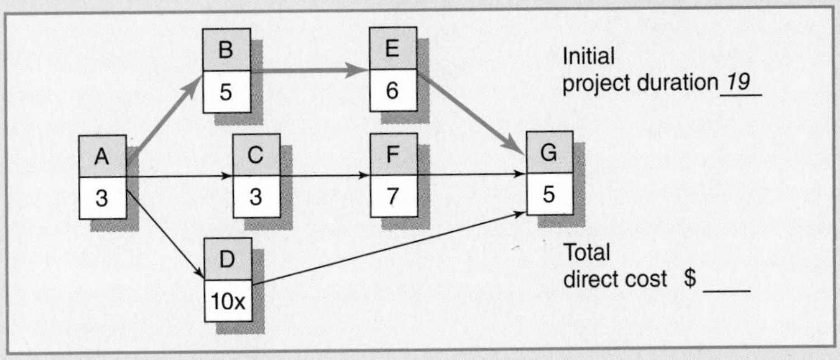

4. Given the data and information that follow, compute the total direct cost for each project duration. If the indirect costs for each project duration are $90 (15 time units), $70 (14), $50 (13), $40 (12), and $30 (11), compute the total project cost for each duration. What is the optimum cost-time schedule for the project? What is this cost?

Act.	Crash Cost (Slope)	Maximum Crash Time	Normal Time	Normal Cost
A	20	1	5	50
B	60	2	3	60
C	0	0	4	70
D	10	1	2	50
E	60	3	5	100
F	100	1	2	90
G	30	1	5	50
H	40	0	2	60
I	200	1	3	200
				$730

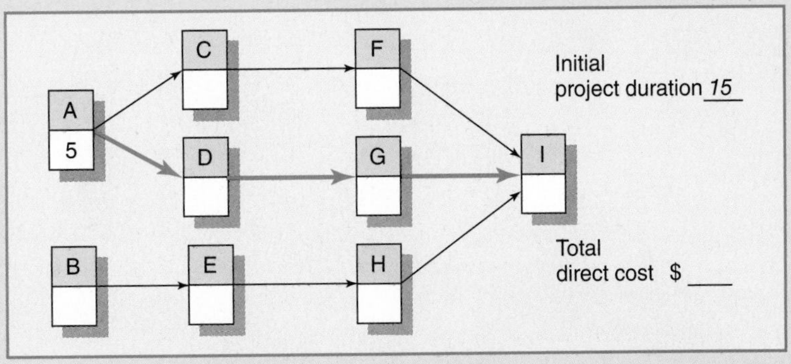

5. If the indirect costs for each duration are $1,200 for 16 weeks, $1,130 for 15 weeks, $1,000 for 14 weeks, $900 for 13 weeks, $860 for 12 weeks, $820 for 11 weeks, and $790 for 10 weeks, compute the total costs for each duration. Plot these costs on a graph. What is the optimum cost-time schedule?

Act.	Crash Cost (Slope)	Maximum Crash Time	Normal Time	Normal Cost
A	10	1	4	30
B	70	2	7	60
C	0	0	1	80
D	20	2	4	40
E	50	3	5	110
F	200	3	5	90
G	30	1	2	60
H	40	1	2	70
I	0	0	2	140
				$680

Time unit = 1 week

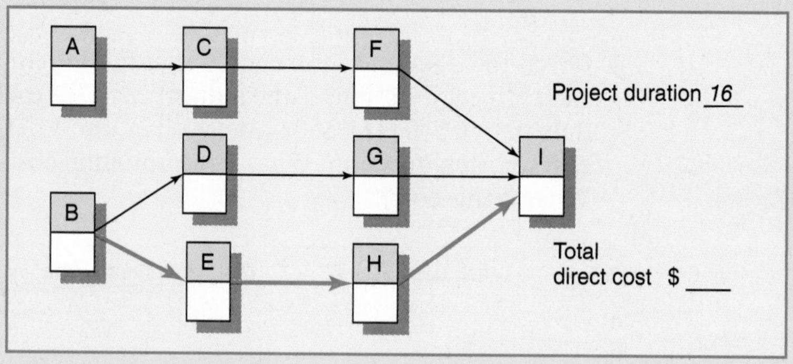

6. If the indirect costs for each duration are \$300 for 27 weeks, \$240 for 26 weeks, \$180 for 25 weeks, \$120 for 24 weeks, \$60 for 23 weeks, and \$50 for 22 weeks, compute the direct, indirect and total costs for each duration. What is the optimum cost-time schedule? The customer offers you \$10 for every week you shorten the project from your original network. Would you take it? If so for how many weeks?

Act.	Crash Cost (Slope)	Maximum Crash Time	Normal Time	Normal Cost
A	80	2	10	40
B	30	3	8	10
C	40	1	5	80
D	50	2	11	50
E	100	4	15	100
F	30	1	6	20
				\$300

Time unit = 1 week

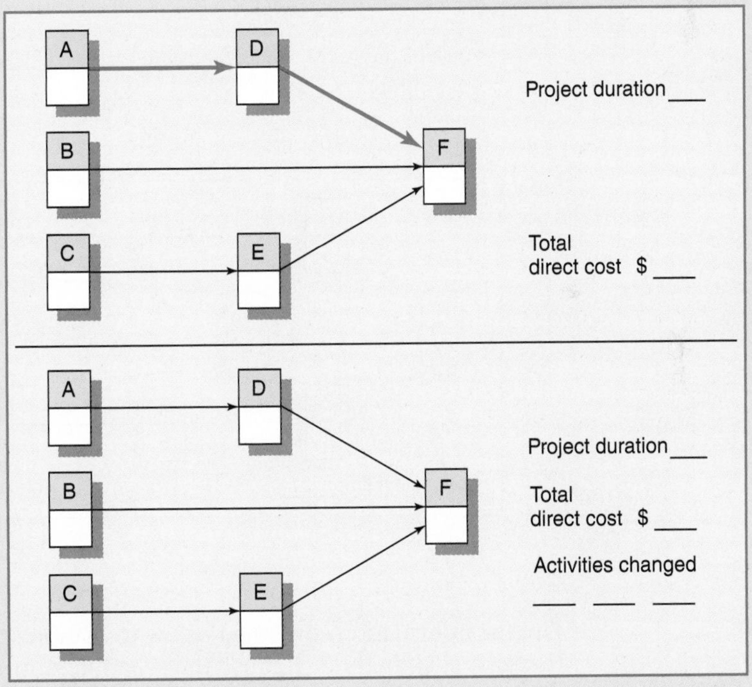

7. Use the information contained below to compress one time unit per move using the least cost method. Reduce the schedule until you reach the crash point of the network. For each move identify what activity(s) was crashed, the adjusted total cost, and explain your choice if you have to choose between activities that cost the same.

   Note: Crash point of the network is the point in which the duration cannot be reduced any further.

Activity ID	Crash Cost (Slope)	Maximum Crash Time	Normal Time	Normal Cost
A	—	0	4	$50
B	$40	3	5	70
C	40	1	5	80
D	40	2	4	40
E	40	2	5	60
F	40	1	5	50
G	30	1	4	70
H	30	1	4	80
I	—	0	3	50

Total direct normal costs—$550

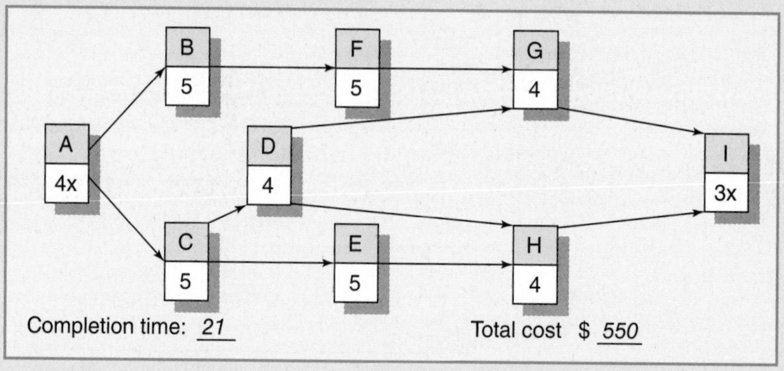

8.* Use the information contained below to compress one time unit per move using the least cost method. Reduce the schedule until you reach the crash point of the network. For each move identify what activity(s) was crashed, the adjusted total cost, and explain your choice if you have to choose between activities that cost the same.

   If the indirect cost for each duration are $1,500 for 17 weeks, $1,450 for 16 weeks, $1,400 for 15 weeks, $1,350 for 14 weeks, $1,300 for 13 weeks, $1,250

* The solution to this exercise can be found in Appendix One.

for 12 weeks, $1,200 for 11 weeks, and $1,150 for 10 weeks, what is the optimum cost-time schedule for the project? What is the cost?

Act.	Crash Cost (Slope)	Maximum Crash Time	Normal Time	Normal Cost
A	0	0	3	150
B	100	1	4	200
C	60	1	3	250
D	40	1	4	200
E	0	0	2	250
F	30	2	3	200
G	20	1	2	250
H	60	2	4	300
I	200	1	2	200

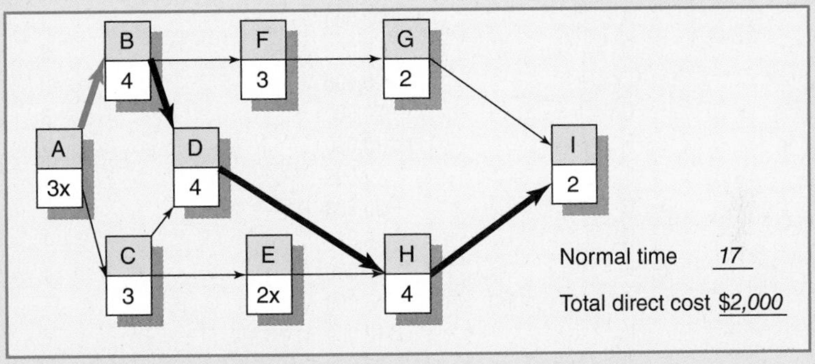

References

Abdel-Hamid, T., and S. Madnick, *Software Project Dynamics: An Integrated Approach* (Englewood Cliffs, NJ: Prentice Hall, 1991).

Baker, B. M., "Cost/Time Trade-off Analysis for the Critical Path Method," *Journal of the Operational Research Society,* 48 (12) 1997, pp. 1241–44.

Brooks, F. P., Jr., *The Mythical Man-Month: Essays on Software Engineering Anniversary Edition* (Reading, MA: Addison-Wesley Longman, Inc., 1994), pp. 15–26.

DeMarco, T., *Slack: Getting Past Burnout, Busywork, and the Myth of Total Efficiency* (New York: Broadway, 2002).

Gordon, R. I. and J. C. Lamb, "A Closer Look at Brooke's Law," *Datamation,* June, 1977, pp. 81–86.

Ibbs, C. W., S. A. Lee, and M. I. Li, "Fast-Tracking's Impact on Project Change," *Project Management Journal,* 29 (4) 1998, pp. 35–42.

Khang, D. B., and M.Yin, "Time, Cost, and Quality Tradeoff in Project Management," *International Journal of Project Management,* 17 (4) 1999, pp. 249–56.

Perrow, L. A., *Finding Time: How Corporations, Individuals, and Families Can Benefit From New Work Practices* (Ithaca, NY: Cornell University Press, 1997).

Roemer, T. R., R. Ahmadi, and R. Wang, "Time-Cost Trade-offs in Overlapped Product Development," *Operations Research,* 48 (6) 2000, pp. 858–65.

Smith, P. G., and D. G. Reinersten, *Developing Products in Half the Time* (New York: Van Nostrand Reinhold, 1995).

Verzuh, E., *The Fast Forward MBA in Project Management,* 4th ed. (New York: John Wiley, 2012).

Vroom, V. H., *Work and Motivation* (New York: John Wiley & Sons, 1964).

Case

International Capital, Inc.—Part B

Given the project network derived in Part A of the case from Chapter 7, Brown also wants to be prepared to answer any questions concerning compressing the project duration. This question will almost always be entertained by the accounting department, review committee, and the client. To be ready for the compression question, Brown has prepared the following data in case it is necessary to crash the project. (Use your weighted average times (t_e) computed in Part A of the International Capital case found in Chapter 7.)

Activity	Normal Cost	Maximum Crash Time	Crash Cost/Day
A	$ 3,000	3	$ 500
B	5,000	2	1000
C	6,000	0	—
D	20,000	3	3,000
E	10,000	2	1,000
F	7,000	1	1,000
G	20,000	2	3,000
H	8,000	1	2,000
I	5,000	1	2,000
J	7,000	1	1,000
K	12,000	6	1,000
Total normal costs =	$103,000		

Using the data provided, determine the activity crashing decisions and best-time cost project duration. Given the information you have developed, what suggestions would you give Brown to ensure she is well prepared for the project review committee? Assume the overhead costs for this project are $700 per workday. Will this alter your suggestions?

Case

Whitbread World Sailboat Race

Each year countries enter their sailing vessels in the nine-month Round the World Whitbread Sailboat Race. In recent years, about 14 countries entered sailboats in the race. Each year's sailboat entries represent the latest technologies and human skills each country can muster.

Bjorn Ericksen has been selected as a project manager because of his past experience as a master helmsman and because of his recent fame as the "best designer of racing sailboats in the world." Bjorn is pleased and proud to have the opportunity to design, build, test, and train the crew for next year's Whitbread entry for his country. Bjorn has picked Karin Knutsen (as chief design engineer) and Trygve Wallvik (as master helmsman) to be team leaders responsible for getting next year's entry ready for the traditional parade of all entries on the Thames River in the United Kingdom, which signals the start of the race.

As Bjorn begins to think of a project plan, he sees two parallel paths running through the project—design and construction and crew training. Last year's boat will be used for training until the new entry can have the crew on board to learn maintenance tasks. Bjorn calls Karin and Trygve together to develop a project plan. All three agree the major goal is to have a winning boat and crew ready to compete in next year's competition at a cost of $3.2 million. A check of Bjorn's calendar indicates he has 45 weeks before next year's vessel must leave port for the United Kingdom to start the race.

THE KICKOFF MEETING

Bjorn asks Karin to begin by describing the major activities and the sequence required to design, construct, and test the boat. Karin starts by noting that design of the hull, deck, mast, and accessories should only take six weeks—given the design prints from past race entries and a few prints from other countries' entries. After the design is complete, the hull can be constructed, the mast ordered, sails ordered, and accessories ordered. The hull will require 12 weeks to complete. The mast can be ordered and will require a lead time of eight weeks; the seven sails can be ordered and will take six weeks to get; accessories can be ordered and will take 15 weeks to receive. As soon as the hull is finished, the ballast tanks can be installed, requiring two weeks. Then the deck can be built, which will require five weeks. Concurrently, the hull can be treated with special sealant and friction-resistance coating, taking three weeks. When the deck is completed and mast and accessories received, the mast and sails can be installed, requiring two weeks; the accessories can be installed, which will take six weeks. When all of these activities have been completed, the ship can be sea-tested, which should take five weeks. Karin believes she can have firm cost estimates for the boat in about two weeks.

Trygve believes he can start selecting the 12-man or woman crew and securing their housing immediately. He believes it will take six weeks to get a committed crew on-site and three weeks to secure housing for the crew members. Trygve reminds Bjorn that last year's vessel must be ready to use for training the moment the crew is on-site until the new vessel is ready for testing. Keeping the old vessel operating will cost $4,000 per week as long as it is used. Once the crew is on-site and housed, they can develop and implement a routine sailing and maintenance training program, which will take 15 weeks (using the old vessel). Also, once the crew is selected and on-site, crew equipment can be selected, taking only two weeks. Then crew equipment can be ordered; it will take five weeks to arrive. When the crew equipment and maintenance training program are complete, crew maintenance on the new vessel can begin; this should take 10 weeks. But crew maintenance on the new vessel cannot begin until the deck is complete and the mast, sails, and accessories have arrived. Once crew maintenance on the new vessel begins, the new vessel will cost $6,000 per week until sea training is complete. After the new ship maintenance is complete and while the boat is being tested, initial sailing training can be implemented; training should take seven weeks. Finally, after the boat is tested and initial training is complete, regular sea training can be implemented—weather permitting; regular sea training requires eight weeks. Trygve believes he can put the cost estimates together in a week, given last year's expenses.

Bjorn is pleased with the expertise displayed by his team leaders. But he believes they need to have someone develop one of those critical path networks to see if they can safely meet the start deadline for the race. Karin and Trygve agree. Karin suggests the cost estimates should also include crash costs for any activities that can be compressed and the resultant costs for crashing. Karin also suggests the team complete the following priority matrix for project decision making:

FIGURE C9.1
Project Priority Matrix: Whitbread Project

	Time	Performance	Cost
Constrain			
Enhance			
Accept			

TWO WEEKS LATER

Karin and Trygve submit the following cost estimates for each activity and corresponding crash costs to Bjorn (costs are in thousands of dollars):

Activity	Normal Time	Normal Cost	Crash Time	Crash Cost
A Design	6	$ 40	2	$ —
B Build hull	12	1,000	2	—
C Install ballast tanks	2	100	0	—
D Order mast	8	100	1	200
E Order sails	6	40	0	—
F Order accessories	15	600	2	100
G Build deck	5	200	0	—
H Coat hull	3	40	0	—
I Install accessories	6	300	1	100
J Install mast and sails	2	40	1	40
K Test	5	60	1	40
L Sea trials	8	200	1	250
M Select crew	6	10	1	10
N Secure housing	3	30	0	—
O Select crew equipment	2	10	0	—
P Order crew equipment	5	30	0	—
Q Routine sail/maintenance	15	40	3	30
R Crew maintenance training	10	100	1	240
S Initial sail training	7	50	2	150
Total direct cost		$2,990		

Bjorn reviews the materials and wonders if the project will come in within the budget of $3.2 million and in 45 weeks. Advise the Whitbread team of their situation.

Case

Nightingale Project—A

You are the assistant project manager to Rassy Brown, who is in charge of the Nightingale project. Nightingale was the code name given to the development of a handheld electronic medical reference guide. Nightingale would be designed for emergency medical technicians and paramedics who need a quick reference guide to use in emergency situations.

Rassy and her project team were developing a project plan aimed at producing 30 working models in time for MedCON, the biggest medical equipment trade show each year. Meeting the MedCON October 25 deadline was critical to success. All the major medical equipment manufacturers demonstrated and took orders for new products at MedCON. Rassy had also heard rumors that competitors were considering developing a similar product, and she knew that being first to market would have a significant sales advantage. Besides, top management made funding contingent upon developing a workable plan for meeting the MedCON deadline.

The project team spent the morning working on the schedule for Nightingale. They started with the WBS and developed the information for a network, adding activities when needed. Then the team added the time estimates they had collected for each activity. Following is the preliminary information for activities with duration time and predecessors:

Activity	Description	Duration	Predecessor
1	Architectural decisions	10	None
2	Internal specifications	20	1
3	External specifications	18	1
4	Feature specifications	15	1
5	Voice recognition	15	2,3
6	Case	4	2,3
7	Screen	2	2,3
8	Speaker output jacks	2	2,3
9	Tape mechanism	2	2,3
10	Database	40	4
11	Microphone/soundcard	5	4
12	Pager	4	4
13	Barcode reader	3	4
14	Alarm clock	4	4
15	Computer I/O	5	4
16	Review design	10	5,6,7,8,9,10,11,12,13,14,15
17	Price components	5	5,6,7,8,9,10,11,12,13,14,15
18	Integration	15	16,17
19	Document design	35	16
20	Procure prototype components	20	18
21	Assemble prototypes	10	20
22	Lab test prototypes	20	21
23	Field test prototypes	20	19,22
24	Adjust design	20	23
25	Order stock parts	15	24
26	Order custom parts	2	24
27	Assemble first production unit	10	25, FS—8 time units 26, FS—13 time units
28	Test unit	10	27
29	Produce 30 units	15	28
30	Train sales representatives	10	29

Use any project network computer program available to you to develop the schedule for activities (see Case Appendix for further instructions)—noting late and early times, the critical path, and estimated completion for the project.

Prepare a short memo that addresses the following questions:

1. Will the project as planned meet the October 25th deadline?
2. What activities lie on the critical path?
3. How sensitive is this network?

Case

Nightingale Project—B

Rassy and the team were concerned with the results of your analysis. They spent the afternoon brainstorming alternative ways for shortening the project duration. They rejected outsourcing activities because most of the work was developmental in nature and could only be done in-house. They considered altering the scope of the project by eliminating some of the proposed product features. After much debate, they felt they could not compromise any of the core features and be successful in the marketplace. They then turned their attention to accelerating the completion of activities through overtime and adding additional technical manpower. Rassy had built into her proposal a discretionary fund of $200,000. She was willing to invest up to half of this fund to accelerate the project, but wanted to hold onto at least $100,000 to deal with unexpected problems. After a lengthy discussion, her team concluded that the following activities could be reduced at the specified cost:

- Development of voice recognition system could be reduced from 15 days to 10 days at a cost of $15,000.
- Creation of database could be reduced from 40 days to 35 days at a cost of $35,000.
- Document design could be reduced from 35 days to 30 days at a cost of $25,000.
- External specifications could be reduced from 18 days to 12 days at a cost of $20,000.
- Procure prototype components could be reduced from 20 days to 15 days at a cost of $30,000.
- Order stock parts could be reduced from 15 days to 10 days at a cost of $20,000.

Ken Clark, a development engineer, pointed out that the network contained only finish-to-start relationships and that it might be possible to reduce project duration by creating start-to-start lags. For example, he said that his people would not have to wait for all of the field tests to be completed to begin making final adjustments in the design. They could start making adjustments after the first 15 days of testing. The project team spent the remainder of the day analyzing how they could introduce lags into the network to hopefully shorten the project. They concluded that the following finish-to-start relationships could be converted into lags:

- Document design could begin 5 days after the start of the review design.
- Adjust design could begin 15 days after the start of field test prototypes.

- Order stock parts could begin 5 days after the start of adjust design.
- Order custom parts could begin 5 days after the start of adjust design.
- Training sales representatives could begin 5 days after the start of test unit and completed 5 days after the production of 30 units.

As the meeting adjourns, Rassy turns to you and tells you to assess the options presented and try to develop a schedule that will meet the October 25th deadline. You are to prepare a report to be presented to the project team that answers the following questions:

1. Is it possible to meet the deadline?
2. If so, how would you recommend changing the original schedule (Part A) and why? Assess the relative impact of crashing activities versus introducing lags to shorten project duration.
3. What would the new schedule look like?
4. What other factors should be considered before finalizing the schedule?

CASE APPENDIX: TECHNICAL DETAILS

Create your project schedule and assess your options based on the following information:

1. The project will begin the first working day in January, 2010.
2. The following holidays are observed: January 1, Memorial Day (last Monday in May), July 4, Labor Day (first Monday in September), Thanksgiving Day (fourth Thursday in November), December 25 and 26.
3. If a holiday falls on a Saturday, then Friday will be given as an extra day off; if it falls on a Sunday, then Monday will be given as a day off.
4. The project team works Monday through Friday, 8 hour days.
5. If you choose to reduce the duration of any one of the activities mentioned, then it must be for the specified time and cost (i.e., you cannot choose to reduce database to 37 days at a reduced cost; you can only reduce it to 35 days at a cost of $35,000).
6. You can only spend up to $100,000 to reduce project activities; lags do not contain any additional costs.

Case

The "Now" Wedding—Part A*

On December 31 of last year, Lauren burst into the family living room and announced that she and Connor (her college boyfriend) were going to be married. After recovering from the shock, her mother hugged her and asked, "When?" The following conversation resulted:

Lauren: January 21.
Mom: What?

* This case was adapted from a case originally written by Professor D. Clay Whybark, University of North Carolina, Chapel Hill, N.C.

Dad: The Now Wedding will be the social hit of the year. Wait a minute. Why so soon?

Lauren: Because on January 30 Connor, who is in the National Guard, will be shipping out overseas. We want a week for a honeymoon.

Mom: But Honey, we can't possibly finish all the things that need to be done by then. Remember all the details that were involved in your sister's wedding? Even if we start tomorrow, it takes a day to reserve the church and reception hall, and they need at least 14 days' notice. That has to be done before we can start decorating, which takes 3 days. An extra $200 on Sunday would probably cut that 14 day notice to 7 days, though.

Dad: Oh, boy!

Lauren: I want Jane Summers to be my maid of honor.

Dad: But she's in the Peace Corps in Guatemala, isn't she? It would take her 10 days to get ready and drive up here.

Lauren: But we could fly her up in 2 days and it would only cost $1,000.

Dad: Oh, boy!

Mom: And catering! It takes 2 days to choose the cake and decorations, and Jack's Catering wants at least 5 days' notice. Besides, we'd have to have those things before we could start decorating.

Lauren: Can I wear your wedding dress, Mom?

Mom: Well, we'd have to replace some lace, but you could wear it, yes. We could order the lace from New York when we order the material for the bridesmaids' dresses. It takes 8 days to order and receive the material. The pattern needs to be chosen first, and that would take 3 days.

Dad: We could get the material here in 5 days if we paid an extra $20 to air-freight it. Oh, boy!

Lauren: I want Mrs. Jacks to work on the dresses.

Mom: But she charges $48 a day.

Dad: Oh, boy!

Mom: If we did all the sewing we could finish the dresses in 11 days. If Mrs. Jacks helped we could cut that down to 6 days at a cost of $48 for each day less than 11 days. She is very good too.

Lauren: I don't want anyone but her.

Mom: It would take another 2 days to do the final fitting and 2 more days to clean and press the dresses. They would have to be ready by rehearsal night. We must have rehearsal the night before the wedding.

Dad: Everything should be ready rehearsal night.

Mom: We've forgotten something. The invitations!

Dad: We should order the invitations from Bob's Printing Shop, and that usually takes 7 days. I'll bet he would do it in 6 days if we slipped him an extra $20!

Mom: It would take us 2 days to choose the invitation style before we could order them and we want the envelopes printed with our return address.

Lauren: Oh! That will be elegant.

Mom: The invitations should go out at least 10 days before the wedding. If we let them go any later, some of the relatives would get theirs too late to come and that would make them mad. I'll bet that if we didn't get them out until 8 days before the wedding, Aunt Ethel couldn't make it and she would reduce her wedding gift by $200.

Dad: Oh, boy!!

Mom: We'll have to take them to the Post Office to mail them and that takes a day. Addressing would take 3 days unless we hired some part-time girls and we can't start until the printer is finished. If we hired the girls we could probably save 2 days by spending $40 for each day saved.

Lauren: We need to get gifts for the bridesmaids. I could spend a day and do that.

Mom: Before we can even start to write out those invitations we need a guest list. Heavens, that will take 4 days to get in order and only I can understand our address file.

Lauren: Oh, Mom, I'm so excited. We can start each of the relatives on a different job.

Mom: Honey, I don't see how we can do it. Why, I've got to choose the invitations and patterns and reserve the church and . . .

Dad: Why don't you just take $3,000 and elope. Your sister's wedding cost me $2,400 and she didn't have to fly people up from Guatemala, hire extra girls and Mrs. Jacks, use airfreight, or anything like that.

1. Using a yellow sticky approach (see p. 153), develop a project network for the "Now" Wedding.
2. Create a schedule for the wedding using MS Project. Can you reach the deadline of January 21 for the "Now" Wedding? If you cannot, what would it cost to make the January 21 deadline and which activities would you change?

Case

The "Now" Wedding—Part B

Several complications arose during the course of trying to meet the deadline of January 20 for the "Now" Wedding rehearsal. Since Lauren was adamant on having the wedding on January 21 (as was Connor for obvious reasons), the implications of each of these complications had to be assessed.

1. On January 1 the chairman of the Vestry Committee of the church was left unimpressed by the added donation and said he wouldn't reduce the notice period from 14 to 7 days.
2. Mother comes down with the three-day flu as she starts work on the guest list January 2.
3. Bob's Printing Shop press was down for one day on January 5 in order to replace faulty brushes in the electric motor.
4. The lace and dress material are lost in transit. Notice of the loss is received on January 10.

Can the wedding still take place on January 21? If not, what options are available?

CHAPTER TEN

Leadership: Being an Effective Project Manager

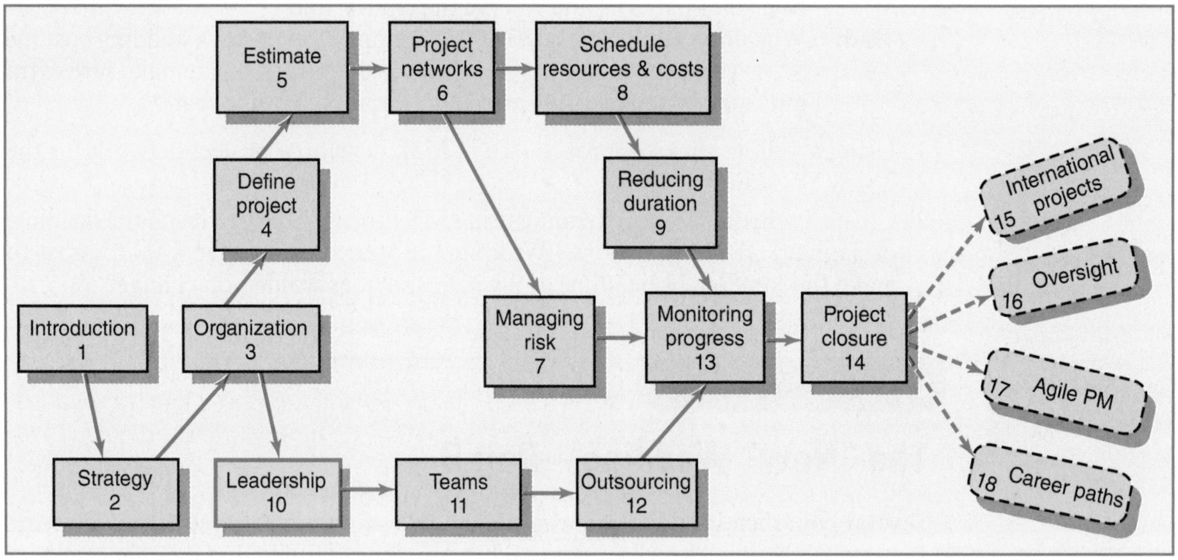

Leadership: Being an Effective Project Manager

Managing versus Leading a Project

Managing Project Stakeholders

Influence as Exchange

Social Network Building

Ethics and Project Management

Building Trust: The Key to Exercising Influence

Qualities of an Effective Project Manager

Summary

I couldn't wait to be the manager of my own project and run the project the way I thought it should be done. Boy, did I have a lot to learn!

—first-time project manager

This chapter is based on the premise that one of the keys to being an effective project manager is building cooperative relationships among different groups of people to complete projects. Project success does not just depend on the performance of the project team. Success or failure often depends on the contributions of top management, functional managers, customers, suppliers, contractors, and others.

The chapter begins with a brief discussion of the differences between leading and managing a project. The importance of managing project stakeholders is then introduced. Managers require a broad influence base to be effective in this area. Different sources of influence are discussed and are used to describe how project managers build social capital. This management style necessitates constant interacting with different groups of people whom project managers depend on. Special attention is devoted to managing the critical relationship with top management and the importance of leading by example. The importance of gaining cooperation in ways that build and sustain the trust of others is emphasized. The chapter concludes by identifying personal attributes associated with being an effective project manager. Subsequent chapters will expand on these ideas in a discussion of managing the project team and working with people outside the organization.

Managing versus Leading a Project

In a perfect world, the project manager would simply implement the project plan and the project would be completed. The project manager would work with others to formulate a schedule, organize a project team, keep track of progress, and announce what needs to be done next, and then everyone would charge along. Of course no one lives in a perfect world, and rarely does everything go according to plan. Project participants get testy; they fail to complement each other; other departments are unable to fulfill their commitments; technical glitches arise; work takes longer than expected. The project manager's job is to get the project back on track. A manager expedites certain activities; figures out ways to solve technical problems; serves as peacemaker when tensions rise; and makes appropriate trade-offs among time, cost, and scope of the project.

However, project managers do more than put out fires and keep the project on track. They also innovate and adapt to ever-changing circumstances. They often have to deviate from what was planned and introduce significant changes in the project scope and schedule to respond to unforeseen threats or opportunities. For example, customers' needs may change, requiring significant design changes midway through the project. Competitors may release new products that dictate crashing project deadlines. Working relationships among project participants may break down, requiring a reformulation of the project team. Ultimately, what was planned or expected in the beginning may be very different from what was accomplished by the end of the project.

Project managers are responsible for integrating assigned resources to complete the project according to plan. At the same time they need to initiate changes in plans and schedules as persistent problems make plans unworkable. In other words, managers want to keep the project going while making necessary adjustments along the way. According to Kotter (1990) these two different activities represent the distinction between management and leadership. Management is about coping with complexity, while leadership is about coping with change.

Good management brings about order and stability by formulating plans and objectives, designing structures and procedures, monitoring results against plans, and taking corrective action when necessary. Leadership involves recognizing and articulating the need to significantly alter the direction and operation of the project, aligning people to the new direction, and motivating them to work together to overcome hurdles produced by the change and to realize new objectives.

Strong leadership, while usually desirable, is not always necessary to successfully complete a project. Well-defined projects that encounter no significant surprises require little leadership, as might be the case in constructing a conventional apartment building in which the project manager simply administrates the project plan. Conversely, the higher the degree of uncertainty encountered on a project—whether in terms of changes in project scope, technological stalemates, breakdowns in coordination between people, and so forth—the more leadership is required. For example, strong leadership would be needed for a software development project in which the parameters are always changing to meet developments in the industry.

It takes a special person to perform both roles well. Some individuals are great visionaries who are good at exciting people about change. Too often though, these same people lack the discipline or patience to deal with the day-to-day drudgeries of managing. Likewise, there are other individuals who are very well organized and methodical but lack the ability to inspire others.

Strong leaders can compensate for their managerial weaknesses by having trusted assistants who oversee and manage the details of the project. Conversely, a weak leader can complement his or her strengths by having assistants who are good at sensing the need to change and rallying project participants. Still, one of the things that make good project managers so valuable to an organization is that they have the ability to both manage and lead a project. In doing so they recognize the need to manage project interfaces and build a social network that allows them to find out what needs to be done and obtain the cooperation necessary to achieve it.

Managing Project Stakeholders

First-time project managers are eager to implement their own ideas and manage their people to successfully complete their project. What they soon find out is that project success depends on the cooperation of a wide range of individuals, many of whom do not directly report to them. For example, during the course of a system integration project, a project manager was surprised by how much time she was spending negotiating and working with vendors, consultants, technical specialists, and other functional managers:

> Instead of working with my people to complete the project, I found myself being constantly pulled and tugged by demands of different groups of people who were not directly involved in the project but had a vested interest in the outcome.

Too often when new project managers do find time to work directly on the project, they adopt a hands-on approach to managing the project. They choose this style not because they are power-hungry egomaniacs but because they are eager to achieve results. They become quickly frustrated by how slowly things operate, the number of people that have to be brought on board, and the difficulty of gaining cooperation. Unfortunately, as this frustration builds, the natural temptation is to exert more pressure and get more heavily involved in the project. These project managers quickly earn the reputation of "micro managing" and begin to lose sight of the real role they play on guiding a project.

Some new managers never break out of this vicious cycle. Others soon realize that authority does not equal influence and that being an effective project manager involves managing a much more complex and expansive set of interfaces than they had previously anticipated. They encounter a web of relationships that requires a much broader spectrum of influence than they felt was necessary or even possible.

For example, a significant project, whether it involves renovating a bridge, creating a new product, or installing a new information system, will likely involve in one way or another working with a number of different groups of stakeholders. First, there is the core group of specialists assigned to complete the project. This group is likely to be supplemented at different times by professionals who work on specific segments of the project. Second, there are the groups of people within the performing organization who are either directly or indirectly involved with the project. The most notable is top management, to whom the project manager is accountable. There are also other managers who provide resources and/or may be responsible for specific segments of the project, and administrative support services such as human resources, finance, etc. Depending on the nature of the project, there are a number of different groups outside the organization that influence the success of the project; the most important is the customer for which the project is designed (see Figure 10.1).

Each of these groups of stakeholders brings different expertise, standards, priorities, and agendas to the project. **Stakeholders** are people and organizations that are actively involved in the project, or whose interests may be positively or negatively affected by the project (PMBOK, 2013). The sheer breadth and complexity of stakeholder relationships distinguish project management from regular management. To be effective, a project manager must understand how stakeholders can affect the project and develop methods for managing the dependency. The nature of these dependencies is identified here:

- The **project team** manages and completes project work. Most participants want to do a good job, but they are also concerned with their other obligations and how their involvement on the project will contribute to their personal goals and aspirations.

FIGURE 10.1
Network of Stakeholders

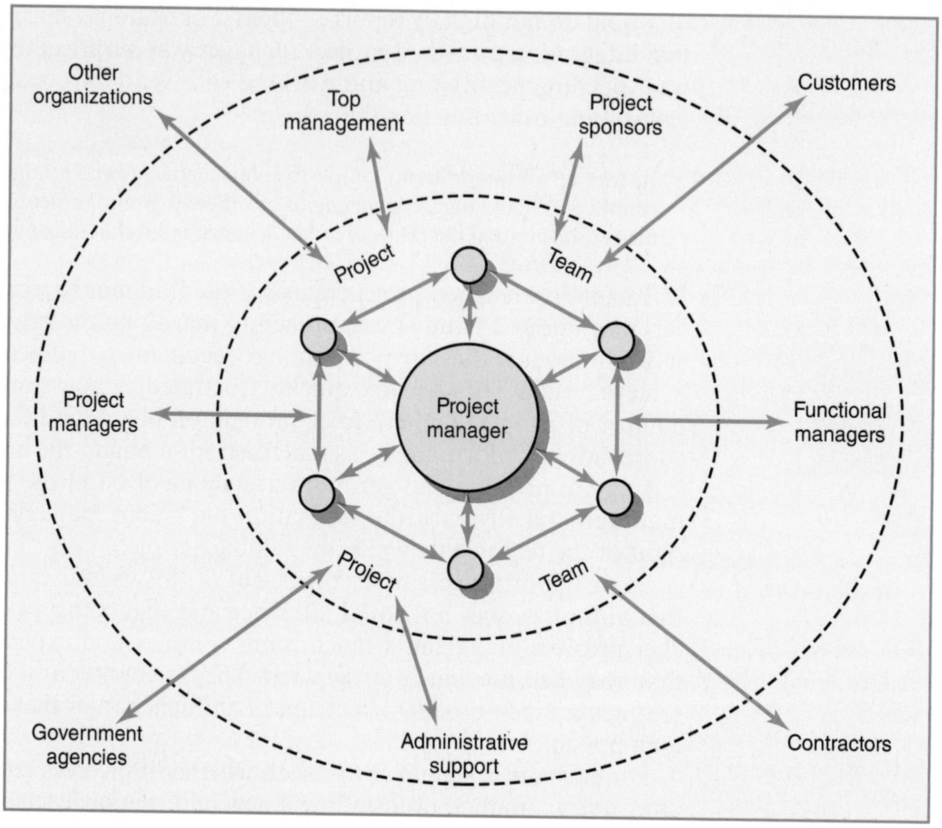

- **Project managers** naturally compete with each other for resources and the support of top management. At the same time they often have to share resources and exchange information.
- **Administrative support** groups, such as human resources, information systems, purchasing agents, and maintenance, provide valuable support services. At the same time they impose constraints and requirements on the project such as the documentation of expenditures and the timely and accurate delivery of information.
- **Functional managers,** depending on how the project is organized, can play a minor or major role toward project success. In matrix arrangements, they may be responsible for assigning project personnel, resolving technical dilemmas, and overseeing the completion of significant segments of the project work. Even in dedicated project teams, the technical input from functional managers may be useful, and acceptance of completed project work may be critical to in-house projects. Functional managers want to cooperate up to a point, but only up to a certain point. They are also concerned with preserving their status within the organization and minimizing the disruptions the project may have on their own operations.
- **Top management** approves funding of the project and establishes priorities within the organization. They define success and adjudicate rewards for

accomplishments. Significant adjustments in budget, scope, and schedule typically need their approval. They have a natural vested interest in the success of the project, but at the same time have to be responsive to what is best for the entire organization.

- **Project sponsors** champion the project and use their influence to gain approval of the project. Their reputation is tied to the success of the project, and they need to be kept informed of any major developments. They defend the project when it comes under attack and are a key project ally.
- **Contractors** may do all the actual work, in some cases, with the project team merely coordinating their contributions. In other cases, they are responsible for ancillary segments of the project scope. Poor work and schedule slips can affect work of the core project team. While contractors' reputations rest with doing good work, they must balance their contributions with their own profit margins and their commitments to other clients.
- **Government agencies** place constraints on project work. Permits need to be secured. Construction work has to be built to code. New drugs have to pass a rigorous battery of U.S. Food and Drug Administration tests. Other products have to meet safety standards, for example, Occupational Safety and Health Administration standards.
- **Other organizations,** depending on the nature of the project, may directly or indirectly affect the project. For example, suppliers provide necessary resources for completion of the project work. Delays, shortages, and poor quality can bring a project to a standstill. Public interest groups may apply pressure on government agencies. Customers often hire consultants and auditors to protect their interests on a project.
- **Customers** define the scope of the project, and ultimate project success rests in their satisfaction. Project managers need to be responsive to changing customer needs and requirements and to meeting their expectations. Customers are primarily concerned with getting a *good deal* and, as will be elaborated in Chapter 11, this naturally breeds tension with the project team.

These relationships are interdependent in that a project manager's ability to work effectively with one group will affect her ability to manage other groups. For example, functional managers are likely to be less cooperative if they perceive that top management's commitment to the project is waning. Conversely, the ability of the project manager to buffer the team from excessive interference from a client is likely to increase her standing with the project team.

The project management structure being used will influence the number and degree of external dependencies that will need to be managed. One advantage of creating a dedicated project team is that it reduces dependencies, especially within the organization, because most of the resources are assigned to the project. Conversely, a functional matrix structure increases dependencies, with the result that the project manager is much more reliant upon functional colleagues for work and staff.

The old-fashioned view of managing projects emphasized directing and controlling subordinates; the new perspective emphasizes managing project stakeholders and anticipating change as the most important jobs. Project managers need to be able to assuage concerns of customers, sustain support for the project

SNAPSHOT FROM PRACTICE The Project Manager as Conductor

Metaphors convey meaning beyond words. For example, a meeting can be described as being difficult or "like wading through molasses." A popular metaphor for the role of a project manager is that of *conductor*. The conductor of an orchestra integrates the divergent sounds of different instruments to perform a given composition and make beautiful music. Similarly, the project manager integrates the talents and contributions of different specialists to complete the project. Both have to be good at understanding how the different players contribute to the performance of the whole. Both are almost entirely dependent upon the expertise and know-how of the players. The conductor does not have command of all the musical instruments. Likewise, the project manager usually possesses only a small proportion of the technical knowledge to make decisions. As such, the conductor and project manager both facilitate the performance of others rather than actually perform.

Conductors use their arms, baton, and other nonverbal gestures to influence the pace, intensity, and involvement of different musicians. Likewise, project managers orchestrate the completion of the project by managing the involvement and attention of project members. Project managers balance time and process and induce participants to make the right decisions at the right time just as the conductor induces the wind instruments to perform at the right moment in a movement. Each controls the rhythm and intensity of work by managing the tempo and involvement of the players. Finally, each has a vision that transcends the music score or project plan. To be successful they must both earn the confidence, respect, and trust of their players.

at higher levels of the organization, quickly identify problems that threaten project work, while at the same time defend the integrity of the project and the interests of the project participants.[1]

Within this web of relationships, the project manager must find out what needs to be done to achieve the goals of the project and build a cooperative network to accomplish it. Project managers must do so without the requisite authority to expect or demand cooperation. Doing so requires sound communication skills, political savvy, and a broad influence base. See the Snapshot from Practice: The Project Manager as Conductor for more on what makes project managers special.

Influence as Exchange

To successfully manage a project, a manager must adroitly build a cooperative network among divergent allies. Networks are mutually beneficial alliances that are generally governed by the **law of reciprocity** (Kaplan, 1984; Grant, 2013). The basic principle is that "one good deed deserves another, and likewise, one bad deed deserves another." The primary way to gain cooperation is to provide resources and services for others in exchange for future resources and services. This is the age-old maxim: "Quid pro quo (something for something)." Or in today's vernacular: "You scratch my back, I'll scratch yours."

Cohen and Bradford (1990) described the exchange view of influence as "currencies." If you want to do business in a given country, you have to be prepared to use the appropriate currency, and the exchange rates can change over time as conditions change. In the same way, what is valued by a marketing manager may be different from what is valued by a veteran project engineer, and you are likely to need to use different influence currency to obtain the cooperation of each individual. Although this analogy is a bit of an oversimplification, the key premise holds

[1] For a systematic treatise on stakeholder management, see: Lynda Bourne, *Stakeholder Relationship Management* (Farnham, England: Gower Publishing Ltd., 2009).

TABLE 10.1
Commonly Traded Organizational Currencies

Source: Adapted from A. R. Cohen and David L. Bradford, *Influence without Authority* (New York: John Wiley & Sons, 1990). Reprinted by permission of John Wiley & Sons, Inc.

Task-related currencies	
Resources	Lending or giving money, budget increases, personnel, etc.
Assistance	Helping with existing projects or undertaking unwanted tasks.
Cooperation	Giving task support, providing quicker response time, or aiding implementation.
Information	Providing organizational as well as technical knowledge.
Position-related currencies	
Advancement	Giving a task or assignment that can result in promotion.
Recognition	Acknowledging effort, accomplishments, or abilities.
Visibility	Providing a chance to be known by higher-ups or significant others in the organization.
Network/contacts	Providing opportunities for linking with others.
Inspiration-related currencies	
Vision	Being involved in a task that has larger significance for the unit, organization, customer, or society.
Excellence	Having a chance to do important things really well.
Ethical correctness	Doing what is "right" by a higher standard than efficiency.
Relationship-related currencies	
Acceptance	Providing closeness and friendship.
Personal support	Giving personal and emotional backing.
Understanding	Listening to others' concerns and issues.
Personal-related currencies	
Challenge/learning	Sharing tasks that increase skills and abilities.
Ownership/involvement	Letting others have ownership and influence.
Gratitude	Expressing appreciation.

true that in the long run, "debit" and "credit" accounts must be balanced for cooperative relationships to work. Table 10.1 presents the commonly traded organizational currencies identified by Cohen and Bradford; they are then discussed in more detail in the following sections.

Task-Related Currencies

This form of influence comes directly from the project manager's ability to contribute to others' accomplishing their work. Probably the most significant form of this currency is the ability to respond to subordinates' requests for additional manpower, money, or time to complete a segment of a project. This kind of currency is also evident in sharing resources with another project manager who is in need. At a more personal level, it may simply mean providing direct assistance to a colleague in solving a technical problem.

Providing a good word for a colleague's proposal or recommendation is another form of this currency. Because most work of significance is likely to generate some form of opposition, the person who is trying to gain approval for a plan or proposal can be greatly aided by having a "friend in court."

Another form of this currency includes extraordinary effort. For example, fulfilling an emergency request to complete a design document in two days instead of the normal four days is likely to engender gratitude. Finally, sharing valuable information that would be useful to other managers is another form of this currency.

Position-Related Currencies

This form of influence stems from the manager's ability to enhance others' positions within their organization. A project manager can do this by giving someone a challenging assignment that can aid their advancement by developing their skills and abilities. Being given a chance to prove yourself naturally generates a strong sense of gratitude. Sharing the glory and bringing to the attention of higher-ups the efforts and accomplishments of others generate goodwill.

Project managers confide that a useful strategy for gaining the cooperation of professionals in other departments/organizations is figuring out how to make these people look good to their bosses. For example, a project manager worked with a subcontractor whose organization was heavily committed to total quality management (TQM). The project manager made it a point in top-level briefing meetings to point out how quality improvement processes initiated by the contractor contributed to cost control and problem prevention.

Another variation of recognition is enhancing the reputation of others within the firm. "Good press" can pave the way for lots of opportunities, while "bad press" can quickly shut a person off and make it difficult to perform. This currency is also evident in helping to preserve someone's reputation by coming to the defense of someone unjustly blamed for project setbacks.

Finally, one of the strongest forms of this currency is sharing contacts with other people. Helping individuals expand their own networks by introducing them to key people naturally engenders gratitude. For example, suggesting to a functional manager that he should contact Sally X if he wants to find out what is really going on in that department or to get a request expedited is likely to engender a sense of indebtedness.

Inspiration-Related Currencies

Perhaps the most powerful form of influence is based on inspiration. Most sources of inspiration derive from people's burning desire to make a difference and add meaning to their lives. Creating an exciting, bold vision for a project can elicit extraordinary commitment. For example, many of the technological breakthroughs associated with the introduction of the original Macintosh computer were attributed to the feeling that the project members had a chance to change the way people approached computers. A variant form of vision is providing an opportunity to do something really well. Being able to take pride in your work often drives many people.

Often the very nature of the project provides a source of inspiration. Discovering a cure for a devastating disease, introducing a new social program that will help those in need, or simply building a bridge that will reduce a major traffic bottleneck can provide opportunities for people to feel good about what they are doing and that they are making a difference. Inspiration operates as a magnet—pulling people as opposed to pushing people toward doing something.

Relationship-Related Currencies

These currencies have more to do with strengthening the relationship with someone than directly accomplishing the project tasks. The essence of this form of influence is forming a relationship that transcends normal professional boundaries and extends into the realm of friendship. Such relationships develop by giving personal and emotional backing. Picking people up when they are feeling down, boosting their confidence, and providing encouragement naturally breed goodwill.

Sharing a sense of humor and making difficult times fun is another form of this currency. Similarly, engaging in non-work-related activities such as sports and family outings is another way relationships are naturally enhanced.

Perhaps the most basic form of this currency is simply listening to other people. Psychologists suggest that most people have a strong desire to be understood and that relationships break down because the parties stop listening to each other. Sharing personal secrets/ambitions and being a wise confidant also creates a special bond between individuals.

Personal-Related Currencies

This last form of currency deals with individual needs and an overriding sense of self-esteem. Some argue that self-esteem is a primary psychological need; the extent to which we can help others feel a sense of importance and personal worth will naturally generate goodwill. A project manager can enhance a colleague's sense of worth by sharing tasks that increase skills and abilities, delegating authority over work so that others experience ownership, and allowing individuals to feel comfortable stretching their abilities. This form of currency can also be seen in sincere expressions of gratitude for the contributions of others. Care, though, must be exercised in expressing gratitude since it is easily devalued when overused. That is, the first *thank you* is likely to be more valued than the twentieth.

The bottom line is that a project manager will be influential only insofar as she can offer something that others value. Furthermore, given the diverse cast of people a project manager depends on, it is important that she be able to acquire and exercise different influence currencies. The ability to do so will be constrained in part by the nature of the project and how it is organized. For example, a project manager who is in charge of a dedicated team has considerably more to offer team members than a manager who is given the responsibility of coordinating the activities of different professionals across different departments and organizations. In such cases, that manager will probably have to rely more heavily on personal and relational bases of influence to gain the cooperation of others.

Social Network Building

Mapping Dependencies

The first step to building a **social network** is identifying those stakeholders on whom the project depends for success. The project manager and his or her key assistants need to ask the following questions:

- Whose cooperation will we need?
- Whose agreement or approval will we need?
- Whose opposition would keep us from accomplishing the project?

Many project managers find it helpful to draw a map of these dependencies. For example, Figure 10.2 contains the dependencies identified by a project manager responsible for installing a new financial software system in her company.

It is always better to overestimate rather than underestimate dependencies. All too often, otherwise talented and successful project managers have been derailed because they were blindsided by someone whose position or power they had not anticipated. After identifying the stakeholders associated with your project, it is important to assess their significance. Here the power/interest matrix introduced

FIGURE 10.2
Dependencies for Financial Software Installation Project

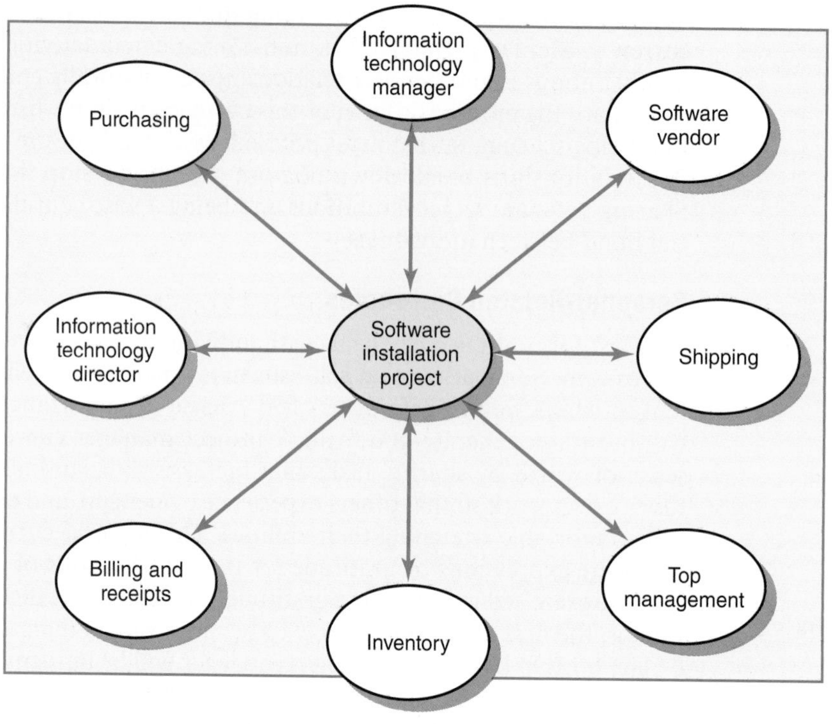

in Chapter 3 becomes useful. Those individuals with the most power over and interest in the project are the most significant stakeholders and deserve the greatest attention. In particular, you need to "step into their shoes" and see the project from their perspective:

- What differences exist between myself and the people on whom I depend (goals, values, pressures, working styles, risks)?
- How do these different people view the project (supporters, indifferents, antagonists)?
- What is the current status of the relationship I have with the people I depend on?
- What sources of influence do I have relative to those on whom I depend?

Once you start this analysis you can begin to appreciate what others value and what currencies you might have to offer as a basis on which to build a working relationship. You begin to realize where potential problems lie—relationships in which you have a current debit or no convertible currency. Furthermore, diagnosing another's point of view as well as the basis for their positions will help you anticipate their reactions and feelings about your decisions and actions. This information is vital for selecting the appropriate influence strategy and tactics and conducting win/win negotiations.

For example, after mapping her dependency network, the project manager who was in charge of installing the software system realized that she was likely to have serious problems with the manager of the receipts department, who would be one of the primary users of the software. She had no previous history of working with this individual but had heard through the grapevine that the manager was upset with the choice of software and that he considered this project to be another unnecessary disruption of his department's operation. Prior to project initiation the project manager arranged to have lunch with the manager, where she sat patiently and listened to his concerns. She invested additional time and attention to educate him and his staff about the benefits of the new software. She tried to minimize the disruptions the transition would cause in his department. She altered the implementation schedule to accommodate his preferences as to when the actual software would be installed and the subsequent training would occur. In turn, the receipts manager and his people were much more accepting of the change, and the transition to the new software went more smoothly than anticipated.

Management by Wandering Around (MBWA)

The preceding example illustrates the next step in building a supportive social network. Once you have established who the key players are that will determine success, then you initiate contact and begin to build a relationship with those players. Building this relationship requires a management style employees at Hewlett-Packard refer to as **"management by wandering around" (MBWA)** to reflect that managers spend the majority of their time outside their offices. MBWA is somewhat of a misnomer in that there is a purpose/pattern behind the "wandering." Through face-to-face interactions, project managers are able to stay in touch with what is really going on in the project and build cooperation essential to project success.

Effective project managers initiate contact with key players to keep abreast of developments, anticipate potential problems, provide encouragement, and reinforce the objectives and vision of the project. They are able to intervene to resolve conflicts and prevent stalemates from occurring. In essence, they "manage" the project. By staying in touch with various aspects of the project they become the focal point for information on the project. Participants turn to them to obtain the most current and comprehensive information about the project which reinforces their central role as project manager.

We have also observed less-effective project managers who eschew MBWA and attempt to manage projects from their offices and computer terminals. Such managers proudly announce an open-door policy and encourage others to see them when a problem or an issue comes up. To them no news is good news. This allows their contacts to be determined by the relative aggressiveness of others. Those who take the initiative and seek out the project manager get too high a proportion of the project manager's attention. Those people less readily available (physically removed) or more passive get ignored. This behavior contributes to the adage, "Only the squeaky wheel gets greased," which breeds resentment within the project team.

Effective project managers also find the time to regularly interact with more distal stakeholders. They keep in touch with suppliers, vendors, top management, and other functional managers. In doing so they maintain familiarity with different parties, sustain friendships, discover opportunities to do favors, and understand the motives and needs of others. They remind people of commitments and champion the cause of their project. They also shape people's expectations (see Snapshot from Practice: Managing Expectations). Through frequent communication they alleviate people's concerns about the project, dispel rumors, warn people of potential problems, and lay the groundwork for dealing with setbacks in a more effective manner.

Unless project managers take the initiative to build a network of supportive relationships, they are likely to see a manager (or other stakeholder) only when there is bad news or when they need a favor (e.g., they don't have the data they promised or the project has slipped behind schedule). Without prior, frequent, easy give-and-take interactions around nondecisive issues, the encounter prompted

SNAPSHOT FROM PRACTICE Managing Expectations*

Dorothy Kirk, a project management consultant and program manager with Financial Solutions Group of Mynd, offers several keen insights about the art of managing stakeholder expectations:

> . . . expectations are hardy. All they need to take root is the absence of evidence to the contrary. Once rooted, the unspoken word encourages growth. They can develop and thrive without being grounded in reality. For this reason, project managers do daily battle with unrealistic expectations.

She goes on to offer several tips for managing expectations:

- The way you present information can either clarify or muddy expectations. For example, if you estimate that a task will take 317 hours, you are setting high expectations by your precision. The stakeholder is likely to be unhappy if it takes 323 hours. The stakeholder will not be unhappy with 323 hours if you quoted an estimate of 300–325 hours.
- Recognize that it is only human nature to interpret a situation in one's best interest. For example, if you tell someone it will be done by January, you are inclined to interpret it to your advantage and assume you have to the end of January, while the other person believes it will be done January 1st.
- Seize every opportunity to realign expectations with reality. Too often we avoid opportunities to adjust expectations because we hold onto a false hope that things will somehow work out.
- Do not ask for stakeholder suggestions for improvement if you do not intend to do something with their input. Asking for their input raises expectations.
- State the obvious. What is obvious to you may be obscure to others.
- Don't avoid delivering bad news. Communicate openly and in person. Expect some anger and frustration. Do not get defensive in return. Be prepared to explain the impact of the problems. For example, never say the project is going to be late without being able to give a new date. Explain what you are doing to see that this does not continue to happen.

All stakeholders have expectations about the schedule, cost, and project benefits. Project managers need to listen for, understand, and manage these expectations.

* D. Kirk, "Managing Expectations," *PM Network,* August 2000, pp. 59–62.

by the problem is likely to provoke excess tension. The parties are more likely to act defensively, interrupt each other, and lose sight of the common problem.

Experienced project managers recognize the need to build relationships before they need them. They initiate contact with the key stakeholders at times when there are no outstanding issues or problems and therefore no anxieties and suspicions. On these social occasions, they engage in small talk and responsive banter. They respond to others' requests for aid, provide supportive counsel, and exchange information. In doing so they establish credit in that relationship, which will allow them to deal with more serious problems down the road. When one person views another as pleasant, credible, and helpful based on past contact, he or she is much more likely to be responsive to requests for help and less confrontational when problems arise.[2]

Managing Upward Relations

Research consistently points out that project success is strongly affected by the degree to which a project has the support of top management.[3] Such support is reflected in an appropriate budget, responsiveness to unexpected needs, and a clear signal to others in the organization of the importance of cooperation.

Visible top management support is not only critical for securing the support of other managers within an organization, but it also is a key factor in the project

[2] This discussion is based on Leonard R. Sayles, *Leadership: Managing in Real Organizations* (New York: McGraw-Hill, 1989) pp. 70–78.

[3] See, for example: J. L. Pinto and S. K. Mantel, "The Causes of Project Failure," *IEEE Transactions in Engineering Management,* Vol. 37, No. 4 (1990), pp. 269–76.

manager's ability to motivate the project team. Nothing establishes a manager's right to lead more than her ability to defend. To win the loyalty of team members, project managers have to be effective advocates for their projects. They have to be able to get top management to rescind unreasonable demands, provide additional resources, and recognize the accomplishments of team members. This is more easily said than done.

Working relationships with upper management is a common source of consternation. Laments like the following are often made by project managers about upper management:

> They don't know how much it sets us back losing Neil to another project.
>
> I would like to see them get this project done with the budget they gave us.
>
> I just wish they would make up their minds as to what is really important.

While it may seem counterintuitive for a subordinate to "manage" a superior, smart project managers devote considerable time and attention to influencing and garnering the support of top management. Project managers have to accept profound differences in perspective and become skilled at the art of persuading superiors.

Many of the tensions that arise between upper management and project managers are a result of differences in perspective. Project managers become naturally absorbed with what is best for their project. To them the most important thing in the world is their project. Top management should have a different set of priorities. They are concerned with what is best for the entire organization. It is only natural for these two interests to conflict at times. For example, a project manager may lobby intensively for additional personnel only to be turned down because top management believes that the other departments cannot afford a reduction in staff. Although frequent communication can minimize differences, the project manager has to accept the fact that top management is inevitably going to see the world differently.

Once project managers accept that disagreements with superiors are more a question of perspective than substance, they can focus more of their energy on the art of persuading upper management. But before they can persuade superiors, they must first prove loyalty.[4] Loyalty in this context simply means that most of the time project managers have to show that they consistently follow through on requests and adhere to the parameters established by top management without a great deal of grumbling or fuss. Once managers have proven loyalty to upper management, senior management is much more receptive to their challenges and requests.

FIGURE 10.3
The Significance of a Project Sponsor

Project managers have to cultivate strong ties with upper managers who are sponsoring the project. As noted earlier, these are high-ranking officials who championed approval and funding of the project; as such, their reputations are aligned with the project. Sponsors are also the ones who defend the project when it is under attack in upper circles of management. They shelter the project from excessive interference (see Figure 10.3). Project managers should *always* keep such people informed of any problems that may cause embarrassment or disappointment. For example, if costs are beginning to outrun the budget or a technical glitch is threatening to delay the completion of the project, managers make sure that the sponsors are the first to know.

Timing is everything. Asking for additional budget the day after disappointing third-quarter earnings are reported is going to be much more difficult than making a similar request four weeks later. Good project managers pick the optimum time to appeal to top management. They enlist their project sponsors to lobby their

[4] Sayles, *Leadership,* pp. 136–45.

Research Highlight

Improving the Performance of New-Product Teams*

Ancona and Caldwell studied the performance of 45 new-product teams in five high-technology companies and produced some startling results. The most significant was that internal team dynamics were not related to performance. That is, high-performance teams were not distinguished by clearer goals, smoother workflow among members, or greater ability to satisfy the individual goals of team members. What related to team performance were level and intensity of external interactions between the project team and the rest of the organization. Ancona and Caldwell identified four key patterns of activity which contribute to creating a high-performance team:

1. *Ambassador* activities are aimed at representing the team to others and protecting the team from interference. The project manager typically takes on this responsibility, which involves buffering the team from political pressures and building support for the project within the hierarchy of the company.
2. *Task coordinator* activities are aimed at coordinating the team's efforts with other units and organizations. Unlike the ambassador role, which is focused upward, these are more lateral activities and involve negotiating and interacting with interested parties within the organization.
3. *Scouts* act as a scout on an expedition; that is, they go out from the team to bring back information about what is going on elsewhere in the organization. This is a much less focused task than task coordinator.
4. *Guard* activities differ from the other activities in that they are intended to keep information and resources inside the team, preventing drainage out of the group. A key guard activity is keeping necessary information secret until it is appropriate to share it.

Ancona and Caldwell found that the importance of these activities varies during the product development life cycle if the project team is to be successful. For example, scouting activities are more critical during the creation phase, when the product idea is being formulated and the team is being developed. Ambassador activities are especially critical during the development phase, when product specifications have been agreed upon and the major task is developing a prototype.

Ancona and Caldwell caution that their findings do not mean that teamwork and the internal operations of a project team are not important to project success. Effective team dynamics are necessary to successfully integrate information from outside sources and coordinate activities across groups. Their research supports the adage that problems and opportunities often lie at the borders of projects, and that one of the primary jobs of a project manager is to manage the interface between his or her team and the rest of the organization.

* D. G. Ancona and D. Caldwell, "Improving the Performance of New-Product Teams," *Research Technology Management,* Vol. 33, No. 2 (March–April 1990), pp. 25–29.

cause. They also realize there are limits to top management's accommodations. Here, the Lone Ranger analogy is appropriate—you have only so many silver bullets, so use them wisely.

Project managers need to adapt their communication pattern to that of the senior group. For example, one project manager recognized that top management had a tendency to use sports metaphors to describe business situations, so she framed a recent slip in schedule by admitting that "we lost five yards, but we still have two plays to make a first down." Smart project managers learn the language of top management and use it to their advantage.

Finally, a few project managers admit ignoring chains of command. If they are confident that top management will reject an important request and that what they want to do will benefit the project, they do it without asking permission. While acknowledging that this is very risky, they claim that bosses typically won't argue with success.

Leading by Example

A highly visible, interactive management style is not only essential to building and sustaining cooperative relationships, it also allows project managers to utilize their most powerful leadership tool—their own behavior (Peters, 1988; Kouznes & Posner, 2012). Often, when faced with uncertainty, people look to others for cues

SNAPSHOT FROM PRACTICE Leading at the Edge*

In 1914, the intrepid explorer Ernest Shackleton embarked on the *Endurance* with his team of seamen and scientists, intent upon crossing the unexplored Antarctic continent. What happened in the two years between their departure and their ultimate incredible rescue has rarely been matched in the annals of survival: a ship crushed by expanding ice pack . . . a crew stranded on the floes of the frozen Weddell Sea . . . two perilous treks in open boats across a raging Southern Ocean . . . a team marooned on the wild, forlorn Elephant Island, stretched to the limits of human endurance.

This adventure provided the basis for the book *Leading at the Edge: Leadership Lessons from the Extraordinary Saga of Shackleton's Antarctic Expedition* written by Dennis Perkins. Perkins provides numerous incidents of how Shackleton's personal example influenced the behavior of his beleaguered crew. For example, from the beginning of the Trans-Atlantic expedition to its end Shackleton consistently encouraged behavior that emphasized caring and respect:

> After the destruction of the *Endurance* Shackleton heated hot milk for the crew and went from tent to tent with the "life giving" drink. After the sail to the island of South Georgia, when the exhausted crew had landed, Shackleton took the first watch, which he kept for three hours instead of the usual one.

Crew members emulated the caring behaviors that Shackleton modeled. A good example of this occurred during one of the most dramatic moments in the *Endurance* saga. The food supply had dwindled to perilously low levels. Less than a week's supply remained, and the tiny ration of seal steak usually served at breakfast was eliminated. The waste meat generally used to feed the dogs was inspected for edible scraps.

Under these wretched conditions, and after a wet sleepless night, an argument broke out among some of the team members. Caught in the middle, one crew member (Greenstreet) spilled his tiny ration of powdered milk and shouted at the biologist (Clark). Alfred Lansing described what happened next:

© Topham/The Image Works

> Greenstreet paused to get his breath, and in that instant his anger was spent and he suddenly fell silent. Everyone else in the tent became quiet, too, and looked at Greenstreet, shaggy-haired, bearded, and filthy with blubber soot, holding his empty mug in his hand and looking helplessly down into the snow that had thirstily soaked up his precious milk. The loss was so tragic he seemed almost on the point of weeping. Without speaking, Clark reached out and poured some milk into Greenstreet's mug. Then Worsely, then Macklin, and Rickerson and Kerr, Orde-Lees, and finally Blackborrow. They finished in silence.

* Adapted from Dennis N. T. Perkins, *Leading at the Edge: Leadership Lessons from the Extraordinary Saga of Shackleton's Antarctica Expedition* (New York: AMACOM Press, 2000), pp. 94–95; and Alfred Lansing, *Endurance: Shackleton's Incredible Voyage* (New York: Carroll & Graf, 1998), p. 127.

as to how to respond and demonstrate a propensity to mimic the behavior of superiors. A project manager's behavior symbolizes how other people should work on the project. Through her behavior a project manager can influence how others act and respond to a variety of issues related to the project. (See Snapshot from Practice: Leading at the Edge for a dramatic example of this.)

To be effective, project managers must "walk the talk" (see Figure 10.4). Six aspects of leading by example are discussed next.

FIGURE 10.4
Leading by Example

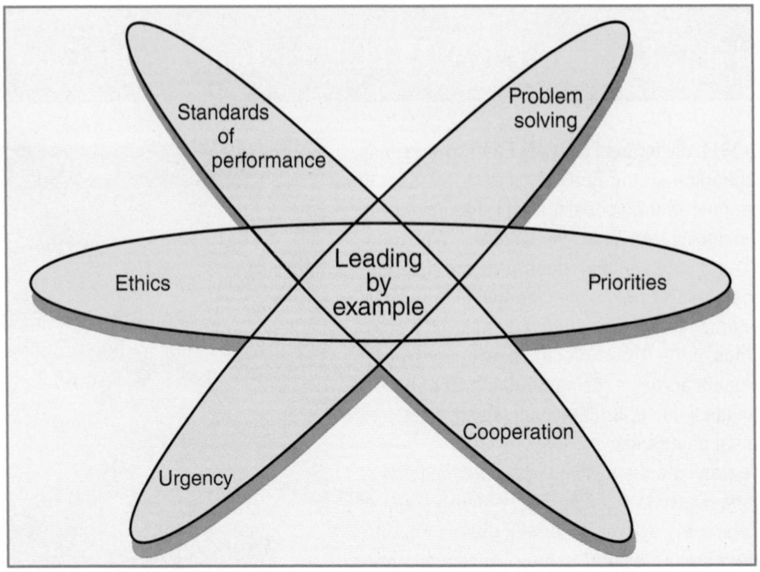

Priorities

Actions speak louder than words. Subordinates and others discern project managers' priorities by how they spend their time. If a project manager claims that this project is critical and then is perceived as devoting more time to other projects, then all his verbal reassurances are likely to fall on deaf ears. Conversely, a project manager who takes the time to observe a critical test instead of simply waiting for a report affirms the importance of the testers and their work. Likewise, the types of questions project managers pose communicate priorities. By repeatedly asking how specific issues relate to satisfying the customer, a project manager can reinforce the importance of customer satisfaction.

Urgency

Through their actions project managers can convey a sense of urgency, which can permeate project activities. This urgency in part can be conveyed through stringent deadlines, frequent status report meetings, and aggressive solutions for expediting the project. The project manager uses these tools like a metronome to pick up the beat of the project. At the same time, such devices will be ineffective if there is not also a corresponding change in the project manager's behavior. If they want others to work faster and solve problems quicker, then they need to work faster. They need to hasten the pace of their own behavior. They should accelerate the frequency of their interactions, talk and walk more quickly, get to work sooner, and leave work later. By simply increasing the pace of their daily interaction patterns, project managers can reinforce a sense of urgency in others.

Problem Solving

How project managers respond to problems sets the tone for how others tackle problems. If bad news is greeted by verbal attacks, then others will be reluctant to be forthcoming.[5] If the project manager is more concerned with finding out who

[5] This is the classic "kill the messenger" syndrome. This and other forces that contribute to distorting information can be found in Erik Larson and Jon King "The Systemic Distortion of Information: An On-going Management Challenge," *Organizational Dynamics*, Winter 1996, pp. 49–62.

is to blame instead of how to prevent problems from happening again, then others will tend to cover their tracks and cast the blame elsewhere. If, on the other hand, project managers focus more on how they can turn a problem into an opportunity or what can be learned from a mistake, then others are more likely to adopt a more proactive approach to problem solving.

Cooperation

How project managers act toward outsiders influences how team members interact with outsiders. If a project manager makes disparaging remarks about the "idiots" in the marketing department, then this oftentimes becomes the shared view of the entire team. If project managers set the norm of treating outsiders with respect and being responsive to their needs, then others will more likely follow suit.

Standards of Performance

Veteran project managers recognize that if they want participants to exceed project expectations then they have to exceed others' expectations of a good project manager. They establish a high standard for project performance through the quality of their daily interactions. They respond quickly to the needs of others, carefully prepare and run crisp meetings, stay on top of all the critical issues, facilitate effective problem solving, and stand firm on important matters.

Ethics

How others respond to ethical dilemmas that arise in the course of a project will be influenced by how the project manager has responded to similar dilemmas. In many cases, team members base their actions on how they think the project manager would respond. If project managers deliberately distort or withhold vital information from customers or top management, then they are signaling to others that this kind of behavior is acceptable. Project management invariably creates a variety of ethical dilemmas; this would be an appropriate time to delve into this topic in more detail.

Ethics and Project Management

Questions of ethics have already arisen in previous chapters that discussed padding of cost and time estimations, exaggerating pay-offs of project proposals, and so forth. Ethical dilemmas involve situations where it is difficult to determine whether conduct is right or wrong. Is it acceptable to falsely assure customers that everything is on track when, in reality, you are only doing so to prevent them from panicking and making matters worse?

In a survey of project managers, 81 percent reported that they encounter ethical issues in their work.[6] These dilemmas range from being pressured to alter status reports, backdate signatures, or shade documentation to mask the reality of project progress to falsifying cost accounts, compromising safety standards to accelerate progress, and approving shoddy work.

Project management is complicated work, and, as such, ethics invariably involve gray areas of judgment and interpretation. For example, it is difficult to distinguish deliberate falsification of estimates from genuine mistakes or the willful exaggeration of project payoffs from genuine optimism. It becomes problematic to

[6] While this survey is a bit old, our conversations with project managers suggest that the results hold true today (J. Cabanis, "A Question of Ethics: The Issues Project Managers Face and How They Resolve Them," *PM Network,* December 1995, pp. 8–28).

SNAPSHOT FROM PRACTICE The Collapse of Arthur Andersen*

AP Photo/Stephen J. Carrera

"Think straight and talk straight" was the principle on which Arthur E. Andersen built his accounting firm in the early 1900s. It was a phrase his mother taught him and became the firm's motto. The commitment to integrity and a systematic, planned approach to work were instrumental in Arthur Andersen becoming one of the largest and best-known accounting firms in the world.

> Working for Arthur Andersen was not for everyone. It could be a tough culture. It was much too hierarchical and top down for the more free spirited. Many people left after less than two years, believing the rewards did not warrant the demands that were made on them. Others learned to play by the rules and some even thrived. To remain in the firm, staff members were expected to work hard, respect authority of rank, and maintain a high level of conformity. In return they were rewarded with support, promotion, and the possibility of making partner. Those individuals who made a career with the firm grew old together, professionally and personally, and most had never worked anywhere else. To these survivors, Andersen was their second family, and they developed strong loyalties to the firm and its culture. (p. 133)

On October 23, 2001, David Duncan told his Enron project team that they needed to start complying with Andersen's new policy on handling audit documents. The policy had been instituted to make sure that the firm's extraneous paperwork could not be used in court cases. Although the document retention policy required that papers supporting the firm's opinions and audit be retained, it allowed a broad category of secondary documents to be destroyed. The team reacted with stunned silence to Duncan's directive. Then everyone got up and began racing to do what they had been told to do. No one asked Duncan to explain further. None asked whether what they were doing was wrong. No one questioned whether what he or she were doing might be illegal. Andersen's Houston staff just reacted, following orders without question.

On November 9, 2001, the day after the Securities Exchange Commission (SEC) issued a subpoena to Andersen, the shredding stopped. More than one ton of documents had been destroyed and 30,000 e-mails and Enron-related computer files erased. According to Andersen's legal defense team, the shredding was business as usual. The lawyers claimed that the shredding was standard practice for eliminating unnecessary files. To the SEC, it appeared to be the start of a deep cover-up operation. Subsequently one of the most respected accounting firms in the world closed its doors.

* Susan E. Squires, Cynthia J. Smith, Lorna McDougall, and William R. Yeak, *Inside Arthur Andersen: Shifting Values, Unexpected Consequences* (Upper Saddle River, NJ: Prentice Hall, 2004).

determine whether unfulfilled promises were deliberate deception or an appropriate response to changing circumstances.

To provide greater clarity to business ethics, many companies and professional groups publish a code of conduct. Cynics see these documents as simply window dressing, while advocates argue that they are important, albeit limited, first steps. In practice, personal ethics do not lie in formal statutes but at the intersection of one's work, family, education, profession, religious beliefs, and daily interactions. Most project managers report that they rely on their own private sense of right and wrong—what one project manager called his "internal compass." One common rule of thumb for testing whether a response is ethical is to ask, "Imagine that whatever you did was going to be reported on the front page of your local newspaper. How would you like that? Would you be comfortable?"

Unfortunately, scandals at Enron, Worldcom, and Arthur Andersen have demonstrated the willingness of highly trained professionals to abdicate personal responsibility for illegal actions and to obey the directives of superiors (see Snapshot from Practice: The Collapse of Arthur Andersen). Top management and the culture of an organization play a decisive role in shaping members' beliefs of what is right and wrong. Many organizations encourage ethical transgressions by creating a "win at all cost" mentality. The pressures to succeed obscure consideration of whether the ends justify the means. Other organizations place a premium on "fair play" and command a market position by virtue of being trustworthy and reliable.[7]

Many project managers claim that ethical behavior is its own reward. By following your own internal compass your behavior expresses your personal values. Others suggest that ethical behavior is doubly rewarding. You not only are able to fall asleep at night but you also develop a sound and admirable reputation. As will be explored in the next section, such a reputation is essential to establishing the trust necessary to exercise influence effectively.

Building Trust: The Key to Exercising Influence

We all know people who have influence but whom we do not trust; these individuals are often referred to as "political animals" or "jungle fighters." While these individuals are often very successful in the short run, the prevalent sense of mistrust prohibits long-term efficacy. Successful project managers not only need to be influential, they also need to exercise influence in a manner that builds and sustains the trust of others.

The significance of trust can be discerned by its absence. Imagine how different a working relationship is when you distrust the other party as opposed to trusting them. When people distrust each other, they often spend inordinate amounts of time and energy attempting to discern hidden agendas and the true meaning of communications and then securing guarantees to promises. They are much more cautious with each other and hesitant to cooperate. Here is what one line manager had to say about how he reacted to a project manager he did not trust:

> Whenever Jim approached me about something, I found myself trying to read between the lines to figure what was really going on. When he made a request, my initial reaction was "no" until he proved it.

[7] For a more in-depth discussion of ethics, see: L. Trevino and K. Nelson, *Managing Business Ethics: Straight Talk about How to Do It Right*, 5th ed. (Hoboken, NJ: John Wiley & Sons, 2011).

Conversely, trust is the "lubricant" that maintains smooth and efficient interactions. When you trust, people are more likely to take your actions and intentions at face value when circumstances are ambiguous. For example, here is what a functional manager had to say about how he dealt with a project manager he trusted:

> If Sally said she needed something, no questions were asked. I knew it was important or she wouldn't have asked.

Trust is an elusive concept. It is hard to nail down in precise terms why some project managers are trusted and others are not. One popular way to understand trust is to see it as a function of character and competence. Character focuses on personal motives (i.e., does he or she want to do the right thing?), while competence focuses on skills necessary to realize motives (i.e., does he or she know the right things to do?).

Stephen Covey resurrected the significance of character in leadership literature in his best-selling *Seven Habits of Highly Effective People*. Covey criticized popular management literature as focusing too much on shallow human relations skills and manipulative techniques, which he labeled the personality ethic. He argues that at the core of highly effective people is a character ethic that is deeply rooted in personal values and principles such as dignity, service, fairness, the pursuit of truth, and respect.

One of the distinguishing traits of character is consistency. When people are guided by a core set of principles, they are naturally more predictable because their actions are consistent with these principles. Another feature of character is openness. When people have a clear sense of who they are and what they value, they are more receptive to others. This trait provides them with the capacity to empathize and the talent to build consensus among divergent people. Finally, another quality of character is a sense of purpose. Managers with character are driven not only by personal ambitions but also for the common good. Their primary concern is what is best for their organization and the project, not what is best for themselves. This willingness to subordinate personal interests to a higher purpose garners the respect, loyalty, and trust of others.

The significance of character is summarized by the comments made by two team members about two very different project managers.

> At first everyone liked Joe and was excited about the project. But after a while, people became suspicious of his motives. He had a tendency to say different things to different people. People began to feel manipulated. He spent too much time with top management. People began to believe that he was only looking out for himself. It was HIS project. When the project began to slip he jumped ship and left someone else holding the bag. I'll never work for that guy again.

> My first impression of Jack was nothing special. He had a quiet, unassuming management style. Over time I learned to respect his judgment and his ability to get people to work together. When you went to him with a problem or a request, he always listened carefully. If he couldn't do what you wanted him to do, he would take the time to explain why. When disagreements arose he always thought of what was best for the project. He treated everyone by the same rules; no one got special treatment. I'd jump at the opportunity to work on a project with him again.

Character alone will not engender trust. We must also have confidence in the competency of individuals before we really trust them (Kanter, 1979). We all know well-intended managers whom we like but do not trust because they have a history of coming up short on their promises. Although we may befriend these managers, we don't like to work with or for them.

Competence is reflected at a number of different levels. First, there is task-related knowledge and skills reflected in the ability to answer questions, solve technical problems, and excel in certain kinds of work. Second, there is competence at an interpersonal level demonstrated in being able to listen effectively, communicate clearly, resolve arguments, provide encouragement, and so forth. Finally, there is organizational competence. This includes being able to run effective meetings, set meaningful objectives, reduce inefficiencies, and build a social network. Too often there is a tendency for young engineers and other professionals to place too much value on task or technical competence. They underestimate the significance of organizational skills. Veteran professionals, on the other hand, recognize the importance of management and place a greater value on organizational and interpersonal skills.

One problem new project managers experience is that it takes time to establish a sense of character and competency. Character and competency are often demonstrated when they are tested, such as when a tough call has to be made or when difficult problems have to be solved. Veteran project managers have the advantage of reputation and an established track record of success. Although endorsements from credible sponsors can help a young project manager create a favorable first impression, ultimately he or she will have to demonstrate character and competence during the course of dealings with others in order to gain their trust.

So far this chapter has addressed the importance of building a network of relationships to complete the project based on trust and reciprocity. The next section examines the nature of project management work and the personal qualities needed to excel at it.

Qualities of an Effective Project Manager

Project management is, at first glance, a misleading discipline in that there is an inherent logic in the progression from formulating a project scope statement, creating a WBS, developing a network, adding resources, finalizing a plan, and reaching milestones. However, when it comes to actually implementing and completing projects, this logic quickly disappears, and project managers encounter a much messier world, filled with inconsistencies and paradoxes. Effective project managers have to be able to deal with the contradictory nature of their work. Some of those contradictions are listed here:

- **Innovate and maintain stability.** Project managers have to put out fires, restore order, and get the project back on track. At the same time they need to be innovative and develop new, better ways of doing things. Innovations unravel stable routines and spark new disturbances that have to be dealt with.
- **See the big picture while getting your hands dirty.** Project managers have to see the big picture and how their project fits within the larger strategy of their firm. There are also times when they must get deeply involved in project work and technology. If they don't worry about the details, who will?
- **Encourage individuals but stress the team.** Project managers have to motivate, cajole, and entice individual performers while at the same time maintaining teamwork. They have to be careful that they are considered fair and consistent in their treatment of team members while at the same time treating each member as a special individual.
- **Hands-off/Hands-on.** Project managers have to intervene, resolve stalemates, solve technical problems, and insist on different approaches. At the same time they have to recognize when it is appropriate to sit on the sidelines and let other people figure out what to do.

no workshop or magic potion that can transform a pessimist into an optimist or provide a sense of purpose when there is not one. These qualities get at the very soul or being of a person. Optimism, integrity, and even being proactive are not easily developed if there is not already a predisposition to display them.

Summary

To be successful, project managers must build a cooperative network among a diverse set of allies. They begin by identifying who the key stakeholders on a project are, followed by a diagnosis of the nature of the relationships, and the basis for exercising influence. Effective project managers are skilled at acquiring and exercising a wide range of influence. They use this influence and a highly interactive management style to monitor project performance and initiate appropriate changes in project plans and direction. They do so in a manner that generates trust, which is ultimately based on others' perceptions of their character and competence.

Project managers are encouraged to keep in mind the following suggestions:

- *Build relationships before you need them.* Identify key players and what you can do to help them before you need their assistance. It is always easier to receive a favor after you have granted one. This requires the project manager to see the project in systems terms and to appreciate how it affects other activities and agendas inside and outside the organization. From this perspective they can identify opportunities to do good deeds and garner the support of others.
- *Trust is sustained through frequent face-to-face contact.* Trust withers through neglect. This is particularly true under conditions of rapid change and uncertainty that naturally engender doubt, suspicion, and even momentary bouts of paranoia. Project managers must maintain frequent contact with key stakeholders to keep abreast of developments, assuage concerns, engage in reality testing, and focus attention on the project. Frequent face-to-face interactions affirm mutual respect and trust in each other.

Ultimately, exercising influence in an effective and ethical manner begins and ends with how you view the other parties. Do you view them as potential partners or obstacles to your goals? If obstacles, then you wield your influence to manipulate and gain compliance and cooperation. If partners, you exercise influence to gain their commitment and support. People who view social network building as building partnerships see every interaction with two goals: resolving the immediate problem/concern and improving the working relationship so that next time it will be even more effective. Experienced project managers realize that "what goes around comes around" and try at all cost to avoid antagonizing players for quick success.

Key Terms

Emotional intelligence (EQ), *361*
Inspiration-related currencies, *346*
Law of reciprocity, *344*
Leading by example, *352*
Management by wandering around (MBWA), *349*
Personal-related currencies, *347*
Position-related currencies, *346*
Proactive, *360*
Relationship-related currencies, *346*
Social network building, *347*
Stakeholder, *341*
Systems thinking, *360*
Task-related currencies, *345*

Review Questions

1. What is the difference between leading and managing a project?
2. Why is a conductor of an orchestra an appropriate metaphor for being a project manager? What aspects of project managing are not reflected by this metaphor? Can you think of other metaphors that would be appropriate?
3. What does the exchange model of influence suggest you do to build cooperative relationships to complete a project?
4. What differences would you expect to see between the kinds of influence currencies that a project manager in a functional matrix would use and the influence a project manager of a dedicated project team would use?
5. Why is it important to build a relationship before you need it?
6. Why is it critical to keep the project sponsor informed?
7. Why is trust a function of both character and competence?
8. Which of the eight traits/skills associated with being an effective project manager is the most important? The least important? Why?

Exercises

1. Do an Internet search for the Keirsey Temperament Sorter Questionnaire and find a site that appears to have a reputable self-assessment questionnaire. Respond to the questionnaire to identify your temperament type. Read supportive documents associated with your type. What does this material suggest are the kinds of projects that would best suit you? What does it suggest your strengths and weaknesses are as a project manager? How can you compensate for your weaknesses?
2. Access the Project Management Institute Web site and review the standards contained in PMI Member Ethical Standards section. How useful is the information for helping someone decide what behavior is appropriate and inappropriate?
3. You are organizing an AIDS benefit concert in your hometown that will feature local heavy metal rock groups and guest speakers. Draw a dependency map identifying the major groups of people that are likely to affect the success of this project. Who do you think will be most cooperative? Who do you think will be the least cooperative? Why?
4. You are the project manager responsible for the overall construction of a new international airport. Draw a dependency map identifying the major groups of people that are likely to affect the success of this project. Who do you think will be most cooperative? Who do you think will be the least cooperative? Why?
5. Identify an important relationship (co-worker, boss, friend) in which you are having trouble gaining cooperation. Assess this relationship in terms of the influence currency model. What kinds of influence currency have you been exchanging in this relationship? Is the "bank account" for this relationship in the "red" or the "black"? What kinds of influence would be appropriate for building a stronger relationship with that person?
6. Each of the following seven mini-case scenarios involve ethical dilemmas associated with project management. How would you respond to each situation, and why?

Jack Nietzche

You returned from a project staffing meeting in which future project assignments were finalized. Despite your best efforts, you were unable to persuade the director of project management to promote one of your best assistants, Jack Nietzche, to a project manager position. You feel a bit guilty because you dangled the prospect of this promotion to motivate Jack. Jack responded by putting in extra hours to ensure that his segments of the project were completed on time. You wonder how

Jack will react to this disappointment. More importantly, you wonder how his reaction might affect your project. You have five days remaining to meet a critical deadline for a very important customer. While it won't be easy, you believed you would be able to complete the project on time. Now you're not so sure. Jack is halfway through completing the documentation phase, which is the last critical activity. Jack can be pretty emotional at times, and you are worried that he will blow up once he finds he didn't get the promotion. As you return to your office, you wonder what you should do. Should you tell Jack that he isn't going to be promoted? What should you say if he asks about whether the new assignments were made?

Seaburst Construction Project

You are the project manager for the Seaburst construction project. So far the project is progressing ahead of schedule and below budget. You attribute this in part to the good working relationship you have with the carpenters, plumbers, electricians, and machine operators who work for your organization. More than once you have asked them to give 110 percent, and they have responded.

One Sunday afternoon you decide to drive by the site and show it to your son. As you point out various parts of the project to your son, you discover that several pieces of valuable equipment are missing from the storage shed. When you start work again on Monday you are about to discuss this matter with a supervisor when you realize that all the missing equipment is back in the shed. What should you do? Why?

The Project Status Report Meeting

You are driving to a project status report meeting with your client. You encountered a significant technical problem on the project that has put your project behind schedule. This is not good news because completion time is the number one priority for the project. You are confident that your team can solve the problem if they are free to give their undivided attention to it and that with hard work you can get back on schedule. You also believe if you tell the client about the problem, she will demand a meeting with your team to discuss the implications of the problem. You can also expect her to send some of her personnel to oversee the solution to the problem. These interruptions will likely further delay the project. What should you tell your client about the current status of the project?

Gold Star LAN project

You work for a large consulting firm and were assigned to the Gold Star LAN project. Work on the project is nearly completed and your clients at Gold Star appear to be pleased with your performance. During the course of the project, changes in the original scope had to be made to accommodate specific needs of managers at Gold Star. The costs of these changes were documented as well as overhead and submitted to the centralized accounting department. They processed the information and submitted a change order bill for your signature. You are surprised to see the bill is 10 percent higher than what you submitted. You contact Jim Messina in the accounting office and ask if a mistake has been made. He curtly replies that no mistake was made and that management adjusted the bill. He recommends that you sign the document. You talk to another project manager about this and she tells you off the record that overcharging clients on change orders is common practice in your firm. Would you sign the document? Why? Why not?

Cape Town Bio-Tech

You are responsible for installing the new Double E production line. Your team has collected estimates and used the WBS to generate a project schedule. You have confidence in the schedule and the work your team has done. You report to top management that you believe that the project will take 110 days and be completed by March 5. The news is greeted positively. In fact, the project sponsor confides that orders do not have to be shipped until April 1. You leave the meeting wondering whether you should share this information with the project team or not.

Ryman Pharmaceuticals

You are a test engineer on the Bridge project at Ryman Pharmaceuticals in Nashville, Tennessee. You have just completed conductivity tests of a new electrochemical compound. The results exceeded expectations. This new compound should revolutionize the industry. You are wondering whether to call your stockbroker and ask her to buy $20,000 worth of Ryman stock before everyone else finds out about the results. What would you do and why?

Princeton Landing

You are managing the renovation of the Old Princeton Landing Bar and Grill. The project is on schedule despite receiving a late shipment of paint. The paint was supposed to arrive on 1/30, but instead arrived on 2/1. The assistant store manager apologizes profusely for the delay and asks if you would be willing to sign the acceptance form and backdate it to 1/30. He says he won't qualify for a bonus that he has worked hard to meet for the past month if the shipment is reported late. He promises to make it up to you on future projects. What would you do and why?

References

Abrashoff, D. M., *It's Your Ship* (New York: Business Plus, 2002).

Ancona, D. G., and D. Caldwell, "Improving the Performance of New-Product Teams," *Research Technology Management,* 33 (2) March-April 1990, pp. 25–29.

Anand, V., B. E. Ashforth, and M. Joshi, "Business as Usual: The Acceptance and Perpetuation of Corruption in Organizations," *Academy of Management Executive,* 19 (4) 2005, pp. 9–23.

Badaracco, J. L., Jr., and A. P. Webb, "Business Ethics: A View from the Trenches," *California Management Review,* 37 (2) Winter 1995, pp. 8–28.

Baker, B., "Leadership and the Project Manager," *PM Network,* December 2002, p. 20.

Baker, W. E., *Network Smart: How to Build Relationships for Personal and Organizational Success* (New York: McGraw-Hill, 1994).

Bennis, W., *On Becoming a Leader* (Reading, MA: Addison-Wesley, 1989).

Bradberry, T., and J. Graves, *The Emotional Intelligence Quick Book: How to Put Your EQ to Work* (New York: Simon & Schuster, 2005).

Bourne, L., *Stakeholder Relationship Management* (Farnham, England: Gower Publishing Ltd., 2009).

Cabanis, J., "A Question of Ethics: The Issues Project Managers Face and How They Resolve Them," *PM Network,* December 1996, pp. 19–24.

Cabanis-Brewin, J., "The Human Task of a Project Leader: Daniel Goleman on the Value of High EQ," *PM Network,* November 1999, pp. 38–42.

Cohen, A. R., and D. L. Bradford, *Influence Without Authority* (New York: John Wiley & Sons, 1990).

Covey, S. R., *The Seven Habits of Highly Effective People* (New York: Simon & Schuster, 1989).

Dinsmore, P. C., "Will the Real Stakeholders Please Stand Up?" *PM Network,* December 1995, pp. 9–10.

Einsiedel, A. A., "Profile of Effective Project Managers," *Project Management Journal,* 31 (3) 1987, pp. 51–56.

Ferrazzi, K., *Never Eat Alone and Other Secrets to Success One Relationship at a Time* (Crown Publishers, 2005).

Gabarro, S. J., *The Dynamics of Taking Charge* (Boston: Harvard Business School Press, 1987).

Grant, A., *Give and Take: A revolutionary Approach to Success,* (New York: Viking Press, 2013).

Hill, L. A., *Becoming a Manager: Mastery of a New Identity* (Boston: Harvard Business School Press, 1992).

Kanter, R. M., "Power Failures in Management Circuits," *Harvard Business review*, July–August, 1979, pp. 65–79.

Kaplan, R. E., "Trade Routes: The Manager's Network of Relationships," *Organizational Dynamics,* 12 (4) Spring 1984, pp. 37–52.

Kirk, D., "Managing Expectations," *PM Network,* August 2000, pp. 59–62.

Kotter, J. P., "What Leaders Really Do," *Harvard Business Review,* 68 (3) May–June 1990, pp. 103–11.

Kouzes, J. M., and B. Z. Posner, *The Leadership Challenge 5th edt.,* (San Francisco: Jossey-Bass, 2012).

Kouzes, J. M., and B. Z. Posner, *Credibility: How Leaders Gain and Lose It. Why People Demand It* (San Francisco: Jossey-Bass, 1993).

Larson, E. W., and J. B. King, "The Systemic Distortion of Information: An Ongoing Management Challenge," *Organizational Dynamics,* 24 (3) Winter 1996, pp. 49–62.

Lewis, M. W., M. A. Welsh, G. E. Dehler, and S. G. Green, "Product Development Tensions: Exploring Contrasting Styles of Project Management," *Academy of Management Journal,* 45 (3) 2002, pp. 546–64.

Peters, L. H., "A Good Man in a Storm: An Interview with Tom West," *Academy of Management Executive,* 16 (4) 2002, pp. 53–63.

Peters, L. H., "Soulful Ramblings: An Interview with Tracy Kidder," *Academy of Management Executive,* 16 (4) 2002, pp. 45–52.

Peters, T., *Thriving on Chaos: Handbook for a Management Revolution* (New York: Alfred A. Knopf, 1988).

Pinto, J. K., and S. K. Mantel, "The Causes of Project Failure," *IEEE Transactions in Engineering Management,* 37 (4) 1990, pp. 269–76.

Pinto, J. K., and D. P. Sleven, "Critical Success Factors in Successful Project Implementation," *IEEE Transactions in Engineering Management,* 34 (1) 1987, pp. 22–27.

Project Management Institute, *PMBOK Guide 5th edt.,* (Newtown Sq., PA: Project Management Institute, 2013).

Posner, B. Z., "What It Takes to Be an Effective Project Manager," *Project Management Journal,* March 1987, pp. 51–55.

Project Management Institute, *Leadership in Project Management Annual* (Newton Square, PA: PMI Publishing, 2006).

Robb, D. J., "Ethics in Project Management: Issues, Practice, and Motive," *PM Network,* December 1996, pp. 13–18.

Sayles, L. R., *Leadership: Managing in Real Organizations* (New York: McGraw-Hill, 1989), pp. 70–78.

Sayles, L. R., *The Working Leader* (New York: Free Press, 1993).

Senge, P. M., *The Fifth Discipline* (New York: Doubleday, 1990).

Shenhar, A. J., and B. Nofziner, "A New Model for Training Project Managers," *Proceedings of the 28th Annual Project Management Institute Symposium,* 1997, pp. 301–6.

Shtub, A., J. F. Bard, and S. Globerson, *Project Management: Engineering, Technology, and Implementation* (Englewood Cliffs, NJ: Prentice Hall, 1994).

Trevino, L. K., and K. A. Nelson, *Managing Business Ethics: Straight Talk about How to Do It Right,* 5th ed. (Hoboken, NJ: John Wiley & Sons, 2011).

Turner, J. R., and R. Müller, "The Project Manager Leadership Style as a Success Factor on Projects: A Literature Review," *Project Management Journal,* 36 (2) 2005, pp. 49–61.

Case

The Blue Sky Project*

Garth Hudson was a 29-year-old graduate of Eastern State University (ESU) with a B.S. degree in management information systems. After graduation he worked for seven years at Bluegrass Systems in Louisville, Kentucky. While at ESU he worked part time for an oceanography professor, Ahmet Green, creating a customized database for a research project he was conducting. Green was recently appointed director of Eastern Oceanography Institute (EOI), and Hudson was confident that this prior experience was instrumental in his getting the job as information services (IS) director at the Institute. Although he took a significant pay cut, he jumped at the opportunity to return to his alma mater. His job at Bluegrass Systems had been very demanding. The long hours and extensive traveling had created tension in his marriage. He was looking forward to a normal job with reasonable hours. Besides, Jenna, his wife, would be busy pursuing her MBA at Eastern State University. While at Bluegrass, Hudson worked on a wide range of IS projects. He was confident that he had the requisite technical expertise to excel at his new job.

Eastern Oceanography Institute was an independently funded research facility aligned with Eastern State University. Approximately 50 full- and part-time staff worked at the Institute. They worked on research grants funded by the National Science Foundation (NSF) and the United Nations (UN), as well as research financed by private industry. There were typically 7 to 9 major research projects under way at any one time as well as 20 to 25 smaller projects. One-third of the Institute's scientists had part-time teaching assignments at ESU and used the Institute to conduct their own basic research.

FIRST YEAR AT EOI

Hudson made a point of introducing himself to the various groups of people upon his arrival at the Institute. Still, his contact with the staff had been limited. He spent most of his time becoming familiar with EOI's information system,

* Prepared by Erik Larson and V. T. Raja, senior instructor at the College of Business, Oregon State University.

The rest of the visit seemed to go well. He helped Shari unload a heavy box and managed to get an appreciative grin from Pinyarat when he almost correctly pronounced her name. Satisfied, Tom went back up to his office thinking that MBWA wouldn't be that tough to do.

After responding to e-mail and calling some vendors, Tom ventured back out to see how things were going downstairs. When he got there, the floor was weirdly quiet. People were busy doing their work and his attempts at generating conversation elicited stiff responses. He left thinking that maybe MBWA is going to be tougher than he thought.

1. What do you think is going on at the end of this case?
2. What should Tom do next and why?
3. What can be learned from this case?

Case

Cerberus Corporation*

Cerberus is a successful producer of specialty chemicals. It operates nine large campus sites in the United States, with a number of different business units on each site. These business units operate independently, with direct reporting to corporate headquarters. Site functions such as safety, environmental, and facilities management report to a host organization—typically the business unit that is the largest user of their services.

SUSAN STEELE

Susan Steele has worked in the Facilities group at the Cerberus Richmond site for the last two years. The Facilities manager, Tom Stern, reports to the General Manager of the largest business unit on site, the highly profitable Adhesives and Sealants Division. Susan started with Cerberus when she graduated with her business degree from Awsum University. She was excited about her new assignment—leading a project for the first time. She remembered Tom saying, "We've got office furniture dating back to the 80s. There are those ugly green-top desks that look like they came from military surplus! I'm especially concerned about computer workstation ergonomics—it's a major issue that we absolutely must fix! I want you to lead a project to transition our office furniture to the new corporate standard."

Susan assembled her project team: Jeff, the site safety/ergonomics engineer; Gretchen, the space planner; Cindy, the move coordinator; and Kari, the accounting liaison for Facilities. At their first meeting, everyone agreed that ergonomics was the most urgent concern. All five business units responded to a workstation survey that identified injury-causing ergonomics. The team was developing a plan to replace old desks with new, ergo-adjustable furniture by the end of the year. Susan asked Kari about the budget, and Kari responded, "Facilities should not pay for this. We want the individual business units to pay so that the costs will show where they are incurred."

* Courtesy of John Sloan, Oregon State University.

Gretchen spoke up: "You know, we've got lots of department moves going on constantly. Everybody is always jockeying for space and location as their business needs change. Besides the ergonomics, could we say that only corporate standard furniture gets moved? That would force changing some of the stuff that's just plain ugly." Everyone agreed that this was a great idea.

Susan presented the project plan to Tom and got a green light to proceed.

JON WOOD

Jon Wood is a planning manager, with 22 years experience at Cerberus. His business unit, Photographic Chemicals Division (PCD), is losing money. Digital photography is continuing to reduce the size of the market, and PCD is having trouble matching the competition's relentless price-cutting. Jon recently transferred to Richmond from corporate headquarters, where he ran the economic forecasting group. He is considered a new broom, and he is determined to sweep clean.

One of Jon's early actions was to negotiate with his general manager for a department move. Money was tight, and the site facilities function charged an arm and a leg for moves (covering all their fixed overhead, the operations people groused). However, Jon felt it was important to move from Building 4, where they were next to Production, to Building 6, where they could be close to Marketing, Forecasting, and Accounting. His General Manager agreed, and there was lots of excitement in his team about their upcoming move. Jon assigned one of his planners, Richard, to work with the Facilities team on the layout and move plan for the group. Things seemed to be going fine—Jon saw Richard sitting down with the move coordinator, and they seemed to be on track.

The day before the move, Jon hung up the phone from a particularly tense teleconference with a Canadian subcontractor. Production was not going well, and product availability would be tight for the rest of the quarter. Clustered around his desk were Richard, Cindy, and a person he hadn't met yet, Susan. After hurried introductions, Susan told Jon that his filing cabinets could not be moved. The cabinets are large lateral files, five feet wide and two feet deep, a combination of both filing cabinets and bookshelves. Jon brought them with him from Corporate because he thought they looked nice with their dark grey steel sides and wood veneer tops. Susan told him that he would have to replace them with new corporate standard cabinets, virtually the same size. Jon said, "You mean you want me to throw away perfectly good filing cabinets and spend another $2,000 on new ones, just so they match? I won't do it!"

Susan replied, "Then I won't authorize the movement of the old cabinets."

Jon said, "You're joking—these cabinets are grey, the new ones are grey—the only difference is the wood top! You'd throw away $2,000 for nothing?"

Susan replied stiffly, "I'm sorry, that's the policy."

Jon said, "I don't care what the policy is. If I have to move them myself, those cabinets are not going to the dump. My division is losing money and I'm not going to throw money away. If you don't like it, you're going to have to get your general manager to convince my general manager to make me do it. Now would you please leave so I can get some work done."

1. If you were Susan, what would you do?
2. What, if anything, could Susan have done differently to avoid this problem?
3. What could the management of Cerberus do to more effectively manage situations like this?

CHAPTER ELEVEN

Managing Project Teams

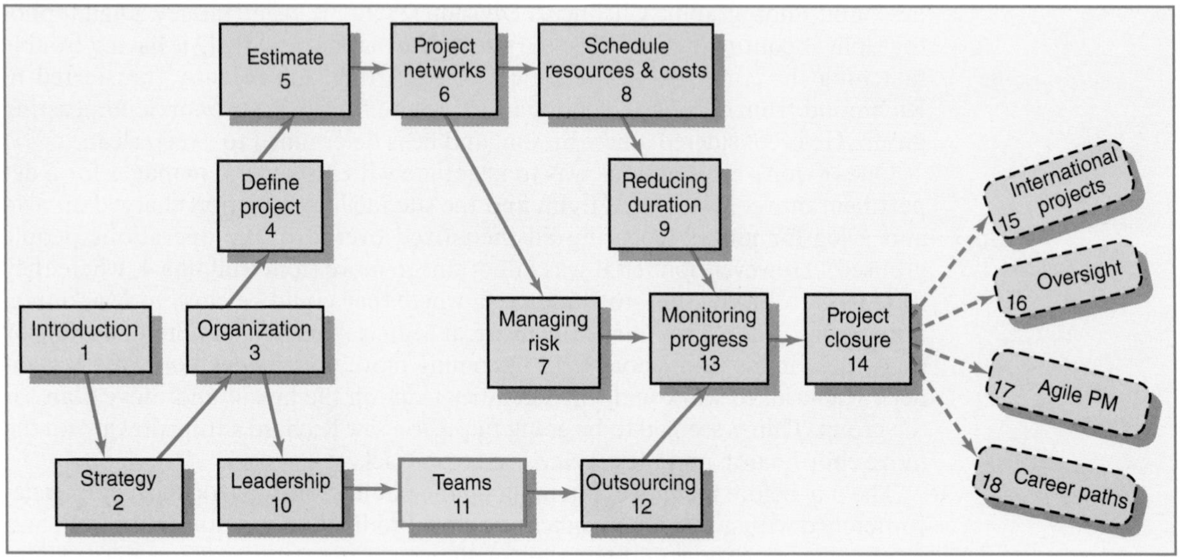

Managing Project Teams

The Five-Stage Team Development Model
Situational Factors Affecting Team Development
Building High-Performance Project Teams
Managing Virtual Project Teams
Project Team Pitfalls
Summary

Coming together is a beginning. Keeping together is progress. Working together is success.

—Henry Ford

The magic and power of teams is captured in the term "synergy," which is derived from the Greek word *sunergos:* "working together." There is positive and negative synergy. The essence of positive **synergy** can be found in the phrase "The whole is greater than the sum of the parts." Conversely, negative synergy occurs when the whole is less than the sum of the parts. Mathematically, these two states can be symbolized by the following equations:

$$\text{Positive Synergy } 1 + 1 + 1 + 1 + 1 = 10$$

$$\text{Negative Synergy } 1 + 1 + 1 + 1 + 1 = 2 \text{ (or even } -2)$$

Synergy perhaps can best be seen on a basketball court, a soccer pitch, or a football field where teammates play as one to defeat a superior foe (see Snapshot from Practice: The 2008 Olympic Redeem Team). Although less visible than in team sports, positive and negative synergy can also be observed and felt in the daily operations of project teams. Here is a description from one team member we interviewed:

> Instead of operating as one big team we fractionalized into a series of subgroups. The marketing people stuck together as well as the systems guys. A lot of time was wasted gossiping and complaining about each other. When the project started slipping behind schedule, everyone started covering their tracks and trying to pass the blame on to others. After a while we avoided direct conversation and resorted to e-mail. Management finally pulled the plug and brought in another team to salvage the project. It was one of the worst project management experiences in my life.

This same individual fortunately was also able to recount a more positive experience:

> There was a contagious excitement within the team. Sure we had our share of problems and setbacks, but we dealt with them straight on and, at times, were able to do the impossible. We all cared about the project and looked out for each other. At the same time we challenged each other to do better. It was one of the most exciting times in my life.

The following is a set of characteristics commonly associated with high-performing teams that exhibit **positive synergy:**[1]

1. The team shares a sense of common purpose, and each member is willing to work toward achieving project objectives.

[1] See E. H. Schein, *Process Consultation,* 2nd ed. (Reading, MA: Addison-Wesley, 1988), pp. 42–43; and R. Likert, *New Patterns of Management* (New York: McGraw-Hill, 1961), pp. 162–77.

SNAPSHOT FROM PRACTICE Managing Martians*

Donna Shirley's 35-year career as aerospace engineer reached a pinnacle in July 1997 when Sojourner—the solar-powered, self-guided, microwave-oven-sized rover—was seen exploring the Martian landscape in Pathfinder's spectacular images from the surface of the red planet. The event marked a milestone in space exploration: No vehicle had ever before roamed the surface of another planet. Shirley, a manager at the Jet Propulsion Laboratory's Mars Exploration Program, headed the mostly male team that designed and built Sojourner. In her insightful memoir, *Managing Martians,* written with Danelle Morton, she makes the following observation about managing creative teams:

Courtesy of NASA.

> When you are managing really brilliant, creative people, at some point you find it's impossible to command or control them because you can't understand what they are doing. Once they have gone beyond your ability to understand them, you have a choice to make as a manager. You can limit them and the project by your intelligence, which I think is the wrong way to do it. Or you can trust them and use your management skills to keep them focused on the goal.
>
> A lot of bad managers get threatened when their "subordinates" know more than they do. They either hire people who are inferior to them so they can always feel in control or they bottleneck people who know something they don't so they can maintain control. The whole project suffers from the manager's insecurities.

* Donna Shirley and Danelle Morton, *Managing Martians* (New York: Broadway Books, 1998), pp. 88–89.

- *Political connections.* Managers are wise to recruit individuals who already have a good working relationship with key stakeholders. This is particularly true for projects operating in a matrix environment in which a significant portion of the work will be under the domain of a specific functional department and not the core project team.
- *Ambition, initiative, and energy.* These qualities can make up for a lot of shortcomings in other areas and should not be underestimated.
- *Familiarity.* Research suggests repeat collaboration stifles creativity and innovation. On challenging, breakthrough projects it is wise to interject the team with experts who have little previous working experience with others (Skilton and Dooley, 2010).

See the Managing Martians snapshot for further advice on recruiting team members.

After reviewing needed skills, the manager should try and find out through the corporate grapevine who is good, who is available, and who might want to work on the project. Some organizations may allow direct interviews. Often a manager will have to expend political capital to get highly prized people assigned to the project.

In matrix environments, the project manager will have to request appointments with functional managers to discuss project requirements for staffing. The following documents should be available at these discussions: an overall project scope statement, endorsements of top management, and a description of the tasks and general schedule that pertain to the people from their departments. Managers need to be precise as to what attributes they are seeking and why they are important.

Conducting Project Meetings

The First Project Team Meeting

Research on team development confirms what we have heard from project managers: The first **project kick-off meeting** is critical to the early functioning of the project team. According to one veteran project manager:

> The first team meeting sets the tone for how the team will work together. If it is disorganized, or becomes bogged down with little sense of closure, then this can often become a self-fulfilling prophecy for subsequent group work. On the other hand, if it is crisply run, focusing on real issues and concerns in an honest and straightforward manner, members come away excited about being part of the project team.

There are typically three objectives project managers try to achieve during the first meeting of the project team. The first is to provide an overview of the project, including the scope and objectives, the general schedule, method, and procedures. The second is to begin to address some of the interpersonal concerns captured in the team development model: Who are the other team members? How will I fit in? Will I be able to work with these people? The third and most important objective is to begin to model how the team is going to work together to complete the project. The project manager must recognize that first impressions are important; her behavior will be carefully monitored and interpreted by team members. This meeting should serve as an exemplary role model for subsequent meetings and reflect the leader's style.

The meeting itself comes in a variety of shapes and forms. It is not uncommon in major projects for the kick-off meeting to involve one or two days, often at a remote site away from interruptions. This retreat provides sufficient time for preliminary introduction, to begin to establish ground rules, and to define the structure of the project. One advantage of off-site kick-off meetings is that they provide ample opportunity for informal interaction among members during breaks, meals, and evening activities; such informal interactions are critical to forming relationships.

However, many organizations do not have the luxury of holding elaborate retreats. In other cases the scope of project does not warrant such an investment of time. In these cases, the key operating principle should be KISS (keep it simple stupid!). Too often when constrained by time, project managers try to accomplish too much during the first meeting; in doing so, issues do not get fully resolved, and members come away with an information headache.

The project manager needs to remember that the primary goal is to run a productive meeting, and objectives should be realistic given the time available. If the meeting is only one hour, then the project manager should simply review the scope of the project, discuss how the team was formed, and provide an opportunity for members to introduce themselves to the team.

Establishing Ground Rules

Whether as part of an elaborate first meeting or during follow-up meetings, the project manager must quickly begin to establish operational ground rules for how the team will work together. These ground rules involve not only organizational and procedural issues but also normative issues on how the team will interact with each other. Although specific procedures will vary across organizations and projects, some of the major issues that need to be addressed include the following:

Planning Decisions

- How will the project plan be developed?
- Will a specific project management software package be used? If so, which one?
- What are the specific roles and responsibilities of all the participants?
- Who needs to be informed of decisions? How will they be kept informed?
- What are the relative importance of cost, time, and performance?
- What are the deliverables of the project planning process?
- Who will approve and sign off at the completion of each deliverable?
- Who receives each deliverable?

Tracking Decisions

- How will progress be assessed?
- At what level of detail will the project be tracked?
- How will team members get data from each other?
- How often will they get this data?
- Who will generate and distribute reports?
- Who needs to be kept informed about project progress, and how will they be informed?
- What content/format is appropriate for each audience?
- Meetings
  - Where will meetings be located?
  - What kind of meetings will be held?
  - Who will "run" these meetings?
  - How will agendas be produced?
  - How will information be recorded?

Managing Change Decisions

- How will changes be instituted?
- Who will have change approval authority?
- How will plan changes be documented and evaluated?

Relationship Decisions

- What department or organizations will the team need to interact with during the project?
- What are the roles and responsibilities of each organization (reviewer, approver, creator, user)?
- How will all involved parties be kept informed of deliverables, schedule dates, expectations, etc.?
- How will the team members communicate among themselves?
- What information will and won't be exchanged?

Checklists like these are only a guide; items should be added or deleted as needed. Many of these procedures will have already been established by precedent and will only have to be briefly reviewed. For example, *Microsoft Project* or *Primavera* may be the standard software tool for planning and tracking. Likewise, a specific firm is likely to have an established format for reporting status information. How to deal with other issues will have to be determined by the project team. When appropriate, the project manager should actively solicit input from the project team members and draw upon their experience and preferred work habits. This process also contributes to their buying into the operational decisions. Decisions should be recorded and circulated to all members.

During the course of establishing these operational procedures, the project manager, through word and deed, should begin working with members to establish the norms for team interaction. Below are examples of some of the norms researchers have found associated with high-performance teams.[3]

- Confidentiality is maintained; no information is shared outside the team unless all agree to it.
- It is acceptable to be in trouble, but it is not acceptable to surprise others. Tell others immediately when deadlines or milestones will not be reached.
- There is zero tolerance for bulling a way through a problem or an issue.
- Agree to disagree, but when a decision has been made, regardless of personal feelings, move forward.
- Respect outsiders, and do not flaunt one's position on the project team.
- Hard work does not get in the way of having fun.

One way of making these norms more tangible is by creating a team charter that goes beyond the scope statement of the project and states in explicit terms the norms and values of the team. This charter should be a collaborative effort on the part of the core team. Project managers can lead by proposing certain tenets, but they need to be open to suggestions from the team. Once there is general agreement to the rules of conduct, each member signs the final document to symbolize commitment to the principles it contains.

Unfortunately, in some cases charters become a meaningless ritual because the charter is signed and filed away, never to be discussed again. To have a lasting effect, the charter has to be a legitimate part of the project monitoring system. Just as the team reviews progress toward project objectives, the team assesses the extent to which members are adhering to the principles in the charter.

Project managers play a major role in establishing team norms through personal example. If they freely admit mistakes and share what they have learned from them, other team members will begin to do the same. At the same time, project managers need to intervene when they believe such norms are being violated. They should talk to offenders privately and clearly state their expectations. The amazing thing about groups is that once a group is cohesive, with well-established norms, the members will police themselves so that the manager doesn't have to be the heavy. For example, one project manager confided that his team had a practice of having a small bean bag present at every meeting. If any one member felt that

[3] See Katzenbach, J. R., and D. K. Smith, *The Wisdom of Teams* (Boston: Harvard Business School Press, 1993); Bolman, L. G. and T. E. Deal, "What Makes Teams Work," *Organizational Dynamics,* vol. 21 (2), pp. 34–45; Katz, R., "How a Team at Digital Equipment Designed the 'Alpha' Chips," *The Human Side of Managing Technological Innovation,* R. Katz, Editor (New York: Oxford Press, 1997) pp. 137–148.

Key Terms

Brainstorming, *394*
Dysfunctional conflict, *396*
Functional conflict, *396*
Groupthink, *403*
Nominal group technique (NGT), *405*
Positive synergy, *375*
Project kick-off meeting, *383*
Project vision, *388*
Team building, *399*
Team rituals, *389*
Virtual project team, *399*

Review Questions

1. What are the differences between the five-stage model of team development and the punctuated equilibrium model?
2. What are the elements of an effective project vision? Why are they important?
3. Why should a project manager emphasize group rewards over individual rewards?
4. What is the difference between functional and dysfunctional conflict on a project?
5. When would it be appropriate to hold a formal team-building session on a project?
6. What are the unique challenges to managing a virtual project team?
7. What can a project manager do to avoid some of the pitfalls of a highly cohesive project team?

Exercises

1. The following activities are based on a recently completed group project that you have been involved in. This project may have been a student project, a work project, or an extracurricular project.
   a. Analyze the development of the team in terms of the five-phase model and the punctuated equilibrium model. Which model does the best job of describing how the team evolved?
   b. Analyze the group in terms of the nine situational factors that influence team development. What factors positively contributed to group performance? What factors negatively contributed to group performance? How did the group try to overcome the negative factors? What could you have done differently to overcome these negative factors?
   c. Analyze how effectively the group managed meetings. What did the group do well? What didn't the group do well? If the group were formed again, what specific recommendations would you make about how the group should manage meetings?
2. Assume that you have the following decision-making options: (1) make the decision on your own with available information, (2) consult others before making a decision, and (3) call a meeting and reach a consensus, seeking to arrive at a final decision everyone can agree on. Which approach would you use to make each of the following decisions and why?
   a. You are the project leader for Casino Night on campus, a charitable event organized by your group to raise money for the homeless. The event was a big success, garnering a net profit of $3,500. Before the event your team researched nearby organizations that support the homeless and to whom the money could be given. You narrowed the choices to the "Chunk of Coal House" and "St. Mary's Soup Kitchen." Eventually your group decided that the funds be given to Chunk of Coal. You are about to write a check to its director when you read in the local newspaper that the Chunk of Coal House has terminated operations. What should you do with the money?

b. You are a golf course designer hired by Trysting Tree Golf Club to renovate their golf course. You have worked closely with the board of directors of the club to develop a new layout that is both challenging and aesthetically pleasing. Everyone is excited about the changes. The project is nearly 75 percent complete when you encounter problems on the 13th hole. The 13th hole at Trysting Tree is a 125-yard par three in which golfers have to hit their tee shots over a lake to a modulated green. During the construction of the new tee box, workers discovered that an underground spring runs beneath the box to the lake. You inspected the site and agreed with the construction supervisor that this could create serious problems, especially during the rainy winter months. After surveying the area, you believe the only viable option would be to extend the hole to 170 yards and create elevated tees on the adjacent hillside.

c. You are the leader of a new product development project. Your team has worked hard on developing a third-generation product that incorporates new technology and meets customer demands. The project is roughly 50 percent complete. You have just received a report from the marketing department detailing a similar product that is about to be released by a competitor. The product appears to utilize radical new design principles that expand the functionality of the product. This poses a serious threat to the success of your project. Top management is considering canceling your project and starting over again. They want you to make a recommendation.

3. The following activities are based on a current or recently completed group project that you have been involved in. This project may be a student project, a work project, or an extracurricular project.
   a. How strong is the team identity on this project and why?
   b. What could participants do to strengthen team identity?
   c. What kind of informal activities could be used to rejuvenate the team? Why would these activities work?

References

Adams, J. R., and S. E. Brandt, "Behavioral Implications of the Project Lifecyle," *Project Management Handbook,* 2nd ed., D. I. Cleland and W. R. King (eds.), (New York: Van Nostrand Reinhold, 1988), pp. 206–30.

Berkun, S., *The Art of Project Management* (Sebastopol, CA: O'Reilly, 2005).

Cleland, D. I., "Team Building: The New Strategic Weapon," *PM Network,* Vol. 11 (1) 1997.

Bowen, K. H., K. B. Clark, C. A. Holloway, and S. C. Wheelwright, *The Perpetual Enterprise Machine,* (New York: Oxford Press, 1994).

Bolman, D. G., and T. E. Deal, What Makes Teams Work," *Organizational Dynamics,* vol. 21 (2), 1992, pp. 34–45.

Coutu, D. L., "Organization Trust in Virtual Teams," *Harvard Business Review,* Vol. 76 (3) 1998, pp. 20–21.

DeMarco, T., and T. Lister, *Peopleware: Productive Projects and Teams,* 2nd ed. (New York: Dorsett House, 1999).

Ericksen, J., and L. Dyer, "Right from the Start: Exploring the Effects of Early Team Events on Subsequent Project Team Performance," *Administrative Science Quarterly*, 49 (3) 2004, pp. 438–71.

Frame, J. D., *Managing Projects in Organizations* (San Francisco: Jossey-Bass, 1995).

Hackman, J. R., *Leading Teams: Setting the Stage for Great Performances* (Cambridge, MA: Harvard Business School Press, 2002).

Homans, G. C., *Social Behavior: Its Elementary Forms* (New York: Harcourt Brace Jovanovich, 1961).

Janis, I. L., *Groupthink* (Boston: Houghton Mifflin, 1982).

Johansen, R., D. Sibbett, S. Benson, A. Martin, R. Mittman, and P. Saffo, *Leading Business Teams: How Teams can use Technology and Group Process Tools to Enhance Performance* (Reading, MA: Addison-Wesley, 1991).

Katz, R., "How a Team at Digital Equipment Designed the 'Alpha' Chip," *The Human Side of Managing Technological Innovation,* 2nd ed. Ed. Ralph Katz (New York: Oxford University Press, 2004), pp. 121–33.

Katzenbach, J. R., and D. K. Smith, *The Wisdom of Teams* (Boston: Harvard Business School Press, 1993).

Kidder, T., *The Soul of a New Machine* (New York: Avon Books, 1981).

Kirkman, B. L., B. Rosen, C. B. Gibson, P. E. Tesluk, and S. O. McPherson, "Five Challenges to Virtual Team Success: Lessons From Sabre, INC.," *Academy of Management Executive,* 16 (2) 2002, pp. 67–79.

Leavitt, H. J., and J. Lipman-Blumen, "Hot Groups," *Harvard Business Review,* Vol. 73 1995, pp. 109–16.

Likert, R., *New Patterns in Management,* (New York: McGraw-Hill, 1961).

Linetz, B. P., and K. P. Rea, *Project Management for the 21st Century* (San Diego: Academic Press, 2001).

Lipsinger, R., and DeRosa D., *Virtual Team Success: A Practical Guide for Working and Leading from a Distance* (San Francisco: Jossey-Bass, 2010).

Maier, N. R. F., *Problem Solving and Creativity in Individuals and Groups* (Belmont, CA: Brooks-Cole, 1970).

Maier, N. R. F., *Problem-Solving Discussion and Conference,* (New York: McGraw-Hill, 1963).

Malhotra, A., A. Majchrzak, and B. Rosen, "Leading Virtual Teams," *Academy of Management Perspectives*, 21 (1) 2007, pp. 60–70.

Maznevski, M. L., and K. M. Chudoba, "Bridging Space over Time: Global Virtual Team Dynamics and Effectiveness," *Organization Science,* Vol. 11 (5), September–October 2000, pp. 473–92.

Posner, B. Z., "What's All the Fighting About? Conflicts in Project Management," *IEEE Transactions in Engineering Management*, EM-33, 1986, pp. 207–211.

Peters, T., *Thriving on Chaos: Handbook for a Management Revolution* (New York: Knopf, 1988).

Ritti, R. R., and S. L. Levy, *The Ropes to Skip and the Ropes to Know: Studies in Organizational Behavior* (New York: Wiley, 2009).

Senge, P. M., *The Fifth Discipline* (New York: Doubleday, 1990).

Seta, J. J., P. B. Paulus, and J. Schkade, "Effects of Group Size and Proximity under Cooperative and Competitive Conditions," *Journal of Personality and Social Psychology,* 98 (2) 1976, pp. 47–53.

Sherif, M., *Group Conflict and Cooperation: Their Social Psychology* (Chicago: Aldine, 1967).

Siebdrat, F., M. Hoegl, and H. Ernst, "How to Manage Virtual Teams," *MIT Sloan Management Review,* http://sloanreview.mit.edu/the-maazine/2009-summer/ 50412/ how-to manage-virtual teams/2009.

Skilton, P. F., and K. J. Dooley, "The Effects of Repeat Collaboration on Creative Abrasion," *Academy of Management Review,* 35 (1) 2010, pp. 118–34.

Smith, B. J., "Buiolding Shared Visions: How to Begin," *The Fifth Discipline Fieldbook: Strategies and Tools for Building a Learning Organization,* eds. P. M. Senge, C. Roberts, R. B. Ross, B. J. Smith, and A. Kleiner (New York: Doubleday, 1994), pp. 312–327.

Smith, P. G., and D. G. Reinertsen, *Developing Products in Half the Time* (New York: Van Nostrand Reinhold, 1995).

Thamhain, H. J., and D. L. Wilemon, "Conflict Management in Project Life Cycle," *Sloan Management Review,* Vol. 16 (3) 1975, pp. 31–41.

Thoms, P., "Creating a Shared Vision with a Project Team," *PM Network,* January 1997, pp. 33–35.

3M, "Leading a Distributed Team," *www.3m.com/meetingnetwork/readingroom/ meetingguide_distribteam.html.* Accessed June 6, 2006.

Tuchman, B. W., "Development Sequence of Small Groups," *Psychological Bulletin,* vol. 63 (1965), pp. 384–399.

Tuchman, B. W., and M. C. Jensen, "Stages of Small Group Development Revisited," *Group and Organizational Studies,* Vol. 2 1977, pp. 419–27.

Vroom, V. H., and A. G. Jago, *The New Leadership* (Englewood Cliffs, NJ: Prentice Hall, 1988).

Zander, A., *Making Groups Effective* (San Francisco: Jossey-Bass, 1994).

Case

Kerzner Office Equipment

Amber Briggs looked nervously at her watch as she sat at the front of a large table in the cafeteria at Kerzner Office Equipment. It was now 10 minutes after 3:00 and only 10 of the 14 members had arrived for the first meeting of the Kerzner anniversary task force. Just then two more members hurriedly sat down and mumbled apologies for being late. Briggs cleared her throat and started the meeting.

KERZNER OFFICE EQUIPMENT

Kerzner Office Equipment is located in Charleston, South Carolina. It specializes in the manufacture and sales of high-end office furniture and equipment. Kerzner enjoyed steady growth during its first five years of existence with a high-water employment mark of more than 1,400 workers. Then a national recession struck, forcing Kerzner to lay off 25 percent of its employees. This was a traumatic period for the company. Justin Tubbs was brought in as the new CEO, and things began to slowly turn around. Tubbs was committed to employee participation and redesigned operations around the concept of self-managing teams. The company soon introduced an innovative line of ergonomic furniture designed to reduce back strain and carpal tunnel. This line of equipment proved to be a resounding success, and Kerzner became known as a leader in the industry. The company currently employs 1,100 workers and has just been selected for the second straight time by the *Charleston Post and Courier* as one of the 10 best local firms to work for in South Carolina.

AMBER BRIGGS

Amber Briggs is a 42-year-old human resource specialist who has worked for Kerzner for the past five years. During this time she has performed a variety of activities involving recruitment, training, compensation, and team building. David Brown, vice president of human resources, assigned Briggs the responsibility for organizing Kerzner's 10th anniversary celebration. She was excited about the project because she would report directly to top management.

CEO Tubbs briefed her as to the purpose and objectives of the celebration. Tubbs stressed that this should be a memorable event and that it was important to celebrate Kerzner's success since the dark days of the layoffs. Moreover, he confided that he had just read a book on corporate cultures and believed that such events were important for conveying the values at Kerzner. He went on to say that he wanted this to be an employee celebration—not a celebration conjured up by top management. As such, she would be assigned a task force of 14 employees from each of the major departments to organize and plan the event. Her team was to present a preliminary plan and budget for the event to top management within three months. When discussing budgets, Tubbs revealed that he felt the total cost should be somewhere in the $150,000 range. He concluded the meeting by offering to help Briggs in any way he could to make the event a success.

FIGURE C11.1
Celebration Task Force

Agenda

3:00	Introductions
3:15	Project overview
3:30	Ground rules
3:45	Meeting times
4:00	Adjourn

Soon thereafter Briggs received the list of the names of the task force members, and she contacted them either by phone or e-mail to arrange today's meeting. She had to scramble to find a meeting place. Her cubicle in human resources was too small to accommodate such a group, and all the meeting rooms at Kerzner were booked or being refurbished. She settled on the cafeteria because it was usually deserted in the late afternoon. Prior to the meeting she posted the agenda on a flipchart (see Figure C11.1) adjacent to the table. Given everyone's busy schedules, the meeting was limited to just one hour.

THE FIRST MEETING

Briggs began the meeting by saying, "Greetings. For those who don't know me, I'm Amber Briggs from human resources and I've been assigned to manage the 10th anniversary celebration at Kerzner. Top management wants this to be a special event—at the same time they want it to be our event. This is why you are here. Each of you represents one of the major departments, and together our job is to plan and organize the celebration." She then reviewed the agenda and asked each member to introduce him/herself. The tall, red-haired woman to the right of Briggs broke the momentary silence by saying, "Hi, I'm Cara Miller from Plastics. I guess my boss picked me for this task force because I have a reputation for throwing great parties."

In turn each member followed suit. Below is a sampling of their introductions:

"Hi, I'm Mike Wales from maintenance. I'm not sure why I'm here. Things have been a little slow in our department, so my boss told me to come to this meeting."

"I'm Megan Plinski from domestic sales. I actually volunteered for this assignment. I think it will be a lot of fun to plan a big party."

"Yo, my name is Nick Psias from accounting. My boss said one of us had to join this task force, and I guess it was my turn."

"Hi, I'm Rick Fennah. I'm the only one from purchasing who has been here since the beginning. We've been through some rough times, and I think it is important to take time and celebrate what we've accomplished."

"Hi, I'm Ingrid Hedstrom from international sales. I think this is a great idea, but I should warn you that I will be out of the country for most of the next month."

"I'm Abby Bell from engineering. Sorry for being late, but things are a bit crazy in my department."

Briggs circled the names of the two people who were absent and circulated a roster so that everyone could check to see if their phone numbers and e-mail addresses were correct. She then summarized her meeting with Tubbs and told the group that he expected them to make a formal presentation to top management within 10 weeks. She acknowledged that they were all busy people and that it was her job to manage the project as efficiently as possible. At the same time, she reiterated the importance of the project and that this would be a very public event: "If we screw up, everyone will know about it."

Briggs went over the ground rules and emphasized that from now on meetings would start on time and that she expected to be notified in advance if someone was going to be absent. She summarized the first part of the project as centering on five key questions: when, where, what, who, and how much? She created a stir in the group when she responded to a question about cost by informing them that top management was willing to pay up to $150,000 for the event. Megan quipped, "This is going to be one hell of a party."

Briggs then turned the group's attention to identifying a common meeting time. After jousting for 15 minutes, she terminated the discussion by requesting that each member submit a schedule of free time over the next month by Friday. She would use this information and a new planning software to identify optimal times. She ended the meeting by thanking the members for coming and asking them to begin soliciting ideas from co-workers about how this event should be celebrated. She announced that she would meet individually with each of them to discuss their role on the project. The meeting was adjourned at 4:00 P.M.

1. Critique Briggs's management of the first meeting. What, if anything, should she have done differently?
2. What barriers is she likely to encounter in completing this project?
3. What can she do to overcome these barriers?
4. What should she do between now and the next meeting?

Case

Ajax Project

Tran was taking his dog Callie on her evening walk as the sun began to set over the coastal range. He looked forward to this time of the day. It was an opportunity to enjoy some peace and quiet. It was also a time to review events on the Ajax project and plot his next moves.

Ajax is the code name given by CEBEX for a high-tech security system project funded by the U.S. Department of Defense (DOD). Tran is the project manager and his core team consisted of 30 full-time hardware and software engineers.

Tran and his family fled Cambodia when he was four years old. He joined the U.S. Air Force when he was 18 and used the education stipend to attend Washington State University. He joined CEBEX upon graduating with a dual degree in mechanical and electrical engineering. After working on a variety of projects for 10 years Tran decided he wanted to enter management. He went to night school at the University of Washington to earn an MBA.

Tran became a project manager for the money. He also thought he was good at it. He enjoyed working with people and making the right things happen. This was his fifth project and up to now he was batting .500, with half of his projects coming ahead of schedule. Tran was proud that he could now afford to send his oldest child to Stanford University.

Ajax was one of many defense projects the CEBEX Corporation had under contract with DOD. CEBEX is a huge defense company with annual sales in excess of $30 billion and more than 120,000 employees worldwide. CEBEX's five major business areas are Aeronautics, Electronic Systems, Information & Technology Services, Integrated Systems & Solutions, and Space Systems. Ajax was one of several new projects sponsored by the Integrated Systems & Solutions division aimed at the homeland security business. CEBEX was confident that it could leverage its technical expertise and political connections to become a major player in this growing market. Ajax was one of several projects directed at designing, developing, and installing a security system at an important government installation.

Tran had two major concerns when he started the Ajax project. The first was the technical risks inherent in the project. In theory the design principles made sense and the project used proven technology. Still the technology had never been applied in the field in this matter. From past experience, Tran knew there was a big difference between the laboratory and the real world. He also knew that integrating the audio, optical, tactile, and laser subsystems would test the patience and ingenuity of his team.

The second concern involved his team. The team was pretty much split down the middle between hardware and electrical engineers. Not only did these engineers have different skill sets and tend to look at problems differently, but generational differences between the two groups were evident as well. The hardware engineers were almost all former military, family men with conservative attire and beliefs. The electrical engineers were a much motlier crew. They tended to be young, single, and at times very cocky. While the hardware engineers talked about the Seattle Mariners, raising teenagers, and going to Palm Desert to play golf, the software engineers talked about Vapor, the latest concert at the Gorge amphitheater, and going mountain biking in Peru.

To make matters worse, tension between these two groups within CEBEX festered around salary issues. Electrical engineers were at a premium, and the hardware engineers resented the new hires' salary packages, which were comparable to what they were earning after 20 years of working for CEBEX. Still the real money was to be made from the incentives associated with project performance. These were all contingent on meeting project milestones and the final completion date.

Before actual work started on the project, Tran arranged a two-day team-building retreat at a lodge on the Olympic peninsula for his entire team as well as key staff from the government installation. He used this time to go over the major objectives of the project and unveil the basic project plan. An internal consultant facilitated several team-building activities that made light of cross-generational issues. Tran felt a real sense of camaraderie within the team.

The good feelings generated from the retreat carried over to the beginning of the project. The entire team bought into the mission of the project and technical challenges it represented. Hardware and electrical engineers worked side by side to solve problems and build subsystems.

The project plan was built around a series of five tests, with each test being a more rigorous verification of total system performance. Passing each test represented a key milestone for the project. The team was excited about conducting the first Alpha test one week early—only to be disappointed by a series of minor technical glitches that took two weeks of problem solving to resolve. The team worked extra hard to make up for the lost time. Tran was proud of the team and how hard members had worked together.

The Alpha II test was conducted on schedule, but once again the system failed to perform. This time three weeks of debugging was needed before the team received the green light to move to the next phase of the project. By this time, team goodwill had been tested, and emotions were a bit frayed. A cloud of disappointment descended over the team as hopes of bonuses disappeared with the project falling further behind schedule. This was augmented by cynics who felt that the original schedule was unfair and the deadlines were impossible to begin with.

Tran responded by starting each day with a status meeting where the team reviewed what they accomplished the previous day and set new objectives for that day. He believed these meetings were helpful in establishing positive momentum and reinforcing a team identity among the engineers. He also went out of his way to spend more time with the "troops," helping them solve problems, offering encouragement, and a sincere pat on the back when one was deserved.

He was cautiously optimistic when the time came to conduct the Alpha III test. It was the end of the day when the switch was turned on, but nothing happened. Within minutes the entire team heard the news. Screams could be heard down the hallway. Perhaps the most telling moment was when Tran looked down at the company's parking lot and saw most of his project team walking by themselves to their cars.

As Callie chased some wild bunnies, Tran pondered what he should do next.

1. How effective has Tran been as a project manager? Explain.
2. What problem(s) does Tran face?
3. How would you go about solving them? Why?

Case

Franklin Equipment, Ltd.*

Franklin Equipment, Ltd. (FEL), with headquarters and main fabrication facilities in Saint John, New Brunswick, was founded 75 years ago to fabricate custom-designed large machines for construction businesses in the Maritime Provinces. Over the years its product lines became strategically focused on creating rock-crushing equipment for dam and highway construction and for a few other markets that require the processing of aggregate. FEL now designs, fabricates, and assembles stationary and portable rock-crushing plants and services its own products and those of its competitors.

In the 1970s, FEL began to expand its market from the Maritime Provinces to the rest of Canada. FEL currently has several offices and fabrication facilities throughout the country. More recently, FEL has made a concerted effort to market its products internationally.

Last month, FEL signed a contract to design and fabricate a rock-crushing plant for a Middle East construction project, called Project Abu Dhabi. Charles Gatenby secured this contract and has been assigned as project manager. This project is viewed as a coup because FEL has wanted to open up markets in this area for a long time and has had difficulty getting prospective customers to realize that FEL is a Canadian firm and not from the United States. Somehow these customers view all North American vendors as the same and are reluctant to employ any of them because of international political considerations.

A project of this scope typically starts with the selection of a team of managers responsible for various aspects of the design, fabrication, delivery, and installation of the product. Manager selection is important because the product design and fabrication vary with the unique needs of each customer. For example, the terrain, rock characteristics, weather conditions, and logistical concerns create special problems for all phases of plant design and operations. In addition, environmental concerns and labor conditions vary from customer to customer and from region to region.

In addition to the project manager, all projects include a design engineer; an operations manager, who oversees fabrication and on-site assembly; and a cost accountant, who oversees all project financial and cost reporting matters. Each of these people must work closely together if a well-running plant is to be delivered on time and within cost constraints. Because international contracts often require FEL to employ host nationals for plant assembly and to train them for operations, a human resource manager is also assigned to the project team. In such cases, the human resource manager needs to understand the particulars of the plant specifications and then use this knowledge to design selection procedures and assess particular training needs. The human resource manager also needs to learn the relevant labor laws of the customer's country.

FEL assigns managers to project teams based on their expertise and their availability to work on a particular project given their other commitments. This typically means that managers without heavy current project commitments will be assigned to new projects. For instance, a manager finishing one project will likely be assigned a management position on a new project team. The project manager typically has little to say about who is assigned to his or her team.

* Courtesy of John A. Drexler Jr., Oregon State University.

Because he secured Project Abu Dhabi and has established positive working relationships with the Abu Dhabi customer, Gatenby was assigned to be project manager. Gatenby has successfully managed similar projects. The other managers assigned to Project Abu Dhabi are Bill Rankins, a brilliant design engineer, Rob Perry, operations manager with responsibility for fabrication and installation, Elaine Bruder, finance and cost accounting manager, and Sam Stonebreaker, human resource manager. Each of these managers has worked together on numerous past projects.

A few years ago, FEL began contracting for team facilitator services from several consulting firms to help new project teams operate effectively. Last month, FEL recruited Carl Jobe from one of these consulting firms to be a full-time internal consultant. A number of managers, including Gatenby, were so impressed with Jobe's skills that they convinced FEL top management of the need to hire a permanent internal facilitator; Jobe was the obvious choice.

Because Gatenby was instrumental in hiring Jobe at FEL, he was excited at the prospect of using Jobe to facilitate team building among Project Abu Dhabi team members. Gatenby was very proud of having secured this project and had expected to be appointed project manager. He knew that this project's success would be instrumental in advancing his own career.

Gatenby told Jobe, "This project is really important to FEL and to me personally. I really need for you to help us develop into a team that works well together to achieve the project's goals within budget. I've observed your success in developing teams on other projects, and I expect you'll do the same for Project Abu Dhabi. I'll take care of you if you help me make this work."

Jobe outlined for Gatenby how he would proceed. Jobe would begin by interviewing team members individually to learn their perceptions of each other and of the promises and pitfalls of being involved in this project. Meetings of the entire team would follow these interviews using the information he collected to help establish a team identity and a shared vision.

Jobe interviewed Bruder first. She expressed skepticism about whether the project could succeed. During the interview, Bruder appeared to be distant, and Jobe could not figure out why he had not established good rapport with her. Bruder intimated that she expected a lot of cost overruns and a lot of missed production deadlines. But not knowing Jobe well, Bruder was reluctant to identify any specific barriers to the project's success. While she would not directly say so, it was clear to Jobe that Bruder did not want to be a part of Project Abu Dhabi. Jobe left this interview confused and wondering what was going on.

Jobe's next interview was with Perry, the operations manager. Perry has worked at FEL for 15 years, and he immediately came to the point: "This project is not going to work. I cannot understand why upper management keeps assigning me to work on projects with Rankins. We simply cannot work together, and we don't get along. I've disliked him from day one. He keeps dropping the fact that he has earned all these advanced degrees from Purdue. And he keeps telling us how things are done there. I know he's better educated than I am, and he's really smart. But I'm smart too and am good at what I do. There's no need for Rankins to make me feel like an idiot because I don't have a degree. Jobe, I'll be honest with you. Rankins has only been here for five years, but I hold him personally responsible for my problem with alcohol, and for its resulting effect on my marriage. I got divorced last year, and it's Rankins's fault."

Jobe next talked with Rankins, who said, "I don't care what you do. Perry and I simply can't work closely together for the nine months it will take to get it done. One of us will kill the other. Ever since I arrived at FEL, Perry has hated my guts and does everything he can to sabotage my designs. We usually worry about customers creating change orders; here it's the fabrication and operations manager who is responsible for them. Perry second-guesses everything I do and makes design changes on his own, and these are always bad decisions. He is out of control. I swear he stays awake at nights thinking up ways to ruin my designs. I don't have this problem with any other manager."

Jobe left these interviews thoroughly discouraged and could not imagine what would come up in his interview with Stonebreaker. But Stonebreaker was quite positive: "I enjoy these international projects where I get to travel abroad and learn about different cultures. I can't wait to get started on this."

Jobe asked Stonebreaker about the ability of various team members to work together. Stonebreaker replied, "No problem! We've all worked together before and have had no problems. Sure, there have been ruffled feathers and hurt feelings between Rankins and Perry. Rankins can be arrogant and Perry stubborn, but it's never been anything that we can't work around. Besides, both of them are good at what they do—both professionals. They'll keep their heads on straight."

Jobe was even more bewildered. Gatenby says this project's success rides on Jobe's facilitation skills. The finance manager appears to want off this project team. The design engineer and operations manager admit they detest each other and cannot work together. And the human resources manager, having worked on projects with Perry and Rankins before, expects a rosy working relationship and anticipates no problems.

Jobe had a second meeting with Gatenby. Before discussing the design of the team-building sessions, he asked questions to learn what Gatenby thought about the ability of team members to work together. Gatenby admitted that there has been very bad blood between Perry and Rankins, but added, "That's why we hired you. It's your job to make sure that the history between those two doesn't interfere with Project Abu Dhabi's success. It's your job to get them to work well together. Get it done."

Their dialogue toward the end of this meeting progressed as follows:

Jobe: "Why do you expect Rankins and Perry to work well together, given their history? What incentives do they have to do so?"

Gatenby: "As you should know, FEL requires formal goal setting between project managers and functional managers at the beginning of each project. I've already done this with Bruder, Stonebreaker, Perry, and Rankins. Perry and Rankins have explicit goals stating they must work well together and cooperate with each other."

Jobe: "What happens if they do not meet these goals?"

Gatenby: "I've already discussed this with top management. If it appears to me after two months that things are not working out between Perry and Rankins, FEL will fire Rankins."

Jobe: "Does Perry know this?"

Gatenby: "Yes."

1. Evaluate the criteria FEL uses to assign managers to project teams. What efficiencies do these criteria create? What are the resulting problems?
2. Why is it even more important that project team members work well together on international projects such as Project Abu Dhabi?
3. Discuss the dilemma that Jobe now faces.
4. What should Jobe recommend to Gatenby?

CHAPTER TWELVE

Outsourcing: Managing Interorganizational Relations

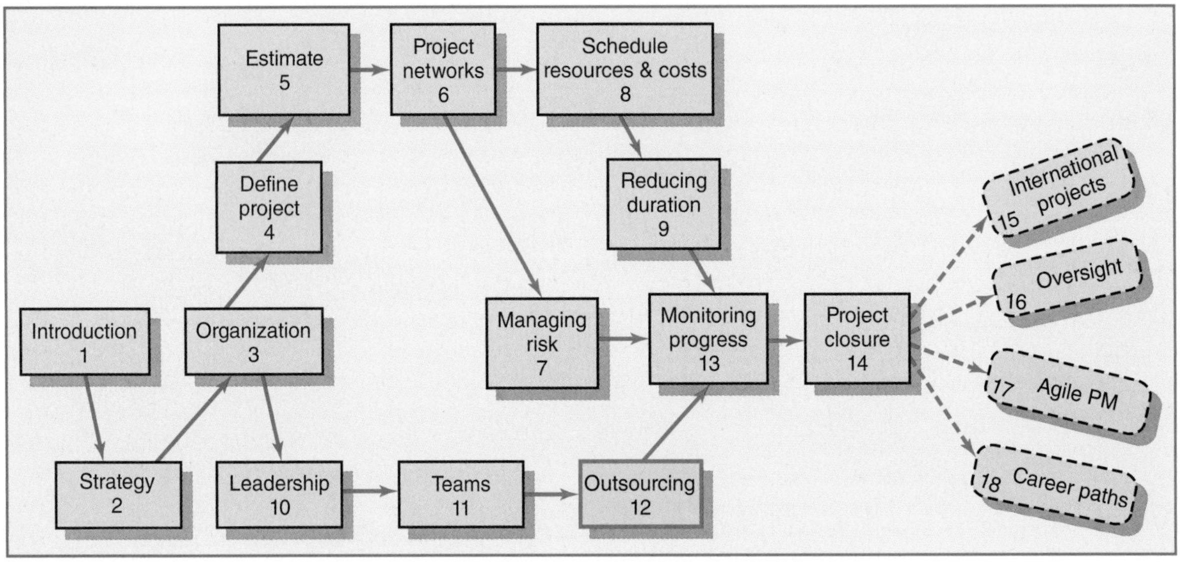

Outsourcing: Managing Interorganizational Relations
Outsourcing Project Work
Best Practices in Outsourcing Project Work
The Art of Negotiating
A Note on Managing Customer Relations
Summary
Appendix 12.1: Contract Management

. . . being a good partner has become a key corporate asset. I call it a company's collaborative advantage. In the global economy, a well-developed ability to create and sustain fruitful collaborations gives companies a significant competitive leg up.

—Rosabeth Moss Kanter, Harvard Business School professor

It is rare in today's flat world to find important projects that are being completed totally in-house. Outsourcing or contracting significant segments of project work to other companies is commonplace. For example, nine states attempting to unify the accounting of all their state agencies did not have the internal resources to implement such a large project. Hence, project teams were formed consisting of personnel from software, hardware, and accounting firms to implement the projects. Small high-tech firms outsource research to determine what features customers value in new products they are developing. Even industry giants such as Microsoft and Intel commonly hire independent firms to test new products they are developing.

Contracting project work has long been the norm in the construction industry, where firms hire general contractors who, in turn, hire and manage cadres of subcontractors to create new buildings and structures. For example, the Chunnel project, which created a transportation tunnel between France and England, involved more than 250 organizations. Contracting is not limited to large projects. For example, an insurance company worked with an outside contractor to develop an answering service that directs customers to specific departments and employees. The trend for the future suggests that more and more projects will involve working with people from different organizations.

This chapter extends the previous two chapters' discussion of building and managing relations by focusing specifically on issues surrounding working with people from other organizations to complete a project. First, the advantages and disadvantages of outsourcing project work are introduced. This is followed by a discussion of *best practices* used by firms to outsource and collaborate with each other on projects. The focus then shifts to the art of negotiating, which is at the heart of effective collaboration. Negotiating skills and techniques for resolving disagreements and reaching optimal solutions are then presented. The chapter closes with a brief, but important, note on managing customer relations. In addition, an appendix on contract management is included to augment our discussion of how organizations work together on projects.

Outsourcing Project Work

The term **outsourcing** has traditionally been applied to the transferring of business functions or processes (e.g., customer support, IT, accounting) to other, often foreign companies. For example, when you call your Internet provider to solve a

FIGURE 12.1
Reclining Chair Project

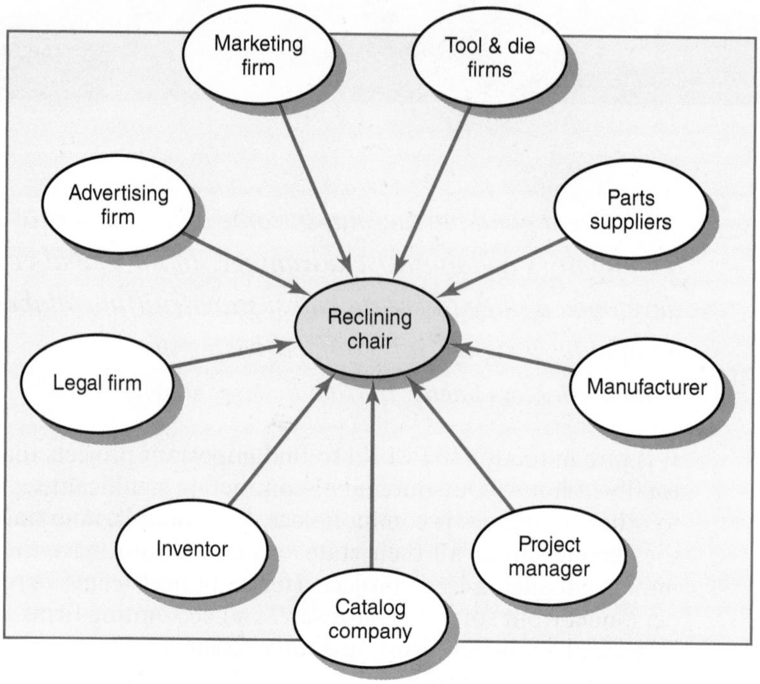

technical problem you are likely to talk to a technician in Bangalore, India, or Bucharest, Romania. Outsourcing is now being applied to contracting significant chunks of project work. For example, Apple and Motorola work closely with manufacturers in China to develop next-generation smartphones. Toyota and DaimlerChrysler collaborate with suppliers to develop new automobile platforms.

The shift toward outsourcing is readily apparent in the film industry. During the golden era of Hollywood, huge, vertically integrated corporations made movies. Studios such as MGM, Warner Brothers, and 20th Century–Fox owned large movie lots and employed thousands of full-time specialists—set designers, camera people, film editors, and directors. Star actors like Humphrey Bogart and Marilyn Monroe were signed to exclusive studio contracts for a set number of films (e.g., six films over three years). Today, most movies are made by a collection of individuals and small companies who come together to make films project-by-project. This structure allows each project to be staffed with the talent most suited to its demands rather than choosing from only those people the studio employs. This same approach is being applied to the creation of new products and services. For example, see Figure 12.1.

Figure 12.1 depicts a situation in which a zero-gravity reclining chair is being developed. The genesis for the chair comes from a mechanical engineer who developed the idea in her garage. The inventor negotiates a contract with a catalog firm to develop and manufacture the chair. The catalog company in turn creates a project team of manufacturers, suppliers, and marketing firms to create the new chair. Each participant adds requisite expertise to the project. The catalog firm brings its brand name and distribution channels to the project. Tool and die firms provide customized parts which are delivered to a manufacturing firm that will produce the chair. Marketing firms refine the design, develop packaging, and test market potential names. A project manager is assigned by the catalog firm to work with the inventor and the other parties to complete the project.

Many outsourced projects operate in a virtual environment in which people are linked by computers, faxes, computer-aided design systems, and video teleconferencing. They rarely, if ever, see one another face-to-face. On other projects, participants from different organizations work closely together, for example, at a construction site or in shared office space. In either case, people come and go as services are needed, much as in a matrix structure, but they are not formal members of one organization, just technical experts who form a temporary alliance with an organization, fulfill their contractual obligations, and then move on to the next project.

The advantages of outsourcing project work are many:

1. *Cost reduction*. Companies can secure competitive prices for contracted services, especially if the work can be outsourced offshore. Furthermore, overhead costs are dramatically cut since the company no longer has to internally maintain the contracted services.
2. *Faster project completion*. Not only can work be done more cheaply, but it can also be done faster. Competitive pricing means more resources for the dollar. For example, you can hire three Indian software engineers for the price of one American software engineer. Furthermore, outsourcing can provide access to equipment that can accelerate completion of project tasks. For example, by contracting a backhoe operater you are able to accomplish in four hours what it would take a landscaping crew four days to complete.
3. *High level of expertise*. A high level of expertise and technology can be brought to bear on the project. A company no longer has to keep up with technological advances. Instead, it can focus on developing its core competencies and hire firms with the know-how to work on relevant segments of the project.
4. *Flexibility*. Organizations are no longer constrained by their own resources but can pursue a wide range of projects by combining their resources with talents of other companies. Small companies can instantly go global by working with foreign partners.

The disadvantages of outsourcing project work are less well documented:

1. *Coordination breakdowns*. Coordination of professionals from different organizations can be challenging, especially if the project work requires close collaboration and mutual adjustment. Breakdowns are exacerbated by physical separation with people working in different buildings, different cities, if not different countries.
2. *Loss of control*. There is potential loss of control over the project. The core team depends on other organizations that they have no direct authority over. While long-term survival of participating organizations depends on performance, a project may falter when one partner fails to deliver.
3. *Conflict*. Projects are more prone to interpersonal conflict since the different participants do not share the same values, priorities, and culture. Trust, which is essential to project success, can be difficult to forge when interactions are limited and people come from different organizations.
4. *Security issues*. Depending on the nature of the project, trade and business secrets may be revealed. This can be problematic if the contractor also works for your competitor. Confidentiality is another concern and companies have to be very careful when outsourcing processes like payroll, medical transcriptions, and insurance information.

SNAPSHOT FROM PRACTICE The Boeing 787 Dreamliner*

BACKGROUND

In 2002 the basic design and plans for Boeing's 787 Dreamliner were accepted and given the charter to "Go." The Dreamliner boasts the latest design and revolutionary technology in the history of commercial air travel. But the project met bumpy weather. The first 787 aircraft, scheduled to be tested in July 2007, was delayed until December 2009. Orders for the advanced 787 grew quickly to over 800 planes. This rosy picture presented Boeing with a giant-sized headache. For various reasons (such as design, outsourcing, and labor issues) delivery dates slipped behind three years or more and costs ballooned to several billion dollars. Many analysts blame outsourcing work to foreign suppliers for a majority of the cost and schedule overruns.

Kyodo via AP Images

KEY FACTORS INFLUENCING OUTSOURCING DECISION

The Dreamliner outsourcing decision that gave 70 percent of plane content to outside suppliers included 30 percent to foreign suppliers. These percentages are greater than any previous commercial plane built by Boeing. Boeing's outsourcing rationale was based on typical economic considerations of cost, sales, and risk. In Boeing's case this meant:

Cost. Establishing partnerships with suppliers to lower risks and development costs, along with gaining some valuable expertise and process innovation.

Sales. Farming out numerous designs and component to foreign countries (e.g., Sweden, Italy, South Korea, and China) with the expectation that these countries will buy planes from Boeing in the future.

Risk. Recognizing the need to balance risk of outsourcing at the organizational and operational levels is crucial. The different levels are co-dependent. Taking gigantic steps away from successful outsourcing small amounts of past aircraft to foreign suppliers increases risk. The complexities in coordinating new technology and advance capabilities are daunting.

Clearly, the outsourcing decision ricocheted. Costs are over budget, some sales have been rescinded, customers are seeking compensation for delays, and potential ROI is reduced.

5. *Political hot potato.* Foreign outsourcing of work is perceived as a major cause of underemployment and U.S. companies are under increased pressure to keep jobs local. Furthermore, companies like Apple have been criticized for the oppressive labor practices of some of their suppliers in China.

Few people disagree that reducing costs is the primary motive behind outsourcing project work. However, there are limits to outsourcing (see Snapshot from Practice: Boeing 787 Dreamliner), and there appears to be a shift away from simply nailing the best low-cost deal to securing services from companies that provide the best value in terms of both cost and performance. Performance is not limited to simply the quality of specific work but also ability to collaborate and work together. Companies are doing their homework to determine "Can we work with these people?"

IMPACTS

Boeing's brand has been seriously tarnished by delays and mismanagement. The process to manage the logistics of outsourcing was not able to handle the volume of logistical problems and change management issues. Chronic delays of a few nonperforming partners induced Boeing to buy out or support partners and consumed cash. Wall Street estimates cost overruns range between 12 and 18 billion dollars over the original planned investment of $5 billion. Lessons learned from outsourcing of the 787 Dreamliner can point the way to bring back the shine to Boeing's reputation as the leader in design, technology, and integration.

LESSONS LEARNED

The lessons learned in the Dreamliner launch have been well documented. A few obvious relevant lessons are noted in suggestion form here:

- Identify and analyze all risks of outsourcing at organization *and* component levels. For example, assess the risks and implications of farming out large portions (30 percent) of the design and manufacture of crucial components to foreign suppliers. Outsourcing tends to work better in non-core areas.
- Thoroughly investigate partnership capabilities and resources. Due diligence reduces problems.
- Develop processes for quickly addressing issues and problems. Increase liaison and supervision of supply chain logistics with outsource partners.
- Reconsider seriously the implications of farming out key expertise. This runs the risk of becoming fully reliant on suppliers and transferring unique intellectual property. Partners get risk free technical knowhow, high margin markets for component parts over the life of the plane, and perhaps the future ability to become a future competitor.
- The risk of outsourcing complex, high technology components carries the burden of careful coordination and liaison.

Boeing executives have acknowledged the problems associated with outsourcing large portions of the 787 Dreamliner. For example, Boeing's Commercial Airplanes Chief, Jim Albaugh, expressed to students at Seattle University, "We spent a lot more money in trying to recover [the project] than we ever would have spent if we'd tried to keep the key technologies closer to home. The pendulum swung too far." He added that, in part, chasing the financial measure of return on assets led Boeing astray. Boeing CEO Jim McNerney noted that the 787 game plan may have been overly ambitious, incorporating too many firsts all at once.

THE FUTURE

Although Boeing's 787 outsourcing experience was very costly, outsourcing will continue and evolve. Lessons learned will prompt aircraft builders to reevaluate future outsourcing and move on. Expect to see emphasis on risk- and cost-sharing partnerships.

The major short-term challenge for Boeing is to ramp up production to satisfy the hundreds of waiting orders. Boeing can recoup by adjusting their integrative outsourcing and logistics model as a top priority.

* http://seattletimes.nwsource.com/html/sundaybuzz/2014125414_sundaybuzz06.html; http://atwonline.com/aircraft-engines-components/news/boeing-commercial-airplanes-ceo-concedes-787-outsourcing-backfired. Accessed: 1/12/2013.

Best Practices in Outsourcing Project Work

This section describes some of the best practices we have observed being used by firms that excel in project management (see Figure 12.2). Although the list is by no means comprehensive, it reflects strategies used by organizations with extensive outsourcing experience. These practices reveal an underlying theme in how firms approach contracted work on projects. Instead of the traditional master–slave relationship between owner and provider or buyer and seller, all parties work together as partners sharing the ultimate goal of a successful project.

FIGURE 12.2
Best Practices in Outsourcing Project Work

- Well-defined requirements and procedures.
- Extensive training and team-building activities.
- Well-established conflict management processes in place.
- Frequent review and status updates.
- Co-location when needed.
- Fair and incentive-laden contracts.
- Long-term outsourcing relationships.

Differences between the traditional approach and the partnering approach to managing contracted relationships are summarized in Table 12.1.[1] Partnering requires more than a simple hand-shake. It typically entails a significant commitment of time and energy to forge and sustain collaborative relations among all parties. This commitment is reflected in the seven best practices which will be discussed next.

Well-Defined Requirements and Procedures

Convincing people from different professions, organizations, and cultures to work together is difficult. If expectations and requirements are fuzzy or open

TABLE 12.1
Key Differences Between Partnering and Traditional Approaches to Managing Contracted Relationships

Partnering Approach	Traditional Approach
Mutual trust forms the basis for strong working relationships.	Suspicion and distrust; each party is wary of the motives for actions by the other.
Shared goals and objectives ensure common direction.	Each party's goals and objectives, while similar, are geared to what is best for them.
Joint project team exists with high level of interaction.	Independent project teams; teams are spatially separated with managed interactions.
Open communications avoid misdirection and bolster effective working relationships.	Communications are structured and guarded.
Long-term commitment provides the opportunity to attain continuous improvement.	Single project contracting is normal.
Objective critique is geared to candid assessment of performance.	Objectivity is limited due to fear of reprisal and lack of continuous improvement opportunity.
Access to each other's organization resources is available.	Access is limited with structured procedures and self-preservation taking priority over total optimization.
Total company involvement requires commitment from CEO to team members.	Involvement is normally limited to project-level personnel.
Integration of administrative systems equipment takes place.	Duplication and/or translation takes place with attendant costs and delays.
Risk is shared jointly among the partners, which encourages innovation and continuous improvement.	Risk is transferred to the other party.

[1] C. Cowan, C. F. Gray, and E. W. Larson, "Project Partnering," *Project Management Journal,* 12 (4) December 1992, pp. 5–15.

SNAPSHOT FROM PRACTICE — Four Strategies for Communicating with Outsourcers*

Dr. Adam Kolawa offers four strategies for overcoming poor communication with offshore project partners.

STRATEGY 1: RECOGNIZE CULTURAL DIFFERENCES

Realize that not everyone you communicate with shares your assumptions. What is obvious to you is not necessarily obvious to your partner. This is especially true with foreign outsourcers. As an American, you likely assume that laws are generally obeyed. Believe it or not, that's generally not true in most of the world, where laws are guidelines that are not necessarily followed. This can lead to major communication problems! You think if you write a contract, everybody is going to adhere to it. For many people, a contract is merely a suggestion.

STRATEGY 2: CHOOSE THE RIGHT WORDS

When you explain your requirements to an outsourcer, word choice is critical. For many outsourcers, English is still a foreign language—even in India, where both outsourcing and the English language are common. No matter how prevalent English has become, your outsourcer might have a basic understanding of each word you utter yet be not completely clear on the exact meaning of the message you're trying to convey. This is why you should speak in a direct manner using short sentences made of basic, simple words.

STRATEGY 3: CONFIRM YOUR REQUIREMENTS

You should take the following steps to confirm that the outsourcer thoroughly understands your requirements:

1. *Document your requirements.* Follow up your conversations in writing. Commit your requirements to paper for the outsourcer. Many people understand written language better than spoken language, probably because they have more time to process the message.
2. *Insist your outsourcer re-document your requirements.* Leave nothing to chance. Require outsourcers to write the requirements in their own words. If outsourcers cannot relay to you what you explained to them, then they didn't understand.
3. *Request a prototype.* After the requirements are written, ask the outsourcer to create a prototype for you. This is a safety net to ensure that your wants and needs are positively understood. Ask the provider to sketch what you want your final product to look like or build a quick, simple program that reflects how the final product will look.

STRATEGY 4: SET DEADLINES

Another important cultural difference relates to schedules and deadlines. To most Americans, a deadline is a set completion date. In many other cultures, a deadline is a suggestion that maybe something will be finished by that indicated date. To ensure that outsourced work is completed on time it is imperative to add a penalty clause to your contract or enforce late fees.

Although these strategies were directed toward working with foreign outsourcers, you would be surprised to find how many project managers use them when working with their American counterparts!

* Adam Kolawa, "Four Strategies for Communicating with Outsourcers," *Enterprise Systems Journal* at www.esj.com, accessed September 13, 2005.

to debate, this is even harder. Successful firms are very careful in selecting the work to be outsourced. They often choose to contract only work with clearly defined deliverables with measurable outcomes. For example, contractors hire electric firms to install heating and air-conditioning systems, electronic firms use design firms to fabricate enclosures for their products, and software development teams outsource the testing of versions of their programs. In all of these cases, the technical requirements are spelled out in detail. Even so, communicating requirements can be troublesome, especially with foreign providers (see the Snapshot from Practice: Four Strategies for Communicating with Outsourcers), and extra care has to be taken to ensure that expectations are understood.

Not only do requirements have to be spelled out, but the different firms' project management systems need to be integrated. Common procedures and terminology need to be established so that different parties can work together. This can be problematic when you have firms with more advanced project management systems working with less developed organizations. Surprisingly, this often is the case when U.S. firms outsource software work to India. We have heard reports that Indian providers are shocked at how unsystematic their U.S. counterparts are in their approach to managing software projects.

The best companies address this issue up front instead of waiting for problems to emerge. First they assess "fit" between providers' project management methods and their own project management system. This is a prime consideration in choosing vendors. Work requirements and deliverables are spelled out in detail in the procurement process. They invest significant time and energy to establishing project communication systems to support effective collaboration.

Finally, whenever you work with other organizations on projects, security is an important issue. Security extends beyond competitive secrets and technology to include access to information systems. Firms have to establish robust safeguards to prevent information access and the introduction of viruses due to less secure provider systems. Information technology security is an additional cost and risk that needs to be addressed up front before outsourcing project work.

Extensive Training and Team-Building Activities

Too often managers become preoccupied with the plans and technical challenges of the project and assume that people issues will work themselves out over time. Smart firms recognize that people issues are as important, if not more important than technical issues. They train their personnel to work effectively with people from other organizations and countries. This training is pervasive. It is not limited to management but involves all the people, at all levels, who interact with and are dependent upon outsourcers. Whether in a general class on negotiation or a specific one on working with Chinese programmers, team members are provided with a theoretical understanding of the barriers to collaboration as well as the skills and procedures to be successful.

The training is augmented by interorganizational team-building sessions designed to forge healthy relationships before the project begins. Team-building workshops involve the key players from the different firms, for example, engineers, architects, lawyers, specialists, and other staff. In many cases, firms find it useful to hire an outside consultant to design and facilitate the sessions. Such a consultant is typically well-versed in interorganizational team building and can provide an impartial perspective to the workshop.

The length and design of the team-building sessions will depend on the experience, commitment, and skill level of the participants. For example, one project, in which the owner and the contractors were relatively inexperienced at working together, utilized a two-day workshop. The first day was devoted to ice-breaking activities and establishing the rationale behind partnering. The conceptual foundation was supported by exercises and minilectures on teamwork, synergy, win/win, and constructive feedback. The second day began by examining the problems and barriers that prevented collaboration in the past. Representatives from the different organizations were separated and each asked the following:

- What actions do the other groups engage in that create problems for us?
- What actions do we engage in that we think create problems for them?
- What recommendations would we make to improve the situation?

The groups shared their responses and asked questions on points needing clarification. Agreements and disparities in the lists were noted and specific problems were identified. Once problem areas were noted, each group was assigned the task of identifying its specific interests and goals for the project. Goals were shared across groups, and special attention was devoted to establishing what goals they had in common. Recognition of shared goals is critical for transforming the different groups into a cohesive team.

The team-building sessions often culminate with the creation of a **partnering charter** signed by all of the participants. This charter states their common goals for the project as well as the procedures that will be used to achieve these goals (see Figure 12.3 for an example of the first page of a project charter).

Well-Established Conflict Management Processes in Place

Conflict is inevitable on a project and, as pointed out in the previous chapter, disagreements handled effectively can elevate performance. Dysfunctional conflict, however, can catch fire and severely undermine project success. Outsourced projects are susceptible to conflicts since people are unaccustomed to working together and have different values and perspectives. Successful firms invest significant time and energy up front in establishing the "rules of engagement" so that disagreements are handled constructively.

Escalation is the primary control mechanism for dealing with and resolving problems. The basic principle is that problems should be resolved at the lowest level within a set time limit (say, 24 hours), or they are "escalated" to the next level of management. If so, the principals have the same time limit to resolve the problem, or it gets passed on to the next higher level. No action is not an option. Nor can one participant force concessions from the other by simply delaying the decision. There is no shame in pushing significant problems up the hierarchy; at the same time, managers should be quick to point out to subordinates those problems or questions that they should have been able to resolve on their own.

If possible, key personnel from the respective organizations are brought together to discuss potential problems and responses. This is usually part of a coordinated series of team-building activities discussed earlier. Particular attention is devoted to establishing the change management control system where problems often erupt. People who are dependent on each other try to identify potential problems that may occur and agree in advance how they should be resolved. See the Snapshot from Practice: "Partnering" a Flu Shot for Projects for the benefits of doing this.

Finally, principled negotiation is the norm for resolving problems and reaching agreements. This approach, which emphasizes collaborative problem solving, is discussed in detail later in this chapter.

Frequent Review and Status Updates

Project managers and other key personnel from all involved organizations meet on a regular basis to review and assess project performance. Collaborating as partners is considered a legitimate project priority which is assessed along with time, cost, and performance. Teamwork, communication, and timely problem resolution are evaluated. This provides a forum for identifying problems not only with the project but also with working relationships so that they can be resolved quickly and appropriately.

FIGURE 12.4
Sample Online Survey

Evaluation of partnering process: attitudes, teamwork, process.
(Collected separately from owner and contractor participants, compared, and aggregated.)

1. Communications between the owner/contractor personnel are

1	2	3	4	5
Difficult, guarded				Easy, open, up front

2. Top management support of partnering process is

1	2	3	4	5
Not evident or inconsistent				Obvious and consistent

3. Problems, issues, or concerns are

1	2	3	4	5
Ignored				Attacked promptly

4. Cooperation between owner and contractor personnel is

1	2	3	4	5
Cool, detached, unresponsive, removed				Genuine, unreserved, complete

5. Responses to problems, issues, or concerns frequently become

1	2	3	4	5
Personal issues				Treated as project problems

budget for the project should contain ample funds to support timely travel to different organizations.

Co-location is less relevant for independent work that does not require ongoing coordination between professionals from different organizations. This would be the case if you are outsourcing discrete, independent deliverables like beta testing or a marketing campaign. Here normal channels of communication can handle the coordination issues.

Fair and Incentive-Laden Contracts

When negotiating contracts the goal is to reach a fair deal for all involved. Managers recognize that cohesion and cooperation is undermined if one party feels he or she is being unfairly treated by others. They also realize that negotiating the best deal in terms of price can come back to haunt them with shoddy work and change order gouging.

Performance-based contracts, in which significant incentives are established based on priorities of the project, are becoming increasingly popular. For example, if time is critical, then contractors accrue payoffs for beating deadlines; if scope is critical, then bonuses are issued for exceeding performance expectations. At the same time contractors are held accountable with penalty clauses for failure to perform up to standard, meet deadlines, and/or control costs. More specific information about different types of contracts is presented in this chapter's appendix on contract management.

SNAPSHOT FROM PRACTICE U.S. Department of Defense's Value Engineering Awards*

As part of an effort to cut costs the United States Department of Defense (DoD) issues annual Value Engineering Awards. Value engineering is a systematic process to analyze functions to identify actions to reduce cost, increase quality, and improve mission capabilities across the entire spectrum of DoD systems, processes, and organizations. The Value Engineering Awards Program is an acknowledgment of outstanding achievements and encourages additional projects to improve in-house and contractor productivity.

In 2012, 48 different individuals and project teams received recognition with the DoD, reporting over $4 billion in savings.

Photo by Sgt. Ken Hammond, U.S. Air Force

One team that received an award was the Defense Intelligence Agency (DIA) Hosted Server Computing (HSC) Virtualization Team. This team was recognized for planning, engineering, implementing and deploying the new HSC Virtual Infrastructure for the DoD Intelligence Information System enterprise and virtualizing more than 300 existing servers and applications residing on those servers. These efforts ensure 100 percent failover and disaster-recovery capability for more than 175 applications critical to the support of the DoD intelligence mission. Additionally, this initiative provides service to customers and mission enablers throughout the intelligence community.

The HSC team also provided a platform service to enable both internal- and external-solution hosting for DIA and its mission partners. Every intelligence business and infrastructure is, or will be, processed by 5,000 virtual servers that this service integrates, tests, deploys and maintains. The platform guarantees resources for tenants, increases agility and operational efficiency, shortens time to market, and provides greater automation and self-service when possible. The HSC service has demonstrated compelling value by increasing capability to customers and end users by more than 40 percent.

* http://www.dia.mil/public-affairs/news/2012-08-06.html. Accessed: 12/2/2012.

Companies recognize that contracts can discourage continuous improvement and innovation. Instead of trying some new, promising technique that may reduce costs, contractors will avoid the risks and apply tried and true methods to meet contracted requirements. Companies that treat contractors as partners consider continuous improvement as a joint effort to eliminate waste and pursue opportunities for cost savings. Risks as well as benefits are typically shared 50/50 between the principals, with the owner adhering to a fast-track review of proposed changes.

How the U.S. Department of Defense reaps the benefits of continuous improvement through value engineering is highlighted in the Snapshot from Practice: Value Engineering Awards.

Long-Term Outsourcing Relationships

Many companies recognize that major benefits can be enjoyed when outsourcing arrangements extend across multiple projects and are long term. For example, Corning and Toyota are among the many firms that have forged a network of long-term strategic partnerships with their suppliers. The average large corporation is involved in around 30 alliances today versus fewer than 3 in the early 1990s.

Among the many advantages for establishing a long-term partnership are the following:

- **Reduced administrative costs**—The costs associated with bidding and selecting a contractor are eliminated. Contract administration costs are reduced as partners become knowledgeable of their counterpart's legal concerns.
- **More efficient utilization of resources**—Contractors have a known forecast of work while owners are able to concentrate their workforce on core businesses and avoid the demanding swings of project support.
- **Improved communication**—As partners gain experience with each other, they develop a common language and perspective, which reduces misunderstanding and enhances collaboration.
- **Improved innovation**—The partners are able to discuss innovation and associated risks in a more open manner and share risks and rewards fairly.
- **Improved performance**—Over time partners become more familiar with each other's standards and expectations and are able to apply lessons learned from previous projects to current projects.

Working as partners is a conscious effort on the part of management to form collaborative relationships with personnel from different organizations to complete a project. For outsourcing to work, the individuals involved need to be effective negotiators capable of merging interests and discovering solutions to problems that contribute to the project. The next section addresses some of the key skills and techniques associated with effective negotiation.

The Art of Negotiating

Effective negotiating is critical to successful collaboration. All it takes is one key problem to explode to convert a sense of "we" into "us versus them." At the same time, negotiating is pervasive through all aspects of project management work. Project managers must negotiate support and funding from top management. They must negotiate staff and technical input from functional managers. They must coordinate with other project managers and negotiate project priorities and commitments. They must negotiate within their project team to determine assignments, deadlines, standards, and priorities. Project managers must negotiate prices and standards with vendors and suppliers. A firm understanding of the negotiating process, skills, and tactics is essential to project success.

Many people approach negotiating as if it is a competitive contest. Each negotiator is out to win as much as he or she can for his or her side. Success is measured by how much is gained compared with the other party. While this may be applicable when negotiating the sale of a house, it is not true for project management. *Project management is not a contest!* First, the people working on the project, whether they represent different companies or departments within the same organization, are not enemies or competitors but rather allies or partners. They have formed a temporary alliance to complete a project. For this alliance to work requires a certain degree of trust, cooperation, and honesty. Second, if conflicts escalate to the point where negotiations break down and the project comes to a halt, then everyone loses. Third, unlike bartering with a street vendor, the people involved on project work have to continue to work together. Therefore, it behooves them to resolve disagreements in a way that contributes to healthy working relationships. Finally, as pointed out in the previous chapter, conflict on a project can be good. When dealt with effectively it can lead to innovation, better decisions, and more creative problem solving.

Project managers accept this noncompetitive view of negotiation and realize that negotiation is essentially a two-part process: The first part deals with reaching an agreement; the second part is the implementation of that agreement. It is the implementation phase, not the agreement itself, that determines the success of negotiations. All too often, managers reach an agreement with someone only to find out later that they failed to do what they agreed to do or that their actual response fell far short of expectations. Experienced project managers recognize that implementation is based on satisfaction not only with the outcome but also with the process by which the agreement was reached. If someone feels bullied or tricked into doing something, this feeling will invariably be reflected by half-hearted performance.

Veteran project managers do the best they can to merge individual interests with what is best for the project and come up with effective solutions to problems. Fisher and Ury from the Harvard Negotiation Project champion an approach to negotiating that embodies these goals.[2] It emphasizes developing win/win solutions while protecting yourself against those who would take advantage of your forthrightness. Their approach is called **principled negotiation** and is based on four key points listed in Table 12.2 and discussed in the following sections.

TABLE 12.2 Principled Negotiation

1. Separate the people from the problem
2. Focus on interests, not positions
3. Invent options for mutual gain
4. When possible, use objective criteria

1. Separate the People from the Problem

Too often personal relations become entangled with the substantive issues under consideration. Instead of attacking the problem(s), people attack each other. Once people feel attacked or threatened their energy naturally goes to defending themselves, and not to solving the problem. The key, then, is to focus on the problem—not the other person—during the negotiation. Avoid personalizing the negotiation and framing the negotiation as a contest. Instead, try to keep the focus on the problem to be resolved. In Fisher and Ury's words: *Be hard on the problem, soft on the people.*

By keeping the focus on the issues and not the personalities, negotiators are better able to let the other person blow off steam. On important problems it is not uncommon for people to become upset, frustrated, and angry. However, one angry attack produces an angry counterattack, and the discussion quickly escalates into a heated argument, an emotional chain reaction.

In some cases people use anger as a means of intimidating and forcing concessions because the other person wishes to preserve the relationship. When people become emotional, negotiators should keep a cool head and remember the old German proverb, "Let anger fly out the window."[3] In other words, in the face of an emotional outburst, imagine opening a window and letting the heat of the

[2] R. Fisher and W. Ury, *Getting to Yes: Negotiating Agreement without Giving In*, 2nd ed. (New York: Penguin Books, 1991).

[3] Ibid.

Summary

Outsourcing has become an integral part of project management. More and more companies are collaborating with each other on projects to compete in today's business world. The advantages of outsourcing include cost reduction, quicker completion times, greater flexibility, and higher level of expertise. Disadvantages include coordination problems, loss of control, conflicts, security issues and political fallout.

A number of proactive best practices have emerged among firms that have mastered the outsourcing process. These practices include establishing well-defined requirements and procedures and utilizing fair and incentive-laden contracts. Team-building sessions are held before the project begins to forge relationships between personnel from different organizations. Escalation guidelines for resolving conflicts are established, as are provisions for process improvement and risk sharing. On highly critical work, arrangements are made so that key personnel work together, face to face. Joint assessments of how well people are collaborating is the norm during status report briefings. Finally, many companies are realizing the benefits of forming long-term alliances with each other on projects. The ultimate goal is to work together as partners.

Effective negotiating skills are essential to working on projects as partners. People need to resolve differences at the lowest level possible in order to keep the project on track. Veteran project managers realize that negotiating is not a competitive game and work toward collaborative solutions to problems. They accomplish this by separating people from the problem, focusing on interests and not positions, inventing options for mutual gain, and relying on objective criteria whenever possible to resolve disagreements. They also recognize the importance of developing a strong BATNA, which provides them with the leverage necessary to seek collaborative solutions.

Customer satisfaction is the litmus test for project success. Project managers need to take a proactive approach to managing customer expectations and perceptions. They need to actively involve customers in key decisions and keep them abreast of important developments. Active customer involvement keeps the project team focused on the objectives of the project and reduces misunderstandings and dissatisfaction.

Key Terms

Best alternative to a negotiated agreement (BATNA), *436*
Co-location, *429*
Escalation, *427*
Met-expectations model, *437*
Outsourcing, *419*
Partnering charter, *427*
Principled negotiation, 433

Review Questions

1. Why do firms outsource project work?
2. What are the best practices used by firms to outsource project work?
3. What does the term "escalate" refer to, and why is it essential to project success?
4. Why is the principled negotiation approach recommended for negotiating agreements on projects?

5. What does the acronym BATNA refer to, and why is it important to being a successful negotiator?
6. How can a project manager influence customer expectations and perceptions?

Exercises

1. Break into groups of four to five students. Assign half of the groups the role of Owner and the other half the role of Contractor.

   Owners: After saving for many years you are about to hire a contractor to build your "dream home." What are your objectives for this project? What concerns or issues do you have about working with a general contractor to build your home?

   Contractors: You specialize in building customized homes. You are about to meet with prospective owners to begin to negotiate a contract for building their "dream home." What are your objectives for this project? What concerns or issues do you have about working with the owners to build their home?

   Each Owner group meets with another Contractor group and shares their objectives, concerns, and issues.

   Identify what objectives, issues, and concerns you have in common and which ones are unique. Discuss how you could work together to realize your objectives. What would be the keys to working as partners on this project?
2. Enter "outsourcing" in an Internet search engine and browse different Web sites. Who appears to be interested in outsourcing? What are the advantages of outsourcing? What are the disadvantages? Does outsourcing mean the same thing to different people? What are future trends in outsourcing?
3. Break into four groups and review the instructions for "Get the most you can" exercise provided by your teacher. Complete the exercise. What was your initial strategy? Did it change? If so, why? What does this exercise tell you about our ability to collaborate with each other?

References

Cowan, C., C. F. Gray, and E. W. Larson, "Project Partnering," *Project Management Journal,* Vol. 12, No. 4, December 1992, pp. 5–15.

Covey, S. R., *The Seven Habits of Highly Effective People* (New York: Simon and Schuster, 1990).

DiDonato, L. S., "Contract Disputes: Alternatives for Dispute Resolution (Part 1)," *PM Network,* May 1993, pp. 19–23.

Drexler, J. A., and E. W. Larson, "Partnering: Why Project Owner-Contractor Relationships Change," *Journal of Construction Engineering and Management,* Vol. 126, No. 4, July/August 2000, pp. 293–397.

Dyer, S., *Partner Your Project* (Warwickshire, UK: Pendulum Pub., 1997).

Economy, P., *Business Negotiating Basics* (Burr Ridge, IL: Irwin Professional Publishing, 1994).

Fisher, R., and W. Ury, *Getting to Yes: Negotiating Agreement without Giving In,* 2nd ed. (New York: Penguin Books, 1991).

Hedberg, B., G. Dahlgren, J. Hansson, and N. Olve, *Virtual Organizations and Beyond* (New York: Wiley, 1997).

Hoang, H., and F. T. Rothaermel, "The Effect of General and Partner-Specific Alliance Experience on Joint R&D Project Performance," *Academy of Management Journal,* Vol. 48, No. 2, 2005, pp. 332–45.

CHAPTER THIRTEEN

Progress and Performance Measurement and Evaluation

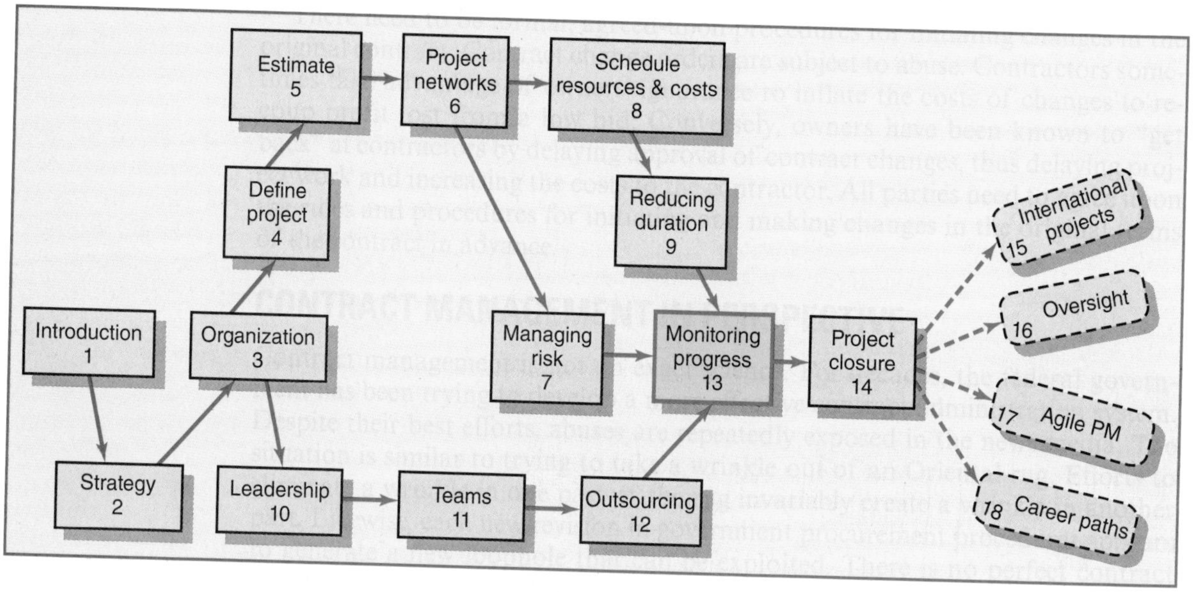

Progress and Performance Measurement and Evaluation
Structure of a Project Monitoring Information System
The Project Control Process
Monitoring Time Performance
Development of an Earned Value Cost/Schedule System
Developing a Status Report: A Hypothetical Example
Indexes to Monitor Progress
Forecasting Final Project Cost
Other Control Issues
Summary
Appendix 13.1: The Application of Additional Earned Value Rules
Appendix 13.2: Obtaining Project Performance Information from MS Project

How does a project get one year late?
. . . One day at a time.
—Frederick P. Brooks, The Mythical Man Month, p. 153

Evaluation and control are part of every project manager's job. Control by "wandering around" and/or "involvement" can overcome most problems in small projects. But large projects need some form of formal control. Control holds people accountable, prevents small problems from mushrooming into large problems, and keeps focus. Except for accounting controls, project control is not performed well in most organizations. Control is one of the most neglected areas of project management. Unfortunately, it is not uncommon to find resistance to control processes. In essence, those who minimize the importance of control are passing up a great opportunity to be effective managers and, perhaps, allow the organization to gain a competitive edge. Neglecting control in organizations with multiple projects is even more serious. For effective control, the project manager needs a single information system to collect data and report progress on cost, schedule, and specifications. The general structure of such a system is discussed next.

Structure of a Project Monitoring Information System

A project monitoring system involves *determining what* data to collect; *how, when,* and *who* will collect the data; *analysis* of the data; and *reporting* current progress.

What Data Are Collected? Data collected are determined by *which* metrics will be used for project control. Typical key data collected are actual activity duration times, resource usage and rates, and actual costs, which are compared against planned times, resources, and budgets. Since a major portion of the monitoring system focuses on cost/schedule concerns, it is crucial to provide the project manager and stakeholders with data to answer questions such as:

- What is the current status of the project in terms of schedule and cost?
- How much will it cost to complete the project?
- When will the project be completed?
- Are there potential problems that need to be addressed now?
- What, who, and where are the causes for cost or schedule overruns?
- What did we get for the dollars spent?
- If there is a cost overrun midway in the project, can we forecast the overrun at completion?

The performance metrics you need to collect should support answering these questions. Examples of specific metrics and tools for collecting data will be discussed in detail later in this chapter.

Gantt charts (bar charts) and control charts are the typical tools used for communicating project schedule status. As suggested in Chapter 6, the Gantt chart is the most favored, used, and understandable. This kind of chart is commonly referred to as a tracking Gantt chart. Gantt and control charts serve well as a means for tracking and trending schedule performance. Their easy-to-understand visual formats make them favorite tools for communicating project schedule status—especially to top management, who do not usually have time for details. Adding actual and revised time estimates to the Gantt chart gives a quick overview of project status on the report date.

Tracking Gantt Chart

Figure 13.1 presents a baseline Gantt chart and a tracking Gantt chart for a project at the end of period 6. The solid bar below the original schedule bar represents the actual start and finish times for completed activities or any portion of an activity completed (see activities A, B, C, D, and E). For example, the actual start time for activity C is period 2; the actual finish time is period 5; the actual duration is three time units, rather than four scheduled time periods. Activities in process show the actual start time; the extended bar represents the expected remaining duration (see activities D and E). The remaining duration for activities D and E are shown with the hatched bar. Activity F, which has not started, shows a revised estimated actual start (9) and finish time (13).

Note how activities can have durations that differ from the original schedule, as in activities C, D, and E. Either the activity is complete and the actual is known, or new information suggests the estimate of time be revised and reflected

FIGURE 13.1
Baseline Gantt Chart

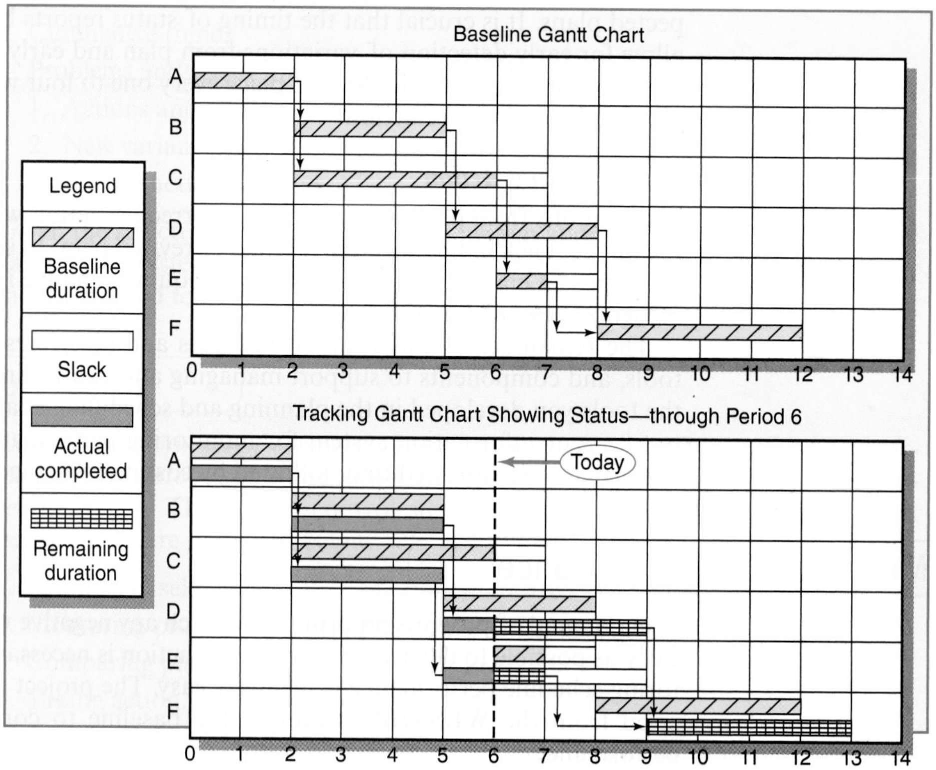

in the status report. Activity D's revised duration results in an expected delay in the start of activity F. The project is now estimated to be completed one period later than planned. Although sometimes the Gantt chart does not show dependencies, when it is used with a network, the dependencies are easily identified if tracing is needed.

Control Chart

This chart is another tool used to monitor past project schedule performance and current performance and to estimate future schedule trends. Figure 13.2 depicts a project control chart. The chart is used to plot the difference between the scheduled time on the critical path at the report date with the actual point on the critical path. Although Figure 13.2 shows the project was behind early in the project, the plot suggests corrective action brought the project back on track. If the trend is sustained, the project will come in ahead of schedule. Because the activity scheduled times represent average durations, four observations trending in one direction indicate there is a very high probability that there is an identifiable cause. The cause should be located and action taken if necessary. Control chart trends are very useful for giving warning of potential problems so appropriate action can be taken if necessary.

Control charts are also frequently used to monitor progress toward milestones, which mark events and as such have zero duration. Milestones are significant project events that mark major accomplishments. To be effective, milestones need to be concrete, specific, measurable events. Milestones must be easily identifiable by all project stakeholders—for example, product testing complete. Critical merge activities are good candidates for milestones. Control charts very similar to the example shown in Figure 13.2 are often used to record and communicate project progress toward a milestone.

Schedule slippage of one day seldom receives a great deal of attention. However, one day here and another there soon add up to large delay problems. It is

FIGURE 13.2
Project Schedule Control Chart

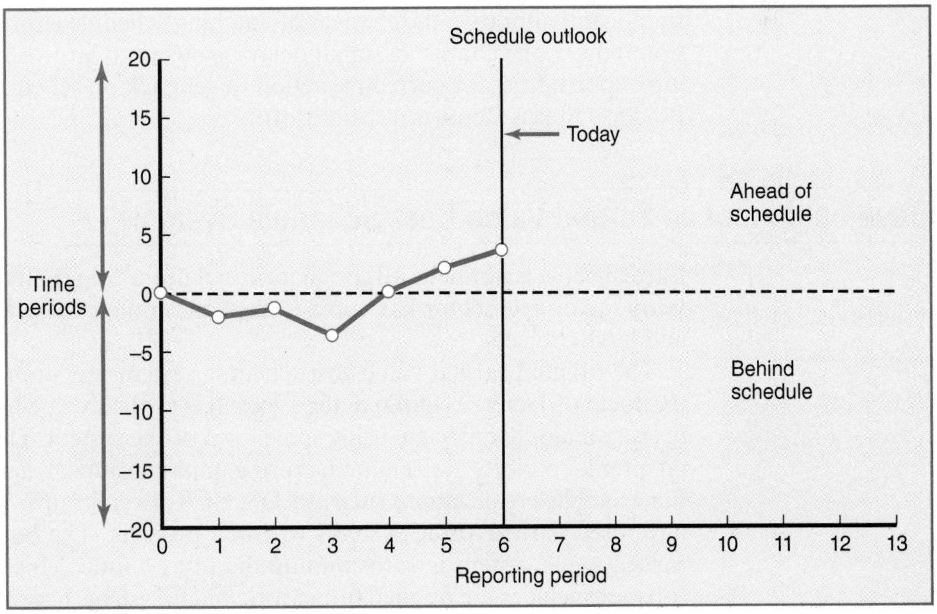

SNAPSHOT FROM PRACTICE — Status Reports at Microsoft*

When Bill Gates was in charge of Microsoft, project teams sent reports each month to top executives, as well as to the managers of all related projects. The status reports were brief and had a standard format. Gates read most of them quickly, and spotted potential delays, or changes he did not want. He especially looked for schedule slips, cutting too many product features, or the need to change a specification. Gates usually responded to the relevant managers or developers directly by electronic mail. Status reports are an important mechanism for communicating between top management and projects. As Gates explained:

"I get all the status reports. Right now there might be a hundred active projects. . . . [The status reports] contain the schedule, including milestones dates, and any change in spec, and any comments about 'Hey, we can't hire enough people,' or 'Jeez, if this OLE (Object Linking and Embedding) 2 Mac release isn't done, we're just going to have to totally slip.' . . . They know [their report] goes up to all the people who manage all the other groups that they have dependencies with. So if they don't raise it in the status report and then two months later they say something, that's a breakdown in communication. . . . The internal group is totally copied on those things, so it's sort of the consensus of the group."

* From *Microsoft Secrets: The World's Most Powerful Software Company Creates Technology.* Copyright © 1995 by Michael A. Cusumano and Richard W. Selby.

AP Photo/Keystone, Alessandro della Valle

well known that once work gets behind, it has a tendency to stay behind because it is difficult to make up. Examples of causes of schedule slippage are unreliable time estimates, minor redesign, scope creep, and unavailable resources. Using slack early in a path may create a problem for someone responsible for a later activity; flexibility and potential opportunities are reduced. For these reasons, having frequent and clearly defined monitoring points for work packages can significantly improve the chances of catching schedule slippage early. Early detection reduces the chance of small delays growing to large ones and thereby reducing opportunities for corrective action to get back on schedule. See Snapshot from Practice: Status Reports at Microsoft.

Development of an Earned Value Cost/Schedule System

Earned value is not new; although its initial use was in military contracts, in recent years the private sector has come to depend on the system for managing multiple and large projects.

The original earned value cost/schedule system was pioneered by the U.S. Department of Defense (DoD) in the 1960s. It is probably safe to say project managers in every major country are using some form of the system. The system is being used on internal projects in the manufacturing, pharmaceutical, and high-tech industries. For example, organizations such as EDS, NCR, Levi Strauss, Tektronics, and Disney have used earned value systems to track projects. The basic framework of the earned value system is withstanding the test of time. Most project management software includes the original framework; many systems have added industry-specific

TABLE 13.1
Glossary of Terms

EV	Earned value for a task is simply the percent complete times its original budget. Stated differently, EV is the percent of the original budget that has been earned by actual work completed. [The older acronym for this value was BCWP—budgeted cost of the work performed.]
PV	The planned time-phased baseline of the value of the work scheduled. An approved cost estimate of the resources scheduled in a time-phased cumulative baseline [BCWS—budgeted cost of the work scheduled].
AC	Actual cost of the work completed. The sum of the costs incurred in accomplishing work [ACWP—actual cost of the work performed].
CV	Cost variance is the difference between the earned value and the actual costs for the work completed to date where CV = EV − AC.
SV	Schedule variance is the difference between the earned value and the baseline line to date where SV = EV − PV.
BAC	Budgeted cost at completion. The total budgeted cost of the baseline or project cost accounts.
EAC	Estimated cost at completion.
ETC	Estimated cost to complete remaining work.
VAC	Cost variance at completion. VAC indicates expected actual over- or underrun cost at completion.

variations to more precisely track progress and costs. This chapter presents the "generic" core of an integrated cost/schedule information system.[1]

The earned value system starts with the time-phased costs that provide the project budget *baseline,* which is called the planned budgeted value of the work scheduled (PV). Given this time-phased baseline, comparisons are made with actual and planned schedule and costs using earned value. The earned value approach provides the missing links not found in conventional cost-budget systems. At any point in time, a status report can be developed for the project.

The earned value cost/schedule system uses several acronyms and equations for analysis. Table 13.1 presents a glossary of these acronyms. You will need this glossary as a reference. In recent years acronyms have been shortened to be more phonetically friendly. This movement is reflected in material from the Project Management Institute, in project management software, and by most practitioners. This text edition follows the recent trend. The acronyms found in brackets represent the older acronyms, which are often found in software programs. To the uninitiated, the terms used in practice appear horrendous and intimidating. However, once a few basic terms are understood, the intimidation index will evaporate.

Following five careful steps ensures that the cost/schedule system is integrated. These steps are outlined here. Steps 1, 2, and 3 are accomplished in the planning stage. Steps 4 and 5 are sequentially accomplished during the execution stage of the project.

1. Define the work using a WBS. This step involves developing documents that include the following information (see Chapters 4 and 5):
   a. Scope.
   b. Work packages.
   c. Deliverables.
   d. Organization units.
   e. Resources.
   f. Budgets for each work package.

[1] See Fleming and Koppelman for a more complete earned value description.

2. Develop work and resource schedule.
   a. Schedule resources to activities (see Chapter 8).
   b. Time-phase work packages into a network.
3. Develop a time-phase budget using work packages included in an activity. The cumulative values of these budgets will become the baseline and will be called the planned budgeted cost of the work scheduled (PV). The sum should equal the budgeted amounts for all the work packages in the cost accounts (see Chapter 8).
4. At the work package level, collect the actual costs for the work performed. These costs will be called the actual cost of the work completed (AC). Collect percent complete and multiply this times the original budget amount for the value of the work actually completed. These values will be called earned value (EV).
5. Compute the schedule variance (SV = EV − PV) and cost variance (CV = EV − AC). Prepare hierarchical status reports for each level of management—from work package manager to customer or project manager. The reports should also include project rollups by organization unit and deliverables. In addition, actual time performance should be checked against the project network schedule.

Figure 13.3 presents a schematic overview of the integrated information system, which includes the techniques and systems presented in earlier chapters. Those who have tenaciously labored through the early chapters can smile! Steps 1 and 2 are already carefully developed. Observe that control data can be traced backward to specific deliverables and organization unit responsible.

The major reasons for creating a baseline are to monitor and report progress and to estimate cash flow. Therefore, it is crucial to integrate the baseline with the performance measurement system. Costs are placed (time-phased) in the baseline exactly as managers expect them to be "earned." This approach facilitates tracking costs to their point of origin. In practice, the integration is accomplished by using the same rules in assigning costs to the baseline as those used to measure progress

FIGURE 13.3
Project Management Information System Overview

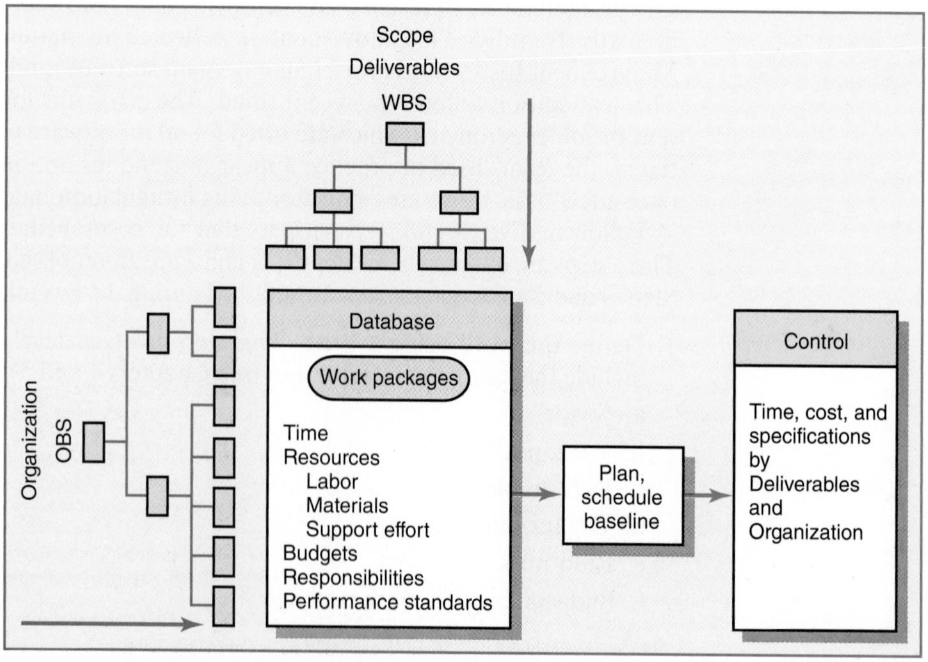

using earned value. You may find several rules in practice, but percent complete is the workhorse most commonly used. Someone familiar with each task estimates what percent of the task has been completed or how much of the task remains.

Percent Complete Rule

This rule is the heart of any earned value system. The best method for assigning costs to the baseline under this rule is to establish frequent checkpoints over the duration of the work package and assign completion percentages in dollar terms. For example, units completed could be used to assign baseline costs and later to measure progress. Units might be lines of code, hours, drawings completed, cubic yards of concrete in place, workdays, prototypes complete, etc. This approach to percent complete adds "objectivity" to the subjective observation approaches often used. When measuring percent complete in the monitoring phase of the project, it is common to limit the amount earned to 80 or 90 percent until the work package is 100 percent complete.

What Costs Are Included in Baselines?

The baseline (PV) is the sum of the cost accounts, and each cost account is the sum of the work packages in the cost account. Three direct costs are typically included in baselines—labor, equipment, and materials. The reason: these are direct costs the project manager can control. Overhead costs and profit are typically added later by accounting processes. Most work packages should be discrete, of short time span, and have measurable outputs. If materials and/or equipment are a significant portion of the cost of work packages, they can be budgeted in separate work packages and cost accounts.

Methods of Variance Analysis

Generally the method for measuring accomplishments centers on two key computations:

1. Comparing earned value with the expected schedule value.
2. Comparing earned value with the actual costs.

These comparisons can be made at the project level or down to the cost account level. Project status can be determined for the latest period, all periods to date, and estimated to the end of the project.

Assessing the current status of a project using the earned value cost/schedule system requires three data elements—planned cost of the work scheduled (PV), budgeted cost of the work completed (EV), and actual cost of the work completed (AC). From these data the schedule variance (SV) and cost variance (CV) are computed each reporting period. *A positive variance indicates a desirable condition, while a negative variance suggests problems or changes that have taken place.*

Cost variance tells us if the work accomplished costs more or less than was planned at any point over the life of the project. If labor and materials have not been separated, cost variance should be reviewed carefully to isolate the cause to either labor or materials—or to both.

Schedule variance presents an overall assessment of *all* work packages in the project scheduled to date. It is important to note schedule variance contains *no* critical path information. Schedule variance measures progress in dollars rather than time units. Therefore, it is unlikely that any translation of dollars to time will yield accurate information telling if any milestone or critical path is early, on time,

TABLE 13.2
Digital Camera Prototype Status Reports: Periods 1–7

Cost Variance CV = EV − AC
Schedule Variance SV = EV − PV

Status Report: Ending Period 1

Task	%Complete	EV	AC	PV	CV	SV
A	50%	10	10	10	0	0
Cumulative Totals		**10**	**10**	**10**	**0**	**0**

Status Report: Ending Period 2

Task	%Complete	EV	AC	PV	CV	SV
A	Finished	20	30	20	−10	0
Cumulative Totals		**20**	**30**	**20**	**−10**	**0**

Status Report: Ending Period 3

Task	%Complete	EV	AC	PV	CV	SV
A	Finished	20	30	20	−10	0
B	33%	5	10	5	−5	0
C	20%	20	30	20	−10	0
D	60%	21	20	15	+1	+6
Cumulative Totals		**66**	**90**	**60**	**−24**	**+6**

Status Report: Ending Period 4

Task	%Complete	EV	AC	PV	CV	SV
A	Finished	20	30	20	−10	0
B	Finished	15	20	15	−5	0
C	50%	50	70	50	−20	0
D	80%	28	30	25	−2	+3
Comulative Totals		**113**	**150**	**110**	**−37**	**+3**

Status Report: Ending Period 5

Task	%Complete	EV	AC	PV	CV	SV
A	Finished	20	30	20	−10	0
B	Finished	15	20	15	−5	0
C	60%	60	100	80	−40	−20
D	80%	28	50	35	−22	−7
Cumulative Totals		**123**	**200**	**150**	**−77**	**−27**

Status Report: Ending Period 6

Task	%Complete	EV	AC	PV	CV	SV
A	Finished	20	30	20	−10	0
B	Finished	15	20	15	−5	0
C	80%	80	110	100	−30	−20
D	Finished	35	60	35	−25	0
Cumulative Totals		**150**	**220**	**170**	**−70**	**−20**

Status Report: Ending Period 7

Task	%Complete	EV	AC	PV	CV	SV
A	Finished	20	30	20	−10	0
B	Finished	15	20	15	−5	0
C	90%	90	120	100	−30	−10
D	Finished	35	60	35	−25	0
E	0%	0	0	30	0	−30
F	0%	0	0	0	0	0
Cumulative Totals		**160**	**230**	**200**	**−70**	**−40**

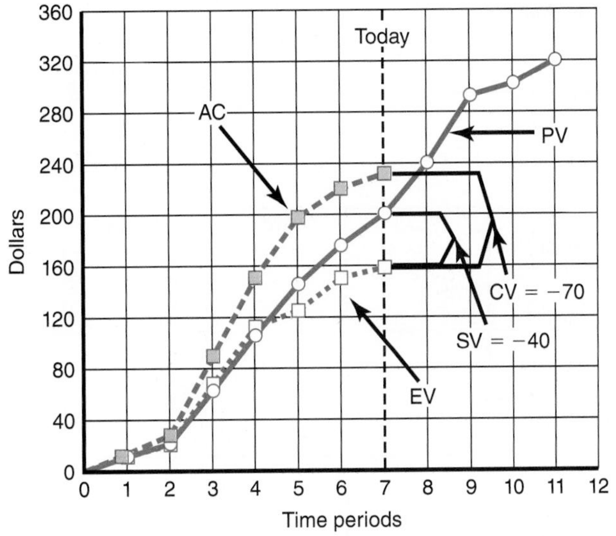

FIGURE 13.9
Digital Camera Prototype Summary Graph ($000)

Figure 13.9 shows the graphed results of all the status reports through period 7. This graph represents the data from Table 13.2. The cumulative actual costs (AC) to date and the earned value budgeted costs to date (EV) are plotted against the original project baseline (PV). The cumulative AC to date is $230; the cumulative EV to date is $160. Given these cumulative values, the cost variance (CV = EV − AC) is negative $70 (160 − 230 = −70). The schedule variance (SV = EV − PV) is negative $40 (160 − 200 = −40). Again, recall that only the project network or Tracking Gantt chart can give an accurate assessment of schedule performance down to the work package level.

A Tracking Gantt bar chart for the Digital Camera Prototype is shown in Figure 13.10. From this figure you can see Task C (Memory/Software), which had an original duration of 4 time units, now is expected to require 6 time units. This delay of 2 time units for Task C will also delay Tasks E and F two time units and result in the project being late 2 time periods.

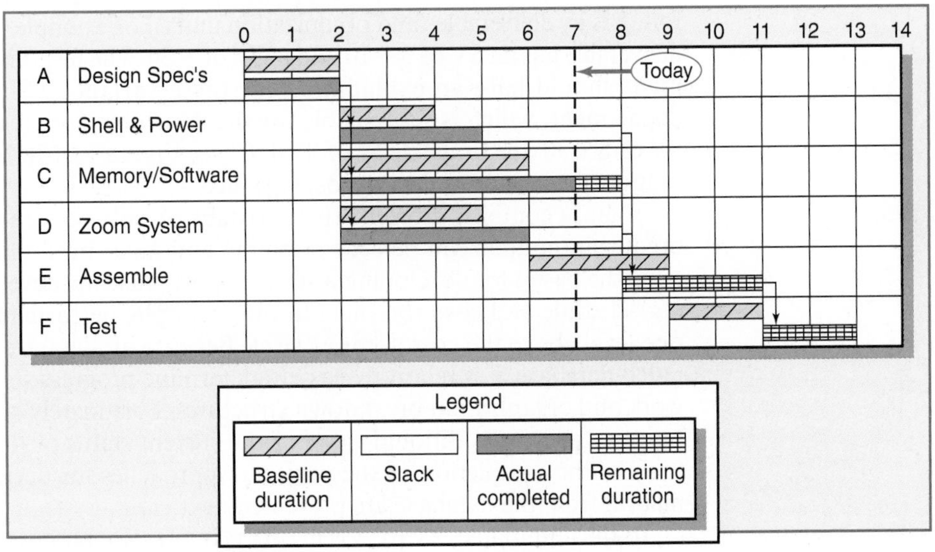

FIGURE 13.10
Digital Camera Project-Tracking Gantt Chart Showing Status—Through Period 7

FIGURE 13.11 Project Rollup End Period 7 ($000)

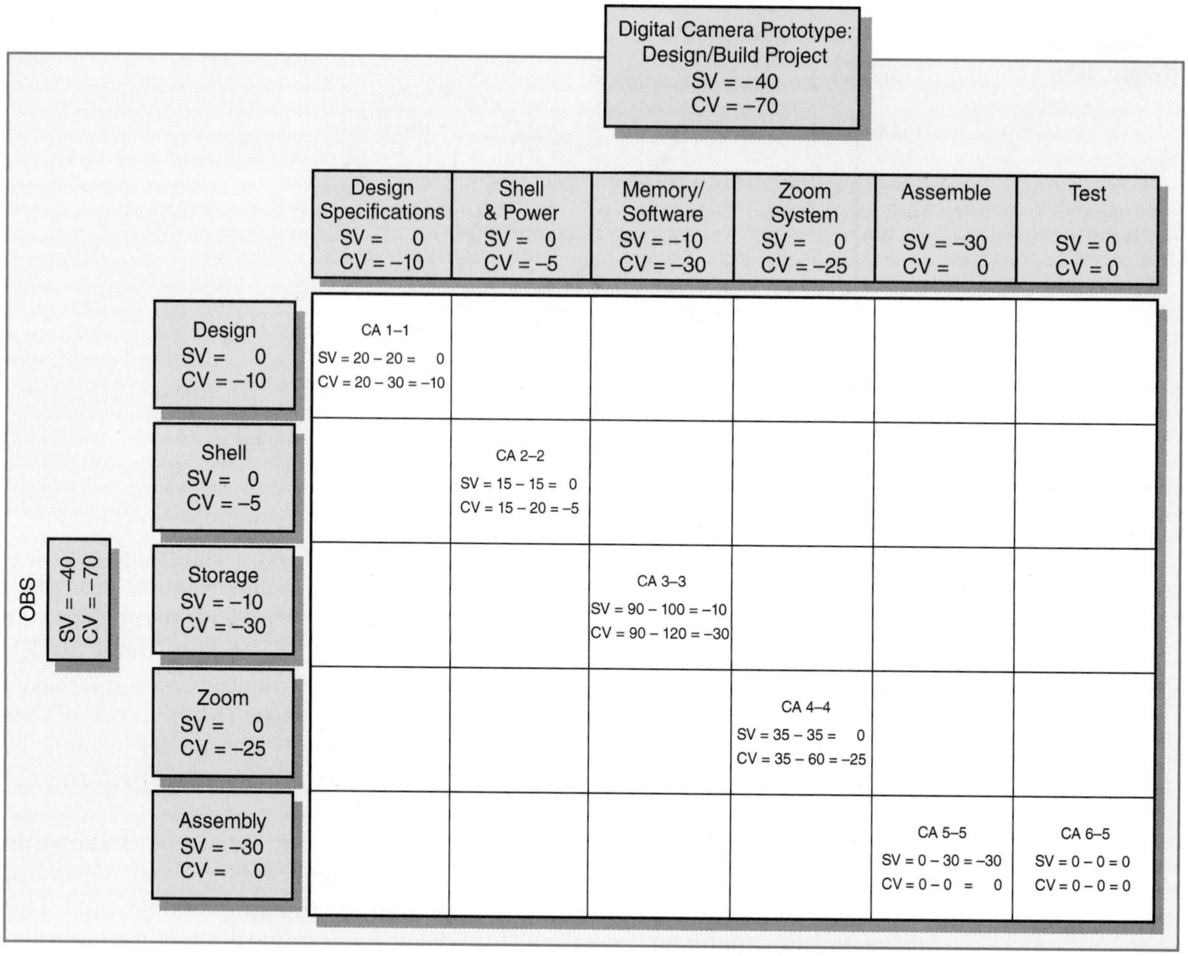

Figure 13.11 shows an oversimplified project rollup at the end of period 7. The rollup is by deliverables and organization units. For example, the Memory/Software deliverable has an SV of $ −10 and a CV of −30. The responsible "Storage" department should have an explanation for these variances. Similarly, the assembly department, which is responsible for the Assemble and Test deliverables, has an SV of $ −30 due to the delay of Task C (see Figure 13.10). Most deliverables look unfavorable on schedule and cost variance.

In more complex projects, the crosstabs of cost accounts by deliverables and organization units can be very revealing and more profound. This example contains the basics for developing a status report, baseline development, and measuring schedule and cost variance. In our example, performance analysis had only one level above the cost account level. Because all data are derived from the detailed database, it is relatively easy to determine progress status at all levels of the work and organization breakdown structures. Fortunately, this same current database can provide additional views of the current status of the project and forecast costs at the completion of the project. Approaches for deriving additional information from the database are presented next.

To the uninitiated, a caveat is in order. In practice budgets may not be expressed in total dollars for an activity. Frequently, budgets are time-phased for materials and labor separately for more effective control over costs. Another common approach used in practice is to use labor hours in place of dollars in the earned value system. Later, labor hours are converted to dollars. The use of labor hours in the earned value system is the *modus operandi* for most construction work. Labor hours are easy to understand and are often the way many time and cost estimates are developed. Most earned value software easily accommodates the use of labor hours for development of cost estimates.

Indexes to Monitor Progress

Practitioners sometimes prefer to use schedule and cost indexes over the absolute values of SV and CV, because indexes can be considered efficiency ratios. Graphed indexes over the project life cycle can be very illuminating and useful. The trends are easily identified for deliverables and the whole project.

Indexes are typically used at the cost account level and above. In practice, the database is also used to develop indexes that allow the project manager and customer to view progress from several angles. An index of 1.00 (100 percent) indicates progress is as planned. An index greater than 1.00 shows progress is better than expected. An index less than 1.00 suggests progress is poorer than planned and deserves attention. Table 13.3 presents the interpretation of the indexes.

Performance Indexes

There are two indexes of performance efficiency. The first index measures *cost* efficiency of the work accomplished to date: (Data from Table 13.2)

Cost performance index (CPI) = EV/AC = 160/230 = .696 or .70

The CPI of .696 shows that $.70 worth of work planned to date has been completed for each $1.00 actually spent—an unfavorable situation indeed. The CPI is the most accepted and used index. It has been tested over time and found to be the most accurate, reliable, and stable. For example, U.S. government studies have shown that the CPI is stable from the 20 percent completion point regardless of contract type, program, or service. The CPI can provide an "early warning signal" as to cost overruns so that adjustments can be made to the budget or scope of a project.[2]

The second index is a measure of scheduling efficiency to date:

Scheduling performance index (SPI) = EV/PV = 160/200 = .80

The schedule index indicates $.80 worth of work has been accomplished for each $1.00 worth of scheduled work to date. Figure 13.12 shows the indexes plotted for our example project through period 7. This figure is another example of graphs used in practice.

TABLE 13.3
Interpretation of Indexes

Index	Cost (CPI)	Schedule (SPI)
>1.00	Under cost	Ahead of schedule
=1.00	On cost	On schedule
<1.00	Over cost	Behind schedule

[2] Cited by Q. W. Fleming and J. M. Koppleman, *Earned Value Project Management* (Newton Square, PA: Project Management Institute, 2010), pp. 39–42.

FIGURE 13.12
Indexes Periods 1–7

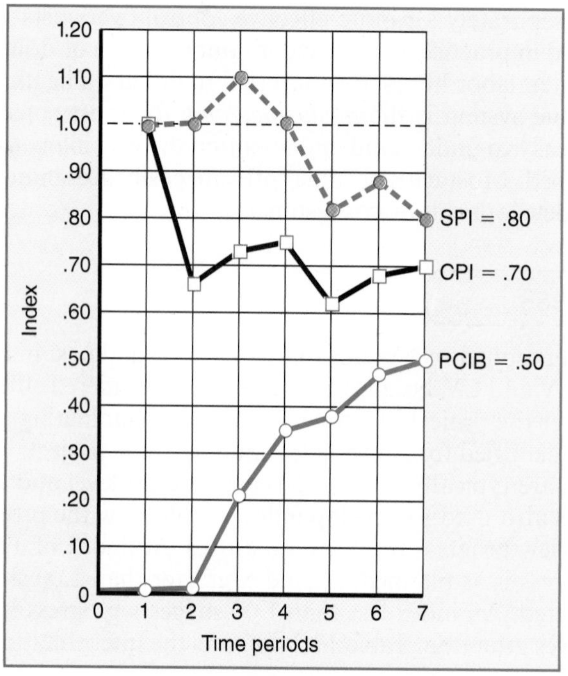

Project Percent Complete Indexes

Two project percent complete indexes are used, depending on your judgment of which one is most representative of your project. The first index assumes the original budget of work complete is the most reliable information to measure project percent complete. The second index assumes the actual costs-to-date and expected cost at completion are the most reliable for measuring project percent complete. These indexes compare the to-date progress to the end of the project. The implications underlying use of these indexes are that conditions will not change, no improvement or action will be taken, and the information in the database is accurate. The first index looks at percent complete in terms of *budget* amounts:

Percent complete index PCIB = EV/BAC = 160/320 = .50 (50%)

This PCIB indicates the work accomplished represents 50 percent of the total budgeted (BAC) dollars to date. Observe that this calculation does not include actual costs incurred. Because actual dollars spent do not guarantee project progress, this index is favored by many project managers when there is a high level of confidence in the original budget estimates.

The second index views percent complete in terms of *actual* dollars spent to accomplish the work to date and the actual expected dollars for the completed project (EAC). For example, at the end of period 7 the staff re-estimates that the EAC will be 575 instead of 320. The application of this view is written as

Percent complete index PCIC = AC/EAC = 230/575 = .40 (40%)

Some managers favor this index because it contains actual and revised estimates that include newer, more complete information.

These two views of percent complete present alternative views of the "real" percent complete. These percents may be quite different as shown above. (Note:

The PCIC index was not plotted in Figure 13.12. The new figures for EAC would be derived each period by estimators in the field.)

Technical Performance Measurement

Measuring technical performance is as important as measuring schedule and cost performance. Although technical performance is often assumed, the opposite can be true. The ramifications of poor technical performance frequently are more profound—something works or it doesn't if technical specifications are not adhered to.

Assessing technical performance of a system, facility, or product is often accomplished by examining the documents found in the scope statement and/or work package documentation. These documents should specify criteria and tolerance limits against which performance can be measured. For example, the technical performance of a software project suffered because the feature of "drag and drop" was deleted in the final product. Conversely, the prototype of an experimental car exceeded the miles per gallon technical specification and, thus, its technical performance. Frequently tests are conducted on different performance dimensions. These tests become an integral part of the project schedule.

It is very difficult to specify how to measure technical performance because it depends on the nature of the project. Suffice it to say, measuring technical performance must be done. Technical performance is frequently where quality control processes are needed and used. Project managers must be creative in finding ways to control this very important area.

Software for Project Cost/Schedule Systems

Software developers have created sophisticated schedule/cost systems for projects that track and report budget, actual, earned, committed, and index values. These values can be labor hours, materials, and/or dollars. This information supports cost and schedule progress, performance measurements, and cash flow management. Recall from Chapter 5 that budget, actual, and committed dollars usually run in different time frames (see Figure 5.6). A typical computer-generated status report includes the following information outputs:

1. Schedule variance (EV − PV) by cost account and WBS and OBS.
2. Cost variance (EV − AC) by cost account and WBS and OBS.
3. Indexes—total percent complete and performance index.
4. Cumulative actual total cost to date (AC).
5. Expected costs at completion (EAC).
6. Paid and unpaid commitments.

The variety of software packages, with their features and constant updating, is too extensive for inclusion in this text. Software developers and vendors have done a superb job of providing software to meet the information needs of most project managers. Differences among software in the last decade have centered on improving "friendliness" and output that is clear and easy to understand. Anyone who understands the concepts and tools presented in Chapters 4, 5, 6, 8, and 13 should have little trouble understanding the output of any of the popular project management software packages.

Additional Earned Value Rules

Although the percent complete rule is the most-used method of assigning budgets to baselines and for cost control, there are additional rules that are very useful for reducing the overhead costs of collecting detailed data on percent complete of individual work packages. (An additional advantage of these rules, of course, is that they remove the often subjective judgments of the contractors or estimators as to how much work has actually been completed.) The first two rules are typically used for short-duration activities and/or small-cost activities. The third rule uses gates before the total budgeted value of an activity can be claimed.

- **0/100 rule.** This rule assumes credit is earned for having performed the work once it is completed. Hence, 100 percent of the budget is earned when the work package is completed. This rule is used for work packages having very short durations.
- **50/50 rule.** This approach allows 50 percent of the value of the work package budget to be earned when it is started and 50 percent to be earned when the package is completed. This rule is popular for work packages of short duration and small total costs.
- **Percent complete with weighted monitoring gates.** This more recent rule uses subjective estimated percent complete in combination with hard, tangible monitoring points. This method works well on long-duration activities that can be broken into short, discrete work packages of no more than one or two report periods. These discrete packages limit the subjective estimated values. For example, assume a long-duration activity with a total budget of \$500. The activity is cut into three sequentially discrete packages with monitoring gates representing 30, 50, and 100 percent of the total budget. The earned amount at each monitoring gate cannot exceed \$150, \$250, and \$500. These hard monitoring points serve as a check on overly optimistic estimates.

Notice the only information needed for the first two rules is that the work package has started and the package has been completed. For those who wish to explore the application of these two rules, or who are studying for certification, Appendix 13.1 presents two exercises that apply these rules along with the percent complete rule.

The third rule is frequently used to authorize progress payments to contractors. This rule supports careful tracking and control of payments; it discourages payment to contractors for work not yet completed.

Forecasting Final Project Cost

There are basically two methods used to revise estimates of future project costs. In many cases both methods are used on specific segments of the project. The result is confusion of terms in texts, in software, and among practitioners in the field. We have chosen to note the differences between the methods.

The first method allows experts in the field to change original baseline durations and costs because new information tells them the original estimates are not accurate. We have used $\mathbf{EAC_{re}}$ to represent revisions made by experts and practitioners associated with the project. The revisions from project experts are almost always used on smaller projects.

The equation for calculating revised estimated cost at completion (EAC_{re}) is as follows:

$$EAC_{re} = AC + ETC_{re}$$

where EAC_{re} = revised estimated cost at completion.
AC = cumulative actual cost of work completed to date.
ETC_{re} = revised estimated cost to complete remaining work.

A second method is used in large projects where the original budget is less reliable. This method uses the actual costs to date plus an efficiency index (CPI = EV/AC) applied to the remaining project work. When the estimate for completion uses the CPI as the basis for forecasting cost at completion, we use the acronym **EAC_f.** The equation is presented here.

The equation for this forecasting model (EAC_f) is as follows:

$$EAC_f = ETC + AC$$

$$ETC = \frac{\text{Work remaining}}{CPI} = \frac{BAC - EV}{EV/AC}$$

where EAC_f = estimated total cost at completion.
ETC = estimated cost to complete remaining work.
AC = cumulative actual cost of work completed to date.
CPI = cumulative cost index to date.
BAC = total budget of the baseline.
EV = cumulative budgeted cost of work completed to date.

The following information is available from our earlier example; the estimate cost at completion (EAC_f) is computed as follows:

Total baseline budget (BAC) for the project	$320
Cumulative earned value (EV) to date	$160
Cumulative actual cost (AC) to date	$230

$$EAC_f = \frac{320 - 160}{160/230} + 230 = \frac{160}{.7} + 230 = 229 + 230$$

$$EAC_f = 459$$

The final project projected cost forecast is $459,000 versus $320,000 originally planned.

Another popular index is the **To Complete Performance Index** (TCPI), which is useful as a supplement to the estimate at complete (EAC_f) computation. This ratio measures the amount of value each *remaining* dollar in the budget must earn to stay within the budget. The index is computed for the Digital Camera project at the end of period 7.

$$TCPI = \frac{BAC - EV}{BAC - AC} = \frac{320 - 160}{320 - 230} = \frac{160}{90} = 1.78$$

The index of 1.78 indicates that each remaining dollar in the budget must earn $1.78 in value. There is more work to be done than there is budget left. Clearly, it would be tough to increase productivity that much to make budget. The work to be done will have to be reduced or you will have to accept running over budget. If the TCPI is less than 1.00, you should be able to complete the project without using all of the remaining budget. A ratio of less than 1.00 opens the possibility of other opportunities such as improving quality, increasing profit, or expanding scope.

Research data indicate that on large projects that are more than 15 percent complete, the model performs well with an error of less than 10 percent (Fleming and Koppleman, 2010; Christensen, 1998). This model can also be used for WBS and OBS cost accounts that have been used to forecast remaining and total costs. It is important to note that this model assumes conditions will not change, the cost database is reliable, EV and AC are cumulative, and past project progress is representative of future progress. This objective forecast represents a good starting point or benchmark that management can use to compare other forecasts that include other conditions and subjective judgments.

Exhibit 13.1 presents an abridged monthly status report similar to one used by a project organization. The form is used for all projects in their project portfolio. (Note that the schedule variance of −$22,176 does not translate directly to days. The 25 days were derived from the network schedule.)

Another summary report is shown in the Snapshot from Practice: Trojan Decommissioning Project. Compare the differences in format.

EXHIBIT 13.1
Monthly Status Report

Project number: 163 **Project manager:** Connor Gage
Project priority now: 4
Status as of: April 1
Earned value figures:

PV	EV	AC	SV	CV	BAC
588,240	566,064	596,800	−22,176	−30,736	1,051,200
EAC	**VAC**	**EAC_f**	**CPI**	**PCIB**	**PCIC**
1,090,640	−39,440	1,107,469	.95	.538	.547

Project description: A computer-controlled conveyor belt that will move and position items on the belt with accuracy of less than one millimeter.

Status summary: The project is approximately 25 days behind schedule. The project has a cost variance of ($30,736).

Explanations: The schedule variance has moved from noncritical activities to those on the critical path. Integration first phase, scheduled to start 3/26, is now expected to start 4/19, which means it is approximately 25 days behind schedule. This delay is traced to the loss of the second design team which made it impossible to start utilities documentation on 2/27 as planned. This loss illustrates the effect of losing valuable resources on the project. The cost variance to date is largely due to a design change that cost $21,000.

Major changes since last report: The major change was loss of one design team to the project.

Total cost of approved design changes: $21,000. Most of this amount is attributed to the improved design of the serial I/O drivers.

Projected cost at completion: EAC_f is estimated to be $1,107,469. This represents an overrun of $56,269, given a CPI of .95. The CPI of .95 causes the forecast to be greater than the VAC −$39,440.

Risk watch: Nothing suggests the risk level of any segments has changed.

SNAPSHOT FROM PRACTICE Trojan Decommissioning Project

AP Photo/Don Ryan

Portland General Electric Company has been charged with decommissioning the Trojan Nuclear Plant. This is a long and complex project extending over two decades. The first segment of the project of moving the used reactors to a storage location is complete and was awarded the Project of the Year, 2000, by the Project Management Institute (PMI). The remainder of the project—decontamination of the remaining structures and waste—is ongoing.

Exhibit 13.2 shows their earned value status report. This report measures schedule and cost performance for monitoring the project. The report also serves as a basis for funding for rate filings with the Public Utilities Commission.

The SPI (0.94) suggests the project schedule is falling behind. Resolving issues with a major vendor and solutions for technical problems should solve these delay problems. The CPI (1.14) for the project is positive. Some of this good cost performance is attributed to partnering and incentive arrangements with vendors and labor unions.

Interview with Michael B. Lackey, general manager, Trojan, PGE.

Other Control Issues

Scope Creep

Large changes in scope are easily identified. It is the "minor refinements" that eventually build to be major scope changes that can cause problems. These small refinements are known in the field as **scope creep.** For example, the customer of a software developer requested small changes in the development of a custom accounting software package. After several minor refinements, it became apparent the changes represented a significant enlargement of the original project scope. The result was an unhappy customer and a development firm that lost money and reputation.

Although scope changes are usually viewed negatively, there are situations when scope changes result in positive rewards. Scope changes can represent significant opportunities.[3] In product development environments, adding a small feature to a product can result in a huge competitive advantage. A small change in the production process may get the product to market one month early or reduce product cost.

Scope creep is common early in projects—especially in new-product development projects. Customer requirements for additional features, new technology, poor design assumptions, etc., all manifest pressures for scope changes. Frequently these changes are small and go unnoticed until time delays or cost overruns are observed. Scope creep affects the organization, project team, and project suppliers. Scope changes alter the organization's cash flow requirements in the form of

[3] See S. Keifer, "Scope Creep ... Not Necessarily a Bad Thing," *PM Network,* 10 (5), 1996, pp. 33–35.

FIGURE 13.13
Scope Changes to a Baseline

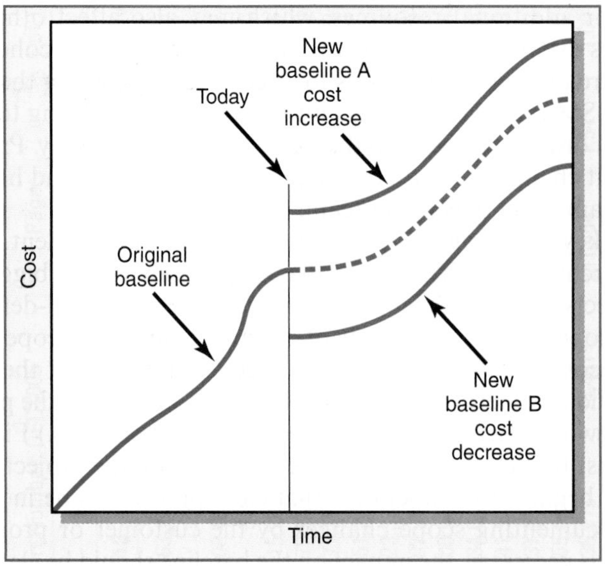

should be accepted and signed off by the project customer. Figure 13.13 depicts the cost impact of a scope change on the baseline at a point in time—"today." Line A represents a scope change that results in an increase in cost. Line B represents a scope change that decreases cost. Quickly recording scope changes to the baseline keeps the computed earned values valid. Failure to do so results in misleading cost and schedule variances.

Care should be taken to not use baseline changes to disguise poor performance on past or current work. A common signal of this type of baseline change is a constantly revised baseline that seems to match results. Practitioners call this a "rubber baseline" because it stretches to match results. Most changes will not result in serious scope changes and should be absorbed as positive or negative variances. Retroactive changes for work already accomplished should not be allowed. Transfer of money among cost accounts should not be allowed after the work is complete. Unforeseen changes can be handled through the contingency reserve. The project manager typically makes this decision. In some large projects, a partnering "change review team," made up of members of the project and customer teams, makes all decisions on project changes.

The Costs and Problems of Data Acquisition

Data acquisition is time consuming and costly. The Snapshot from Practice: A Pseudo-Earned Value Percent Complete Approach captures some of the frequent issues surrounding resistance to data collection of percent complete for earned value systems. Similar pseudo-percent complete systems have been used by others. Such pseudo-percent complete approaches appear to work well in multiproject environments that include several small and medium-sized projects. Assuming a one-week reporting period, care needs to be taken to develop work packages with a duration of about one week long so problems are identified quickly. For large projects, there is no substitute for using a percent complete system that depends on data collected through observation at clearly defined monitoring points.

In some cases data exist but are not sent to the stakeholders who need information relating to project progress. Clearly, if the information does not reach the right people in a timely manner, you can expect serious problems. Your communication

SNAPSHOT FROM PRACTICE
A Pseudo-Earned Value Percent Complete Approach

A consultant for the U.S. Forest Service suggested the use of earned value to monitor the 50-plus timber sale projects taking place concurrently in the district. As projects were completed, new ones were started. Earned value was tried for approximately nine months. After a nine-month trial, the process was to be reviewed by a task force. The task force concluded the earned value system provided good information for monitoring and forecasting project progress; however, the costs and problems of collecting timely percent complete data were unacceptable because there were no funds available to collect such data.

The level of detail dilemma was discussed, but no suggestions satisfied the problem. The discussion recognized that too little data fail to offer good control, while excessive reporting requires paperwork and people, which are costly. The task force concluded progress and performance could be measured using a pseudo-version of percent complete while not giving up much accuracy for the total project. This modified approach to percent complete required that very large work packages (about 3 to 5 percent of all work packages in a project) be divided into smaller work packages for closer control and identification of problems sooner. It was decided work packages of about a week's duration would be ideal. The pseudo-version required only a telephone call and "yes/no" answers to one of the following questions to assign percent complete:

Has work on the work package started?	No = 0%
Working on the package?	Yes = 50%
Is the work package completed?	Yes = 100%

Data for the pseudo-earned value percent complete system was collected for all 50-plus projects by an intern working fewer than eight hours each week.

plan developed in the project planning stage can greatly mitigate this problem by mapping out the flow of information and keeping stakeholders informed on all aspects of project progress and issues. See Figure 13.14 for an internal communication plan for a WiFi Project. The information developed in this chapter contributes significant data to support your communication plan and ensures correct dissemination of the data.

FIGURE 13.14
Conference Center WiFi Project Communication Plan

What Information	When?	Mode?	Responsible?	Recipient?
Milestone report	Bimonthly	E-mail	Project office	Senior management
Time/cost report	Weekly	E-mail	Project office	Staff and customer
Risk report	Weekly	E-mail	Project office	Staff and customer
Issues	Weekly	E-mail	Anyone	Staff and customer
Team meeting times	Weekly	Meeting	Project manager	Staff and customer
Outsourcing performance	Bimonthly	Meeting	Project manager	Project office, staff, and customer
Change requests	Anytime	Document	Project manager, customer, design	Project office, staff, and customer
Stage gate decisions	Monthly	Meeting	Project office	Senior management

Summary

The best information system does not result in good control. Control requires the project manager to *use* information to steer the project through rough waters. Control and Gantt charts are useful vehicles for monitoring time performance. The cost/schedule system allows the manager to have a positive influence on cost and schedule in a timely manner. The ability to influence cost decreases with time; therefore, timely reports identifying adverse cost trends can greatly assist the project manager in getting back on budget and schedule. The integrated cost/schedule model provides the project manager and other stakeholders with a snapshot of the current and future status of the project. The benefits of the cost/schedule model are as follows:

1. Measures accomplishments against plan and deliverables.
2. Provides a method for tracking directly to a problem work package and organization unit responsible.
3. Alerts all stakeholders to early identification of problems, and allows for quick, proactive corrective action.
4. Improves communication because all stakeholders are using the same database.
5. Keeps customer informed of progress, and encourages customer confidence that the money spent is resulting in the expected progress.
6. Provides for accountability over individual portions of the overall budget for each organizational unit.

With your information system in place, you need to use your communication plan to keep stakeholders informed so timely decisions can be made to ensure the project is managed effectively.

Key Terms

Baseline budget, *468*
Budget at completion (BAC), *463*
Control chart, *461*
Cost performance index (CPI), *473*
Cost variance (CV), *463*
Earned value (EV), *459*
Estimated cost at completion—Forecasted (EAC_f), *477*
Estimated cost at completion—Revised estimates (EAC_{re}), *476*
Percent complete index—budget costs (PCIB), *474*
Percent complete index—actual costs (PCIC), *474*
Schedule performance index (SPI), *473*
Schedule variance (SV), *463*
Scope creep, *479*
To complete performace index (TCPI), *477*
Tracking Gantt chart, *460*
Variance at completion (VAC), *463*

Review Questions

1. How does a Tracking Gantt chart help communicate project progress?
2. How does earned value give a clearer picture of project schedule and cost status than a simple plan versus actual system?
3. Schedule variance (SV) is in dollars and does not directly represent time. Why is it still useful?
4. How would a project manager use the CPI?
5. What are the differences between BAC and EAC?
6. Why is it important for project managers to resist changes to the project baseline? Under what conditions would a project manager make changes to a baseline? When would a project manager not allow changes to a baseline?

Exercises

1. In month 9 the following project information is available: actual cost is $2,000, earned value is $2,100, and planned cost is $2,400. Compute the SV and CV for the project.
2. On day 51 a project has an earned value of $600, an actual cost of $650, and a planned cost of $560. Compute the SV, CV, and CPI for the project. What is your assessment of the project on day 51?

3. Given the project network and baseline information below, complete the form to develop a status report for the project at the end of period 4 and the end of period 8. From the data you have collected and computed for periods 4 and 8, what information are you prepared to tell the customer about the status of the project at the end of period 8?

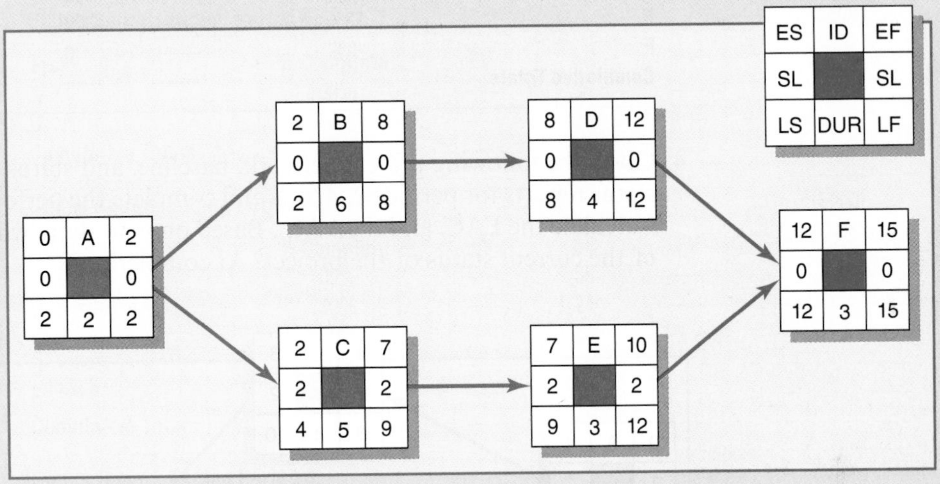

Project baseline (PV) (in $)

Task	DUR	ES	LF	SL	Budget (PV)	1	2	3	4	5	6	7	8	9	10	11	12	13	14	15
A	2	0	2	0	400	200	200													
B	6	2	8	0	2400			200	600	200	600	200	600							
C	5	2	9	2	1500			200	400	500	100	300								
D	4	8	12	0	1600									400	400	400	400			
E	3	7	12	2	900								300	400	200					
F	3	12	15	0	600													200	100	300
					Period PV total	200	200	400	1000	700	700	500	900	800	600	400	400	200	100	300
					Cumulative PV total	200	400	800	1800	2500	3200	3700	4600	5400	6000	6400	6800	7000	7100	7400

End of Period 4

Task	Actual % Complete	EV	AC	PV	CV	SV
A	Finished	—	300	400	—	—
B	50%	—	1000	800	—	—
C	33%	—	500	600	—	—
D	0%	—	0	—	—	—
E	0%	—	—	—	—	—
Cumulative Totals		—	—	—	—	—

5. Given the following project network, baseline, and status information, develop status reports for periods 1–4 and complete the project summary graph (or a similar one). Report the final SV, CV, CPI, and PCIB. Based on your data, what is your assessment of the current status of the project? At completion?

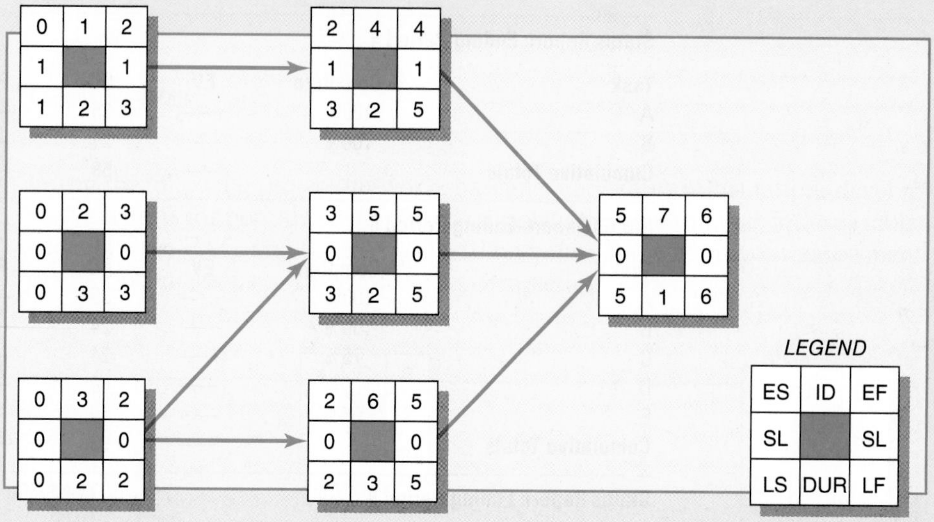

Schedule information						Baseline budget needs ($ 000)					
ACT/ WP	DUR	ES	LF	SL	Total PV	Time period 0–1	1–2	2–3	3–4	4–5	5–6
1	2	0	3	1	12	4	8				
2	3	0	3	0	15	3	7	5			
3	2	0	2	0	8	4	4				
4	2	2	5	1	6			3	3		
5	2	3	5	0	10				6	4	
6	3	2	5	0	9			3	3	3	
7	1	5	6	0	5						5
					Total PV by period	11	19	11	12	7	5
					Cumulative PV by period	11	30	41	53	60	65

Status Report: Ending Period 1 **($000)**

Task	%Complete	EV	AC	PV	CV	SV
1	50%	___	6	4	___	___
2	40%	___	8	3	___	___
3	25%	___	3	___	___	___
Cumulative Totals		___	**17**	___	___	___

Status Report: Ending Period 2 **($000)**

Task	%Complete	EV	AC	PV	CV	SV
1	Finished	___	13	___	___	___
2	80%	___	14	___	___	___
3	75%	___	8	___	___	___
Cumulative Totals		___	**35**	___	___	___

Status Report: Ending Period 3 **($000)**

Task	%Complete	EV	AC	PV	CV	SV
1	Finished	12	13	___	___	___
2	80%	___	15	___	___	___
3	Finished	___	10	___	___	___
4	50%	___	4	___	___	___
5	0%	___	0	___	___	___
6	33.3%	___	4	___	___	___
Cumulative Totals		___	___	___	___	___

Status Report: Ending Period 4 **($000)**

Task	%Complete	EV	AC	PV	CV	SV
1	Finished	12	13	___	___	___
2	Finished	15	18	___	___	___
3	Finished	___	10	___	___	___
4	Finished	___	8	___	___	___
5	30%	___	3	___	___	___
6	66.7%	___	8	___	___	___
7	0%	___	0	___	___	___
Cumulative Totals		___	___	___	___	___

Summary Graph

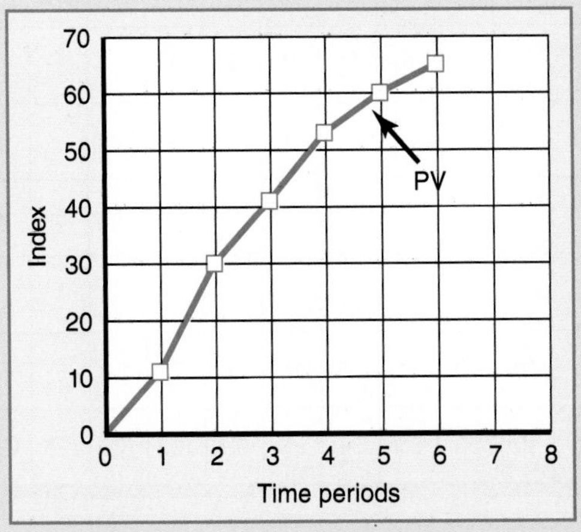

6. The following labor hours data have been collected for a nanotechnology project for periods 1 through 6. Compute the SV, CV, SPI, and CPI for each period. Plot the EV and the AC on the summary graph provided (or a similar one). Plot the SPI, CPI, and PCIB on the index graph provided (or a similar one). What is your assessment of the project at the end of period 6?

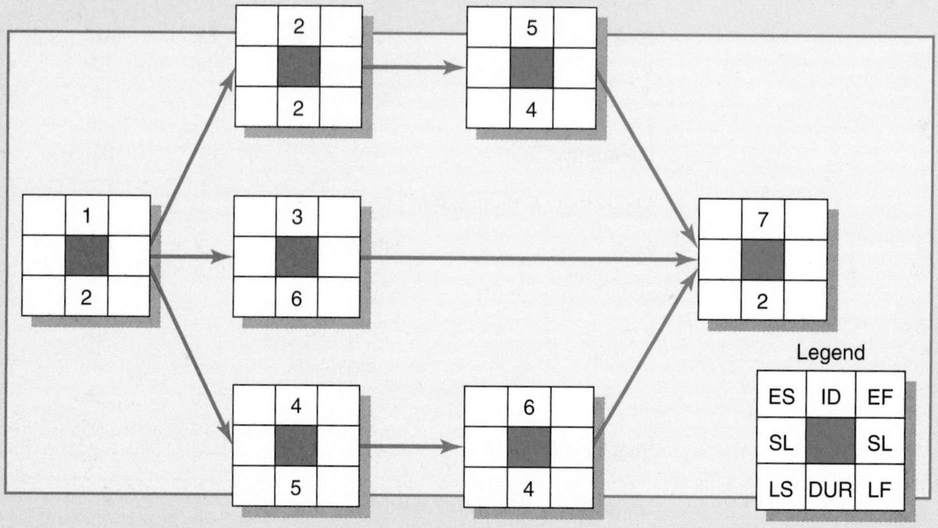

Schedule information						Baseline budget needs–labor hours (00)												
ACT/WP	DUR	ES	LF	SL	Total PV	Time period 0 1 2 3 4 5 6 7 8 9 10 11 12 13 14												
1	2	0	2	0	20	10	10											
2	2	2	7	3	24			16	8									
3	6	2	11	3	30			5	5	10	3	2	5					
4	5	2	7	0	25			10	10	2	2	1						
5	4	4	11	3	16					4	4	4	4					
6	4	7	11	0	20								5	5	6	4		
7	2	11	13	0	10												5	5
Total PV by period						10	10	31	23	16	9	7	14	5	6	4	5	5
Cumulative PV by period						10	20	51	74	90	99	106	120	125	131	135	140	145

Status Report: Ending Period 1

Task	%Complete	EV	AC	PV	CV	SV
1	50%	——	500	1000	——	——
Cumulative Totals		——	**500**	**1000**	——	——

Status Report: Ending Period 2

Task	%Complete	EV	AC	PV	CV	SV
1	Finished	——	1500	2000	——	——
Cumulative Totals		——	**1500**	**2000**	——	——

Status Report: Ending Period 3

Task	%Complete	EV	AC	PV	CV	SV
1	Finished	2000	1500	2000	——	——
2	0%	——	0	——	——	——
3	10%	——	200	——	——	——
4	20%	——	500	——	——	——
Cumulative Totals		——	**2200**	——	——	——

Status Report: Ending Period 4

Task	%Complete	EV	AC	PV	CV	SV
1	Finished	2000	1500	2000	——	——
2	50%	——	1000	——	——	——
3	30%	——	800	——	——	——
4	40%	——	1500	——	——	——
Cumulative Totals		——	**4800**	——	——	——

Status Report: Ending Period 5

Task	%Complete	EV	AC	PV	CV	SV
1	Finished	2000	1500	2000	——	——
2	Finished	——	2000	——	——	——
3	50%	——	800	——	——	——
4	60%	——	1500	——	——	——
5	25%	——	400	——	——	——
Cumulative Totals		——	**6200**	——	——	——

Status Report: Ending Period 6

Task	%Complete	EV	AC	PV	CV	SV
1	Finished	2000	1500	2000	——	——
2	Finished	——	2000	——	——	——
3	80%	——	2100	——	——	——
4	80%	——	1800	——	——	——
5	50%	——	600	——	——	——
Cumulative Totals		——	**8000**	——	——	——

Period	**SPI**	**CPI**	**PCIB**
1	____	____	____
2	____	____	____
3	____	____	____
4	____	____	____
5	____	____	____
6	____	____	____

SPI = EV/PV
CPI = EV/AC
PCIB = EV/BAC

Summary Graph

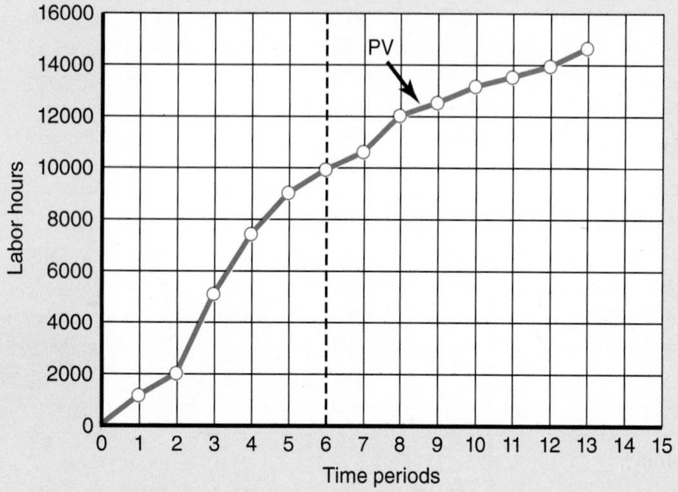

Indexes Periods 1–6

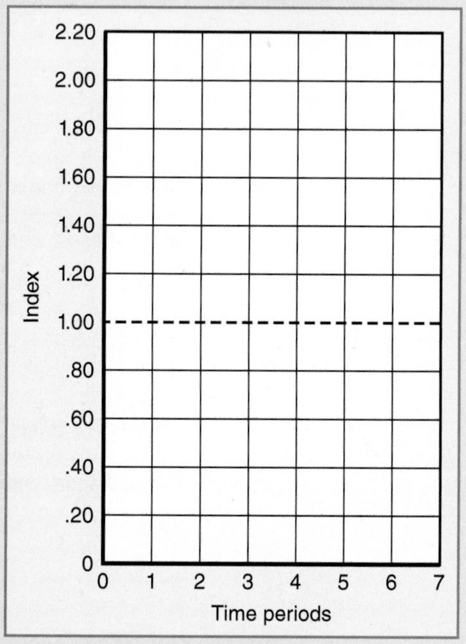

7. The following data have been collected for a British health care IT project for two-week reporting periods 2 through 12. Compute the SV, CV, SPI, and CPI for each period. Plot the EV and the AC on the summary graph provided. Plot the SPI, CPI, and PCIB on the index graph provided. (You may use your own graphs.) What is your assessment of the project at the end of period 12?

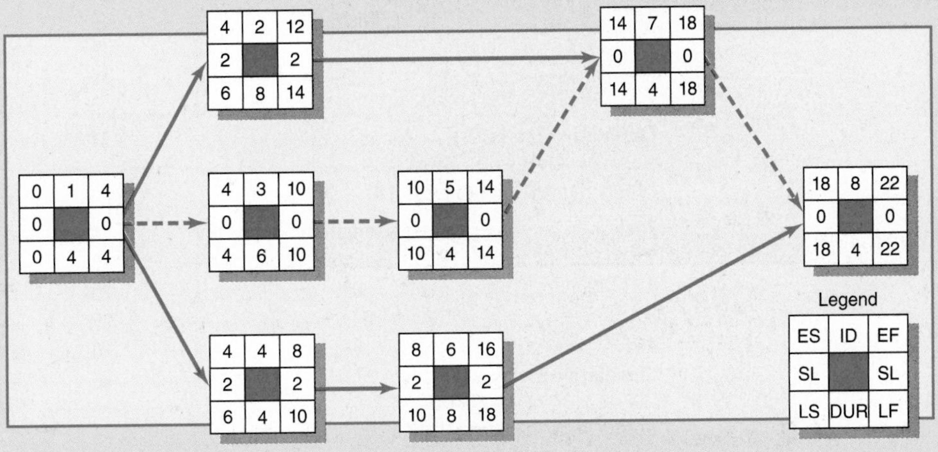

Baseline (PV) ($00)

Task	DUR	ES	LF	SL	PV ($00)	0–2	2–4	4–6	6–8	8–10	10–12	12–14	14–16	16–18	18–20	20–22
1	4	0	4	0	8	4	4									
2	8	4	14	2	40			10	10	10	10					
3	6	4	10	0	30			10	15	5						
4	4	4	10	2	20			10	10							
5	4	10	14	0	40						20	20				
6	8	8	18	2	60					20	20	10	10			
7	4	14	18	0	20								10	10		
8	4	18	22	0	30										20	10
					Period PV total	4	4	30	35	35	50	30	20	10	20	10
					Cumulative PV total	4	8	38	73	108	158	188	208	218	238	248

Status Report: Ending Period 2 ($00)

Task	**%Complete**	**EV**	**AC**	**PV**	**CV**	**SV**
1	50%	___	4	___	___	___
Cumulative Totals		___	4	___	___	___

Status Report: Ending Period 4 **($00)**

Task	%Complete	EV	AC	PV	CV	SV
1	Finished	—	10	—	—	—
Cumulative Totals		—	**10**	—	—	—

Status Report: Ending Period 6 **($00)**

Task	%Complete	EV	AC	PV	CV	SV
1	Finished	—	10	—	—	—
2	25%	—	15	—	—	—
3	33%	—	12	—	—	—
4	0%	—	0	—	—	—
Cumulative Totals		—	**37**	—	—	—

Status Report: Ending Period 8 **($00)**

Task	%Complete	EV	AC	PV	CV	SV
1	Finished	—	10	—	—	—
2	30%	—	20	—	—	—
3	60%	—	25	—	—	—
4	0%	—	0	—	—	—
Cumulative Totals		—	**55**	—	—	—

Status Report: Ending Period 10 **($00)**

Task	%Complete	EV	AC	PV	CV	SV
1	Finished	—	10	—	—	—
2	60%	—	30	—	—	—
3	Finished	—	40	—	—	—
4	50%	—	20	—	—	—
5	0%	—	0	—	—	—
6	30%	—	24	—	—	—
Cumulative Totals		—	**124**	—	—	—

Status Report: Ending Period 12 **($00)**

Task	%Complete	EV	AC	PV	CV	SV
1	Finished	—	10	—	—	—
2	Finished	—	50	—	—	—
3	Finished	—	40	—	—	—
4	Finished	—	40	—	—	—
5	50%	—	30	—	—	—
6	50%		40	—	—	—
Cumulative Totals		—	**210**	—	—	—

Period	SPI	CPI	PCIB
2	—	—	—
4	—	—	—
6	—	—	—
8	—	—	—
10	—	—	—
12	—	—	—

SPI = EV/PV
CPI = EV/AC
PCIB = EV/BAC

Summary Graph

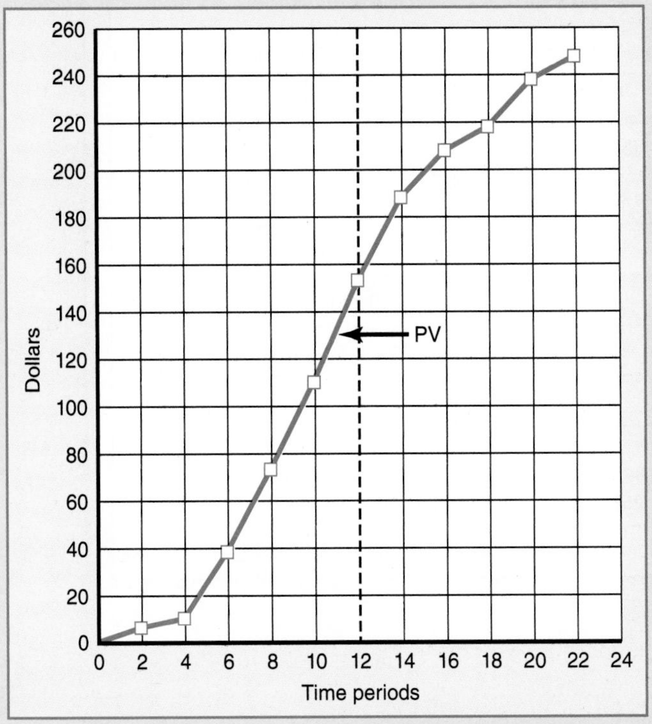

Indexes Periods 2–12

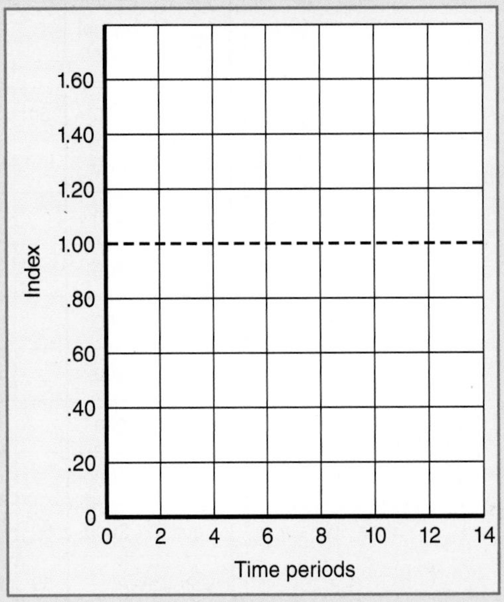

8.*Part A. You are in charge of the Aurora Project. Given the following project network, baseline, and status information, develop status reports for periods 1–8 and complete the performance indexes table. Calculate the EAC_f and VAC_f. Based on your data, what is the current status of the project? At completion?

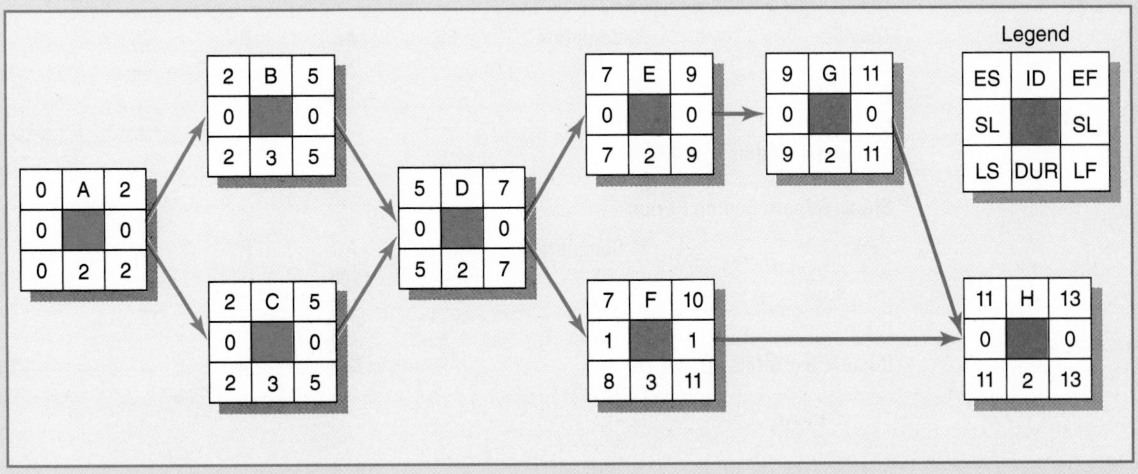

* The solution to this exercise can be found in Appendix 1.

ID	Budget ($000)	0–1	1–2	2–3	3–4	4–5	5–6	6–7	7–8	8–9	9–10	10–11	11–12	12–13
A	100	50	50											
B	250			100	50	100								
C	450			150	150	150								
D	200						100	100						
E	300								200	100				
F	300								100	50	150			
G	200										150	50		
H	200												100	100
Total	2000	50	50	250	200	250	100	100	300	150	300	50	100	100
Cumulative		50	100	350	550	800	900	1000	1300	1450	1750	1800	1900	2000

Status Report: Ending Period 1 **($000)**

Task	**% Complete**	**EV**	**AC**	**PV**	**CV**	**SV**
A	25%	___	50	___	___	___
Cumulative Totals		___	**50**	___	___	___

Status Report: Ending Period 2 **($000)**

Task	**% Complete**	**EV**	**AC**	**PV**	**CV**	**SV**
A	50%	___	100	___	___	___
Cumulative Totals		___	___	___	___	___

Status Report: Ending Period 3 **($000)**

Task	**% Complete**	**EV**	**AC**	**PV**	**CV**	**SV**
A	100%	___	200	___	___	___
B	0%	___	0	___	___	___
C	0%	___	0	___	___	___
Cumulative Totals		___	___	___	___	___

Status Report: Ending Period 4 **($000)**

Task	**% Complete**	**EV**	**AC**	**PV**	**CV**	**SV**
A	100%	___	200	___	___	___
B	60%	___	100	___	___	___
C	50%	___	200	___	___	___
Cumulative Totals		___	**500**	___	___	___

Status Report: Ending Period 5 **($000)**

Task	% Complete	EV	AC	PV	CV	SV
A	100%	___	200	___	___	___
B	100%	___	200	___	___	___
C	100%	___	400	___	___	___
Cumulative Totals		___	**800**	___	___	___

Status Report: Ending Period 6 **($000)**

Task	% Complete	EV	AC	PV	CV	SV
A	100%	___	200	___	___	___
B	100%	___	200	___	___	___
C	100%	___	400	___	___	___
D	75%	___	100	___	___	___
Cumulative Totals		___	**900**	___	___	___

Status Report: Ending Period 7 **($000)**

Task	% Complete	EV	AC	PV	CV	SV
A	100%	___	200	___	___	___
B	100%	___	200	___	___	___
C	100%	___	400	___	___	___
D	100%	___	150	___	___	___
E	20%	___	100	___	___	___
F	5%	___	50	___	___	___
Cumulative Totals		___	**1100**	___	___	___

Status Report: Ending Period 8 **($000)**

Task	% Complete	EV	AC	PV	CV	SV
A	100%	___	200	___	___	___
B	100%	___	200	___	___	___
C	100%	___	400	___	___	___
D	100%	___	150	___	___	___
E	100%	___	350	___	___	___
F	10%	___	100	___	___	___
Cumulative Totals		___	**1400**	___	___	___

Performance Indexes Summary

Period	EV	AC	PV	SPI	CPI	PCI-B
1	___	___	___	___	___	___
2	___	___	___	___	___	___
3	___	___	___	___	___	___
4	___	___	___	___	___	___
5	___	___	___	___	___	___
6	___	___	___	___	___	___
7	___	___	___	___	___	___
8	___	___	___	___	___	___

EAC_f = ______________ VAC_f = ______________

Part B. You have met with your Aurora project team and they have provided you with the following revised estimates for the remainder of the project:

- Activity F will be completed at the end of period 12 at a total cost of 500.
- Activity G will be completed at the end of period 10 at a total cost of 150.
- Activity H will be completed at the end of period 14 at a total cost of 200.

Calculate the EAC_{re} and VAC_{re}. Based on the revised estimates, what is the expected status of the project in terms of cost and schedule? Between the VAC_f and the VAC_{re}, which one would you have the greatest confidence in?

EAC_{re} = __________ VAC_{re} = __________

References

Abramovici, A., "Controlling Scope Creep," *PM Network,* Vol. 14, No. 1, January 2000, pp. 44–48.

Anbari, F. T., "Earned Value Project Management Method and Extensions," *Project Management Journal,* Vol. 34, No. 4, December 2003, pp. 12–22.

Brandon, D. M., Jr., "Implementing Earned Value Easily and Effectively," *Project Management Journal,* Vol. 29, No. 3, June 1998, pp. 11–17.

Bowles, M. "Keeping Score," *PMNetwork,* May 2011, pp. 50–59.

Christensen, D. S., and S. Heise, "Cost Performance Index Stability," *National Contract Management Association Journal,* 25, 1993, pp. 7–15.

Christensen, D. S., "The Cost and Benefits of the Earned Value Management Process," *Acquisition Review Quarterly,* 5 (1998), pp. 373–86.

Fleming, Q., and Joel M. Koppelman, *Earned Value Project Management,* 4th ed. (Newton Square, PA: Project Management Institute, 2010).

Kerzner, H., "Strategic Planning for a Project Office," *Project Management Journal,* Vol. 34, No. 2, June 2003, pp. 13–25.

Kim, E. H., W. G. Wells, and M. R. Duffey, "A Model for Effective Implementation of Earned Value Methodology," *International Journal of Project Management,* 21 (5), 2003, pp. 375–82.

Naeni, L., S. Shadrokh, and A. Salehipour, "A Fuzzy Approach to the Earned Value Management," *International Journal of Project Management,* 9 (6), 2011, pp. 764–72.

Webb, A., *Using Earned Value: A Project Manager's Guide* (Aldershot, UK: Gower Publishing Co., 2003).

Case

Tree Trimming Project

Wil Fence is a large timber and Christmas tree farmer who is attending a project management class in the fall, his off season. When the class topic came to earned value, he was perplexed. Isn't he using EV?

Each summer Wil hires crews to shear fields of Christmas trees for the coming Holiday season. Shearing entails having a worker use a large machete to shear the branches of the tree into a nice, cone shaped tree.

Will describes his business as follows:

A. I count the number of Douglas Fir Christmas trees in the field (24,000).

B. Next, I agree on a contract lump sum for shearing with a crew boss for the whole field ($30,000).

C. When partial payment for work completed arrives (5 days later), I count or estimate the actual number sheared (6,000 trees). I take the actual as a percent of the total to be sheared, multiply the percent complete by total contract amount for the partial payment [(6,000/$30,000 = 25%), (.25 × $30,000 = $7500)].

1. Is Wil over, on, or below cost and schedule? Is Wil using earned value?
2. How can Wil set up a scheduling variance?

Case

Scanner Project

You have been serving as Electroscan's project manager and are now well along in the project. Develop a narrative status report for the board of directors of the chain store that discusses the status of the project to date and at completion. Be as specific as you can using numbers given and those you might develop. Remember, your audience is not familiar with the jargon used by project managers and computer software personnel; therefore, some explanation may be necessary. Your report will be evaluated on your detailed use of the data, your total perspective of the current status and future status of the project, and your recommended changes (if any).

Appendix 13.1

The Application of Additional Earned Value Rules

The following example and exercises are designed to provide practice in applying the following three earned value rules:

- Percent complete rule
- 0/100 rule
- 50/50 rule

See the chapter for an explanation of each of these rules.

Electroscan, Inc. 555 Acorn Street, Suite 5 Boston, Massachusetts			29 In-store Scanner Project (thousands of dollars) Actual Progress as of January 1				
Name	PV	EV	AC	SV	CV	BAC	EAC_f
Scanner project	420	395	476	−25	−81	915	1103
H 1.0 Hardware	92	88	72	−4	16	260	213
H 1.1 Hardware specifications (DS)	20	20	15	0	5	20	15
H 1.2 Hardware design (DS)	30	30	25	0	5	30	25
H 1.3 Hardware documentation (DOC)	10	6	5	−4	1	10	8
H 1.4 Prototypes (PD)	2	2	2	0	0	40	40
H 1.5 Test prototypes (T)	0	0	0	0	0	30	30
H 1.6 Order circuit boards (PD)	30	30	25	0	5	30	25
H 1.7 Preproduction models (PD)	0	0	0	0	0	100	100
OP 1.0 Operating system	195	150	196	−45	−46	330	431
OP 1.1 Kernel specifications (DS)	20	20	15	0	5	20	15
OP 1.2 Drivers	45	55	76	10	−21	70	97
OP 1.2.1 Disk drivers (DEV)	25	30	45	5	−15	40	60
OP 1.2.2 I/O drivers (DEV)	20	25	31	5	−6	30	37
OP 1.3 Code software	130	75	105	−55	−30	240	336
OP 1.3.1 Code software (C)	30	20	40	−10	−20	100	200
OP 1.3.2 Document software (DOC)	45	30	25	−15	5	50	42
OP 1.3.3 Code interfaces (C)	55	25	40	−30	−15	60	96
OP 1.3.4 Beta test software (T)	0	0	0	0	0	30	30
U 1.0 Utilities	87	108	148	21	−40	200	274
U 1.1 Utilities specifications (DS)	20	20	15	0	5	20	15
U 1.2 Routine utilities (DEV)	20	20	35	0	−15	20	35
U 1.3 Complex utilities (DEV)	30	60	90	30	−30	100	150
U 1.4 Utilities documentation (DOC)	17	8	8	−9	0	20	20
U 1.5 Beta test utilities (T)	0	0	0	0	0	40	40
S 1.0 System integration	46	49	60	3	−11	125	153
S 1.1 Architecture decisions (DS)	9	9	7	0	2	10	8
S 1.2 Integration hard/soft (DEV)	25	30	45	5	−15	50	75
S 1.3 System hard/software test (T)	0	0	0	0	0	20	20
S 1.4 Project documentation (DOC)	12	10	8	−2	2	15	12
S 1.5 Integration acceptance testing (T)	0	0	0	0	0	30	30

SIMPLIFYING ASSUMPTIONS

The same simplifying assumptions used for the chapter example and exercises will also be used here.

1. Assume each cost account has only one work package, and each cost account will be represented as an activity on the network.
2. The project network early start times will serve as the basis for assigning the baseline values.
3. Except when the 0/100 rule or 50/50 rule is used, baseline values will be assigned linearly, unless stated differently. (Note: In practice estimated costs should be applied "exactly" as they are expected to occur so measures of schedule and cost performance are useful and reliable.)

4. For purposes of demonstrating the examples, from the moment work on an activity begins, some actual costs will be incurred each period until the activity is completed.
5. When the 0/100 rule is used, the total cost for the activity is placed in the baseline on the early finish date.
6. When the 50/50 rule is used, 50 percent of the total cost is placed in the baseline on the early start date and 50 percent on the early finish date.

APPENDIX EXERCISES

1. Given the information provided for development of a product warranty project for periods 1 through 7, compute the SV, CV, SPI, and CPI for each period. Plot the EV and the AC on the PV graph provided. Explain to the owner your assessment of the project at the end of period 7 and the future expected status of the project at completion. Figure A13.1A presents the project network. Figure A13.1B presents the project baseline noting those activities using the 0/100 (rule 3) and 50/50 (rule 2) rules. For example, activity 1 uses rule 3, the 0/100 rule. Although the early start time is period 0, the budget is not placed in the time-phased baseline until period 2 when the activity is planned to be finished (EF). This same procedure has been used to assign costs for activities 2 and 7. Activities 2 and 7 use the 50/50 rule. Thus, 50 percent of the budget for each activity is assigned on its respective early start date (time period 2 for activity 2 and period 11 for activity 7) and 50 percent for their respective finish dates. Remember, when assigning earned value as the project is being implemented, if an activity actually starts early or late, the earned values must shift with the actual times. For example, if activity 7 actually starts in period 12 rather than 11, the 50 percent is not earned until period 12.

FIGURE A13.1A

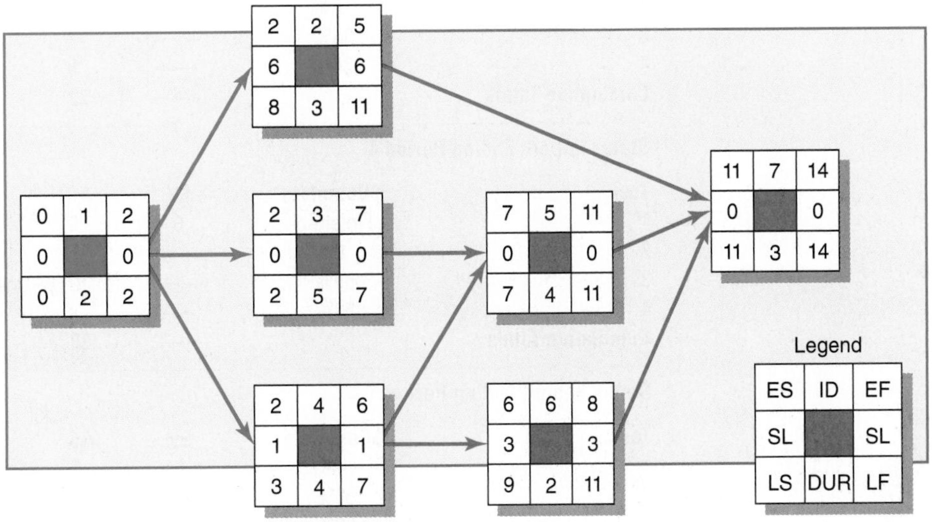

FIGURE A13.1B

Schedule information							Baseline budget needs													
							Time period													
EV Rule	ACT/WP	DUR	ES	LF	SL	Total PV	0–1	1–2	2–3	3–4	4–5	5–6	6–7	7–8	8–9	9–10	10–11	11–12	12–13	13–14
③	1	2	0	2	0	6		6												
②	2	3	2	11	6	20			10		10									
①	3	5	2	7	0	30			9	6	6	6	3							
①	4	4	2	7	1	20			8	2	5	5								
①	5	4	7	11	0	16								4	4	4	4			
①	6	2	6	11	3	18							9	9						
②	7	3	11	14	0	8												4		4
Total PV by period							0	6	27	8	21	11	12	13	4	4	4	4	0	4
Cumulative PV by period							0	6	33	41	62	73	85	98	102	106	110	114	114	118

Rule
1 = %complete
2 = 50/50
3 = 0/100

Status Report: Ending Period 1

Task	%Complete	EV	AC	PV	CV	SV
1	0%	—	3	0	—	—
Cumulative Totals		—	**3**	**0**	—	—

Status Report: Ending Period 2

Task	%Complete	EV	AC	PV	CV	SV
1	Finished	6	5	—	—	—
Cumulative Totals		**6**	**5**	—	—	—

Status Report: Ending Period 3

Task	%Complete	EV	AC	PV	CV	SV
1	Finished	6	5	—	—	—
2	0%	—	5	—	—	—
3	30%	—	7	—	—	—
4	25%	—	5	—	—	—
Cumulative Totals		—	**22**	—	—	—

Status Report: Ending Period 4

Task	%Complete	EV	AC	PV	CV	SV
1	Finished	6	5	—	—	—
2	0%	—	7	—	—	—
3	50%	—	10	—	—	—
4	50%	—	8	—	—	—
Cumulative Totals		—	**30**	—	—	—

Status Report: Ending Period 5

Task	%Complete	EV	AC	PV	CV	SV
1	Finished	6	5	—	—	—
2	50%	—	8	—	—	—
3	60%	—	12	—	—	—
4	70%	—	10	—	—	—
Cumulative Totals		—	**35**	—	—	—

Status Report: Ending Period 6

Task	%Complete	EV	AC	PV	CV	SV
1	Finished	6	5	___	___	___
2	50%	___	10	___	___	___
3	80%	___	16	___	___	___
4	Finished	___	15	___	___	___
Cumulative Totals		___	**46**	___	___	___

Status Report: Ending Period 7

Task	%Complete	EV	AC	PV	CV	SV
1	Finished	6	5	___	___	___
2	Finished	___	14	___	___	___
3	Finished	___	20	___	___	___
4	Finished	___	15	___	___	___
5	0%	___	0	___	___	___
6	50%	___	9	___	___	___
Cumulative Totals		___	**63**	___	___	___

Period	SPI	CPI	PCIB
1	___	___	___
2	___	___	___
3	___	___	___
4	___	___	___
5	___	___	___
6	___	___	___
7	___	___	___

SPI = EV/PV
CPI = EV/AC
PCIB = EV/BAC

FIGURE A13.1C

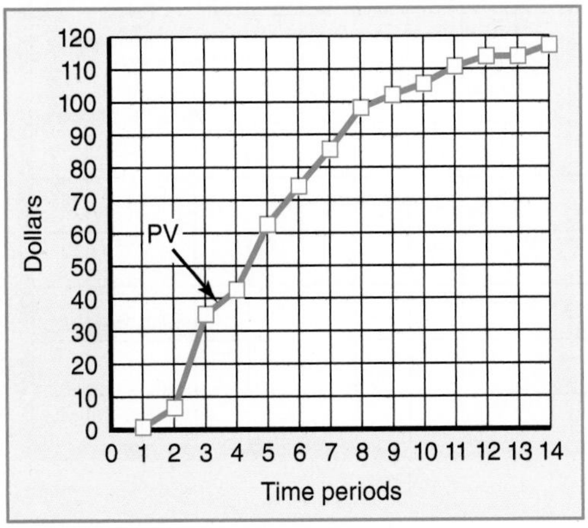

FIGURE A13.1D

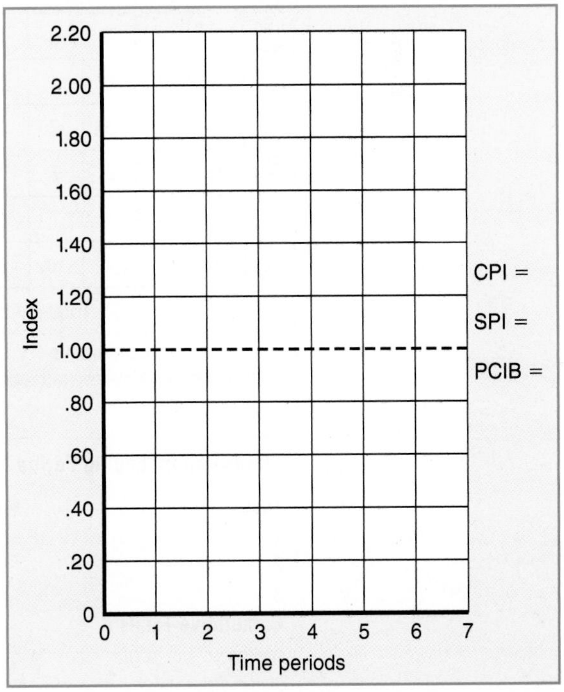

2. Given the information provided for development of a catalog product return process for periods 1 through 5, assign the PV values (using the rules) to develop a baseline for the project. Compute the SV, CV, SPI, and CPI for each period. Explain to the owner your assessment of the project at the end of period 5 and the future expected status of the project at the completion.

FIGURE A13.2A

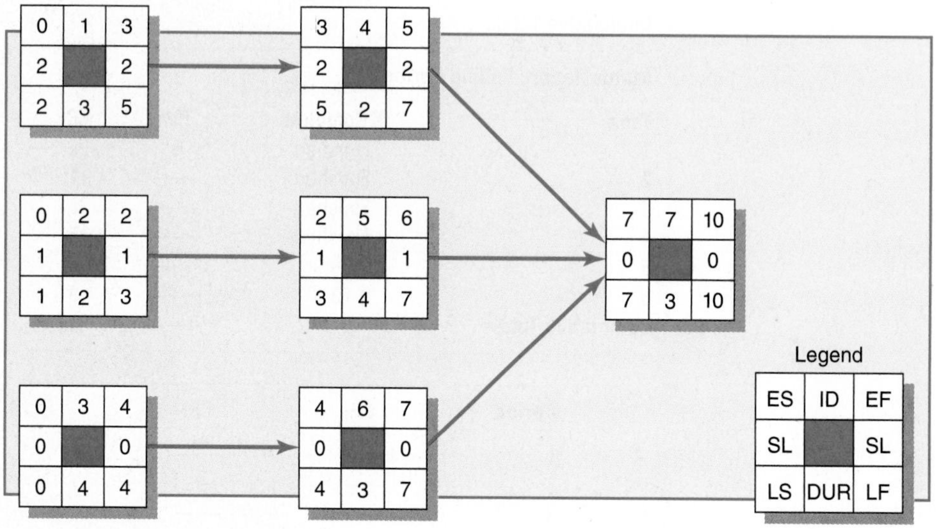

FIGURE A13.2B

Schedule information							Baseline budget needs									
							Time period									
EV Rule	ACT/ WP	DUR	ES	LF	SL	Total PV	1	2	3	4	5	6	7	8	9	10
(2)	1	3	0	5	2	30										
(3)	2	2	0	3	1	20										
(2)	3	4	0	4	0	30										
(3)	4	2	3	7	2	10										
(2)	5	4	2	7	1	40										
(1)	6	3	4	7	0	30										
(1)	7	3	7	10	0	60										
Total PV by period																
Cumulative PV by period																

Rule
1 = %complete
2 = 50/50
3 = 0/100

Status Report: Ending Period 1

Task	**%Complete**	**EV**	**AC**	**PV**	**CV**	**SV**
1	40%	___	8	___	___	___
2	0%	___	12	___	___	___
3	30%	___	10	___	___	___
Cumulative Totals		___	**30**	___	___	___

Status Report: Ending Period 2

Task	%Complete	EV	AC	PV	CV	SV
1	80%	——	20	——	——	——
2	Finished	——	18	——	——	——
3	50%	——	12	——	——	——
Cumulative Totals		——	**50**	——	——	——

Status Report: Ending Period 3

Task	%Complete	EV	AC	PV	CV	SV
1	Finished	——	27	——	——	——
2	Finished	——	18	——	——	——
3	70%	——	15	——	——	——
4	0%	——	5	——	——	——
5	30%	——	8	——	——	——
Cumulative Totals		——	**73**	——	——	——

Status Report: Ending Period 4

Task	%Complete	EV	AC	PV	CV	SV
1	Finished	——	27	——	——	——
2	Finished	——	18	——	——	——
3	Finished	——	22	——	——	——
4	0%	——	7	——	——	——
5	60%	——	22	——	——	——
Cumulative Totals		——	**96**	——	——	——

Status Report: Ending Period 5

Task	%Complete	EV	AC	PV	CV	SV
1	Finished	——	27	——	——	——
2	Finished	——	18	——	——	——
3	Finished	——	22	——	——	——
4	Finished	——	8	——	——	——
5	70%	——	24	——	——	——
6	30%	——	10	——	——	——
Cumulative Totals		——	**109**	——	——	——

FIGURE A13.2C

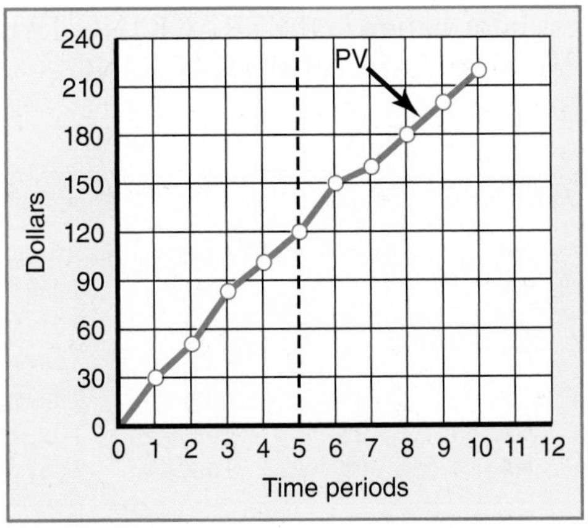

Period	SPI	CPI	PCIB
1	___	___	___
2	___	___	___
3	___	___	___
4	___	___	___
5	___	___	___

SPI = EV/PV
CPI = EV/AC
PCIB = EV/BAC

Appendix 13.2

Obtaining Project Performance Information from MS Project 2010[4]

The objective of this appendix is to illustrate how one can obtain the performance information discussed in Chapter 13 from MS Project 2010. One of the great strengths of MS Project is its flexibility. The software provides numerous options for entering, calculating, and presenting project information. Flexibility is also the software's greatest weakness in that there are so many options that working with the software can be frustrating and confusing. The intent here is to keep it simple and present basic steps for obtaining performance information. Students with more ambitious agendas are advised to work with the software tutorial or consult one of many instructional books on the market.

For purposes of this exercise we will use the Digital Camera project, which was introduced in Chapter 13. In this scenario the project started as planned on March 1 and today's date is March 7. We have received the following information on the work completed to date:

Design Spec.s took 2 days to complete at a total cost of $20.

Shell & Power took 3 days to complete at a total cost of $25.

Memory/Software is in progress with 4 days completed and two days remaining. Cost to date is $100.

Zoom System took 2 days to complete at a cost of $25.

All tasks started on time.

STEP 1 ENTERING PROGRESS INFORMATION

We enter this progress information in the TRACKING TABLE from the GANTT CHART VIEW ▶ VIEW ▶ TABLES ▶ TRACKING:

TABLE A13.2A Tracking Table

ID	Task Name	Act. Start	Act. Finish	% Comp.	Act. Dur.	Rem. Dur.	Act. Cost	Act. Work
1	**Digital Camera Prototype**	**3/1**	**NA**	**61%**	**6.72 days**	**4.28 days**	**$170.00**	**272 hrs**
2	Design Spec.s	3/1	3/2	100%	2 days	0 days	$20.00	32 hrs
3	Shell & Power	3/3	3/7	100%	3 days	0 days	$25.00	40 hrs
4	Memory/Software	3/3	NA	67%	4 days	2 days	$100.00	160 hrs
5	Zoom System	3/3	3/4	100%	2 days	0 days	$25.00	40 hrs
6	Assemble	NA	NA	0%	0 days	3 days	$0.00	0 hrs
7	Test	NA	NA	0%	0 days	2 days	$0.00	0 hrs

[4] For MS Project 2007 users the instructions are very similar except you can access the Tables option directly from Gantt View.

Note that the software automatically calculates the percent complete and actual finish, cost, and work. In some cases you will have to override these calculations if they are inconsistent with what actually happened. **Be sure to check** to make sure the information in this table is displayed the way you want it to be.

The final step is to enter the current status date (March 7). You do so by clicking PROJECT ▶ PROJECT INFORMATION and inserting the date into the status date window.

STEP 2 ACCESSING PROGRESS INFORMATION

MS Project provides a number of different options for obtaining progress information. The most basic information can be obtained from PROJECT ▶ REPORTS ▶ COSTS ▶ EARNED VALUE. You can also obtain this information from GANTT CHART view. Click VIEW ▶ TABLE ▶ MORE TABLES ▶ EARNED VALUE.

TABLE A13.2B Earned Value Table

ID	Task Name	PV	EV	AC	SV	CV	EAC	BAC	VAC
2	Design Spec.s	$20.00	$20.00	$20.00	$0.00	$0.00	$20.00	$20.00	$0.00
3	Shell & Power	$15.00	$15.00	$25.00	$0.00	($10.00)	$25.00	$15.00	($10.00)
4	Memory/Software	$100.00	$70.00	$100.00	($30.00)	($30.00)	$153.85	$100.00	($53.85)
5	Zoom System	$35.00	$35.00	$25.00	$0.00	$10.00	$25.00	$35.00	$10.00
6	Assemble	$0.00	$0.00	$0.00	$0.00	$0.00	$120.00	$120.00	$0.00
7	Test	$0.00	$0.00	$0.00	$0.00	$0.00	$30.00	$30.00	$0.00
		$170.00	$140.00	$170.00	($30.00)	($30.00)	$373.85	$320.00	($53.85)

When you scale this table to 80 percent you can obtain all the basic CV, SV and VAC information on one convenient page.

Note: Older versions of MS Project use the old acronyms:

BCWS = PV

BCWP = EV

ACWP = AC

and the EAC is calculated using the CPI and is what the text refers to as EAC_f.

STEP 3 ACCESSING CPI INFORMATION

To obtain additional cost information such as CPI and TCPI click from the GANTT CHART view click VIEW ▶ TABLE ▶ MORE TABLES ▶ EARNED VALUE COST INDICATORS, which will display the following information:

TABLE A13.2C Earned Value Cost Indicators Table

ID	Task Name	PV	EV	CV	CV%	CPI	BAC	EAC	VAC	TCPI
1	**Digital Camera Prototype**	**$170.00**	**$140.00**	**($30.00)**	**−21%**	**0.82**	**$320.00**	**$373.85**	**($53.85)**	**1.2**
2	Design Spec.s	$20.00	$20.00	$0.00	0%	1	$20.00	$20.00	$0.00	
3	Shell & Power	$15.00	$15.00	($10.00)	−66%	0.6	$15.00	$25.00	($10.00)	
4	Memory/Software	$100.00	$70.00	($30.00)	−42%	0.7	$100.00	$153.85	($53.85)	
5	Zoom System	$35.00	$35.00	$10.00	28%	1.4	$35.00	$25.00	$10.00	
6	Assemble	$0.00	$0.00	$0.00	0%	0	$120.00	$120.00	$0.00	
7	Test	$0.00	$0.00	$0.00	0%	0	$30.00	$30.00	$0.00	

Note: For MS Project 2007 users the instructions are very similar except you can access the Tables option directly from Gantt View.

STEP 4 ACCESSING SPI INFORMATION

To obtain additional schedule information such as SPI from the GANTT CHART view, click VIEW ▶ TABLE ▶ MORE TABLES ▶ EARNED VALUE SCHEDULE INDICATORS, which will display the following information:

TABLE A13.2D **Earned Value Schedule Indicators Table**

ID	Task Name	PV	EV	SV	SV%	SPI
1	**Digital Camera Prototype**	**$170.00**	**$140.00**	**($30.00)**	**−18%**	**0.82**
2	Design Spec.s	$20.00	$20.00	$0.00	0%	1
3	Shell & Power	$15.00	$15.00	$0.00	0%	1
4	Memory/Software	$100.00	$70.00	($30.00)	−30%	0.7
5	Zoom System	$35.00	$35.00	$0.00	0%	1
6	Assemble	$0.00	$0.00	$0.00	0%	0
7	Test	$0.00	$0.00	$0.00	0%	0

STEP 5 CREATING A TRACKING GANTT CHART

You can create a Tracking Gantt Chart like the one presented on page 460 by simply clicking TASK ▶ GANTT CHART (upper left hand corner) ▶ TRACKING GANTT ▶ TRACKING GANTT.

FIGURE A13.2E **Tracking Gantt Chart**

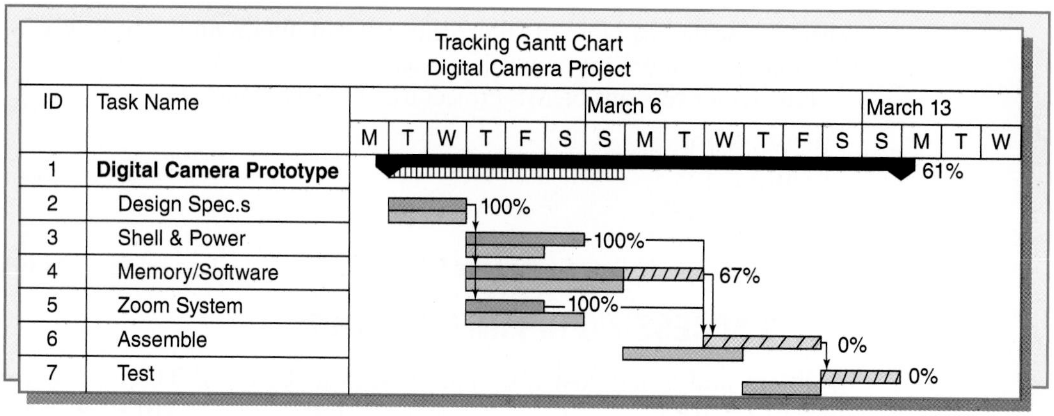

CHAPTER FOURTEEN

Project Closure

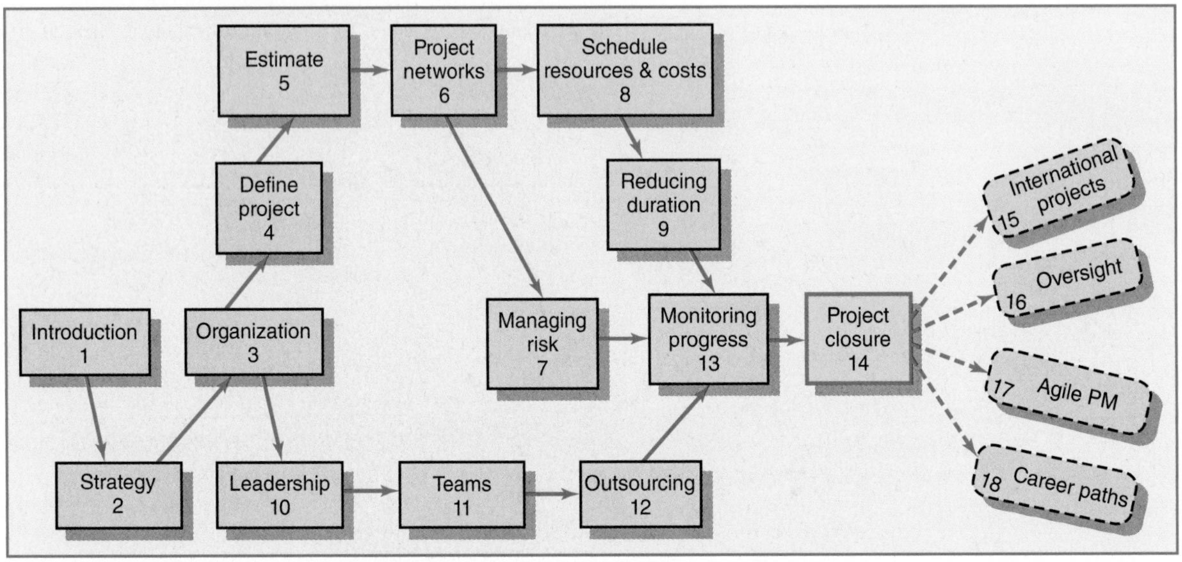

Project Closure

Types of Project Closure

Wrap-up Closure Activities

Post-Implementation Evaluation

Retrospectives

Summary

Appendix 14.1: Project Closeout Checklist

Appendix 14.2: Euro Conversion

Those who cannot remember the past are condemned to relive it.

—*George Santayana, 1863–1952*

Every project comes to an end eventually. But how many project participants get excited about closing out a project? The deliverables are complete. Ownership is ready to be transferred. Everyone's focus is what's next—hopefully a new, exciting project. Carefully managing the closure phase is as important as any other phase of the project. Observation tells us that organizations that manage closure and review well prosper. Those who don't tend to have projects that drag on forever and repeat the same mistakes over and over.

Closing out a project includes a daunting number of tasks. In the past and on small projects the project manager was responsible for seeing all tasks and loose ends were completed and signed off. This is no longer true. In today's project-driven organizations that have many projects occurring simultaneously, the responsibility for completing closure tasks has been parsed among the project manager, project teams, project office, an oversight "review committee," and an independent retrospective facilitator. Many tasks overlap, occur simultaneously, and require coordination and cooperation among these stakeholders.

The three major deliverables for **project closure** are described below (see Figure 14.1):

1. *Wrapping up the project.* The major wrap-up task is to ensure the project is approved and accepted by the customer. Other wrap-up activities include closing accounts, paying bills, reassigning equipment and personnel, finding new opportunities for project staff, closing facilities, and the final report. Checklists are used extensively to ensure tasks are not overlooked. In many organizations, the lion's share of closure tasks are largely done by the project office in coordination with the project manager. The final report writing is usually assigned to one project office staff member, who assembles input from all

FIGURE 14.1
Project Closure and Review Deliverables

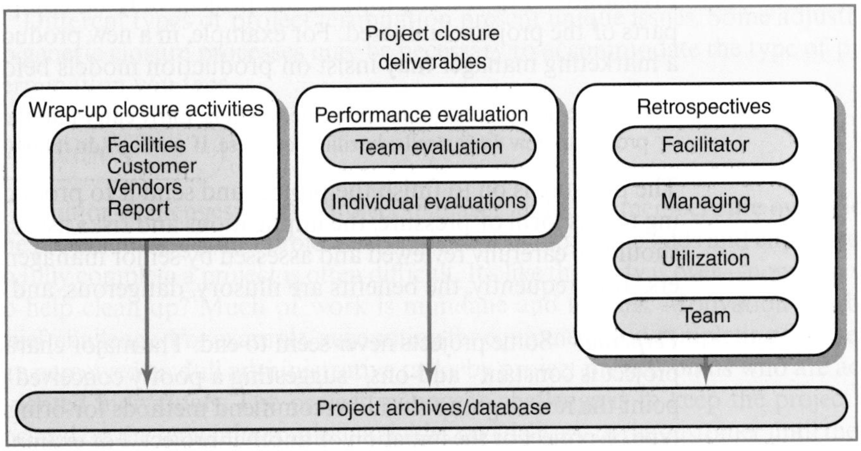

SNAPSHOT FROM PRACTICE Lessons Learned from Katrina*

On August 25, 2005, winds of 145 miles per hour and rains covered 80 percent of New Orleans with some areas under 20 feet of water. Hurricane Katrina dispersed havoc on every corner of New Orleans. In its trail it left over 1,300 people dead in Louisiana and Mississippi. Katrina will long be remembered as the costliest and most deadly hurricane ever recorded in the United States.

Response came from many different groups from within the country and from other countries. Katrina also drew the largest response of The National Guard to a national emergency in history. Governors from every state sent National Guard troops to support and assist the state of Mississippi. By September 8, 51,000 troops were responding to the emergency. Many other nonprofit groups offered help in a variety of ways—food, shelter, financial, health care, and transportation. Groups that contributed support have reviewed their efforts to see what lessons learned can be used to improve future emergency efforts. The results of the review of The National Guard efforts follow here:

Three of the key lessons from The National Guard retrospective are described.

- *Lack of equipment was one of the biggest problems—especially communication equipment. Ability to communicate among the many different support groups (e.g., civilian and military) was thwarted by incompatible systems or simple lack of availability.*

  Action Item: $1.3 billion has been authorized for new equipment that is compatible across major emergency groups.

- *Lack of protocols and standardization of reports, graphics, and communication caused delays and poor coordination among the many support groups.*

  Action Item: A single standard protocol for all states is now being applied.

- *The National Guard is under state control. Guard troops integrated quickly into the host-state command structures and cooperation ensued.*

  Action Item: Maintain status quo.

Because Guard soldiers are controlled by the states, they were empowered to enforce civil laws, something federal troops are prohibited from doing, except under the provisions of the insurrection laws. Fortunately, coordination and cooperation among state and federal troop command work reasonably well. However, the federal agencies (e.g., Homeland Security) need to incorporate the Guard into planning and preparation for the federal response to catastrophic disasters.

Lessons learned from the Katrina disaster are not limited to the military. Almost every agency and support group, such as individuals, communities, churches, and other groups, have developed lessons learned from their project response experience. For example, the Red Cross and state guard have better plans for handling thousands of people problems involving shelter, evacuation, and medical assistance. These lessons learned from Katrina are ready to go and should be enormously helpful in future hurricane situations.

* Les A. Melnyk, "Katrina Lessons Learned," *Soldiers Magazine*, June 20, 2006 and "Lessons Learned from Katrina: Preparing Your Institution for a Catastrophic Event." Federal Deposit Insurance Corporation is the source of this information. 1/20/08

process, effectiveness of group decision and problem-solving processes, group cohesion, trust among team members, and quality of information exchanged. Measurement of customer and user satisfaction with project deliverables (i.e., the project results) is often missed completely. Yet, project success depends significantly on satisfying these two very important groups. The quality of the deliverables is the responsibility of the team.

Before an evaluation of the project team can be effective and useful, a minimum core of conditions needs to be in place before the project begins (see Chapter 11). Some typical conditions are listed here in the form of questions:

1. Do standards for measuring performance exist? (You can't manage what you can't measure.) Are the goals clear for the team and individuals? Challenging? Attainable? Lead to positive consequences?
2. Are individual and team responsibilities and performance standards known by all team members?

Research Highlight

Measures of Team Performance*

If team evaluation is not done well in practice, how bad is it? Joseph Fusco surveyed 1,667 project managers representing 134 different projects. Fifty-two percent of the respondents indicated their team received no collective evaluation of their team performance. Of the 22 percent who indicated their team was evaluated, further probing found their evaluation was informal, lasting little more than 20 minutes. This apparent lack of team evaluation practices may be sending the wrong signal. Individual team members can slough off poor team performance by relying on the old saying, "I did my job." Strong team evaluation practices need to emphasize team members are "in this together," while minimizing individual performance. Nearly every company in Fusco's survey lacked an effective project management reward system.

* Joseph Fusco, "Better Policies Provide the Key to Implementing Project Management," *Project Management Journal*, Vol. 28, No. 3, September 1997, p. 38.

3. Are team rewards adequate? Do they send a clear signal that senior management believes that the synergy of teams is important?
4. Is a clear career path for successful project managers in place?
5. Is the team empowered to manage short-term difficulties?
6. Is there a relatively high level of trust emanating from the organizational culture?
7. Team evaluation should go beyond time, cost, and specifications. Are there criteria beyond the constraint criteria? Creation of project deliverables would be a good place to start. The "characteristics of highly effective teams" from Chapter 11 can easily be adapted as measurements of team performance.

The "in-place conditions" will support any evaluation approach for teams and their members.

In practice, the actual team evaluation process takes many forms—especially when evaluation goes beyond time, budget, and specifications. The typical mechanism for evaluation of teams is a survey administered by a consultant, a staff member from the human resources department, or through computer e-mail. The survey is normally restricted to team members, but in some cases, other project stakeholders interacting with the team may be included in the survey. An example of a partial survey is found in Table 14.2. After the results are tabulated, the team meets with the facilitator and/or senior management, and the results are reviewed.

This session is comparable to the team-building sessions described in Chapter 11, except that the focus is on using the survey results to assess the development of the team, its strengths and weaknesses, and the lessons that can be applied to future

TABLE 14.2
Sample Team Evaluation and Feedback Survey

	Disagree				Agree
Using the scale below, assess each statement.					
1. The team shared a sense of common purpose, and each member was willing to work toward achieving project objectives.	1	2	3	4	5
2. Respect was shown for other points of view. Differences of opinion were encouraged and freely expressed.	1	2	3	4	5
3. All interaction among team members occurred in a comfortable, supportive atmosphere.	1	2	3	4	5

- Be consistent and fair in your treatment of all team members. Nothing breeds resentment more than if, through the grapevine, individuals feel they are being held to a different standard than are other project members.
- Treat the review as only one point in an ongoing process. Use it to reach an agreement as to how the individual can improve his or her performance.

Both managers and subordinates may dread a formal performance review. Neither side feels comfortable with the evaluative nature of the discussion and the potential for misunderstanding and hurt feelings. Much of this anxiety can be alleviated if the project manager is doing her job well. Project managers should be constantly giving team members feedback throughout the project so that individual team members can have a pretty good idea how well they have performed and how the manager feels before the formal meeting. Post-project angst can be avoided if pre-project expectations are discussed before the project and regularly reenforced during project performance.

While in many cases the same process that is applied to reviewing the performance of team members is applied to evaluating the project manager, many organizations augment this process, given the importance of the position to their organization. This is where conducting the **360-degree review** is becoming more popular. In project-driven organizations, the project office typically will be responsible for collecting information on a specific project manager from customers, vendors, team members, peers, and other managers. This approach has tremendous promise for developing more effective project managers (Cochran, 2000).

In addition to performance reviews, data are collected for project retrospectives, which can present situations that may influence performance. In these situations performance evaluations should recognize and note the unusual situation.

Retrospectives

Why Retrospectives?

Lessons learned represent *an analysis carried out during and shortly after the project life cycle; they attempt to capture positive and negative project learning.* That is, "what worked and what didn't?" Lessons learned (postmortems, post-project review, or whatever name you choose to use) have long been part of project management. Peter Senge's *The Fifth Discipline: The Art and Practice of the Learning Organization* (1990) drew attention to institutionalizing organizational learning.

Although the past processes have been useful for closure and lessons learned, sadly their real value has not been exploited. Large, multinational companies with projects spread across the globe have been disappointed in their failure to effectively mine lessons learned. Smaller organizations observed, they too were not reaping the golden rewards of lessons learned. The same mistakes continue year after year. In the words of one executive: "Lessons learned are worth their weight in gold. I do not understand why we don't do a better job nurturing, dispersing, and implementing lessons learned." The processes for capturing lessons learned continue to evolve, but there are still many barriers to effectively mining the lessons learned that have been identified by practitioners. A few of the most ubiquitous barriers are noted here.

- The most common reason given for not creating lessons learned is lack of time.
- Most lessons learned are captured when the project is complete; teams get little direction or support after the lessons are reported.

- Lessons learned often degenerate into blame sessions that became emotionally damaging.
- Lessons learned are not being used across different locations.
- Lessons learned while implementing the project are seldom used to improve the remaining work in the project.
- Too often the lessons learned are not used in future projects because the organizational culture fails to recognize the value of learning.

What is needed to overcome these barriers is a methodology and management philosophy to ensure lessons learned are identified, utilized, and become a significant part of the project management organizational culture. The keys are to turn lessons learned into actions taken and to have someone own the lesson. One effort that appears to address the barriers and offer a solution is retrospectives. The military has long used retrospectives to improve their operations (e.g., after each maneuver). Retrospectives have emerged as a strong process and management philosophy used by project-driven organizations around the world to mine the gold that lessons learned can provide. Retrospectives are championed by Norman Kerth in his text *Project Retrospectives* (2001).

*A **retrospective** is a methodology that analyzes a past project event to determine what worked and what didn't, develops lessons learned, and creates an action plan that ensures lessons learned are used to improve management of future projects.*

The major goals of retrospectives are to reuse solutions and stop repetitive mistakes across the organization.

Retrospectives methodology has several embedded, distinguishing characteristics to ensure its effectiveness and value:

- Uses an independent facilitator.
- Includes a minimum of three in-process learning gates during the project life cycle.
- Has an owner.
- Develops a repository that is easy to use.
- Mandates a discipline that ensures retrospectives are used.

Initiating the Retrospective Review

The review process depends primarily on organization size and project size. Every effort should be made to make the project review a normal process rather than a surprise notice. In small organizations and projects where face-to-face contact at all levels is prevalent, the closure may be informal and only represent another staff meeting. But even in these environments the content of a formal project review should be examined and covered with notes made of the lessons learned. In some organizations, review initiation comes from a formal project review group or can be automatic. For example, in the latter case, all projects are reviewed at specific stages in the project life cycle—perhaps when a project is 10 to 20 percent complete in time or money, 50 percent complete, and after completion. In most other multiproject organizations, reviews (called stage gates) are planned for the completion of major milestones. The review is not linked to percent complete. Milestones are binary; either you have reached requirements completion or you have not. Regardless of how reviews are set up, they should be set up in the project planning stage—before the project begins.

Research Highlight

Chaos: Software Projects*

The Standish Group International is a market research and advisory firm specializing in mission-critical software and electronic commerce. They have conducted and published extensive research on the success and failure of software development/application projects. Their research, code name "CHAOS," shows that a staggering 31 percent of software projects will be canceled before they are ever completed. In addition, 53 percent of projects will cost 189 percent of their original estimates. In terms of success, on the average only 16 percent of software projects are completed on time and within budget. In larger companies, the success rate is much worse—9 percent. The Standish Group estimated that in 1995 American companies and government agencies spent $81 billion for canceled software projects.

The CHAOS research is based on "key findings" from research surveys and personal interviews. The respondents were information technology (IT) executive managers. The sample included large, medium, and small companies across major industry segments, for example, banking; securities; manufacturing; retail; wholesale; health care; insurance service; and local, state, and federal organizations. The total sample size was 365 respondents and represented 8,380 projects.

Based on an in-depth comparison of successful versus unsuccessful software projects, the Standish Group created a success potential chart that identifies key factors associated with project success. The success criteria were weighted based on the input from the surveyed IT managers. The most important criterion, "user involvement," was given 19 success points, while the least important, "hard-working, focused staff," was given 3 success points. The following chart lists the criteria in order of importance:

* Used by permission of the Standish Group International, Inc., 196 Old Town House Rd., West Yarmouth, MA 02673. The CHAOS report was updated in 2001 and 2009. Although improvement was noted (e.g., cost overruns were reduced to 145 percent), the magnitude of the core problems remains the same.

Success Criteria	Points
1. User involvement	19
2. Executive management support	16
3. Clear statement of requirements	15
4. Proper planning	11
5. Realistic expectations	10
6. Smaller project milestones	9
7. Competent staff	8
8. Project team ownership	6
9. Clear vision and objectives	3
10. Hard-working, focused staff	3
Total	100

encouraging its use is normally the responsibility of the project office or oversight committee. See Research Highlight: CHAOS: Software Projects.

Overseeing a Post-Project Retrospective

In the past, lessons learned were primarily collected from a post-project survey. Someone reviewed the answers, summarized the results, and filed the document. In retrospective methodology, the facilitator uses several questionnaires as a starting point to conduct the post-project retrospective. These surveys often offer clues to unrecognized deeper problems. A facilitator relates that clues to areas needing improvement are often found by checking the changes running through the project's change management system. For example, change management in multiple design changes might suggest poor freeze rules for design. These hard data can point directly to areas that hold potential for improvement. In some cases the data direct the facilitator to the area where a problem was solved.

TABLE 14.3
Project Process Review Questionnaire

	Item	Comments
1.	Were the project objectives and strategic intent of the project clearly and explicitly communicated?	
2.	Were the objectives and strategy in alignment?	
3.	Were the stakeholders identified and included in the planning?	
4.	Were project resources adequate for this project?	
5.	Were people with the right skill sets assigned to this project?	
6.	Were time estimates reasonable and achievable?	
7.	Were the risks for the project appropriately identified and assessed before the project started?	
8.	Were the processes and practices appropriate for this type of project? Should projects of similar size and type use these systems? Why/why not?	
9.	Did outside contractors perform as expected? Explain.	
10.	Were communication methods appropriate and adequate among all stakeholders? Explain.	
11.	Is the customer satisfied with the project product?	
12.	Are the customers using the project deliverables as intended? Are they satisfied?	
13.	Were the project objectives met?	
14.	Are the stakeholders satisfied their strategic intents have been met?	
15.	Has the customer or sponsor accepted a formal statement that the terms of the project charter and scope have been met?	
16.	Were schedule, budget, and scope standards met?	
17.	Is there any one important area that needs to be reviewed and improved upon? Can you identify the cause?	

Process and Methods Review

Process review begins with a review of the strategic intent of the project, selection criteria, project charter, project objectives, project scope, and acceptance criteria. This starting point reinforces and clarifies the business case for the project and the final project deliverables. Additional data gathering for process review is initiated through a questionnaire that is distributed to all major project stakeholders for responses. Some typical questions used are shown in Table 14.3. Although this questionnaire has some areas of omission, it can be used to initiate developing a questionnaire for your project.

Organizational Review

One of the themes of this text is that project performance is strongly influenced by organizational culture. It is therefore important to assess what fundamental organizational culture properties affect project successes and failures or become a hindrance to project teams. Again, survey questionnaires are easy, quick, and inexpensive to develop and collect data. Table 14.4, Organizational Culture Review, shows a partial organizational survey found in practice.

It is rare that important problems or successes will not show up in answers to a well-developed questionnaire.

TABLE 14.4 Organizational Culture Review Questionnaire

	Item	Comments
1.	Was the organizational culture supportive for this type of project?	
2.	Was senior management support adequate?	
3.	Were people with the right skills assigned to this project?	
4.	Did the project office help or hinder management of the project? Explain.	
5.	Did the team have access to organizational resources (people, funds, equipment)?	
6.	Was training for this project adequate? Explain.	
7.	Were lessons learned from earlier projects useful? Why? Where?	
8.	Did the project have a clear link to organizational objectives? Explain.	
9.	Was project staff properly reassigned?	
10.	Was the Human Resources Office helpful in finding new assignments? Comment.	

With survey information in hand, the facilitator then visits one-on-one with project team members, the project manager, and other stakeholders to dive deeper into cause-effect impacts. Fundamentally, the attempt is to isolate "the lack of *x* resulted in *y*." It is important to stay with the big lessons. For example, the facilitator might ask team members, "What was the biggest pain point in the project?" From these discussions the facilitator synthesizes collective wisdom.

Armed with the information gleaned from one-on-one sessions and other sources, the facilitator leads a team retrospective session. This session first reviews the facilitator's report and attempts to add key information. In fact, one of the roles of the facilitator is to lead the team in exploring new ways for solving a problem. Once the team reaches consensus of the key retrospective(s), the team develops and documents an action plan for improving future projects. Each retrospective should have at least one lesson that will improve current or future projects. One person needs to be assigned "owner" of the lesson learned and serve as the go-to person for more information. If possible, the facilitator should get senior management's commitment to implement the lesson.

An additional task of a facilitator is a review of the archived lessons to identify any trends across similar projects. For example, are there affinities between problems and successes among many projects? Have resources been inadequate? Has senior management visibly supported mining lessons learned? What fundamental organizational culture dimensions affect project successes and failures or become a hindrance to project teams?

In a conversation with one project office manager, she related that a facilitator found that the same problem across most multicountry projects had been occurring for over four years! It is difficult to believe no one picked up on such an obvious problem on so many projects. In this organization, U.S. managers were too focused on schedules, performance, and the bottom line; they neglected to establish a personal relationship with their foreign counterparts—e.g., the counterpart's key interests, family, holiday celebrations, and many other cultural aspects. Relationships were often strained and performance suffered. The result was that the project participants in each country are now required to attend a culture awareness class of the country of their counterparts to learn of customs, culture, and mores. Results improved dramatically.

Utilization of Retrospectives

Each retrospective is assigned an owner, typically a team member who is very interested in and familiar with the retrospective. This team member/owner will serve as the contact point for anyone needing information (expertise, contacts, templates, etc.) relating to the retrospective.

Another task of the retrospective facilitator is to guarantee there is a clear process to ensure retrospectives are used to improve management of future projects. Where retrospective methodology is used, some organizations mandate that the team of a new project review the retrospectives of similar projects. This mandate is one tactic that ensures that the most significant lessons are institutionalized. There is no excuse for not using past best practices and avoiding past mistakes. If the project managers before your project had completed retrospectives more effectively, your project might have avoided many mistakes. Of course, a requirement is archiving the lessons in a repository/library. But beyond a retrospective lessons learned library, a simple, easy to use, consistent format is necessary to ensure that information is easily found, used, and updated over time. A blog can be used to receive user comments on how helpful the retrospective is in improving a process or product.

Archiving Retrospectives

If retrospectives are to be used, it is critical to have a repository where reports and retrospective/lessons learned are accessible and easily retrieved. This is usually done using a Web site or other electronic means. For example, a round table of project office directors estimated that among their group of companies, 60–70 percent of their projects are global and virtual; all use some version of a Web-based system to collaborate and archive learning (e.g., Basecamp, SharePoint, Net Meeting, Voice Over IP). The responsibility for maintaining a repository for retrospectives and encouraging their use is normally the responsibility of the project office or oversight committee. Encouraging use of the repository depends on the ease of searching for information that is relevant to your project. Utilizing the information is defeated if information is difficult to find. For example, one project manager reported to your authors, "There are so many lessons learned items in the retrospectives library, I can't find information that applies to my project." This manager either wasn't interested in learning from others or the archive was poorly arranged.

At a minimum the repository should classify projects by type or characteristics. Each project review is categorized because there are differences in the way projects with different characteristics are managed and handled in an organization. A prospective project manager of a software coding project will have little interest in the construction of a clean room or recycling of inkjet reservoirs for printers. A prospective project manager of a small project will not be as interested in a computer project planning and control system as a project manager who is going to manage a very large project. The classification of projects by characteristics allows prospective readers, teams, and project managers to be selective in the search and use of report content.

One repository search engine uses the following classification scheme to allow prospective project stakeholders to start their search for information related to their prospective project:

- Project type—e.g., development, marketing, systems, construction.
- Size—monetary.
- Number of staff.
- Technology level—low, medium, high, new.
- Strategic or support.

Other classifications relevant to the organization could be included to drill further in search of projects that match the features of the prospective project. For example, another classification system indexes retrospectives by issues and problems.

Celebration A final wrap-up activity for the facilitator is the project closure celebration. An upbeat, festive celebration brings closure to the enjoyable experiences everyone has had and the need to say good-bye. Celebration is an opportunity to recognize the effort project stakeholders contributed. Even if the project did not reach its objectives, recognize the effort and goals that were achieved. If the project was a success, invite everyone who in some way contributed to project success. Thank the team and each one individually. The spirit of the celebration should be one in which the stakeholders are thanked for a job well done and leave with a good feeling of accomplishment and success.

Concluding Retrospective Notes

The retrospective methodology is more inclusive and disciplined than past lessons learned approaches. The impetus for its success has been accompanied by greater recognition of the real value of lessons learned in improving the management of projects. For example, Intel, which has project teams dispersed over 290 locations in 45 countries, has found using trained facilitators to be highly effective in mining and using retrospectives. Intel continues to train 15 new facilitators each year. Retrospective methodology is now standard operating procedure in many project-driven organizations. The lessons learned are often the single best source of information a project manager or team can use in planning their next project. Retrospectives are a main change agent for developing best project-management practices across the organization. Retrospective methodology is one positive step toward ensuring lessons learned are developed and implemented.

Summary

The goals of project closure are to complete the project and to improve performance of future projects. Implementing closure and review has three major closure deliverables: wrap-up, evaluation, and retrospectives. Wrap-up closure activities include delivering the final project deliverable, closing accounts, finding new opportunities for project staff, closing facilities, and creating the final report. Project evaluation verifies and documents project performance. The retrospectives methodology promises lessons learned are identified and used. Too often we spend massive dollars planning a project and little to nothing learning from the experience of completing the project. Failure to review, assess, and record successes and failures has consistently proven to be a costly waste. Retrospective methodology addresses this waste.

Key Terms

Lessons learned, *522*
Performance review, *520*
Project closure, *511*
Project evaluation, *517*
Project facilitator, *524*
Retrospective, *523*
Team evaluation, *517*
360-degree review, *522*

Review Questions

1. How does the project closure review differ from the performance measurement control system discussed in Chapter 13?
2. What major information would you expect to find in a project review?
3. Why is it difficult to perform a truly independent, objective review?
4. Comment on the following statement: "We cannot afford to terminate the project now. We have already spent more than 50 percent of the project budget."
5. Why should you separate performance reviews from pay reviews? How do you do this?
6. Advocates of retrospective methodology claim there are distinguishing characteristics that increase its value over past lessons learned methods. What are they? How does each characteristic enhance project closure and review?

Exercises

1. Consider a course that you recently completed. Perform a review of the course (the course represents a project and the course syllabus represents the project plan).
2. Imagine you are conducting a review of the International Space Station project. Research press coverage and the Internet to collect information on the current status of the project. What are the successes and failures to date? What forecasts would you make about the completion of the project, and why? What recommendations would you make to top management of the program, and why?
3. Interview a project manager who works for an organization that implements multiple projects. Ask the manager what kind of closure procedures are used to complete a project and whether lessons learned are used.
4. What are some of the lessons learned from a recent project in your organization? Was a retrospective done? What action plans were generated to improve processes as a result of the project?

References

Anonymous, "Annual Survey of Business Improvement Architects," Toronto, Canada, in *PM Network,* "Deliverables," Vol. 21, No. 4, April 2007, p. 18.

Cochran, D., "Finally, a Way to Completely Measure Project Manager Performance," *PM Network,* September 2000, pp. 75–80.

Cooke-Davies, T., "Project Management Closeout Management: More than Simply Saying Good Bye and Moving On," in J. Knutson (Ed.), *Project Management for Business Processionals* (Indianapolis, IN: John Wiley and Sons, 2001), pp. 200–14.

Fretty, P., "Why Do Projects Really Fail?" *PM Network,* March 2006, pp. 45–48.

Gobeli, D., and E. W. Larson, "Barriers Affecting Project Success," in *1986 Proceedings Project Management Institute: Measuring Success* (Upper Darby, PA: Project Management Institute, 1986), pp. 22–29.

Hoffman, R., "Ten Reasons You Should Be Using 360 Degree Feedback," *HR Magazine,* April 1995, pp. 82–85.

Jedd, Marcia, "Standing Guard," *PM Network,* Vol. 21, No. 1, January 2007, pp. 73–77.

Kendrick, Tom, *Identifying and Managing Project Risk,* 2nd ed. ANACOM, New York, NY 2009.

Kerth, Norman L., *Project Retrospectives: A Handbook for Team Reviews* (New York: Dorset House, 2001).

Kwak, Y. H., and C. W. Ibbs, "Calculating Project Management's Return on Investment," *Project Management Journal,* Vol. 31, No. 2, March 2000, pp. 38–47.

Ladika, S., "By Focusing on Lessons Learned, Project Managers Can Avoid Repeating the Same Old Mistakes," *PM Network,* Vol. 22, No. 2, February 2008, pp. 75–77.

Lavell, Debra, and Russ Martinelli, "Program and Project Retrospectives: An Introduction," *PM World Today,* Vol. 10, No. 1, January 2008, p. 1.

Latham, G. P., and K. N. Wexley, *Increasing Productivity through Performance Appraisal,* 2nd ed. (Reading, MA: Addison-Wesley, 1994).

Marlin, Mark, "Implementing an Effective Lessons Learned Process in a Global Project Environment," *PM World Today,* Vol. 10, No. 11, November 2008, pp. 1–6.

Nelson, Ryan R., "Project Retrospectives: Evaluating Project Success, Failure, and Everything in Between," *MIS Quarterly Executive,* Vol. 4, No. 3, September 2005, p. 372.

Pippett, D. D., and J. F. Peters, "Team Building and Project Management: How Are We Doing?" *Project Management Journal,* Vol. 26, No. 4, December 1995, pp. 29–37.

Romanoff, T. K., "The Ten Commandments of Performance Management," *Personnel,* Vol. 66, No. 1, 1989, pp. 24–26.

Royer, I., "Why Bad Projects Are So Hard to Kill," *Harvard Business Review,* February 2003, pp. 49–56.

Senge, P., *The Fifth Discipline: The Art and Practice of the Learning Organization* (New York: Doubleday, 1990).

Sheperd, D. A., H. Patzelt, and M. Wolfe, "Moving Forward from Project Failure: Negative Emotions, Affective Commitment, and Learning from the Experience," *Academy of Management Journal,* Vol. 54, No. 6, 2011, pp. 1229–60.

Staw, Berry M., and Jerry Ross, "Knowing When to Pull the Plug," *Harvard Business Review,* March-April 1987, pp. 68–74.

Wheatly, M., "Over the Bar," *PM Network,* Vol. 17, No. 1, January 2003, pp. 40–45.

Yates, J. K., and S. Aniftos, "ISO 9000 Series of Quality Standards and the E/C Industry," *Project Management Journal,* Vol. 28, No. 2, June 1997, pp. 21–31.

Zaitz, Les, "Rail Car Deal Snags Tri Met for Millions," *Oregonian,* December 14, 2008, p. 1, and January 7, 2009, p. D4.

Appendix 14.1

Project Closeout Checklist

Section 5: Project Closeout

Project Closeout Transition Checklist

Provide basic information about the project including: Project Title—The proper name used to identify this project; Project Working Title—The working name or acronym that will be used for the project; Proponent Secretary—The Secretary to whom the proponent agency is assigned or the Secretary that is sponsoring an enterprise project; Proponent Agency—The agency that will be responsible for the management of the project; Prepared by—The person(s) preparing this document; Date/Control Number—The date the checklist is finalized and the change or configuration item control number assigned.

Project Title:	____________	*Project Working Title:*	____________
Proponent Secretary:	____________	*Proponent Agency:*	____________
Prepared by :	____________	*Date/Control Number:*	____________

Complete the Status and Comments columns. In the Status column indicate: Yes, if the item has been addressed and completed; No, if the item has not been addressed, or is incomplete; N/A, if the item is not applicable to this project. Provide comments or describe the plan to resolve the item in the last column.

	Item	**Status**	**Comments/Plan to Resolve**
1	Have all the product or service deliverables been accepted by the customer?		
1.1	Are there contingencies or conditions related to the acceptance? If so, describe in the Comments.		
2	Has the project been evaluated against each performance goal established in the project performance plan?		
3	Has the actual cost of the project been tallied and compared to the approved cost baseline?		
3.1	Have all approved changes to the cost baseline been identified and their impact on the project documented?		
4	Have the actual milestone completion dates been compared to the approved schedule?		
4.1	Have all approved changes to the schedule baseline been identified and their impact on the project documented?		

(Continued)

following among the questions it uses to evaluate vulnerability to terrorism: Have you included possible terrorist targets (facilities and personnel) in your hazard and vulnerability analysis? Have you conducted a counterterrorism exercise complete with law enforcement, fire, medical, and emergency management participation? What should your organization's policy be on negotiating with a person threatening a terrorist act?[2]

Managing projects in a dangerous world is a tough assignment. Security precautions are major cost considerations not only in dollars and cents, but also in the psychological well-being of personnel sent abroad. Effective risk management is critical to success.

Geography

One factor that is often underestimated until project personnel actually arrive at a foreign destination is the geography of the country. Imagine what it is like to deplane from a modern aircraft and encounter the 105- degree heat and 90 percent humidity of Jakarta, Indonesia, or three feet of fresh snow and −22 degree temperatures in Kokkla, Finland. Whether it is the wind, the rain, the heat, the jungle, or the desert, more than one project manager has asserted that their greatest challenge was overcoming the "elements." Mother Nature cannot be ignored.

The planning and implementation of a project must take into account the impact the country's geography will have on the project. For example, a salvage operation off the coast of Greenland can only be scheduled one month out of the year because the waterway is frozen over during the remainder of the year. Construction projects in Southeast Asia have to accommodate the monsoon season when rainfall can be as high as 50 inches per month. Geography does not just affect outdoor projects. It can have an indirect effect on "indoor" projects. For example, one information systems specialist reported that his performance on a project in northern Sweden declined due to sleep deprivation. He attributed his problems to the 20 hours of daylight this part of the world experiences during summer months. Finally, extreme weather conditions can make extraordinary demands on equipment. Projects can grind to a halt because of equipment breakdown under the brunt of the elements. Working under extreme conditions typically requires special equipment, which increases the costs and complexity of the project.

Before beginning a project in a foreign land, project planners and managers need to study carefully the unique characteristics of the geography of that country. They need to factor into project plans and schedules such items as climate, seasons, altitude, and natural geographical obstacles. See the Snapshot from Practice: The Filming of *Apocalypse Now* for an example of a poorly planned endeavor in the Philippines.

Economic

Basic economic factors in foreign countries and regions influence choices of site selection and project success. The gross domestic product (GDP) of a country suggests the level of development of a country. A faltering economy may indicate fewer sources of capital funding. Changes in protectionist strategies of

[2] Contingency Planning and Management.com, "Strohl Systems Offers Terrorism Readiness Questionnaire," September 24, 2001.

SNAPSHOT FROM PRACTICE The Filming of *Apocalypse Now**

In February 1976, Francis Ford Coppola took his Hollywood film crew to the Philippines to shoot *Apocalypse Now,* a film adaptation of Joseph Conrad's *Heart of Darkness* within the context of the Vietnam conflict. The Philippines was chosen because the terrain was similar to Vietnam's, and the government was willing to rent its helicopter force for the movie. At the time, the U.S. military was unwilling to cooperate on a film about Vietnam. An additional advantage was cheap labor. Coppola was able to hire more than 300 laborers at $1 to $3 per day to construct elaborate production sets, including an impressive Cambodian temple. *Apocalypse Now* was scheduled for 16 weeks of shooting at a budget of $12 to $14 million.

Months earlier, George Lucas, of *Star Wars* fame, warned Coppola against filming the movie in the Philippines. He said, "It's one thing to go over there for three weeks with five people and scrounge some footage with the Filipino Army, but if you go over there with a big Hollywood production, the longer you stay the more in danger you are of getting sucked into the swamp." His words turned out to be prophetic.

A civil war was going on between government forces and communist rebels. Shooting was repeatedly interrupted because the Philippine military ordered their helicopter pilots to leave the set and fly to the mountains to fight the rebels.

In May 1976, a typhoon struck the Philippine Islands, destroying most of the movie sets. The film team was forced to shut down production and returned to the United States for two months.

The lead character was played by Martin Sheen, who suffered a serious heart attack under the stress and heat of the filming and had to return to the United States. Coppola scrambled to film the scenes that did not require Sheen, but eventually production came to a standstill until Sheen's return nine weeks later.

The entire project proved to be a traumatic experience for Coppola, who had enjoyed Academy Award success with his previous *Godfather* movies. "There were times when I thought I was going to die, literally, from the inability to move the problems I had. I would go to bed at four in the morning in a cold sweat."

Film production ended in May 1977 after more than 200 days of shooting. The final cost was about $30 million. To date, *Apocalypse Now* has earned more than $150 million throughout the world.

* *Hearts of Darkness: A Filmmaker's Apocalypse* (Paramount Pictures, 1991).

a host country, such as import quotas and tariffs, can quickly alter the viability of projects. Other factors such as balance of payments, taxation, labor laws, safety regulations, and market size can influence project choices and operations.

Skills, educational level, and labor supply prevalent in a host country can determine the choice of a project site. Is project selection driven by low wage levels or availability of technically skilled talent? For example, you can hire three computer programmers in Ukraine for the price of one programmer in the United States. Conversely, many high-tech companies are willing to endure the additional expense of setting up joint projects in Switzerland and Germany to take advantage of their engineering prowess.

Financial exposure is a significant risk for many international projects. Let's look first at the potential impact of currency fluctuations on project success. For example, a U.S. contractor agrees to build a customized product for a German client. The product will be built in the United States. The contractor estimates that the project will cost $925,000, and, in order to earn a nice profit, prices the project at $1,000,000. To accommodate the German buyer the price is converted to euros. Suppose at the time of the contract, the exchange rate is $1.15 per Euro, and the price specified in the contract is €869,566.

SNAPSHOT FROM PRACTICE River of Doubt*

After his crushing election defeat in 1912 as a third-party candidate, former president Theodore ("Teddy") Roosevelt set his sights on a grand adventure, the first descent of an unmapped rapids-choked tributary of the Amazon aptly titled the "River of Doubt." Together with Brazil's most famous explorer, Candido Mariano da Silva Rondon, Roosevelt accomplished a feat that belongs in the annals of great expeditions.

© Fotomas/Topham/The Image Works

Along the way, Roosevelt and his men faced an unbelievable series of hardships, losing their canoes and supplies to crushing whitewater rapids, and enduring starvation, Indian attacks, disease, drowning, and even murder within their ranks. Candice Millard brings alive these extraordinary events in her nonfiction thriller *The River of Doubt.* While her account details the ill-fated journey it also reveals insights into international project management as it describes the collaboration between the American and Brazilian cohorts. While each party ultimately earned the respect and admiration of the other, friction between the two parties simmered from the outset.

One source of consternation was the amount of supplies and luggage that the Americans required for the journey. Warned that the luggage requirements of the former president and his party would be extensive, the Brazilian commodore Rondon ordered 110 mules and 17 pack oxen to be used for the expedition's overland journey across the Brazilian highland to the great river. Surely, he felt, this would be more than necessary for such a trip.

The Brazilians were astounded by the sheer volume of baggage that was unloaded from Roosevelt's ship, the *Vandycks.* There were mountains of crates: guns and ammunition, chairs and tables, tents and cots, equipment for collecting and preserving specimens, surveying the river, and cooking meals. An exhausted stevedore elicited a roar of laughter from the onlooking crowd when he announced, "Nothing lacking but the piano!"

Rather than risk embarrassment by telling Roosevelt that they were not prepared to take so much luggage, Rondon scrambled to find additional animals. Extra oxen and mules were located, but they were far from tame. Loaded with supplies, the oxen would buck and throw off the packs. The expedition was delayed as gauchos (South American cowboys) endeavored to "break" the animals as quickly as possible.

Within days of finally setting off across the vast highlands, Roosevelt and his men began to experience the harsh realities that were to plague the expedition. After crossing a bone-strewn graveyard of oxen and mules that had starved to death or been eaten during previous expeditions, they were stunned by the sight of unopened supply crates, all clearly marked "Roosevelt South American Expedition." The pack animals, still making their weary away across the plateau ahead of them, had begun bucking off their heavy loads!

As the officers rode slowly past the boxes, they wondered what they were leaving behind and how precious it might become in the months ahead. Little did they know how true those fears would be.

* Candice Millard, *The River of Doubt* (New York: Doubleday), 2005.

water desalination plant from sea water in a Middle East country. She was restricted to the living compound for families of foreign guest workers. Going outside the compound to a nearby city meant covering her head, arms, and legs and being accompanied by another woman or, preferably, a man. A physical altercation in the city concerning her clothing was traumatic for her. She left the country and returned home. Her husband requested a transfer back home three months later. The loss of the original project manager from the project required the assigned project manager to establish relationships with the project team and host country's nationals to get the project moving smoothly again.

Not only do project managers have to adapt to the culture of the host country, but often times overseas projects require working with people from different countries. For example, on a light rail project in the Philippines, an American firm was hired to oversee the interests of local real estate companies who were funding the project. The American project manager had to work with Czech representatives who were providing the rail equipment, Japanese engineers responsible for building the rail, Australian bankers who were providing additional financing, an Indian firm that were the principal architects, as well as the native Filipinos.

Of all the factors, working within a multicultural environment is most often the greatest challenge for project managers. It will be dealt with in detail later in this chapter.

Project Site Selection

As the project manager studies the factors contributing to site selection, he will see that inherent in all of these factors is the risk level senior management and directors are willing to accept for the potential rewards of a successful international project. One approach for the project manager to digest, clarify, and understand the factors leading to the selection of a specific project is to use a risk matrix similar to those found in Chapter 7. The major difference lies in the selection of the risk factors for different project sites.

Figure 15.2 presents a truncated matrix for project site selection of the construction of a laser printer factory in Singapore, India, or Ireland. In this example, political stability, worker skill and supply, culture compatibility, infrastructure, government support, and product-to-market advantage were the major assessment factors. Each project site is compared against each factor. Figure 15.3 depicts a further breakdown of the infrastructure evaluation factor. In this example, transportation, educated workforce, utilities, telecommunications, and vendor suppliers are considered important to evaluating the infrastructure for

FIGURE 15.2
Assessment Matrix Project Site Selection

Score legend

5 = excellent
3 = acceptable
1 = poor

	Political stability	Worker skill, supply	Culture compatibility	Infrastructure	Government support	Product-to-market advantage
Singapore	5	4	4	4	4	3
India	3	4	3	3	3	3
Ireland	5	4	5	5	5	5

Research Highlight

Cross-Cultural Orientations*

Anthropologists Kluckhohn and Strodtbeck assert that cultural variations reflect how different societies have responded to common issues or problems throughout time (see Figure 15.4). Five of the issues featured in their comparative framework are discussed here.

- *Relationship to nature*—This issue reflects how people relate to the natural world around them and to the supernatural. Should people dominate their environment, live in harmony with it, or be subjugated to it? North Americans generally strive to harness nature's forces and change them as they need. Other societies, as in India, strive to live in harmony with nature. Still other societies see themselves at the mercy of physical forces and/or subject to the will of a supreme being. Life in this context is viewed as predetermined, preordained, or an exercise in chance.
- *Time orientation*—Does the culture focus on the past, present, or future? For example, many European countries focus on the past and emphasize maintaining tradition. North Americans, on the other hand, are less concerned with tradition and tend to focus on the present and near future. Paradoxically, Japanese society, while rich with tradition, has a much longer time horizon.
- *Activity orientation*—This issue refers to a desirable focus of behavior. Some cultures emphasize "being" or living in the moment. This orientation stresses experiencing life and seeking immediate gratification. Other cultures emphasize "doing" and emphasize postponing immediate gratification for greater accomplishment. A third alternative is the "control" orientation, where people restrain their desires by detaching themselves from objects. The activity dimension affects how people approach work and leisure and the extent to which work-related concerns pervade their lives. It is reflected in the age-old question, "Do we live to work or work to live?"
- *Basic nature of people*—Does a culture view people as good, evil, or some mix of these two? In many Third World countries, people see themselves as basically honest and trustworthy. Conversely, some Mediterranean cultures have been characterized as taking a rather evil view of human nature. North Americans are somewhere in between. They see people as basically good but stay on guard so as not to be taken advantage of.
- *Relationships among people*—This issue concerns the responsibility one has for others. Americans, for instance, tend to be highly individualistic and believe everyone should take care of him- or herself. In contrast, many Asian societies emphasize concern for the group or community he or she is a member of. A third variation is hierarchical, which is similar to the group except that in these societies groups are hierarchically ranked, and membership is essentially stable over time. This is a characteristic of aristocratic societies and caste systems.

The Kluckhohn and Strodtbeck framework provides a basis for a deeper understanding of cultural differences. At the same time, they warn that not all members of a culture practice the same behavior all the time, and, as in the United States, there is likely to be considerable variation within a given culture.

* F. Kluckhohn and F. L. Strodtbeck, *Variations in Value Orientations* (Evanston, IL: Row, Peterson, 1961).

FIGURE 15.4
Kluckhohn-Strodtbeck's Cross-Cultural Framework

Note: The line indicates where the United States tends to fall along these issues.

Cultural issue	Variations		
Relationship to nature	Domination	Harmony	Subjugation
Time orientation	Past	Present	Future
Activity orientation	Being	Doing	Controlling
Nature of people	Good	Evil	Mixed
Relationships among people	Individualist	Group	Hierarchical

Research Highlight

Hofstede Framework*

The Hofstede framework grew from a study of 88,000 people working in IBM subsidiaries in 50 countries and 3 multicountry regions. Based on responses to a 32-item questionnaire, Dutch social scientist Geert Hofstede developed different dimensions for examining cultures:

1. Individualism versus collectivism. Identifies whether a culture holds individuals or the group responsible for each member's welfare.
2. Power distance. Describes the degree to which a culture accepts status and power differences among its members.
3. Uncertainty avoidance. Identifies a culture's willingness to accept uncertainty and ambiguity about the future.
4. Masculinity-femininity. Describes the degree to which the culture emphasizes competitive and achievement-oriented behavior or displays concerns for relationships.

Figure 15.5 shows how he ranked selected countries according to collectivism-individualism and power distance. Wealth appears to influence both factors. Power distance is correlated with income inequality in a country while individualism is correlated with national wealth (Per Capita Gross National Product). As a result high power distance and collectivism are often found together, as are low power distance and individualism. This can affect decision making on project teams. For example, while the high collectivism may lead a project team in Thailand to operate consensually, the high power distance may cause decisions to be heavily influenced by the desires of the project manager. Conversely, a similar team operating in more individualistic and low power distance such as Great Britain or America might make decisions with more open debate including challenging the preferences of the project manager.

* G. Hofstede, *Culture's Consequences: Comparing Values, Behaviors, Institutions and Organizations Across Nations,* 2nd Edition (Thousand Oaks, CA: Sage Publications, 2001). http://www.geerthofstede.nl

FIGURE 15.5
Sample Country Clusters on Hofstede's Dimensions of Individualism-Collectivism and Power Distance

Collectivism		Colombia, Peru, Thailand, Singapore, Mexico, Turkey, Indonesia
Individualism	Israel, Finland, Germany, Ireland, New Zealand, Canada, Great Britain, United States	Spain, South Africa, France, Italy, Belgium
	Low power distance	High power distance

slower pace of life. They can't understand why Americans are always in such a hurry. Punctuality varies across cultures. For example, Americans will generally tolerate someone being 5 to 10 minutes late. In contrast, among Peruvians, the period before an apology or explanation for being late is expected might be 45 minutes to an hour!

While working on multicultural projects, managers sometimes encounter ethical dilemmas that are culturally bound. For example, the 1999 Olympic site selection scandal featured the sordid details of committee members peddling their votes for a wide range of gifts (i.e., university scholarships for their children, extravagant trips). In many societies such "bribes" or "tributes" are expected and the only way to conduct meaningful business. Moreover, many cultures will not grant a female project manager the same respect they will a male project manager. Should U.S. management increase project risk or violate its own sex-discrimination policy?

These cultural differences are just the tip of the iceberg. There are numerous "How to Do Business in . . ." books written by people who have traveled and worked abroad. Although these books may lack rigor, they typically do a good job of identifying local customs and common mistakes made by outsiders. On the other hand, anthropologists have made significant contributions to our understanding of why and how the cultures of societies are different (see the accompanying Research Highlights). Students of international project management are encouraged to study these works to gain a deeper understanding of the root causes of cultural diversity.

So what can be said to prepare people to work on international projects? The world is too diverse to do justice in one chapter to all the cultural variations managers are likely to encounter when working on international projects. Instead, a sample of some of these differences will be highlighted by discussing working on projects in four different countries: Mexico, France, Saudi Arabia, and China. We apologize to our readers outside the United States because briefings are presented from the viewpoint of a U.S. project manager working in these countries. Still, in an effort not to be too ethnocentric, we present a fifth scenario for foreign project managers assigned to working in the United States. Although by no means exhaustive, these briefings provide a taste of what it is like to work in and with people from these countries.

Working in Mexico

America developed historically in an environment where it was important for strangers to be able to get along, interact, and do business. On the American frontier almost everyone was a stranger, and people had to both cooperate and keep their distance. The New England Yankee sentiment that "Good fences make good neighbors" expresses this American cultural value well. Conversely, Mexico developed historically in an environment where the only people to trust were family and close friends—and by extension, people who were known to those whom you knew well. As a consequence, personal relationships dominate all aspects of Mexican business. While Americans are generally taught not to do business with friends, Mexicans and other Latin Americans are taught to do business with no one but friends.

The significance of personal relationships has created a *compadre* system in which Mexicans are obligated to give preference to relatives and friends when hiring, contracting, procuring, and sharing business opportunities. North Americans often complain that such practices contribute to inefficiency in Mexican firms. While this may or may not be the case, efficiency is prized by Americans, while Mexicans place a higher value on friendship.

Mexicans tend to perceive Americans as being "cold." They also believe that most Americans look down on them. Among the most effective things an American can do to prevent being seen as a typical *Gringo* is to take the time and effort in the beginning of a working relationship to really get to know Mexican counterparts. Because family is all-important to Mexicans, a good way for developing a personal relationship is exchanging information about each other's family. Mexicans will often gauge people's trustworthiness by the loyalty and attention they devote to their family.

The *mañana* syndrome reflects another cultural difference between Americans and Mexicans. Mexicans have a different concept of time than Americans do. Mexicans feel confined and pressured when given deadlines; they prefer open-ended schedules. They generally consider individuals to be more important than sticking to a schedule. If a friend drops in at work, most Mexicans will stop and talk, regardless of how long it takes, and even if chatting makes their work late. This sometimes contributes to the erroneous perception that Mexicans lack a work ethic. Quite the contrary; given a minimal incentive, Mexicans can be quite industrious and ambitious.

Finally, as in many other cultures, Mexicans do not share Americans' confidence that they control their own destiny. While Americans are taught, "When the going gets tough, the tough get going," Mexicans are taught, "Taking action without knowing what is expected or wanted can have dangerous consequences." Mexicans tend to be more cautious and want to spend more time discussing risks and potential problems that Americans might dismiss as improbable or irrelevant.

Other useful guidelines for working with Mexicans on projects include the following:

1. Americans tend to be impersonal and practical when making arguments; Mexicans can be very passionate and emotional when arguing. They enjoy a lively debate.
2. Where Americans tend to use meetings as the place to work things out publicly, Mexicans tend to see meetings as the place where persons with authority ratify what has been decided during informal private discussions.
3. While Mexicans can be emotional, they tend to shy away from any sort of direct confrontation or criticism. A long silence often indicates displeasure or disagreement.
4. Speech in Mexico is often indirect. People rarely say no directly but are more likely to respond by saying maybe *(quizas),* or by saying "I will think about it" or changing the subject. Yes *(si)* is more likely to mean "I understand you" than "yes."
5. Titles are extremely important in Mexico and are always used when a person is introducing him- or herself or being introduced. Pay as much attention to remembering a person's title as to remembering his or her name.

Today, with NAFTA and increased international business activity in Mexico, old traditions are disappearing. American managers report that cultural differences are less evident in northern Mexico where many multinational firms operate. Here *hora americana* (American time) rather than *hora mexicana* tends to be used when dealing with foreigners. Project managers should devote up-front effort to understanding how much older mores of Mexican culture apply to their project.[4]

Working in France

Some Americans consider the French the most difficult to work with among Europeans. This feeling probably stems from a reflection of the French culture, which is quite different from that in the United States.

[4] Adapted from E. Kras, *Management in Two Cultures: Bridging the Gap between U.S. and Mexican Managers,* rev. ed. (Yarmouth, ME: Intercultural Press, 1995); L. W. Tuller, *An American's Guide to Doing Business in Latin America* (Avon, MA: Adams Business, 2008).

In France, one's social class is very important. Social interactions are constrained by class standing, and during their lifetimes most French people do not encounter much change in social status. Unlike an American, who through hard work and success can move from the lowest economic stratum to the highest, a successful French person might, at best, climb one or two rungs up the social ladder. Additionally, the French are very status conscious and like to provide signs of this status, such as knowledge of literature and arts; a well-designed, tastefully decorated house; and a high level of education.

The French tend to admire or be fascinated with people who disagree with them; in contrast, Americans are more attracted to those who agree with them. As a result, the French are accustomed to conflict and, during negotiations, accept the fact that some positions are irreconcilable and must be accepted as such. Americans, on the other hand, tend to believe that conflicts can be resolved if both parties make an extra effort and are willing to compromise. Also, the French often determine a person's trustworthiness based on their first-hand, personal evaluation of the individual's character. Americans, in contrast, tend to evaluate a person's trustworthiness on the basis of past achievements and other people's evaluations.

The French are often accused of lacking an intense work ethic. For example, many French workers frown on overtime and on average they have one of the longest vacations in the world (four to five weeks annually). On the other hand, the French enjoy a reputation for productive work, a result of the French tradition of craftsmanship. This tradition places a greater premium on quality rather than on getting things accomplished quickly.

Most French organizations tend to be highly centralized with rigid structures. As a result, it usually takes longer to carry out decisions. Because this arrangement is quite different from the more decentralized organizations in the United States, many U.S. project managers find the bureaucratic red tape a source of considerable frustration.

In countries like the United States, a great deal of motivation is derived from professional accomplishments. The French do not tend to share this same view of work. While they admire American industriousness, they believe that quality of life is what really matters. As a result they attach much greater importance to leisure time, and many are unwilling to sacrifice the enjoyment of life for a dedication to project work.

Cautions to remember with the French include these:

1. The French value punctuality. It is very important to be on time for meetings and social occasions.
2. Great importance is placed on neatness and taste. When interacting with French businesspeople, pay close attention to your own professional appearance and appear cultured and sophisticated.
3. The French can be very difficult to negotiate with. Often, they ignore facts, no matter how convincing they may be. They can be quite secretive about their position. It is difficult to obtain information from them, even in support for their position. Patience is essential for negotiating with them.
4. French managers tend to see their work as an intellectual exercise. They do not share the American view of management as an interpersonally demanding exercise, where plans have to be constantly "sold" upward and downward using personal skills.

5. The French generally consider managers to be experts. They expect managers to give precise answers to work-related questions. To preserve their reputation, some French managers act as if they know the answers to questions even when they don't.[5]

Working in Saudi Arabia

Project management has a long tradition in Saudi Arabia and other Arab countries. Financed by oil money, European and American firms have contributed greatly to the modernization of Arab countries. Despite this tradition, foreigners often find it very hard to work on projects in Saudi Arabia. A number of cultural differences can be cited for this difficulty.

One is the Arabian view of time. In North America, it is common to use the cliché, "The early bird gets the worm." In Saudi Arabia, a favorite expression is, "Bukra insha Allah," which means, "Tomorrow if God wills," an expression that reflects the Saudis' approach to time. Unlike Westerners, who believe they control their own time, Arabs believe that Allah controls time. As a result, when Saudis commit themselves to a date in the future and fail to show up, there is no guilt or concern on their part because they have no control over time in the first place. In planning future events with Arabs, it pays to hold lead time to a week or less, because other factors may intervene or take precedence.

An associated cultural belief is that destiny depends more on the will of a supreme being than on the behavior of individuals. A higher power dictates the outcome of important events, so individual action is of little consequence. As a result, progress or the lack of progress on a project is considered more a question of fate than effort. This leads Saudis to rely less on detailed plans and schedules to complete projects than Americans do.

Another important cultural contrast between Saudi Arabians and Americans is emotion and logic. Saudis often act on the basis of emotion; in contrast, those in an Anglo culture are taught to act on logic. During negotiations, it is important not only to share the facts but also to make emotional appeals that demonstrate your suggestion is the right thing to do.

Saudis also make use of elaborate and ritualized forms of greetings and leave-takings. A businessperson may wait far past the assigned meeting time before being admitted to a Saudi office. Once there, the individual may find a host of others present; one-on-one meetings are rare. Moreover, during the meeting there may be continuous interruptions. Visitors arrive and begin talking to the host, and messengers may come in and go out on a regular basis. The businessperson is expected to take all this activity as perfectly normal and to remain composed and ready to continue discussions as soon as the host is prepared to do so.

Initial meetings are typically used to get to know the other party. Business-related discussions may not occur until the third or fourth meeting. Business meetings typically conclude with an offer of coffee or tea. This is a sign that the meeting is over and that future meetings, if there are to be any, should now be arranged.

[5] Adapted from R. Hallowell, D. Bowen, and C. I. Knoop, "Four Seasons Goes to Paris," *Academy of Management Executive,* 16 (4) November 2002, pp. 7–24; J. Hooker, *Working across Cultures* (Stanford, CA: Stanford Business Books, 2003); T. Morrison and W. A. Conaway, *Kiss, Bow, or Shake Hands (The Bestselling Guide to Doing Business in More than 60 Countries*), 2nd ed. (New York: Adams Media, 2006).

Saudis attach a great deal of importance to status and rank. When meeting with them, defer to the senior person. It is also important never to criticize or berate anyone publicly. This causes the individual to lose face; the same is true for the person who makes these comments. Mutual respect is expected at all times.

Other useful guidelines for working in an Arab culture such as Saudi Arabia include the following:

1. It is important never to display feelings of superiority because this makes the other party feel inferior. No matter how well someone does something, the individual should let the action speak for itself and not brag or draw attention to himself.
2. A lot of what gets done is a result of going through administrative channels in the country. It is often difficult to sidestep a lot of this red tape, and efforts to do so can be regarded as disrespect for legal and governmental institutions.
3. Connections are extremely important in conducting business. More important people get fast service from less important people. Close relatives take absolute priority; non-relatives are kept waiting.
4. Patience is critical to the success of business negotiations. Time for deliberations should be built into all negotiations to prevent a person from giving away too much in an effort to reach a quick settlement.
5. Important decisions are usually made in person and not by correspondence or telephone. While Saudis seek counsel from many people, the ultimate power to make a decision rests with the person at the top, and this individual relies heavily on personal impressions, trust, and rapport.[6]

Working in China

In recent years the People's Republic of China (PRC, or China, for short) has moved away from isolation to encourage more business with the rest of the world. While China holds tremendous promise, many Western firms have found working on projects in China to be a long, grueling process that often results in failure. One of the primary reasons for problems is the failure to appreciate Chinese culture.

Chinese society, like those of Japan and Korea, is influenced by the teachings of Confucius (551–478 B.C.). Unlike America, which relies on legal institutions to regulate behavior, in Confucian societies the primary deterrent against improper or illegal behavior is shame or loss of face. Face is more than simply reputation. There is a Chinese saying that, "Face is like the bark of a tree; without its bark, the tree dies." Loss of face not only brings shame to individuals but also to family members. A member's actions can cause shame for the entire family, hampering that family from working effectively in Chinese society.

In China, "whom you know is more important than what you know." The term *guanxi* refers to personal connections with appropriate authorities or individuals. China observers argue that *guanxi* is critical for working with the Chinese. Chinese are raised to distrust strangers, especially foreigners. Trust is transmitted via *guanxi*. That is, a trusted business associate of yours must pass you along to his trusted business associates. Many outsiders criticize *guanxi*, considering it to be like nepotism where decisions are made regarding contracts or problems based on family ties or connections instead of an objective assessment of ability.

[6] Adapted from R. T. Moran, P. R. Harris, and S. V. Moran, *Managing Cultural Differences*, 5th ed. (Houston, TX: Gulf Publishing, 2010); and J. Hooker, *Working across Cultures* (Stanford, CA: Stanford Business Books, 2003).

Many believe that the quickest way to build *guanxi* relationships is through tendering favors. Gift-giving, entertainment at lavish banquets, questionable payments, and overseas trips are common. While Westerners see this as nothing short of bribery, the Chinese consider it essential for good business. Another common method for outsiders to acquire *guanxi* is by hiring local intermediaries, who use their connections to create contacts with Chinese officials and businesspeople.

In dealing with the Chinese, you must realize they are a collective society in which people pride themselves on being a member of a group. For this reason, you should never single out a Chinese for specific praise because this is likely to embarrass the individual in front of his peers. At the same time, you should avoid the use of "I" because it conveys that the speaker is drawing attention to himself or herself.

Chinese do not appreciate loud, boisterous behavior, and when speaking to each other they maintain a greater physical distance than is typical in America. Other cautions include the following:

1. Once the Chinese decide who and what is best, they tend to stick to their decisions. So while they may be slow in formulating a plan, once they get started they make good progress.
2. Reciprocity is important in negotiations. If Chinese give concessions, they expect some in return.
3. The Chinese tend to be less animated than Americans. They avoid open displays of affection and physical contact; they are more reticent and reserved than Americans.
4. The Chinese place less value on the significance of time and often get Americans to concede concessions by stalling.
5. In Confucian societies those in position of power and authority are obligated to assist the disadvantaged. In return they gain face and a good reputation.[7]

For more insights on Chinese culture see the Snapshot from Practice: Project Management X-Files.

Working in the United States

In the world of international projects, professionals from other countries will come to the United States to manage projects. To them, the United States is a foreign assignment. They will have to adapt their management style to the new environment they find in the States.

Immigration has made the United States a melting pot of diverse cultures. While many are quick to point out the differences between North and South, Silicon Valley and Wall Street, social anthropologists have identified certain cultural characteristics that shape how many Americans conduct business and manage projects.

Mainstream Americans are motivated by achievement and accomplishment. Their identity and, to a certain extent, their self-worth are measured by what they have achieved. Foreigners are often astounded by the material wealth accumulated by Americans and the modern conveniences most Americans enjoy. They are also quick to point out that Americans appear too busy to truly enjoy what they have achieved.

[7] Adapted from J. L. Graham and N. M. Lam, "The Chinese Negotiation," *Harvard Business Review,* October 1, 2003, pp. 82–91; I. Yeung and R. L. Tung, "Achieving Business Success in Confucian Societies: The Importance of Guanxi (Connections)," *Organizational Dynamics,* 25 (2) Autumn 1996, pp. 54–65; and Hooker, *Working across Cultures.*

SNAPSHOT FROM PRACTICE Project Management X-Files

Americans tend to discount the significance of luck and believe that good fortune is generally a result of hard work. In other cultures, luck takes on greater significance and has supernatural ramifications. For example, in many Asian cultures certain numbers are considered lucky, while others are unlucky. In Hong Kong the numbers 7, 3, and especially 8 (which sounds like the word for prosperity) are considered lucky, while the number 4 is considered unlucky (because it is pronounced like the word "death"). Hong Kong businesspeople go to great lengths to avoid the number 4. For example, there is no fourth floor in office and hotel buildings. Business executives have been known to reject ideal sites in heavily congested Hong Kong because the address would contain the number 4. They pay premium prices for suitable sites containing addresses with the lucky numbers. Likewise, Hong Kong business managers avoid scheduling important events on the fourth day of each month and prefer to arrange critical meetings on the eighth day.

Hong Kong is also a place where the ancient art of *Feng shui* (literally "wind water") is practiced. This involves making sure a site and buildings are aligned in harmony with the earth's energy forces so that the location will be propitious. Feng shui practitioners are often called in on construction projects to make sure that the building is aligned correctly on the site. In some cases, the technical design of the building is changed to conform to the recommendations of such experts. Similarly, Feng shui experts have been known to be called in when projects are experiencing problems. Their recommendations may include repositioning the project manager's desk or hanging up mirrors to deflect the flow of unharmonious influences away from the building or site of the project.

© Rob Brimson/Taxi/Getty Images

In cultures where luck is believed to play a role in business, people who discount luck may not only insult the luck seekers, they may risk being thought negligent in not paying enough attention to what is viewed as a legitimate business concern.

Americans tend to idolize the self-made person who rises from poverty and adversity to become rich and successful. Most Americans have a strong belief that they can influence and create their future, that with hard work and initiative, they can achieve whatever they set out to do. Self-determination and pragmatism dominate their approach to business.

Although Americans like to set precise objectives, they view planning as a means and not an end. They value flexibility and are willing to deviate from plans and improvise if they believe change will lead to accomplishment. Obstacles on a project are to be overcome, not worked around. Americans think they can accomplish just about anything, given time, money, and technology.

Americans fought a revolution and subsequent wars to preserve their concept of democracy, so they resent too much control or interference, especially by governments. While more an ideal than practice, there is deep-rooted belief in

American management philosophy that those people who will be affected by decisions should be involved in making decisions. Many foreign businesspeople are surprised at the amount of autonomy and decision-making authority granted to subordinates. Foreign personnel have to learn to interact with American professionals below their rank in their own organizations.

Businesspeople from different African, Asian, and Latin American countries are amazed and often somewhat distressed at the rapid pace of America. "Getting things done" is an American characteristic. Americans are very time-conscious and efficient. They expect meetings to start on time. They tinker with gadgets and technological systems, always searching for easier, better, more efficient ways of accomplishing things. American professionals are often relentless in pursuing project objectives and expect that behavior of others also.

Americans in play or business generally are quite competitive, reflecting their desire to achieve and succeed. Although the American culture contains contradictory messages about the importance of success (i.e., "It's not whether you win or lose but how you play the game" versus "nice guys finish last"), winning and being number one are clearly valued in American society. Foreigners are often surprised at how aggressively Americans approach business with adversarial attitudes toward competitors and a desire to not just meet but to exceed project goals and objectives.

Other guidelines and cautions for working with Americans on projects include:

1. More than half of U.S. women work outside the home; females have considerable opportunity for personal and professional growth, guaranteed by law. It is not uncommon to find women in key project positions. Female professionals expect to be treated as equals. Behavior tolerated in other countries would be subject to harassment laws in the States.
2. In the United States, gifts are rarely brought by visitors in a business situation.
3. Americans tend to be quite friendly and open when first meeting someone. Foreigners often mistake this strong "come-on" for the beginning of a strong reciprocal friendship. This is in contrast to many other cultures where there is more initial reserve in interpersonal relations, especially with strangers. For many foreigners, the American comes on too strong, too soon, and then fails to follow up with the implicitly promised friendship.
4. Although in comparison to the rest of the world Americans tend to be informal in greeting and dress, they are a noncontact culture (e.g., they avoid embracing in public usually) and Americans maintain certain physical/psychological distance with others (e.g., about two feet) in conversations.
5. American decision making is results oriented. Decisions tend to be based on facts and expected outcomes, not social impact.[8]

Summary Comments about Working in Different Cultures

These briefings underscore the complexity of working on international projects. It is common practice to rely on intermediaries—often natives who are foreign educated—to bridge the gap between cultures. These intermediaries perform a variety of functions. They act as translators. They use their social connections to

[8] Adapted from Moran et al., *Managing Cultural Differences;* and D. Z. Milosevic, "Echoes of the Silent Language of Project Management," *Project Management Journal,* 30 (1) March 1999, pp. 27–39.

SNAPSHOT FROM PRACTICE Dealing with Customs

Will corruption influence the project? Bribes are illegal in the United States, but in some countries they are the usual way to do business. For example, one American project manager in a foreign country requested that a shipment of critical project equipment be sent "overnight rush." Two days later, inquiries to the sender confirmed the materials had been delivered to the nearby airport. Further inquiries to the port found the shipment "waiting to pass customs." Locals quickly informed the American that money paid to the chief customs inspector would expedite clearance. The American project manager's response was, "I will not be held hostage. Bribes are illegal!" Two more days of calling government officials did not move the shipment from customs. The manager related his problem to a friendly businessman of the host nation at a social affair. The local businessman said he would see if he could help. The shipment arrived the next morning at 10:00 A.M. The American called his local business friend and thanked him profusely. "I owe you one." "No," replied the local. "You owe me a $50 dinner when I visit you in the States." The use of an intermediary in such situations may be the only avenue available to a manager to reduce the stress and personal conflict with the U.S. value system.

expedite transactions and protect the project against undue interference. They are used to sidestep the touchy bribery/gift dilemma (see the Dealing with Customs Snapshot from Practice). They serve as cultural guides, helping outsiders understand and interpret the foreign culture. In today's world, there are a growing number of consulting firms that perform these functions by helping foreign clients work on projects in their country.

The international briefings also highlight the importance of project managers doing their homework and becoming familiar with the customs and habits of the host country they are going to be working in. As far as possible, the project should be managed in such a way that local-country norms and customs are honored. However, there are limits to the extent to which you should accommodate foreign cultures. *Going native* is generally not an alternative. After all, it took a Russian his entire life to learn how to be a Russian. It would be foolish to think an outsider could learn to be one in six months, two years, or perhaps ever.

The remainder of this chapter focuses on the selection and training of project personnel for international projects. But before these issues are discussed, this section concludes with a discussion of the phenomenon of culture shock, which can have a profound effect on a foreigner's performance on a project in a strange culture.

Culture Shock

> My first few weeks in Chiang Mai [Thailand] were filled with excitement. I was excited about the challenge of building a waste treatment plant in a foreign country. I was fascinated with Thai customs and traditions, the smells and sights of the night market. Soon I noticed a distinct change in my attitude and behavior. I started having problems sleeping and lacked energy. I became irritable at work, frustrated by how long things took to accomplish, and how I couldn't seem to get anything accomplished. I started staying up late at night watching CNN in my hotel room.

This engineer is experiencing what many would call "culture shock." *Culture shock* is a natural psychological disorientation that most people suffer when they move

FIGURE 15.6
Culture Shock Cycle

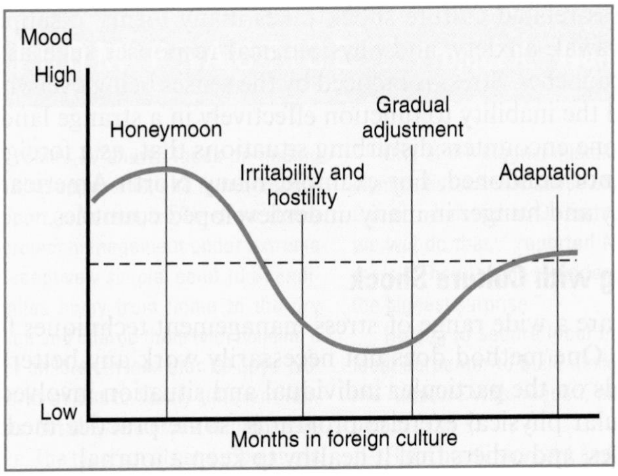

into a culture different from their own. The culture shock cycle has four stages (see Figure 15.6):

1. *Honeymoon*—You start your overseas assignment with a sense of excitement. The new and the unusual are welcomed. At first it is amusing not to understand or be understood. Soon a sense of frustration begins to set in.
2. *Irritability and hostility*—Your initial enthusiasm is exhausted, and you begin to notice that differences are greater than you first imagined. You become frustrated by your inability to get things done as you are accustomed to. You begin to lose confidence in your abilities to communicate and work effectively in the different culture.
3. *Gradual adjustment*—You begin to overcome your sense of isolation and figure out how to get things done in the new culture. You acquire a new perspective of what is possible and regain confidence in your ability to work in the culture.
4. *Adaptation*—You recover from your sense of psychological disorientation and begin to function and communicate in the new culture.

Culture shock is not a disease but a natural response to immersing yourself in a new environment. Culture shock results from a breakdown in your selective perception and effective interpretation system. At a subliminal level, your senses are being bombarded by a wide variety of strange sounds, sights, and smells. At the same time, the normal assumptions you are accustomed to using in your home culture to interpret perceptions and to communicate intentions no longer apply. When this happens, whether in a business context or in normal attempts to socialize, confusion and frustration set in. The natives' behavior does not seem to make sense, and, even more importantly, your behavior does not produce expected results. Frustration occurs because you are used to being competent in such situations and now find you are unable to operate effectively.

Culture shock is generally considered a positive sign that the professional is becoming involved in the new culture instead of remaining isolated in an expatriate ghetto. The significant question is how best to manage culture shock, not how to avoid it. The key appears to be managing the stress associated with culture shock.

selection of personnel for international projects. Organizations examine a number of characteristics to determine whether an individual is suitable for overseas work. They may look for work experience with cultures other than one's own, previous overseas travel, good physical and emotional health, a knowledge of a host nation's language, and even recent immigration background or heritage. Prospective candidates and their family members are often interviewed by trained psychologists, who assess their ability to adapt and function in the new culture.

While there is growing appreciation for screening people for foreign assignments, the number one reason for selection is that the personnel assigned are the best people available for the technical challenges of the project (Mendenhall et al., 1987). Technical know-how takes precedence over cross-cultural sensitivity or experience. As a consequence, training is critical to fill in the cultural gaps and prepare individuals to work in a foreign land.

Training varies widely, depending on the individual, company, nature of the project, and cultures to work with. Project professionals assigned to foreign countries should have a minimal understanding of the following areas:

- Religion.
- Dress codes.
- Education system.
- Holidays—national and religious.
- Daily eating patterns.
- Family life.
- Business protocols.
- Social etiquette.
- Equal opportunity.

An example of a short-term training program is the one developed by Underwriter Laboratories, Inc., to train staff who travel to Japan to work with clients on projects. The program is designed around a series of mini-lectures that cover topics ranging from how to handle introductions to the proper way to exchange gifts to the correct way of interpreting Japanese social and business behavior. The two-day program consists of lectures, case studies, role plays, language practice, and a short test on cultural terminology; it concludes with a 90-minute question-and-answer period. At the end of the program, participants have a fundamental understanding of how to communicate with the Japanese. More importantly, they know the types of information they lack and how to go about learning more to become effective intercultural communicators.

Other training programs are more extensive. For example, Peace Corps volunteers undergo an intense two- to four-month training program in their country of service. The training includes classes on the history and traditions of the country, intensive language instruction, and cross-cultural training as well as home-stays with local families. Many companies outsource training to one of the many firms specializing in overseas and intercultural training.

Figure 15.7 attempts to link the length and type of training with the cultural fluency required to successfully complete the project. Three different learning approaches are highlighted (Mendenhall et al., 1987):

1. The "information-giving" approach—the learning of information or skills from a lecture-type orientation.

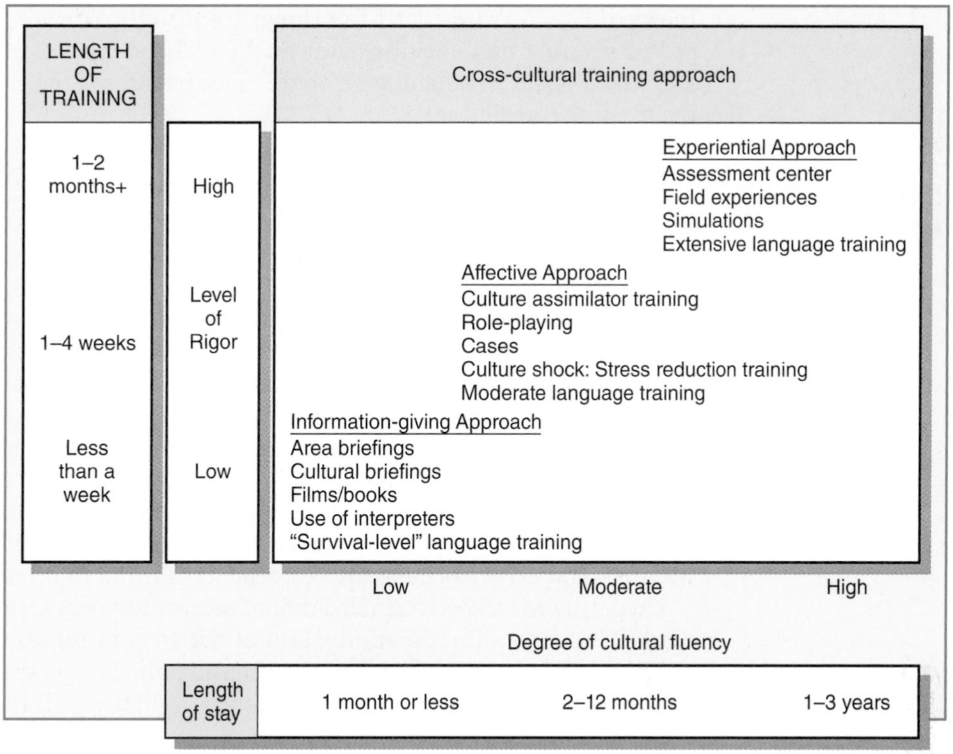

FIGURE 15.7
Relationship between Length and Rigor of Training and Cultural Fluency Required

2. The "affective" approach—the learning of information/skills that raise the affective responses on the part of the trainee and result in cultural insights.
3. The "behavioral/experiential" approach—variant of the affective approach technique that provides the trainee with realistic simulations or scenarios.

According to this framework, the length and level of training would depend on the degree of cultural fluency required to be successful. In general, the longer the person is expected to work in the foreign country, the more intensive the training should be. Length of stay should not be the only consideration; high levels of cultural fluency, and therefore more extensive training, may be required to perform short-term, intense projects. In addition, location is important. Working in Australia will likely require less cultural fluency than working on a project in Pakistan.

While English is rapidly becoming the international language for business in many parts of the world, you should not underestimate the value of being able to speak the language of the host country. At a minimum you should be able to exchange basic pleasantries in the native tongue. Most foreigners consider this a sign of respect, and even if you stumble they appreciate the effort.

In many situations translators are used to facilitate communication. While time-consuming, this is the only way to communicate with non-English-speaking personnel. Be careful in the selection of translators, and do not just assume they are competent. For example, one of the authors enlisted the help of a Polish translator to conduct a meeting with some Polish managers. After the meeting the translator, who taught English at a local university, asked if the author "had good time." I responded that I felt things went well. The translator repeated her question.

Puzzled, I reaffirmed that I felt things went well. After the interchange was repeated several times, the translator finally grabbed my wrist, pointed at my watch, and asked again if I "had good time?" Doubts arose concerning the accuracy of the meeting translation!

Summary

The number of international projects continues to increase, and nothing on the horizon suggests things will change in the new millennium. More and more project managers will be needed to implement international projects. There are few guidelines for the fledgling international project manager. Preparing for international projects can be enhanced through training. As a general background, potential international project managers can benefit from a basic international business course that sensitizes them to the forces of change in the global economy and to cultural differences. Learning a foreign language is also strongly recommended.

Further training specific to the host country is a very useful preproject endeavor. The length and type of training usually depend on the duration of the project manager's assignment. Review Figure 15.7. Still, self-learning, on-the-job training, and experience are the best teachers for international project managers.

Preparing for a specific international project requires serious preproject homework. Understanding the motivation of the firm in selecting the project and its site provides important insights. What basic political, geographic, economic, and infrastructure factors were key considerations? How will they impact the implementation of the project?

Finally, preparation and understanding the cultural differences of the host country go a long way toward making positive first impressions with the nationals and managing the project. International projects have distinct personalities. All people are not the same. Differences within and among countries and cultures are numerous and complex. Project managers need to accept these differences and treat them as real—or live with the consequences. What works at home may not work in the foreign country. Americans are regarded as friendly by our neighbors in the global village, but Americans are also noted to be insensitive to differences in local cultures and customs and awkward in our use of languages other than English. Although most attention in foreign projects is focused on technical efforts and their cost, the project must be carried out within the environment of the country's social customs, work practices, government controls, and religious beliefs. In most cultures, sincerity and flexibility will pay off.

Key Terms

Cross-cultural orientations *550*
Culture *545*
Culture shock *561*
Infrastructure *544*

Review Questions

1. How do environmental factors affect project implementation?
2. What role do local intermediaries play in helping an outsider complete a project?
3. Why is it important to honor the customs and traditions of a country when working on an international project?

4. What is culture shock? What can you do to reduce the negative effects of culture shock?
5. How should you go about preparing yourself for an international project?

Exercises

1. Interview someone who has worked or lived in a foreign country for more than six months.
   a. What was his experience with culture shock?
   b. What did he learn about the culture of the country he lived in?
   c. What advice would he give to someone who would be working on a project in that country?
2. Try as best you can to apply the Kluckhohn-Strodtbeck cross-cultural framework to the four countries discussed in this chapter: Mexico, France, Saudi Arabia, and China. Where do you think these countries lie on each of the cultural issues?
3. Place in order the following countries in terms of what you would think would be the least to most corrupt:

   United States, Denmark, Saudi Arabia, Russia, Australia, Hong Kong, Nepal, China, Kenya, Indonesia, Botswana, Greece, Chile.

   Use an Internet search engine to find the most recent International Corruptions Perceptions Index (CPI) released by the Berlin-based organization Transparency International.
   a. Check your predictions with the Index.
   b. How well did you do? What countries surprised you? Why?
4. Safety is a major concern when working on projects abroad. Select a country that you would consider dangerous to work in and look up the travel advisory provided for that country by the U.S. State Department (http://travel.state.gov/). How safe is it to work in that country?

References

Ackoff, R. L., *Ackoff's Fables: Irreverent Reflections on Business and Bureaucracy* (New York: Wiley, 1991), p. 221.

Adler, N., and A. Gunderson, *International Dimensions of Organizational Behavior,* 5th ed. (Mason, OH: Thomson Publishing, 2007).

Arms, P. B. and E, Lucas, "How do Foreign Clients Really See American Project Managers?," *Proceedings of the 1978 Annual Seminar/Symposium on Project Management* (Newtown, PA: Project Management Institute, 1978), pp. 11K 1–7.

Borsuk, R., "In Indonesia, a Twist on Spreading the Wealth: Decentralization of Power Multiplies Opportunities for Bribery, Corruption," *The Wall Street Journal,* January 29, 2003, p. A16.

Cahill, T., "Deadly Business in Moscow," *Bloomberg Businessweek,* March 1, 2010, pp. 22–23.

Chen, M., and D. Miller, "West Meets East: Toward an Ambicultural Approach to Management," *The Academy of Management Perspectives,* 24 (4) November 2010, pp. 17–24.

Contingency Planning and Management.com, "Strohl Systems Offers Terrorism Readiness Questionnaire," September 24, 2001.

Deneire, M., and M. Segalla, "Mr. Christian Pierret, Secretary of State for Industry (1997–2002), on French Perspectives on Organizational Leadership and Management," *Academy of Management Executive,* 16 (4) November 2002, pp. 25–30.

CHAPTER SIXTEEN

Oversight

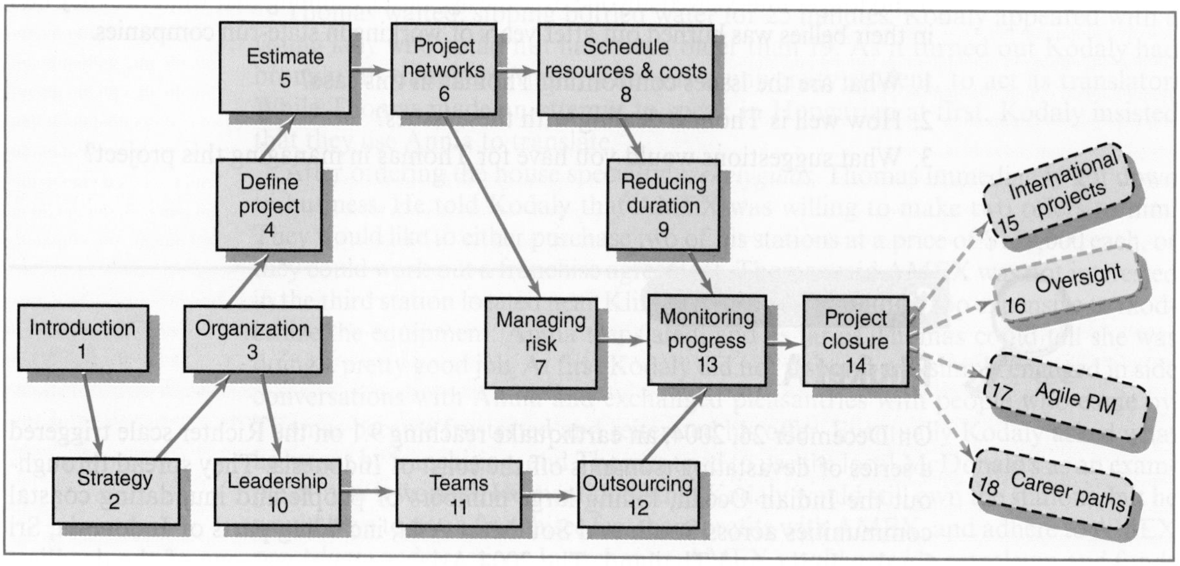

Oversight

Project Oversight

Organization Project Management in the Long Run

Summary

Without continual growth and progress, such words as achievement and success have no meaning.
—Benjamin Franklin

Project Oversight

In the recent years the paradigm shift to project oversight/governance has been profound. **Project oversight** can be defined as *a set of principles and processes to guide and improve the management of projects.* The intent is to ensure projects meet the needs of the *organization* through standards, procedures, accountability, efficient allocation of resources, and continuous improvement in the management of projects. A second purpose is to support the project manager. We estimate over 95 percent of project-driven organizations have been implementing some form of oversight for several years. Progress has been rapid and steady. The typical activities of project oversight cover two dimensions: organization and project. Here are some of the major oversight activities used in practice:

At the Organization Level

- Project selection.
- Portfolio management.
- Improving the way all projects are managed over time.
- Assessing and elevating the maturity level of the organization's project management system.
- Using the balanced scorecard approach to review progress on strategic priorities.

At the Project Level

- Review projects' objectives.
- Decide on issues raised by the project manager such as resource needs and escalation.
- Track and assist the project to resolve bottlenecks.
- Review status reports from the project manager.
- Audit and review lessons learned.
- Authorize any major deviations from the original scope.
- Cancel the project.

All of these activities are designed to bring consistency, structure, accountability, and improvement to the management of projects. Today, project oversight, through an executive committee, oversight team, or a project office, covers every aspect of managing projects in the organization.

Importance of Oversight to the Project Manager

What does this solid paradigm shift mean to a project manager who is normally in charge of only one or two projects? Four things. First, in almost all cases oversight is interested in supporting and helping the project manager where needed. This is an improvement over the past. Second, the oversight function determines the environment in which the project manager will implement his or her project. This can affect the management of a project in a positive or negative manner. Third, depending on the size and complexity of the project, methods used to hold the project manager responsible and accountable will influence how performance is measured. Finally, the project manager, who is responsible for day-to-day management, will probably be reporting to this oversight group at predetermined phases in the project. In short, project oversight supports project management at the organization and project levels.

As a project manager you need to be aware of how these oversight activities can and will influence management of your projects. A short description of two significant organizational oversight structures of these oversight activities follows.

Portfolio Project Management

Portfolio project management is the centralized oversight of projects ensuring that allocation of resources to projects is directed toward projects that contribute the greatest value to organization goals. Portfolio management is becoming more common and important in project organizations. A PMI global survey of over 1,000 project practitioners and leaders over a variety of industries found that 72 percent of high-performing organizations use portfolio management compared to only 39 percent of low performers.[1]

A senior executive oversight committee ensures the project portfolio includes a balance of projects to best utilize the organization's resources and competencies and represent the organization's risk tolerance level. Managing the organization project portfolio includes several key responsibilities:

- Review project options available by type (new, operational, compliance)
- Confirm business case and linkage to organizational strategy
- Select, prioritize, and balance risk of all organizational projects
- Ensure availability of resources
- *Set macro time, cost, and requirements
- *Review gating outcomes (see next section on "Gating")

Bringing these responsibilities of portfolio management under one umbrella provides benefits not available from managing them individually. Some responsibilities of portfolio project management are often delegated to the project management office—especially the last two responsibilities marked with an asterisk.

Project Office

A PMI study found 65 percent of project organizations have a project office.[2] The project office is used as the vehicle to support and manage oversight activities. Here is one definition:

> The *project office (PO)* is the unit responsible for the continued support of consistent application of selection criteria, standards, and processes; training of and general assistance to project managers; and continued improvement and use of best practices.

[1] "PMI's Pulse of the Profession," March 2012, *Project Management Institute Report,* p. 7, www.pmi.org.

[2] Ibid.

SNAPSHOT FROM PRACTICE The Project Office*

As more and more companies embrace project management as a critical vehicle for realizing corporate objectives, they are creating centralized project offices (POs) to oversee and improve the management of projects. PO functions vary widely by organization and need. In some cases, they serve as a simple clearinghouse for project management information. In other cases, they recruit, train, and assign managers to specific projects. As POs mature and evolve over time, they become full-service providers of project management expertise within a firm. The different services POs may provide include the following:

- Creating and maintaining the internal project management information system.
- Recruiting and selecting project managers both within and outside the organization.
- Establishing standardized project planning and reporting methodologies.
- Training personnel in project management techniques and tools.
- Auditing ongoing and recently completed projects.
- Developing comprehensive risk management programs.
- Providing in-house project management consulting and mentoring services.
- Maintaining an internal project management library containing critical documents, including project plans, funding papers, test plans, audit reports, and so forth.
- Establishing and benchmarking best practices in project management.
- Maintaining and tracking the portfolio of projects within an organization.

© Cliff Gray

A good example of how project offices evolve is the global project office (GPO) at Citibank's Global Corporate Bank. GPO originated at the grassroots level within the small world of Operations and Technology for Global Cash Management. Committed to bringing order to the chaos of managing projects, GPO instituted training programs and professional project management practices on a very small scale. Soon the success of GPO-supported projects caught the eye of upper management. Within three years the department was expanded to offer a full range of PO services across Citibank's entire banking operation. GPO's mission is to establish project management as a core competency throughout the entire Citibank organization.

* T. R. Block and J. D. Frame, "Today's Project Office: Gauging Attitudes," *PM Network,* August 2001; W. Gradante and D. Gardner, "Managing Projects from the Future, Not from the Past," *Proceedings of the 29th Annual Project Management Institute 1998 Seminars and Symposium* (Newtown Square, PA: Project Management Institute, 1998), pp. 289–94.

The project office frequently includes project portfolio management. Project portfolios and project offices both result in an integration function for planning and control. The PO also supports the integration of the processes of managing projects within the social/cultural environment of the organization. High-tech firms such as Hewlett-Packard (HP), International Business Machines (IBM), and Dell all use project offices to coordinate projects and to ensure best practices are being used to manage projects.[3] For example, HP has project offices in Europe/Middle East, Americas, Asia Pacific, and Japan with several others planned. Because projects are used to implement strategy, HP has created a new position—vice president of project offices. Project offices ensure a consistent approach to all projects in all locations. See Snapshot from Practice: The Project Office.

[3] D. Kingsberry and Jake Steward, "Implementing a Global Program Management Office," PMI Global Conference, 2003.

FIGURE 16.1 Project Portfolio Cost Summary Report for Top Management

Net Services, Inc. — View: Cost — Project Portfolio Cost Summary ($ 000) — Date:

Gantt · Network · Resource · Status · WBS · Sponsor · Team · Priority · Issues

Location	Project ID	Description	PV	EV	AC	CPI	SPI	PCIB	BAC	EAC	VAC
Summary	All	Portfolio							$18,120		
United States									$10,500		
○	01-003	Digitize Fingerprints-FBI	3,000	3,500	3,230	1.08	1.17	97.2%	3,600	3,322	278
◍	01-011	Encryption	270	250	250	1.00	0.93	71.4%	350	350	0
◍	01-002	Internet Protocol--CIA						0.0%	950		
◍	01-009	Supply Chain Partners	90	90	90	1.00	1.00	16.7%	540	540	0
	01-012	Bonus Mileage Awards						0.0%	630		
●	01-005	E-sales Claims	150	140	150	0.93	0.93	35.0%	400	429	-29
●	01-011	Procurement Net	400	340	380	0.89	0.85	27.6%	1,230	1,375	-145
◍	01-008	Smart Tag Tracking	850	900	900	1.00	1.06	32.1%	2,800	2,800	0
Asia/Pacific									$2,800		
◍	02-007	Currency Conversion	125	120	120	1.00	0.96	80.0%	150	150	0
◍	02-002	Billing System	280	280	280	1.00	1.00	70.0%	400	400	0
○	02-005	Web-Based Cash Flow	210	220	200	1.10	1.05	73.3%	300	273	27
	02-004	Olympic Simulation						0.0%	1,950		
EEC									$4,820		
●	03-008	Smart Card	145	110	140	0.79	0.76	18.3%	600	764	-164
	03-003	Warranty						0.0%	70		
	03-004	Simulation--ESA						0.0%	800		
●	03-005	Air Reservation Net	510	490	520	0.94	0.96	35.0%	1,400	1,486	-86
●	03-007	Pilot Internet Log Syst.	540	490	550	0.89	0.91	57.6%	850	954	-104
◍	03-006	Internet Telephone Syst.	850	850	860	0.99	1.00	77.3%	1,100	1,113	-13

LEGEND
○ Under Budget
◍ On Budget
● Over Budget

Figures 16.1 and 16.2 provide an example of a report the project office provides senior management of an international organization. Note that such a report requires a standard format for all projects. Figure 16.1 depicts a project portfolio cost summary report developed for top management. Figure 16.2 presents the same summary for project schedules. Additional detailed information for any specific highlighted project—such as the project schedule, cost status report, project team—is only a double click away. For example, the Smart Card project in the European Economic Community (EEC) appears to be behind schedule. The cause can be identified by "drilling down" to the project schedule, WBS, resources, or issues. Standard project formats such as these provide a wealth of information in multiproject organizations.

Project offices are known to result in positive benefits such as the following:

- They serve as a bridge between senior management and project managers.
- They support integration of all project management processes from selection through project closure and lessons learned.
- Through training they support the movement of the organization to a higher level of project management maturity.

The growth in the application of portfolio project management and project offices will continue. Portfolio management and project offices strongly influence how a project manager will manage his or her respective project. A more recent oversight activity has been the quick implementation of phase gate reviews.

FIGURE 16.2 **Project Portfolio Schedule Summary Report for Project Schedules**

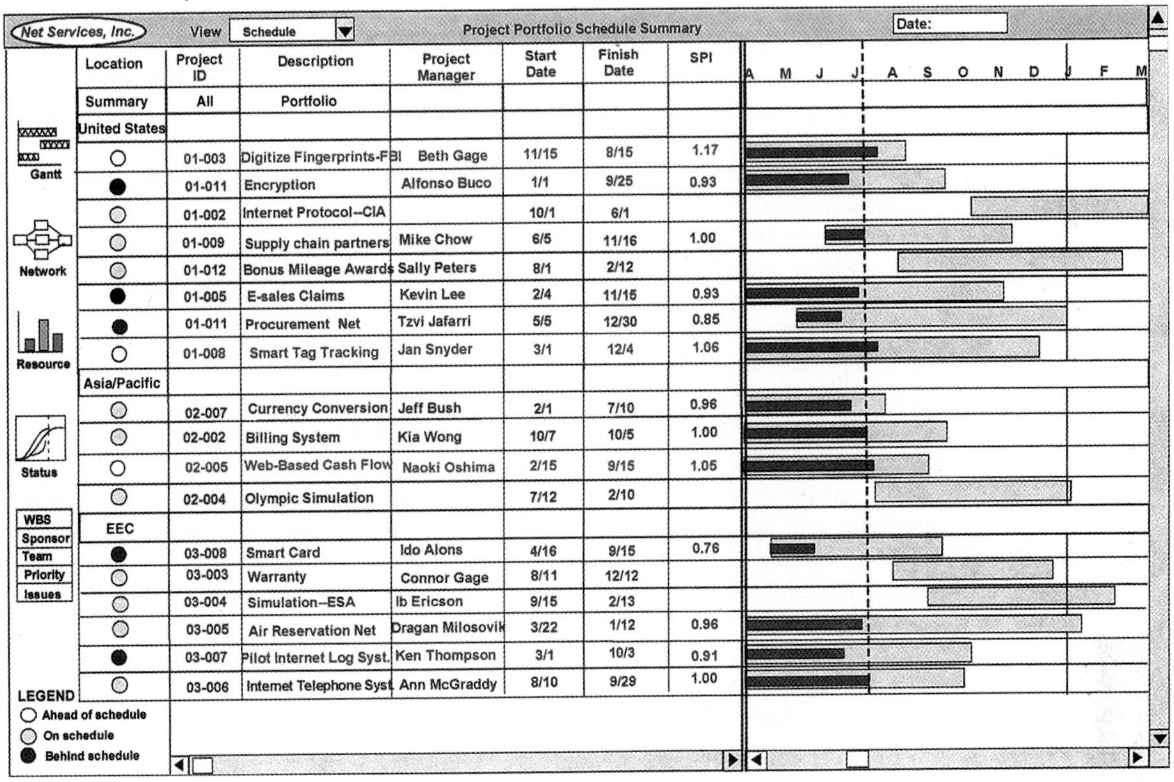

Location	Project ID	Description	Project Manager	Start Date	Finish Date	SPI
Summary	All	Portfolio				
United States						
○	01-003	Digitize Fingerprints-FBI	Beth Gage	11/15	8/15	1.17
●	01-011	Encryption	Alfonso Buco	1/1	9/25	0.93
○	01-002	Internet Protocol--CIA		10/1	6/1	
○	01-009	Supply chain partners	Mike Chow	6/5	11/16	1.00
○	01-012	Bonus Mileage Awards	Sally Peters	8/1	2/12	
●	01-005	E-sales Claims	Kevin Lee	2/4	11/15	0.93
●	01-011	Procurement Net	Tzvi Jafarri	5/5	12/30	0.85
○	01-008	Smart Tag Tracking	Jan Snyder	3/1	12/4	1.06
Asia/Pacific						
○	02-007	Currency Conversion	Jeff Bush	2/1	7/10	0.96
○	02-002	Billing System	Kia Wong	10/7	10/5	1.00
○	02-005	Web-Based Cash Flow	Naoki Oshima	2/15	9/15	1.05
○	02-004	Olympic Simulation		7/12	2/10	
EEC						
●	03-008	Smart Card	Ido Alons	4/16	9/15	0.76
○	03-003	Warranty	Connor Gage	8/11	12/12	
○	03-004	Simulation--ESA	Ib Ericson	9/15	2/13	
○	03-005	Air Reservation Net	Dragan Milosovik	3/22	1/12	0.96
●	03-007	Pilot Internet Log Syst.	Ken Thompson	3/1	10/3	0.91
○	03-006	Internet Telephone Syst	Ann McGraddy	8/10	9/29	1.00

Phase Gate Methodology

Phase gates provide an in-depth review of individual projects at *specific phases* in the project life cycle. These reviews cover assessments to continue or kill the project, reassess resource allocation, reassess prioritization, and evaluate execution progress, as well as strategic alignment decisions. The phase review process serves the organization by having gatekeepers (usually selected from several areas of the firm) perform the review. The phase gate process is also designed to support the project manager on decisions and other issues such as escalation and resource needs. The idea of phase gate methodology fits effortlessly into the oversight function of the project office. Phase gate methodology was originally developed for product development, but the application of the methodology has grown beyond new product development to include all projects in the portfolio. One study by Morris and Jamieson showed 85 percent of those surveyed use phase review gates, while 85 percent who did not thought they should.

The original *Stage-Gate*™ model was pioneered by Robert G. Cooper (2000) several decades ago to improve management of new product development. The original model incorporates five stages: preliminary investigation, detailed investigation, development, testing and validation, and full production and market launch. Stages precede gates and represent information developed to enable gatekeepers to make the right decision at the next gate. These decision points at each gate are known as go, kill, hold, or recycle decisions. Given the information developed for each stage, the gatekeepers (the oversight team) can decide to continue with the project, abort the project, or revise/recycle.

Today, variations of the original model are being used across all industries to help manage project portfolios. These variations are not limited to new product development. The number of stages and gates varies. But the idea of oversight review several times throughout the project life cycle appears in all models. Each gate check will always, at a minimum, check the project against alignment with current strategic goals.

Phase gate methodology has appeal because it provides a clean-cut, structured process that can be consistently applied across all projects in the portfolio. Distinct review stages and go/kill gates comprise this oversight function. The major goals for phase gating are to ensure oversight and support for the project manager and the project team, to direct organization resources toward strategic goals, and to reduce the number of projects that do not support the forward direction of the organization. A multiproject organization having employees spread across many time zones that does not use some form of phase review methodology is rare. For example, companies such as 3M, General Motors, Northern Telecom, DuPont, Intel, Hewlett-Packard, and Dell all use some form of phase gating to manage projects.

The **phase gate** review process can be defined as a *structured process to review, evaluate, and document outcomes in each project phase and to provide management with information to guide resource deployment toward strategic goals.* This oversight activity begins with project selection and tracking the project life cycle through closure and lessons learned. Phase gates need to occur at consistent points in the project life cycle so each project encounters similar gates at predefined authorization points.

The phase review process may appear similar to the project audit discussed in an earlier chapter. Some overlap does occur, but the focus here is more integrated and holistic. Individual projects are reviewed as part of a total portfolio. For example, have strategic priorities changed the importance of the project? If the priorities of the organization have changed, a project that is executing on time, on budget, and meeting the project goals may have to be "killed." Phase review takes place at each phase from project selection through lessons learned as opposed to the audit, which often takes place at the end of the project. Phase gating provides a larger perspective to managing multiple projects in a project portfolio. Gatekeepers first focus on organization needs, with individual project needs second.

Figure 16.3 is a flow diagram of an abridged, generic variation of phase gate methodology that has application across all types of projects. Another practice used during the implementation phase is to create gates at significant milestones.

The decision gates focus on go/kill decisions based on major questions such as those shown in Gates 1 and 2 below. At a minimum each gate should include three components:

1. Required deliverables (e.g., project goals, progress, variances).
2. Gate criteria and specific outputs (e.g., adjusting project scope, schedule).
3. A clear yes/no decision on whether to go ahead.

The criteria for all of the gates during the project are selected *before* the start of the project.

The value of phase gating methods rests firmly on having enough information to support the gate decision. Significant amounts of support data must be gathered to answer critical gate questions. Using the best practices shown in earlier chapters will prepare you to easily answer critical gate questions. Frequent questions from practice for each gate are presented here.

FIGURE 16.3
Abridged Generic Phase Gate Process Diagram

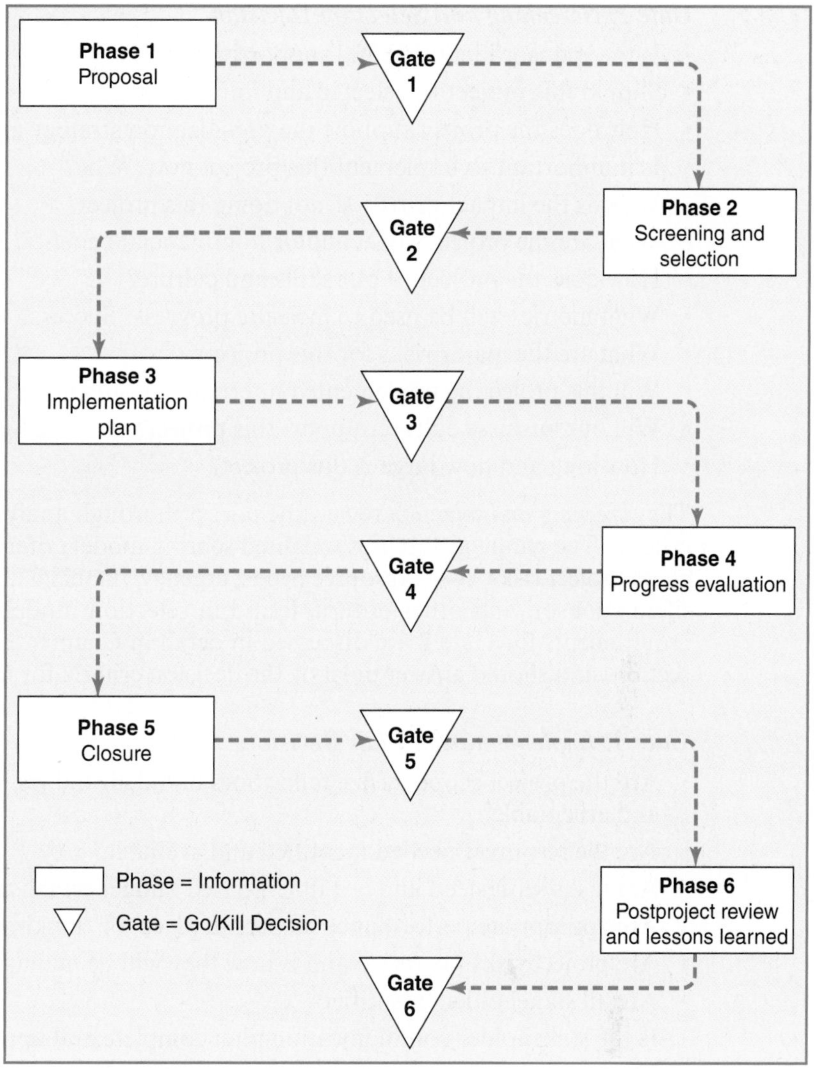

Gate 1: Proposal Decision

- What business problem does the proposed project solve?
- Does this project align with our strategic direction?
- What type of project is this? Strategic, organization maintenance, "must," etc.?
- Should the project be considered?

This *proposal* phase answers a fundamental question: Is the project a good idea and does it solve a business problem or issue? Basically, anyone can propose a project. However, the proposal should provide enough key information to allow an oversight team to decide if the proposal should be considered further. For example, the information might include the business problem the proposed project will solve, the urgency of the project, and clear, relevant project objectives. Gate 1 provides information at a minimal expenditure of cost and resources and in a short time, so the project can be reevaluated more thoroughly if it is perceived to have merits.

Gate 2: Screening and Selection Decision

- Is the sponsor identified and supportive?
- Should this project be selected and implemented?
- How does the project support the organization strategy and goals?
- Is it important to implement this project now? Why?
- What is the impact or risk of not doing this project?
- What are the project's ROI and/or nonfinancial benefits?
- How does the project fit our skills and culture?
- What metrics will be used to measure progress? Success?
- What are the major risks for this project?
- Will this project be implemented internally or outsourced?
- Will our business culture support this project?
- How long and how large is this project?

The *screening and selection* review includes a thorough analysis based on selection criteria. The gating group uses weighted scoring model criteria, which typically include project risks, costs, resource needs, urgency, financial analysis, benefits, identified sponsor, and other criteria found in selection models. Many information requirements for Gate 2 are discussed in detail in Chapter 2 (see project selection section) and should answer most of the decision criteria for this phase review.

Gate 3: Implementation Plan Decision

- Are the project scope, tasks, milestones and deliverables, and gates established and acceptable?
- Are the resources needed identified and available?
- Are tasks sequenced and is a time-phased budget established?
- Are appropriate performance metrics in place for tracking the project?
- Are project risks identified and is how they will be managed clearly stated?
- Are all stakeholders identified?
- Is the stakeholder communication plan complete and appropriate?
- Is a formal change management system in place?
- Are accountability metrics in place and is responsibility assigned?

The *implementation plan* review information should include the planning document developed in earlier chapters. For example, what are the specific goals for the project and what are the major deliverables (scope)? What tasks will be performed to complete the deliverables (WBS)? How are tasks sequenced (network)? When will the tasks be performed (schedule)? What resources are needed to complete the tasks (resource schedule)? What are the estimated costs for the tasks (time-phased budget)? What and how will performance be measured (variance metrics)? How will information be collected and distributed (communication plan)? What and how will project risks be identified and handled (risk plan)? What vendors will be used for procurement?

Gate 4: Progress Evaluation Decision

- Is the project still aligned with business requirements?
- Are activities completed according to the project plan?

- Are the technical requirements of the project being met?
- Are contractors meeting defined performance requirements?
- Are there urgent corrective actions that must be done quickly?
- Are time, costs, and scope performances within acceptable limits?
- Have the project objectives changed?
- What risks can be retired?

Your *progress evaluation* review covers the control activities of tracking progress, identifying variances from your plan, and taking corrective action. A major chunk of the data requirements for the phase review are simply measures against the project plan. Tracking progress and identifying variances against scope, time, budget, and control of changes and identified risks are easily accomplished using available software (see Chapters 7 and 13). For example, if the project is not going according to plan, your risk assessment plan may help you decide an action to be taken. Beyond these quantitative measures, there are always "issues" that deserve attention. Moreover, project priority must be checked against strategy to determine whether this measure is still valid. If not, a change in scope or killing the project may be necessary. Don Kingsberry, director of HP's Global Program Management Office, describes HP's progress phase review succinctly: "We have 42 health checks on current projects. We look at risks, issues, critical path analysis, resource analysis, sponsorship, alignment with strategy, earned value metrics, dependency, and other factors impacting the triple constraints of project management: time, cost, and scope." (See Boyer [2003] for more on HP's efforts.)

Gate 5: Closure

- Did the project deliver the business outcomes? Were the metrics and benefits used to justify the project met?
- Were project scope objectives met?
- Were project cost and schedule met?
- Are contracts closed out?
- Are the end users satisfied?
- Have staff been recognized and reassigned?
- Was the organization culture right for this type of project?
- Was senior management support adequate?
- Were the right people assigned to the project?
- Were project risks identified and assessed realistically?
- Did technology overextend our competencies?
- How will the project be delivered?

The *closure* and lessons learned activities closely follow the closure activities found in the audit chapter. Some organizations have wrapped phases 5 and 6—closure, post project review and lessons learned—into a single gate.

Gate 6: Post Project Review and Lessons Learned

- Have we identified what went wrong and what contributed to success?
- Have changes to improve delivery of future projects been communicated and archived?
- Has an owner of each retrospective been identified?

SNAPSHOT FROM PRACTICE Phase Gate Side Benefits

One manager from a high-tech firm related to your authors that "phase-gating is the best thing that has ever happened to [his] firm—better than apple pie. We rotate middle managers to serve on the project oversight committee to give them as much exposure as possible." Serving on the oversight committee has great rewards for the organization and individual. The following relates the core of his conversation:

First, the process itself gets everyone on the same menu. Everyone is constantly reminded of the strategic vision of the firm and how the project supports the vision. Second, serving on a review or oversight committee provides a more holistic insight that creates more understanding and tolerance of changes that need to occur. Serving on the oversight committee is the cheapest, most rewarding training vehicle we have ever had. Best of all, the training lasts and the learned holistic view is transferred to others. The cost of serving on the oversight committee is near zero. Members are more likely to support and help see a project through to a speedy, successful completion. Next, using the phased approach limits scope creep, which has been a constant issue in all our projects. Finally, the bottom line is that the number of useless projects has practically disappeared—pet projects are out in the open, resources are used more efficiently, and most projects come in on time and within budget. Phase gating has changed the whole culture of our firm and the way projects are managed.

- What hindered or contributed to delivering the expected ROI or business outcomes?
- Can others learn from this experience?
- What changes in scope or quality were made?
- Who will be responsible for archiving the lessons learned?

The questions shown above for each phase only touch the surface of those found in practice. Some are formalized, others very porous and less structured, but all phase review models are designed to check management of a project from selection to lessons learned. Key benefits of using phase gating are:

- Provides excellent training for functional staff who serve on oversight review groups.
- Encourages a larger perspective and role of projects within the organization.
- Is a clear-cut process, easily understood, and applicable to all projects in a portfolio.
- Provides a structured process for a project office to follow on all projects.
- Eliminates poor value projects.
- Supports faster decision making with predefined deliverables for each gate.

See Snapshot from Practice: Phase Gate Side Benefits for a project manager's opinion on the benefits of phase gating.

Another key oversight function is benchmarking your project management maturity against others in your industry.

Organization Project Management in the Long Run

Organization Project Management Maturity

Individual audits and phase gate reviews can yield valuable lessons that team members can apply to future project work. A more encompassing look, from an organizationwide point of view, uses a project maturity model that strives for a never-ending goal to continuously improve the management of projects. It is well established that project-driven companies with higher maturity levels are more successful in managing projects than those lacking project maturity programs. Project maturity has become a competitive edge. Companies are increasingly using outsourcing or external contractors and RFPs (Request for proposals) to look for contractors that have reached high maturity levels. Harold Kerzner, a project management consultant and professor, eloquently states why a company should pursue maturity:

> Given the fact that many executives today view their company as a stream of projects, project management permeates the entire organization, mandating that maturity is necessary. So only those companies that want to stay in business and remain competitive should pursue maturity. The alternative is rather unpleasant. (Quoted in Mueller, 2005)

The purposes of all maturity models, and many are available, are to enable organizations to assess their progress in implementing the best practices in their industry and continuously move to improvement. It is important to understand that the model does not ensure success; it serves only as a measuring stick and an indicator of progress.

The term *maturity model* was coined in the late 1980s from a research study by the United States government and the Software Engineering Institute (SEI) at Carnegie Mellon University. The government wanted a tool to predict successful software development by contractors. The outcome of this research was the Capability Maturity Model (CMMI). The model focuses on guiding and assessing organizations in implementing concrete best practices of managing software development projects. Since its development, the model is used across all industries.

CMMI was retired and in 2004 replaced with, the Project Management Institute (PMI) version of the Organizational Project Management Maturity Model. The latest version is called OPM3 (See *www.pmi.org/opm3*). Typically, these models are divided into a continuum of growth layers: initial, repeatable, defined, managed, and optimized. Figure 16.4 presents our version, which borrows liberally from other models.

FIGURE 16.4
Project Management Maturity Model

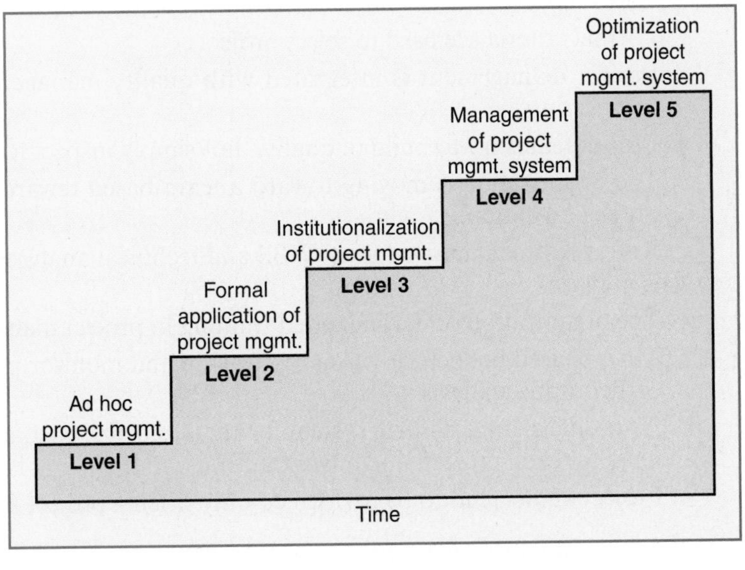

Level 1: Ad Hoc Project Management No consistent project management process is in place. How a project is managed depends upon the individuals involved. Characteristics of this level include:

- No formal project selection system exists—projects are done because people decide to use them or because a high-ranking manager orders them done.
- How any one project is managed varies by individual and thus is unpredictable.
- No investment is made in project management training.
- Working on projects is a struggle because it goes against the grain of established policies and procedures.

Level 2: Formal Application of Project Management The organization applies established project management procedures and techniques. This level is often marked by tension between project managers and line managers who need to redefine their roles. Features of this level include:

- Standard approaches to managing projects, including scope statements, WBS, and activity lists, are used.
- Quality emphasis is on the product or outcome of the project and is inspected instead of built in.
- The organization is moving in the direction of a stronger matrix with project managers and line managers working out their respective roles.
- Recognition of the need for cost control, not just scope and time management, is growing.
- No formal project priority selection system is established.
- Limited training in project management is provided.

Level 3: Institutionalization of Project Management An organizationwide project management system, tailored to specific needs of the organization with the flexibility to adapt the process to unique characteristics of the project, is established. Characteristics of this level include:

- An established process for managing projects is evident by planning templates, status report systems, and checklists for each stage of the project life cycle.
- Formal criteria are used to select projects.
- Project management is integrated with quality management and concurrent engineering.
- Project teams try to build in quality, not simply inspect it.
- The organization is moving toward a team-based reward system to recognize project execution.
- Risk assessment derived from WBS and technical analyses and customer input is in place.
- The organization offers expanded training in project management.
- Time-phased budgets are used to measure and monitor performance based on earned value analysis.
- A specific change control system for requirements, cost, and schedule is developed for each project, and a work authorization system is in place.
- Project audits tend to be performed only when a project fails.

Level 4: Management of Project Management System The organization develops a system for managing multiple projects that are aligned with strategic goals of the organization. Characteristics of this level include:

- Portfolio project management is practiced; projects are selected based on resource capacity and contribution to strategic goals.
- A project priority system is established.
- Project work is integrated with ongoing operations.
- Quality improvement initiatives are designed to improve both the quality of the project management process and the quality of specific products and services.
- Benchmarking is used to identify opportunities for improvement.
- The organization has established a Project Management Office or Center for Excellence.
- Project audits are performed on all significant projects and lessons learned are recorded and used on subsequent projects.
- An integrative information system is established for tracking resource usage and performance of all significant projects.

Level 5: Optimization of Project Management System The focus is on continuous improvement through incremental advancements of existing practices and by innovations using new technologies and methods. Features include:

- A project management information system is fine-tuned; specific and aggregate information is provided to different stakeholders.
- An informal culture that values improvement drives the organization, not policies and procedures.
- There is greater flexibility in adapting the project management process to demands of a specific project.

Progress from one level to the next will not occur overnight. The Software Engineering Institute estimates the following median times for movement:

- Maturity level 1 to 2 is 22 months.
- Maturity level 2 to 3 is 29 months.
- Maturity level 3 to 4 is 25 months.
- Maturity level 4 to 5 is 13 months.

Why does it take so long? One reason is simply organizational inertia. It is difficult for social organizations to institute significant changes while at the same time maintaining business efficacy. "How do we find time to change when we are so busy just keeping our heads above water?"

A second significant reason is that one cannot leapfrog past any one level. Just as a child cannot avoid the trials and tribulations of being a teenager, people within an organization have to work through the unique challenges and problems of each level to get to the next level. Learning of this magnitude naturally takes time and cannot be avoided by using quick fixes or simple remedies.

Our best-guess estimates are that most companies are in the throes of moving from level 2 to level 3 and that fewer than 10 percent of those firms that actively practice project management are at either level 4 or 5. Remember, project maturity is not an end; project maturity is a never-ending process of continuous improvement. An additional view of the success of the projects you have selected over time is discussed next.

The Balanced Scorecard Model

Project priority selection models select which actions (projects) best support organizational strategy. The balanced scorecard model differs from selection models by reviewing projects over a longer horizon—5 to 10 years after the project is implemented. It is more "macro" in perspective than project selection models. This model measures the results of major activities taken to support the overall vision, mission, and goals of the organization. It helps answer two questions: Did we select the right projects? Did the projects contribute to long-range strategic direction of the firm? American Express, the U.S. Department of Transportation, ExxonMobil, Kaiser Permanente, National Semiconductor, and others are known to be using their own customized models of the balanced scorecard. (See Kaplan and Norton, 1992.)

The scorecard model limits measures of performance to goals in four main areas: *customer, internal, innovation and learning,* and *financial measures.* For example, a performance measure for a customer might be industry ranking for sales, quality, or on-time projects. Internal measures that influence employees' actions could mean time to market or reduction of design time to final product. Innovation and learning measures frequently deal with process and product innovation and improvement. For example, the percentage of sales or profit from new products is often used as a performance goal and measure. Project improvement savings from partnering agreements are another example of an innovation and learning measure. Finally, financial measures such as ROI, cash flow, and projects on budget reflect improvement and actions that contribute value to the bottom line.

These four perspectives and performance measures keep vision and strategy at the forefront of employees' actions. The basic assumption underlying the balanced scorecard model is that people will take the necessary actions to improve the performance of the organization on the given measures and goals. The balanced scorecard model and priority selection models should never conflict with each other. If a conflict exists, both models should be reviewed and conflicts eliminated. When both models are used in project-driven organizations, focus on vision, strategy, and implementation are reinforced. Both models encourage employees to determine the actions needed to improve performance.

Summary

Oversight practices are directed to improving the way the organization manages all projects. Oversight or governance in multiproject organizations supports the trend of integration over the last three decades. Centralization of project management activities became imperative as projects became more numerous and became the means to implement organization strategy. Project portfolios and project offices serve to gain centralized control over all projects in the organization. The multiproject environment also assists as an impetus for phase gate checks at several points over the project life cycle. Benchmarking your project management maturity quickly surfaced as large organizations realized the amount of organization resources devoted to projects and the importance of projects to meeting competition. The need for assessing the long-run value of selected projects over several years continues to increase each year. The balance score card methodology appears to be meeting this need. Succinctly, the major goals of project oversight are to ensure the effective allocation of organization resources and to improve the management of projects. Oversight activities continue to be adopted by most organizations participating in the global economy. Oversight activities are not limited to only large organizations; oversight activities continue to move down the size ladder to smaller organizations where successful project management can be a significant competitive edge.

How projects are managed in your organization will depend heavily on the level of project oversight and maturity. As oversight continues to evolve, you will need to view your job as a project manager from a broader, top-down view of project management in your organization and even in the total field of project management.

Key Terms

Balanced scorecard, *586*
Oversight, *573*
Phase gating, *578*
Portfolio management, *574*
Project management maturity, *582*
Project office (PO), *575*

Review Questions

1. What are the major economic forces that serve as an impetus for using oversight/governance tools and processes?
2. The Super Web Design president asked you to justify present and future oversight activities. Answer her request.
3. What are the three major advantages to an organization using a maturity model?
4. "We aren't big enough to have a project office, but we need the discipline of project management methods and standards." What advice would you give the CEO of this organization? Justify.
5. Explain to a fellow student the major benefits of project management oversight to the organization.

Exercise

1. Reread the "Day in a Life" case in Chapter 1. How would you assess her effectiveness now that you have studied project management? What part of Rachel's experience contributes to her success?

References

Archibald, Russell D., "The Interfaces between Strategic Management of an Enterprise and Project Portfolio Management within the Enterprise," *Proceedings of 22nd IPMA World Congress,* "Project Management to Run," Rome, Italy, November 2008, pp. 9–11.

Archibald, Russell D., "Five Decades of Modern Project Management: Where It Came From—Where It's Going," *PM World Today,* Vol. XI, Issue X, October 2009.

Baker, B., "The Nominees Are . . . ," *PM Network,* Vol. 18, No. 6, June 2004, p. 23.

Boyer, C., "Make Profit Your Priority," *PM Network,* Vol. 17, No. 10, October 2003, p. 40.

Cooper, R. G., *Product Leadership: Creating and Launching Superior New Products* (Cambridge, MA: Perseus Publishing, 2000).

Cooper, R. G., S. J. Edgett, and E. J. Kleinschmidt, *Portfolio Management for New Products* (Reading, MA: Addison-Wesley, 1998).

Ibbs, C. W., and Y. H. Kwak, "Assessing Project Maturity," *Project Management Journal,* Vol. 31, No. 1, March 2000, pp. 32–43.

Jafari, Ali, "Bridging the Gap," *The Project Manager (The Magazine of the Australian Institute of Project Management),* Vol. 29, No. 4, June/July 2010, pp. 24–26.

Kaplan, R. S., and D. Norton, "The Balanced Scorecard—Measures that Drive Performance," *Harvard Business Review,* January–February 1992, pp. 73–79. Note: A CD simulation is available from Harvard Customer Service, Product 8387. This interactive simulation provides hands-on experience for learning more about the method.

Morris, P. W., and A. Jamieson, "Moving from Corporate Strategy to Project Strategy," *Project Management Journal,* Vol. 36, No. 4, December 2005, pp. 5–18.

Mueller, E., "Maturity, Do or Die?" *PM Network,* Vol. 20, No. 2, February 2006, p. 32.

Norrie, J., and D. H. T. Walker, "A Balanced Scorecard Approach to Project Management Leadership," *Project Management Journal,* Vol. 35, No. 4, December 2004, pp. 47–56. "Pull the Plug," *PM Network,* Vol. 20, No. 6, June 2006, pp. 39–42.

PMI Report, "PMI's Pulse of the Profession," March 2012, Project Management Institute, p. 7.

Rover, I., "Why Bad Projects Are So Hard to Kill," *Harvard Business Review,* February 2003, pp. 49–56.

Stewart, W. E., "Balanced Scorecard for Projects," *Project Management Journal,* Vol. 32, No. 1, March 2001, pp. 38–47. (2000 International Student Paper Award Winner.)

Case

Don't Tell Me What You Have Done. Tell Me What You Are Going to Do

The firm has been merged with a larger firm carrying a similar product line of information technology consumer and industry products. One major goal of the merger was to save costs by eliminating duplication and improving management. Weeks before the merger, Lauren (not her real name) had just been promoted to project office director of the smaller firm. She assumed her position would be absorbed into the project office of the large firm. Mentally, Lauren was prepared to start job hunting. Maybe she should change careers and go back to a job that used her bachelor's degree in political science. Two weeks after the merger was finalized, others, including herself, received a letter to report for an interview with the new company senior management "conversion" vice president. Lauren spent three days gathering materials to substantiate all of her past accomplishments, to demonstrate her management skills, and to show her potential value to the new firm. When the big day came, Lauren entered the office of the interviewer with approximately nine inches of substantiating material. She was prepared!

The first few minutes were spent explaining her past roles in the firm, the new project office, and other niceties. She explained to the VP she had all of the materials with her to back up her statements and he could take them if he wished. He replied, "I am not as interested in your past accomplishments as I am in your possible future accomplishments. Here is the need. Projects eat up about 40 percent of our yearly expenses. We need to cut 10 million off those expenses. In five minutes tell me how you will do it and how it will be verified."

Her last statement at the end of four minutes was: "I can give you five million within the next year. Ten million is too big a stretch."

His retort was, "Lauren, can you get five in six months?"

(Gulp.) "I'm pretty sure I can."

"Congratulations, Lauren, you are now the new project office director of this continental division."

In 500 words or less, write what you believe Lauren could have used as key points to get the position.

CHAPTER SEVENTEEN

An Introduction to Agile Project Management

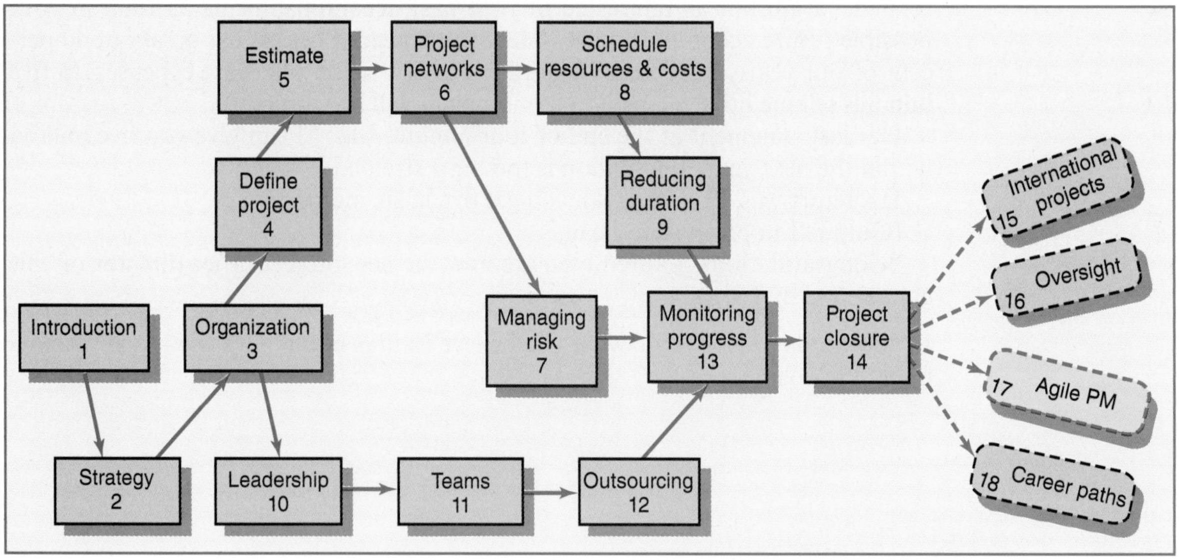

An Introduction to Agile Project Management

Traditional versus Agile Methods

Agile PM

Agile PM in Action: Scrum

Applying Agile PM to Large Projects

Limitations and Concerns

Summary

We know less about the project today than at any time in the future.

—Chet Hendrickson

As project management entered the new millennium, many professionals recognized that one-size fits all project management methods did not meet their needs. This recognition was especially true for those working on software and product development projects in which the end product is not well defined and evolves over time. This project environment requires flexibility and the ability to manage changes as more information and learning take place. Enter **Agile Project Management** (Agile PM). Instead of attempting to plan the entire project up front, Agile PM relies on incremental, iterative development cycles to complete projects.

Ken Schwaber uses the analogy of building a house to explain the difference between incremental, iterative development and traditional project management.[1] The traditional approach would be that the buyers could not move into the house until the entire house is completed. The iterative approach would build the house room by room. The plumbing, electrical, and infrastructure would be built for the most important room (i.e., kitchen) first and then extended to each room as it was constructed. Each time a room is completed, the builders and the buyers would assess progress and make adjustments. In some cases, the buyers would realize that they didn't need that extra room they felt they had to have. In other cases, they would add features they didn't realize they needed to have. Ultimately the house is built to fit the customer's wishes.

Agile PM is ideal for exploratory projects in which requirements need to be discovered and new technology tested. It focuses on active collaboration between the project team and customer representatives, breaking projects into small functional pieces, and adapting to changing requirements. While iterative development principles have been around for some time, it is only recently that agile methodologies have taken root within the project management profession.

In this chapter the core principles of Agile PM are discussed and compared with traditional project management methods. A specific agile methodology called Scrum is used to describe these principles in action. The chapter concludes with a discussion of limitations and concerns. The goal is not to provide a comprehensive account of all the methods associated with Agile PM but to provide a primer on how agile works.

Traditional versus Agile Methods

Traditional approaches to project management concentrate firmly on thorough planning up front. The rationale is that if you plan, execute your plan, and take corrective action on deviations from plan, you have a high probability of success.

[1] Schwaber, K., *Agile Project Management with Scrum*, (Seattle: Microsoft, 2004) p. xviii.

Agile PM

Fundamentally, Agile PM is related to the rolling wave planning and scheduling project methodology (see Chapter 5). That is, the final project design is not known in great detail and is continuously developed through a series of incremental iterations over time. Iterations are short time frames ("time boxes") that typically last from one to four weeks. The goal of each iteration is to develop a workable product that satisfies one or more desired product features to demonstrate to the customer and other key stakeholders. At the end of each iteration, stakeholders and customers review progress and re-evaluate priorities to ensure alignment with customer needs and company goals. Adjustments are made and a different iterative cycle begins. Each new iteration subsumes the work of the previous iterations and adds new capabilities to the evolving product (see Figure 17.3) to produce a next, expanded version of the product. See the Snapshot from Practice: IDEO for an example of iterative development in action.

Iterative development processes provide the following important advantages:

- Continuous integration, verification, and validation of the evolving product.
- Frequent demonstration of progress to increase the likelihood that the end product will satisfy customer needs.
- Early detection of defects and problems.

There is growing evidence that iterative and evolutionary development is superior to traditional plan-driven project management when it comes to creating new products. (See Research Highlight: Product Development Practices That Work.)

It should be noted that Agile PM is not one set method, but a family of methods designed to respond to the challenges of unpredictable projects. A few of the more popular ones are listed here:

Scrum	RUP (Rational Unified Process)
Extreme Programming (XP)	Crystal Clear
Agile Modeling	Dynamic Systems Development Method (DSDM)
Lean Development	Rapid Product Development (RPD)

FIGURE 17.3 Iterative, Incremental Product Development

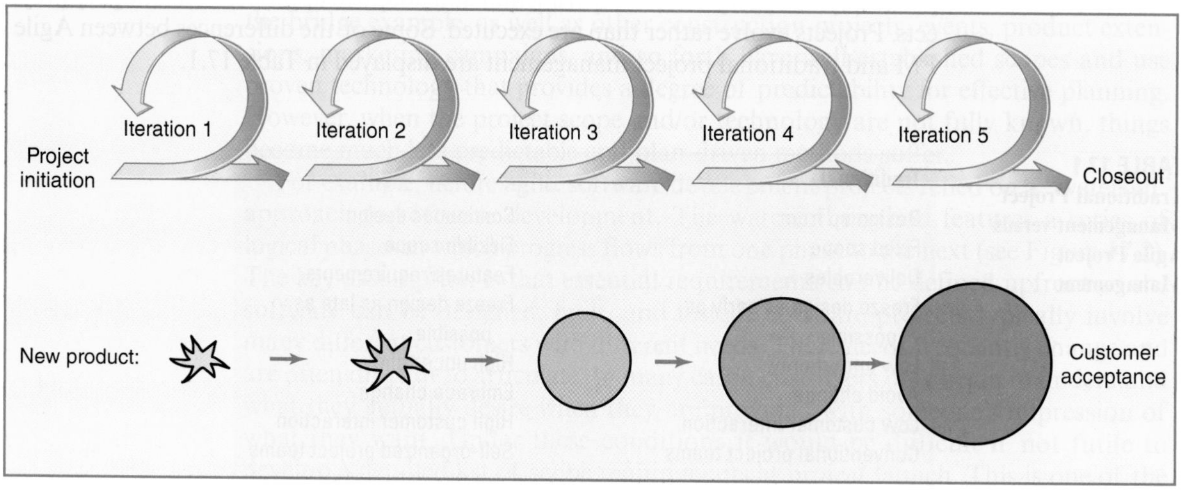

SNAPSHOT FROM PRACTICE IDEO: Masters of Design*

IDEO, headquartered in Palo Alto, California, is one of the premier design firms in the world. They are responsible for a wide range of product innovations including the first Apple mouse, Head's Airflow Tennis Racket, Zyliss Salad Spinner, and Nokia N-Gage Smartphones. IDEO's many clients include Pepsi-Cola, 3M, Logitech, Nike, and HBO. IDEO has won more of the *BusinessWeek/IDSA Industrial Design Excellence Awards* than any other firm.

IDEO's approach to product design relies heavily on an iterative development process in which product prototypes are used to explore and further refine product ideas. CEO Tim Brown states that the goal of prototyping "is to learn about the strengths and weaknesses of the idea and identify new directions that the prototype might take."

© Mark Richards/PhotoEdit

For example, IDEO worked with Procter and Gamble to develop a new Crest toothpaste tube. The challenge was to improve the traditional screw-on cap, which always gets gunked up with toothpaste. IDEO's first solution was a pop-on, pop-off cap. However, when designers created rough prototypes and watched people use them, they quickly noticed that users kept trying to unscrew the cap even though they were told how it worked. The designers concluded that the action was a well-ingrained habit that would probably be impossible to break. So they came up with a hybrid: a twist-off cap that had a short thread but would still be easy to clean.

Focused prototyping resolves critical problems one by one. Brown recommends that prototypes should only take as much time and effort needed to generate useful feedback and evolve an idea.

For example, IDEO was working on a chair for Vecta, a high-end office furniture manufacturer. The project had evolved to the point where the height adjustment lever that tilted with the chair became critical. The team didn't build the whole chair or even the tilt mechanism. They just built the little lever and its interface with the tilt mechanism. It took only a couple of hours. When finished the prototype quickly demonstrated that the principle would work.

"It doesn't matter how clever you are, your first idea about something is never right," Brown says, "so the great value of prototyping—and prototyping quickly and inexpensively—is that you learn about the idea and make it better."

* J. M. Pethokoukis, "The Deans of Design: From the Computer Mouse to the Newest Swiffer, IDEO is the Firm behind the Scenes," *U.S. News & World Report,* Posted 9-24-2008; T. Brown, "Design Thinking," *Harvard Business Review,* June 2008, pp. 84–95.

While each of these methods has unique elements and applications, most are based on the following Agile principles:

- Focus on customer value—Employ business-driven prioritizations of requirements and features.
- Iterative and incremental delivery—Create a flow of value to customers by "chunking" project delivery into small, functioning increments.
- Experimentation and adaptation—Test assumptions early and build working prototypes to solicit customer feedback and refine product requirements.
- Self-organization—Team members decide amongst themselves who and what should be done.
- Continuous improvement—Teams reflect, learn, and adapt to change; work informs the plan.

The first phase is analysis and review of functional requirements that will be needed to complete the feature. The team commits to meet these requirements. The second phase is the development of a design that meets the requirements of the feature. The third phase is to build the feature so that it is functional. Finally, the feature is tested and documented. At the end of each sprint, features are demonstrated. Within this sprint framework, Scrum relies on specific roles, meetings, and documents/logs to manage the project.

Roles and Responsibilities

There are three key roles to the scrum process: Product owner, development team, and scrum master.

Product Owner This person acts on behalf of customers/end users to represent their interests. For commercial development projects the product owner may be the product manager. For internal projects, the product owner could be the manager of the business group that will benefit from the software. In other cases, the product owner could be a representative of the client organization. They are responsible for ensuring that the development team focuses their efforts on developing a product that will fulfill the business objective of the project.

The product owner in consultation with others establishes the initial list of product requirements and prioritizes them in the product backlog. Owners often work with the development team to refine features through stories and end user cases (e.g., when the user clicks the F2 key an option drop down window appears). The product owners negotiate sprint goals and backlog items with the development team. Owners have the option to change features and priorities at the end of each sprint if desired. *However, no changes should be made once a sprint has started.* Product owners are the final arbiter on requirements questions and are empowered to accept or reject each product increment. They ultimately decide whether the project is completed. Product owners are the keeper of the product vision and the watchdog on project cost.

Development Team The team is responsible for delivering the product. A team is typically made up of five to nine people with cross-functional skill sets. There are no designated roles or titles; people take on different responsibilities depending on the nature of the work. The team is **self organizing** in the sense they decide both who and how the work is to be accomplished. Team members should be co-located so that intense face-to-face collaboration occurs. They are responsible for the achieving commitments they make at the sprint planning and sprint review meetings.

Scrum Master (aka Project Manager) The Scrum master facilitates the scrum process and resolves impediments at the team and organization level. The Scrum master is not the leader of the team (the team leads itself!) but acts as a buffer between the team and outside interference. They have no formal authority. Instead, they are responsible for making sure that the Scrum process is adhered to. They help the product owner with planning and try to keep the team energized. The Scrum master serves more as a coach than a manager.

Scrum Meetings

Scrum uses a series of coordinated meetings to manage the development process (see Figure 17.5).

FIGURE 17.5 Scrum Meetings

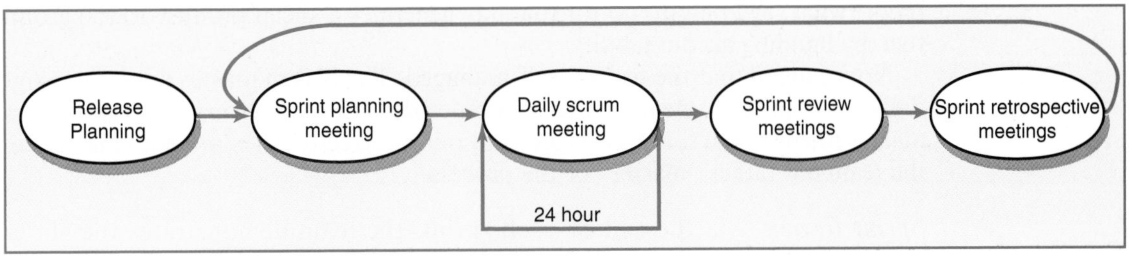

Release Planning The purpose of release planning is to establish the goals and general plan for the project. The product owner works with the team, Scrum master, and others to address the question on how the project can meet or exceed the desired customer expectations and return on investment. Outcomes of this meeting include establishing highest priority product backlog, the major risks, and the overall features and functionality that the released product will contain. The meeting also produces a probable delivery date and initial cost estimates if nothing changes. Management can then monitor progress and make changes to the release plan on a sprint-by-sprint basis.

Sprint Planning At the start of each sprint, the product owner and development team negotiate which product backlog items the team will attempt this sprint. The product owner is responsible for identifying which features are most important, and the team is responsible for determining what is possible within the sprint. If it is impossible to complete a certain key item within four weeks, the team works with the product owner to break the feature down into doable pieces. All committed items are recorded in a product backlog. The team uses this backlog to prioritize specific work to be done and assign initial responsibilities. These tasks are recorded in the sprint backlog. Once the meeting has adjourned the goals for the sprint cannot be changed.

Daily Scrum The heartbeat of an Agile project is the daily meetings which are commonly referred to as the "Scrum." Each work day at the same time and place, team members stand in a circle and take turns answering the following key questions:

1. What have you done since the last Scrum?
2. What will you do between now and the next Scrum?
3. What is getting in the way (blocks) you from performing your work as effectively as possible?

The Scrum, which typically lasts 15 minutes, is held next to a whiteboard, at which time all tasks and blocks are recorded. The Scrum master erases blocks once they have been removed.

The meetings must start on time. A late fine (e.g., $1) collected by the Scrum master and donated to charity, is a popular rule. The meeting is limited to just those three core questions. Members stand to create a sense of urgency. Immediately afterwards, specific members may meet to resolve issues that surfaced.

The value of the Scrum is that it creates a daily mechanism to quickly inform the team about the state of the project. It sustains a sense of team identity that encourages openness and resolution of problems in real time. Having everyone report what they plan to do for that day generates a social promise to the group, thereby building accountability.

Notice again that the team is self-managed. The Scrum master does not assign daily tasks to team members; the team decides amongst themselves. The Scrum master role is to see that the Scrum is running correctly. They are not "master" of the team but rather "master" of the process.

Sprint Review At the end of each sprint, the team demonstrates the actual work product increments they have built to the product owner and other relevant stakeholders. Feedback is solicited from the product owner and other relevant stakeholders. The product owner declares which items are "done" and which items need further work and are returned to the product backlog. The team can take this opportunity to suggest improvements and new features for the product owner to accept or reject. The sprint review meeting is an opportunity to examine and adapt the product as it emerges and iteratively refine key requirements. Such refinements will be the subject of the next sprint planning meeting.

Sprint Retrospective The purpose of the retrospective meeting is to reflect on how well the previous sprint went and identify specific actions that can improve future sprints. The Scrum master typically facilitates this meeting and the team decides which changes will be made in how they work together for the next sprint. The retrospective reflects Scrum's commitment to continuous improvement and the value it places on improving not only products but team interactions.

Product and Sprint Backlogs

Each project has a product backlog and a sprint backlog. The product owner controls the product backlog and the team controls the sprint backlog. The **product backlog** is the customer's prioritized list of key features desired when the project is completed. The product backlog usually defines each feature and estimates of time, cost, and work remaining. See Figure 17.6 for a partial product backlog for a software project.

The **sprint backlog** is developed and controlled by the team. It represents the amount of work the team commits to complete during the next sprint. The sprint backlog lists the tasks (activities) that must be completed to deliver a functional feature or segment of a feature. The sprint backlog also serves as a status

FIGURE 17.6
Partial Product Backlog

	A	B	C	D	E	F	G
1		Phone-In Prescription Software Project					
2		Product Backlog					
3							
4	ID	Product	Priority	Status	Estimate	Actual	
5					Hours	Hours	
6							
7	1	Customer Information	2	Complete	100	90	
8	2	Insurance Information	1	Complete	160	180	
9	3	Drug Information	3	Started	80		
10	4	Doctor Information	5	Not started	40		
11	5	Inventory status	4	Started	120		
12							

FIGURE 17.7
Partial Sprint Backlog

Phone-In Prescription Software Project
Sprint Backlog

Sprint Description	Responsible	Actual Hours	Remaining Hours	Defined	In Progress	Tested	Accepted
Drug categories	RT	16	0	X	X	X	●
Generics	CG	32	0	X	X	X	●
Branded	AL	24	8	X	X	X	
Design drug inventory system	EL	40	0	X	X	X	●
Code inventory availability	CE		32				
Code manufacture order	MC		32				
Integrate all inventory systems	LE	4	16	X			

document by listing the person responsible for each task, remaining hours of work, and recording the task as *finished, in process*, or *not yet started.* See Figure 17.7 for a partial example of a sprint backlog.

Scrum does not use any of the conventional project management tools like Gantt charts or network diagrams. Instead it relies on the daily scrums and the active involvement of the product owner to manage work flow. Risk is mitigated by short developmental cycles and rigorous testing.

Sprint and Release Burndown Charts

Scrum uses "burndown" charts which focus on the work remaining are used to track progress. **Sprint Burndown Charts** are used to track progress on a daily basis (See Figure 17.8). The axis on the left shows the remaining effort required to complete the sprint backlog and the axis on the bottom contains the number days

FIGURE 17.8
Sprint Burn Down Chart

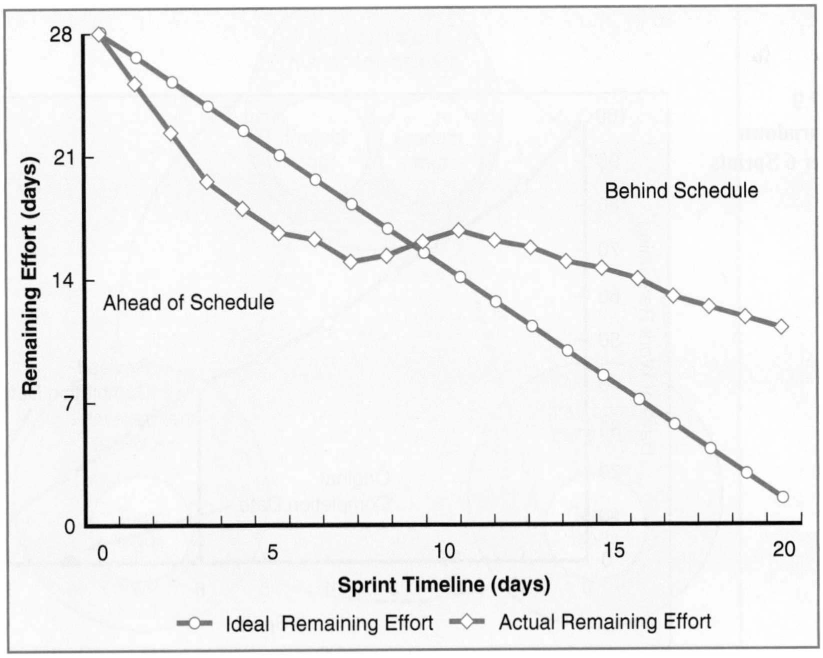

SNAPSHOT FROM PRACTICE Agile Alliance

On February 11–13, 2001, at The Lodge at Snowbird ski resort in the Wasatch mountains of Utah, 17 representatives of various new software methodologies (such as Extreme Programming, Scrum, Adaptive Software Development, and Crystal Clear) met to discuss the need for lighter alternatives to the traditional, documentation-driven project management methodology. They were united by a desire to free themselves of Dilbert manifestations of make-work and arcane policies and spark a revolution in the software industry. By the end of two days they formed the Agile Alliance to champion change and published a manifesto that declared four core values.

> We are uncovering better ways of developing software by doing it and helping others do it. Through this work we have come to value:
>
> Individuals and interactions over processes and tools
> Working software over comprehensive documentation
> Customer collaboration over contract negotiation
> Responding to change over following a plan

These four values were expanded upon by a set of 12 guiding principles.

1. Our highest priority is to satisfy the customer through early and continuous delivery of valuable software.
2. Welcome changing requirements, even late in development.
3. Deliver working software frequently, from a couple of weeks to a couple of months, with a preference to the shorter timescale.
4. Businesspeople and developers must work together daily throughout the project.
5. Build projects around motivated individuals. Give them the environment and support they need, and trust them to get the job done.
6. The most efficient and effective method of conveying information to and within a development team is face-to-face conversation.
7. Working software is the primary measure of progress.
8. Agile processes promote sustainable development.
9. Continuous attention to technical excellence and good design enhances agility.
10. Simplicity—the art of maximizing the amount of work not done—is essential.
11. The best architectures, requirements, and designs emerge from self-organizing teams.
12. At regular intervals, the team reflects on how to become more effective, then turns and adjusts its behavior accordingly.

To find a wealth of information on Agile PM, log onto the Agile Alliance website at: http://www.agilealliance.org/.

Limitations and Concerns

Agile methods in the software industry grew at a grass roots level. Many engineers saw traditional plan-driven project management as stifling effective development with too much emphasis on processes and documentation and not enough on creativity and experimentation. Early on there was a rebellious tone to the Agile movement, so much so, that several of the key founders published an *Agile Manifesto* (see Snapshot from Practice on Agile Alliance). The manifesto affirmed a different set of values than those currently being applied by management to projects they were working on.

The revolutionary nature of Agile is reflected in the story one IT manager told the authors about her efforts several years ago at using Agile PM. She worked for a large, multinational high-tech firm that had spent five years rigidly institutionalizing a set of traditional project management policies and procedures. Despite their best efforts, her department consistently completed projects behind schedule with several cancellations. Out of desperation she started secretly using Agile methods to complete software projects. By using Agile PM her project teams were able to not only meet but beat project schedules—a rarity within her company. When top management confronted her for not conforming to procedure, she pointed to her recent success rate to defend being left alone. Ultimately management couldn't argue with success, and she was allowed to expand her efforts.

The repeated success and improvement in software development projects have led to key elements of Agile PM being incorporated in the Project Management Body of Knowledge (PMBOK). In 2011 the Project Management Institute began offering a certification in Agile PM along with the traditional Project Management Professional (PMP).

Agile PM does not satisfy top management's need for budget, scope, and schedule control. Remember the new house analogy. The buyers got exactly what they wanted but did not know how much it would cost. Nor did they know how long it would take or even what it would look like when it was done. While ballpark estimates are provided, Agile methods by their very nature do not provide the detail estimates of time and costs that management likes. No matter how realistic "it depends" is, management as well as customers are accustomed to working with a greater level of certainty than Agile provides. In response to the financial concerns, many organizations establish "ceilings," which is the maximum budget that should not be exceeded in the development of a given product or service.

Even if management totally buys into the value of Agile PM, one cannot simply install it into an organization over night, it needs to evolve over time. Many of the Agile principles, including self-organizing teams and intense collaboration, are incompatible with corporate cultures. For example, the principle of self-organizing teams, in which members decide who should do what, regardless of rank or title, contradicts command and control structures. Likewise, intense collaboration is not for everyone. One Agile manager confessed that she had to let several of her top engineers go because their lone-wolf personalities were not compatible with collaboration. Most companies report gradual introduction of Agile project management. For example, Siemens Medical Systems started with one Scrum team in 2004, then 10 Scrum teams in 2005, 70 teams in 2006, and over 97 teams in 2007.

As noted earlier, Agile methods appear to work best on small projects that require only five to nine dedicated team members to complete the work. Here face-to-face communication replaces time-consuming documentation and informal coordination supplants top-down control.

Although some companies have successfully applied Agile PM to large projects, others have struggled with the scaling challenge. Too often coordination requirements undermine the adaptability of small teams, which is a chief strength of Agile PM. This has led many companies to use hybrid models that combine Agile and waterfall methods. For example, IPC Media, a subsidiary of Time Inc., uses an iterative waterfall approach in which large projects are broken down into subprojects performed by different teams in parallel. Short sprints and additional check points are used within a structured planned process. A recent survey of more than 800 software engineers reported that 40 percent were using a hybrid approach on their projects.[2]

Companies that enjoy success on large projects tend to have had a strong history of using Agile on smaller projects, and Agile principles are part of their product development culture.

[2] http://www.jamasoftware.com/media/documents/State_of_Requirements_Management_2011.pdf.

Agile requires active customer involvement. Involvement comes in different shapes and forms. Designating an internal person to act as a product owner to represent the interests of customers is relatively easy. Soliciting the active participation of external customers can be more problematic. Even though there is consistent evidence that customer participation enhances project success, not all customers want to be that actively involved. Many are simply too busy. Others believe that they hired the project team so they would not have to be involved. Securing the cooperation of customers to devote the requisite time to support Agile PM is a common source of frustration in the field.

Agile PM frameworks, like Scrum, are used exclusively to complete software development projects from beginning to end. Other companies are using Agile PM only during the early exploratory phase of a project. Agile PM is used to develop critical breakthrough technology or define essential features. Once the features and technology are known then traditional project management is applied to complete the project.

Summary

Agile project management has emerged as a response to the challenges of managing projects with loosely defined scopes and high levels of uncertainty. Agile relies on an iterative development process in which the scope of the project evolves over time. Development teams create feature-driven working products at the end of each development cycle. Active customer involvement is used to guide this process. Here are some of the key advantages of Agile methods:

- Work is divided into smaller and smaller chunks that are more easily scheduled and controlled.
- Collaboration between the customer and designers is increased leading to solid change control.
- Methods demand that features be tested and functional when completed.

Agile PM is still evolving. While much of the attention in this chapter has been devoted to software development, Agile PM is being successfully applied to a wide range of unpredictable projects. New methods and approaches will continue to be developed and adapted to meet the specific needs of projects. Stay tuned.

Key Terms

Agile PM *591*
Feature *596*
Iterative incremental development (IID) *594*
Product backlog *600*
Product owner *598*
Release burndown chart *602*
Scaling *601*
Scrum master *598*
Scrum meeting *598*
Self-organizing team *598*
Sprint backlog *601*
Sprint burndown chart *601*

Review Questions

1. Why is the traditional project management approach less effective when project scope and technology are not well known?
2. What is iterative incremental development? Why is it useful for developing new products?

3. What are the advantages of Agile PM? What are the disadvantages of Agile PM?
4. What similarities and differences exist between a traditional project manager and a Scrum master?
5. What are the differences between a self-organizing team and a conventional project team?
6. Why is it difficult to apply Agile PM to large scale projects?

Exercises

1. Break into small groups and identify at least two real-life examples of projects in which:
   a. The scope and technology are well known.
   b. The scope is well known but the technology is less well known.
   c. The scope is not well known but the technology is known.
   d. Neither the scope nor the technology is well known.
2. Break into small groups and discuss the following question:

   What organizational, group, individual, and project factors do you think would promote the successful adoption of Agile PM methodologies like Scrum? Why?
3. Use a project you are currently working on to hold a Scrum meeting according to the guidelines on page 599. Designate one member to act as the Scrum master and hold a standing meeting that lasts no longer than 15 minutes. Assess the value of such meetings.
4. Below are four mini-cases from practice. Break into small groups and (1) analyze the case and (2) provide five recommendations for the IT department.

Project A

You've just taken over a project from another project manager and have come back from a very uncomfortable meeting with your business sponsor. In the meeting, the sponsor told you how dissatisfied he is with the project's performance to date and that he's getting ready to pull the plug on the project entirely. Deadlines keep slipping, the application isn't complete, and the sponsor feels like he can't get in touch with anyone to give him an update on the project's status and progress.

From conversations with your project team, you learn that requirements still haven't been finalized, and the team is waiting for input before being able to proceed on several key parts of the application. Despite that, they've been able to push forward in other areas, and are quite proud of the work they've done. However, they haven't had a chance to show it to the sponsor.

To complicate matters further, your boss has made it clear that this project must be completed on schedule, because he needs the resources for another project.

What do you do? What impact do your decisions have on the project's cost, schedule, and performance?

Project B

Your project team has finished gathering the requirements and developing the solution design. Your team is broken into two main groups: The first group consists of the project manager, business analysts, and management and is located in the United States. The second group consists of the development and QA teams and they are located in India.

The WBS was developed based on estimates from the teams in India. The development team agreed to provide daily updates to you about progress against the WBS to make sure that the project's milestones are going to be met.

However, by the time the development team got close to the first milestone, it became obvious that they were behind even though their daily updates indicated that they are on track. In addition, the team adopted a different design approach than the one agreed upon at the beginning of the project.

The lack of meaningful updates from the development team along with a different design track has jeopardized the whole project by rendering the whole plan obsolete. Your team is now at risk of not delivering the project.

What do you do? What is the impact to cost, schedule, and performance?

Project C

You have just taken over as the program manager of a large program with multiple tracks and a go-live scheduled in three months. At the first meeting with the project sponsors and key stakeholders, you find out that the business requirements are not complete and in some cases not started, project scope is not realistic to meet the upcoming go-live and overall the project teams are confused due to lack of communication and understanding of priorities.

What do you do? What impact do your decisions have on the project's cost, schedule, and performance?

Project D

You've just been assigned to take over a new project from an outgoing project manager. The project is a high-visibility project that is using a development methodology that is new to you and to your company. In your transition meetings with the outgoing project manager, he assures you that development is complete, and all you have to do is shepherd the project through acceptance testing and release. As a result, several project team members were released as scheduled.

The acceptance testing does not go as smoothly as planned. The application has more defects than anticipated, and some core functionality is not able to be tested. The project team doesn't feel like they are getting the direction they need to continue moving forward, and the business sponsor has asked you when he can expect to test application functionality you didn't know is in scope. In addition, your project's deadline is rapidly approaching, and interproject dependencies make it unlikely that you will be able to push your launch date.

What do you do? What impact do your decisions have on cost, schedule, and performance?

References

Boulter, M., *Smart Client Architecture and Design Guide* (Seattle: Microsoft Press, 2004).

Decarlo, D., *eXtreme Project Management* (Jossey-Bass, 2004).

Faris, R., and I. Abdelshafi, "Project Management and Agile: Perfect Fit," 2006 PMI Global Congress Proceedings, Seattle, Washington.

Griffiths, M., *Using Agile Principles Alongside: A Guide to the Project Management Body of Knowledge,* PMI Global Proceedings, Anaheim, California, 2004.

Highsmith, J., *Agile Project Management* (Boston: Addison Wesley, 2004).

Hildebrand, C., *Full Speed Ahead, PM Network,* Vol. 21, No. 10, October 2007. pp. 36–41.

Jackson, M. B., "Step by Step," *PM Network,* 26 (6), June 2012, pp. 57–61.

James, M., "Scrum" (Download PDF @ *http://refcardz.dzone.com/* on 5/18/2009), 2009.

Jonasson, Hans, *Determining Project Requirements* (Boca Raton, FL: Auerback Publications, 2008).

Kruchten, P., *The Rational Unified Process: An Introduction,* Third Edition. (Upper Saddle River, NJ: Pearson Education, 2004).

Larman, C., *Agile & Iterative Development: A Manager's Guide* (Boston: Addison-Wesley, 2004).

McConnel, S., *Rapid Development: Taming Wild Software Schedules* (Redmond, WA: Microsoft Press, 1996).

Schwaber, K., *Agile Project Management with Scrum* (Redmond, WA: Microsoft Press, 2004).

Takeuchi, H., and I. Nonaka, "The New Product Development Game," *Harvard Business Review,* January–February 1986.

Vanderjack, B., "21 Methods to Engage and Retain Your Product Owner in an Agile Project," www.pmworldjournal.net, Vol. 1, No. 4, November 2012, pp. 1–6.

Worthen, B., "Try Software on Workers First, Fix It Later," *The Wall Street Journal,* September 25, 2007, pp. B1 and B4.

Case

Introducing Scrum at P2P

PART A

Kendra Hua had worked for six years as a software engineer in the IT department at Point 2 Point (P2P), a large freight moving company. She liked her job and the people she worked with. While she did some maintenance work, she worked primarily on projects, usually full time. Her work covered a wide range of projects including system upgrades, inventory control, GPS tracking, billing, and customer databases. These projects were typically able to meet project requirements but were consistently late. Within the IT department it was common practice for a betting pool to emerge regarding completion dates. The rule of thumb was to take the original schedule and multiply it by 1.5 and start guessing from then on.

Management decided to try to turn things around by changing the way P2P completed IT projects. Instead of the traditional waterfall approach in which all the requirements were defined upfront, the IT department was to start using Agile project management, and more specifically Scrum, to complete their projects.

Kendra had just been assigned to the Big Foot project, which involved developing a system for monitoring P2P's carbon footprint. To prepare for this project, Kendra and her entire team of software engineers would attend a two-day Scrum workshop.

The team was shocked because one of the principles they had been taught is that you don't change course midway through a sprint. Prem did his best to explain this to Isaac, but he was insistent. He kept saying that these changes had to be made, otherwise much of the sprint output would be a waste of time. He kept repeating that the team needed to be flexible, "After all isn't that what the Agile approach is all about." The meeting came to an impasse until Prem came forward with a compromise. The team would agree to do the new work, but the sprint needed to be extended by two weeks. Everyone agreed and Kendra went back to work.

Up till the end of the second sprint, Prem continued to direct project work. When it came for the sprint review meeting four of the five new features were completed as well as most of the original features. However, the feature demonstrations did not go well. Isaac and several of the end users that were present were critical of the user friendliness of several of the completed features. Kendra and other team members defended their work by saying, "Why didn't you tell us you wanted it to perform that way?" Prem did his best to keep the meeting under control, but the team had little to say when an important feature simply did not work. In the end, only half of the features were accepted as being done.

Kendra walked out of the sprint review discouraged. Tomorrow morning was the sprint retrospective meeting. She had a lot on her mind, but wasn't sure what she should say or how to say it at the meeting.

1. How well is Scrum working?
2. What are the issues confronting the Big Foot project?
3. Assume you are Kendra. What would you want to say at the retrospective? How would you say it?
4. What improvements or changes need to be made?

PART B

Prem opened the retrospective by saying he had gotten a call from his boss and she was not happy with the progress. Prem said that he and the team were under the gun to get back on track. The list of things that went well during the second sprint was short and when it came time to discuss improvements there was an awkward silence. Kendra spoke up and began by saying she had gone back and reviewed the Scrum book. She went on to say that she thought the whole idea behind Scrum was that the team was to work to solve their own problems and it wasn't Prem's role to play task master. A couple of other team members murmured agreement. Prem became defensive and said if he had not intervened it would have taken days for the team to solve the problem.

Another member said he thought it was a mistake allowing Isaac to change the sprint commitments. Prem agreed that in principle that was true, but said sometimes you have to bend the rules to do what is right. He admonished the team by saying that they had to practice being more agile. The retrospective ended with few specific recommendations other than that in order to get back on track, Prem felt he would have to get even more involved in the execution of the project.

The subsequent sprint 3 planning meeting was more of a formality. Isaac updated the product backlog with revised priorities and Prem signed off for the team as to what they would commit to. There was little interaction between the team and Isaac except seeking clarification on performance requirements for specific features.

The team met under Prem's leadership for their daily Scrums. Sometimes the Scrums went beyond the normal 15 minutes as Prem reviewed progress and described in detail what needed to be done that day. Isaac would occasionally show up, change priorities, review work and answer questions. Kendra worked hard on her assignments and often received praise from Prem for work well done.

One evening when the team got together for a few beers and sushi, one of the team members pulled out a spreadsheet and asked who wanted to make the first bet on when they thought the project would be done.

After several sprints, Isaac finally signed off on the last feature and declared the project completed. A collective "yahoo" sprang from the team. After the meeting Kendra went around collecting money from each of her teammates—she had predicted that the project would take 12 weeks longer than planned.

1. How would you assess P2P effort at introducing Scrum?
2. What challenges does an organization face when adopting an Agile approach like Scrum?
3. What could P2P have done to enhance success?

CHAPTER EIGHTEEN

Project Management Career Paths

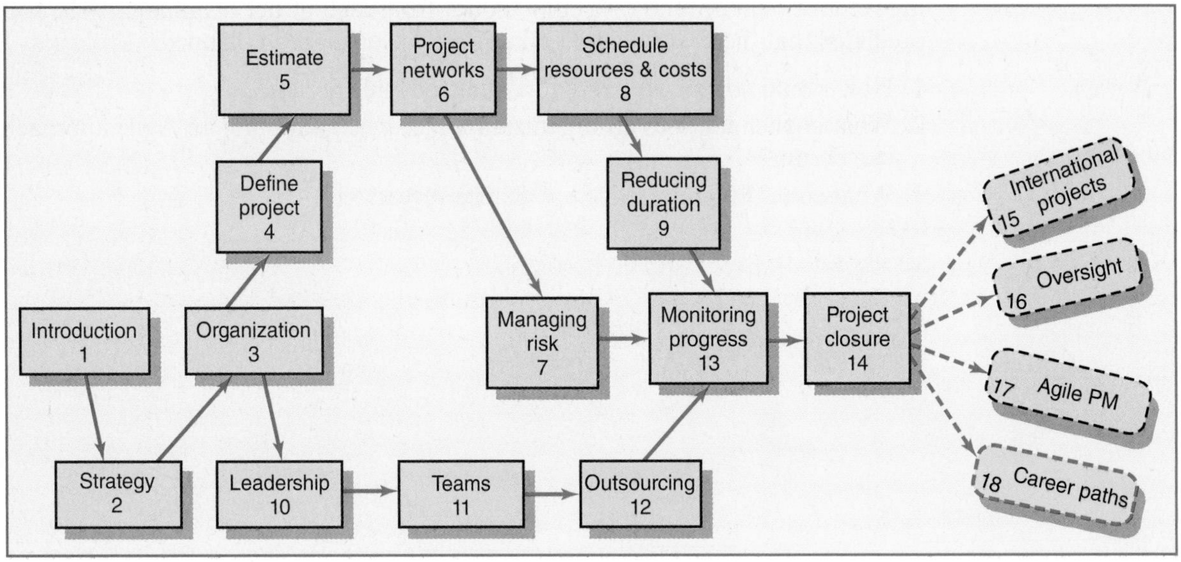

Project Management Career Paths

Career Paths

Pursuing a Career

Professional Training and Certification

Gaining Visibility

Mentors

Success in Key Projects

Summary

Eighty percent of success is showing up.

—Woody Allen

This chapter discusses basic issues regarding a career in project management. One point to remember is that pursuing a career in project management does not necessarily mean you will ever have the title of project manager. Yes, there are growing numbers of fields in which project manager is a career path, but there are many more jobs in which project management is not a title but a job requirement. This underscores a major advantage to being good at managing projects; and that is the basic project management methodology you have been exposed to in this text is transferable across most businesses and professions. Think back to the Snapshots from Practice contained in the different chapters. They were not limited to one or two industries or professions, but rather entailed a smorgasbord of industries and professions! So, whether you are interested in a formal career in project management or just see managing projects as being important for your aspirations, this chapter provides advice for further developing your project management skills and know-how.

Career Paths

There is no set career path for becoming a project manager. Career avenues vary from industry to industry, organization to organization, and from profession to profession. What can be said is that advancement occurs incrementally. You don't simply graduate and become a project manager. As in other careers, you have to work your way up to the position. For example, in project-based organizations such as construction firms, you may begin by working on several projects as an assistant engineer, then take an assignment as a project analyst. From there you are promoted to principal engineer, advance to assistant project manager, assume the role of project manager over a small project, and then continue to bigger, riskier projects. In other organizations, project management careers run parallel with functional advancement with many crossovers. For example, at Intel a management information systems (MIS) specialist might start his career as a designer, then take an assignment as a project specialist, later work as a project manager, and then return to a functional position as head of a department or as a product manager. See the Rod Gwinn Snapshot from Practice for an example of how a former student launched a career in project management.

Other people find that their project management responsibilities expand as they move up the organization's hierarchy. For example, a former marketing student began her career as an assistant buyer for a large retail company. She then became area sales manager at a specific store and became involved on a part-time basis in a series of projects, acting as a facilitator of focus groups. She was promoted to buyer and eventually became a store manager. In her current position, she coordinates a variety of projects ranging from improving the sales acumen of

SNAPSHOT FROM PRACTICE Rod Gwinn

1988–2002	Information Technology Professional
2002–2006	B.S. Business Administration–Oregon State University
2005–2006	Project Management Intern–Symantec Inc.
2006–2008	IT Manager–ECOS Consulting
2008–Pres	IT Project Manager–State of Oregon

Over the years I have worked on, and managed, many technology projects. Some of these went well, others did not. In retrospect, I see that the projects that went smoothly were the ones that were well organized and had some sort of a plan to follow. I did not realize at the time how much project management played a role in even the smallest IT project.

After working in the IT field for almost 20 years, I decided it was time to head back to college to finish my elusive degree. In my junior year, our MIS class took on a project to assist Symantec Corporation with a small development project. This allowed me to directly utilize the skills I had acquired during my early career, plus my learning experiences from the College of Business. One of the outcomes of this project was that the representative from Symantec mentioned an intern program that may be of interest to us.

As we were nearing our summer break, I pursued the opportunity at Symantec. I started as an intern shortly before the end of my junior year, and worked with them through the end of 2005. This proved to be a tremendous opportunity. I was directly working on IT projects for one of the largest software organizations in the world. I was exposed to their very formal process for project management and had the chance to apply my recent classroom experience in a meaningful way.

After graduation, I accepted a position at ECOS, a small environmental consulting company, where I applied my newly developed skills to help shape their technology strategic plan. I continued to explore opportunities in project management and was made aware of a position with the state of Oregon that seemed to be a very good fit for my experience and education. In April 2008, I accepted the position of enhancement project manager. My primary responsibility was to oversee the enhancement phase (Version 1.5) of the new MMIS (Medicaid Management Information System). I am very satisfied to have a new career path, as an IT project manager, which allows me to utilize both my past experiences and my recent education. One of the things I enjoy most about this type of work is the sense of accomplishment in delivering a project that is useful, usable, and meets, or even exceeds, expectations.

her salesforce to altering the physical layout of the store. Although the title of project manager does not appear in her job description, almost 50 percent of her work involves managing projects.

One aspect of project managing that is unique is the temporary nature of assignments. With line appointments, promotions are for the most part permanent and there is a natural, hierarchical progression to positions with greater authority and responsibility. In the example of the former marketing student, she progressed from assistant buyer to sales manager to buyer to store manager. Only under very unusual circumstances would she regress to being a buyer. Conversely, tenure is rarely granted to project managers. Once the project is completed, the manager may return to his previous department, even to a lesser position. Or, depending on the projects available, he may be assigned to manage a more or less significant project. Future work depends on what projects are available at the time the individual is available and how well the last project went. See the Ron Parker Snapshot for another example of a former student who leveraged his ability to manage projects into a successful career in the glass products industry.

SNAPSHOT FROM PRACTICE Ron Parker

1986	B.S. Business Administration–Oregon State University
1986–1990	Food Products Manufacturing
1990–1994	Wood Products Manufacturing
1994–Current	Glass Products Manufacturing

Upon completion of my business degree at OSU, I was recruited by a Fortune 100 food products company for a first line production supervisor position. In that role, an opportunity came up for me to manage a project that involved rolling out a new statistical package-weight-control program throughout the factory. Successfully completing that project was instrumental in accelerating my career within the company, advancing from supervisor to product manager in less than three years.

After four years in food products I accepted an offer to join a wood products manufacturing company. Initially my role in this company was Human Resources Manager. My HR responsibilities included managing several projects to improve safety and employee retention. Successful completion of these projects led to a promotion to Plant Manager. In the Plant Manager role, I was tasked with building and managing a new wood door manufacturing factory. After successfully taking that factory to full production, I was promoted again to Corporate Manager of Continuous Improvement. This "culture change" project involved implementing Total Quality Management throughout 13 different manufacturing factories as well as all the indirect and support functions within the corporation. Shortly after we successfully ingrained this new culture in the company, the owner passed away, leading me to look for other employment.

I was able to leverage my previous experience and success to convince the owner of a struggling glass fabrication company to hire me. In this new role as General Manager, I was tasked with turning the company around. This was my largest project yet. Turning a company around involves a myriad of smaller improvement projects spanning from facilities and equipment improvements to product line additions and deletions to sales and marketing strategy and everything in between. In four years, we successfully turned the company around to the extent that the owner was able to sell the company and comfortably retire.

Successfully turning that glass company around got the attention of a much larger competitor of ours, resulting in an offer of employment. This new offer involved the start-up of a $30M high-tech glass manufacturing facility in another state. We were able to take that facility from a dirt field to the highest volume manufacturing facility of its kind in the world in just three years. After building and operating this factory at a world-class benchmark level for 8 years, I came across a new and exciting opportunity to help expand a strong glass fabrication company in Canada. I spent four years successfully transitioning this Canadian company from a medium size glass fabrication facility to one of the largest and most successful of its kind in North America.

After tiring of the "Great White North," I found an opportunity to tackle the largest and most impactful project of my career. I'm currently VP of Operations in a venture-funded high-tech start-up company. In this role, I'm overseeing the construction and start-up of the first full-scale, high-volume electrochromic glass fabrication factory in the world. This new project involves building a company from the ground up and taking an exciting new technology from the lab to full-scale commercialization. Success in this role, although still far from being certain, will eventually revolutionize the glass industry through the introduction of a product that dramatically improves the energy efficiency and occupant comfort of buildings around the world.

Looking back on my career, it is apparent that my degree of success has largely been the result of taking on and successfully completing successively larger and increasingly impactful projects.

There's a saying that's always resonated with me: "If your only tool is a hammer, all your problems look like nails." Good tools are hard to come by and heavy to carry around. I like my tool bag filled with generalist tools; things like communication skills, leadership, common sense, judgment, reasoning, logic and a strong sense of urgency. I often wonder how much more I could have accomplished had I actually studied project management and had more of that toolset in my bag. With a bag full of strong generalist tools, you can tackle any problem in any business. Project management is clearly one of those skills where the better you are at it, the higher your chances of success in any business environment. Having the tools is only part of the equation though. To be successful, you must also be willing to run at problems/opportunities when everyone else is running away from them.

TABLE 18.1
PMI Certification Requirements

	CAPM	PMP
Full Name:	Certified Associate in Project Management	Project Management Professional
Project Role:	Contributes to project team	Leads and directs project teams
Eligibility Requirements:	High school diploma/global equivalent **AND** 1,500 hours experience **OR** 23 hours project management education	High school diploma/global equivalent **5** years project management experience **35** hours project management education **OR** Bachelor's degree/global equivalent **3** years project management experience **35** hours project management education
Exam Information:	3 hours; 150 multiple-choice questions	4 hours; 200 multiple-choice questions

students in taking the examinations. These books provide useful tips as well as practice exams.

Passing the exam and being certified as either a CAPM or PMP is a clearly visible way to signal your competence and interest. See the Ginger Butler Snapshot from Practice for an example of how one former student used the CAPM to launch a career in project management.

More on Certification

The benefit of earning certification lies in adding value to your degree. You may find being certified opens a door to an interview. Levinson reports that certified project managers may have greater access to jobs and higher salaries. According to the Seventh Edition of the PMI Project Management Salary Survey, individuals with certain credentials like the PMP earn at least $10,000 more than those without. IBM reports that some of their customers request a certified project manager. However, Steve DelGrosso, director of IBM's Project Management Center of Excellence, points out: "Being a certified project manager doesn't necessarily make you better than any other project manager. It just indicates that you have a certain level of knowledge and expertise, and that you can work proficiently in a project environment." If seven of ten projects fail, customers may believe a certified manager will bring a project in on time and on budget. However, many factors affect the success of a project. The best that can be said is that hiring a certified project manager may increase the odds of success (Levinson, 2010).

Interviews of IT executives show that many of the so-called "soft" skills of leadership, communication skills (oral and writing), and ability to deal with ambiguity and change are more valuable than certification (Stevenson and Starkweather, 2010). PMI certification indicates that you have learned the processes of project management along with the common terms used in the field (e.g., scope, requirements, work breakdown structure, project network, risk, earned value, critical chain, agile). On the inside front cover of this text, you

SNAPSHOT FROM PRACTICE Ginger Butler

2000 B.S. Business Administration
2000-07 Software Analyst
2007 Master Business Administration (MBA) CAPM PMI Project Management Certification
2007 Project Manager
2008 Director Project Management Office
2009 Vice President, Products & Operations

After 10 years of bookkeeping, I decided to return to college to complete a bachelor's degree in business administration–management information systems. It was in my junior year that I took a project management (PM) course. I was impressed with how PM methods can break down the most complicated projects into steps that could then be turned into processes that would likely result in successful projects. The next seven years were spent as a software analyst. Time and time again, I could see the need for effective PM in our software development shop. Slowly, I started to apply what I had learned and began to realize how useful project management tools and techniques were to getting things done.

I knew that I needed to learn more. I was contemplating whether to take a project management course to acquire PM certification or make a bolder move and earn an MBA. I made the decision to earn the MBA and, once again, had the opportunity to take an advanced course in PM. Before I graduated, I orchestrated a PM certification prep course in which I and 11 other graduate students ultimately earned their certification.

One week after graduation, I took a project management position at Avant Assessment. PM certification was a requirement for the job. Avant Assessment (founded in 2001) designs, develops, and delivers four-skill language proficiency assessments that are standards-based, validated, and delivered in a Web environment. The company embraced the science of PM and provided an amazing opportunity for me to make a significant impact as a project manager. Within two years, I was promoted to director of our PM office. From there I was able to create cohesive and effective processes in our production department and have repeated the process development successes in our products department.

Recently, I was promoted to director of operations. This is a direct result of what I have been able to accomplish with the education and continued learning about project management. By coupling the MBA with PM, I was prepared to take on significant challenges and produce tactical, operational, and strategic improvements within and across departments. Granted, I was in the right place at the right time to get such a great opportunity at Avant Assessment. This company is an innovative thinking, action-oriented company that has been very rewarding to work for. Avant recognizes and encourages personal and professional growth and development. Thanks to the spark of interest found years ago in project management, and to Avant Assessment for igniting a passion for improvement, my career has skyrocketed.

can find a chart that correlates sections of the text to the accrediting exam. In summary, PMI certification exams are very process oriented and may help you pass a hiring filter.

Gaining Visibility

As you accumulate knowledge and techniques, you need to apply them to your immediate job situation. Most people's jobs entail some form of project work, whether realizing a mandated objective or simply figuring out ways to improve the quality of performance. Gantt charts, responsibility matrixes, CPM networks, and other project management tools can be used to plan and implement these endeavors. It may also be wise to look outside the workplace for opportunities to develop project management skills. Active involvement in your local community can provide numerous opportunities to manage projects. Organizing a local soccer tournament, managing a charitable fund-raising event, or coordinating the renovation of the neighborhood park can allow you to practice project management. Furthermore, given the volunteer nature of most of these projects, they can provide you with an excellent training ground to sharpen your ability to exercise influence without formal authority.

Regardless of how competent and worthy you are, your project management skills must be visible to others for them to be recognized. Many project managers' careers began by volunteering for task forces and small projects. Ideally you should select task forces and projects that allow you access to higher-ups and other departments within your organization, providing you with opportunities to develop contacts.

This was certainly true for a former student of ours named Bob who escaped the trenches of a large corporation by volunteering to lead the organization's annual United Way campaign. While an important cause, directing the United Way campaign was generally given to someone who was expendable. This was true for Bob whose career had bottomed out. Bob took advantage of the United Way task force to show off his project management skills. Through recruiting key participants, establishing a shared vision, managing milestones, and contagious enthusiasm the campaign was a resounding success shattering previous records. Bob's efforts caught the attention of top management, and he was rewarded with more project work.

Mentors

In pursuing your ambition you should continually be on the lookout for a mentor. Most fast-track managers acknowledge that mentors played a significant role in their advancement. **Mentors** are typically superiors who take a special interest in you and your career. They use their clout to champion your ambitions and act as a personal coach, teaching you "the ropes to skip and the ropes to know." This special treatment does not come without a price. Mentors typically require fervent loyalty and superior performance; after all, the mentor's reputation rests on your performance. How do you find a mentor? Most people say it just happens. But it doesn't happen to everyone. Mentors typically seek A+ workers, not C workers, and you must make your abilities known to others.

Many organizations have instituted formal mentoring programs in which experienced project managers are assigned to promising young managers (see Snapshot: Grooming the Next Generation at Intel). Although the relationship may not evolve to the personal level experienced with an informal mentor, designated mentors play a very similar role in coaching and championing one's professional progress. You should take advantage of this opportunity to learn as much as you can from these seasoned veterans.

Since much project work is temporary and contractual in nature, it is important to develop professional contacts that may lead to future work. Attending conferences, trade fairs, and workshops provides good opportunities to "network" and develop social connections that might precipitate project assignments. These social/professional networks can provide a safety net for project work during times of downsizing and layoffs.

SNAPSHOT FROM PRACTICE Grooming the Next Generation at Intel*

"Mentoring is how we groom the next generation of talent," asserts Jeff Hodgkinson, senior program manager at IT giant Intel. A 30-year Intel veteran, he has mentored dozens of people across the corporation—from new recruits to project managers looking for help as they transition to new roles.

"I had great mentors and managers over the years, and now I'm at the age where I feel obligated to pass the knowledge on to the next generation," Mr. Hodgkinson says. "Besides I want to make sure the next generation of Intel employees keep our stock up and keep putting out good products."

Even seasoned professionals can benefit from mentoring. Hodgkinson was assigned to be a mentor for Bill Crider, a senior program manager in the engineering computing program office at Intel in Austin, Texas. Crider was in the midst of managing a massive five-year IT upgrade project that involved 48 sub-teams, more than 85,000 computers, and 24 project managers who reported to him.

"There were many times on that project where I felt completely in over my head," Crider admits.

Mentoring helped Crider improve his project management style, teaching him to focus on the big picture and delegate more of the daily tasks. "I was heading toward a classic burnout situation. I was working 12-hour days, but I couldn't complain to anyone over or under me," Crider says, "Jeff helped me see that I was taking too much on and how to worry less about the little things."

Crider now mentors and coaches about 15 project managers. He admits mentoring takes time, but he says it's worth the effort—both to the mentee and to the organization. "You need to mentor because it's wrong not pass on what you know," he says.

For Hodgkinson, mentoring has expanded his social network and established him as a project management go-to guy. "When you mentor other people, you earn respect," he says. "They come to you for help, which establishes your reputation as an expert."

* S. F. Gale, "Building Leaders," *PM Network,* October 2010, pp. 34–37.

Success in Key Projects

Ultimately your goal is to accumulate a portfolio of project management experiences that broaden your skill base and reputation. Early on you should choose, when possible, projects with the greatest learning opportunities. Pick projects more for the quality of the people working on them than for the scope of the projects. There is no better way to learn how to be an effective project manager than by watching one at work. Keep a diary of your observations and review and refine lessons learned. Later, as your confidence and competency grow, you should try to get involved in projects that will enhance your reputation within the firm. Remember the comments about customer satisfaction. You want to exceed your superior's expectations. Avoid run-of-the-mill projects or assignments. Seek high-profile projects that have some risks and tangible payoffs. At the same time, be careful to be involved in projects commensurate with your abilities.

Finally, despite your efforts you may find that you are not making satisfactory progress toward your career goals. If this is your appraisal, you may wish to seriously consider moving to a different company or even a different industry that might provide more project management opportunities. Hopefully, you have managed to accumulate sufficient project management experience to aid in your job search. One advantage of project work over general management is that it is typically easier to highlight and "sell" your accomplishments.

Summary

It is rare to find a job or a career path that would not benefit from being good at managing projects. Students starting their careers should take advantage of every opportunity to continue to develop and expand their project management skills. They should volunteer to work on task forces, take advantage of training opportunities, and apply project management tools and techniques to their work. They should signal to their superiors their interest in project management and garner project assignments. Over time they should accumulate a portfolio of project management experiences that establishes their skill base and reputation as someone who gets things done quickly and done right.

As you pursue your career we leave you two suggestions as a project manager:

1. Maintain a sense of the big picture. Engage regularly in what some have called "helicopter management," which means expand your perspective beyond immediate concerns and assess how the project fits in the larger scheme of things. Project managers need to constantly assess how the project fulfills the mission and strategy of the firm, how the project is affecting the rest of the organization, whether the expectations of stakeholders are changing, and what key project interfaces have to be managed.
2. Remember that successful project management is essentially a balancing act. Project managers need to balance the soft (people) side of project management with the hard (technical) side, the demands of top management with the needs of team members, short-term gain with long-term need, and so forth.

Key Terms

CAPM, *619*   Mentor, *622*   PMP, *619*

Review Questions

1. Why are project management knowledge and skills transferable across industries? Professions?
2. Is there a set career path in project management? Explain.
3. How can a mentor help someone pursue a career in project management?

Exercises

1. Interview someone who has worked as a project manager or project management professional.
   a. How did they get started in the field?
   b. How has their career progressed?
   c. What advice would they give someone wishing to pursue a career in project management?
2. Interview someone who works in a field you are interested in pursuing.
   a. How did they get started in the field?
   b. How important is project management in the field? In their current job?
   c. What advice would they give someone wishing to pursue a career in their field?

3. Use an Internet job search engine (e.g., Monster.com) and search for jobs in the field of project management. What did this search reveal about
   a. the demand for project managers?
   b. the importance of certification?
   c. different industries looking for project managers?

References

Ferrazzi, K., and T. Rhaz, *Never Eat Alone: And Other Secrets to Success, One Relationship at a Time* (New York: Broadway Business, 2005).

Gray, C., "Accelerating Management Maturity in Project-Oriented Organizations," *PM World Today,* May 2011, pp. 1–4.

Lientz, B. P., and K. P. Rea, *Project Management for the 21st Century* (San Diego: Academic Press, 1995).

Hölzle, K., "Designing and Implementing a Career Path for Project Managers," *International Journal of Project Management,* 28 (8), 2010, pp. 779–786.

Levinson, M., "Why Project Management Certifications Matter," *Networkworld.com* (retrieved November 17, 2010).

Martin, P., and K. Tate, *Getting Started in Project Management* (New York: Wiley, 2004).

Pant, L., and B. Baroudi, "Project Management Education: The Human Skills Imperative," *International Journal of Project Management,* Vol. 26, 2008, pp. 124–128.

Project Management Institute, *Project Management Salary Survey, 7th ed.* (Newton Sq., PA: PMI Publications, 2012).

Stevenson, D. H., and Jo A. Starkweather, "IT Critical Competency Index: IT Execs Prefer Soft Skills," *International Journal of Project Management,* Vol. 7, October 2010, pp. 663–671.

Project: **Voyagers**

Year	Inflows	Outflows	Net flow	Discount Factor	NPV
0		75,000	(75,000)	1.00	(75,000)
1	15,000		15,000	0.81	12,150
2	25,000		25,000	0.66	16,500
3	50,000		50,000	0.54	27,000
4	50,000		50,000	0.44	22,000
5	150,000		150,000	0.36	54,000
					Total: $(56,650)
				If calculated in EXCEL:	$(55,714)

Chapter 6

6-3. Activity C is a burst activity. Activity G is a merge activity.

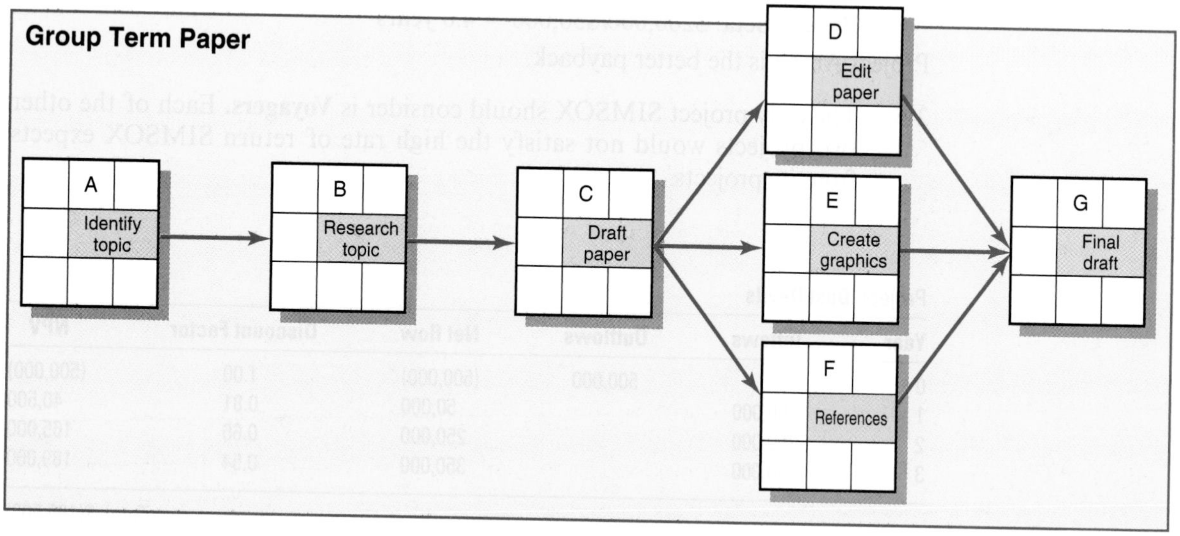

6-11.

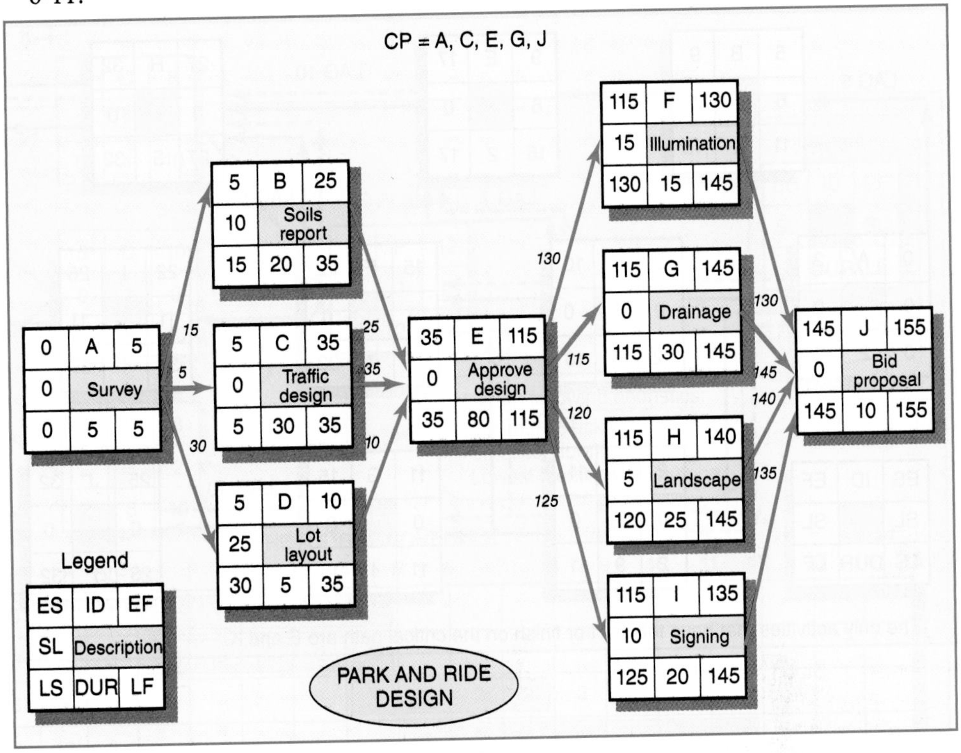

CP = A, C, E, G, J
0 A 5
0 Survey
0 5 5
5 B 25
10 Soils report
15 20 35
5 C 35
0 Traffic design
5 30 35
5 D 10
25 Lot layout
30 5 35
35 E 115
0 Approve design
35 80 115
115 F 130
15 Illumination
130 15 145
115 G 145
0 Drainage
115 30 145
115 H 140
5 Landscape
120 25 145
115 I 135
10 Signing
125 20 145
145 J 155
0 Bid proposal
145 10 155
Legend
ES ID EF
SL Description
LS DUR LF
PARK AND RIDE DESIGN

6-13.

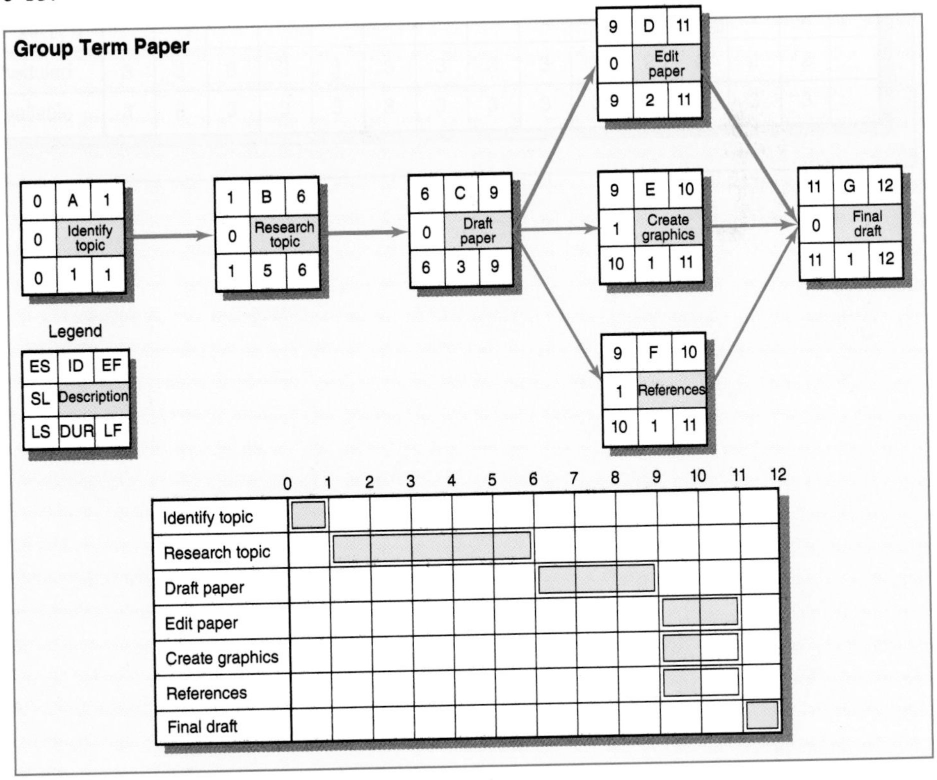

Group Term Paper
0 A 1
0 Identify topic
0 1 1
1 B 6
0 Research topic
1 5 6
6 C 9
0 Draft paper
6 3 9
9 D 11
0 Edit paper
9 2 11
9 E 10
1 Create graphics
10 1 11
9 F 10
1 References
10 1 11
11 G 12
0 Final draft
11 1 12
Legend
ES ID EF
SL Description
LS DUR LF
0 1 2 3 4 5 6 7 8 9 10 11 12
Identify topic
Research topic
Draft paper
Edit paper
Create graphics
References
Final draft

8-7. You should not spend time planning how you are going to spend your bonus. The schedule will take 16 days.

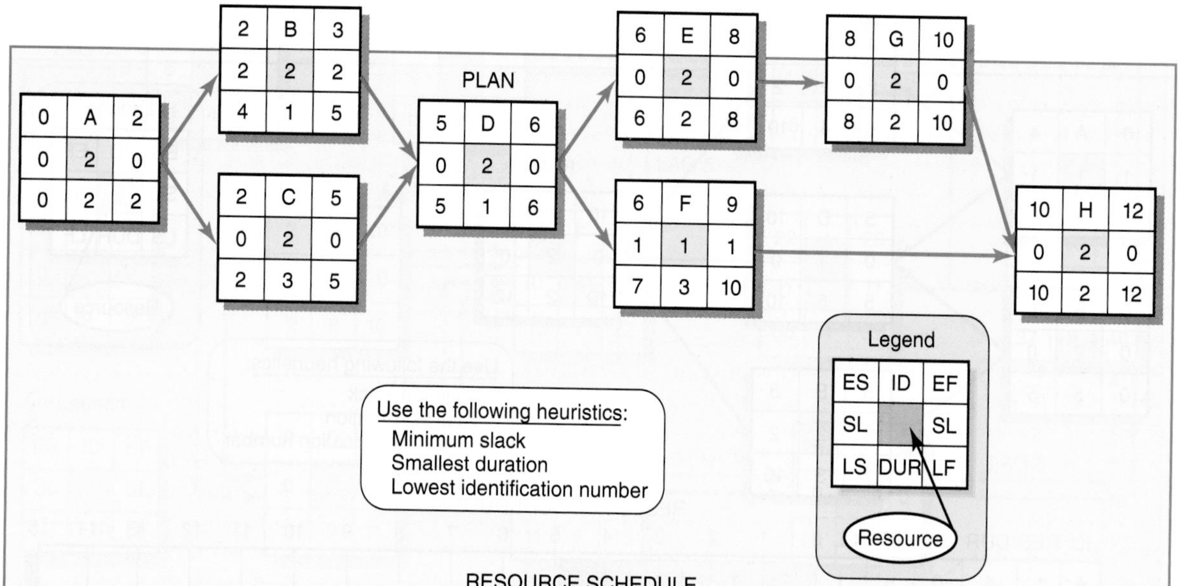

RESOURCE SCHEDULE

ID	RES	DUR	ES	LF	SL	0	1	2	3	4	5	6	7	8	9	10	11	12	13	14	15	16	17	18
A	2	2	0	2	0	2	2																	
B	2	1	5	6	0						2													
C	2	3	2	5	0			2	2	2														
D	2	1	6	7	0							2												
E	2	2	7	9	0								2	2										
F	1	3	9	12	0										1	1	1							
G	2	2	12	14	0													2	2					
H	2	2	14	16	0															2	2			
Resources scheduled						2	2	2	2	2	2	2	2	2	1	1	1	2	2	2	2			
Resources available						2	2	2	2	2	2	2	2	2	2	2	2	2	2	2	2			

8-10.

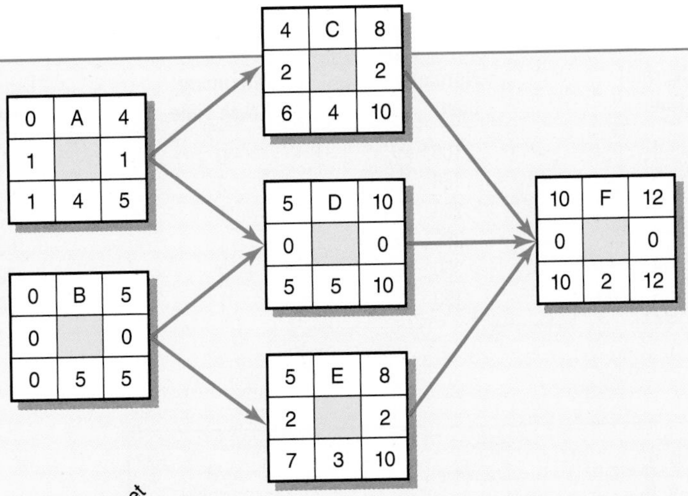

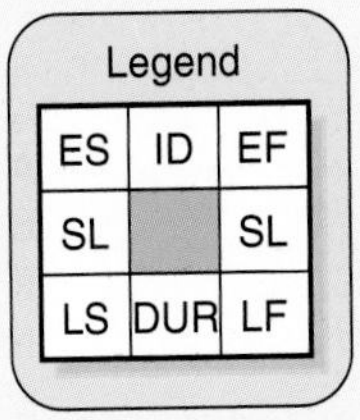

Cost by Week

A	10	10	10	10	
B	8	4	8	4	8
C	12	12	12	12	
D	6	2	2	2	6
E	8	8	12		
F	20	20			

ID	Budget 0	1	2	3	4	5	6	7	8	9	10	11	12
A	40	10	10	10	10								
B	32	8	4	8	4	8							
C	48					12	12	12	12				
D	18						6	2	2	2	6		
E	28						8	8	12				
F	40											20	20
Total	206	18	14	18	14	20	26	22	26	2	6	20	20
Cumulative		18	32	50	64	84	110	132	158	160	166	186	206

Chapter 9

9-2.

Activity	Normal Time	Normal Cost	Maximum Crash Time	Crash Cost
A	1	100	0	0
B	3	150	2	100
C	4	200	1	50
D	3	200	1	60
E	4	200	2	70
F	3	150	1	90

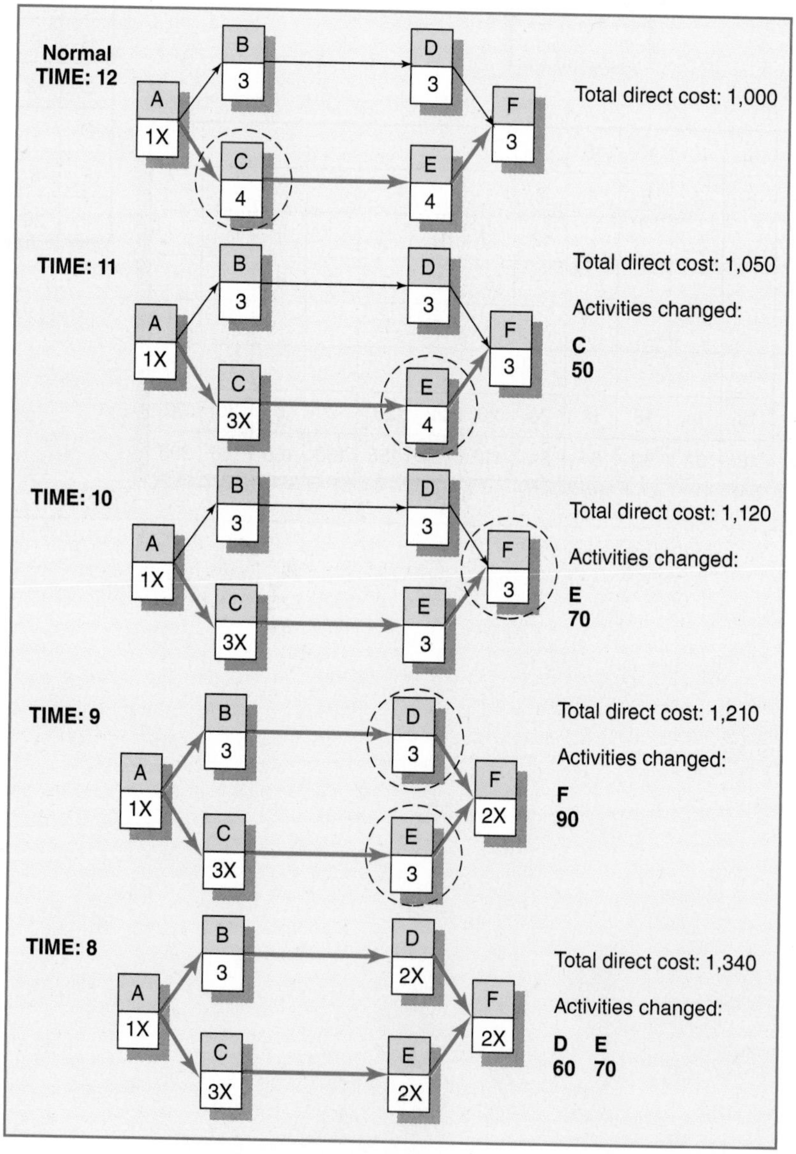

9-8.

Activity	Normal Time	Normal Cost	Maximum Crash Time	Crash Cost
A	3	150	0	0
B	4	200	1	100
C	3	250	1	60
D	4	200	1	40
E	2	250	0	0
F	3	200	2	30
G	2	250	1	20
H	4	300	2	60
I	2	200	1	200

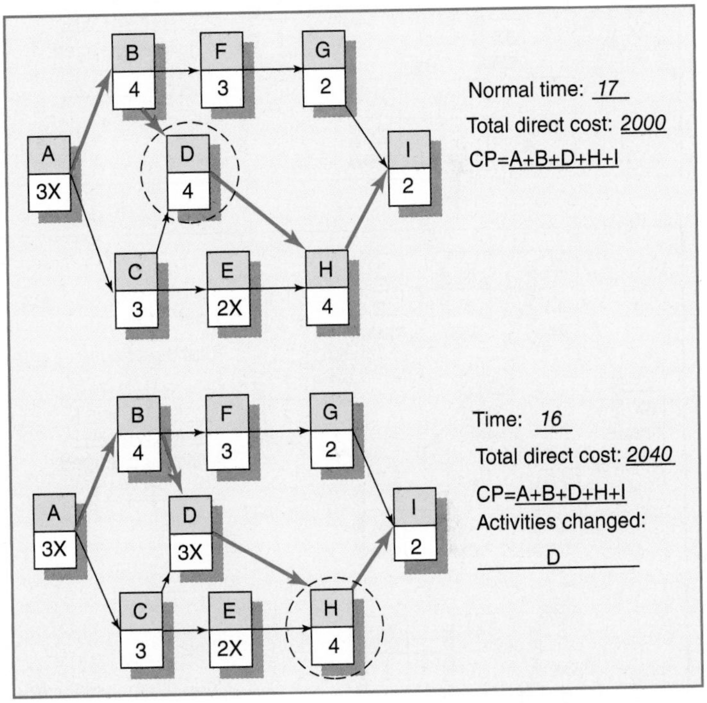

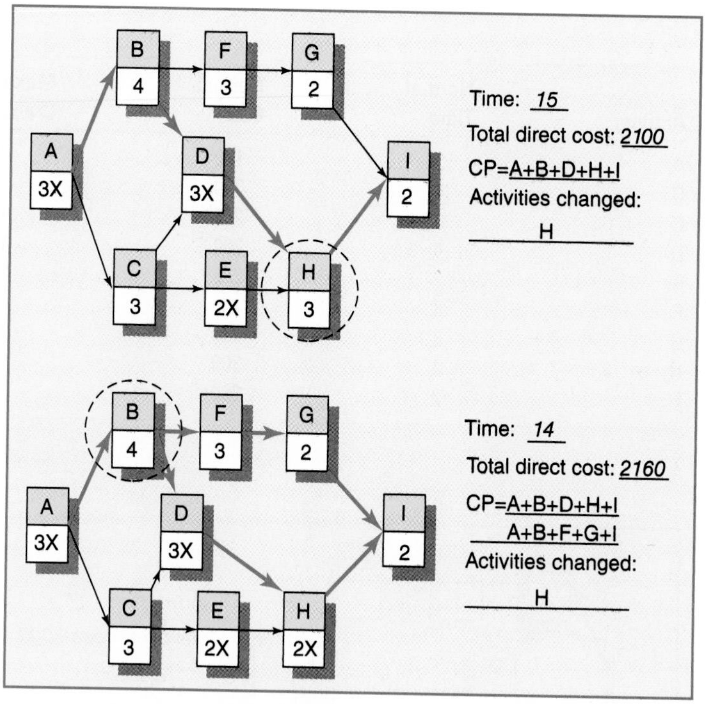
B
4
F
3
G
2
A
3X
D
3X
I
2
C
3
E
2X
H
3
Time: 15
Total direct cost: 2100
CP=A+B+D+H+I
Activities changed:
H
B
4
F
3
G
2
A
3X
D
3X
I
2
C
3
E
2X
H
2X
Time: 14
Total direct cost: 2160
CP=A+B+D+H+I
A+B+F+G+I
Activities changed:
H

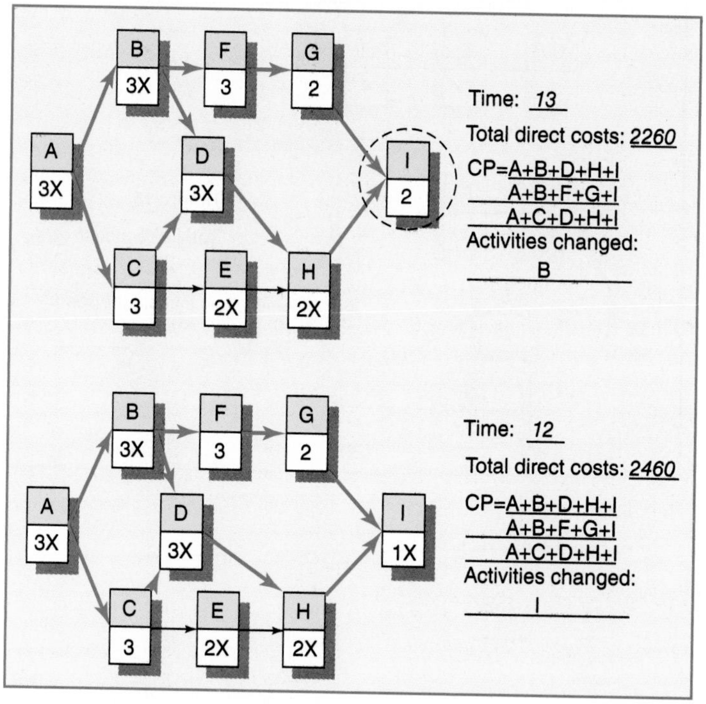
B
3X
F
3
G
2
A
3X
D
3X
I
2
C
3
E
2X
H
2X
Time: 13
Total direct costs: 2260
CP=A+B+D+H+I
A+B+F+G+I
A+C+D+H+I
Activities changed:
B
B
3X
F
3
G
2
A
3X
D
3X
I
1X
C
3
E
2X
H
2X
Time: 12
Total direct costs: 2460
CP=A+B+D+H+I
A+B+F+G+I
A+C+D+H+I
Activities changed:
I

Duration	Direct Cost	Indirect Cost	Total Cost
17	2000	1500	3500
16	2040	1450	3490
15	2100	1400	3500
14	2160	1350	3510
13	2260	1300	3560
12	2460	1250	3710

The optimum time cost schedule would be 16 weeks at a cost of $3490.

Chapter 13

13-4.

Status Report: **Ending Period 2** **($000)**

Task	% Complete	EV	AC	PV	CV	SV
A	75%	30	25	20	5	10
B	50%	16	12	12	4	4
Cumulative Totals		46	37	32	9	14

Status Report: **Ending Period 4** **($000)**

Task	% Complete	EV	AC	PV	CV	SV
A	100%	40	35	40	5	0
B	100%	32	24	24	8	8
Cumulative Totals		72	59	64	13	8

Status Report: **Ending Period 6** **($000)**

Task	% Complete	EV	AC	PV	CV	SV
A	100%	40	35	40	5	0
B	100%	32	24	32	8	0
C	75%	36	24	24	12	12
D	0%	0	0	6	0	−6
E	50%	14	10	8	4	6
Cumulative Totals		122	93	110	29	12

Status Report: **Ending Period 8** **($000)**

Task	% Complete	EV	AC	PV	CV	SV
A	100%	40	35	40	5	0
B	100%	32	24	32	8	0
C	100%	48	32	48	16	0
D	33%	6	20	10	−14	−4
E	100%	28	20	28	8	0
Cumulative Totals		154	131	158	23	−4

Performance Indexes Summary ($000)

Period	EV	AC	PV	SPI	CPI	PCIB
2	46	37	32	1.44	1.24	22%
4	72	59	64	1.13	1.22	35%
6	122	93	110	1.11	1.31	59%
8	154	131	158	.97	1.18	75%

Forecast Costs at Completion

$$\begin{aligned} EAC_f &= \frac{(BAC - EV)}{(EV/AC)} + AC \\ &= \frac{(206 - 154)}{(154/131)} + 131 \\ &= 175 \\ VAC_f &= BAC - EAC_f \\ VAC_f &= 206 - 175 \\ VAC_f &= 31 \end{aligned}$$

At the end of the 8th period, three-quarters of the project has been completed at a savings of $23,000. If the project continues to get $1.18 worth of work for each dollar spent the project will be $31,000 under budget at completion. The project appears to be slightly behind of schedule.

13-8. Part A

Status Report: **Ending Period 1** ($000)

Task	% Complete	EV	AC	PV	CV	SV
A	25%	25	50	50	−25	−25
Cumulative Totals		25	50	50	−25	−25

Status Report: **Ending Period 2** ($000)

Task	% Complete	EV	AC	PV	CV	SV
A	50%	50	100	100	−50	−50
Cumulative Totals		50	100	100	−50	−50

Status Report: **Ending Period 3** ($000)

Task	% Complete	EV	AC	PV	CV	SV
A	100%	100	200	100	−100	0
B	0%	0	0	100	0	−100
C	0%	0	0	150	0	−150
Cumulative Totals		100	200	350	−100	−250

Status Report: **Ending Period 4** **($000)**

Task	% Complete	EV	AC	PV	CV	SV
A	100%	100	200	100	−100	0
B	60%	150	100	150	50	0
C	50%	225	200	300	25	−75
Cumulative Totals		475	500	550	−25	−75

Status Report: **Ending Period 5** **($000)**

Task	% Complete	EV	AC	PV	CV	SV
A	100%	100	200	100	−100	0
B	100%	250	200	250	50	0
C	100%	450	400	450	50	0
Cumulative Totals		800	800	800	0	0

Status Report: **Ending Period 6** **($000)**

Task	% Complete	EV	AC	PV	CV	SV
A	100%	100	200	100	−100	0
B	100%	250	200	250	50	0
C	100%	450	400	450	50	0
D	75%	150	100	100	50	50
Cumulative Totals		950	900	900	50	50

Status Report: **Ending Period 7** **($000)**

Task	% Complete	EV	AC	PV	CV	SV
A	100%	100	200	100	−100	0
B	100%	250	200	250	50	0
C	100%	450	400	450	50	0
D	100%	200	150	200	50	0
E	20%	60	100	0	−40	60
F	5%	15	50	0	−35	15
Cumulative Totals		1075	1100	1000	−25	75

Status Report: **Ending Period 8** **($000)**

Task	% Complete	EV	AC	PV	CV	SV
A	100%	100	200	100	−100	0
B	100%	250	200	250	50	0
C	100%	450	400	450	50	0
D	100%	200	150	200	50	0
E	100%	300	350	200	−50	100
F	10%	30	100	100	−70	−70
Cumulative Totals		1330	1400	1300	−70	30

Performance Indexes Summary **($000)**

Period	EV	AC	PV	SPI	CPI	PCIB
1	25	50	50	.50	.50	2%
2	50	100	100	.50	.50	3%
3	100	200	350	.29	.50	5%
4	475	500	550	.86	.95	24%
5	800	800	800	1.00	1.00	40%
6	950	900	900	1.06	1.06	48%
7	1075	1100	1000	1.08	.98	54%
8	1330	1400	1300	1.02	.95	67%

$$EAC_f = \frac{(BAC - EV)}{(EV/AC)} + AC \qquad VAC_f = BAC - EAC_f$$

$$2105 = \frac{(2000 - 1330)}{(1330/1400)} + 1400 \qquad -105 = 2000 - 2105$$

With two-thirds of the project completed the forecast is that the project will be $105,000 over budget at completion.

13-8 Part B.

Revised Estimates: **Ending Period 14**

Task	% Complete	EV	AC	PV	CV	SV
A	100%	100	200	100	−100	0
B	100%	250	200	250	50	0
C	100%	450	400	450	50	0
D	100%	200	150	200	50	0
E	100%	300	350	300	−50	0
F	100%	300	500	300	−200	0
G	100%	200	150	200	50	0
H	100%	200	200	200	0	0
Cumulative Totals		2000	2150	2000	−150	0

$$EAC_{re} = AC + ETC_{re} \qquad 2150 = 1400 + 750$$

$$VAC_{re} = BAC - EAC_{re} \qquad -150 = 2000 - 2150$$

Revised estimates indicate that the project will be one period behind schedule and $150,000 over budget.

APPENDIX TWO

Computer Project Exercises

In developing the exercises, trade-offs had to be made to enrich the learning experience. One of the major problems students initially encounter is data and detail overload. This reduces their ability to identify project and data problems and to compare alternatives. Although the project found in the exercises is real, it has been reduced and detail has been eliminated many times to concentrate on applying project management principles and understanding linkages. In addition, other simplifying assumptions have been made so that students and instructors can trace problems and discuss outcomes. These assumptions detract from reality, but they keep the focus on the objectives of the exercises and reduce student frustration with software intricacies. Moving from these exercises to real projects is primarily one of increasing detail. The simplifying assumptions are given below (make sure they are included in "default," "preferences," and/or "options" sections of the software used):

The POM+ Project*

Big Kola Company has been concerned that specialized fruit drinks have been eroding their cola market. The CEO mandates that "If you can't beat them, join them." Grape juice was the first product that was successful after an advertising blitz claiming the antitoxin benefits. Lately, competition is compressing grape juice margins and profits. Months of additional market surveys and focus groups have resulted in three potential high-margin drinks: cranberry, blueberry, and pomegranate. All these choices represent antitoxins. The decision is to produce the pomegranate drink that has many health claims. For example, the relative ability of these juices to eliminate harmful free radicals (antitoxins) is 71 percent for pomegranate, 33 percent for blueberry, and 20 percent for cranberry (Technion Institute of Technology). The market potential appears very attractive and should have a higher profit margin than the other potential juice products. Another appeal for pomegranate juice is its familiarity in the Middle East and Asia.

The Priority Matrix for the POM+ Project is:

	Time	Scope	Cost
Constrain			X
Enhance		X	
Accept	X		

* Cliff Gray, Erik Larson, & Pinyarat Sirisomboonsuk, doctoral candidate at Rawls College of Business, Texas Tech University.

Connor Gage, the project manager, has formed his project team and the members have come up with the following work breakdown structure.

1.0 POM+Project
1.1 R&D product development
    1.1.1 Need survey
    1.1.2 Set product specs
    1.1.3 Shelf life report
    1.1.4 Nutrition report
1.2 Secure fruit suppliers
1.3 Initial Production
    1.3.1 Equipment rehab
    1.3.2 Production trials
    1.3.3 Quality trials
    1.3.4 Quality metrics
    1.3.5 Quality training
1.4 Distribution
    1.4.1 Market testing
    1.4.2 Package design
    1.4.3 Select distributors
1.5 Legal
    1.5.1 Complete FDA certification
    1.5.2 Register trademark
1.6 Prepare product launch

Part 1

1. Develop the WBS outline using the software available (save your file).
2. Use this file and the information provided below to create a project schedule.
3. The following holidays are observed: January 1, Martin Luther King Day (third Monday in January), Memorial Day (last Monday in May), July 4th, Labor Day (first Monday in September), Thanksgiving Day (4th Thursday in November), December 25 and 26.
4. If a holiday falls on a Saturday then Friday will be given as an extra day off, and if it falls on a Sunday then Monday will be given off.
5. The project team works eight-hour days, Monday through Friday.
6. The project will begin on January 3, 2012.
7. Based on this schedule, submit a memo that answers the following questions:
    a. When is the project estimated to be completed? How many working days will it take?
    b. What is the critical path?
    c. Which activity has the most total slack?
    d. How sensitive is this network?
    e. Identify two sensible milestones and explain your choice.

Include the following (one page) printouts:

- A Gantt chart.
- A network diagram highlighting the critical path.
- A schedule table reporting ES, LS, EF, LF, and slack for each activity.

Hints: Change the timescale to months and weeks. The estimated duration of the project is 135 days.

Remember: Save your files for future exercises!

The following information has been derived from the WBS. *Note* that the activity number is what appears in the software with the complete WBS entered.

#*	Activity	Duration	Predecessor(s)
3	Need survey	20	None
4	Set product specs	15	3
5	Shelf life report	10	4
6	Nutrition report	5	4
7	Select fruit suppliers	20	5, 6
9	Equipment rehab	30	4
10	Production trials	15	7, 9
11	Quality trials	20	10
12	Quality metrics	5	11
13	Quality training	15	12
15	Market testing	30	5, 6
16	Package design	15	15
17	Select distributors	25	5, 6
19	Complete FDA certification	15	7, 15
20	Register trademark	5	7, 15
21	Prepare product launch	15	13, 16, 17, 19FS + 25 days, 20FS + 15 days

FS = Finish to Start lag

Part 2

Remember the old saying, "A project plan is not a schedule until resources are committed." This exercise illustrates this sometime subtle, but important point.

Using your files from Part 1, input resources and their costs if you have not already done so. All information is found in Tables A2.1 and A2.2.

Prepare a memo that addresses the following questions:

1. Which if any of the resources are overallocated?
2. Assume that the project is time constrained and try to resolve any overallocation problems by leveling within slack. What happens?
3. What is the impact of leveling within slack on the sensitivity of the network?

   Include a Gantt chart with the schedule table after leveling within slack.

4. Assume the project is resource constrained and resolve any overallocation problems by leveling outside of slack. What happens?

TABLE A2.1
Resource Assignments

Activity	Resources
Need survey	MRKT (500%)
Set product specs	R&D (400%), MRKT (200%)
Shelf life report	R&D (300%)
Nutrition report	R&D (300%)
Select fruit suppliers	PURCH (100%)
Equipment rehab	ENG (1,000%), PROD (2,000%)
Production trials	PROD (1,500%), PURCH (100%), ENG (1,000%)
Quality trials	QUAL (300%), PROD (500%)
Quality metrics	QUAL (300%), PROD (100%)
Quality training	QUAL (300%), PROD (1,500%)
Market testing	MRKT (500%)
Package design	DESIGN (300%), MRKT (100%)
Select distributors	MRKT (500%)
Complete FDA certification	LEGAL (300%)
Register trademark	LEGAL (300%)
Prepare product launch	QUAL (300%), PURCH (200%), PROD (1,500%), MRKT (500%), ENG (500%), R&D (100%)

TABLE A2.2
Resources Availability and Pay Rates

Resource	Abbrev	Available	Hourly rate
Marketing staff	MRKT	5	$ 80/hr
R&D	R&D	5	$ 80/hr
Engineering	ENG	10	$100/hr
Purchasing	PURCH	2	$ 60/hr
Quality engineers	QUAL	3	$ 80/hr
Designers	DESIGN	3	$ 60/hr
Legal staff	LEGAL	3	$120/hr
Production	PROD	20	$ 60/hr

Include a Gantt chart with the schedule table after leveling outside of slack.

Note: No splitting of activities is allowed.

Note: No partial assignments (e.g., 50 percent). All resources must be assigned 100 percent.

Part 3

Top management has accepted the July 19th completion schedule created at the end of Part 2. Prepare a brief memo that addresses the following questions:

1. How much will the project cost? What is the most expensive activity?
2. What does the cash flow statement tell you about how costs are distributed over the life span of the project?

Include a monthly cash flow for the project.

Once you are confident that you have the final schedule, save the file as a baseline. **Hint:** Save a backup file just in case without baseline!

TABLE A2.3
Status Report March 31, 2012

Activity	Actual Start	Actual Finish	Actual Duration	Remaining Duration
Need survey	1/3/12	2/2/12	22	0
Set product specs	2/3/12	2/28/12	18	0
Shelf life report	2/29/12	3/13/12	10	0
Nutrition report	3/14/12	3/19/12	4	0
Equipment rehab	2/29/12		23	12

Part 4 A

Assume that today is March 31, 2012, and Table A2.3 contains the tracking information for the project up till now. Enter this information into your saved baseline file and prepare a status report for the first three months of the POM+ project.

Your status report should also address the following questions:

1. How is the project progressing in terms of cost and schedule?
2. What activities have gone well? What activities have not gone well?
3. What do the PCIB and PCIC indicate in terms of how much of the project has been accomplished to date?
4. What is the forecasted cost at completion (EAC_f)? What is the predicted VAC_f?
5. Report and interpret the TCPI for the project at this point in time.
6. What is the estimated date of completion?
7. How well is the project doing in terms of its priorities?

Try to present the above information in a form worthy of consideration by top management.

Include an Earned Value table and a Tracking Gantt Chart.

Note: Insert March 31, 2012, as the status date in the Project Information box.

Part 4 B

Assume that today is May 31, 2012, and Table A2.4 contains the tracking information for the project up till now. Enter this information into your saved baseline file and prepare a status report for the POM+ project.

Your status report should address the following questions:

1. How is the project progressing in terms of cost and schedule?
2. What activities have gone well? What activities have not gone well?
3. What do the PCIB and PCIC indicate in terms of how much of the project has been accomplished to date?
4. What is the forecasted cost at completion (EAC_f)? What is the predicted VAC_f?
5. Report and interpret the TCPI for the project at this point in time.
6. What is the estimated date of completion?
7. How well is the project doing in terms of its priorities?

Try to present the above information in a form worthy of consideration by top management.

Include an Earned Value table and a Tracking Gantt Chart.

Note: Insert May 31, 2012, as the status date in the Project Information box.

TABLE A2.4
Status Report
May 31, 2012

Activity	Actual Start	Actual Finish	Actual Duration	Remaining Duration
Need survey	1/3/12	2/2/12	22	0
Set product specs	2/3/12	2/28/12	18	0
Shelf life report	2/29/12	3/13/12	10	0
Nutrition report	3/14/12	3/19/12	4	0
Select fruit suppliers	4/3/12	4/30/12	20	0
Equipment rehab	2/29/12	4/11/12	31	0
Production trials	4/17/12	5/4/12	14	0
Quality trials	5/7/12	5/31/12	18	0
Market testing	4/4/12	5/9/12	26	0
Package design	5/10/12	5/25/12	12	0
Select distributors	5/28/12		4	18
Complete FDA certification	5/11/12	5/31/12	14	0

Red Zuma Project

The ARC Company specializes in developing and selling a wide range of high-quality scooters. Sales representatives report that there is a growing demand for racing scooters. ARC's president, Robin Lane, is excited about the possibilities and predicts that one day these kinds of razor scooters will be featured in X-Game events. ARC is a small company and uses a strong matrix to optimally utilize limited manpower.

The Project Priority Matrix for the Red Zuma Project is:

	Time	Scope	Cost
Constrain		X	
Enhance	X		
Accept			X

Part 1

You are a member of a project team assigned to develop the new razor scooter code named "Red Zuma." Table A2.5 contains the information necessary to create a project schedule. For the purpose of this case assume the following:

1. The project begins January 2, 2015.
2. The following holidays are observed: January 1, Martin Luther King Day (third Monday in January), Memorial Day (last Monday in May), July 4th, Labor Day (first Monday in September), Thanksgiving Day (4th Thursday in November), December 25.
3. If a holiday falls on a Saturday, then Friday will be given as an extra day off, and if it falls on a Sunday, then Monday will be given as a day off. If December 25th falls on a Friday then Monday will not be given a day off.
4. The project team works eight-hour days, Monday through Friday.

TABLE A2.5
Red Zuma: Project Schedule

ID	Task Name	Duration	Predecessors
1	**1 Red Zuma Project**	260 days	
2	1.1 Market Analysis	25 days	
3	1.2 Product Design	30 days	2
4	1.3 Manufacturing Study	20 days	2
5	1.4 Product Design Selection	10 days	3, 4
6	1.5 Detailed Marketing Plan	15 days	5
7	1.6 Manufacturing Process	30 days	5
8	1.7 Detailed Product Design	45 days	5
9	1.8 Build Prototypes	25 days	8
10	1.9 Lab Test Prototypes	10 days	9
11	1.10 Field Test Prototypes	15 days	9
12	1.11 Finalized Product Design	20 days	7,10,11
13	1.12 Final Manufacturing Process	10 days	12
14	1.13 Order Components	7 days	12
15	1.14 Order Production Equipment	14 days	13
16	1.15 Install Production Equipment	35 days	14FS+20 days,15FS+30 days
17	1.16 Celebrate	1 days	6, 16

Note: FS refers to a Finish-to-Start lag.

Construct a network schedule for this project and prepare a memo that answers the following questions:

1. When is the project estimated to be completed? How long will the project take?
2. What is the critical path for the project?
3. Which activity has the greatest amount of slack?
4. How sensitive is this network?
5. Identify two sensible milestones and explain your choices.

Include the following printouts:

- A Gantt chart.
- A network diagram highlighting the critical path.
- A schedule table reporting ES, LS, EF, LF, and slack for each activity.

Part 2

The following personnel have been assigned full-time to the Red Zuma project team:

4 marketing specialists
4 design engineers
4 development engineers
4 industrial engineers
4 test riders
2 purchasing agent

Use the file from Part 1 and the information contained in Tables A2.6 and A2.7 to assign resources to the project schedule.

TABLE A2.6
Red Zuma Project Resources

	$	Number available
Marketing specialist	$80,000/yr	4
Design engineer	$125,000/yr	4
Development engineer	$110,000/yr	4
Industrial engineer	$100,000/yr	4
Purchasing agent	$75,000/yr	2
Test rider	$70/hr	4

Note: MS Project considers resources in terms of percentages with one full-time worker being 100%.

TABLE A2.7 Red Zuma Resource Assignments

Task Name	Resource Names
Red Zuma Project	
Market Analysis	Marketing Specialist [400%]
Product Design	Marketing Specialist, Design Engineer [400%], Development Engineer [200%], Industrial Engineer, Purchasing Agent
Manufacturing Study	Industrial Engineer [400%], Development Engineer [200%]
Product Design Selection	Marketing Specialist [200%], Design Engineer [300%], Development Engineer [200%], Industrial Engineer [200%], Purchasing Agent [25%]
Detailed Marketing Plan	Marketing Specialist [400%]
Manufacturing Process	Design Engineer, Development Engineer [200%], Industrial Engineer [300%]
Detailed Product Design	Marketing Specialist [200%], Design Engineer [400%], Development Engineer [200%], Industrial Engineer [200%], Purchasing Agent [25%]
Build Prototypes	Design Engineer [200%], Development Engineer [200%], Industrial Engineer [400%]
Lab Test Prototypes	Design Engineer [200%], Development Engineer [200%], Test Rider
Field Tests	Marketing Specialist, Design Engineer [200%], Development Engineer, Industrial Engineer, Test Rider [300%]
Finalized Product Design	Marketing Specialist [200%], Design Engineer [300%], Development Engineer [300%], Industrial Engineer [200%], Purchasing Agent [25%]
Final Manufacturing Process	Industrial Engineer [300%], Design Engineer, Purchasing Agent [25%]
Order Components	Purchasing Agent
Order Production Equipment	Purchasing Agent
Install Production Equipment	Design Engineer, Development Engineer [300%], Industrial Engineer [400%]
Celebration	Design Engineer [400%], Development Engineer [400%], Industrial Engineer [400%], Marketing Specialist [400%], Purchasing Agent [200%]

Note: Resource assignments without brackets is 100%.

Part A

Prepare a memo that addresses the following questions:

1. Which if any of the resources are overallocated?
2. Assume that the project is time constrained and try to resolve any overallocation problems by leveling within slack. What happens?
3. What is the impact of leveling within slack on the sensitivity of the network?

Include a Gantt chart with the schedule table after leveling within slack.

4. Assume that the project is resource constrained and no additional personnel are available. How long will the project take given the resources assigned? (Hint: Undo leveling performed in Part A before answering this question.)

Note: No splitting of activities is allowed.

5. How does the new duration compare with the estimated completion date generated from Part 1? What does this tell you about the impact resources can have on a schedule?

Include a Gantt chart with a schedule table displaying free and total slack depicting the resource-constrained schedule.

Part B

Top management is not happy with the resource-constrained schedule. Robin Lane, the president, has promised retailers that ARC will begin production in time for the major trade show in Las Vegas on January 22, 2016, which means the project needs to be completed by January 17, 2016. She has authorized working the first available Saturday of each month to help the project get completed sooner. She realizes that this will only reduce the project duration by 12–13 days.

After talking to the engineers, everyone agrees that they do not have to wait for the Detailed Product Design to be 100% completed before starting to build the prototype. The consensus is that Building the Prototype can start 30 days after the start of the Detailed Product Design. Likewise the Final Manufacturing Process can start 15 days after the start of Finalized Product Design.

Dewey Martin, director of product development, is also willing to add personnel to the project. He is willing to make available at least one more Development, Design, and/or Industrial Engineer to the project as well as Marketing Specialist. Since there is an acute shortage of personnel at ARC he requests that you only use additional manpower that will help meet the deadline. Your objective is to develop a schedule which will satisfy the deadline with minimum additional resource usage.

Prepare a memo that addresses the following questions:

1. What was the impact of introducing Start-to-Start lags to the schedule and budget?
2. Which, if any additional personnel assignments, would you choose to complete the project before the January 17th deadline? Explain your choices as well as the reasons for not choosing other options.
3. How have these changes affected the sensitivity of the network and the critical path?

Include a Gantt chart with a schedule table displaying free and total slack for the new schedule.

Note: Do not assign new personnel to specific tasks, simply add them to the Resource Sheet. All new personnel are available full time (100%).

At first glance—this appears to be a very complicated, difficult assignment, but if you enter the information correctly, the computer is able to generate the answers with a few simple clicks.

Part 3

Top management has accepted the schedule created at the end of Part 2. Prepare a brief memo that addresses the following questions:

1. How much will the project cost? What is the most expensive activity?
2. What does the cash flow statement tell you about how costs are distributed over the life span of the project?

Include a monthly cash flow for the project.

Once you are confident that you have the final schedule, save the file as a baseline. **Hint:** Save a backup file just in case without baseline!

Part 4

Part A

Today's date is July 8, 2015, the milestone date for the completion of the Prototype. You are charged with preparing a status report for top management. Table A2.8 summarizes progress on the Red Zuma project:

Submit a professional status report to Robin Lane that addresses the following questions:

1. How is the project progressing in terms of cost and schedule?
2. What activities have gone well? What activities have not gone well?
3. How much of the project has been accomplished (PCIB)?
4. What is the forecasted cost at completion (EAC_f)?
5. What is the estimated completion date?
6. How is the project doing in terms of priorities (see Part 1)?

Report and interpret relevant Earned Value metrics in your report.

Include a Tracking Gantt chart as well as an Earned Value Table with your memo.

TABLE A2.8 Red Zuma Project Update

	Task Name	Act. Start	Act. Finish	% Comp.	Phys. % Comp.	Act. Dur.	Rem. Dur.
1	**1 Red Zuma**	**Fri 1/9/15**	**NA**	**46%**	**0%**	**125.85 days**	**146.4 days**
2	1.1 Market Analysis	Fri 1/9/15	Thu 2/12/15	100%	0%	25 days	0 days
3	1.2 Product Design	Fri 2/13/15	Wed 4/1/15	100%	0%	35 days	0 days
4	1.3 Manufacturing Study	Fri 2/13/15	Fri 3/6/15	100%	0%	16 days	0 days
5	1.4 Product Design Selection	Thu 4/2/15	Fri 4/17/15	100%	0%	13 days	0 days
6	1.5 Detailed Marketing Plan	NA	NA	0%	0%	0 days	15 days
7	1.6 Manufacturing Process	NA	NA	0%	0%	0 days	30 days
8	1.7 Detailed Product Design	Mon 4/20/15	Wed 6/24/15	100%	0%	49 days	0 days
9	1.8 Build Prototypes	Wed 6/10/15	NA	39%	0%	9 days	14 days
10	1.9 Lab Test Prototypes	NA	NA	0%	0%	0 days	10 days
11	1.10 Field Test Prototypes	NA	NA	0%	0%	0 days	15 days
12	1.11 Finalized Product Design	NA	NA	0%	0%	0 days	20 days
13	1.12 Final Manufacturing Process	NA	NA	0%	0%	0 days	10 days
14	1.13 Order Components	NA	NA	0%	0%	0 days	7 days
15	1.14 Order Production Equipment	NA	NA	0%	0%	0 days	14 days
16	1.15 Install Production Equipment	NA	NA	0%	0%	0 days	35 days
17	1.16 Celebrate	NA	NA	0%	0%	0 days	1 days

Part B

You have told Robin Lane that based on what you know now you need to revise the estimates for some of the remaining activities. Detailed Product Design is expected to take 3 days longer than planned. Build Prototypes is expected to take 2 days less than planned and Finalized Product Design is expected to take 3 days longer than planned. Final Manufacturing Process is expected to take 2 days less than planned, while Install Production Equipment is now expected to take only 30 days. You also report that Detailed Marketing plan will be completed before the end of the New Year. She is insisting that the project be completed by January 17th in order to be ready for the Las Vegas show. She is willing to spend $50,000 from Management Reserves to expedite shipping if necessary. $25,000 would reduce the shipping of components by 5 days and/or $25,000 would reduce the shipping of manufacturing parts by 5 days (Hint: Adjust lag). Prepare a memo to Robin that addresses the following questions:

1. What is the impact of the revised estimates for Finalized Product Design and Install Production Equipment on the project schedule and cost?
2. Would you recommend authorizing the expenditure of $50,000? Explain.
3. What, if any other recommendations, would you make so that the project can achieve Robin's deadline? Justify your recommendations.

Include a Tracking Gantt chart with variance schedule that depicts your final recommendations and revised schedule.

Hint: After adjusting the Installation of Production Equipment and Finalized Product Design, level outside of slack to eliminate any resource over allocation problems.

Conveyor Belt Project

Part 1

Project Description

The new computer-controlled conveyor belt is an exciting project that moves and positions items on the conveyor belt within <1 millimeter. The project will produce a new system for future installations, and for replacement of those in the field, at a low cost. The computer-controlled conveyor belt has the potential to be a critical unit in 30 percent of the systems installed in factories. The new system is also easier to update with future technologies.

The Project Priority Matrix for the Conveyor Belt Project (CBP) is:

	Time	Scope	Cost
Constrain	X		
Enhance		X	
Accept			X

Table A2.9 has been developed for you to use in completing the project exercises.

Assignment

Develop the WBS outline using the software available to you.

Question

Does this information (WBS) allow you to define any milestones of the project? Why or why not? What are they?

Remember: Save your file for future exercises!

TABLE A2.9
Conveyor Belt Project; WBS

Conveyor Belt Project	
Hardware	Hardware specifications
	Hardware design
	Hardware documentation
	Prototypes
	Order circuit boards
	Assemble preproduction models
Operating system	Kernel specifications
	Drivers
	Disk drivers
	Serial I/O drivers
	Memory management
	Operating system documentation
	Network interface
Utilities	Utilities specifications
	Routine utilities
	Complex utilities
	Utilities documentation
	Shell
System integration	Architectural decisions
	Integration first phase
	System hard/software test
	Project documentation
	Integration acceptance testing

Part 2

Use your file from Part 1 and the information provided below to complete this exercise. (See Table A2.10.)

1. Each work package will represent an activity.
2. The project begins January 4, 2010.
3. The following holidays are observed: January 1, Memorial Day (last Monday in May), July 4th, Labor Day (first Monday in September), Thanksgiving Day (4th Thursday in November), December 25 and 26.
4. If a holiday falls on a Saturday then Friday will be given as an extra day off, and if it falls on a Sunday, then Monday will be given as a day off.
5. The project teams work eight-hour days, Monday through Friday.

Warning: Experience has taught students to frequently make separate backup files for each exercise. The software is never as friendly as users expect!

Construct a network schedule for the conveyor belt project and prepare a memo that addresses the following questions:

1. When is the project estimated to be completed? How long will the project take?
2. What is the critical path(s) for the project?
3. Which activity has the greatest amount of slack?
4. How sensitive is this network?
5. Identify two sensible milestones and explain your choices.
6. Compare the advantages/disadvantages of displaying the schedule as a network versus a Gantt chart.

TABLE A2.10 Conveyor Belt Project; Schedule

Activity	Description	Resource	Duration (days)	Preceding Activity
1	Architectural decisions	Design	25	—
2	Hardware specifications	Development, design	50	1
3	Kernel specifications	Design	20	1
4	Utilities specifications	Development, design	15	1
5	Hardware design	Design, development	70	2
6	Disk drivers	Assembly, development	100	3
7	Memory management	Development	90	3
8	Operating system documentation	Design, documentation	25	3
9	Routine utilities	Development	60	4
10	Complex utilities	Development	80	4
11	Utilities documentation	Documentation, design	20	4
12	Hardware documentation	Documentation, design	30	5
13	Integration first phase	Assembly, development	50	6,7,8,9,10,11,12
14	Prototypes	Assembly, development	80	13
15	Serial I/O drivers	Development	130	13
16	System hard/software test	Assembly	25	14,15
17	Order circuit boards	Purchasing	5	16
18	Network interface	Development	90	16
19	Shell	Development	60	16
20	Project documentation	Documentation, development	50	16
21	Assemble preproduction models	Assembly, development	30	17F-S, lag 50 days
22	Integrated acceptance testing	Assembly, development	60	18,19,20,21

Note: F-S refers to a Finish-to-Start lag.

Include the following printouts:

- A Gantt chart.
- A network diagram highlighting the critical path.
- A schedule table reporting. ES, LS, EF, LF, and slack for each activity.

Hint: the project should be completed in 530 days.
Remember: Save your file for future exercises!

Part 3

Remember the old saying, "A project plan is not a schedule until resources are committed." This exercise illustrates this subtle, but very important, difference.

Part A

Using your files from Part 2 input resources and their costs if you have not already done so. All information is found in Tables A2.10 and A2.11.

TABLE A2.11 Organization Resources

Name	Group	Cost ($/hr)
Design	R&D (2 teams)	$100
Development	R&D (2 teams)	70
Documentation	R&D (1 team)	60
Assembly/test	R&D (1 team)	70
Purchasing	Procurement (1 team)	40

Prepare a memo that addresses the following questions:

1. Which if any of the resources are overallocated?
2. Assume that the project is time constrained and try to resolve any overallocation problems by leveling within slack. What happens?
3. What is the impact of leveling within slack on the sensitivity of the network?

Include a Gantt chart with the schedule table after leveling within slack.

4. Assume the project is resource constrained and resolve any overallocation problems by leveling outside of slack. What happens? What are the managerial implications?
5. What options are available at this point in time?

Include a Gantt chart with the schedule table after leveling outside of slack.

Note: No splitting of activities is allowed.
Note: No partial assignments (e.g., 50 percent). All resources must be assigned 100 percent.

Part B

When you show the resource-constrained network to top management, they are visibly shaken. After some explanation and negotiation they make the following compromise with you:

- The project must be completed no later than February 2, 2012 (530 days).
- You may assign two additional development teams.
- If this does not suffice, you may hire other development teams from the outside. Hire as few external teams as possible because they cost $50 more per hour than your inside development people.

Internal Development

Add as many development units (teams) as needed to stay within the 530 days. If you need more than two internal development units, then hire as few external teams as necessary. Select the cheapest possibility! Change as few activities as possible. It is recommended you keep work packages which require cooperation of several organizational units inside your company. You decide how best to do this. **Hint:** Undo leveling prior to adding new resources.

Once you have obtained a schedule that meets the time and resource constraints, prepare a memo that addresses the following questions:

1. What changes did you make and why?
2. How long will the project take?
3. How did these changes affect the sensitivity of the network?

Include a Gantt chart with a schedule table presenting the new schedule.

Part 4

Based on the file created at the end of Part 3, prepare a memo that addresses the following questions:

1. How much will the project cost?

2. What does the cash flow statement tell you about how costs are distributed over the life span of the project?

Include a monthly cash flow and a cost table for the project.

Once you are confident that you have the final schedule, save the file as a baseline.

Hint: Save a backup file just in case without baseline!

Part 5

Prepare status reports for each of the first four quarters of the project given the information provided here. This requires saving your resource schedule as a baseline and inserting the appropriate status report date in the program. Assume that no work has been completed on the day of the status report.

Your status report should include a table containing the PV, EV, AC, BAC, EAC, SV, CV, and CPI for each activity and the whole project. The report should also address the following questions:

1. How is the project progressing in terms of cost and schedule?
2. What activities have gone well? What activities have not gone well?
3. What do the PCIB and PCIC indicate in terms of how much of the project has been accomplished to date?
4. What is the forecasted cost at completion (EAC_f)? What is the predicted VAC_f?
5. Report and interpret the TCPI for the project at this point in time.
6. What is the estimated date of completion?
7. How well is the project doing in terms of its priorities?

Try to present the above information in a form worthy of consideration by top management.

Include a Tracking Gantt chart with each report.

First Quarter, April 1, 2010

Table A2.12 summarizes the information regarding activities accomplished to date.

Be sure to save your file after each quarterly report and use it to build the next report!

TABLE A2.12
April 1, 2010

Activity	Start Date	Finish Date	Actual Duration	Remaining Duration
Hardware specifications	2/9/10		37	8
Kernel specifications	2/8/10	3/12/10	25	0
Disk drivers	3/15/10		13	87
Memory management	3/15/10		13	77
Op. systems documentation	3/15/10		13	7
Utilities specifications	3/8/10	3/29/10	16	0
Complex utilities	3/30/10		2	85
Architectural decisions	1/4/10	2/5/10	25	0

TABLE A2.13
July 1, 2010

Activity	Start Date	Finish Date	Actual Duration	Remaining Duration
Hardware specifications	2/9/10	4/12/10	45	0
Hardware design	4/13/10		56	11
Kernel specifications	2/8/10	3/12/10	25	0
Disk drivers	3/15/10		77	33
Memory management	3/15/10		77	19
Op. systems documentation	3/15/10	4/16/10	25	0
Utilities specifications	3/8/10	3/29/10	16	0
Routine utilities*	4/26/10		47	18
Complex utilities	3/30/10		66	25
Utilities documentation	5/3/10	6/2/10	22	0
Architectural decisions	1/4/10	2/5/10	25	0

* The project manager for the external development team that was hired to perform routine utilities reported that due to commitments to other clients they would be able to start on that activity 4/26/10.

Second Quarter, July 1, 2010

Table A2.13 summarizes the information regarding activities accomplished since the last report.

Third Quarter, October 1, 2010

Table A2.14 summarizes the information regarding activities accomplished since the last report.

Fourth Quarter, January 1, 2011

Table A2.15 summarizes the information regarding activities accomplished since the last report.

Part 6

You have received revised estimates for the remaining activities at the end of the fourth quarter:

- Prototypes will be completed on 3/8/11.
- Serial I/O drivers will be completed on 6/30/11.

TABLE A2.14
October 1, 2010

Activity	Start Date	Finish Date	Actual Duration	Remaining Duration
Hardware specifications	2/9/10	4/12/10	45	0
Hardware design	4/13/10	7/16/10	67	0
Hardware documentation	7/19/10	8/24/10	27	0
Kernel specifications	2/8/10	3/12/10	25	0
Disk drivers	3/15/10	8/17/10	110	0
Memory management	3/15/10	7/30/10	98	0
Op. systems documentation	3/15/10	4/16/10	25	0
Utilities specifications	3/8/10	3/29/10	16	0
Routine utilities	4/26/10	7/27/10	65	0
Complex utilities	3/30/10	8/11/10	95	0
Utilities documentation	5/3/10	6/2/10	22	0
Architectural decisions	1/4/10	2/5/10	25	0
Integration 1st phase	8/25/10		26	24

TABLE A2.15
January 1, 2011

Activity	Start Date	Finish Date	Actual Duration	Remaining Duration
Hardware specifications	2/9/10	4/12/10	45	0
Hardware design	4/13/10	7/16/10	67	0
Hardware documentation	7/19/10	8/24/10	27	0
Prototypes	11/11/10		34	44
Kernel specifications	2/8/10	3/12/10	25	0
Disk drivers	3/15/10	8/17/10	110	0
Serial I/O drivers	11/11/10		34	119
Memory management	3/15/10	7/30/10	98	0
Op. systems documentation	3/15/10	4/16/10	25	0
Utilities specifications	3/8/10	3/29/10	16	0
Routine utilities	4/26/10	7/27/10	65	0
Complex utilities	3/30/10	8/11/10	95	0
Utilities documentation	5/3/10	6/2/10	22	0
Architectural decisions	1/4/10	2/5/10	25	0
Integration 1st phase	8/25/10	11/10/10	55	0

- System hardware/software test will start on 7/1/11 and take 25 days.
- Order circuit boards will start on 8/8/11 and take 5 days.
- Assemble preproduction model will begin on 10/14/11 and take 18 days.
- Project documentation is expected to start on 8/8/11 and will take 55 days.
- Network interface is expected to start on 8/8/11 and will take 99 days.
- Shell is expected to start on 8/8/11 and will take 55 days.
- Integrated acceptance testing is expected to start on 12/29/11 and will take 54 days.

Prepare a memo that addresses the following questions:

1. What is the new EAC for the project? How long should the project take given these revised estimates?
2. How happy will top management be with these forecasts given the priorities of the project?
3. What recommendations would you make?

Include a revised schedule, a Tracking Gantt chart, and cost table with your memo.

A

activity Task(s) of the project that consumes time while people/equipment either work or wait.

activity duration Estimate of time (hours, days, weeks, months, etc.) necessary to complete a project task.

actual cost of the work completed (AC) The sum of the cost incurred in accomplishing work. Previously this was called the actual cost of the work performed (ACWP).

actual cost of the work performed (ACWP) Actual cost of the work performed in a given time period. The sum of the costs incurred in accomplishing work.

Agile Project Management (Agile PM) A family of incremental, iterative development methods for completing projects.

analysis Data are collected to record the project history, management performance, and lessons learned to improve future projects. Analysis examines in detail the underlying causes of problems, issues, and successes.

AOA Activity-on-arrow method for drawing project networks. The activity is shown as an arrow.

AON Activity-on-node method for drawing project networks. The activity is on the node (rectangle).

apportionment method Costs allocated to a specific segment of a project by using a percentage of planned total cost—for example, framing a house might use 25 percent of the total cost, or coding a teaching module 40 percent of total cost.

avoiding risk Elimination of the risk cause before the project begins.

B

backward pass The method used to compute the late start and finish times for each activity in the project network.

balanced matrix A matrix structure in which the project manager and functional managers share roughly equal authority over the project. The project manager decides what needs to be done; functional managers are concerned with how it will be accomplished.

balanced scorecard method Model that measures the long-run results of major program activities in four areas—customer, internal, innovation and learning, and financial.

bar chart A graphic presentation of project activities depicted as a time-scaled bar line (also called a Gantt chart).

baseline A concrete document and commitment; it represents the first real plan with cost, schedule, and resource allocation. The planned cost and schedule performance are used to measure actual cost and schedule performance. Serves as an anchor point for measuring performance.

BATNA Best alternative to a negotiated agreement. Strong or weak BATNA indicates your power to negotiate with the other party.

bottom-up estimates Detailed estimates of work packages usually made by those who are most familiar with the task (also called micro estimates).

brainstorming Generating as many ideas/solutions as possible without critical judgment.

budget at completion (BAC) Budgeted cost at completion. The total budgeted cost of the baseline or project cost accounts.

budget reserve Reserve setup to cover identified risks that may occur and influence baseline tasks or costs. These reserves are typically controlled by the project manager and the project team. See management reserve.

budgeted cost of the work performed (BCWP) The value for completed work measured in terms of the planned budget for the work. The earned value or original budgeted cost for work actually completed.

build-own-operate-transfer (BOOT) A risk management provision in which the prime contractor not only builds the facility, but also takes over ownership until its operation capacity has been proven before final transfer of ownership to the client.

burst activity An activity that has more than one activity immediately following it.

C

capability maturity model (CMM) A framework which describes the evolutionary stages of project management systems.

change control The process of documenting, reviewing, accepting or rejecting change, and documenting any change to the project baseline.

change management system A defined process for authorizing and documenting changes in the scope of a project.

chart of accounts A hierarchical numbering system used to identify tasks, deliverables, and organizational responsibility in the work breakdown structure.

co-location A situation in which project members including those from different organizations work together in the same location.

communication plan A plan that defines information to be collected and distributed to stakeholders based on their requirements.

concurrent engineering or simultaneous engineering Cross-functional teamwork in new-product development projects that provides product design, quality engineering, and manufacturing process engineering all at the same time.

consensus decision making Reaching a decision that all involved parties basically agree with and support.

contingency fund See contingency reserve.

contingency plan A plan that covers possible identified project risks that may materialize over the life of the project.

contingency reserve Usually an amount of money or time set aside to cover identified and unforeseen project risks.

contract A formal agreement between two parties wherein one party (the contractor) obligates itself to perform a service and the other party (the client) obligates itself to do something in return, usually in the form of a payment to the contractor.

cost account A control point of one or more work packages used to plan, schedule, and control the project. The sum of all the project cost accounts represents the total cost of the project.

cost performance index (CPI) The ratio of work performed to actual costs (EV/AC).

cost-plus contract A contract in which the contractor is reimbursed for all direct allowable costs (materials, labor, travel) plus an additional fee to cover overhead and profit.

cost variance (CV) The difference between EV and AC (CV = EV − AC). Tells if the work accomplished cost more or less than was planned at any point over the life of the project.

crash cost The direct cost of completing an activity in its crash time.

crash point The most a project activity time can realistically be compressed with the resources available to the organization.

crash time The shortest time an activity can be completed (assuming a reasonable level of resources).

crashing Shortening an activity or project.

critical path The longest activity path(s) through the network. The critical path can be distinguished by identifying the collection of activities that all have the same minimum slack.

critical path method (CPM) A scheduling method based on the estimates of time required to complete activities on the critical path. The method computes early, late, and slack times for each activity in the network. It establishes a planned project duration, if one is not imposed on the project.

culture The totality of socially transmitted behavior patterns, beliefs, institutions, and all other products of human work and thought characteristic of a community or country.

culture shock A natural psychological disorientation that most people suffer when they move to a culture different from their own.

D

daily Scrum meeting A short status meeting held daily by each team during which the team members synchronize their work and progress as well as report any impediments for removal by the Scrum master.

dedicated project team An organizational structure in which all of the resources needed to accomplish a project are assigned full time to the project.

deliverable A major product or result that must be finished to complete the project.

Delphi technique A group method to predict future events—e.g., time, cost.

direct costs Costs that are clearly charged to a specific work package—usually labor, materials, or equipment.

dummy activity An activity that does not consume time; it is represented on the AOA network as a dashed line. A dummy activity is used to ensure a unique identification number for parallel activities and used to maintain dependencies among activities on the project network.

duration (DUR) The time needed to complete an activity, a path, or a project.

dysfunctional conflict Disagreement that does not improve project performance.

E

early finish (EF) The earliest an activity can finish if all its preceding activities are finished by their early finish times (EF = ES + DUR).

early start (ES) The earliest an activity can start. It is the largest early finish of all its immediate predecessors (ES = EF − DUR).

earned value (EV) The physical work accomplished plus the authorized budget for this work. Previously this was called the budgeted cost of work performed (BCWP).

emotional intelligence (EQ) The ability or skill to perceive, assess, and manage the emotions of one's self and others.

escalation A control mechanism for resolving problems in which people at the lowest appropriate level attempt to resolve a problem within a set time limit or the problem is "escalated" to the next level of management.

estimated cost at completion (EAC) The sum of actual costs to date plus revised estimated costs for the work remaining in the WBS. The text uses EAC_{re} to represent revisions made by experts and practitioners associated with the project. A second method is used in large projects where the original budget is less reliable. This method uses the actual costs to date plus an efficiency index (CPI = EV/AC) applied to the remaining project work. When the estimate for completion uses the CPI as the basis for forecasting cost at completion, we use the acronym EAC_f, where $\mathbf{EAC_f}$ = estimated costs at completion. Includes costs to date plus revised estimated costs for the work remaining. (Uses formula to compute EAC.)

ETC_f Estimated cost to complete (uses formula to compute estimates).

ETC_{re} Estimated cost to complete (uses expert estimates).

event A point in time when an activity(s) is started or completed. It does not consume time.

F

failure mode and effects analysis (FMEA) Each potential risk is assessed in terms of severity of impact, probability of the event occurring, and ease of detection.

fast-tracking Accelerating project completion typically by rearranging the network schedule and using start-to-start lags.

feature A piece of a product that delivers some useful functionality to a customer.

fixed-price or "lump sum" contract A contract in which the contractor agrees to perform all the work specified in the contract at a predetermined, fixed price.

float See slack.

forecasted estimated cost to complete (ETC_f) Estimated total cost of a project based on CPI. Uses formula to compute estimates.

forward pass The method for determining the early start and finish times for each activity in the project network.

free slack The maximum amount of time an activity can be delayed from its early start (ES) without affecting the early start (ES) of any activity immediately following it.

function points Points derived from past software projects to estimate project time and cost, given specific features of the project.

functional conflict Disagreement that contributes to the objectives of the project.

functional manager A manager responsible for activities in a specialized department or function (e.g., engineering, marketing, finance).

functional organization A hierarchical organizational structure in which departments represent individual disciplines such as engineering, marketing, purchasing.

G

Gantt chart See bar chart.

going native Adopting the customs, values, and prerogatives of a foreign culture.

Golden Rule Do unto others as you would wish them to do unto you.

groupthink A tendency of members in highly cohesive groups to lose their critical evaluative capabilities.

H

hammock activity A special-purpose, aggregate activity that identifies the use of fixed resources or costs over a segment of the project—e.g., a consultant. Derives its duration from the time span between other activities.

heuristic A rule of thumb used to make decisions. Frequently found in scheduling projects. For example, schedule critical activities first, then schedule activities with the shortest duration.

I

implementation gap The lack of consensus between the goals set by top management and those independently set by lower levels of management. This lack of consensus leads to confusion and poor allocation of organization resources.

incremental, iterative development (IID) A cyclical development process in which a project gradually evolves over time.

indirect costs Costs that cannot be traced to a particular project or work package.

infrastructure Basic services (i.e., communication, transportation, power) needed to support project completion.

in-process project audit Project audits early in projects that allow for corrective changes if they are needed on the audited project or others in progress.

insensitive network A network in which the critical path is likely to remain stable during the life of the project.

inspiration-related currencies Influence based on inspiration (opportunity to do good, be the best, etc.).

international project A project that includes tasks that will be completed in different countries.

ISO 9000 A set of standards governing the requirements for documentation of a quality program.

J

joint evaluation A process in which different parties involved in a project evaluate how well they work together.

L

lag The amount of time between the end of one activity and the start of another. A duration assigned to the activity dependency. The minimum amount of time a dependent activity must be delayed to begin or end.

lag relationship The relationship between the start and/or finish of a project activity and the start and/or finish of another activity. The most common lag relationships are (1) finish-to-start, (2) finish-to-finish, (3) start-to-start, and (4) start-to-finish.

late finish (LF) The latest an activity can finish and not delay a following activity ($LF = LS + DUR$).

late start (LS) The latest an activity can start and not delay a following activity. It is the largest late finish (LF) of all activities immediately preceding it ($LS = LF - DUR$).

law of reciprocity People are obligated to grant a favor comparable to the one they received.

leading by example Exhibiting the behaviors you want to see in others.

learning curves A mathematical curve used to predict a pattern of time reduction as a task is performed over and over.

leveling Techniques used to examine a project for an unbalanced use of resources, and for resolving resource over-allocations.

M

management by wandering around (MBWA) A management style in which managers spend the majority of their time outside their offices interacting with key people.

management reserve A percentage of the total project budget reserved for contingencies. The fund exists to cover unforeseen, new problems—not unnecessary overruns. The reserve is designed to reduce the risk of project delays. Management reserves are typically controlled by the project owner or project manager. See budget reserve.

matrix Any organizational structure in which the project manager shares responsibility with the functional managers for assigning priorities and for directing the work of individuals assigned to the project.

maturity model A model used to assess project management practices against others in the same industry and to guide and continuously strive to improve the management of projects. Most maturity models recognize levels of maturity so organizations can gauge their relative maturity against others in their industry.

mentor Typically a more experienced manager who acts as a personal coach and champions a person's ambitions.

merge activity An activity that has more than one activity immediately preceding it.

met-expectations model Customer satisfaction is a function of the extent to which perceived performance exceeds expectations.

milestone An event that represents significant, identifiable accomplishment toward the project's completion.

mitigating risk Action taken to either reduce the likelihood that a risk will occur and/or the impact the risk will have on the project.

Monte Carlo simulation A method of simulating project activity durations using probabilities. The method identifies the percentage of times, activities, and paths that are critical over thousands of simulations.

N

negative reinforcement A motivational technique in which negative stimuli are removed once desired behavior is exhibited.

net present value (NPV) A minimum desired rate of return discount (e.g., 15 percent) is used to compute present value of all future cash inflows and outflows.

network A logic diagram arranged in a prescribed format (e.g., AOA or AON) consisting of activities, sequences, interrelationships, and dependencies.

network organization An alliance of several organizations created for the purpose of creating products and services for customers.

network sensitivity The likelihood that the critical path will change on a project.

nominal group technique (NGT) A structured problem-solving process in which members privately rank-order preferred solutions.

O

objective An end you seek to create or acquire. Should be specific, measurable, realistic, assignable, and include a time frame for accomplishment.

organization breakdown structure (OBS) A structure used to assign responsibility for work packages.

organizational culture A system of shared norms, beliefs, values, and assumptions held by an organization's members.

organizational currencies A set of currencies used as a medium of exchange within organizations to influence behavior.

organizational politics Actions by individuals or groups of individuals to acquire, develop, and use power and other resources to obtain preferred outcomes when there is uncertainty or disagreement over choices.

outsourcing Contracting for the use of external sources (skills) to assist in implementing a project.

overhead costs Typically organization costs that are not directly linked to a specific project. These costs cover general expenses such as upper management, legal, market promotion, and accounting. Overhead costs are usually charged per unit of time or as a percentage of labor or material costs.

oversight A set of principles and processes to guide and improve the management of projects. The intent is to ensure projects meet the needs of the organization through standards, procedures, accountability, efficient allocation of resources, and continuous improvement in the management of projects.

P

padding estimates Adding a safety factor to a time or cost estimate to ensure the estimate is met when the project is executed.

parallel activity One or more activities that can be carried on concurrently or simultaneously.

partnering See project partnering.

partnering charter A formal document that states common goals as well as cooperative procedures used to achieved these goals which is signed by all parties working on a project.

path A sequence of connected activities.

payback method The time it takes to pay back the project investment (investment/net annual savings). The method does not consider the time value of money or the life of the investment.

performance review In general, all review methods of individual performance center on the technical and social skills brought to the project and team. These reviews stress personal improvement and are frequently used for salary and promotion decisions.

personal-related currencies Influence based on enhancing another person's self-esteem.

phase estimating This estimating method begins with a macro estimate for the project and then refines estimates for phases of the project as it is implemented.

phase gating A structured process to review, evaluate, and document outcomes at each project phase and to provide management with information to guide resource deployment toward strategic goals.

phase project delivery Delivering useful parts of a project in phases instead of when the project is entirely completed.

plan of record The current official plan for the project in terms of scope, budget, and schedule.

planned value (PV) The planned time-phased baseline of the value of the work scheduled. Previously this was called budgeted cost of work scheduled (BCWS).

portfolio management Centralized selection and management of a portfolio of projects to ensure that allocation of resources is directed and balanced toward the strategic focus of the organization.

position-related currencies Influence based on the ability to enhance someone else's position within an organization.

positive synergy A characteristic of high-performance teams in which group performance is greater than the sum of individual contributions.

precedence diagram method A method used to construct a project network that uses nodes (e.g., a rectangle) to represent activities and connecting arrows to indicate dependencies.

principled negotiation A process of negotiation that aims to achieve win/win results.

priority matrix A matrix that is set up before the project begins that establishes which criterion among cost, time, and scope will be enhanced, constrained, or accepted.

priority system The process used to select projects. The system uses selected criteria for evaluating and selecting projects that are strongly linked to higher-level strategies and objectives.

priority team The group (sometimes the project office) responsible for selecting, overseeing, and updating project priority selection criteria.

proactive Working within your sphere of influence to accomplish something.

process breakdown structure (PBS) A phase-oriented grouping of project activities that defines the total scope of the project. Each descending level represents an increasingly detailed description of project work.

product backlog A prioritized list of project requirements with estimated time to turn them into complete product functionality.

product owner The person responsible for managing the product backlog in Scrum so as to maximize the value of the project. The product owner represents all stakeholders.

project A temporary endeavor undertaken to create a unique product, service, or result.

project audit report A report that includes classification of the project, analysis of information gathered, recommendations, lessons learned, and an appendix of backup information.

project charter A document that authorizes the project manager to initiate and lead a project.

project closure All of the activities of shutting down a project. The major activities are evaluation of project goals and performance, developing lessons learned, releasing resources, and preparing a final report.

project cost—duration graph A graph that plots project cost against time; it includes direct, indirect, and total cost for a project over a relevant range of time.

project evaluation The process of assessing, verifying, and documenting project results.

project facilitator A guide who leads the project team through an analysis of project activities that went well, what needs improvement, and development of a follow-up action plan with goals and accountability.

project interfaces The intersections between a project and other groups of people both within and outside the organization.

project kick off meeting Typically the first meeting of the project team.

project life cycle The stages found in all projects—definition, planning, execution, and delivery.

project management The application of knowledge, skills, tools, and techniques to project activities to meet the project requirements.

Project Management Professional (PMP) An individual who has met specific education and experience requirements set forth by the Project Management Institute, has agreed to adhere to a code of professional conduct, and has passed an examination designed to objectively assess and measure project management knowledge. In addition, a PMP must satisfy continuing certification requirements or lose the certification.

project manager The individual responsible for managing a project.

project office (PO) A centralized unit within an organization or department that oversees and improves the management of projects.

project organization An organizational structure in which core work is accomplished by project teams.

project oversight See oversight.

project partnering A nonbinding method of transforming contractual relationships into a cohesive, cooperative project team with a single set of goals and established procedures for resolving disputes in a timely manner.

project portfolio Group of projects that have been selected for implementation balanced by project type, risk, and ranking by selected criteria.

project screening matrix A matrix used to assess and compare the relative value of projects being considered for implementation.

project sponsor Typically a high-ranking manager who champions and supports a project.

project vision An image of what the project will accomplish.

projectized organization A multi-project organization in which project managers have full authority to assign priorities and direct the work of persons assigned to their project.

R

ratio (parametric) methods Uses the ratio of past actual costs for similar work to estimate the cost for a potential project. This macro method of forecasting cost does not provide a sound basis for project cost control since it does not recognize differences among projects.

reference class forecasting A sophisticated forecasting method in which you take an external view and forecast project costs based on actual outcomes of similar projects.

relationship-related currencies Influence based on friendship.

release burndown chart The trend of work remaining across time. In a release or product, the source of data is the product backlog with work remaining tracked on the vertical axis and number of sprints on the horizontal axis.

release meeting An Agile project meeting that occurs before the project gets underway which focuses on the goals, priorities, risks, and timeline of a project.

requirements Define capabilities, features, or attributes of the project's deliverables. They are usually defined through user stories or user cases that represent the users' perspective of what they expect from the project.

resource Any person, groups, skill, equipment or material used to accomplish a task, work package, or activity.

resource-constrained project A project that assumes resources are limited (fixed) and therefore time is variable.

resource profile A chart showing the usage of a resource in a project over time. It is common to try to reduce the peak of the resource usage by leveling or smoothing, thereby improving the utilization of the resource.

responsibility matrix A matrix whose intersection point shows the relationship between an activity (work package) and the person/group responsible for its completion.

retrospective A methodology that analyzes a past project event to determine what worked and what didn't, develops lessons learned, and creates an action plan that ensures lessons learned are used to improve management of future projects.

revised estimated cost to complete (ETC_{re}) Estimated total cost based on revised estimates made by experts and actual costs to date.

risk The chance that an undesirable project event will occur and the consequences of all its possible outcomes.

risk breakdown structure (RBS) A hierarchical depiction of the identified project risks arranged by risk category and subcategory that identifies the various areas and causes of potential risks.

risk profile A list of questions that addresses traditional areas of uncertainty on a project.

risk severity matrix A tool used to assess the impact of risks on a project.

S

"sacred cow" A project that is a favorite of a powerful management figure who is usually the champion for the project.

scaling Adapting Agile PM to large, multi-team projects.

scenario planning A structured process of thinking about future possible environments that would have potential high impact to disrupt the way you do business, and then developing potential strategies to compete in these altered environments.

schedule performance index (SPI) The ratio of work performed to work scheduled (EV/PV).

schedule variance (SV) The difference between the planned dollar value of the work actually completed and the value of the work scheduled to be completed at a given point in time (SV = EV − PV). Schedule variance contains no critical path information.

scope creep The tendency for the scope of a project to expand once it has started.

scope statement A definition of the end result or mission of a project. Scope statements typically include project objectives, deliverables, milestones, specifications, and limits and exclusions.

Scrum An incremental, iterative development approach to managing projects with a well-defined set of roles and processes.

Scrum master The person responsible for the Scrum process and its correct application.

self-organizing team A semi-autonomous team that manages itself.

sensitivity of a network The likelihood that the critical path(s) will change once the project begins to be implemented.

sharing risk Allocating proportions of risk to different parties.

slack (SL) Time an activity can be delayed before it becomes critical.

social network building The process of identifying and building cooperative relationships with key people.

sociotechnical perspective A focus on the interaction between tools/methods and people.

splitting A scheduling technique in which work is interrupted on one activity and the resource is assigned to another activity for a period of time, then reassigned to work on the original activity.

sprint A fixed period of time during which a Scrum teams works to turn the product backlog it has selected into an increment of product functionality.

sprint backlog A list of tasks that defines a Scrum team's work for a sprint. Each task identifies those responsible for doing the work and the estimated amount of work remaining on the task on any given day during the sprint.

sprint burndown chart The trend of work remaining across time in a sprint. The source of data is the sprint backlog with work remaining tracked on the vertical axis and days of a sprint on the horizontal axis.

sprint planning meeting A Scrum meeting divided into two segments. During the first segment the product owner presents the highest priority product backlog to the team. The team and product owner collaborate to determine how much of the product backlog it can turn into functionality during the upcoming sprint. During the second segment, the team plans how it will meet his commitment by detailing its work as a plan in the sprint backlog.

sprint retrospective meeting A Scrum meeting in which the team discusses the just concluded sprint and determines what could be changed that might make the next sprint more enjoyable and productive.

sprint review meeting A Scrum meeting in which the team demonstrates to the product owner and any other interested parties what it was able to accomplish during the sprint.

stakeholders Individuals and organizations that are actively involved in the project, or whose interests may be positively or negatively affected as a result of project execution or completion. They may also exert influence over the project and its results.

strong matrix A matrix structure in which the project manager has primary control over project activities and functional managers support project work.

systems thinking A holistic approach to viewing problems that emphasizes understanding the interactions among different problem factors.

T

task See activity.

task-related currencies Influence based, helping someone else do their work.

team-building A process designed to improve the performance of a team.

team evaluation Evaluating the performance of the project team using a minimum core of conditions in place before the project began. Evaluation practices should emphasize the team as a whole, while minimizing individual performance.

team rituals Ceremonial actions that reinforce team identity and values.

template method Use of a prepared form to develop project networks, costs, and time estimates.

360-degree feedback A multirater appraisal system based on performance information that is gathered from multiple sources (superiors, peers, subordinates, customers).

time and cost databases Collection of actual versus estimated times and costs of work packages over many projects that are used for estimating new project tasks and their expected possible error.

time buffer A contingency amount of time for an activity to cover uncertainty—for example, availability of a key resource or merge event.

time-constrained project A project that assumes time is fixed and, if resources are needed, they will be added.

time-phased baseline A cost baseline that is derived from the WBS and project schedule. The budgeted costs are distributed to mirror the project schedule.

time-phased budgets Planned costs that are broken down by distinct time periods (e.g., $5,000 per week) for a work package, as opposed to a budget for a whole job/project (6 months for a total of $130,000). Time phasing allows better cost control by measuring the actual rate of expenditure versus the planned expenditure rate over small pieces of the project.

top-down estimates Rough estimates that use surrogates to estimate project time and cost (also called macro estimates).

total slack (TS) The amount of time an activity can be delayed and not affect the project duration (TS = LS − ES or LF − EF).

Tracking Gantt A Gantt chart that compares planned versus actual schedule information.

transferring risk Shifting responsibility for a risk to another party.

triple constraint The competing demands of time, cost, and scope. These constraints frequently represent trade-off decisions to be dealt with by the project manager and/or sponsor.

V

variance at completion (VAC) Indicates expected actual cost over- or underrun at completion (VAC = BAC − EAC).

virtual project team Spatially separated project team whose members are unable to communicate face to face. Communication is usually by electronic means.

W

weak matrix A matrix structure in which functional managers have primary control over project activities and the project manager coordinates project work.

work breakdown dictionary Provides detailed information about each element in the WBS. The dictionary typically includes the work package level (code), name, and functional description.

work breakdown structure (WBS) A hierarchical method that successively subdivides the work of the project into smaller detail.

work package A task at the lowest level of the WBS. Responsibility for the package should be assigned to one person and, if possible, limited to 80 hours of work.

ACRONYMS

AC	Actual cost of work completed
ACWP	Actual cost of work performed
AOA	Activity-on-arrow
AON	Activity-on-node
BAC	Budget at completion
BATNA	Best alternative to a negotiated agreement
BCWP	Budgeted cost of work performed
BCWS	Budgeted cost of work scheduled
BOOT	Build-own-operate-transfer
CAPM	Certified Associate in Project Management
CCPM	Critical-chain approach to project planning and management
CPI	Cost performance index
CPM	Critical path method
CV	Cost variance
DUR	Duration
EAC	Estimate at completion (with revised cost estimates)
EF	Early finish
EQ	Emotional intelligence
ES	Early start
ETC	Estimate to complete
EV	Earned value
FAC	Forecast at completion
FF	Free float
IFB	Invitation for bid
KISS	Keep it simple, stupid
LF	Late finish
LS	Late start
MBWA	Management by wandering around
NIH	Not invented here
NPV	Net present value
OBS	Organization breakdown structure
PCI	Percent complete index
PCIB	Percent complete index—budget costs
PCIC	Percent complete index—actual costs
PDM	Precedence diagramming method
PERT	Project evaluation review technique
PMP	Project Management Professional
PO	Project office
PV	Planned value of work scheduled
RBS	Risk breakdown structure
RM	Responsibility matrix
SL	Slack
SPI	Schedule performance index
SV	Schedule variance
TCPI	To complete performance index
VAC	Variance at completion
WBS	Work breakdown structure

$$\text{PCIB} = \frac{\text{EV}}{\text{BAC}}$$

$$\text{CV} = \text{EV} - \text{AC}$$

$$\text{CPI} = \frac{\text{EV}}{\text{AC}}$$

$$\text{EAC}_\text{f} = \frac{(\text{BAC} - \text{EV})}{\left(\frac{\text{EV}}{\text{AC}}\right)} + \text{AC}$$

$$\text{EAC}_\text{re} = \text{AC} + \text{ETC}_\text{re}$$

$$t_e = \frac{a + 4m + b}{6}$$

$$\sigma_{t_e} = \left(\frac{b - a}{6}\right)$$

$$\text{TCPI} = \frac{(\text{BAC} - \text{EV})}{(\text{BAC} - \text{AC})}$$

$$\text{PCIC} = \frac{\text{AC}}{\text{EAC}}$$

$$\text{SV} = \text{EV} - \text{PV}$$

$$\text{SPI} = \frac{\text{EV}}{\text{PV}}$$

$$\text{VAC}_\text{f} = \text{BAC} - \text{EAC}_\text{f}$$

$$\text{VAC}_\text{re} = \text{BAC} - \text{EAC}_\text{re}$$

$$\sigma_{T_E} = \sqrt{\Sigma\sigma_{t_e}^2}$$

$$Z = \frac{T_S - T_E}{\sqrt{\Sigma\sigma_{t_e}^2}}$$

INDEX

Note: Page numbers followed by n indicate material in source notes and footnotes.

A

Abdel-Hamid, T., 329
Abdelshafi, I., 608
Abramovici, A., 498
Abrashoff, D. M., 365
Acceleration options, 307–312
Accounting services, 356
Ackoff, Russell L., 539, 567
Activity
  basic relationships, 166–167
  burst, 164, 167, 172–173
  defined, 162, 164
  hammock, 186–187
  level of detail, 176
  merge, 164, 167, 171
  numbering, 176–177
  parallel, 164, 167
  in project networks, 162, 164, 166–169
  splitting, 268–269, 299–300
Activity-on-arrow (AOA), 165–169
Activity-on-node (AON), 165–169
  versus activity-on-arrow (AOA), 165–166
  automated warehouses, 168, 177–179
  backward pass, 171–173
  basic relationships, 166–169
  computers in developing, 177–179
  forward pass, 170–171
  fundamentals, 166
  laddering, 180, 181
  lag relationship, 180–186
    combinations, 184
    finish-to-finish, 184, 185
    finish-to-start, 181
    start-to-finish, 184
    start-to-start, 181–184
    use in forward and backward pass, 185–186
Activity orientation, 550
Actual cost (AC)
  defined, 463
  variance analysis, 465
Adams, A. M., 231
Adams, J. R., 395, 407
Adaptive Software Development, 604
Adjourning stage of teams, 377, 378
Adler, N., 545, 563, 567
Adler, P. S., 53
Administrative support, dependencies of, 342
Aerospace industry, 72, 382
Agile Alliance, 604
Agile Manifesto, 604
Agile PM, 590–606
  examples of, 595, 596, 597, 604
  iterative incremental development processes (IIDs), 594–596
  with large projects, 603–604
  limitations and concerns, 604–606
  nature of, 591
  process breakdown structure (PBS), 596
  scrum, 596–603
  traditional methods versus, 591–593
Ahmadi, R., 329
Airlines, 441
Airplane production, 296, 422–423
Albaugh, Jim, 423
Alegi, Peter, 220n
Alexander, R. C., 34n, 55
Allen, Roger F., 101n
Allen, Stephen D., 101n
Allen, Woody, 615
All-or-nothing projects, 221
Alternatives, in group decision making, 393–394
Ambassador activities, 352
American Express, 586
American Planning Association (APA), 148
Anand, V., 365
Anbari, F. T., 498
Ancona, D. G., 352, 352n, 365
Andersen, Arthur E., 356
Angus, R. B., 454
Aniftos, S., 532
Apocalypse Now (film), 542, 543
Apotheker, Leo, 30
Apple, 15, 30, 31, 34, 74, 306, 420, 422
Applebaum, Jeffrey, 429
Apportionment, for estimating project times and costs, 137
Arbitrating conflict, 397
Archibald, Russell D., 587
Archives, of retrospectives in closing stage, 529–530
Arenas, Gilbert, 515
Arms, P. B., 549, 567
Arrow, K. J., 258, 291
Arthur Andersen, 356, 357
Ashforth, B. E., 365
Ashley, D. B., 102, 125
Association for the Advancement of Cost Engineering (AACE), 148
Atkinson, W., 231
AT&T, 25, 67, 138, 520
Automated warehouses, 168, 177–179
Automotive industry, 13, 386
Autonomy Corporation, 30
Avant Assessment, 621
Avatar (film), 404n
Avoiding risk, 215–216

B

Backward pass-latest times, 171–173, 185–186
  lag relationships, 185–186
  using backward pass information, 175–176
Badaracco, J. L., Jr., 365
Baker, B., 588
Baker, B. M., 231, 329, 365
Baker, W. E., 365
Balanced matrix, 76, 78–79
Balanced scorecard model, 586
Banking, 575
Bank of America, 138
Bard, J. F., 367
Barnes, M., 152
Barnes, R., 303
Baroudi, B., 625
Baseline budget, 467–468, 469
Baselines
  changes in, 481–482
  developing, 273–278, 459, 463–465, 467–468
  project cost, 251, 273–278
  project monitoring information system, 459, 465, 467–468, 481–482
  time-phased budget, 176, 251, 273–278, 464
Basic nature of people, 550
BATNA (best alternative to a negotiated agreement), 436–437
Baxter, Jerry B., 308n

Bay of Pigs invasion (Cuba), 403
Bedeian, A. G., 231
Behavior, in organizational culture, 85
BellAircraft, 221
Benko, C., 21, 53
Bennis, W., 360, 365
Benson, S., 404, 408
Berkun, S., 388n, 407
Best alternative to a negotiated agreement (BATNA), 436–437
Best practices in outsourcing, 423–432
- co-location, 429–430
- conflict management processes, 427
- fair and incentive-laden contracts, 430–431
- frequent review and status updates, 427–429
- long-term outsourcing relationships, 431–432
- training and team-building activities, 426–427
- well-defined requirements and procedures, 424–426

Beta distribution, PERT, 239–240
Beyer, J. M., 82n, 92
"Big Dig" (Boston), 148
Bigelow, D., 53
Bill & Melinda Gates Foundation, 13
Biotechnology, 309
Black, J. H., 157
Block, T. R., 92, 575n
Bloom, Howard, 515n
Boeing, 149, 300, 422–423
Bogart, Humphrey, 420
Bolman, L. G., 385n, 407
Bonar, Robert, 14
Bonuses, 391
Borsuk, R., 567
Bottom-up estimates, 133–143
- nature of, 134–135
- parametric procedures, 139–140
- range estimating, 140–141
- template methods, 139

Boulter, M., 608
Bourne, Lynda, 120n, 344n, 365
Bowen, D., 555n, 568
Bowen, H. K., 75, 88, 92, 388, 390, 407
Bowles, M., 498
Boyer, C., 53, 581, 588
Bradberry, T., 361n, 365
Bradford, David L., 344, 345, 345n, 365
Brainstorming
- of cost savings options, 322–323
- in generating alternatives, 393–394
- options for mutual gain, 435

Brandon, D. M., Jr., 498
Brandt, S. E., 395, 407
Brazil, 546
Breashears, David, 219
Bribery, 551, 560
Brin, Sergey, 84
Brooks, Frederick P., Jr., 309, 309n, 329, 457
Brown, S., 92
Brown, Tim, 595
Brucker, P., 291
Bruzelius, N., 152
Bryant, Kobe, 376
Budd, C. S., 302
Budget at completion (BAC), 463
Budget reserves, 223
Budgets
- budget reserves, 223
- percent complete index—budgeted costs (PCIB), 474–475
- Project Baseline Budget, 467–468, 469
- time-phase budget baselines, 176, 274–278

Buehler, R., 148n, 152
Buffers
- feeder, 295
- project, 295
- resource, 295
- time, 224

Build-Own-Operate-Transfer (BOOT) provisions, 216, 515
Bureaucratic bypass syndrome, 404
Burgess, A. R., 291
Burst activities, 164, 167, 172–173
Butler, Ginger, 621

C

C. C. Myers, Inc., 308
Cabanis, J., 365
Cabanis-Brewin, J., 361n, 365
Cahill, T., 541, 567
Caldwell, D. F., 82n, 93, 352, 352n, 365
Calendar dates, for project activities, 180
Calhoun, Chad, 312
California Department of Transportation (CalTrans), 308
Callaway Golf Equipment, 104
Cameron, K. S., 92
Canan, Crystal, 429
Capability Maturity Model (CMM), 583
CAPM (Certified Associate in Project Management), 4, 619–620
Career paths. *See* Project management career paths
Carlton, J., 74n, 92
Carnegie Mellon University, 583
Carr, M. J., 231
Carrier Transicold, 218
Cases
- The Accounting Software Installation Project, 444–448
- Advantage Energy Technology Data Center Migration, 200–202
- Advantage Energy Technology Data Center Migration—Part B, 245–248
- Ajax Project, 411–413
- Alaska Fly-Fishing Expedition, 231–232
- AMEX, Hungary, 569–571
- The Blue Sky Project, 367–371
- Cerberus Corporation, 372–373
- A Day in the Life, 21–23
- Don't Tell Me What You Have Done. Tell Me What You Are Going to Do, 588–589
- Film Prioritization, 57–60
- Franklin Equipment, Ltd., 413–416
- Fund Raising Project Selection, 61–62
- Goldrush Electronics Negotiation Exercise, 448–449
- Greendale Stadium Case, 202–203
- Hector Gaming Company, 56–57
- Horizon Consulting, 97–99
- International Capital, Inc.—Part A, 244–245
- International Capital, Inc.—Part B, 330
- Introducing Scrum at P2P, 609–613
- Kerzner Office Equipment, 409–411
- Manchester United Soccer Club, 126–127
- Maximum Megaherz Project, 536
- Moss and McAdams Accounting Firm, 94–96
- Nightingale Project—A, 333–334
- Nightingale Project—B, 334–335
- The "Now" Wedding—Part A, 335–337
- The "Now" Wedding—Part B, 337
- Post Graduation Adventure, 154–155
- Power Train, Ltd., 291–293
- Scanner Project, 499

Cases—*Cont.*
Sharp Printing, AG, 153–154
Shell Case Fabricators, 442–444
Silver Fiddle Construction, 233–234
Sustaining Project Risk Management during Implementation, 237–239
Tom Bray, 371–372
Trans LAN Project, 234–235
Tree Trimming Project, 499
Whitbread World Sailboat Race, 330–332
XSU Spring Concert, 235–236
Casey, W., 80n, 92
Castro, Edson de, 389
Cavendish, J., 454
CCPM. *See* Critical-chain project management (CCPM)
Celebration, in closing stage, 530
Certification programs, 4, 619–621
Certified Associate in Project Management (CAPM), 4, 619–620
Change management systems, 225–228
change request forms and logs, 226–228
integration of, 227–228
Chaparral Steel, 80–81, 88
Character, trust and, 358, 359
Charnes, A., 291
Chatman, J., 82n, 93
Checklists
closing stage, 514, 533–535
project scope, 102–106
in project selection, 39–40
Chen, M., 549, 567
Chermack, T. J., 54
Chilmeran, A. H., 125
China
cross-cultural factors in, 540–541, 556–557
legal/political factors in, 540–541
China Sunergy Co., Ltd., 13
Christensen, D. S., 478, 498
Chudoba, K. M., 408
Chunnel project, 148, 419
Cigna, 133
Cisco, 30
Citibank Global Corporate Bank, 575
Citigroup, 541
Clark, K. B., 92, 388, 389, 407
Cleland, D. I., 407
Cleveland Cavaliers, 515
Closing stage, 510–530
adjourning stage of teams, 377, 378
dedicated project teams and, 74
Closing stage—*Cont.*
evaluation, 512, 517–522
functional organization and, 69
matrix management and, 78
phase gate methodology, 581
post-implementation evaluation, 512, 517–522
project closeout checklists, 514, 533–535
of project life cycle, 9, 396
retrospectives, 512, 522–530
sources of conflict in, 396
types, 512–513
wrap-up activities, 511–512, 513–517, 533–535
Coady, Gerry, 41
Cochran, Dick, 520n, 522, 531
Cohen, A. R., 344, 345, 345n, 365
Cohen, D. J., 21, 53
Colangelo, Jerry, 376
Collins, J. C., 87, 92, 568
Co-location
in outsourcing, 429–430
team identity and, 387
Combination of lag relationships, 184
Communication
cultural factors in, 565–566. *See also* Cultural factors
in international projects, 565–566
in outsourcing, 425, 432
project communication plan, 118–122
virtual project teams and, 402–403
Compadre system, 552
Competency, trust and, 358–359
Compliance/emergency projects, 36–37
Computer industry, 27, 30, 74, 271, 389, 399–400, 623
Computer-related products and services, 84
Conaway, W. A., 555n, 568
Concurrent engineering, 182–184
Conductor metaphor, 344
Conference calls, virtual project teams and, 402
Conflict management, 394–398
dedicated project teams and, 73, 74
dysfunctional conflict, 396, 397–398
functional conflict, 396–397
low-priority projects, 395
matrix management and, 78
in outsourcing, 427
resource conflicts, 34–35
virtual project teams and, 403
Confucius, 556
Consensus methods
consensus testing in group decision making, 394
for estimating project times and costs, 135–136
Consistency, trust and, 358
Construction/demolition industries, 148, 215, 254, 308, 312
Consultants, external
as independent project facilitators, 524–525
in rejuvenating the project team, 398–399
Contingencies, in project estimation, 133
Contingency funding, 222–224
Contingency planning, 216–221
cost risks, 220–221
funding risks, 221
schedule risks, 220
technical risks, 218–220
Contract change control system, 453–454
Contract management
contract change control system, 453–454
cost-plus contracts, 64, 452–453
fixed-price contracts, 64, 451–452
nature of contracts, 450
in outsourcing, 430–431, 449–454
in perspective, 454
procurement management and, 63–65, 450, 583
Contractors. *See also* Outsourcing
dependencies of, 343
incentive contracts, 307, 308, 430–431
selection from bid proposals, 65
Control. *See also* Project monitoring information system
in conflict management, 397–398
contract change control, 453–454
defined, 458
project control process, 458–459
risk response control, 224–228
Control charts, in project monitoring information system, 460, 461–462
Controlled Demolition Inc., 215
Control Tower project office, 80
Conway, 525
Cooke-Davies, T., 531
Cooper, M. J., 302
Cooper, Robert G., 577, 588
Cooper, W. W., 291

Cooperation. *See also* Project teams
in leading by example, 355
in negotiations for outsourcing, 432–433
Coppola, Francis Ford, 543
Core project team, in accelerating project completion, 310
Corning, 431
Corporate downsizing, 12–13
Cost accounts, 113
Cost and Optimization Engineering (Jelen and Black), 157
Cost estimates, 130–149
apportion methods, 137
consensus methods, 135–136
factors influencing quality of, 130–131
forecasting final project cost, 476–478
function point methods, 137–139
guidelines for, 131–133
learning curves, 139, 155–159
level of detail, 143–144
for mega projects, 148
parametric procedures, 139–140
phase estimating, 141–143
range estimating, 140–141
ratio methods, 136
refining, 146–149
template methods, 139
time and cost database, 149
top-down versus bottom-up, 133–143
types of costs, 144–145
Cost performance index (CPI), 473
Cost-plus contracts, 64, 452–453
Cost risks, in contingency planning, 220–221
Cost/schedule graph, 466
Cost-sharing ratio (CSR), 452
Cost variance (CV)
computing, 464
defined, 463
variance analysis, 465, 466–467
Countercultures, 83, 88
Coutu, D. L., 402, 407
Covance, 309
Covey, Stephen R., 358, 360n, 365, 435, 435n, 441
Cowan, C. C., 424n, 441
Crashing, 314–321
Crash point, 315–316
Crash times, 314–316, 319–321
Crawford, Lynn, 21, 36, 53
Credibility, in recruiting project members, 381–382
Crider, Bill, 623
Crime, 541
Critical-chain project management (CCPM), 293–303
accelerating project completion, 311, 312
in action, 295–296, 300–301
impact on project schedule, 299
monitoring project performance, 300
splitting tasks, 299–300
time estimates, 294–295
traditional scheduling approach versus, 296–299
Critical path method (CPM), 161, 164, 174, 176, 177, 239, 317. *See also* PERT (program evaluation and review technique)
Cross-cultural orientations, 550
Cross-functional integration, 73
Crystal Clear, 604
Cubanis, J., 355n
Cullinane, T. P., 454
Cultural factors. *See also* Communication; Organizational culture
adjustments, 549–552
in China, 540–541, 556–557
cross-cultural orientations, 550
culture, defined, 545, 548
culture shock, 560–563
in France, 553–555
Hofstede Framework, 551
in Hong Kong, 558
in international projects, 545–547, 548–563
Kluckhohn-Strodtbeck Cross-Cultural Framework, 550
in Mexico, 552–553
in Namibia, Africa, 563
in outsourcing, 425
in Saudi Arabia, 555–556
summary comments, 559–560
in the United States, 549–551, 557–559
Culture shock, 560–563
coping with, 562–563
culture shock cycle, 561
nature of, 560–562
stress-related, 562
Culver, Irvin, 72
Currency fluctuations, 543–544
Customer relations
increased customer focus and, 14
met expectations in, 437–439
in outsourcing, 437–439
Customer relations—*Cont.*
project managers as client account executives, 439
Customers
assumption of project responsibilities, 322
dependencies of, 343
scope checklist review with, 103

D

Dahlgren, G., 441
Daily scrum, 599–600
DaimlerChrysler, 420
Dalkey, N. C., 152
Dangler paths, 180
Daniel, Tim, 541
Darnell, R., 21
Databases
project monitoring information system, 457–458, 482–483
time and cost, 149
Data General Corporation, 389
Deadlines
imposed, 307
in outsourcing, 425
Deal, T. E., 81, 92, 385n, 407
Decarlo, D., 608
Decision-making process, 392–394
facilitating, 393–394
importance of, 392–393
nominal group technique (NGT) in, 405
in project meetings, 383–386
Dedicated project teams, 70–74, 88
advantages and disadvantages, 72–74
examples of, 71–74
nature of, 71–72
Defining stage, 100–123
establishing project priorities, 106–108
organization breakdown structure (OBS), 113
process breakdown structure (PBS), 101, 116–117, 596
project communication plan, 118–122
in project life cycle, 8, 9, 396
project scope, 102–106
responsibility matrices (RM), 117–118, 119
sources of conflict in, 396
work breakdown structure (WBS), 101, 108–116
Dehler, G. E., 366
De Laat, P. B., 92

Delbeeq, Andrew, 405n
Delegation, 360
DelGrosso, Steve, 620
Deliverables
in closing stage, 511–512
project scope, 64, 103
Dell, 575, 578
Dell Children's Medical Center, 14
Deloitte Consulting, 33
Delphi Method, 135, 136, 210n
DeMarco, T., 310, 329, 407
Demeulemeester, E. L., 291, 302
Deneire, M., 567
Dependencies
mapping, 347–349
stakeholder, 341–344
Derby, Charles, 21
DeRosa, D., 401, 408
Descamps, J. P., 53
Design firms, 594, 595
Developing Products in Half the Time (Smith and Reinertsen), 218–219
Dexter, Susan, 309
DiDonato, L. S., 441
Digital Equipment Corporation, 385n, 388, 389
Dinsmore, P. C., 365
Direct costs, 144–145
project, 314
project overhead, 145
Dish Network, 13
DiStefano, J. J., 549n, 568
Documentation. *See also* Reports and reporting
in outsourcing, 425
public documents in organizational culture, 85
Doh, J. P., 568
Doing it twice, in accelerating project completion, 310
Dooley, K. J., 382, 409
Doran, G. T., 31, 31n, 54
Dreamliner (Boeing), 422–423
Drexl, A., 291
Drexler, John A., Jr., 413n, 441, 442
Dropped baton, 294
Duffey, M. R., 498
Dunbar, E., 568
Duncan, David, 356
Duncan, J., 231
DuPont, 138, 578
Duration of project. *See* Project duration
Dvir, Dov, 26n, 80n, 94, 303
Dworatschek, S., 92
Dyer, L., 407
Dyer, S., 441
Dysfunctional conflict, 396, 397–398

E

EAC_f (estimated cost at completion, forecast), 477
EAC_{re} (estimated cost at completion, revised), 476–477
Early and late times, 163
Earned value (EV)
additional earned value rules, 476, 499–506
defined, 276, 459, 463
development of earned value cost/schedule system, 459, 462–467, 499–506
50/50 rule, 476
percent complete rule, 465
percent complete with weighted monitoring gates, 476
pseudo-earned value percent complete approach, 483
in status report, 469
in time-phased budgets, 276
variance analysis, 465
0/100 rule, 476
Eastman Kodak, 149, 390
Economic factors, 542–544
Eden, L., 568
Edgett, S. J., 588
EDS, 462
Edward, K. A., 442
Einsiedel, A. A., 365
Eisenhardt, K. R., 92
Eiteman, D. K., 568
Electrical utilities, 479
Electronic bulletin boards, virtual project teams and, 402
Electronics industry, 13
Eliyahu Goldratt Institute, 300n, 301
E-mail, virtual project teams and, 402
Emerson, Ralph Waldo, 305
Emhjellenm, K., 152
Emotional intelligence (EQ), 361
Emotional Intelligence (Goleman), 361
Empathy, 361, 435
Energy production, 13
Englund, R. L., 92
Enron, 356, 357
Entrepreneurial culture, 87
Environmental factors, 540–547
culture, 545–547. *See also* Cultural factors
economy, 542–544
geography, 542, 543
infrastructure, 544–545
Environmental factors—*Cont.*
legal/political, 382, 422, 540–541
security, 541–542
Equipment factor, as resource constraint, 254–255
Ericksen, J., 407
Ernst, H., 409
Errors
as acceptable, 225
network logic, 176
project estimation, 133
reporting, 225
Escalation, 427
Estimated cost at completion (EAC)
defined, 463
EAC_f (forecast), 477
EAC_{re} (revised), 476–477
Estimated cost to complete (ETC), 463
Estimation. *See* Project estimation
Ethics, 355–357
bribery, 551, 560
codes of conduct, 357
collapse of Arthur Andersen, 356
in leading by example, 355
European Economic Community (EEC), 576
Evaluation. *See* Project evaluation
Everest (IMAX film), 219
Excessive multitasking, 294–295
Exchange rate fluctuations, 543–544
Exclusions from scope, 103
Executing stage. *See also* Implementation
of project life cycle, 9, 396
sources of conflict in, 396
Expectations
managing, 350
met-expectations model, 437–439
Extreme Programming, 604
ExxonMobil, 586

F

Facilitators, 524–525
Faerman, S. R., 442
Failed projects, 513
Failure Mode and Effects Analysis (FMEA), 213
Faris, R., 608
Fast-tracking, 183, 310–311
Features, 596
Feeder buffers, 295
Fendly, L. G., 258, 291
Ferrazzi, K., 366, 625
Fiat, 13
FIFA (Federation Internationale de Football Association), 220

Fifth Discipline, The (Senge), 522
Filipczak, B., 92
Film industry, 13, 543
Final project report, 516–517
  appendix, 517
  executive summary, 516
  forecasting, 476–478
  lessons learned, 517, 522–523, 581–582
  recommendations, 517
  review and analysis, 516–517
Financial selection models, 37–39
  net present value (NPV), 37–39, 213
  payback, 37, 38
Financial Solutions Group of Mynd, 350
Finish-to-finish lag relationship, 184, 185
Finish-to-start lag relationship, 181
Fischer, Randy, 429
Fisher, R., 433–437, 441
Fixed-price contracts, 64, 451–452
Fleming, Q. W., 455, 473n, 478, 498
Float, 173–175
  free, 175
  total, 173–175
Flow diagrams, phase gate methodology, 578–579
Floyd, S. W., 54
Flyvbjerg, Bent, 148, 148n, 152
FMEA (Failure Mode and Effects Analysis), 213
Folklore, in organizational culture, 85–86
Follow-on contracts, 157–159
Follow-up, in group decision making, 394
Food industry, 206
Ford, E. C., 231
Ford, Henry, 375
Ford Motors, 138, 386
Forecasting
  of final project cost, 476–478
  Reference Class Forecasting, 148
Forming stage of teams, 377
Fortune 500, 33
Forward exchange/contract, 544
Forward pass-earliest times, 169–171
  lag relationships, 185–186
  with slack times, 173
  using forward pass information, 175–176
Foti, R., 36, 54
Frame, J. D., 92, 387, 408, 575n
France, cross-cultural factors in, 553–555
Frank, L., 54
Frankel, Rob, 515
Franklin, Benjamin, 573
Fraser, J., 455
Free float, 175
Free slack (FS), 175
Fretty, Peter, 296n, 532
Friedman, Thomas L., 54
Fritz, Robert, 388
Frontier Airlines Holdings, 41
Fuji, 390
Functional conflict, 396–397
Functional managers
  dependencies of, 342
  project managers versus, 75, 78
Functional organization, 68–70
  advantages and disadvantages, 69–70
  nature of, 68
"Function points", for estimating project times and costs, 137–139
Funding risks, in contingency planning, 221
Fusco, Joseph C., 33, 33n, 54, 519, 519n

G

Gabarro, S. J., 366
Gale, S. F., 623n
Gallagher, R. S., 92
Gamble, John E., 104n
Gantt, H. L., 200
Gantt charts, 177, 179
  baseline, 460
  in critical-chain project management (CCPM), 299
  in project monitoring information system, 460–461
  tracking, 460–461, 471, 508
Gardner, D., 575n
Garside, J., 306n
Gary, L., 125
Gates, Bill, 462
GE Appliances, 405
Geary, L. K., 93
Gene Codes, 597
General and administrative (G&A) overhead costs, 145
General Electric (GE), 8, 15, 25, 138, 405, 520
General Motors (GM), 183, 300, 578
Geographical factors, 542, 543
Germany
  project cancellation procedures, 513
  truck toll-collection system, 513
Gersick, Connie J., 379, 379n
Ghani, Saud Abdul, 220
Gibson, C. B., 408
Ginter, P. M., 231
Globerson, S., 125, 367
Goal, The (Goldratt), 293–303
Gobeli, D. H., 75, 77, 79, 92, 93, 102, 125, 532
Going native, 404, 560
Gold, Dan, 309
Goldberg, Aaron I., 74, 93
Golden Gate Bridge (San Francisco), 254
Goldratt, Eliyahu, 268, 291, 293–302
Goldsman, L. P., 455
Goleman, Daniel, 361
Goo, S. K., 84n
Google Inc., 15, 30, 84
Gordon, R. I., 309n, 329
Governance. *See* Project governance
Government agencies. *See also names of specific government agencies*
  dependencies of, 343
Gradante, W., 575n
Graham, J. L., 557n, 568
Graham, R. J., 21, 53, 92
Grant, A., 344, 366
Graves, J., 361n, 365
Gray, Clifford F., 8, 21, 79, 92, 231, 424n, 441, 625
Gray, N. S., 152
Green, S. G., 366
Greetings, 555
Griffen, D., 148n, 152
Griffiths, M., 608
Gringos, 552
Gross domestic product (GDP), 542
Groupthink, 403–404
Gryglak, Adam, 386
Guanxi, 556–557
Guard activities, 352
Gundersen, N. A., 454
Gunderson, A., 545, 563, 567
Gustafson, D. H., 405n
Gwinn, Rod, 615, 616

H

Habitat for Humanity, 312, 312n
Hackman, J. R., 408
Halliburton, 515
Hallowell, R., 555n, 568
Hamburger, D. H., 231
Hammock activities, 186–187

Hansson, J., 441
Harris, P. R., 556n, 568
Harrison, M. T., 82n, 92
Harvard Business School, 596
Harvard Negotiation Project, 433
HBO, 595
Health care industry, 14
Hedberg, B., 441
Hedging, 544
Heise, S., 498
Helm, J., 54
Hendrickson, Chet, 591
Hendrix, K., 125
Henricks, Paul, 309
Henry, R. A., 207–208, 231
Hermida Quintella, Rogério, 55
Herroelen, W. S., 291, 302
Heuristics, 258, 259
Hewlett-Packard (HP), 30, 67, 138, 399–400, 405, 520, 575, 578, 581, 619
Highsmith, J., 608
Hildebrand, C., 609
Hill, L. A., 366
Hoang, H., 441
Hobbs, B., 36, 53, 79–80, 93
Hobday, M., 93
Hodgetts, R. M., 568
Hodgkinson, Jeff, 623
Hoegl, M., 409
Hoffman, Robert, 520n, 532
Hofstede, Geert, 551, 551n, 568
Hofstede Framework, 551
Holloway, C. A., 92, 388, 389, 407
Hölzle, K., 625
Homans, G. C., 378n, 408
Home care products, 12
Honesty, in negotiations for outsourcing, 432–433
Hong Kong, cross-cultural factors in, 558
Hooker, J., 555n, 557n, 568
Hubris, 74
Hulett, D. T., 231
Hurowicz, L., 258, 291
Hurricane Katrina, 518
Hutchens, G., 54

I

Ibbs, C. W., 329, 532, 588
IBM, 27, 30, 88, 138, 149, 309, 400, 575, 620
IDEO, 594, 595
Implementation
  implementation gap in project portfolio system, 32–33, 35
  phase gate methodology, 580
  projects in organization strategy, 32
Incentives, 320
  incentive contracts, 307, 308, 430–431
  project reward systems, 391–392
Independence
  in project estimation, 132–133
  project facilitators, 524–525
Indexes to monitor progress, 473–476
  additional earned value rules, 476, 499–506
  performance indexes, 473
  project percent complete indexes, 474–475, 483
  software for project cost/schedule systems, 475, 506–508
  technical performance measurement, 475
India, infrastructure factors in, 544–545
Indirect costs, project, 313–314
Individual reviews, 521–522
Inflation, 544
Information system. *See also* Project monitoring information system
  coding work breakdown structure for, 113–116
  in project communication plan, 121
Infrastructure factors, 544–545
Ingebretsen, M., 125, 231
Innovation, in outsourcing, 432
Inspiration-related currencies, 345, 346
Integrity, 360
Intel, 25, 300, 419, 525, 530, 578, 615, 622, 623
Internal staff specialists, in rejuvenating the project team, 398–399
International Business Machines (IBM), 27, 30, 88, 138, 149, 309, 400, 575, 620
International projects, 538–566
  cross-cultural factors in, 545–547, 548–563
  environmental factors in, 540–547
  outsourcing, 419–420, 425, 426
  personnel selection and training for, 563–566
  project site selection, 547–548, 551
  virtual global teams in, 400–401
International SOS Assistance, Inc., 541
Into Thin Air (Krakauer), 219
Invitation for bid (IFB), 451
IPC Media, 605
Irix Pharmaceuticals, 309
Iterative incremental development processes (IIDs), 594–596

J

Jackson, M. B., 609
Jafari, Ali, 588
Jago, A. G., 393, 409
James, LeBron, 376, 515
James, M., 609
Jamieson, A., 54, 577, 588
Janis, I. L., 403, 408
Japan, training in, 564
Jassawalla, A. R., 93
Jedd, Marcia, 532
Jeffery, R., 152
Jelen, F. C., 157
Jensen, M. C., 377, 409
Jet Propulsion Laboratory, 382
Jobs, Steve, 74
Johansen, R., 404, 408
Johnson, Clarence L. "Kelly," 72, 93
Johnson, Magic, 376
Johnson, R. E., 54
Jonas, D., 21
Jonasson, Hans, 609
Jones, Claude, 152, 291
Jordan, Michael, 376
Joshi, M., 365

K

Kahneman, D., 148n, 152
Kaiser Permanente, 586
Kalaritis, Panos, 309
Kanter, Rosabeth Moss, 358, 366, 419, 442
Kaplan, R. E., 344, 366
Kaplan, Robert S., 54, 586, 588
Katz, D. M., 125
Katz, Ralph, 388, 408
Katzenbach, J. R., 385n, 408
Keifer, S., 479n
Kellebrew, J. B., 291
Kelly, J. E., 200
Kendrick, Tom, 532
Kennedy, A. A., 81, 92
Kenny, J., 54
Kerth, Norman L., 523, 532

Kerzner, Harold, 81n, 93, 125, 498, 583
Kezsbom, D. S., 442
Khang, D. B., 329
Kharbanda, O. P., 54, 129n, 152
Kidd, Jason, 376
Kidder, Tracy, 389, 389n, 391, 391n, 408
Kim, E. H., 498
King, Jon B., 354n, 366
Kingsberry, Don, 575n, 581
Kipling, Rudyard, 161
Kirk, Dorothy, 350, 350n, 366
Kirkman, B. L., 408
Kleiner, A., 409
Kleinschmidt, E. J., 588
Kluckhohn, F., 550, 550n, 568
Knoepfel, H., 92
Knoop, C. I., 555n, 568
Knowledge explosion, 11
Koh, Aileen, 21
Kolawa, Adam, 425, 425n
Konda, S. L., 231
Koppelman, Joel M., 473n, 478, 498
Korte, R. F., 54
Kotter, J. P., 340, 366
Kouzes, J. M., 352, 366
Krakauer, Jon, 219, 219n
Krane, J., 568
Kras, E., 553n, 568
Krause, Melissa, 597n
Kruchten, Philippe, 609
Krupp, Goran, 219
Kryzewski, Mike, 376
Kwak, Y. H., 532, 588

L

Lackey, Michael B., 479n
Laddering, 180, 181
Ladika, S., 532
Lags, 180–186
  in forward and backward pass procedures, 185–186
  to reduce schedule detail, 180–184
Lam, N. M., 557n, 568
Lamb, J. C., 309n, 329
Landau, E., 207n
Lane, H. W., 549n, 568
Lange, Merete, 563
Lansing, Alfred, 353, 353n
Large projects, 147, 148, 603–604
Larman, Craig, 609
Larson, Erik W., 21, 69, 72, 75, 77, 79, 92, 93, 102, 125, 354n, 366, 367n, 424n, 441, 442, 532
Larsson, U., 93
Laslo, Z., 93
Latham, G. P., 521, 532
Lavell, Debra, 532
Law of reciprocity, 344–347
  inspiration-related currencies, 345, 346
  personal-related currencies, 345, 347
  position-related currencies, 345, 346
  relationship-related currencies, 345, 346–347
  task-related currencies, 345
Lawrence, P. R., 93
Leach, L. P., 296n, 302
Leadership, 338–362. *See also* Project managers
  ethics and, 355–357
  law of reciprocity and, 344–347
  leading at the edge, 353
  leading by example, 352–355
  managing versus leading a project, 339–340
  project stakeholders and, 340–344
  qualities of effective project manager, 359–362
  social network building, 347–355
  trust and, 357–359
Leading at the Edge (Perkins), 353
Leading by example, 352–355
Learning curves, for estimating project times and costs, 139, 155–159
Leave-takings, 555
Leavitt, H. J., 404, 408
Lechler, T., 94
Lee, S. A., 329
LEED (Leadership in Energy & Environmental Design), 14
Legal/political factors, 382, 422, 540–541. *See also* Organization politics
Leifer, R., 54
Lenovo, 30
Lerner, Mathew, 309n
Lessons learned
  final project report, 517, 522–523, 581–582
  from Hurricane Katrina, 518
  phase gate methodology, 581–582
Letters of commendation, 392
Leus, R., 302
Leveling, 252, 255–257
Level of detail
  for project activities, 176
  in project estimation, 143–144
  in project networks, 176
Levine, H. A., 302
Levinson, Meredith, 620, 625
Levi Strauss, 462
Levy, F. K., 200
Levy, S. L., 391, 392n, 408
Lewis, J. P., 125
Lewis, M. W., 366
Lewis, R., 152
Li, M. I., 329
Lieberthal, G., 568
Lieberthal, K., 568
Lientz, B. P., 625
Likert, R., 375n, 408
Lilly, Bonnie, 312
Limits of scope, 103
Lindberg, Mike, 135
Linetz, B. P., 408
Lipman-Blumen, J., 404, 408
Lipsinger, R., 401, 408
Listening, empathic, 435
Lister, T., 407
Loch, C. H., 231
Lockheed Martin, 71, 72, 205–206, 207
Lodge at Snowbird (Utah), 604
Logitech, 595
Loizeaux, Mark, 215
Lone Ranger analogy, 352
Long-term relationships
  organization project management maturity, 582–586
  in outsourcing, 431–432
Lonza Biologics, 309
Looping, 176
Lorsch, J. W., 93
Lovallo, D., 148n, 152
Low, G. C., 152
Lowe, D., 455
Loyalty, 351
Luby, R. E., 125
Lucas, E., 549, 567
Lucas, George, 543
Lucasfilm, 13, 543
Lucent Technologies, 300
Luthans, F., 568

M

MacCormack, Alan, 596, 596n
MacIntyre, Jeff, 33, 33n, 54
Mackey, J., 303
Madnick, S., 329
Magenau, J. M., 442
Magne, E., 152
Magretta, Joan, 54
Maier, N. R. F., 393n, 408
Majchrzak, A., 93, 408

Malhotra, A., 408
"Management by wandering around" (MBWA), 349–350, 393, 457
Management reserves, 223–224
Managing expectations, 350
Managing Martians (Shirley and Morton), 382
Managing upward relations, 350–352
Mañana syndrome, 552–553
Mannakau, 312
Mantel, S. K., 366
Marlin, Mark, 532
Marriott Corp., 405
Martin, A., 404, 408
Martin, M., 454
Martin, P., 625
Martinelli, Russ, 532
Mass Fatality Identification System (M-FISys), 597
Materials factor, as resource constraint, 254
Matheson, David, 49, 49n, 54
Matheson, Jim, 49, 49n, 54
Matrix management, 74–79
  advantages and disadvantages, 77–78
  Balanced matrix, 76, 78–79
  example of, 89
  nature of, 74–75
  performance reviews, 521
  project versus functional manager responsibilities, 75, 78
  recruiting project members, 381, 382–383
  Strong matrix, 76–79
  Weak matrix, 75–76, 78
Maturity model, 582–586
Maurer, I., 442
Maznevski, M. L., 408
MBWA ("management by wandering around"), 349–350, 393, 457
McConnel, S., 609
McDermott, C. M., 54
McDougall, Lorna, 356n
McFarlan, F. W., 21, 53
McGrath, M. R., 442
McLeod, G., 153
McNerney, Jim, 423
McPherson, S. O., 408
Mediating conflict, 397
Médicins Sans Frontières (Doctors Without Borders), 541
Meetings. *See* Project meetings
Mega projects, estimation for, 147, 148
Melnyk, Les A., 518n
Ménard, P., 79–80, 93
Mendenhall, M. E., 564–565, 568
Menon, R., 231
Mentors, 622–623
Merge activities, 164, 167, 171
Merritt, G. M., 231
Met-expectations model, 437–439
Methods review, 527
Mexico, cross-cultural factors in, 552–553
Meyer, A. D., 231
MGM, 420
Miami Heat, 515
Micro managing, 341
Microsoft, 30, 107, 419, 462
Microsoft Office, 139–140
Microsoft Project, 187n, 262–268, 385, 450, 506–508
Middle management. *See also* Top management
  implementation gap in project portfolio system, 33, 35
  level of detail in project estimates, 143
  managing versus leading a project, 339–340
Milestones, in project scope, 103
Millard, Candice, 546, 546n
Miller, D., 549, 567
Miller, J., 72n, 93
Mills, E., 84n
Milosevic, D. Z., 54, 153, 568
Mission of organization
  project manager understanding of, 26
  in strategic management process, 29
Mitchel, Russ, 271n
Mitigating risk, 214–215
Mittman, R., 404, 408
Mobil Oil, 520
Moffett, M. H., 544, 568
Mohring, R., 291
Monarch, I., 231
Monroe, Marilyn, 420
Montol, S. K., 350n
Moran, James, 200n
Moran, R. T., 556n, 559n, 568
Moran, S. V., 556n, 568
Morgan, Pat, 386
Morigeau, Stuart, 231n
Morris, P. W., 54, 577, 588
Morrison, T., 555n, 568
Morton, Danielle, 382, 382n
Motivation
  for extraordinary performance, 320
  incentives in, 307, 308, 320, 391–392, 430–431
Motorola, 306, 420
Motta, Silva, 55
Mueller, E., 583, 588
Müller, R., 360, 367
Multi-criteria selection models, 39–42, 43
Multiproject environments
  project networks in, 180
  resource scheduling in, 271–273
Multiproject resource schedules, 271–273
Multitasking, 34–35, 294–295
Multi-weighted scoring models, 40–42, 43
Murch, R., 125
Mutual gain, in negotiation process, 435

N

Nabisco, 520
Naeni, L., 498
Nambisan, S., 442
Namibia, Africa, cross-cultural factors in, 563
NASA Mars Climate Orbiter, 205–206, 207
National Basketball Association (NBA), 376, 515
National Semiconductor, 586
Natural hedging, 544
Navistar, 386
NCR, 462
NEC, 25
Negotiation
  components of principled, 433–437
  in outsourcing, 432–437
Nellenbach, Joanita M., 18n
Nelson, K. A., 357n, 367
Nelson, Ryan R., 532
Net present value (NPV)
  in project selection, 37–39
  in risk assessment, 213
Network logic errors, 176
Newbold, R. C., 268–269, 291, 302
Newmann, L., 291
New products
  concurrent engineering, 182–184
  improving performance of new-product teams, 352
NIH (not invented here) culture, 380
Nike, 525, 595
Nissen, M. E., 442
Nofziner, B., 360, 367
Nokia, 306
Nominal group technique (NGT), 405
Nonaka, Ikujiro, 596, 609

Nonfinancial selection models, 39–42
- checklist models, 39–40
- multi-weighted scoring models, 40–42, 43

Nonproject factors, in project estimation, 131
Noreen, E., 303
Normal closing stage, 512
Normal conditions, in project estimation, 132
Norming stage of teams, 377, 378
Norrie, J., 588
Nortel Networks Corp., 541
Northern Telecom, 578
Northridge Earthquake (California), 308, 453
Norton, D. P., 54, 586, 588
Novell, 271
Numbering activities, 176–177

O

Oakland A's, 12
Objectives
- characteristics of, 31
- in project scope, 102–103
- strategy formulation to meet, 29–31
- in supporting organization strategy, 31

Objectivity, in negotiation process, 435–436
OBS (organization breakdown structure), 109, 113, 114, 274–278
O'Connor, G. C., 54
Oddou, G. R., 568
Olson, E. M., 93
Olve, N., 441
Olympic Games, 376, 551
O'Neal, Shaquille, 515
Operational projects, 36–37
OPM3, 583–585
Opportunity management, 221–222
- opportunity, defined, 221–222
- responses to opportunity, 222

Optimism, 361
Oracle, 30
Oregon Health Sciences University (OHSU), 135
O'Reilly, Brian, 520n
O'Reilly, C. A., 82n, 93
Organizational culture, 67, 81–89. *See also* Cultural factors
- characteristics of, 82, 83–86
- countercultures and, 83, 88
- diagnosis worksheet, 85
- ethics in, 355–357
- functions of, 82–83
- implications for organizing projects, 86–88
- nature of, 81–83
- in project estimation, 131
- relationship with project structure, 88

Organizational Project Management Maturity Model (OPM3), 583–585
Organizational review, 527–529
Organization breakdown structure (OBS), 109
- integrating with organization, 113, 114
- time-phased budget and, 274–278

Organization politics
- project managers and, 361
- in project portfolio system, 33–34, 35
- in recruiting project members, 382
- trust and, 357–359

Organization strategy, 24–50
- implementation through projects, 32
- managing portfolio system, 48–49
- project alignment with, 16, 25
- project manager understanding of, 26
- project portfolio management system, 32–37
- project selection criteria, 37–42
- project selection models, 42–47
- revising, 30
- strategic management process overview, 26–32
- strategy, defined, 25

Osmundsen, P., 152
Outdoor experiences/retreats, 399
Outsourcing, 418–440
- in accelerating project completion, 309, 322
- advantages and disadvantages, 421–422
- best practices, 423–432
- co-location, 429–430
- communication in, 425, 432
- conflict management processes, 427
- contract management, 430–431, 449–454
- customer relations, 437–439
- defined, 309, 419–420
- examples of, 422–423, 429, 431, 439
- long-term relationships, 431–432
- negotiation in, 432–437
- in resource allocation, 272–273
- review and status updates, 427–429
- team-building activities, 426–427
- traditional approach versus partnered approach, 423–424
- training activities, 426–427
- well-defined requirements and procedures, 424–426

Overhead costs
- direct, 145
- general and administrative (G&A), 145

Oversight, 572–587
- balanced scorecard model, 586
- defined, 573
- importance to project manager, 574
- at organization level, 573, 582–586
- organization project management maturity, 582–586
- phase gate methodology, 577–582
- portfolio management, 574
- at project level, 573
- project office, 80, 574–576

Overtime
- in accelerating project completion, 308, 309–310
- cross-cultural attitudes toward, 554

Ownership, in team building, 399

P

Pace of life, 549–551
Padding estimates, 130–131
Pant, L., 625
Parallel activities, 164, 167
Parametric procedures, for estimating project times and costs, 139–140
Parker, Ron, 616, 617
Parkinson's law, 294
Partnering charters, 427, 428
Pascoe, T. L., 258, 291
Past experience, in project estimation, 130, 139, 155–159
Path, 164
Patheon Inc., 309
Patterson, J. H., 258, 291
Patzelt, H., 532
Paulus, P. B., 378n, 408
Pavlik, A., 231
Payback model, 37, 38
PBS (process breakdown structure), 101, 116–117, 596
Peace Corps, 564

Peck, W., 80n, 92
Peel, D., 125
People factor
in assigning project work, 270–271
dealing with unreasonable people, 436–437
in negotiation process, 433–434, 436–437
in project estimation, 130
as resource constraint, 253–254
separating people from problem, 433–434
People's Republic of China (PRC). *See* China
Pepsi-Cola, 595
Percent complete index—actual costs (PCIC), 474–475
Percent complete index—budgeted costs (PCIB), 474–475
Percent complete rule, 465
Percent complete with weighted monitoring gates, 476
Performance-based contracts, 430
Performance indexes, 473
Performance measurement. *See* Project monitoring information system
Performance reviews, 520–522
individual, 521–522
project manager, 522
team member, 521–522
360-degree reviews, 520–522, 525
Performing stage of teams, 377, 378
Perkins, Dennis N. T., 353, 353n
Perpetual closing stage, 512
Perrow, L. A., 329
Personal-related currencies, 345, 347
PERT (program evaluation and review technique), 140, 213, 239–244
development of, 239–240
hypothetical example of, 240–243
Pesch, E., 291
Peters, J. F., 532
Peters, L. S., 54
Peters, Lawrence H., 352, 366, 389, 389n
Peters, T., 21, 366, 408
Pethokoukis, J. M., 595n
Pettegrew, A. M., 93
Phase estimating, for project times and costs, 141–143
Phase gate methodology, 577–582
flow diagram, 578–579
gate 1: proposal decision, 579
gate 2: screening and selection decision, 580
Phase gate methodology—*Cont.*
gate 3: implementation plan decision, 580
gate 4: progress evaluation decision, 580–581
gate 5: closure, 581
gate 6: lessons learned, 581–582
phase gate review process, 578
side benefits, 582
Philippines, 543
Physical characteristics, in organizational culture, 84–85
Pich, M. T., 231
Pinto, J. K., 54, 102, 125, 129n, 152, 231, 350n, 366, 442
Pippett, D. D., 532
Pitagorsky, G., 125
Planned value (PV)
costs included in, 465
defined, 276, 463
in time-phased budgets, 276
variance analysis, 465
Planning decisions, 384
Planning horizon, in project estimation, 130
Planning stage. *See also* Project estimation; Resource scheduling
of project life cycle, 8, 9, 396
sources of conflict in, 396
PMBOK (Project Management Body of Knowledge), 231, 341, 605, 619–620
PMI. *See* Project Management Institute (PMI)
PMI Project Management Salary Survey, 620
PMI Standards Committee, 125
PM Network, 619
PMP (Project Management Professional), 4, 605, 619–620
Poli, M., 94
Porras, J. I., 87, 92
Portfolio management, 574
Portfolio risks, balancing, 48–49
Portland General Electric Company, 479, 525
Position-related currencies, 345, 346
Positive synergy, 375–377
Posner, B. Z., 125, 352, 360, 366, 395, 408
Post-implementation evaluation, 512, 517–522
performance reviews, 520–522
phase gate methodology, 580–581
team evaluation, 517–520
Post-project retrospectives, 526–529
organizational review, 527–529
process and methods review, 527
Powell, M., 93
Premature closing stage, 512
Pressman, R. S., 153
Price, M., 54
PricewaterhouseCoopers, 541
Primavera, 385
Principled negotiation, 433–437
Priorities
changed priority closing stage, 513
in leading by example, 354
low-priority projects, 395
priority matrix, 106–108
priority system in project selection, 32, 47
project reward systems and, 391–392
responsibility for prioritizing projects, 47
Priority changes, 513
Priority matrix, 106–108
Priority system, 32, 47
Priority team, 40–42
Proactive approach, 360
Probability analysis, in risk assessment, 213
Problem identification, in group decision making, 393
Problem solving
in leading by example, 354–355
in recruiting project members, 381
Process breakdown structure (PBS), 101, 116–117, 596
Process review, 527
Procrastination, 295
Procter and Gamble, 12, 595
Procurement management
components of, 450
Request for Proposal (RFP), 43, 44, 63–65, 450, 583
Product backlogs, 600–601
Product life cycle, compression of, 11, 25
Product owner, 598
Program(s)
defined, 7–8
projects versus, 7–8
Program evaluation and review technique (PERT), 140, 213, 239–244
Program management, 8
Progress evaluation decision, phase gate methodology, 580–581

Progress measurement. *See* Project monitoring information system
Project(s), 6–11
characteristics of, 7
classification of, 36–37, 49
defined, 6–7
everyday work versus, 7, 8
examples of for college students, 5
implementing organization through, 32
programs versus, 7–8
Project Baseline Budget, 467–468, 469
Project buffers, 295
Project charters, 10–11, 105
Project classification
in project selection, 42
types of projects, 36–37, 49
Project closure, 511. *See also* Closing stage
wrap-up closure activities, 511–512, 513–517, 533–535
Project communication plan, 118–122
Project control process, 458–459, 461–462
Project cost baselines, 251, 273–278
Project Cost-Duration Graph, 313–321
crashing, 314–321
determining activities to shorten, 314–316
project direct costs, 314
project indirect costs, 313–314
simplified example, 316–318
time reduction decisions, 320–321
using, 318–319
Project definition. *See* Defining stage
Project duration, 304–323
acceleration options when resources are constrained, 310–312
acceleration options when resources are not constrained, 308–310
cost as issue in, 321–323
lags and, 180–186
practical considerations, 318–321
Project Cost-Duration Graph, 313–321
in project estimation, 130
rationale for reducing, 305–307
Project estimation, 128–150. *See also* Cost estimates; Resource estimates; Time estimates
accuracy, 142
adjusting estimates of specific tasks, 147–149
Project estimation—*Cont.*
error reduction, 133
factors influencing quality estimates, 130–131
guidelines for times, costs, and resources, 131–133
importance of, 129
learning curves in, 139, 155–159
level of detail, 143–144
mega projects, 147, 148
refining estimates, 146–149
time and cost databases, 149
top-down versus bottom-up, 133–143
types of costs, 144–145
Project evaluation
in closing stage, 512, 517–522
statement of criteria, 64
Project facilitators, 524–525
roles, 524
selecting, 524
Project governance, 15–16
alignment of projects and organizational strategy, 16
governance team in portfolio system, 48
nature of, 15–16
Projectitis, 74
Projectized Organization, 72–73
Project kick-off meeting, 383
Project life cycle, 8–9
defined, 8
project cycle times, 25
sources of conflict over, 395–396
stages of, 8–9. *See also* Closing stage; Defining stage; Executing stage; Planning stage
Project management. *See also* Project teams
critical-chain project management (CCPM) and, 300
current drivers of, 11–15
current examples of, 5, 12–13
importance of, 3–6
integration of, 15–16, 25
leadership versus, 339–340
old-fashioned view of, 343–344
project size and, 15, 147, 148, 603–604
socio-technical approach to, 17–18
Project Management Body of Knowledge (PMBOK), 231, 341, 605, 619–620
Project management career paths, 614–624
examples of, 616, 617, 621, 623
Project management career paths—*Cont.*
gaining visibility, 621–622
mentors, 622–623
nature of, 615–616
professional training and certification, 4, 619–621
projects given to recent college graduates, 5
pursuing a career, 618–619
success in key paths, 623
Project Management Consultants, 429
Project Management Institute (PMI), 3, 4, 6–7, 21, 34, 366, 463, 479, 574, 583–585, 605, 620, 625
Project Management Journal, 619
Project management maturity, 582–586
Project Management Professional (PMP), 4, 605, 619–620
Project management software
in developing project networks, 177–180
Microsoft Project, 187n, 262–268, 385, 450, 506–508
Primavera, 385
for project cost/schedule systems, 475, 506–508
Project management structures, 67–81
dedicated teams, 70–74, 88
functional organization, 68–70
matrix arrangement, 74–79, 89
organization considerations, 79
project considerations, 79–81
relationship with organizational culture, 88
Project managers, 338–362. *See also* Leadership; Project teams
building trust, 357–359
career paths. *See* Project management career paths
certification and training, 4, 605, 619–620
as client account executives, 439
conductor metaphor and, 344
dependencies of, 342
ethics and, 355–357
importance of project oversight to, 574
improving performance of new-product teams, 352
law of reciprocity and, 344–347
leading at the edge, 353
leading by example, 352–355
"management by wandering around" (MBWA), 349–350, 393, 457

Project managers—*Cont.*
managing expectations, 350
managing upward relations, 350–352
motivating for extraordinary performance, 320
nature of, 9–10
performance reviews, 522
project leadership versus, 339–340
project teams, 10–11
qualities of effective, 359–362
role of, 9–10
scrum masters as, 598
social network building, 347–355
stakeholders and, 340–344
understanding strategy, 26
work breakdown structure (WBS) and, 109
Project meetings, 383–387
establishing ground rules, 383–386
project kick-off meeting, 383
scrum, 598–600
subsequent meetings, 386–387
team identity and, 387
Project monitoring information system, 456–484
baseline changes, 481–482
costs and problems of data acquisition, 482–483
critical-chain project management (CCPM) in, 300
data collected in, 457–458, 482–483
earned value cost/schedule system, 459, 462–467, 499–506
examples of use, 462, 479
forecasting final project cost, 476–478
indexes to monitor progress, 473–476
Microsoft Project and, 506–508
process overview, 464
project control process, 458–459, 461–462
reports and reporting in, 458, 467–473
scope creep, 479–481, 482
status report, 468–473, 478
structure of, 457–458
time performance, 459–462
Project networks, 160–187
activities in, 162, 164, 166–169
activity numbering, 176–177
activity-on-arrow (AOA), 165–169
activity-on-node (AON), 165–169
activity-on-arrow (AOA) versus, 165–166
Project networks—*Cont.*
backward pass, 171–173
forward pass, 170–171
backward pass-latest times in, 171–173, 175–176, 185–186
basic rules for developing, 164–165
calendar dates, 180
computers in developing, 177–179
concurrent engineering, 182–184
critical activities in, 161–162
critical path method (CPM), 161, 164, 174, 176, 177, 239, 317
development
basic rules, 164
from work breakdown structure (WBS), 162–163
yellow sticky-note approach to, 165
extended network techniques, 180–187
forward pass-earliest times in, 169–171, 173, 175–176, 185–186
hammock activities, 186–187
laddering, 180, 181
lags, 180–186
in forward and backward pass procedures, 185–186
to reduce schedule detail, 180–184
level of detail for activities, 176
multiple starts/multiple projects, 180
nature of, 161
network computation process, 169–175
backward pass-latest times, 169, 171–173
forward pass-earliest times, 169–171
network logic errors, 176
practical considerations, 176–180
project schedules and, 162
sensitivity, 174–175, 320–321
slack/float in, 173–175
free, 175
total, 173–175
terminology, 164
Project offices (POs), 574–576
benefits of, 576
defined, 80
example of report, 576–577
services of, 575
types of, 80
Project oversight. *See* Oversight
Project plans. *See* Project networks
Project portfolio management system, 32–49
benefits of, 35
classification of projects, 36–37, 49
implementation gap, 32–33, 35
managing the system, 47–49
organization politics, 33–34, 35
priority system in, 32, 47
project portfolio in, 32
project selection, 37–47
resource conflicts and multitasking, 34–35
Project proposals. *See* Proposals
Project queue systems, 272
Project Retrospectives (Kerth), 523
Project reward systems, 391–392
Project rollup, 472
Project schedules. *See also* Time estimates
acceleration options, 307–312
constrained resources, 310–312
unconstrained resources, 308–310
in critical-chain project management (CCPM), 299. *See also* Critical-chain project management (CCPM)
deadlines, 307, 425
development of earned value cost/scheduling system, 459, 462–467, 499–506
early and late times, 163
project networks and, 162
schedule variance (SV), 463–465, 467
slippage in, 272, 461–462
statement of, 64
time buffers, 224
Project scope, 102–106
changes in, 147, 311, 322
checklist, 102–106
reducing, 311, 322
scope statement, 10–11, 17, 64, 105
Project screening
financial selection models, 37–39
multi-criteria selection models, 39–42
nonfinancial selection models, 39–42
overview of project screening process, 46
phase gate methodology, 580
project screening matrix, 40–42, 43
Project screening matrix, 40–42, 43
Project selection, 37–47
financial criteria, 37–39
international projects, 563–564

Project selection—*Cont.*
multi-criteria selection models, 39–42, 43
nonfinancial criteria, 39–42
phase gate methodology, 580
prioritizing proposals, 32, 47
project classification, 42
ranking proposals, 44–47
selecting a model, 42–43
solicitation of project proposals, 43
sources of project proposals, 43
Project site selection, 547–548, 551
Project-specific risk. *See* Risk management process
Project sponsors
dependencies of, 343
managing upward relations, 351
Project structure
organizational culture and, 88
in project estimation, 130
Project teams, 10–11, 374–405
building high-performance, 380–399
conflict management, 394–398
decision-making process, 392–394
dedicated. *See* Dedicated project teams
dependencies of, 341–344
five-stage team development model, 377–378
importance of teamwork, 18
international project, 563–566
low-priority projects, 395
meetings, 383–387, 598–600
pitfalls, 403–405
project synergy, 375–377
punctuated equilibrium and, 379
recruitment process, 380–383
rejuvenating, 398–399
reward systems, 391–392
shared vision, 388–391, 396
situational factors in team development, 378–380
team identity, 387–388
virtual project teams, 399–403, 421
Project vision, 388–391, 396
Proposals
contractor selection from, 65
phase gate methodology, 579
ranking, 44–47
Request for Proposal (RFP), 43, 44, 63–65, 450, 583
sources of, 43, 44
Prototypes, in outsourcing, 425
Pseudo-earned value percent complete approach, 483
Public documents, in organizational culture, 85
Public recognition, 392
Punctuality, 549–551, 554
Punctuated equilibrium, 379

Q

Quality
options for accelerating projects, 311
in project estimation, 130–131
total quality management (TQM), 36, 346
Quinn, R. E., 92, 442

R

Radcliffe, Lauren, 206
Raja, V. T., 367n
Randall, Doug, 55
RAND Corporation, 136
Range estimating, for estimating project times and costs, 140–141
Raskin, P., 55
Ratio methods, for estimating project times and costs, 136
Raz, T., 125, 303
Rea, K. P., 408, 625
Rebello, K., 93
Recruitment process, 380–383
considerations in, 381–382
international projects, 563–566
in matrix management, 381, 382–383
Redetermination contracts, 451–452
Reference Class Forecasting, 148
Refining estimates, 146–149
Reinertsen, D. G., 88, 94, 218–219, 231, 291, 329, 391
Reinman, R., 231
Relationship nature, 550
Relationship-related currencies, 345, 346–347
Relationships among people, 550
Release burndown charts, 602
Release planning, 599
Religious factors, 545–547
Relyea, Dave, 597
Remington, K., 54
Reports and reporting
change request forms and logs, 226–228
errors, 225
final project report, 516–517
Reports and reporting—*Cont.*
in outsourcing, 425
project monitoring information system, 458, 467–473
by project offices (POs), 576–577
status report, 468–473, 478
Request for Proposal (RFP), 43, 44, 63–65, 450, 583
Reserves, 222–224
budget, 223
management, 223–224
Resorts, 604
Resource bottlenecks, 295
Resource buffers, 295
Resource conflicts, 34–35
Resource-constrained projects, 252–253, 255, 257–268, 269
acceleration options, 310–312
computer demonstration, 262–268
EMR project example, 262–268
impacts of, 268
nature of, 255, 257–262
parallel method of applying heuristics, 258, 259
resource allocation methods, 257–268
resource conflicts and multitasking, 34–35
Resource estimates, 130–149
factors influencing quality of, 130–131
guidelines for, 131–133
level of detail, 143–144
phase estimating, 141–143
refining, 146–149
top-down versus bottom-up, 133–143
Resource Pool project office, 80
Resource scheduling, 250–279
assessing resource allocation, 269
assigning project work, 270–271
benefits of, 270
critical-chain project management (CCPM), 293–303
to develop project cost baseline, 251, 273–278
multiproject resource schedules, 271–273
process overview, 251–253
resource-constrained projects, 252–253, 255, 257–268, 269
resource smoothing in, 252, 255–257
splitting activities, 268–269
time-constrained projects, 253, 255–257

Resource scheduling—*Cont.*
time-phased budget baseline, 176, 251, 273–278, 464
types of resource constraints, 253–255
Resource smoothing, 252, 255–257
Responsibilities
client assumption of, 322
in project communication plan, 121
in project estimation, 131–132
project scope, 64
in risk response control, 225
Responsibility matrix (RM), 117–118, 119
Retaining risk, 216
Retrospectives in closing stage, 512, 522–530
archiving, 529–530
concluding retrospective notes, 530
independent facilitators, 524–525
initiating retrospective review, 523
lessons learned, 517, 522–523, 581–582
managing, 525–526
overseeing post-project retrospective, 526–529
process overview, 525
utilizing, 529
Reviews, in outsourcing, 427–429
Reward systems, 391–392. *See also* Incentives
RFP (Request for Proposal), 43, 44, 63–65, 450, 583
Rhaz, T., 625
RHI Consulting, 18
Ricks, D. A., 568
RIM, 306
Risk
avoiding, 215–216
defined, 205
retaining, 216
sources of project, 207
transferring, 216
Risk assessment, 207, 210–213
Failure Mode and Effects Analysis (FMEA), 213
probability analysis, 213
in project estimation, 133
risk severity matrix, 212–213
scenario analysis, 210–212
Risk avoidance, 215–216
Risk breakdown structure (RBS), 208–210
Risk event graph, 206
Risk identification, 207–210
Risk management process, 204–229
balancing portfolio risks, 48–49
cost of mismanaged risk, 205–207
examples of, 205–207, 215, 219
international projects and, 541–542
process overview, 207
risk, defined, 205
risk assessment, 207, 210–213
risk identification, 207–210
risk response control, 207, 224–228
risk response development, 207, 214–224
sources of project risk, 207
Risk mitigation, 214–215
Risk profile, 209–210
Risk register, 224–225
Risk response control, 207, 224–228
change control management, 225–228
risk register, 224–225
Risk response development, 207, 214–224
avoiding risk, 215–216
contingency funding, 222–224
contingency planning, 216–221
mitigating risk, 214–215
opportunity management, 221–222
retaining risk, 216
time buffers, 224
transferring risk, 216
Risk response matrix, 217–218
Risk retention, 216
Risk severity matrix, 212–213
Risk transfer, 216
Ritti, R. R., 391, 392n, 408
River of Doubt (Millard), 546
Rizova, Polly S., 89, 89n, 93
Robb, D. J., 366
Rodriguez, P., 568
Roemer, T. R., 329
Romanoff, T. K., 521, 532
Rondon, Candido Mariano da Silva, 546
Roosevelt, Theodore "Teddy," 546
Rosen, B., 408
Rosenblatt, A., 200
Ross, Jerry, 532
Ross, M., 148n, 152
Rothaermel, F. T., 441
Rothengatter, W., 152
Rourke, D. L., 152
Rousculp, M. D., 231
Rover, I., 588
Royer, I., 532
Ruekert, R. W., 93
Russia, legal/political factors in, 541

S

"Sacred cows," 33–34, 41
Safio, P., 404, 408
Salehipour, A., 498
Samsung, 306
Santayana, George, 511
Sashittal, H. C., 93
Saudi Arabia, cross-cultural factors in, 555–556
Saunders, C. C., 568
Sayles, Leonard R., 350n, 351n, 360, 366, 367
Scaling, 603–604
Scenario analysis, 210–212
Schedule performance index (SPI), 473, 508
Schedule risks. *See also* Resource scheduling
in contingency planning, 220
Schedules. *See* Project schedules
Schedule variance (SV)
computing, 464
defined, 463
variance analysis, 463–465, 467
Schein, E. H., 82n, 94, 375n
Schilling, D. L., 442
Schkade, J., 378n, 408
Schmidt, Eric, 271
Schuler, J. R., 231
Schultzel, H. J., 442
Schwaber, Ken, 591, 591n, 609
Schwalbe, K., 455
Schwartz, Peter, 55
Scileppi, Greg, 18
Scope creep, 105–106, 479–481, 482
Scope statements, 10–11, 17, 64, 105
Scout activities, 352
Scown, M. J., 541, 541n, 568
Scrum, 596–603
features, 596
meetings, 598–600
origins of, 596
process overview, 597
product and sprint backlogs, 600–601
roles and responsibilities, 598
sprint and release burndown charts, 601–602
Scrum master, 598
Scrum meeting, 598–600
Sculley, John, 74, 74n, 94
Sears Roebuck, 138

Seattle Kingdome, 215
Secret of Success, The (Rizova), 89
Security factors, 541–542
Segalla, M., 567
Selection. *See* Project selection
Self-awareness, 361
Self-motivation, 361
Self organizing teams, 598
Self-protection, 294
Self-regulation, 361
Senge, Peter M., 360n, 367, 388n, 408, 522, 532
Senior management. *See* Top management
Sensitivity, of project network, 174–175, 320–321
September 11, 2001 terrorist attacks, 541, 597
Seta, J. J., 378n, 408
Seven Habits of Highly Effective People (Covey), 358, 435
Shackleton, Ernest, 353
Shadrokh, S., 498
Shanahan, S., 258, 291
Shared vision, 388–391, 396
Shareware, virtual project teams and, 402
Sheen, Martin, 543
Shell, G. R., 442
Shenhar, Aaron J., 26, 26n, 55, 80n, 94, 360, 367
Shepherd, D. A., 532
Sherif, M., 378n, 408
Shirley, Donna, 382, 382n
Shtub, A., 367
Sibbett, D., 404, 408
Siebdrat, F., 409
Siemens Medical Systems, 605
Singer, Carl A., 400, 400n
Site selection, 547–548, 551
Situational factors, in team development, 378–380
Skilton, P. F., 382, 409
Skunk works. *See* Dedicated project teams
Slack, 173–175
  free, 175
  total, 173–175
Sleeping Dictionary, The (film), 404n
Slevin, D. P., 102, 125, 366
Slippage, 272, 461–462
Sloan, John, 372n
Small projects, 15
Smith, B. J., 390, 408
Smith, Cynthia J., 356n
Smith, D. K., 34n, 55, 153, 303, 385n, 390, 408
Smith, M., 88, 93
Smith, P. G., 94, 218–219, 231, 329, 409
Snapple Company, 206
Snizek, J. A., 207–208, 231
Snyder, D., 152
Social network building, 347–355
  leading by example, 352–355
  "management by wandering around" (MBWA), 349–350, 393, 457
  managing upward relations, 350–352
  mapping dependencies, 347–349
  social network, defined, 347
Social skills, 361
Socio-technical approach to project management, 17–18
Software Engineering Institute (SEI), 583
Sony, 13, 15
Sood, S., 303
Soul of a New Machine, The (Kidder), 389, 391
Spalding, 515
Spirit Aero Systems, 296
Splitting activities
  critical-chain project management (CCPM) and, 299–300
  in resource scheduling, 268–269
Sports and recreation, 12, 104, 219, 220, 376, 391, 515, 546, 551
Sprint backlogs, 600
Sprint burndown charts, 601–602
Sprint planning, 599
Sprint retrospective, 600
Sprint review, 600
Squires, Susan E., 356n
Srivannaboon, S., 54
Stage-Gate™ model, 577
Stakeholders, 340–344
  defined, 341
  dependencies of, 341–344
  stakeholder analysis in project communication plan, 120–121
  types of, 341–343
Standards of performance, in leading by example, 355
Standish Group International Inc., 21, 102, 125, 526, 526n
Starkweather, Jo Ann, 620, 625
Start-to-finish lag relationship, 184
Start-to-start lag relationship, 181–184
Star Wars films, 13, 543
Statement of work (SOW), 10–11, 17, 64, 105
Status report, 468–473
  assumptions, 467
  baseline development, 467–468
  development of, 468–473
  example of monthly, 478
Status updates, in outsourcing, 427–429
Staw, Berry M., 532
Stern, David, 376, 515
Stevenson, Deborah H., 620, 625
Steward, Jake, 575n
Stewart, T. A., 21
Stewart, W. E., 588
Stonehill, I., 568
Storming stage of teams, 377, 378
Strategic management process, 26–49
  analyze and formulate strategies, 29–31
  defined, 26, 28
  implementing strategies through projects, 32
  objectives support strategy, 31
  portfolio system management, 48–49
  process overview, 28
  project portfolio management system, 32–37
  project selection, 37–47
  review and define organizational mission, 29
Strategic projects, 36–37
Strategy
  defined, 25
  understanding, 26
Stress-related culture shock, 562
Strickland, A. J., 104n
Strodtbeck, F. L., 550, 550n, 568
Strohl Systems Group, 541–542
Strong matrix, 76–79
Stuckenbruck, L. C., 94
Sullivan, Stacy Savides, 84
Sun Microsystems, 271
Swahl, W., 125
Swanson, S., 55, 133n
SWOT (strengths, weaknesses, opportunities, and threats) analysis, 31
Sydney Opera House (Australia), 148
Symons, C. R., 153
Synergy, 375–377
Systems thinking, 360

T

Takeuchi, Hirotaka, 596, 609
Talbot, B. F., 258, 291

Tanzania, 544
Task coordinator activities, 352
Task-related currencies, 345
Tate, K., 125, 625
Team building, 380–399
  five-stage team developmental model, 377–378
  in outsourcing, 426–427
  punctuated equilibrium and, 379
  recruiting project members, 380–383
  rejuvenating the project team, 398–399
  team-building techniques in, 399
Team charters, 385
Team evaluation, 517–520
Team identity, 387–388
Team rituals, 387–388
Team spirit, 404
Technical performance measurement, 475
Technical requirements, in project scope, 103
Technical risks, in contingency planning, 218–220
Technological expertise
  outsourcing and, 421
  in recruiting project members, 381
Tektronics, 462
Telephone industry, 306
Television, 563
Template methods, for estimating project times and costs, 139
Terrorist attacks of 2001, 541, 597
Tesluk, P. E., 408
Thamhain, H. J., 395, 409
Thompson, A. A., 104n
Thompson, G. L., 200
Thompson, Hine, & Flory, 429
Thompson, M. P., 442
Thoms, P., 409
3M, 40, 87, 300, 402, 409, 578, 595
360-degree review, 520–522, 525
Time and cost databases, 149
Time buffers, 224
Time-constrained projects, 253, 255–257
  nature of, 255
  scheduling interval in applying heuristics, 258–262
  smoothing resource demand, 252, 255–257
Time estimates, 130–149. *See also* Project schedules
  apportion methods, 137
  consensus methods, 135–136
Time estimates—*Cont.*
  in critical-chain project management (CCPM), 299
  factors influencing quality of, 130–131
  function point methods, 137–139
  guidelines for, 131–133
  learning curves, 139, 155–159
  level of detail, 143–144
  parametric procedures, 139–140
  phase estimating, 141–143
  range estimating, 140–141
  ratio methods, 136
  refining, 146–149
  template methods, 139
  time and cost database, 149
  top-down versus bottom-up, 133–143
Time Inc., 605
Time management, 361
Time orientation, 550
Time performance, in project monitoring information system, 459–462
Time-phased budget baselines, 176, 251, 273–278, 464
  creating, 274–278
  need for, 276–278
Timer industry, 270, 483
To Complete Performance Index (TCPI), 477–478
Top-down estimates, 133–143
  apportion methods, 137
  consensus methods, 135–136
  "function points," 137–139
  learning curves, 139
  nature of, 134
  ratio methods, 136
Top management. *See also* Middle management
  dependencies of, 342–343
  ethics and, 357
  functional organization and, 68
  implementation gap in project portfolio system, 33, 35
  level of detail in project estimates, 143
  managing upward relations, 350–352
  in portfolio system, 48
  in project portfolio management, 48–49
  responsibility for prioritizing projects, 47
Torti, M. T., 439, 439n
Total quality management (TQM), 36, 346
Total slack/float, 173–175
Toyota, 420, 431
Tracking decisions, 384
Tracking Gantt charts, 460–461, 471, 508
Training
  in international projects, 563–566
  in outsourcing, 426–427
  professional training and certification, 4, 619–621
Transferring risk, 216
Transportation services, 135, 308
Trevino, L. K., 357n, 367
Triple bottom line, 11–12
Trojan Nuclear Plant decommission, 479
Trust
  leadership and, 357–359
  in negotiations for outsourcing, 432–433
  virtual project teams and, 401–402
Tuchman, B. W., 377, 409
Tuller, L. W., 553n
Tung, R. L., 557n, 562, 568
Turner, J. R., 36, 53, 360, 367
Turtle, Q. C., 184, 200
20th Century-Fox, 420

U

"Ugly American," 548–549
Uhlenbruck, K., 568
Ulrich, F. C., 231
Underwriter Laboratories, Inc., 564
United States, cross-cultural factors in, 549–551, 557–559
U.S. Air Force, 300
U.S. Army, 221
U.S. Defense Intelligence Agency (DIA), 431
U.S. Department of Agriculture, 270
U.S. Department of Defense, 3, 221, 431, 462
U.S. Department of Transportation, 586
U.S. Federal Housing Authority (FHA), 137
U.S. Food and Drug Administration (FDA), 343
U.S. Forest Service (USFS), 270, 483
United States Golf Association (USGA), 104
U.S. Green Building Council, 14
U.S. Navy, 300
U.S. West, 405

A Socio-Technical Approach to Project Management

The Technical and Sociocultural Dimensions of the Project Management Process

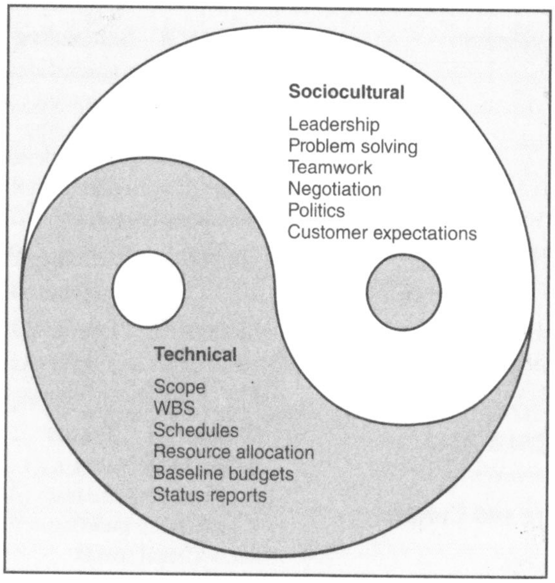

Project Life Cycle

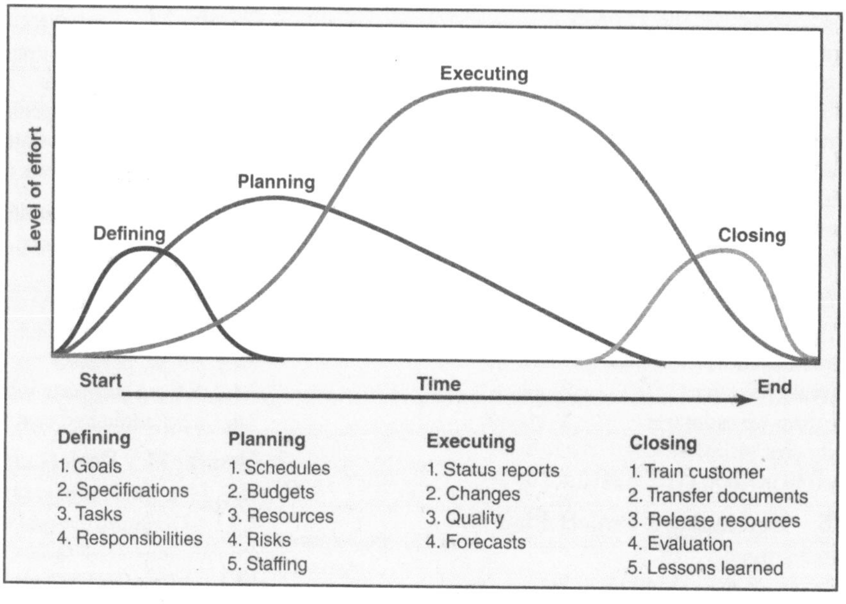